INFORMATION
WARFARE

Second trade paperback edition 1996
Copyright © 1994, 1996 by Winn Schwartau
All rights reserved

First edition
First printing, 1994

Published by
Thunder's Mouth Press
632 Broadway, 7th Floor
New York, NY 10012

Library of Congress Cataloging-in-Publication Data

Schwartàu, Winn.
    Information warfare : cyberterrorism: protecting your personal
security in the electronic age / Winn Schwartau.
        p.   cm.
    Includes index.
    ISBN 1-56025-132-8 : $16.95
    1. Computer security. 2. Computer crimes. I. Title.
QA76.9.A25S354   1994
302.2—dc20   94-2412
                                                            CIP

Printed in the United States of America

Distributed by
Publishers Group West
4065 Hollis Street
Emeryville, CA 94608
(800) 788-3123

2-20-97

ALSO BY WINN SCHWARTAU

The Complete Internet Business Toolkit

Terminal Compromise
A novel about Information Warfare

Security Insider Report

A monthly information security and
personal privacy newsletter.

Over 400 Pages of New Material!

In addition to significant new chapters by Winn Schwartau, the following industry luminaries have contributed works:

Mark Aldrich, *GRCI*

Dr. John Alger, *Dean, School of Information Warfare and Strategy, National Defense University, Washington, D.C.*

Stuart A. Baker, Esq., *Steptoe and Johnson, former general counsel to the NSA*

John Perry Barlow, *Cognitive Dissident; Co-Founder, Electronic Frontier Foundation*

Dr. Phillipe Baumard, *Professor of Strategic Management. University of Paris-XII*

Jim Bell, *CEO Optigreen*

Dr. Frederick Cohen, *President, Management Analytics, Incorporated*

Simon Davies, *Director, Privacy International, UK; Research Fellow, Computer Security Research Centre, London School of Economics; Visiting Fellow, Department of Law, University of Essex, UK*

John M. Deutch, *Director of Central Intelligence*

Matthew G. Devost, *Systems Analyst*

Colonel Charles J. Dunlap, Jr., *Staff Judge Advocate, USAF*

Ronald Eward, *Founder and President, MarTech Strategies*

Lieutenant Commander Robert J. Garigue, *Deputy Program Director, Joint Strategic Information Systems, DISOA-NDHQ, Department of National Defence, Canada; Decision Analysis Laboratory Carleton University, Ottawa*

Matthew Gaylor, *Freematt's Alerts and Electronic Frontier Foundation*

Beth Givens, *Project Director of the Privacy Rights ClearingHouse, University of San Diego Center for Public Interest Law*

Mike Godwin, *Internet World*

Bertil Haggman, *Center for Research on Geopolitics, Helsingborg, Sweden*

Dr. Houston T. Hawkins, *Los Alamos National Laboratory*

Henry M. Kluepfel, CPP, *VP for Corporate Development, Science Applications International Corporation*

Carlo Kopp, *Multiprocessor Research Group, Department of Computer Science, Monash University, Australia*

Martin C. Libicki, *National Defense University*

David F. Linowes, *Boeschenstein Professor Emeritus of Political Economy and Public Policy, University of Illinois, Urbana-Champaign*

Wayne Madsen, *Security Analyst, Computer Science Corporation*

Betty G. O'Hearn, *Interpact Incorporated*

Peter V. Radatti, *President, CyberSoft, Incorporated*

Marcus J. Ranum, *Chief Scientist, V-One Corporation*

Howard Reingold, *Author, Parent, Columnist*

Colonel John Rothrock (Ret.), USAF, *Director, SRI International Center for Global Strategic Planning*

Daniel J. Ryan, *Vice President, Science Applications International Corporation*

Julie J. C. H. Ryan, *Senior Associate, Booz Allen and Hamilton*

General John J. Sheehan, USMC, *Supreme Allied Commander, Atlantic (SACLANT); Commander in Chief, U.S. Atlantic Command*

Charles L. Smith

Charles Swett, *Office of the Assistant Secretary of Defense for Special Operations and Low-Intensity Conflict (Policy Planning)*

Colonel Richard Szafranski, *USAF, AWC National Military Strategy Chair*

Captain Roger D. Thrasher, USAF

Elizabeth Weise, *Associated Press Cyberspace Writer*

Dr. Ira Winkler, *Directory of Technology, NCSA*

Contents

Introduction to *Information Warfare*, 2nd Edition

When Winn Schwartau was writing the first edition of *Information Warfare—Cyberterrorism: Protecting Your Personal Security in the Electronic Age,* the nation was just awakening to an understanding of new threats to its national security interests . . . from Cyberspace. In fact, if there was a single year when awareness of the concerns associated with Information Warfare became focused, it was 1993. In that year, Heidi and Alvin Toffler published *War and Anti-War: Survival at the Dawn of the Twenty-First Century;* retired Air Force Colonel Al Campen published *The First Information War: The Story of Communications, Computers, and Intelligence Systems in the Persian Gulf War;* the Chairman of the Joint Chiefs of Staff published Memorandum of Policy (MOP) No. 30, "Command and Control Warfare"; and the Department of Defense (DOD) published its first version (Top Secret) of Directive 3600.1, "Information Warfare."

The Tofflers, struck by the success of the U.S. war machine in the Persian Gulf, hypothesized that a new form of war, paralleling a new way of making wealth, would dominate a new wave, the information wave, of civilization. Al Campen wrote of the Gulf War as one that was fundamentally different from any previous conflict, and for which the key role of information systems would likely be overlooked, misrepresented, or deprecated by historians. MOP 30 declared command and control warfare to be the implementation of Information Warfare on the battlefield, and that this type of warfare derived from modern military forces' reliance on timely and accurate information.

A final event capped the ascendance of the concept of Information Warfare in 1993. In November, the president of the National Defense University sent a memorandum to the Director of the Joint Staff calling for the establishment of the School of Information Warfare and Strategy, which would conduct a 44-week senior-level program of study in the information component of national power.

If 1993 was the set-up, 1994 was the sting. The School of Information Warfare and Strategy opened its doors to 16 students in August; shortly thereafter, *Information Warfare* appeared. Neither the school nor the book was able to answer all the questions that quickly coalesced within the wide community of interests affected by the concept of Information

Warfare. But both the school and the book emerged as sources of ideas and energy upon which ensuing debates could be based.

The first question that individuals new to the concept of information war generally ask is, "What is it?" Winn Schwartau and the defense community came to similar conclusions to this question, but from different starting points and via different routes. The DOD, for example, focused initially on concepts of command and control warfare that most greatly affected forces on the traditional battlefield. Schwartau saw the threat directed primarily against the economic infrastructure of the nation: as "dangerous international economic competition supplants megaton military intimidation," he wrote in the first edition, "offensive pugnacity will be aimed at the informational and financial infrastructure upon which our Western economy depends." As scholars and staff officers focused on definition, an awareness emerged that the threats of the Information Age would affect the means of warfare as well as global economic and political competition.

The existence, possibilities, and vulnerabilities of Information Warfare have been questioned by many. Two of the most frequently raised objections are forms of the following: (1) if we cannot define it, then it cannot exist; and (2) if information war is everything, then it is nothing.

The second objection can be dismissed quickly with an analogy: If life is everything, then it is nothing. True, information is everywhere. Although it was always everywhere, now more than ever it is in digitized form, which makes it far more accessible to more individuals and far more easily transported from source to user and between users. Returning to the analogy, life is important; and it has goodness and badness. It is comprehensive and vast in its dimensions, and in order to understand it, we must understand its components, subcomponents, microcomponents, and so forth. A taxonomy is necessary. Life is divided among the plant world and the animal world. Each world is further subdivided into phyla, phyla are divided into classes, classes into subclasses, and so forth. Information warfare, in large measure because of its ubiquity, is similarly complex. Like life, it can be defined in many ways. But one can grasp neither the meaning of life nor the meaning of Information Warfare by being exposed to a single definition. And one can understand neither life nor Information Warfare by attending a single lecture, by participating in a single course, or by reading a single book. Yet, as the Chinese tell us, the journey of a thousand miles does begin with a single step. Winn Schwartau's *Information Warfare* is the step. And his taxonomy of Class 1, 2, and 3 Information Warfare is a meaningful organization of ideas upon which to base a serious study of the concept of Information Warfare—particularly with concern to economic infrastructure.

Class 1 Information Warfare, according to Schwartau, is personal Information Warfare. It includes the study of all sources of information about each of us as individuals. Class 2 is corporate Information Warfare. It embraces the study of information as it affects business, commercial, or economic interests. Class 3 is global Information Warfare. It is intended to define those aspects of Information Warfare that affect the national interest. These classes have proved extremely useful in defining issues associated with the Information Age.

Other taxonomies do exist. For example, it is not hard to imagine that breaches of privacy surrounding individual information could become serious enough as to threaten the viability of the government of a nation-state. Similarly, threats to corporations, particularly if they are from outside a nation-state, could become serious enough to threaten the interests of the host nation.

Another taxonomy, focusing more on national security concerns, suggests that Information Warfare can be best understood from the context of the intent of the perpetrator of the attack. The first element in this taxonomy is the hacker. As Schwartau points out in his chapter on hackers, the term usually connotes something bad, but he is quick to point out that the connotations are not always negative. He speaks of the relationship between the hack—a cab driver—and his hack—the cab. It is a relationship of affection, and one in which the hack wants to know all there is to know about his hack. So it is with computer hackers. They want to know everything there is to know about Cyberspace. They are curious and smart, and they adhere to an absolute ethic—do no harm. Their ethic recalls the Hippocratic oath in the early days of medicine when the quest began to better understand the human body. The hacker is an Information Warrior only in the broadest sense. He or she can be a nuisance, but as long as the intent is to do no harm, the hacker is of little concern to law enforcement or the nation-state.

The second element in the national security taxonomy is the cracker, an individual whose objective in Cyberspace is to do harm that is not directed against the nation-state. The cracker uses Cyberspace to confound, to steal, to destroy, to carry out vendettas, to disrupt, to demand attention or ransoms, to gain competitive advantage, to gain wealth, or to gain power in illegal or marginally legal ways. Crackers are the responsibility of traditional law enforcement agencies, but these agencies must be trained in techniques that are most untraditional. One challenge for law enforcement in Cyberspace is that laws are often outdated, untried, and ambiguous. A second challenge is the ease with which an evidence trail can lead from jurisdiction to jurisdiction, and indeed from nation to nation, bringing into play a dizzying array of often conflicting laws.

The final element in the national security taxonomy is defined by those who use information to project power. This group is not limited to nation-state players, but also applies to a wide range of state and nonstate actors. Foreign intelligence services and state-sponsored terrorists are among the state actors in this category. Nonstate actors include religiously motivated terrorists, drug cartels, anarchists, organized crime, ideologically motivated groups, and psychopaths. The common element of these potential actors is that each intends to project power via information means to influence or alter decisions of the established political order or to actually change the political order. The threats from those who use information to project power are the responsibility of the nation-state. The challenge lies in the difficulty of having adequate warning to protect against the threat and adequate response options to counter the intent of the perpetrator. Business as usual is not the answer to the protection of the nation from information projectors of power: the means of information attack are too varied and very difficult to detect; the number of potential targets is nearly limitless; and traditional organizations with traditional skills are inadequate to the task.

A third taxonomy of Information Warfare originated in the DOD. It is based on the most basic of military missions and perhaps unintentionally divides responsibility for Information Warfare among existing staff elements. The first of the categories in the DOD taxonomy encompasses the offensive aspects of information war. It is what the United States is capable of doing against other projectors of power—provided they can be (1) identified so the national command can take decisive action and (2) located precisely enough that a counterattack can be launched with a reasonable chance of success. An advantage of separating offensive from defensive information is that offensive capabilities can be guarded by a veil of secrecy. In the traditional military organization, offensive aspects of information thus fall to the operations staff: the G-3 of general staffs and the J-3 of joint staffs.

The second element of the DOD taxonomy is defensive aspects. Defensive Information Warfare acknowledges that the protection of one's own information is essential. The difficulty in protection is that the nation's information resources extend far beyond those that are owned or controlled by the government. Indeed, much of the infrastructure handling the nation's information assets are privately owned. Government control is hardly an option, particularly when there is considerable bipartisan pressure for less government intervention. Thus, the responsibility for defense is shared, requiring close cooperation between the public and private sectors. And whereas defense is a shared responsibility among all staff elements, commands, and elements within the DOD, the lead rests with the J-6: command, control, communications, and computer systems.

The final element of the DOD taxonomy is the infrastructure that both perpetrates and protects against Information Warfare and allows friendly information systems to function as designed. The purpose of the infrastructure is to exploit, or leverage, friendly information assets. Like defensive Information Warfare, the staff proponent for building and leveraging friendly information systems is the J-6.

These three taxonomies each reflect a bias regarding the definition or understanding of Information Warfare. None is right and none is wrong. Collectively, they illustrate the complex nature of this Information Age phenomena.

Winn Schwartau has long favored a relatively terse definition of Information Warfare: "the use of information and information systems as both weapons and targets in a conflict." After nearly a year of debate, discussion, and staff work, the DOD has promulgated the following definition: "actions taken to achieve information superiority by affecting adversary information, information-based processes, information systems, and computer-based networks while defending one's own information, information-based processes, information systems, and computer-based networks." This definition requires a further definition for *information superiority,* which DOD has also provided: "that degree of dominance in the information domain which permits the conduct of operations without effective opposition." The difficulty with these definitions is that they tend to limit their applicability to the traditional concept of the battlefield by tying information superiority to the conduct of operations. Such a definition is not broad enough to include the economic and political information targets that Schwartau and many others see as the real threat to our national interests.

Perhaps concerns about the official DOD definition led to the U.S. Air Force defining Information Warfare in a different way in its *Cornerstones of Information Warfare* document: "any action to deny, exploit, corrupt, or destroy the enemy's information and its functions; protecting ourselves against those actions; and exploiting our own military information functions." This definition reflects the DOD triad of offensive, defensive, and exploitive elements as well as attacks against political and economic targets, although its final clause belies its prejudice to exploit military information functions.

A better definition encompasses the breadth of the Information Warfare environment, the elements of the three taxonomies presented above, and the critical target sets that must be protected:

> Information warfare consists of those actions intended to protect, exploit, corrupt, deny, or destroy information or information resources in order to achieve a significant advantage, objective, or victory over an adversary.

This definition works for the cracker intent on moving money from one account to another. It works for the intelligence service that is gathering information. It works for the terrorist who threatens a nation's electrical system in exchange for the release of a political prisoner. It works for the nation that gains control of an adversary's aircraft control system to force that nation to withdraw troops from a disputed territory. It works for the commander who gains from national sensors the information needed to counter an enemy effort to isolate his command. It works for the hacker who wants to embarrass his rival hacker gang. It works for psychological operations. It works for electronic warfare.

The dimensions of this definition and the examples offered call atten-

tion to an important distinction between the concept of Information Warfare as it applies to the traditional battlefield and beyond it. On the
battlefield, the task of attaining political objectives primarily requires
killing and destruction of materiel. Information and information resources greatly affect the outcome and always have. Since the widespread introduction of the silicon chip, however, a new and dramatically
improved quality and quantity of information can be collected, communicated, analyzed, fused, and exploited in a variety of ways: in guidance
systems, position location, management, planning, logistics, and a host
of other functional areas. This technology can be used to enhance traditional methods of war. It can help find targets. It can help direct fire to
targets. It can confound the enemy. It can facilitate planning and communications. Such uses of information chip technology in traditional forms
of war are aptly called "information in war."

When information itself becomes the means of conflict, that is, when
information becomes the target of nonlethal techniques or when information attacks other information targets, particularly targets like the enemy
population's beliefs, enemy leadership beliefs, economic information
systems, or political information systems, a purer form of Information
Warfare, or simply "information war," results. This purer form removes
the dominance of Industrial Age components from warfare and is fought
not on the traditional battlefield but in the global realm of battlespace.

The purer form of information war can serve as a deterrent to traditional forms of war, but if deterrence fails, traditional forms and forces
must be called upon to fight. These traditional forces will have the advantages gained through information in war. During the traditional
battlefield fight, national resources and some theater assets will continue
their information war in battlespace. Some take comfort in the knowledge that the United States retains the most powerful conventional force.
But since the buy-in costs of the purer forms of information war are
relatively low and the potential consequences are relatively high (and in
some scenarios extremely insidious), potential enemies of the United
States are likely to eschew the traditional battlefield for the potential of a
battlespace attack.

Winn Schwartau's second edition of *Information Warfare* examines
Information Warfare in its broadest context. While Winn has worked
tirelessly to bring the diverse aspects of this burgeoning field to the
attention of the general public, he has also helped to eliminate the arrogance and ignorance that have interfered with scholarly and professional
discussions of this new means, increased scope, and old ends of war. He
has recognized that the world is changing in significant ways: the nuclear
brinksmanship of the Cold War is largely history; communications and
common interests are creating new centers of power and influence—
religious, ecological, and sadly, criminal and anarchistic as well; the old
sciences are giving way to the nonlinear concepts of chaos and complexity; and global media networks are changing both popular and diplo-

matic views of the world. Without doubt, the concerns and capabilities of the future can best be addressed through the continued sharing of information and insights between the private and public sectors and the hard work of individuals dedicated to the American way. This edition of *Information Warfare* admirably contributes to those ends.

John I. Alger
Dean, School of Information Warfare and Strategy
National Defense University

Dedication and Acknowledgments

My wife, Sherra, tolerates the endless hours. We've made it through 18 years of rock 'n' roll (my former life as a record engineer and producer, but that's another story) and InfoWar. She allowed me to buy the boat that I wired up for my computers and a network. My 11-year-old daughter Ashley, who won the science fair, and the math contest, and the speech competition, and who takes a college writing course and graduated as valedictorian, yet still finds time to see me when I get off the airplane. And to my son, the Adam Bomb, who conquered the deep end of the pool in between two trips overseas. Eternal thanks for the support.

And to my mom. She told me as a young lad, and I never forgot, what the Red Queen said to Alice: "You've got to believe in one unbelievable thing before breakfast every day." I do. I never fell into the box.

I would also like to thank the countless people who have helped me in the last three years, through their verbal and overt public support. To those who have brought me in behind the barbed wires and Marine guards to speak and exchange ideas and to those in the private sector who sometimes don't want to hear what I have to say. Thanks. Most of them know who they are, but my publisher is ripping this sheet out of my hands as I type it . . . sorry.

And for this very special update of *Information Warfare,* I'd like to thank all of the people who contributed to the book: those of you whose work is included and those whose work could not appear due to space limitations. You have made this book all the more valuable to readers worldwide.

But perhaps more than anyone, one person has helped make the update/revision of this book possible. That's Betty O'Hearn, my invaluable assistant. She took over the project a scant few months ago when it was still inchoate in my brain. She saw to it that the contributors contributed, apologized for me to those who didn't make it past the final cut (the publisher's, not mine!) and in general kept my life in better disorder than it would have been without her. Thank you.

Lastly, I want to thank the tens of thousands of people who have followed my work, supported it, helped massage it, criticized it, and evolved the field. Without you, all of you, none of this would have been possible.

We still have a long way to go. Let's do it.

Winn Schwartau
October 1, 1996

Prologue to the Second Edition

Let me set the stage.

The first edition of *Information Warfare* was sent to the publisher in late 1993—yeah, I know, almost three years ago—and it took another six months to hit the streets. But I didn't have a clue, not an earthly clue what was waiting for me.

I did not know that much of the military and intelligence establishment considered the term *Information Warfare* to be classified and unsuitable for the ears of a mere civilian. I did not know that much of the miliary complex was beginning a struggle to come to grips with the convergence of information systems—the military and the private sector. I just didn't know, and it didn't occur to me to ask anyone, either.

My visions of Information Warfare date back to March 1990, when I saw, in a moment of mental kundalini-like clarity (I do my best thinking standing in the shower or at the beach) the power of the individual in many ways overshadowing that of the nation-state and military. The vision crystallized and I spent the next few days outlining on paper what I had seen in my mind; how the increased complexity of our technical society breeds inherent vulnerabilities, and how those weaknesses could be exploited. I also saw how in many ways the U.S. military could be made irrelevant if an attacker chose the right weapons and methods.

It wasn't until 1994, though, that those same ideas, once criticized as being "too far out," became part of mainstream thinking within the military and even in some political circles. I recall being told by a certain former editor of a major magazine (he was fired, for good cause) that my belief in cyber-terrorism was a figment of my distorted imagination and a useless exercise in futility. Six months later he ran a cover story on Cyber Terror using my words and phrases, but he told the writers, "Don't talk to Winn." He was wrong and just afraid to admit it.

The original *Information Warfare* challenged and still challenges "in the box thinking" that so typifies the officialdom of Washington. It challenges corporate America and the world to shift its paradigm, look at things differently than they have in the past, and search for new solutions to new problems.

The challenges to new thinking I have offered sometimes find themselves right back on my doorstep. My publisher put me on a promotional tour, and I hit 17 cities in 42 hours (or so it felt). I ended up in Seattle doing some local TV show—damned if I remember which one. I talked about how Boeing had been the victim of industrial espionage attacks by the French. (See Chapter 15.) It was standard fare. I was used to it, but the federal law enforcement agencies apparently weren't.

The next week, I was home with my three-year-old, Adam (the Adam Bomb!). My wife Sherra had casually escaped with her best friend Teresa for a ladies day out. The doorbell rang. "Adam, go see who it is." I was on the phone and the Internet, and sending a fax.

He returned and said, "Bee eye."

"Huh?" I asked.

"Bee eye," he repeated.

"Hold on a sec," I barked into the phone, and I ran to the front door of my middle class ranch-style stucco home (in deparate need of a paint job) and cracked it open. "Who is it?"

"[Name withheld], FBI." He flashed a badge. My mind whirled. Joke. Friend. Hmmm. Real. Who. What did I do. Joke. Friend. I hollered, "Wait a second!" and slammed the door in his face.

I went back to my office, clicked off the Net, said goodbye to my caller, all the while wondering what the hell the FBI wanted with me. Vietnam was over and I had cut my hair. It hit me that I must have looked guilty of something. Slam the door in the face of the FBI, hide four tons of crack under my son's bed, and act casual.

Hustling back. "Hey, c'mon in," feeling guilty as sin of nothing in particular.

He came in, scanning every inch of my living room, as he had been trained. I wished *I* had read that book on how to scan and case and the one on how to look casual—my heart was pounding as if I had run 15 red lights afer committing a felony. He wanted ice water, I obliged. We sat on my white quasi-leather couch next to the blue wall my wife called "sexy," and my pulse raced. He sat there trying to make small talk, and I didn't buy it.

I knew who Name Withheld was. A Russian-chasing FBIer. What did I have to do with that? His chitchat got to be annoying already. Skirting issues, looking me in the eye for signs of deception, checking my body language for nervouness—I exhibited them all.

"WHAT THE HELL DOES HE WANT?!" my mind screamed. A half hour later, I finally asked, "Is this social or professional?" Some of my friends had been under investigation.

"Professional."

I blew a cork. "So what is it? Arrest me! What?"

He took a measured breath. The consummate pofessional. "You just did a TV show in Seattle?"

"Yeah."

"And you talked about Boeing . . ."

My blood pressure dropped 50 points. "You're here for that?" I laughed. He nodded. He didn't laugh.

"That's on page 271. Be right back." I jumped over to my office for a copy of the book. "Here!" I threw it at him. "Read it. I have a call to make."

He flipped pages.

I got off the phone. "Is this what this is all about?" Name Withheld asked.

"Boeing-wise, yes."

"Who are your sources?"

"Can't tell ya."

He nodded.

"Who sent you?" I asked.

"Some security folks. An agency who cares."

"The CIA," I suggested.

Stone silence.

"Would I be wrong if I said the CIA?"

More silence.

"Bye, Name Withheld. I have to get back to work."

He left, but we stayed friends. See what happens when you write a book?

So here's the second edition (or whatever the publisher has decided to call it). Let's bring you up to speed on a few things that have occurred in the last couple of years; sort of a high-speed time tunnel.

In the first edition, I covered a wide range of events in multiple areas, addressing the whole gamut of capabilities. At that time, late 1993, everyone still needed convincing that such things were real and were actually taking place. Even today, the vast majority of people who are not in the information security or Information Warfare fields have little knowledge of how widespread the effects of the three classes of InfoWar are.

Hackers taking down the Net. Hundreds of thousands of business, educational, governmental passwords all stolen and compromised using network sniffers and Trojan Horses. Pentagon realizes that their machines connected to the Internet are wide open (250,000+ attacks in one year), and an unclassified NATO memo underscores the military vulnerability to Computers Everywhere. OSI cowboy investigation crosses over into Secret Service areas and blows up in their faces. Phil Zimmerman, under continued scrutiny for alleged export violations, stopped and harassed by U.S. Customs for returning to his country; now he's no longer a suspect. Congresswoman Maria Cantwell (D-Microsoft) attempts to add sanity to the export issue and then loses her seat. U.S. Postal Service tries to make FedEx deliveries a crime and thinks about getting in the e-mail business. First CD-ROMS with viruses. Bombs land in the financial sector of London.

Aldrich Ames—Le Carre spy extraordinaire—is a professional hacker who broke through CIA's security systems. (It seems possible that the FBI investigation into Ames's treasonous indiscretions was successful in part because of the techniques described in Chapter 7.) In January 1994 over 100,000 New Yorkers are charged twice for their ATM withdrawals by Chemical Bank, and Lotus gets nailed for poor security in cc:mail.

1994. Hate e-mail becomes all the rage with Nazis on the Net. New York Jewish Defense League asks hackers for help to put the anti-Semites in their place—freedom of speech means nothing to the hate-monger-haters. Professional German hackers from Kohl's Project Rahab want to know more about techno-savvy hate neo-Nazi Thule Network. Al Gore, Clinton's quasi-technical mouthpiece, semi-sorta kinda maybe backpedals a little bit on Clipper. Too much fear and loathing among the voters. Then Clipper II (95) and Clipper III (96) and they still don't get it. Cyberpolitics is felt for the first time and the forever media-sensitive Ted

Kennedy shuts down his Internet connection so as not to violate campaigning ethics. (Jeez, so don't post, already!)

Hacker conventions are more fun than ever, and my latest quasifictional character, CyberChrist, shows up everywhere: I got to write two novelettes: *CyberChrist Meets Lady Luck* and *CyberChrist Bites the Big Apple.* Read 'em; they're almost X-rated but terrific insight and fun.

Mark Ludwig of virus-writing contest fame holds yet another overblown-by-the-media-without-a-clue competition; Bob Bales, head honcho of the virulently antivirus National Computer Security Association wins, even though he isn't one of the three entries. He uses the $100 prize for a romantic evening with Linda.

Not a bad start, eh?

My World War II fighter-ace/hero and cousin Bill Wells is nailed by criminal goofballs who adopt his electronic identity, run up huge bills, and leave him on the hook. He dies shortly thereafter. The ballsy wanted-by-the-FBI cyber-outlaw Kevin Mitnick assumes my electronic identity from the "we have no security Well" in California to carry out his mean-spirited diatribes and a man named Bob is thrashed about with unsubstantiated accusations of rape. The details are plentiful but the accuser remains anonymous. Bob's reputation? Shot to hell.

In June, Sherra, gets hit in a traffic incident and within days we are solicited by over 120 ambulance-chasing, bottom-sucking lawyers, who would work for a mere third of the $2 million she was sure to get. Turns out there's a list of accident victims for sale weekly. Can you believe the gall?

Two incorrigible, opportunistic attorneys arrogantly inundate the Net with 13 gazillion unwanted advertisements pitching their "Help your local immigrant get a Green Card" lawyerly services. They set back the 1995 "Lawyers Are People, Too" campaign by at least 40 years with that stunt.

Hackers contemplate declaring war on foreign countries who wage industrial espionage against the United States . . . the first shots allegedly to be fired in June 1995. Software piracy up to almost $8 billion a year and now India and China (2+ billion people) getting PCs. Think they're gonna pay a hundred bucks a crack for the privilege of using Mr. Bill's Word 6.0? Employees of the INS get caught selling thousands of work permits to illegal aliens. The Florida traffic computers have me incorrectly labeled as a criminal, thereby supporting the thesis that in Cyberspace, you are guilty until proven innocent.

Ex-CIA Officer and intelligence guru Robert Steele calls hackers a "national resource," but FBI Director Louis Freeh says it might, maybe, one day be necessary to outlaw cryptography. That goes over real well. MCI gets hit for $50 million in toll fraud by one disgruntled ex-employee who double whammies everybody by reselling the stolen telephone access codes to folks from Redondo Beach to Russia.

Phew—a very good year. But Cyber-nuts are appearing everywhere. Chapter 9 correctly predicts more chipping: some jokers make one company's keyboards display an unwanted message when typing stops, and

BIOSs are becoming suspect. The Pentium debacle. Several dozen missing transistors prove that a 586 can't divide and the IRS rejects the argument as a failure to compute taxes properly. Accidental or digital sabotage?

These bits and pieces are just a sampling of the fun and games we got to play in Cyberspace in 1994. And then there was 1995!

Media-created superhacker Kevin Mitnick is apprehended by the FBI on the East Coast. Upon arrest, he vomits on the floor. Critics and hackers alike vomit on the Tsutomu Shimamura book detailing his chase of Mitnick. There's going to be a movie deal. We'll see.

Hackers, for reasons still unknown, target me, my family, and my neighbors. Disconnected phones; changed long distance carriers; pulled telephone records at the start. They penetrate GTE's security so many times there remote access seems like a revolving door. From the hackers, I receive copies of GTE's internal networks and other confidential documents and security programs, including one called "Catch the Hacker." Then they break into jewelry store computers to screw around in credit databases. And they don't forget Florida Power. They pull up my electricity records and post them on the Internet. They unmarry my wife and me. (Silver lining? Nah.) It goes on for months and months. Then, the coup de grace. While at an adult Disney outing (there's an oxymoron), we call in to see how grandma (80), daughter (10), and son (4) are doing. Find out that someone has rewired GTE's telephone switches so that all emergency calls to the local 911 appear to come from my house. My mother and children are face-to-face with a phalanx of police, ambulance, and fire services looking for the dead or dying person or persons who had placed the emergency calls. Grandma and granddaughter look at the surprised police officer and fire marshall and say in unison, "Hackers!" The FBI is now handling the matter.

Department of Defense studies show that less than 0.25 percent of all computer break-ins are detected and reported. This suggests that for every computer break-in we know about, there are at least 400 more we don't know about. According to other government studies, the number is more like 1 in 1,000.

The Church of Scientology is embroiled in its own Information War. After ex-churchmembers post confidential, copyrighted written materials on the Net, the CoS goes after the offenders with a vengeance—legal actions in the U.S. and overseas. Someone creates "cancel poodle" to remove Usenet messages posted to alt.religion.scientology (a.r.s.) in an attempt to silence the anti-Church movement. In late May 1996, someone launched a massive Denial of Service attack against a.r.s. by spamming voluminous e-mail at it.

The Feds decide not to prosecute Phil Zimmermann for allegedly putting his cryptographic PGP code on a U.S.-based Internet server. They never give a reason why they choose not to pursue this high-profile case.

The Clinton administration flies a Clipper II flag, and it is shot full of holes well before the top of the mast. Secret FBI documents released through the Freedom of Information Act, show that internal Department of Justice thinking concurs with the majority of Net-sensitive Americans: in order for Clipper or any key escrow system to work, private encryption would have to be banned. As of June 1996 no such action takes place, but word is that such may be a next step.

Some members of Congress have grown up. Legislation for the unregulated export of commercially available cryptography is popping up all over and support is growing. Over 50 percent of DES-based products are made outside of the United States. Estimates vary, but current export rules may cost U.S. businesses several billion dollars each year.

Put on your NSA hat. Your charter is to listen in on the world to help out the U.S. Why on earth would you want to make your job any more difficult by letting cryptography loose? No, you won't stop all exports, but for all of those you do succeed in stopping (by intimidation, law, coercion, whatever) your job is that much easier.

Way back when (1989), I wrote a dissertation on how the next wave of computer viruses were going to be data viruses, not the executable ones we were used to. I showed how they would work, propagate, and so on. I was pooh-poohed, but I maintained it would come. It's no surprise in 1995 that along comes the Word for Windows Macro Virus, which infects the templates of a Word document, not the executable portion of the program. As of June 1996, this macro or data virus is the most prevalent virus around, by a factor of 10 to 50, and is spreading at least 10 times faster than any virus in history. Told you so. :-)

And then there's Java, the magnificent scripting language meant to improve performance and enhance the Web. Sounded like a great idea until you really thought about it. The premise is you access a Web site, and instead of just looking at data, Java will send you a little bitty or bigger program called an applet. These applets will then run on your machine and do whatever they were told to do when they were created. Smell a rat? How about applets that release malicious code and trash your machine? Or steal passwords? Or look at all of your activities and send the results back to Marketing Central?

Microsoft ends up in a stink because Windows 95 is supposed to scan the contents of your hard disk and send the results back to Redmond. "To provide better service only." Class I InfoWar. In May 1996, a new software program at a Chicago Bank causes a nearly $1 trillion error by accidentally depositing $824 million each into hundreds of people's accounts.

Netscape's security is cracked three times in the winter of 1995-1996 by researchers and students. The company does a terrific job of recovering and re-instilling customer confidence each time, but the events underscore that there is no such thing as perfect security. (Netscape is smart, though; it now offers rewards for cracking their schemes.) The biggest lesson, perhaps, is that if a bad guy wants to steal your credit card number, breaking the crypto on an Internet connection is not the most efficient way to go about it. The most effficient way (in the criminal sense) is to get to a database that contains thousands of credit cards; the database will probably not be encrypted. Why should I worry, about using my credit card on the Net? My liability maxes out at 50 bucks.

In April 1996, the People's Republic of China decides that the best way to protect itself against the spread of the Internet is to pass laws prohibiting pornography and social unrest on the Net. Anyone violating these laws is subject to long prison terms. Mainland Chinese Internet subscribers are forced to register with the police, and the PRC Postal Authority is to be the only distributor of Internet subscriptions. Subscribers must sign an agreement not to engage in activities "hostile to the state." The government is also banning advertising on Internet in PRC, but they will maintain Internet connections which they believe are beneficial to mainland economic development.

Singapore hopes to maintain its rigid societal control by filtering all information coming into the country. As long as there is only a single pipeline, they stand a chance. As soon as a separate connection is established, or when a satellite download capability is offered, those hopes are out the window.

At the rate things are going, the '90s are going to make the '60s look like the '50s. (*Flashback* with Dennis Hopper.)

It was two very good years. For Information Warfare, that is.

This updated version of *Information Warfare* is an important book for two reasons. (No, not because I wrote it, although I do have kids to feed.)

First, it will challenge readers to expand their thinking farther than before. I've taken the original material and supplemented it with new ideas that I hope will do what the first edition did almost three years ago: an eternity in this field.

Second, we have gotten some of the finest thinkers to submit their ideas and thoughts about Information Warfare—and not all of them agree with me. The purpose is to give you a wider view of the field without having to buy three dozen books. Some of the contributions are militarily oriented, some are op-ed pieces, some are about personal privacy . . . you'll see. The aggregate provides a wealth of opinion and facts on a subject matter that has literally exploded in the last two years.

So welcome to the challenge; please do not read *Information Warfare* and blindly accept the conclusions automatically. Go through the process. Take out a piece of paper. Make some notes. Draw arrows and lines and add your own thoughts. Use this as a starting point for your own ideas. But if you really feel the need to agree with me, feel free.

Thanks for thinking.

Winn Schwartau   http://www.info-sec.com
October 1, 1996   http://www.info-security.com
http://www.infowar.com   http://www.information-security.com

Summary of Views on IW in the IW Forum

Dr. Frederick B. Cohen, President, Management Analytics

See Info-Sec Heaven at URL http://all.net.

- The "control" leg of the C3 stool actions which inhibit the ability of an adversary to respond/react/retaliate to the actions of another relating to electronic warfare.
- Corporate/government espionage
- False information, stolen information, spoofed information, etc.
- Information-based defense planning
- Information-based gaining competitive advantage
- Information-based gaining economic advantage
- Information-based gaining political advantage
- Information-based undermining trust in religious authority
- Information-based undermining trust in government authority
- The use of information as a weapon
- Manipulate/influence/affect/disrupt
- Tool for propaganda
- Attack or defense based on a foundation of information
- Organized attacks by people with definite financial or political objectives.
- Electronic conflict in which information is a strategic asset.
- Information-based violent and nonviolent warfare/conflict
- Deliberate attempts to break stuff and kill people to further a cause
- Achieving information superiority by affecting adversary information an integrating strategy
- Warfare using intellectual capital
- Control of information
- Collection of strategies, tactics, and operations
- Controlling and securing information that can be used against others
- Day-to-day struggle to stay one step ahead of hackers
- One of the three pillars of future warfare
- Ability to make decisions and create actions at all levels of warfare
- Achieving an information advantage in the application of force
- Use of information as a weapon to wage war
- New "targets" and "weapons" in war
- Manipulate knowledge or perception
- War relating to lines of communication

TECHNOLOGIES

- EMP bombs
- Viruses
- New communications technology
- Electronic intercept

23

- False/misleading data
- Computer code
- Information and information systems
- Sniffing
- Man-in-the-middle attacks

METHODS

- C4I, EW, PSYOPS, space warfare, deception, security
- Covert activities
- Intelligence activities
- State-sponsored terrorism
- Industrial espionage
- Deception (including social engineering, masquerade, spoofing)
- Propaganda
- Hacking and phreaking
- Cracking systems
- Researching public information
- Trash diving
- Intelligence activities

GOALS

- Denial, corruption, disclosure
- Confuse enemy
- Give enemy incorrect picture of battlefield
- Manipulate enemy into making a desired decision
- Cause enemy to implement non-optimum tactics or strategy
- Confuse or disable opponent
- Subtle breaking, entering, copying, trojanizing, etc.
- Protect IT from interception, disruption, and modification
- {corrupt, disrupt, leak} enemy {information, IT}
- Procure economic advantages over opposing sides
- Compromise info systems
- Tactical/strategical advantage over enemy/competition
- Manipulate decision-making process of opponent
- Bring about "political" change
- Improve mission effectiveness
- Bring operational and support elements closer together
- Gain strategic, competitive, or personal superiority over adversary
- Impact on collection and application of information in combat
- Gather and process information that could be used to better secure position in world affairs
- Gain dominance over current or anticipated opponents
- Physical, economic, political, social, racial, religious, etc.
- War on society, governments, industries, or corporations
- Affect balance of power

- Optimize use of info, info systems, and info processes
- Control information
- Obtain advantage in quest for information
- Physical, psychological, economic impact

TARGETS

- "Enemy" information systems
- Infrastructure
- Society
- C3I systems
- C4 loop of current or potential enemy
- Communications and information collection, analysis, and dissemination
- Computers and other communications and information systems
- Data and systems to analyze data
- Information-based processes
- Information systems
- Tactical information

NEW FEATURES OF INFORMATION AND IT

- We have become highly dependent
- A strategic asset to be attacked or protected
- Information dominance, dominating maneuver, and precision strike

LEVELS OF WARFARE (STRATEGIC, OPERATIONAL, TACTICAL)

- IW is simply a way to apply the evolving doctrine of warfare (primarily maneuver and unconventional/low intensity theory) to an information-based economy.
- IW is using information to one's advantage while denying it to the adversary and protecting our own systems.

Model Disclaimer to Be Added to All Candid Communications Between Former Adults

Matthew Gaylor, Electronic Frontier Foundation

In an effort to protect all who were previously considered to be adults, from those who have decided that they Are Our Parents, who have legislated Purity of Thought, you may wish to add the following to your standard message-header.

V-CHIP CONTENT WARNING: THIS POST IS RATED: R, V, NPC, RI, S, I13. [For processing by the required-by-1998 V-chips, those reading this post from an archive must set their V-chip to "42-0666." I will not be held responsible for posts incorrectly filtered out by a V-chip that has been bypassed, hot-chipped, or incorrectly programmed.]

WARNING! It has become necessary to warn potential readers of my messages before they proceed further. This warning may not fully protect me against criminal or civil proceedings, but it may be treated as a positive attempt to obey the various and increasing numbers of laws.

Under the Telecom Act of 1996, minor children (under the age of 18) may not read or handle this message under any circumstances. If you are under 18, delete this message NOW. Also, if you are developmentally disabled, irony-impaired, emotionally traumatized, schizophrenic, suffering PMS, affected by Humor Deprivation Syndrome (HDS), or under the care of a doctor, then the Telecom Act of 1996 may apply to you as well, even if you are 18. If you fall into one of these categories and are not considered competent to judge for yourself what you are reading, DELETE this message NOW.

Under the Utah Protection of Children Act of 1996, those under the age of 18 may not read this post. All residents of Utah, and Mormons elsewhere, must install the M-Chip.

Under the Protection of the Reich laws, residents of Germany may not read this post.

Under the Merciful Shielf of Allah (Praise be to Him!) holy interpretations of the Koran of the following countries (but not limited to this list), you may not read this post if you are a female of any age: Iran, Iraq, Saudi Arabia, Kuwait, United Arab Emirates, Qatar, Egypt, Jordan, Sudan, Libya, Pakistan, Afghanistan, Algeria, Lebanon, Morocco, Tunisia, Yemen, Oman, Syria, Bahrain, and the Palestinian Authority. Nonfemale persons may also be barred from reading this post, depending on the settings of your I-Chip.

Under the proposed Chinese Internet laws, covering the People's Republic of China, Formosa, Hong Kong, Macao, Malaysia, and parts of several surrounding territories, the rules are so nebulous and unspecified that I cannot say whether you are allowed to read this. Thus, you must submit any post you wish to read to your local authorities for further filtering.

In Singapore, merely by receiving this post you have violated the will of Lee Kwan Yu. Report to your local police office to receive your caning.

Finally, if you are barred from contact with the Internet, or protected by court order from being disturbed by thoughts which may disturb you, or covered by protective orders, it is up to you to adjust the settings of your V-Chip to ensure that my post does not reach you.

THANK YOU FOR YOUR PATIENCE IN COMPLYING WITH THESE LAWS.

An Introduction to Information Warfare

> *"What we have is technology, organization, and administration out of control, running for their own sake. . . . And we have turned over to this system the control and direction of everything—the natural environment, our minds, our lives."*
>
> —CHARLES REICH,
> *The Greening of America*

AT ONE POINT, if not already, you will be the victim of Information Warfare. If not you, then a member of your family or a close friend.

Your company will become a designated target of Information Warfare. If not yesterday or today, then definitely tomorrow. You will be hit.

Why? Because the United States is at war, a war that few of us have bothered to notice. The twentieth century information skirmishes, which are the prelude to global Information Warfare, have begun. Information Warfare is coming. For some, it has already arrived.

This book is about how we as citizens of both the United States and Cyberspace must come to terms with our electronic destiny, leading the world into the twenty-first century and the Information Age. We have some tough choices to make. The information revolution will not be an easy transition and the proposed National Information Infrastructure illuminates the complexity of the third generation of American dreams. But the opportunities are too great and the alternatives too grave for us to ignore. This book provides an overview defining where we are today, where we are going, and what issues we must directly confront if we wish to design our future, not be consumed by it.

As the specter of apocalyptic global warfare recedes into the history books (and stays there!), a collective sigh of complacency is replacing the bomb-shelter hysteria of the midcentury. Despite the fact that nearly 175 million people were killed in the twentieth century from the effects of war and war-related politics, Strangelovian predictions thankfully never came to pass. However, as equally dangerous international economic competition supplants megaton military intimidation, offensive pugnacity will be aimed at the informational and financial infrastructure upon which our Western economy depends.

The Cold War is over and has been replaced by economic warfare, a competition between what is shaping up to be three major trading blocks: North America, Europe, and the Asian Pacific Rim. Richard Nixon was fond of saying in the 1970s and 1980s that World War III had already begun and that it was an economic war; perhaps one that the United States was destined to lose. In retrospect, we might have been more attentive to his prescience.

These three huge economic forces account for about one quarter of the population and eighty percent of the GNP of planet Earth. The stakes are enormous and everyone wants a piece.

The foundation of modern society is based on the availability of an access to information that will drive a thriving economy upward on its course or propel a weak one into a position of power. In today's electronically interconnected world, information moves at the speed of light, is intangible, and is of immense value. Today's information is the equivalent of yesterday's factories, yet it is considerably more vulnerable.

Right now, the United States is leading the world into a globally networked society, a true Information Age where information and economic value become nearly synonymous.

With over 125 million computers inextricably tying us all together through complex land- and satellite-based communications systems, a major portion of our domestic $6 trillion economy depends upon their consistent and reliable operation. Information Warfare is an electronic conflict in which information is a strategic asset worthy of conquest or destruction. Computers and other communications and information systems become attractive first-strike targets.

As I told a Congressional Committee on June 27, 1991, "Government and commercial computer systems are so poorly protected today that they can essentially be considered defenseless—an electronic Pearl Harbor waiting to happen. As a result of inadequate security planning on the part of both the government and the private sector, the privacy of most Americans has virtually disappeared."[1]

Computers at Risk, a report published in October of 1990 by the National Research Council, clearly echoed my sentiments. The authors concluded, "The modern thief can steal more with a computer than with a gun. Tomorrow's terrorist may be able to do more damage with a keyboard than with a bomb."[2] In a recent study, two-thirds of Americans polled said that computer usage should be curtailed if their personal privacy was at risk. As a country, we are only now beginning to recognize and accept the fact that our personal and economic interests are indeed merging with our national security interests.

Information Warfare is an integral component of the new economic and political world order. Economic battles are being fought and will continue to be fought, ultimately affecting every American citizen and company as well as the national security of the United States. As terrorism now invades our shores, we can expect attacks upon not only airliners and water supplies, but upon the money supply, a sure way to strike terror into millions of people with a single keystroke.

Since World War II the United States has based its defensive position on our adversaries' capabilities, not their intentions. Voila! The arms race. However, we have not kept up with the Joneses. The world is moving into Cyberspace, but our nation's economically competitive defensive posture is still firmly landlocked.

Cyberspace is a brave new world that only luminaries such as Marshall McLuhan and Arthur C. Clarke glimpsed in their mind's eyes, but not even they could presage the uncertainties unleashed in the last two decades.

Imagine a world where information is the medium of exchange and cash is used only for pedestrian trade. A world where information, not English, German, Japanese, or Russian, is the common language. A world where the power of knowledge and information usurp the strength of military might. A world totally dependent upon new high-tech tools that make information available instantaneously to anyone, anywhere, at any time. A world where he who controls the information, controls the people. A world where electronic privacy no longer exists.

Now imagine a conflict between adversaries in which information is the prize, the spoils of war. A conflict with a winner and a loser. A conflict which turns computers into highly effective offensive weapons. A conflict which defines computers and communications systems as primary targets forced to defend themselves against deadly, invisible bullets and bombs.

Imagine rival economies battling for a widening sphere of global influence over the electronic financial highways, sparing no expense to ensure victory.

Then imagine a world made up of companies that compete and settle disputes by regularly blitzkrieging each other's information infrastructure. A world where electronic and competitive espionage are the expected manner of conducting business.

Or imagine a world in which personal revenge, retribution, getting even is only a keystroke away.

"What kind of world is this? This is the world of Information Warfare. And we, as individuals and as a country, are not prepared for the future we are creating.

In Information Warfare, Information Age weaponry will replace bombs and bullets. These weapons are no longer restricted to the Government or the CIA or KGB. Computer and communications weapons are available from catalogs, retail store fronts, and trade shows. Many can be built from hobbyist parts at home. And, of course, the military is developing its own arsenal of weapons with which to wage Information Warfare.

Information Warfare is about money. It's about the acquisition of wealth, and the denial of wealth to competitors. It breeds Information Warriors who battle across the Global Network in a game of cyberrisk.

Information Warfare is about power. He who controls the information controls the money.

Information Warfare is about fear. He who controls the information can instill fear in those who want to keep their secrets a secret. It's the fear that the Bank of New York felt when it found itself $23 billion short of cash in only one day.

Information Warfare is about arrogance, the arrogance that comes from the belief that one is committing the perfect crime.

Information Warfare is about politics. When the German government sponsors intelligence-agency hacking against U.S. computers, the concept of *ally* needs to be redefined. Or when Iran takes aim at the U.S. economy by state-sponsored counterfeiting, we should have a glimmer that conflict is not what it once was.

Information Warfare is about survival. France and Israel developed their respective economies and based entire industries on stealing American secrets. Japan and Korea purloin American technology as it comes off the drawing boards with the help of their governments.

Information Warfare is about defiance and disenfranchisement in both modern and Third World societies. From the inner cities of Cyberspace come fringe-element hackers with nothing to lose. Some will band together to form Cyberspace's gangs, Cyberspace's organized crime. They recognize the economic benefits of waging Information Warfare.

Information Warfare is about the control of information. As a society we maintain less and less control as Cyberspace expands and electronic anarchy reigns. Given global conditions of the late 1980s and 1990s, Information Warfare is inevitable. Today's planet offers ripe conditions for Information Warfare, conditions which could not have been foreseen even a few short years ago.

Information Warfare currently costs the United States an estimated $100–300 billion per year, and the financial impact on our economy increases every year. Almost 5% of our GNP slithers through the Global Network and out of our control, thereby hurting deficit reduction efforts and impacting our export base and the current trade imbalance. With billions less in commerce, lower taxable revenues and taxable assets deprive the government of its fair share of profits. As a country, more than our image is tarnished by our role as victim in the Information Wars. Our credit is less credit-worthy; our ability to buy and trade suffers; our political and diplomatic impact is reduced because our economic strength is no longer that of the unquestioned leader. We're not the only tough guy on the block anymore.

But an annual $200-plus billion loss is mainly about people, some three to eight million Americans who might otherwise be working. They, too, are the victims of Information Warfare. Information Warfare takes advantage of our reliance on, indeed our addiction to, automation and modern computerized niceties. Information Warfare attacks our very way of life.

The threat of a future computer Chernobyl is not an empty one. It is only a question of who and when. Information Warfare is available to anyone with an agenda and an attitude, and can be waged at three distinct levels of intensity, each with its own goals, methods, and targets.

Class 1: Personal Information Warfare

There is no such thing as electronic privacy. The essence of our very being is distributed across thousands of computers and data bases over which we have little or no control. From credit reports to health records, from Department of Motor Vehicles computers to court records to video rentals, from law enforcement computers to school transcripts to debit card purchases, from insurance profiles to travel histories to our personal bank finances, everything we do and have done is recorded somewhere in a digital repository.

The sad fact is that these very records which define us as an individual remain unprotected, subject to malicious modification, unauthorized disclosure, or out-and-out destruction. Social Security Administration employees have sold our innermost secrets for twenty-five dollars per name. Worse yet, as of today, there is nothing you can do to protect the digital you. You are not given the option or the opportunity to keep yourself and your family protected from electronic invasions of privacy.

Your life can be turned absolutely upside down if the digital you ceases to exist. Electronic murder in Cyberspace: You are just gone. Try proving you're alive; computers don't lie. Or if the picture of the digital you is electronically redrawn just the right way, a prince can become a pauper in microseconds. In Cyberspace, you are guilty until proven innocent.

Class 2: Corporate Information Warfare

Corporate management has little feel for just how weak and defenseless their corporate assets have become. Although the wealth of corporations is increasingly measured in the timeliness and value of their information, no company lists information assets on its balance sheet. Yet without that information, the economic stability of that company is called into question. Putting a company out of business by attacking its information systems may soon become a preferred method of economic and political competition and retribution. The weapons and techniques of Information Warfare are now as common as spreadsheets and calculators.

Corporate board rooms often take elaborate precautions to protect themselves against the statistical probability that a tornado will blow away their operations centers. The one-in-a-million chance that a flood will rage through downtown Denver prompts companies to dig into nearby mountains to build underground vaults, expected to survive a direct fifty megaton hit. What companies have not prepared themselves for, however, is a well organized offensive assault against their information systems—not by Mother Nature, but by man.

We shall discover that it is difficult to indict corporate America alone on all of these counts. The last fifteen years of spiraling growth in information processing has been and is a world-shaking revolution driven by heady technical successes and evangelical visions. Meanwhile, diligence in weighing the risks associated with placing our entire faith on a technical infrastructure remains in short supply.

As we shall see, the federal government must shoulder much of the blame for our current posture. In fact, it is often not in the government's best interest to assist us in protecting our computers and networks. Their noncommittal attitudes have even harmed efforts now under way to enhance personal privacy and commercial national economic security.

Nonetheless, inane antique policies continue unabated, and in some cases, overt attempts on the part of the federal government have further undermined the electronic privacy of every American citizen. Even President Clinton's proposal to address personal privacy and protect American businesses was met with nearly universal derision, suspicion, and doubt. No matter how hard they try, politicians just don't get it.

Class 3: Global Information Warfare

Collective Capitol Hill and White House wisdom has not yet realized that information is a vital national asset. Still thinking in terms of military throw-weight, oil reserves, Japanese cars, and illegal aliens, they miss the fundamental concepts behind the New World Order, the National Information Infrastructure, and our place in the econotechnical Global Network.

Outside of a forward-thinking few in the bowels of the Pentagon and related intelligence services, national security assets are viewed as those tangible items with a value that is concrete, quantifiable, and replaceable. Information, on the other hand, is intangible and does not have an immediately quantifiable monetary worth—unless you lose it. Then it costs a great deal more than you ever thought.

As we move into Cyberspace, we must not ignore the possibilities that an unknown future may bring. We must take off the blinders and accept—not deny—that the New World Order is full of bad guys as well as good guys. We must prepare ourselves for contingencies that we might prefer not to consider, but such planning will be necessary to our national well-being. We have to accept that as the wealth of our nation shifts from smokestack to cybercash, our once well-defined borders are now ethereal concepts with hazy delineations at best.

We will find that it is our job to prepare ourselves and future generations for a world filled with hope and possibilities we couldn't have envisioned only a decade ago, but equally fraught with dangers and obstacles also never considered. Both will be as commonplace and normal for our descendants as hot running water is for us.

In our explorations, we will unfortunately find that a well financed, dedicated adversary has the capability—and I emphasize the word capability—to wage war against nation-states and political or economic spheres of influence as never before. We will find that international conflict may well be waged on the world's information highways or on our own National Information Infrastructure. We must begin to defend ourselves now.

We must ask, then, why will information warfare be fought? Is it a foregone conclusion? A necessary component of our future? The answers are timely and unique to the Information Age and the promise of a National Information Infrastructure. We will see that Information Wars are inevitable for many reasons, given our place in history:

1. The incredibly rapid proliferation of high-quality, high-performance electronic information systems have created the Global Network—Cyberspace—thus redefining how we conduct business. Not only did business and government buy into technology, but tens of millions of individuals were, within less than a decade, suddenly empowered with tools and capabilities previously limited to a select few. The comparatively simple technology required for Information Warfare is universally available. Technological anarchy is the result.

The Global Network is a historically unprecedented highway system that defies nationalism and borders. It places the keys to the kingdom, to our wealth and our digital identity, within equal reach of everyone with a computer. *Capability* as distinct from motivation or intent is a key theme that will be repeated many times throughout this book.

2. While we as a planet withdraw from a bipolar militaristic stand off, we unexpectedly find ourselves joined by dozens of new nation-states filled with unique nation-state histories, each competing for its own identity. The failure of communism does not mean that our system of democratic capitalism automatically wins and that every newly created nation-state will adapt. There are other alternatives, and not all of them are compatible. Self-interest rides high in the early part of this decade.

The rules of the competition for global economic and political influence aren't the same for everyone. We as Americans play by an old rule book in which goodness, Mom, and apple pie define our competitive ethos. Others are less likely to stick to the outmoded Puritan ethic by which we won the Industrial Revolution. Some will willingly beg, borrow, or steal what they want, in any way that they can. Others will resort to physical violence in the pursuit of their agendas, but Americans just don't work that way. America and Americans are still often viewed as spoiled, self-indulgent brats demanding instant gratification. That image makes us inviting targets.

3. Only twenty-five percent of the planet can be considered developed, leaving several billion inhabitants in the unenviable position of being the Have Nots. The Haves are the comparatively rich countries in Western Europe, Japan, some of the Pacific Rim, and, of course, North America. The Have Nots are everyone else. With the Global Network pouring avalanches of information in the forms of text, sound, and especially visual images, across the borders to the Have Nots, the Have Nots very quickly want to become Haves. Through CNN and *Dynasty* and upscale sitcoms and global programming, the Have Nots see for themselves how we, the other half, live, and they want their share of the pie. When there's nothing to lose, there's nothing to fear. The only way is up; going after the King of the Hill—America—is an obvious route.

4. Greed is in no short supply, and few individuals, businesses, or countries are exempt. Business and governments constantly jockey for advantage over each other, often relying on less-than-legal techniques to gain an edge. With the Global Network in place, and the proliferation of technology for everyone, greed has found its way into the fingertips of people who might otherwise never commit a crime. Greed operates at all levels, and due to the vulnerability of most information systems, provides ample opportunity to exploit their weaknesses for stupendous profits. Information Warfare offers tremendous financial gain to the winner and devastation to the loser.

5. The effects of Information Warfare are unique in the annals of conflict. InfoWars can be fought by remote control,

the ringleaders comfortably invisible behind a keyboard ten thousand miles away. No longer is it necessary to intrude physically upon the intended victim's turf. The Global Network offers a million points of entry.

The computer terrorist can inflict indiscriminate damage on millions of people with a single keystroke, sowing fear, suspicion, and doubt. Information Warfare is a low-budget, high-tech vehicle for mass destruction.

6. Information Warfare is a low risk/high reward endeavor. The odds of getting caught are low, of being prosecuted lower still, and of being convicted almost nil. On the international front, countries cannot agree what to do with nuclear weapons, much less an Information Warrior sitting behind a keyboard.

7. Essentially, we don't trust computers. They process information far too fast for us to comprehend, hence we perceive them as being out of our control. Most of us don't have a clue what goes on inside of them. Yet we need computers to sustain our society. Information Warriors leverage our inherent fear and distrust of computers—Binary Schizophrenia, digital addiction, and approximation anxiety—to their advantage.

8. Last, and perhaps most important, Information Warfare will be waged because it can be. History clearly shows that any new technology, regardless of its original intentions, soon finds its way into the arsenals of the warriors; in this case, computer technology has fallen into the hands of the Information Warriors.

Information Warriors come in all shapes and colors. On the global front, the Japanese and their cameras represent the equivalent of the Army scout providing headquarters with valuable strategic information. Hackers and phone phreaks have been waging InfoWar skirmishes against corporate America and the telephone companies for years, but the recent generation of young cybernauts is more aggressive, patently echoing the ills of the society as a whole.

The Soviets, of course, were Information Warriors par excellence. Now, tens of thousands of ex-Iron Curtain intelligence agents seek to ply their trade for the highest bidder; some going as far as offering their services in the classified sections of daily newspapers.

Power-hungry dictators, radical fundamentalists, and a score of international political sects are candidates to use Cyberspace to effect their agendas. The narcoterrorists are well-financed, armed with a bevy of technical advisors, and have already taken aim at the Drug Enforcement Administration with Information Weapons.

Radical environmental groups have shown their willingness to be physically provocative and Information Warfare offers them the ability to strike out in a new, imaginative, and less personally dangerous way at oil companies, logging companies, and other groups unsympathetic to endangered species.

Information brokers and data bankers sell your name, your upper-middle-class zip code, and the date of your last underwear purchase to anyone with a floppy disk—all without your permission. Banks and credit bureaus allow computers to make decisions that affect our lives and our livelihoods based upon information that contains as much as thirty percent erroneous data—all with virtual impunity.

Anyone can be an Information Warrior. Publications such as *2600: The Hacker Quarterly* and *Phrack* provide the basic training for inductees. Cyberspace itself offers safe havens for Information Warriors to build their armies, develop their weapons, and deploy them. An unhappy worker can suddenly turn against his employer with little chance of prosecution. A government employee may moonlight as an Information Warrior, or a teenager may live in Cyberspace twenty hours a day, alighting on Earth only for Coke and pizza. A hundred million potential Information Warriors, some less friendly than others, are out there waiting, honing their skills.

Information Warfare is about capabilities, the potential

power of the individual and the potential power of an organized group. The capabilities of kids, the capabilities of
technological mercenaries, and the capabilities of nation-
states are all threats we must face. Their intentions are
secondary. If a group or an individual chooses to wreak havoc,
today they have the weapons to do exactly as they please.

What will Information Warfare look like? How will we
recognize it? How will it be waged? Who are the Information
Warriors? Where are they? What are the weapons used in
waging Information Warfare? What can they do? Where can
you buy them? What steps are the government and industry
taking to prepare for upcoming Information Wars? This book
presents disturbing answers to some very simple questions
about our personal, corporate, and national future in the
Global Network.

But *Information Warfare* also provides hope, a way out of
the technocratic quagmire in which we find ourselves. The
first step is the admission of the problem and a willingness to
apply available solutions. Personal electronic privacy can be
achieved, and national economic security is possible—if we
think these issues are important enough to address. Cyberspace is a new place to live, and one way or another, we're all
moving in. We might as well figure out how to get along, since
both our individual successes and our national strength depend upon it.

Yes, this book is about Information Warfare—how it's
waged and who will be waging it. It's also about why Information Warfare is a necessary part of our technical evolution,
especially in these troubled international times. And it is
about a proposed solution that allows us to take control of our
electronic destiny.

Outline of a National Information Policy

That solution is a National Information Policy. At present,
life in Cyberspace is subject to few rules or common sets of

accepted behavior delineating right from wrong, good from bad, or legal from illegal. We really don't even know what the definition of information is, yet our economy is based upon it. We futilely attempt to jury-rig existing old, even archaic guidelines which simply will not work in Cyberspace.

Most of us don't even know what questions need to be asked in order to create a national information policy, and that is especially true in Washington. Cyberspace is, at its purest, absolute technological anarchy, and anarchists traditionally reject government control, preferring self-restraint.

Unfortunately, self-restraint and moral responsibility are not hallmarks of the last twenty years, and as technology and information further intertwine with our existences, rules are required. But even before the rules must come the ethos and morals, and before the ethos must come the thesis.

The National Information Policy is not a specific legislative proposal for Congress to debate, but instead it is a series of substantive issues and questions that must be asked, considered, and answered satisfactorily before we can live in the Information Age with any sense of security, stability, or trust.

Who will own and operate Cyberspace and the National Information Infrastructure? How will government and industry coexist during its birth and growth? Will they or should they function as partners in the economic interest of the United States, or is that too socialistic for our taste? Is an attack against U.S. industry or economic interests the same as an attack against the country itself? On the international front, how isolationist a stance should we adapt as part of the global electronic village? And should we have the right to personal electronic privacy as we evolve in this country's third century?

The answers to these and other questions will determine how we live in the next ten to one hundred years. The answers will tell the world what kind of country we are and want to be. The answers may well define the long-term success of the U.S. economic system. Indeed, the answers will tell us who we are.

The National Information Policy provides an outline by

which to create a foundation for the future: A Constitution for Cyberspace.

Information Warfare is real; it's about time we learn what we're up against.

Let us design our future, not be its victim.

Electronic Civil Defense

Winn Schwartau

While reading this book, or reading around it from area to area, I'd like the reader to keep a thought or two in mind.

In June 1991, while testifying before Congress, I said that the United States faced a potential electronic Pearl Harbor if we didn't begin to develop policy and implement defensive procedures. I described how it would occur, and that testimony became the philosophical basis for this book.

Five years later, Attorney General Janet Reno was tasked by President Clinton to oversee efforts to create a National Policy on Cyberspace Security. In concert and cooperation with the Cabinet and intelligence leaders and a few civilians, the Department of Justice will deliver recommendations sometime in mid-1997. Their concern is what this book is all about: the electronic civil defense of the United States from electronic attack. (Other countries have or should have the same concerns.) On July 15, 1996, the President signed an executive order establishing the Commission on Critical Infrastructure Protection.

Modern societies are composed of four critical, highly interrelated, and symbiotic infrastructures upon which their national and personal survival depends:

- The power grid is the foundation of it all. We run it all on electricity, no matter how it is generated, and distribute it over a huge web of overhead wires and underground cables.
- The communications infrastructure requires power and provides the ability to distribute information content for news, education, entertainment, business transactions, and global interdependance.
- The financial infrastructure requires power and communications to permit the electronic movement of money. America's GNP is about $7 trillion, and less than 3 percent of that is in hard currency within our borders. The rest is cybercash—electronic money. Our station in the global marketplace not only rests with the reliability of U.S. systems, but also that of our trading partners worldwide.
- The transportation infrastructure requires the power, communications, and financial infrastructures to function.

So intertwined are these four foundations of American third-wave society and other late-second-wave nation-states that a hiccough in one ripples through the others. The so-called "damping factor" is a function of the resiliency and redundancy of the others and their interconnection.

Unfortunately, our built-in security and protection mechanisms are weak, to put it politely.

As Jim Settle, a friend and retired director of the FBI computer crime squad, said in a *USA Today* banner headline on June 5, 1996, "You bring me a select group of hackers and within 90 days I'll bring this country to its knees." We've all been saying this for years, and finally, the popular media is hearing what we have to say.

As you will learn in these pages, from my words and those of the experts who contributed to this work, the means to make Jim's words true are why we have to develop a National Information Policy which offers electronic civil defense.

Thank the deity of choice that we have not yet seen such an electronic Pearl Harbor launched against us or anyone else, but I maintain that our position has grown more precarious in the three years since this book was first introduced:

- There is greater connectivity.
- There is greater reliance upon the four key infrastructures.
- More people and more countries are connected.
- There are smarter people and more distributed knowledge.
- The United States has fewer friends around the globe.

In the 1950s-1960s we had a civil defense program. While we watched in horror as the atomic bombs went off on TV, we were assured that if we bent over, didn't look at the blast, grabbed our ankles, and kissed our asses goodbye, we might survive. Get into the subways. Cower by a sidewalk gutter and shield your eyes.

Today, though, we have no civil defense program to counter the vulnerabilities and threats that are either here today or on the near horizon.

Let's think about electronic civil defense for a second. Historically, for the bad guys to come after the United States, their first obstacle was formidable: the U.S. military. But how many nation-states are going to attack with a submarine in the Potomac or fly an offensive plane into San Francisco? It was not so long ago, in fact, that the model created by Colonel John Warden reigned. (See Figure 1.)

The defense of the United States was primarily conducted by the military, which protected the population and then the physical infrastructure (which would have to be bombed conventionally). Only if those were effectively bypassed could the organic essentials of the country be affected, and the leaders were the hardest to attack.

But today, that model has changed. In Figure 2, I offer an alternative model to consider.

The first attack point of the smart information warrior is going to be the weakest point, one that will collapse through attacks on its nexus affecting domino-like responses: the econo-technical infrastructure. Immediately affected thereafter is the population. Shut down, disable, or cripple components of the econo-technical infrastructure and the people

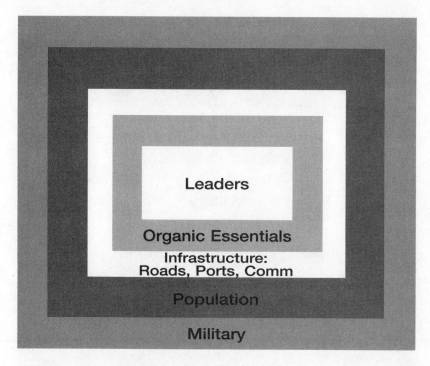

Figure 1. Warden Defensive Model

who depend upon it are immediate collateral victims. And still the military is not even in the game. In the proposed model, through other Information Warfare techniques you will learn about, the leaders are the next targets and victims. Only if the attackers so desire do they bother to go to the physical infrastructure, which brings in the military response. Why would the information warrior do it any other way?

So, meaning no offense, in this new model, unless we change our policies, the military is rendered irrelevant. In this paradigm, they have no immediate role to play in the defense of the United States. Part of our effort here, I believe, is to assist in bringing back the relevance of the military in areas which have traditionally been off limits.

Let us suppose, for the moment, that we do decide that the econotechnical infrastructure and our economic well being has been designated a national security asset worthy of protection. How do we do it, and who is responsible for taking charge? Who is to defend? Who is to protect? Who is to respond? (Too often we think that an attack against us—at the corporate or national level—is Internet-centric. I hope that after reading this book you will see that this view is myopic. There are many more efficient ways to assault a third-wave society and its econo-technical infrastructure.)

The argument as to who's in charge is a deep and potentially divisive

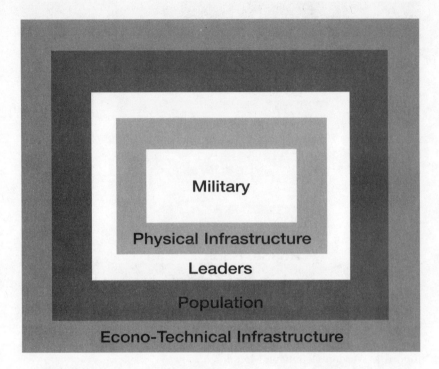

Figure 2. New Defensive Model

one, especially as the military and law enforcement and other civilian agencies fight for budgetary survival.

My belief is that electronic civil defense must be a multi-pronged program. Corporate America must step up to the plate and play as much as we might expect the government to. If we are all in this game together—which we are!—then providing for the common defense cannot be purely relegated to the government or any one agency. As citizens and corporate entities, we must accept responsibility for our own safety and security and not ask "Mother Government" to do it all.

But, from the government view, who takes the lead?

The FBI is stretched to the max. Underfunded, overworked, and with increasing caseloads, they have enough trouble handling their day-to-day tasks; and then along comes the Unabomber or Oklahoma City. Something has to give, and the threshold of pain for defense and response is raised higher and higher as more and more cyber-events occur.

FEMA cannot take it on themselves, although it has a strong history of policy and response process development. The CIA is supposed to deal with external events, the NSA is a communications powerhouse but isn't supposed to listen domestically. Similar arguments can be made against giving the lead to other agencies, including Commerce, Treasury, and so on.

From my perspective, the military is the appropriate organization to be the central coordinator for electronic civil defense. Some people within the military agree, many don't, and all make good arguments. One major hurdle that will have to be overcome is the Posse Comitatus law of 1878:

> From and after the passage of this act it shall not be lawful to employ any part of the Army of the United States, as a posse comitatus, otherwise, for the purpose of executing the laws, except in such cases and under such circumstances as such employment of said force may be expressly authorized by the Constitution or by act of Congress; and no money appropriated by this act shall be used to pay any of the expenses incurred in the employment of any troops in violation of this section and any person willfully violating the provisions of this section shall be deemed guilty of a misdemeanor and on conviction thereof shall be punished by fine not exceeding ten thousand dollars or imprisonment not to exceed two years or by both such fine and imprisonment. (From the United States Statutes at Large, Chapter 263, Sec. 15, June 18, 1878.)

The military is generally prohibited from operating within U.S. borders. But who else is there? The armed forces have huge budgets (although they may argue otherwise) and have decades of experience in organizing responses. They do, however, traditionally think in terms of bombs and bullets and bayonets, and that mental roadblock must be bypassed to create an adequate electronic civil defense.

The military has countless centers of excellence with respect to the tools and techniques outlined in this book. They have, all services added together, the best-trained, most-disciplined, and best-equipped men and women in the world to deal with domestic Information Warfare and electronic Pearl Harbors.

We have to collectively decide if we really mean that the DoD's job is to provide for the common defense of the United States and to redefine what we mean by the common defense. What portion of the common defense is the DoD responsible for?

I would argue that the DoD is the place to create a defensive cyber-force and to launch counteroffensives when deemed appropriate by the legislative and executive branches. They have the infrastructure and organization to coordinate masses of manpower and operate successfully on an interagency basis. So, in my ideal model, the Department of Justice, FEMA, and other governmental entities would function as operative arms of the DoD—under certain special conditions. I do not advocate soldiers marching through the streets with M-16s slung on their soldiers, but I do think that the Posse Comitatus Act needs revision to meet the real and future threats that we face.

The Defense Information Systems Agency has learned a tremendous amount about defensive Information Warfare; for the common defense, that knowledge and experience needs to be transferred to the private sector. But we must also ask and answer, how far into the econo-technical infrastructure does or should DoD responsibility go?

We have to keep in mind that the convergence of the military and private sectors is a reality, and that the convergence becomes more complete every day. The government and the DoD depend upon the financial infrastructure as much as the average citizen or company does. They too need water and power, and we know that 95 percent of their communications run over private lines. At what point does a domestic infrastructure attack become a direct (or indirect) assault upon the military itself, perhaps even invoking some of Colonel Warden's model?

Electronic civil defense takes on another facet when we consider how, as a country, we should operate in this new realm: reactively or proactively. Do we wait for an electronic Pearl Harbor or a minicomputer Chernobyl to occur and then react, or do we plan for it ahead of time and know what we will do under various scenarios? Our current corporate model is definitely reactive and I have heard many military leaders maintain that reactive postures are our only alternative. The econo-technical infrastructure was not built with security in mind; security is an afterthought that affects bottom-line earnings. But at what cost? Reactive or proactive defense and security will be a prime consideration in our future thinking.

I believe we need to seriously examine proactive electronic civil defense and that it requires two major leaps forward:

1. A fundamental change in thinking. We have to shift our paradigm from the physical to the virtual and operate conceptually on that level to design policy.
2. New technologies to detect and defend, which reflect the policy. Work is being done in this area, but alas, not enough yet.

Again, back to the convergence issue from the DoD perspective. In a conflict, will our adversary ignore the military front lines and instead strike at the electronic supply lines that permit our troops to operate? Perhaps our adversary might choose to cut off the unclassified communications that permit toilet paper and food to reach the front; or he might wage a denial of service attack against support infrastructures, or use a PsyOps campaign by assaulting the news and information disseminatiom mechanisms?

I do not pretend to have the answers: I merely have ideas, suggestions, and viewpoints, like all the others who are involved in this debate. And I have a lot of the questions that must be answered if we are to successfully maintain the twenty-first-century equivalent of civil defense.

Please keep these questions and conundra in mind when reading *Information Warfare*. The answers we arrive at, both policy-wise and technically, are key to our national well being.

1

The Econo-Politics of Information Warfare

"Economics is a continuation of war by other means."

—DANIEL BELL,
PARAPHRASING CLAUSEWITZ

LIKE ALL WAR, Information Warfare needs a stage, and the stage is being set as the world changes daily.

Since World War II, the United States has been the greatest military power in history, but that's just not good enough anymore. The New World Order, post August 1991, has changed all of that.

We are now the world's only superpower, having placed the former bipolar militaristic world into history. It just doesn't make sense for an enemy to assemble an assault on New York City or an air strike against Los Angeles. The stakes are too high and the rewards much too low. NORAD, our military detection system operating out of Cheyenne Mountain, Colorado, would know within seconds, and the Pentagon's response would be swift and deliberate. America would cheer loudly at the victory, again proving our invincibility. The Russians aren't coming . . . at least in the way we used to fear. We won the Cold War and now we have to help the former Evil Empire develop a healthy economy, much as we did with Germany and Japan a half century ago. The Russians no longer want to bury us. They need us too much.

China, often cited as Nostradamus's "Sleeping Giant", although a nuclear power and 1.3 billion citizens strong, is an unlikely military adversary. The Chinese just don't have the throw-weight to successfully take us on. And neither does anyone else. No person or country in their right mind—would take on the United States militarily. Nuclear annihilation or a global conflagration becomes more unlikely as each day passes. The Doomsday clock, the timepiece that measured our Cold War date with Armageddon, has all but wound down.

A military attack against France, England, or Germany would again unite forces greater than those pointed at Baghdad in 1991. NATO would then put aside political differences and crush the foolhardy opposing force. Potential global conflict between two superpowers has been replaced by regional conflicts between comparatively small ethnic and political groups. The constant upheavals in Latin America do not present a military danger to the U.S. Cuba's greatest threat is the exodus of its population to our shores. The potential exists for a nuclear exchange between Pakistan and India, indeed terrifying unto itself, but one that we could militarily handle. Similarly, any conflict with North Korea, while unthinkable to the Koreans, would be localized, nuclear weapons notwithstanding.

Even the most radical fundamentalists in the Middle East have to know that a direct assault on any of the Good Guys could mean national suicide. Saddam Hussein, with the world's fourth largest army, showed us all what the Mother of All Defeats looked like. According to historical observer David Halberstam, Winston Churchill predicted "a wizard war" for technology and the military, yet the Iraqis were stilled because they were buried in World War II mindsets. Halberstam observes, "We knew where they were, we knew who they were, and . . . we even knew how many times a day their commanders went to the bathroom."[1]

Now the U.S. has to prepare for a number of smaller wars, spread apart by oceans and continents. But the solution to regional conflicts is not a simple Bombs Away to victory. The civil war in Bosnia is a Pentagon planner's nightmare with no right answer, only the smell of another Vietnam. Washington will pick and choose our conventional conflicts and interventions very carefully. Essentially, we only go in when we know we can win quickly because America doesn't have the stomach for drawn-out wars any more. There's too much else to do.

The Pentagon faces the unenviable task of figuring out just how to successfully launch these miniwars all at the same time. A few years ago all we had to worry about was a major Soviet move; either through Europe, to the warm waters of the Arabian Gulf, or from over the North Pole with thousands of missiles. Today, while our soldiers support humanitarian efforts in Somalia, the Pentagon must worry about Cuba's civil war, Macedonia and Greece getting it on, or a dictator of the week from Latin America making a move on Mexico. All the while, we have to sustain the capability to participate in a huge desert war in the Middle East. Given the media's axiom, "If it bleeds, it leads," CNN would have trouble figuring out which war to choose for its lead story.

The Pentagon is not only redefining its role, but is thinking up new ones. The push for budget cuts in the supposedly peaceful post-Cold War era makes the military's nearly $300 billion per annum spending habits as an obvious place to slash waste.

While no one recommends closing the doors of the Pentagon, big changes are coming; it's their turn to reduce size. Spending tens of billions of dollars for B-2 bombers is of questionable value. Strategic smart bombs are in; one hundred megaton thermonuclear warheads are out. An evolution toward an interservice centralized military command is gaining momentum for good reason: it will cost less to maintain a hierarchal command structure than redundant, overlapping, and competing forces. A single command, its proponents argue, will also be more efficient when called up to take action. The military is having to adapt to the New World Order, and it will probably be the better for the change.

The New World Order, however, is not all it was cracked up

to be. In many ways, the world was a safer place when the United States and the Soviets had their differences. The lines were clearly drawn. We had our puppets, they had theirs, and we battled over which econo-political philosophy was better.

With dozens of new countries emerging, the battle lines are no longer as clear. With no more Soviet-sponsored client-states trading ideology for financial support, everyone is on his own. Marshall McLuhan predicted almost three decades ago that as the world became smaller and boundaries ceased to be clear-cut, ethnic identification would increase dramatically. The New World Order is full of nations that haven't existed in generations, many now pounding their drums of nationalism and cultural history, decrying years of enslavement, or making religious and historical claims to territory. Countries once glued together by political agreement, terror, and intimidation splinter before our eyes. The USSR alone spawned fifteen discrete nation-states, each of which is trying to recreate its heritage, develop its economy, and stand alone and proud in the world community. The break-ups of Czechoslovakia and Yugoslavia created still more separatist groups claiming sovereignty. Meanwhile African nations yo-yo between names and governments as coups mar the sub-Saharan landscape. Rand McNally must be running our of erasers.

The terrain of a country like Yugoslavia is ideal for guerrilla warfare, and our experiences in Vietnam sensitized us to the potential political fallout from embarking on a military mission where no-win scenarios abound. Occasional American military impotence is also a recognized part of the New World Order.

The New World Order is complicated, much more complicated than the world has ever been. Alliances are made and alliances are broken, with governments playing a real-life game of Risk in which the stakes are enormous. The game is less about who gets the most land than it is about pure and simple survival.

For the first time in almost two hundred years, the United States is defending its own soil. The recent spread of terrorism in the United States is causing the government to rethink dozens of policies instituted to fight the Cold War; we are, in fact, much better prepared to protect our interests overseas than on our own soil. Theodore Sorenson wrote, ". . . non-military developments can pose genuine threats to the long-term security and quality of life of American citizens as surely as armed aggression—but cannot be repelled militarily."[2]

Perhaps it is better from a public relations standpoint for the government not to talk about all of the terrorist activities occurring here, but the ones we know about are bad enough. For example, one cell of the terrorist group Abu Nidal operated in the Midwest until early 1993, when enough evidence was collected to make arrests.[3]

The World Trade Center bombing, despite early administration denials, was soon traced to Iranian-sponsored terrorism by Islamic fundamentalists. The planned bombings of the United Nations and New York City tunnels, and the assassinations of political leaders, were found to have similar religious connections. The FBI recently thwarted several little-publicized attacks by terrorists. One group was planning to shoot rocket launchers at planes coming in and out of Chicago's O'Hare airport. Another planned to poison the water supply of a major Northeastern city. Outside CIA headquarters in Langley, Virginia, a Muslim Pakistani went on a shooting spree, killing several people, in alleged retaliation for perceived American indifference to Bosnia.[4]

According to Bruce Hoffman of the Rand Corporation, terrorism "is going to join the omnipresence of crime as one of the things we have to worry about in American cities."[5] Unfortunately, he's probably right. Understanding terrorism is difficult for the Western mind. Barrages of bullets in Rome's airport, suicide missions, the murder of athletes—it just doesn't compute to us. That's why it is difficult to respond effectively without turning the United States into an armed military camp that requires identification papers to get on the subway.

In *The Anatomy of Terrorism*, David Long, a State Department expert, writes, "politically motivated terrorism invariably involves a deeply held sense of grievance over some form of injustice. . . . The immediate objective of the terrorist group is to create terror—not destruction—and then use the unreasonable fear and the resulting political disaffection it has generated among the public to intimidate governments into making political concessions in line with its political goals."[6] Most of us would agree that the World Trade Center bombing created terror, as does the threat of more such events. Long maintains that "terrorism is basically a psychological tactic, with fear and publicity two of its most important elements."[7] Killing is often merely an ancillary result, viewed by the terrorist as a necessary, understandable, and acceptable side effect. There's no arguing that had the perpetrators succeeded in destroying the Holland or Lincoln Tunnels in New York, these goals would have been met.

The motivation for domestic terrorism can be purely political. In some cases the motive is merely that the United States is a strong ally of Israel. Iraq suffered another cruise missile strike by the U.S. for plotting against the life of former President George Bush. Libya is still mad because we took them to task over their Line of Death in 1986, and we're mad because of their involvement in the bombing of the Pan Am plane downed over Lockerbee, Scotland.

International terrorism has finally landed on American soil. It's not just a headline about a European city struck again by the fanatic of the week, but about terrorists working in Denver and Des Moines, New York and Nashville, Boston, Atlanta, and San Francisco. It turns out that America's open-door policy to immigrants is part of the problem, for terrorist groups have established themselves throughout the country. In addition, American universities are hosts to tens of thousands of students, some of whom are here functioning as intelligence operatives for their governments, who may regard the United States with less than friendly intentions.

According to the FBI, two hundred former Afghan fighters

make the New York-New Jersey area home, and many of them may be doing the bidding of the anti-West Iranian government. A *New York Times* report states, "Hundreds of radical operatives live in the U.S., making up a possible loose terrorist network that includes highly trained Islamic mercenaries."[8]

Terrorists plan ahead. They move into their target-host country and establish a comprehensive network of resources, manpower, communications, and intelligence. The House Task Force on Terrorism and Unconventional Warfare has been investigating domestic terrorism for years, and their report *Terrorism in the USA* brings the subject sharply into focus. "Since the early 1980's," the report says, "there has been a concentrated effort by Iran and Syria, and to a lesser extent Libya, with extensive professional help from Cuba and North Korea, to consolidate the terrorist infrastructure in the U.S., namely, intelligence apparatus, logistical and operational support systems."[9]

The U.S. is considered a *Kufr*—a heretic infidel—and a crusading imperialist state in bed with Israel. In the *Jihad*, or Holy War, the radical Muslims view the battle with the West as one between "evil and falsehood, and truth and justice." Guess who is who.

In fact, dedicated and motivated groups of terrorists are now working within our borders. That they may strike at airports or power stations or bridges is a terrifying thought, but apparently one we will have to accept. The department of Immigration is reviewing policy that has permitted the likes of cleric Sheik Omar Abdel Rahman, the alleged link between the World Trade Center bombing and intended tunnel bombings, to enter the U.S. when his past was less than pristine. A computer error was the only Government defense.

As the specter of the Soviet Union fades, we have our work cut out for us. The FBI is reassigning its counterintelligence agents from former Iron Curtain countries to antiterrorist activities, and it's a damn good thing they are. As one Pentagon official said, "we need to improve our capabilities, to try to out-think them, to out-imagine them."[10] They are way ahead of us. David Long concurs, "The highly developed skills of many terrorist organizations in avoiding detection have made the task of carrying our criminal investigations of terrorists acts particularly difficult."[11]

According to Long, "terrorism, first and foremost, is a political problem,"[12] but upon analysis of the New World Order, it could be argued that financial considerations rank almost as high on the terrorist's list. Money fuels international terrorist activities, and has been the primary focus of some efforts. A *New York Post* headline reported "Iran's Plot to Bankrupt America."[13] According to the House Task Force on Terrorism and Unconventional Warfare, Iran and Syria printed billions of dollars in $100 bills in an attempt to bolster their own faltering economies and "to destabilize the United States's economy by undermining confidence in the dollar."[14] And the U.S. government taught them exactly how to do it. The task force noted, "The high quality $100 bills are printed in the Iranian official mint in Teheran, using equipment and know-how purchased from the United States during the reign of the Shah."[15] The task force concluded, "The governments of Iran and Syria are actively engaged in economic warfare against the United States."[16]

We find an even more unlikely partnership in the New World Order; another one aimed at the United States and the Western World. Drugs account for about forty percent of the gross national product of Lebanon, as well as a huge portion of Syria's and a significant part of Iran's. Members of the highest levels of the Syrian government are believed to have used the huge illicit drug industry in Lebanon to finance their own stability. Using their intelligence agencies and their military, these officials smuggle drugs, particularly to Europe, as a highly lucrative endeavor.

However, the Middle East is not an ideal place to grow coca leaves, which yield both cocaine and crack. Enter the Medellín drug cartel and Pablo Escobar. In 1989, at high level meetings in Cyprus, a deal was struck whereby the Colombians would provide raw materials and expertise to the Syrians and their representatives. In return, the Syrians would teach the drug cartels all about terrorism: provide the training, the tricks, and equipment so they could assume the nom-de-guerre of narcoterrorist. One of their first acts was to blow up an Avianca plane moments after it took off from Bogota Airport, killing all 107 passengers on board. The explosive used was SEMTEX, and the detonator was similar to the one used on Pan Am 103. The House task force said, "The United States has been given an ominous warning of what impact Syrian narcoterrorism may have on the West."[17]

So who or what is the target of narcoterrorism? According to Long, "Terrorism always has victims, if not physically, then through severe damage or threat to people's psychological, social, political, or economic well-being. In most instances the victims are not the real target of the terrorist attack—that is the governing authorities the terrorists are trying to intimidate—but rather symbolic targets or merely innocent bystanders who happened to be in the wrong place at the wrong time."[18]

The drug cartels are all about money. It takes billions of dollars yearly to feed America's and Europe's drug habits. In varying degrees, the DEA and the War on Drugs both threaten to interrupt the flow of cash south of the border, to which the cartels have responded angrily, instituting reigns of terror in Colombia. Even though drug dealers are summarily executed in the Muslim states, the Syrians and Iranis are happy to assist in the moral downfall of the West as part of the *Jihad*, and they can use the financial profits, too.

In this case, the two groups have found a workable synergy, a means to double their attack on the West. Their motivations and chosen methods may not necessarily be the same as other terrorists. Strategically, says Long, "each group must choose a mix of specific terrorist operations that collectively are deemed to be the most advantageous in terms of effectiveness and risk. The mix could be called the terrorist strategy of that particular group, and the operations seen as tactics in that strategy."[19]

The Economic Battlefield

The New World Order accentuates disparities in quality of life around the world, breeding two distinct and potentially adversarial groups, the Haves and the Have Nots. East-West military tensions are rapidly being replaced with Have/Have Not tensions.

In the period immediately after World War II, the U.S. economy represented fifty percent of the world's gross national product, and today it still commands a respectable twenty-five percent of same. With less than five percent of the world's population, the United States stands as both an economic and military superpower, and the West in general represents a high standard of living unattainable by seventy-five percent of the global population.[20] We are among the Haves. As a single country, we are still the world's most powerful economic force by a factor of two, but that situation is rapidly deteriorating.

Much of the New World Order is defined by the efforts by the Second and Third World countries to graduate to First World status. In the most broad terms, that means money, and of course, the money is controlled by a select few.

For true Third World countries in Africa, Asia, and Latin America, the vision of the imperialistic *yanqi* breeds envy and resentment. Global communications systems allow the poorest seventy-five percent of the world to see how America lives, and resentment runs deep. Immigrants come to us by slave boat, open dinghy, or the wheel compartment of a jumbo jet—generally at great personal risk. They want a piece of the pie that has been denied them by happenstance of birth. People who risk death to improve their station in life, and the countries they flee from, are not to be treated lightly or ignored. We cannot solve all of their problems, but they have the capacity to make their problems ours.

The planet's Have Nots feel they have little to lose, so an engagement with the West is a no-lose option. They don't want a military confrontation, but rather an economic one, and they play by their rules, not ours. The Have Nots want to become Haves at any cost. The people of South America care little about the cocaine and crack problems in American cities. Coca production is their only means of support. Offer them an alternative, and maybe they'll change their ways; but few businesses are as profitable as drugs. The late Pablo Escobar allegedly put hundreds of millions of dollars into Colombia's rural infrastructure as a means of maintaining popular support for his operations. It's about the money; it's about survival.

In *The Fourth World War*, Count de Marenches, former head of the French intelligence services, maintains that the Cold War was really World War III, and World War IV is now under way, full of new enemies. He predicts, "The Fourth World War will be a terrorist war."[21]

He views the Haves versus Have Nots from a more geographical perspective and, as is his style, without minicing words. "In the starkest terms, it [the Fourth World War] is one of South against North, poor and disorganized nations against rich, organized ones. Soon, there will be more than four billion people in these Southern nations, one billion in Africa alone, against one billion in all of the North."[22] According to Count de Marenches, the current conflict will be less polite, more violent, and less comprehensible than the recently closed chapters on the Cold War; a conflict we may soon view with fond nostalgia, just as we look back on the 1950s.

The Cold War was about money as much as it was about weapons. The United States spent trillions of dollars to defeat an erstwhile ally, but at what cost? Did we merely outspend them? Perhaps we even forced the issue. Padgett Peterson, Information Integrity specialist at Martin Marietta, a defense contractor, believes that we may have forced the Soviets to spend their economy into ruin. For example, he thinks it possible that the U.S. may have instigated the Toshiba submarine propeller incident (Toshiba was internationally censured for selling the Soviets sophisticated computer-controlled equipment that allowed their submarine propellors to operate almost silently) to force the Soviets to spend more than they could. In response, of course, the Pentagon's budget needed to be adjusted upward to counter the threat.

"History is clear," writes Lester Thurow in *Head to Head*. "While military power can sometimes outlast economic power for centuries, eventually military power depends upon having a successful economic base. America's success in the Gulf War proves that it is, and will be, a military superpower in the century to come. But its success in the Gulf in no way guarantees that it will be an economic superpower in the twenty-first century."[23]

As the world evolves into the New World Order, we must expect entirely new challenges. According to Thurow, "Economic arrangements that work in a unipolar world simply do not work in a multipolar world." What he is referring to of course, is that the United States is no longer the singular force driving the world economy. While we won the Cold War, the rest of the world prepared itself for round two—economic warfare. Richard Nixon has been making such predictions for almost twenty years.

Japan lost World War II militarily. In 1950, the Japanese economy was one twentieth the size of the U.S. In 1991 it was more than one half as large! Japan is host to the world's second largest economy and eight of the world's ten largest banks.[24] Who really won that conflict?

Europe was militarily, economically, politically, and socially devastated at the end of World War II. The Marshall Plan, however, financed by a few billion U.S.-supplied dollars succeeded beyond its designers' wildest imagination. We created our own competition. The American way: Beat 'em and build 'em.

Since 1986 the original twelve members of the European Economic Community (EEC) have been designing a New Europe, one in which trade barriers are removed between all countries, one in which an eventual monetary union will tie independent currencies together, thus lessening the disparity of its members. Western Europe's $8 trillion GNP and its 340 million people, combined with those from Middle and Eastern

Europe, create a single market in excess of 850 million people and an estimated $12-14 trillion. On the economic front, America will be dwarfed.

The New Europe is a formidable force that will have profound effects on the U.S. economy, for the rules that the Europeans and the Japanese play by aren't the same ones we use. In France, Airbus has received $20 billion in government subsidies, an advantage that Boeing and other U.S. airplane manufacturers do not share.[25] The closest American parallel to a subsidy is Pentagon spending on new military aeronautical and electronics technology. The difference is that European companies spend their government subsidies on civilian projects that benefit their people and improve their lives. We don't.

No one doubts that the emergence of three dominant economic competitors—the Far East, Europe, and the United States (with Canada and Mexico)—is a giant leap forward for mankind. Thurow writes,

> "From everyone's perspective, replacing military confrontation with an economic contest is a step forward. No one gets killed; vast resources don't have to be devoted to negative-sum activities. The winner builds the world's best product and enjoys the world's highest standard of living. The loser gets to buy some of those best products—but not as many as the winner. Relative to the military confrontations of the past century, both the winners and the losers are winners in the economic game ahead."[26]

Indeed the rules are changing.

Analyst and writer Peter Drucker says that the economic realities of the New World Order require a substantial shift in our concepts of trade and value. He refers to this as postcapitalist society which "is more likely to resemble a liquid"[27] than its crystalline forebearers such as central planning and rigid Western capitalism. The global nature of business will require a new interdependency, where alliances and panoceanic ventures become the norm. Drucker's vision for the future implies vast and almost total shifts in attitudes and perceptions. "That the new society will be both nonsocialist and a postcapitalist society is practically certain. And it is certain that its primary resource will be knowledge."[28]

NATO's presence and necessity in Europe gave the U.S. immense influence over European political and economic affairs. The Soviet threat resulting from the Warsaw Pact indirectly helped U.S. interests. Now the role historically played by NATO is not so clear. Nixon writes, "Without a military presence in Europe, we will have no voice in Europe."[29] Experts and planners have been exploring alternate NATO missions for the twenty-first century to keep America's foot in the door and our influence intact. Drucker suggests that "under conditions of modern technology, defense means a permanent wartime society and a permanent wartime economy. It means the Cold War State."[30]

On the Pacific front, the United States effectively defended Japan after World War II. According to Japan's U.S.-approved constitution the nation's $30 billion defense budget and 250 thousand-man army isn't permitted to leave Japanese soil, leaving it an impotent show of pomp without muscle. Thus, they begrudgingly paid $11 billion for the privilege of not sending troops to Desert Storm. Outside of similar regional events with United Nations or U.S. involvement, such as a conflict with North Korea, Japan doesn't need much military protection.

But bonds and alliances are formed from fear. Once the threat is gone, the alliance tends to weaken, the friendly bonds become less cohesive, perhaps more curt, less congenial. Japan and the United States have been exchanging particularly undiplomatic barbs regarding trade imbalances. We say they employ unfair trade practices; they say we haven't learned how to play the economic game where we don't have a monopoly.

Sintaro Ishihara, author of *The Japan That Can Say No*, predicts that military warfare will be replaced by economic wars in which Japan will, of course, be the winner.[31] An old Japanese adage succinctly sums up the attitude of their economically pugilistic society: **Business is War.**

German Chancellor Helmut Kohl threw down the gauntlet and essentially declared economic war against the Japanese in a televised speech in which he maintained, "The 1990's will be the decade of the Europeans and not that of the Japanese."[32]

The three schools of capitalism will also be competing in style as much as in form. The Japanese business style is monopolistic in nature. Interlocking and mutually supporting business relationships controlled by a few megacorporations are known as *keiretsu*. A handful of companies, in concert with MITI, the Japanese government's trade organization, run the industrial sector of the country with market domination and economic control as a highly focused aim. Recent downturns in the Japanese economy, though, have shown their wealth is as much a function of world economic health as ours. Time will tell.

In Europe, banks own businesses and defend their industries from undesirable foreign ownership. In the United States, both of these activities are illegal. They are violations of both antitrust and banking laws. Foreign governments invest heavily in their domestic industries, whereas the U.S. is weak in such direct investment. Our system is more of a free-for-all, a Wild West competition until it gets too wild and the federal government steps in. However, it tends to do so very selectively. It will only get involved when the going gets real rough, as it did when it came to the aid of the nearly-bankrupt Chrysler in the early 1980s, when it broke up AT&T, or when it investigated possible antitrust action against Microsoft. Otherwise, the concept of a centrally managed economy or centralized national policies have not been part of Washington's lexicon since the Great Depression. How Bill Clinton fares with his centrist views on federal economic stimuli has yet to be seen. In the meantime, the three systems of practicing healthy capitalism are vastly different, the rules of the game are not consistent, the playing field is not level, and the outcome is suddenly not so sure as we would like to pretend.

Not only are the published rules of the economic game skewed against the United States (the European and the Japanese systems are philosophically closer to each others than to ours), but the not often discussed rules of engagement are different. The morals and ethics of business vary widely from country to country, company to company, and from individual to individual. As we will see, industrial espionage is real. Just because you wear a white hat doesn't mean that you can't cheat. And in the global economy, cheating is more widespread than crib sheets in high school.

Lester Thurow quotes France's Edith Cresson as saying, "Japan is an adversary that doesn't play by the rules and has an absolute desire to conquer the world. You have to be naive or blind not to recognize that."[33] What she doesn't say is that the French break quite a few rules themselves. We have been blind, as Cresson suggests. We have been so preoccupied with immediate military invincibility that, with relatively few exceptions, we have allowed our economy to erode without noticing until it has reached a critical point. Outspending the Soviets may be viewed as a very stupid move by future historians.

Nonetheless, the United States needs to make a fundamental decision; a decision which will set the tone for the next century. We need to decide if the American economy is a strategic asset of the United States. We must decide if domestic economic concerns are an issue of national security. Do we have the political flexibility, the acute foresightedness, to realize and act upon the premise that a defensive economic posture is as critical to this country as is our military defensive posture? If not, our two formidable competitors will likely have a field day buying up America, just as Japan bought Rockefeller Center and Michael Jackson.

Occasionally, Congress will get involved and question the sale of Fairchild to Fujitsu or Loral to the French. But a thorough and complete laissez-faire regard—or disregard—for the importance of the economy to our national security bodes ill for the future. Our style of individualistic capitalism, largely free from socialistic-smelling government intervention, may be inadequate for the challenge.

The economic battlefield, as we will learn, is unique. Gun-toting armies will not sail into San Francisco Bay and announce victory. We know how to deal with that contingency. Rather, business-suited visitors invade with better products at cheaper prices. The guy who can build the best mousetrap at the best price sells the most mousetraps, yet now we're importing the mousetraps that we originally invented. We discover that we have indiscriminately given away industry after industry to foreign interests; from steel to electronics to home entertainment to automobiles, we have lost countless trillions of dollars due to political and fiscal mismanagement.

Any domestic business that has been hard hit by imported products has learned this lesson well, yet it seems to have escaped the notice of Washington. Extreme political positions such as those espoused by presidential also-ran Pat Buchanan reek of the fiascoes caused by historically damned protectionism. According to former President Nixon, "Had we engaged in Europe, rather than sulking in isolation after World War I, we could have tipped the balance of power against the aggressors, possibly deterring rather than fighting World War II."[34] We face similar questions today that require better answers than those provided in the past. We must be aggressive players on the global economic field if we are to maintain power and influence on the world scene in the future.

So which is right? Are we going to be constantly battling in regional military conflicts, thereby justifying large expenditures to maintain America's national security? Or should we realign our priorities and concentrate on economic competition instead? I believe that you will find, as I have, that the two are synonymous and, if we are to be successful, we have to address both as part of a more comprehensive world view. We need to identify and maintain that delicate balance which reflects the realities of the New World Order and the economic dynamics that will increasingly drive successes and failures across all national, cultural, or ideological boundaries.

That new reality should certainly include the obvious but by no means trivial observation that we can expect a lot of cheating by everyone involved. Generally speaking both Japanese and European organizations have admitted that they cheat for economic survival. The Soviets have admitted extensive cheating. Their space shuttle, for example, bears striking resemblance to ours. And well it should, considering they acquired (both legally and illegally) the results of billions of dollars of U.S. taxpayer-sponsored space research. The Russians, when asked if they are still cheating, offer circumspect and suspect answers. Of course they are; it's in their economic interest to do so.

And what is the goal of all of this cheating?

Information.

Information is what makes both the Old and the New World Order go around. Information is what gives one player an advantage over the others. In military-speak, information about the enemy's capabilities, positions, strengths, and weaknesses is crucial in determining political stances and military responses.

On a global scale, knowing what the other guy is planning gives you a leg up; you are better prepared to respond or react or subvert. With KH-series spy satellites that can read a license plate from high in orbit, the U.S. knows which training camp in the Sahara Desert is preparing terrorists for which organization. Our satellite surveillance is second to none.

For decades, spies from the CIA, the KGB, MI6, and from other groups who don't "officially" exist have lived in the pursuit of a single commodity: information. Information is a commodity to be bartered for a comrade's freedom or exchanged for other information. We're in a giant game of Monopoly, in which information is the medium of exchange.

The Cold War generated war stories and tall tales of cloak and dagger adventures that spawned an industry of spy thrillers from the likes of John LeCarre, Ian Fleming, and Robert Ludlam. Yet again, the key was information, as readers of *Mad* magazine, which regularly satired the antics of government espionage in its comic department "Spy Vs. Spy" may recall.

Spies have been around forever, gathering information for the other side. During the Revolutionary War, Benedict Arnold sold out West Point for twenty thousand British pounds. Two hundred years later, John Walker sold priceless military information to the Soviets over a period of seventeen years for mere thousands of dollars. Russian spying once maintained an active entourage of 900,000 for the KGB and GRU, both of which were tasked with stealing different types of information. Almost a million people were keeping tabs on anything and everything they deemed valuable.

Writer Ronald Kessler said in *Spy Versus Spy*, "Unlike the KGB, which seeks economic, political, military, and scientific information, the GRU or Chief Intelligence Directorate of the Soviet General Staff . . . focuses only on military secrets."[35] The Soviets were dead serious in their aim to get hold of sensitive U.S. information.

The U.S. spying machine is anemic in comparison. Richard Nixon ought to know. "The entire U.S. intelligence community—which includes not only the CIA but also the Defense Intelligence Agency, the National Security Agency, parts of the Federal Bureau of Investigation, and other agencies—employs approximately 35,000 people."[36]

So what does this say about our preparedness for an economic competition where spying is the dominant form of cheating? It suggests that we are sadly ill-prepared. Perhaps the Lone Ranger syndrome is at fault. As a people, we want to win, but we want to do it honestly. We want to see ourselves as the good guys, the white hats, the cavalry to the rescue. We can't resort to the same dastardly techniques that the bad guys use. It's not sporting; it's not next to Godliness. Such out-

moded and self-denying attitudes invite failure in the economic battleground of the New World Order.

Despite secret intelligence operatives and so-called "black"
budgets, our intelligence services are vastly outnumbered and
outspent by not only the Russians, but by intelligence services
from every major country from Israel to Korea. No wonder
U.S.-developed technology shows up in every corner of the
planet. Nixon comments, "In the 1930's, the Kremlin sought to
boost the Soviet economy by stealing scientific knowledge and
technologies—from basic research to blueprints for turnkey
factories—through spies."[37] It seems that whatever we build,
someone else wants—and gets—for free. That's where it all
begins.

In the truest sense of the word, the CIA and other domestic
and international alphabet soup intelligence agencies wage a
distinct form of Information Warfare. Spies are the original
Information Warriors, and membership in their club is indeed
exclusive. The Soviets were obviously less picky but more
motivated; they recruited twenty-five times as many active
participants as we did.

The Soviet spying machine was well-financed, and was
clear and concise in its mission. "The CIA reported that in the
early 1980s, Soviet intelligence services targeted 3,500 items
annually. The KGB Directorate T orchestrated efforts that
secured about one-third of these items every year."[38]

On the espionage front, a transition was and is still
occurring. The information being sought now focuses less on
the military than in the confrontational past. Nonmilitary,
civilian technologies, products, and processes are now the
targets. And it seems like everyone wants to play.

But herein is a difficult conundrum to resolve.

Since World War II, the Pentagon has based the U.S.
defensive posture on a single overriding premise, a potential
adversary's capabilities, not their presumed intention. National Security Advisor Brent Scowcroft, former-President
Nixon, and a host of others may use slightly different words to
describe that thinking, but essentially the U.S. continues to

structure its defense policies upon that premise. While we have successfully implemented that dogma militarily, our obviously fatal flaw is in failing to expand that strategy to include our national economic interests. We can contend with a madman in the desert (sort of) and build invisible aircraft (sort of), but we have done precious little to aggressively protect the economic well-being of this country.

We tend to think in either military or economic terms instead of recognizing the synergy of the two, and treating them as a single concept as our adversaries have. William Sessions, former director of the FBI, addressed the need to do so when he said to a House Justice subcommittee, "Now and in the future, the collection strategies of adversaries and allies alike will not only focus on defense-related information, but also include scientific, technological, political, and economic information. [Soviet and Russian] defectors . . . predicted that the new independent states will escalate industrial espionage activities in the years ahead to bolster their economies and foster increased technological progress."[39]

If we apply military thinking to economic competition, cheating covers a much wider scope than industrial espionage. Information, disinformation, extortion, blackmail, destruction, or other means of overt economic disruption must be anticipated. The weapons that will be used to effect a national or corporate economic advantage are ideally tailored to their purpose and we again find ourselves on the short end of the stick. Simply put, the United States is not ready to defend itself or its economic interests against a dedicated Information Warrior or economic aggressor. From a military perspective, our economic vulnerability is patently unacceptable.

As we meander through the world of Information Warfare, we shall see that the government and its nonelected guardians of information have been entirely too protective of their turfs. Under the guise of national security, they have kept critical basic information out of the hands of the American public. This information can be used to defend a business or a technology or to provide the means by which a U.S. company can level the playing field with a few dirty tricks of its own.

But first, we need to understand just how dependent we are upon computers, just how incredibly and invisibly prevalent they are in our everyday lives. Only then can we appreciate the attractiveness of information systems as targets and the magnitude of our personal, corporate, and national vulnerability to Information Warfare.

2

Computers Everywhere and the Global Network

"I see a world wide market for about three computers."

—JAMES T. WATSON, 1947, CHAIRMAN OF IBM

"There is no reason for any individual to have a computer in their home."

—KEN OLSEN, FORMER PRESIDENT OF DIGITAL EQUIPMENT CORP.
AT THE WORLD FUTURE SOCIETY IN 1977.[1]

DESPITE THE PREDICTIONS ABOVE, there are 125 million computers out there and more coming.

With the world's econo-political situation neatly providing the required ingredients for Information Warfare, what we need now is a battlefield, the place where rivals wage the skirmishes and full-scale attacks.

That battlefield is call Cyberspace.

Cyberspace is that intangible place between computers where information momentarily exists on its route from one end of the global network to the other. When little Ashley calls Grandmother, they are speaking in Cyberspace, the place between the phones. Cyberspace is the ethereal reality, an infinity of electrons speeding down copper or glass fibers at the speed of light from one point to another. Cyberspace includes the air waves vibrating with cellular, microwave, and satellite communications. We are all wired together in dozens of ways on the Global Network and are thus an integral part of Cyberspace. According to John Perry Barlow, cofounder of Electronic Frontier Foundation, Cyberspace is where all of our money is, except for the cash in our pocket.

Putting aside for a moment the business, government, and econotechnical infrastructure, let's see just how computerized our life has become.

An estimated three billion computers run every aspect of our lives. These computers aren't quite so obvious to us because they tend to be invisibly enmeshed into the fabric of daily chores. These billions of computers, plus the hundred million-plus business-oriented computer systems, are what we call Computers Everywhere. They are indeed everywhere. You can't ride an elevator, microwave food, or watch Vanna White flip letters without interacting with a computer. There's a little computer running nearly everything we touch these days. How many tens of millions of VCRs have been made? TV sets aren't just a couple of knobs and an antenna anymore. Programming your viewing habits is crucial to their operation and your mental well-being. Specialized computers run them as well as their companion video cameras and their brethren, the automatic no-need-to-focus-just-press-the-button point-and-shoot still cameras. Washers and dryers are programmed by Mr. or Mrs. or Ms. Mom at an exact temperature to the microsecond, and the appliances' internal computers respond on command. Mortgages, utility bills, Home Shopping Network—it's all done by computer. Computers run the Department of Motor Vehicles, Social Security, hospitals, doctors. Even our family vet is fully networked. Book an airline, reserve a hotel room, or go to Disneyland, and you talk to a computer. We can no longer ignore the impact of Computers Everywhere on Everyman and Everywoman.

Wherever we go, there's a computer somewhere inside. Have you ridden in a taxi and asked for a receipt lately? The computerized meters have calculators with tiny little printers and are so simple to use that they don't require an instruction manual. Even cash registers are driven by a powerful computer chip. Credit cards are read for authorization by a digital reader, just like bank cards are read by the ATM machine.

Here is an interesting exercise to try. Sit back and think about how much in your life is computerized. How often do you interact with a computer? Fax machines? Electronic car ignitions? High-end digital cassette machines? What about hand held calculators? Home security systems? God knows how many of the kids' toys are computerized. I count nineteen computers in my family and we don't even have Nintendo. (Nintendo alone accounts for almost ten percent of Japan's chip production.) How many hundreds of millions of computers does that make? If you add clock radios, Mr. Coffees, digital watches, sprinkler timers, oven timers, and street lights, you add a billion or so additional computers to your list.

My mother has three VCRs, each run by its own internal computer. Her new five-disc CD player can do a random search and is programmable for hours of customized listening pleasure. She has two programmable clock radios, an answering machine, a digital microwave, two remote control televisions, an automatic 35mm camera, a digital water-softening system, "smart" hot water heater cycling, a programmable sprinkler system, and her own 286-class computer. Let's see, that's fifteen computer-controlled devices in her two-bedroom condo and that doesn't even include her assortment of calculators.

Her interaction with Computers Everywhere doesn't stop there. Mom had to learn how to use an ATM machine. In retirement communities, the ATMs actually speak in English to help customers find their way through all of the options. Weights and measures at the grocery store are measured to the nearest 1/1000 of a pound on digital scales, and bar codes tell the cash register how much to charge for Charmin. When she purchases an item from the Home Shopping Network, she interacts with "Tootie," the order-taking computer, instead of a live person. Billions of computers are invisibly embedded in almost everything we do.

Computers Everywhere

On the other hand, some pretty humongous computers live in Cyberspace, ones with which we communicate every day.

Our telephone system—The Phone Company, henceforth TPC for short—is just a huge computer-controlled electronic switch, albeit a fancy one, with hundreds of millions of terminals (phones) worldwide. The telephone gives you incredible power. You can tell this immense computer to make anybody's phone ring, anywhere in the whole world. And how many people do you know who went to school to learn how to use a phone? The biggest computer system in the world is also the easiest to use.

The telephone is not marketed as a computer. It is sold as a tool, a necessity of life. There is no computer phobia to overcome. Telephones just work, most of the time. Just plug it in and dial away. Nonetheless, at the heart of it all lie super powerful computers. (Of course transitions, such as to touch-tone dialing in the 1960s, were not entirely painless for everybody. Touchtones didn't have the same weight and feel as the older phones, creating some generational resistance.)

Is there a major company in the world that doesn't force you to talk to its computer before you can speak with a real live human being? The miracle of voice mail has produced more disgusted hang-ups than all of the telephone answering machines ever built, which, we must remember, were also originally met with horror due to their impersonality. Making airline reservations can be a frustrating exercise for those of us with fewer brain cells than we were born with: "Thank you for calling Honest-We'll-Be-Here-Tomorrow Airlines. To speed your request, please use this automated attendant. Press 1 for international flight arrival times; Press 2 for international flight departures, Press 3 for domestic flight arrival times, Press 4 for domestic . . ." and by the time 9 comes around, you have forgotten what 1 was, and you either have to call back or figure out which button will start the whole list over again. So what do you do the next time? Write it all down on paper. With a pencil. Rather ironic, isn't it? Once that gauntlet is traversed, selecting flight information is a breeze if you know the flight number, the date, and the airline city codes. Just type them into your phone. . . .

I still prefer a polite voice which, in three seconds or less, can tell me how late the eight o'clock flight from New York is going to be. Call me old fashioned.

Customer service organizations are the worst. They never give you the option you want. It never fails: "Thank you for calling Appliance Conglomerate of America. This is your automated information attendant. Please wait until you have heard all of the options before making your selection. Press 1 for toasters, Press 2 for microwave ovens, Press 3 for convection ovens, Press 4 for popcorn poppers . . . Press 64 for refrigerator condensers. . . ."

Then they put you on hold.

And what about "smart cards"? A smart card is about the size and shape of your favorite American Express card with a little tiny computer built into each one. Our wallets will soon be filled with half-a-dozen or more of these little computers that will allow us, as humans, to interact with the computers that run the companies and organizations with whom we deal: Go to the grocery store and whip out a Computerized Winn Dixie Debit Card that will immediately debit the correct amount from your bank account. (Better keep track of that sucker!) A Nynex Computer Phone Card will soon be required, as both a cost-saving measure and a deterrent to crime, to make a call from a pay phone.

Smart cards will become the electronic equivalent of a social security number, which by the way, will be emblazoned in the silicon guts of your personal smart cards. The memory circuits will know all about you, perhaps including a medical history, personal and family information, driving records, identification for all of the financial institutions with which you deal, and an emergency savings account.

At the heart of President Clinton's health plan is a smart card that has privacy advocates up in arms fearing even further erosion of what little remains of our personal electronic privacy.

Computers Everywhere will only increase.

The Global Network

Sometime in the last few years—we have no exact date—
the Global Network was born.

The Global Network is the offspring of Computers Everywhere. Some cybernauts maintain that the existence of Computers Everywhere begat the union of information systems to
each other, that the Global Network was a foregone evolutionary conclusion. Others might argue that the Global Network
is an interspecies offspring: one parent is the do-nothing-
without-being-told silicon life form of digital electronics and
the other is the highly evolved, cognizant, carbon-based cybernaut. Others hold a purely technocratic view and think that
attributing personality to information systems is the mark of a
madman. In any event, at one point, the Global Network
started to take on a form, a shape, a texture—a look and a feel,
if you will. The exact date of birth is immaterial, for today the
Global Network, still in its formative infancy, is a living,
breathing entity on planet Earth as much as we are.

Our reliance on the Global Network has become so immense that if the entire Network were turned off, we would
literally die. From that perspective, we and the Global Network have become symbiotic. We need it to survive and it
wants to grow.

The Global Network is the interconnecting tissue of Computers Everywhere. The Global Network is a form of Cyberspace, a place where one can travel electronically, projecting
one's being to any place on the planet. The Global Network is
the ability to connect any computer to any other computer or
connect any person to any other person. The Global Network
is instantaneous communications anywhere—by voice, video,
or data. The Global Network is The Phone Company. It is
satellites, modems, faxes, cable television, interactive television, dial-a-poll politics, home shopping, cellular phones and
Wrist-Man television. The Global Network is instant feedback
and instant gratification.

The concept of "life" for computers and software was first

conceived in automaton theory, which was pioneered by the early computer genius John Von Neumann. Its simple, albeit controversial, premise is that software and computing machines are really life forms with whom we cohabit on planet Earth.

Artificial life (or "a-life") researchers have been trying for years to come up with schemes to create a workable silicon-based imitation of the human brain, thus the intense work today on brainlike neural networks that have the ability to learn. But, is that life?

One argument maintains it is only human prejudice that insists life forms must be carbon-based, breathing creations. A more liberal view would include crystals, which do indeed meet a broader definition of life. Software programs definitely exhibit attributes of life. A self-running graphics program can be instructed to behave in certain ways. It can be told to move one inch to the left, then one to the right, add an arm or leg to the image, or whatever the programmer dreams up. When left to run on its own, the antics on the screen do in fact echo many of nature's life forms, such as reef growth.

To most a-life researchers, life can be based on mathematical formulas and software programs, as well as on carbon or silicon. What matters is the activity, not the materials involved.[2] Although images of Frankensteinian software running amok down Main Street are the products of over-active imaginations, a-life certainly does conjure up some possibilities for the Information Warrior.

Robotics will most assuredly contain arguable degrees of a-life, and perhaps that is where the Mary Shelley parallel is most likely to arise. No one can tell where a-life is going, but groups such as the Santa Fe Institute in New Mexico spend a great deal of time thinking about such things.

A clear distinction between artificial life and artificial intelligence must be made. True AI, Artificial Intelligence, can be considered a form of artificial life, but artificial life would not necessarily be considered artificial intelligence. Douglas

Hofstadter condenses the salient requirements for life to exist quite admirably.

> No one knows where the borderline between non-intelligent and intelligent behavior lies; in fact, to suggest that a sharp borderline exists is probably silly. But essential abilities for intelligence are certain:
>   to respond to situations with flexibility;
>   to take advantage of fortuitous circumstances;
>   to make sense out of ambiguous or contradictory messages;
>   to recognize the relative importance of different elements of a situation;
>   to find similarities between situations despite differences which might separate them;
>   to draw distinctions between situations despite similarities which may link them;
>   to synthesize new concepts by taking old concepts and putting them together in new ways;
>   to come up with ideas which are novel.[3]

No one classes an amoeba with a Mensa member (there's a joke there somewhere), but no one would deny that an amoeba is a life form. One must then look at the Global Network for a moment and ask: are any of these capabilities applicable to a computer network? Those cybernauts who assign the attributes of living beings to the Global Network would say yes, the Global Network is in its infancy and it is still learning.

The biological parallels are quite evident. Each individual element of a network can perform certain tasks alone without the help of its neighbors. Each tentacle of the Global Network, after all, is a computer in its own right, each designed to execute specific tasks in specific ways. In addition, much like its biological counterpart, when vast numbers of computers are interconnected, Buckminster Fuller's concept of synergy applies:

Synergy means behavior of whole systems unpredicted by the behavior of their parts taken separately. Synergy means behavior of integral, aggregate, whole systems unpredicted by behaviors of any of their components or subassemblies of their components taken separately from the whole.[4]

Two heads are better than one. Brainstorming, think tanks, free association—all are forms of mental synergy. In a synergistic world, 2 plus 2 could equal 5 or 6 or 300 or 3.14159 or whatever. Synergy plays a vital part in the development of Information Warfare.

When the personal computer was invented, there was no way to predict that the world would be transformed as dramatically as it has in a mere decade. A very few academics and futurists certainly had a glimmer of the possibilities, but even today, mainstreamers have trouble realizing that new technologies and the continued expansion of the Global Network will have even more profound effects on modern society, in ways we cannot begin to fathom.

Thus, the Network-is-a-Lifeform cybernauts maintain it was impossible a decade ago to predict that Cyberspace would be populated with millions of people spanning the globe. It was impossible to predict that various new subcultures would arise, many of which are distinctly at odds with the establishment's way of thinking. Chaos at work.

Today's Global Network is like a baby's brain, an evolving neural network in which the connections grow and multiply. Indeed, a neural network that grows connections is said to "learn," and the same argument can be made for the Global Network.

In the novel *Terminal Compromise,* a Dutch hacker makes the point:

"Ya," Dutchman laughed. "So as the millions of neural connections are made, some people learn skills that others don't and some computers are better suited to certain tasks than others. And now there's a global neural network growing across the face of the planet. Millions more computers are added and we connect them together, until any computer can talk to any other computer. Ya, the Spook is very much right. The Network is alive, and it is still learning.[5]

A first-time mother soon finds out that her new baby doesn't come with a user manual. She has to figure it out herself—determine what's right, what's wrong, what's best for the child—but she can get help by asking others and learning from their experiences.

The same goes for the Global Network.

No one knows what the infant Global Network will look like when it grows up, but we can hypothesize for a moment.

An Apple II cost $3,000 in 1980. The first IBM personal computer with no hard disk and a mere 64K of memory also cost $3,000. The first 286 class machines cost $3,000. Computers double in power roughly every eighteen months. So, eighteen months from now, a computer costing $1,000 will be twice as powerful as a similarly priced machine today. In a decade, the same $1,000 will likely buy a computer 128 times as powerful as you can buy today.

What can we expect? Virtual reality piped into every home computer. Cyberpsych, an electronic noningestible drug that rings of Woody Allen's orgasmatron in *Sleeper*. "Reach out and touch someone" morphs into the twenty-first century. Meanwhile Marshall McLuhan's adage, "The medium is the message" is the cybernauts' motto. The medium, of course, is Cyberspace and most of us haven't gotten the message yet.

On the downside, all of this computerization can cause a severe headache, Carpal Tunnel Syndrome, the need for bifocals, or a number of other maladies that are only now being associated with the incredible proliferation of computers and the number of people who sit at their terminals for hours and weeks and years on end.

The psychological impact of Computers Everywhere and the Global Network on society and individuals is not quite so obvious. We have to learn to live with the new life forms that the cybernauts proclaim exist. Or at least, we must learn to coexist with information systems that are impossible to avoid.

Welcome to the Information Age

It is easy to make a strong case that the Information Age is here and it is also easy to argue that the best is yet to come. "Wait till you see what we come up with next!" the silicon saviors accurately promise. But we have to admit we have already arrived in the Information Age, that magically mysterious era that provides our daily amenities, our pleasures, and our livelihoods at the push of a button, and that it is no longer a distant goal. The first day of the Information Age was that day when our dependence upon computers and communications systems and high-tech gadgetry exceeded our ability to live without them.

Our graduation into the Information Age, whenever that was, spawned complex reactions. For a society whose very existence requires the reliable and continued operation of countless millions of interconnected computers, communications systems, networks, and satellites, we have been derelict in technointrospection.

The technological evangelists of the 1980s promised fabulous futures, with smaller and friendlier and ever more powerful calculating machines, machines which would enrich our lives beyond the wildest dreams of the previous generation. So we bought in, we plunged enthusiastically into the uncharted realms of Cyberspace. We invested hundreds of billions of dollars in a twenty-first century utopian vision shaped by Apple Computers founder Steve Jobs, Microsoft's Bill Gates, and a handful of others—the rightful heirs of English computer patriarch Charles Babbage. The American captivation with successful entrepreneurship and sexy-high-tech toys, as well as Baby Boomer desire for self-indulgence and instant gratification, permitted virtually unbridled growth of systems which we handed control of our day-to-day lives. We didn't see what was happening because the evangelists neglected the downside of their vision. What we didn't hear then, and still don't hear today, is that omnipresent automation may not be all it's cracked up to be.

Since the fifties, automated systems have crept into big business, causing a very subtle shift to occur, one that we still do not fully understand. Value used to be based exclusively upon tangible assets. The company had desks and inventory and buildings and a factory, and those established its worth. Wealth was based upon the gold standard and could be established internationally with little division.

But a mere forty years later, the value of a company is now in its information. The formula for Coca-Cola is worth a whole lot more than one hundred Coke bottling plants. The plants can be replaced. The formula cannot. Think about it: Coke's formula and countless company secrets are kept in Cyberspace, a place we still don't fully comprehend.

American business is as much in the information business as it was in the industrialization business a century ago. Dr. George A. Keyworth, II, science advisor to President Reagan and now a distinguished fellow at the Hudson Institute, wrote in a 1992 briefing paper, "We're moving increasingly toward a business environment in which information itself is the product, and in which the strategies by which businesses use information become critical elements of their success or failure."[6]

As we learn more about Information Warfare, business's reliance upon unprotected Computers Everywhere represents the largest potential threat to the economy of the United States in our history.

Computers Everywhere and the Global Network have taken their place alongside homo sapiens as residents of Planet Earth but along the way, we also transformed the essence of value, what we think of as money, into a new commodity which no one even fifty years ago would recognize.

Cybercash

Individual wealth and worth is now determined by endless zeros and ones entered into, stored upon, analyzed within, and retrieved from hundreds of computers. Virtual money, or as Joel Kurtzman calls it in his book *The Death of Money,* "megabyte money," has replaced real hard cash as the valued medium of exchange. According to Kurtzman, "Money is the network that comprises hundreds of thousands of computers of every type, wired together in places as lofty as the Federal Reserve . . . and as mundane as the thousands of gas pumps around the world outfitted to take credit and debit cards."[7] Money is stored on disk drives and tape drives where the proper combination of 1s and 0s determines one's degree of wealth.

The world's gross national product is about $27 trillion with the New World Order's tripolar economic superpowers controlling the vast amount of the planet's wealth. The United States generates about twenty-five percent of it, Japan and the Far East between seventeen and twenty-three percent, and Europe about forty percent, depending upon whom you include. A disproportionately low twenty-five percent of the population controls nearly ninety percent of the world's goods, services, and money.

One trillion dollars is a lot of money. One thousand billionaires or one million millionaires. A trillion dollars could just about build a brand new New York City, buy two thousand B2 bombers, or provide every American with $4,000. Iran's war with Iraq cost it nearly $600 billion, not quite a trillion, but an incredible amount of money nonetheless. A trillion dollars would pay off twenty-five percent of the national deficit—a start—or get Chrysler out of trouble nine hundred more times.

The $27 trillion planetary output, though, is dwarfed by a parallel economic system that is only two decades old. Behind the $27 trillion "real" economy of goods and services is a hidden, mysterious "financial" economy that rewards speculation, legalized international hedging and fudging for hundredths of a percentage point gain or loss. The financial economy is between twenty and fifty times as large as the real economy: one quadrillion dollars.

The financial economy was created on August 15, 1971, when President Richard Nixon altered the structure of global commerce to such an extent that it "represented the greatest challenge to the world economy since the Great Depression."[8] Nixon, in one swift, bold, and almost unnoticed stroke, removed the American greenback from the gold standard to which it had adhered for decades, permitting the dollar to fluctuate along with the rest of the world's currencies.

The post-World War II monetary system was based upon the July 22, 1944, Bretton Woods Agreement at which the world's major currencies were locked to the dollar, which in turn was locked to the price of gold. This historic agreement stabilized the world's financial systems for almost thirty years. At the time of Bretton Woods, the U.S. necessarily assumed the role of global policeman and the world's financial manager. Nixon changed all of that.

Thus the financial economy was born, and, as it turns out, it could never have grown up without Computers Everywhere and the Global Network. The financial economy consists of the stock options and futures markets. Its global nature is emphasized by the incessant, twenty-four-hour trading of the world's major currencies as they fluctuate by the microsecond. Financial speculators gamble on whether the dollar will go up or down when a hurricane strikes Florida or when we whip Iraq. Floods in the Midwest affect the price of corn and thus soy beans and beef in Texas. A freeze in Southern California drives orange prices higher, and thus the speculator who gambled correctly lands a windfall for his accurate predictions. During September of 1992, one investor alone made an estimated $1 billion by correctly gambling in the financial economy. Good guess or good information? Political events in the U.S., Europe, and the Far East drive the markets wild while Wall Street prognosticators base their careers and fortunes on their analyses. There are winners, and there are losers.

Megabyte money in the financial economy exists primarily in Cyberspace. Computers do the trading, the guessing, and the analysis based upon never-ending volumes of information that must be collected, sorted, analyzed, and evaluated. Computers which are part of the Global Network instruct other computers to buy, sell, trade, or hold to investments and positions based upon instantaneous decisions made often without the intervention of a human mind or a live finger on the keyboard.

The hidden financial world of options, futures, and global hedges is a legal and erudite form of gambling. The world's financial economy, in excess of $1 quadrillion ($1,000 trillion), dwarfs the power of any single country or sphere of influence, and, with the proper incentives, could bankrupt any nation on Earth. Speculation breeds volatility. For every real dollar, speculators manipulate the markets with twenty to fifty financial dollars. Writes Kurtzman, "As a consequence, speculation holds far more sway over each nation's economic livelihood than we generally give it credit for."[9]

Behind the financial economy is a dizzying array of technology designed specifically to keep track of the 1s and the 0s, the dollars and the cents. There has been massive investment in the technology to manage thousands of trillions of dollars. Wall Street firms spent between $30 to 40 billion in the 1980s on Computers Everywhere, with $7.5 billion spent in 1991 alone.[10]

The trading rooms on Wall Street are as complex as a NASA facility. Thousands of computer terminals spread across acres of high-rise floor space offer on-line, real-time, dynamic sources of easy-to-interpret information presented in graphs, charts, three-dimensional models, and just about any other conceivable format. These systems all have a single goal: give the trader or stockbroker or currency rooms enough information to make a decent bet.

Wall Street in many ways is even more demanding than the

military for advances in computer and communications technology. The first Stock Exchange computer was installed by Burroughs (now part of Unisys) in 1964. Prior to that all transactions were done by hand. The financial economy's investment in technology is a relatively small amount compared with the value of the transactions that occur daily. The New York brokerage and trading houses alone pass $1.9 trillion over their computer networks every single day. That's almost $800 trillion per year, which doesn't include Tokyo, London, Frankfurt, Hong Kong, or other international trading centers. One New York brokerage house, Solomon Brothers, trades $2 trillion every year. The Federal Reserve System transfers $1 trillion every day over the Fed Wire. The world's other networks move another $2 trillion-plus every day.[11]

Incredibly vast sums of money, most of it real only in Cyberspace, offer the owners control and power over the destiny of companies, countries, and people. I think it becomes terribly obvious at this point that the Information Warrior has a terrific interest in the financial economy and its underlying technical infrastructure.

So far we have identified four of the components necessary to wage high-level Information Warfare:

- The New World Order
- Computers Everywhere
- The Global Network
- Megabyte Money in a Financial Economy

The last ingredient that the Information Warrior needs to achieve his goals is to understand the psychology of his potential victims. Given the state of technology versus man, the Information Warrior finds a fertile breeding ground to fully exploit and leverage his activities.

Strategic Assessment: The Internet

Charles Swett, Office of the Asst. Secretary of Defense

The views expressed in this paper are those of the author and do not necessarily represent the policies or positions of the Department of Defense. This is a much-condensed version of a longer paper available from the author (703-693-5208 or http://www.fas.org/pub/gen/fas/cp/ swett.html).

Current Trends

In the last few years, the Internet has become a household word. After a long period of relative obscurity when it was solely the domain of technically oriented individuals, the Internet has burst onto the national scene and is playing an increasingly important role in an ever-widening spectrum of activities involving an exponentially increasing number of people. It is now in the mainstream. Having a tangible effect on the social, cultural, economic, and political lives of millions, the evolution of the Internet is taking it into roles completely unanticipated by its original designers. Rather than merely "fitting in" to pre-existing social processes, the Internet is actually transforming the nature of the processes themselves. It is a catalyst.

The Internet has been increasingly involved in politics and international conflict. Local, state, and national governments are establishing a presence on the Internet, both for disseminating information to and receiving feedback from the public. Candidates for elective office are conducting debates over the Internet. Organizers of domestic and international political movements are using the Internet. It has played a key role in Desert Storm, the Tiananmen Square massacre, the attempted coup in Russia, the conflict in the former Yugoslavia, and challenges to authoritarian control in Iran, China, and other oppressive states. The Internet is playing an increasingly significant role in international security, a role that is potentially important to DoD.

Some Predictions

The following predictions offered by the author cover the next five to twenty years.

New political parties operating through the Internet will emerge. The convergence of large numbers of people of similar political persuasion through the Internet eventually will cause the development of political blocs, or parties, whose only means of interaction is the Internet. Virtual conventions will be held over the Internet, where party platforms are agreed upon and candidates for office are determined by vote. These activists will then interface with the physical world by running for elective office, representing an electronic constituency. Virtual political parties of every type will be ad hoc and may not be institutionalized like conventional parties; they may be oriented toward single issues or just a few issues, and so may dissolve once the issues are resolved to their satisfaction. They will also not recognize any political or geographic boundaries. Electronic parties will transcend local, state, and even national borders. Membership in and activism on behalf of these parties will occur on a global scale. They will increasingly make their presence felt in the internal political affairs of nations and in international affairs. The proliferation of these parties will also make the political scene much more complex, and multiple simultaneous political wars will occur in Cyberspace. Due to the almost instantaneous transmission of news about current events to members and the very rapid development of responses to them via e-mail, these parties will be able to react almost immediately to developments that relate to their interests. This reactive speed will afford them a degree of influence that is disproportionately strong relative to their actual numbers.

Although it will be essentially impossible to enforce party discipline in these semi-formal, loosely defined organizations, considerable political momentum will be achieved when large numbers of members support particular positions. Single-issue coalitions between different parties with common interests will add to their potency. Financing would also be problematic, since members may be reluctant to transmit funds to a virtual treasurer for a party that might go out of existence without warning. However, these parties will have modest financial requirements compared to conventional political parties, since most of their operations will occur over the Internet. The only significant costs will be incurred by activities through which party leaders interface with the world of Congress and the White House. Lobbying, advertising, membership drives, polling, and most other party activities will occur almost exclusively on the Internet at almost negligible cost.

Political groups whose operations are coordinated through the Internet will be vulnerable to disruption by false messages inserted by opposing groups. This will encourage the proliferation of encrypted messages. However, these groups will face the dilemma that encrypting their messages excludes the wider audience, from which they hope to elicit sympathy and support.

The monopoly of the traditional mass media will erode. No longer will the news editors and anchors of television networks and newspapers solely determine what the mass audience learns and thinks about current events. Raw news reports from local, national, and international newswires and alternative news sources, and from unaffiliated individual observers on the scene acting alone, will be accessible by all Internet users. The filtering and slanting of the news by traditional media will give way to some extent to direct consumption of unanalyzed information by the mass audience, diminishing the influence now enjoyed by those media. An increasingly skeptical audience will be able to compare raw news reports with the predigested, incomplete, out-of-context, and sometimes biased renditions offered by television and newspapers. Some of the mass media will attempt to reassert their traditional roles on the Internet, and they will fail, because they will not have any advantage over their audience. The average consumer of news on the Internet will have a much wider cognizance of current developments worldwide than currently, and will be more likely to have an opinion on overseas situations.

This is not to say that the traditional mass media will lose their audience and become insignificant. They will continue to play a major role in the national news flow. However, they will lose considerable ground to alternative sources and alternative interpretations circulating on the Internet.

Members of Congress and federal agency officials will be inexorably drawn onto the Internet. When members of Congress who do not currently have a presence on the Internet realize that other members (who may be political competitors or enemies) do have a presence, they will want to join themselves, particularly when they understand they are being attacked in electronic political debates with no one in Cyberspace to defend them (or even worse, that they are not being discussed at all). Remaining out of the Internet will increasingly be recognized as a strategic weakness and a sign of being behind the times. The same phenomenon will affect officials in the executive branch of the federal government. Increasing demands for public accountability will draw them onto the Internet too, beyond simply posting news releases and other documentation online. Members of Congress and senior federal officials will require staffs just to monitor and respond to the traffic.

Text-oriented e-mail will be replaced by video/audio messages. As a result of reductions in the size and cost of high-quality video cameras and improvements in video data compression technology, all personal computers in the future will be equipped with small video cameras, much as each computer today has a mouse. At the same time, the capacity of the communication link connecting personal computers to the Internet will greatly expand, due to replacement of twisted-pair copper telephone wires with fiber-optic cables. These two trends will allow Internet users to compose messages consisting of compressed full-motion color video images of themselves speaking. When a user wants to send a message, he or she will first prepare a script and then speak the words for the camera while reading them from the computer screen like a teleprompter. The resulting data file will then be uploaded into the Internet and played back by all recipients using standard video playback hardware/software with which all computers will be equipped. Although some users will prefer the anonymity of text-oriented e-mail, many others will find the urge to let the world see what they look like and hear what they sound like irresistible. The addition of the visual and audio dimensions to computer-mediated communications will greatly expand the content of messages, since facial expression, tone of voice, body language, race, nationality, gender, and age all convey much information that is lost when flat text is used. Even today, a type of sign language has evolved in e-mail that attempts to make up for this. For example, the icon ;-) resembles a sideways face winking and smiling; the symbol <g> is used to connote *grin*, a good-natured addition to signify that the message is sent in friendship, even if it is critical or sarcastic. When this iconography is replaced by full-motion color video with sound, the emotional impact and intensity of political debate on the Internet will be greatly magnified.

Politically oriented groups will realize the propaganda potential of video on the Internet, and will produce and disseminate video clips supporting their point of view. Internet users will have available to them a wide variety of political advertisements in the form of video files. Opposing groups will engage in video propaganda wars entirely within the Internet medium.

The Internet will be used as a tool of statecraft by national governments. The use of the World Wide Web portion of the Internet by the Peruvian and Ecuadorian governments to pursue their goals in their long-standing border dispute is highly significant. Those nations, not renowned for their technological sophistication, have been the first to bring international diplomacy officially into the online world. Although many governments have an official presence on the Internet, they provide only standard embassy-type public affairs statements, with information about their populations, cultures, industries, and businesses. In the future, as more governments recognize the strategic value of this new medium for conveying their message, they will use it as an additional tool in the political process. That is, the current information placed on the Internet by official government organizations will be supplemented by politically oriented material conveying argumentation favorable to their respective positions on issues important to them. When one country involved in a dispute with others begins to use the Internet in this way, and the other countries become aware of this, the catalytic effect will be that all involved countries enter into the electronic debate in an official way.

The Internet will play an increasingly significant role in international conflict. Political discussions among the members of the online public at large, and real-world activities of national leaders, representatives of electronic political parties and interest groups, world bodies such as the UN, commercial enterprises, and individual political activists will be energized by the Internet. Current information about conflicts placed on the Internet in real time by on-the-scene observers and alternative news sources will be voraciously devoured by the world audience and will have an immediate and tangible impact on the course of events. Video footage of military operations will be captured by inexpensive, hand-held digital video cameras operated by local individuals, transformed unedited into data files, and then uploaded into the global information flow, reaching millions of people in a matter of minutes. Public opinion and calls for action (or calls to terminate actions) may be formed before national leaders have a chance to develop positions or to react to developments. These factors will greatly add to the burden on military commanders, whose actions will be subjected to an unprecedented degree of scrutiny.

Assessment

POLITICAL ROLES

While there is already a great deal of political use of the Internet domestically and internationally, there is likely to be a significant increase in its scale and sophistication in the coming years. Due to the differences in concentration of Internet use in different areas of the world, the direct influence of the Internet on public opinion is likely to be heaviest in the United States, less in other parts of the developed world such as Europe, and still less in the undeveloped world. Individual activists operating in less-developed countries, though, are likely to bring the Internet with them in the form of laptop computers that can access the Internet through any telephone line. Information brought into those countries through the small numbers of Internet access points can be spread locally through more traditional methods such as print, radio broadcast, and word of mouth. The activists will also be able to use the Internet to disseminate information to the rest of the world and to help coordinate their activities.

The Internet is clearly a significant long-term strategic threat to authoritarian regimes, one that they will be unable to counter effectively. News from the outside world brought by the Internet into nations subjugated by such regimes will clash with the distorted versions provided by their governments, eroding the credibility of their positions and encouraging unrest. "Personal" contact between people living under such governments and people living in the free world, conducted via e-mail, will also help achieve a more accurate understanding on both ends and further undermine authoritarian controls. Information about violations of human rights and other forms of oppression will be increasingly conveyed to the outside world by the Internet, helping mobilize external political forces on behalf of the oppressed.

It is thought by some analysts that the concepts of "national sovereignty" and "nation state" are becoming less relevant due to greatly increased economic, political, and cultural linkages that cut across national boundaries. To the extent that this is true, the Internet will play an important role, since it is the medium through which an increasing volume of these types of linkages will take place.

INTELLIGENCE

The Internet is a potentially lucrative source of intelligence useful to DoD. This intelligence can include:

- Reports on current events
- Analytic assessments by politically astute observers on or near the scene of those events, many of whom offer unique insights
- Information about the plans and operations of politically active groups.

The Internet can be used to provide early warning of impending security threats. Internet message traffic about developing situations tends to precede news and intelligence reporting, since the individuals who originate that traffic are not constrained by the resource limitations to which news and intelligence organizations are subject. Those organizations must prioritize their efforts, focusing on what appears to be the most important items of the moment. Individual observers overseas who have access to the Internet can write about anything that interests them. It is likely that routine monitoring of messages originating in other countries would help provide strategic warning of developing security threats that would be of concern to the United States.

At the same time, it should be noted that a great deal of the message traffic on the Internet is idle chit-chat with no intelligence value whatsoever, a veritable "Tower of Babble." Monitoring of that traffic would need to be supported by automated filters that pass through for human analysis only those messages that satisfy certain relevance criteria. Of course, the accuracy of much of the information on the Internet would be suspect, and therefore new means of validating information received this way would be needed. Alternatively, news reports on the Internet could be used to cue higher-confidence means of U.S. intelligence collection by alerting us to potentially important factors and allowing us to orient and focus our collection more precisely.

Beside being used to develop early warning of developing conflicts or the beginnings of new global trends or sea changes, the Internet can be used at the opposite end of the spectrum: to obtain pinpoint information about specific matters of interest. Networks of human sources with access to the Internet could be developed in areas of security concern to the United States, and these sources could be oriented to seek specific information. If constructed and managed correctly, such a system could be much more responsive and efficient than the current complex, unwieldy intelligence tasking and collection processes we must use. We might even consider cultivating the capability to perform strategic reconnaissance by modem. This approach could never replace official DoD intelligence collection systems or services, but could be a useful adjunct.

The Internet can also serve counterintelligence purposes. For example, a message posted recently in an Internet discussion group for left-wing political activists repeated for their benefit an Associated Press article about an upcoming U.S. Army Special Operations Command training exercise directed at the (empty) St. Moritz Hotel in Miami Beach.

If it became widely known that DoD were monitoring Internet traffic for intelligence or counterintelligence purposes, individuals with personal agendas or political purposes in mind, or who enjoy playing pranks, would deliberately enter false or misleading messages. Our analysis function would need to account for this.

SUPPORT TO POLICY-MAKING

Beyond intelligence, the insights and analyses of thoughtful overseas observers such as educators, former politicians, local journalists, and officials of other governments could be very useful to U.S. policymaking. E-mail discussions about the likely consequences of various policy approaches to security problems could help improve the quality of U.S. policymaking. A great deal of brainpower exists on the Internet, and if it could be harnessed and channeled for productive purposes, it might be a useful addition to DoD's informational and political assets. Any such use, of course, would have to be protected by appropriate security measures.

OFFENSIVE USES

Just as the United States could be vulnerable to disinformational e-mail, politically active groups using the Internet could be vulnerable to deceptive messages introduced by hostile persons or groups. Far-right groups and far-left groups tend to watch each other, and it is likely that moles will obtain access to the other camps' networks for the purpose of disrupting their operations. This would tend to weaken the protection afforded by coding or encrypting messages.

Increasingly, officials in national governments, foreign military officers, businesspeople, and journalists are obtaining access to the Internet and establishing individual e-mail addresses. There is even a commercial service that offers access to an online database of the names, organizational titles, phone/fax numbers, and Internet e-mail addresses of virtually all government officials in all countries. Using this information, it would be possible to employ the Internet as an additional medium for psychological operations (Psyops) campaigns. E-mail conveying the U.S. perspective on issues and events could be efficiently and rapidly disseminated to a very wide audience.

The United States might be able to employ the Internet offensively to help achieve unconventional warfare objectives. Information could be transmitted over the Internet to sympathetic groups operating in areas of concern that allows them to conduct operations themselves that we might otherwise have to send our own special forces to accomplish. Although such undertakings would have their own kinds of risks, they would have the benefit of reducing the physical risks to our special forces personnel, and limiting the direct political involvement of the United States since the actions we desire would be carried out by indigenous groups.

ROLES DURING CONFLICT

Even if the actual presence of the Internet in the location of a conflict is very limited, the widespread access to Internet available in the United States and other parts of the developed world will provide a medium over which political debate and activism related to that conflict can occur. Thus the Internet can indirectly play an important role in the way the world deals with a conflict, without having substantial physical presence within the conflict.

The Internet can play an important positive role during future international crises and conflicts. In the chaotic conditions usually present in such situations, normal government and commercial reporting channels are often unreliable or unavailable, and the Internet might be one of the few means of communication present. Some of its uses might include:

- Getting news out of the region and into the U.S. government
- Getting information from the United States and other nations into the region Cultivating political and even operational support for the U.S. side and opposition to the other side

Conclusions

In order to use the Internet most productively for such purposes, it would be necessary for DoD to address it directly and explicitly as an integral asset, rather than as an uncontrollable element of the environment whose role is determined by happenstance or as an afterthought. If viewed as a resource and systematically integrated into our planning and operations, the Internet can make some important contributions to conflict management and assuring the success of U.S. foreign policy.

3

Binary Schizophrenia

JUST LIKE THE TERRORIST, the Information Warrior wants to mess with our minds.

As a society, we pretend that we are sophisticated enough to deal with just about any situation that life offers. We tend to project a cavalier nonchalance when incredible technological achievements leave the lab and arrive at the mall. Who watches space shuttle launches or is impressed by Dick Tracy watches anymore? What technology and Computers Everywhere have precipitated is a complex set of psychological ills which permeates our culture. The bottom line is, we really aren't comfortable with what the technical wizards and gurus have wrought and what their evangelists have sold to us.

The same argument could have been made over a half millennium ago when the first of four stunning social and technological achievements cracked open the door which would eventually lead us into the Information Age. In 1450, German inventor Johann Gutenberg invented the printing press. For the first time in history, the human race had the ability to mass produce and distribute information. Gutenberg was a visionary who believed he would change the world with his one invention. According to historian Daniel Boorstein, "He was a prophet of newer worlds where machines would do the work of scribes, where the printing press would displace the scriptorium, and knowledge would be diffused to countless unseen communities."[1] I seem to remember Steve Jobs being described in similar terms a mere five hundred years later.

Prior to the printing press, the literate few controlled what was read and written. The Bible, during the fifteen hundred years prior to Gutenberg, was meticulously and arduously copied and translated one page at a time. The political implications are inescapable. Indeed, some historians maintain that the Bible was translated according to the religious-political mores of the day; the high priests would meet with the Charlemagnes or the Vatican and decide how best to alter the contents and wording of the Bible to keep the masses in line. Few people checked the Bible for information integrity, and fewer still were willing to be burned at the stake (or worse) for announcing any errors in translation.

As it is today, those in control of the information were in control of society. The Soviet Union, for all of its impressive technological achievements, had strict bans on copy machines and typewriters—not to mention computers of any sort. Stalin's paranoiac preoccupation with restricted information flow—"only tell them what we want them to know"—continued until *perestroika*, and ultimately until the collapse of the Soviet Union. It wasn't that Russian and Ukrainian citizens didn't want access to information, or want to distribute their ideas to others. It was just that they could go to a labor camp for that sort of thing. Giving voice to free thought was treated as a criminal act of sedition against the state. Maybe we can credit Xerox and CNN for the final downfall of the Soviet Union.

After Gutenberg turned the world upside down, the great Venetian scholar Aldus Manutius (1450–1515) pioneered portable books, to the chagrin of many in the church. "We can't have them reading the Bible on their own," Church officials objected. "They might start thinking and come up with different interpretations than those we tell them about." Right. That's the whole idea.

The pen is mightier than the sword. Maybe, maybe not. But without doubt, the availability of information to the masses would evolve over the centuries into a formidable political and economic weapon. The Magna Carta, the Declaration of Independence, the Bill of Rights, the Emancipation Proclamation—they all set the tone for this nation's beliefs and tenets before there was a fax machine in sight.

The second technological development destined to change the way in which information was exchanged was the telephone, invented and first used by Alexander Graham Bell on March 10, 1876. Originally conceived as a mere ancillary tool for businesses, telephones proliferated in the homes of the more well-to-do within little more than a decade. According to author Bruce Sterling, "The telephone was not managed from any centralized broadcast center. It was to be a personal, intimate technology."[2] Eventually anyone with a few pennies could traipse down to their local corner drug store and use a pay phone. All they had to do was ask the operator to dial the number for them.

In 1876, the U.S. was wired with 214,000 miles of telegraph wire connecting 8,500 telegraph offices. Despite the opportunity before them, Western Union dismissed the telephone as a parlor toy, failing to purchase the rights to the invention.[3] Big mistake.

By 1904, the emerging telephone system crisscrossed the American continent, offering the general populace an easier means of communication than the telegraph. In a parallel to today's technology, Western Union attempted to centralize control over their communications systems. The Bell Company and its holding company, AT&T, gave the power to the people—the consumer—to do with the telephone service as they pleased, when they pleased, and from wherever they pleased. AT&T wanted to control the network, the wires that connected businesses, governments, and people in a century-old manifestation of Cyberspace.

The third explosion for information exchange was the radio, which sent electromagnetic communications through the air. Portable information exchange—without wires—set the tone for the century's opening decades and indeed, the entire century. Nikolai Tesla invented the technology, but because his poor business skills and personal idiosyncrasies distanced him from contemporary industrial giants such as George Westinghouse, Marconi has received history's credit for the invention of the radio.

Satellite communications, accurately predicted years earlier by science pundit and author Arthur C. Clarke, changed the face of information exchange when the expensive, time consuming, and occasionally dangerous laying of transatlantic telephone cables was replaced with an orbiting satellite, launched from Cape Canaveral, Florida. Telstar expanded the concept of the network, the phone system, and primitive Cyberspace.

In under thirty years, satellite communications became an absolute necessity for international transactions. Today, the demand is such that hundreds of new satellite launches are being planned. Motorola's Iridium Project, for example, will ring the planet with sixty-six satellites, permitting portable phone users to talk to anyone, anywhere, at any time.[4] A true multinational effort is under way, including Japanese money and manufacturing and Russian orbital launch capabilities. Two competing consortiums have also begun staging their own satellite-based competitive global communications efforts.

The fourth major revolution in information technology was the personal computer. The power of information was further shifted from those in centralized position of power to everyman and everywoman. Prior to the personal computer (circa 1950–1970) early cyberpriests hunched over paper-tape readers, punch cards, and massive clunky disk drives, changing vacuum tubes to keep their behemoth systems crunching.

Only the largest companies—and the government of course—could afford to keep a computer running, and the entire computer industry was basically owned and operated by IBM. It wasn't well until the 1970s, when pioneering companies like Intel and Apple made computers small and affordable enough for any home or office, that the makings for the personal computer revolution were complete. And now we have Computers Everywhere and the Global Network. The Information Age is here—but we've been saying that since the fifteenth century.

In 1964, the French philosopher Jacques Ellul contended that technology had reduced man, its inventor, to a mere cog serving a global megamachine. Politics and the state have been surpassed by the importance of technology, he argued. Economics, whether capitalistic or socialist, no longer matter in the grander scheme of machine over man. Man had little will left, and even the political system which promulgated the machine was a scripted component of the inevitable bureaucracy required to support the machine.[5] All of this thirty years ago. What would he say today?

Seven years later, in *The Greening of America*, Charles Reich also noticed that technology and society were at odds. "What we have is technology, organization, and administration out of control, running for their own sake. . . . And we have turned over to this system the control and direction of everything—the natural environment, our minds, our lives."[6] This was a decade before the personal computer.

Americans, perhaps more so than our better educated technological planetary neighbors, are distinctly schizophrenic about Computers Everywhere. Now, I have no desire to enter into a foray about clinical terminology with the American Psychiatric Association; I am using the term schizophrenia, and more specifically Binary Schizophrenia, only to make a point. By and large, as a culture, we suffer from the pressure caused by two opposing and very strong forces pressing for our attention. Very few of us indeed would disagree strongly with these simple statements:

I Need Computers
I Don't Trust Computers

When these two conditions are forced to coexist, an internal conflict arises. I refer to this technologically-created conflict between preference and cultural necessity as Binary Schizophrenia.

Let's see how this condition manifests itself.

You are a very important person with important things to do (should be easy to imagine). Your importance requires that you travel a lot to see other important people, so you can do important things together. A meeting in Las Vegas requires that you be there, rarin' to go, at 9:00 AM PST. It is absolutely essential that you be there—this will be the most important thing you will have ever done.

No problem. Your secretary talks to the travel agency, takes care of all of your travel needs, and presents you with a neat, prepackaged itinerary with everything covered down to the last detail. In order to fulfill your needs as quickly as possible, your secretary and the travel agent need to use computers: computerized airline, car rental, and hotel reservations; fax machines to confirm those reservations; credit card authorization for immediate payment. You need to be in Vegas. To do this you need computers. Condition one of Binary Schizophrenia is met.

You arrive at the gate ten minutes before departure—as is your usual habit—carrying a bulging briefcase and an expensive leather garment bag. First class is the only way to go: a big seat and a drink in hand before take off. But wait; your seat is occupied. Two clone airline tickets with duplicate seat assignments. Damn computers.

The gate manager can't figure it out. "Oops. But since the other gentleman was here first, he should have the seat. Terribly sorry." They try to negotiate with other passengers, but the flight is full and there are standbys. No one will trade seats with you, not even in coach and not even with the added incentive of compensation. You *have* to be in Vegas.

"Sorry, there's nothing we can do . . . but we will pay for your ticket. . . ." The only way to Las Vegas tonight routes you from La Guardia to O'Hare Chicago for a two-hour layover and then into McCarran Vegas at 1:00 AM instead of 8:30 PM. You needed to get to Las Vegas early so you will be in shape for your meeting. Worst of all? No first class available. Ecch. Damn computers.

So you arrive in Vegas at 1:00 AM, but the good news is that the car rental firm is open all night—as is everything else in the desert mecca of indulgence. You are tired, but looking forward to the drive to your hotel in a Jaguar convertible to give you a much needed buzz.

"What do you mean you never got the reservation . . . ?" You are staggered.

"Our computers were down for a while . . . and I guess the records got a little screwed up . . . but don't worry, we still have cars." Maybe there is a God, you think, only He's having a bad hair day and taking it out on you. "We still have a couple of Volkswagen Vanagons and a selection of Yugos," the young lady says pertly.

A Yugo? For an important meeting? "Never mind. I'll call for a limo." One long, embarrassing, limoless hour later, you begrudgingly choose the bright yellow Yugo because it was the only one without red and orange flames painted on its side and hood. Damn computers. You don't trust 'em. Condition two for Binary Schizophrenia has been met.

At least Caesar's will treat you right.

"I'm sorry, sir, there must have been some mistake. We just don't have any record of your reservation and we just don't have any rooms, none at all. No suites either. You see, there's a computer convention in town."

Damn computer convention.

By 3:30 AM, Caesar's is kind enough (they really are sorry about your problem) to have found you a room. It's only a few blocks down the strip. The rates are $17 for every three hours. Cash only.

Damn computers.

Now I don't know about your level of tolerance, but if you haven't blown your cork by now, only one more thing could completely ruin your year.

Phew! You made it. Tired, but you made it. 9 AM. Your important meeting with important people. On the twenty-third floor with a big view. The secretary is very pretty and very congenial, but you sense something amiss in her kindness.

"I'm sorry, sir, I guess you didn't get the message. That meeting was moved to Tuesday, next week."

Shock. Rage. Denial. Disbelief. Fury. Heavy sigh.

"Why wasn't I called?" you ask, pulling out your combination Skypager and "Star Trek" cellular phone. Unfortunately, the back-lit LCD display on your three-and-a-half-ounce personal communicator is flashing a message:

ERROR 21 NO SERVICE AVAILABLE

Damn Phones. Damn Computers.

Such a chain of crises is thankfully very rare, but most of us have been encumbered by similar detours and they are frustrating to say the least. We can readily appreciate the increasing level of internal panic that comes from being out of control. (Prozac fans can relate.) The unpredictable next-steps taken by those who are out of control after exceeding their tolerance levels to constant roadblocks is entirely up to the reader's imagination. But I don't believe I've yet heard of a court case where the defense is based on the premise that "The computer made me do it." But the computer gets blamed for just about everything, doesn't it?

We have an inherent need for computers, yet at the slightest sign of error, they instantly become the target of our vehemence. The computer is wrong. The computer must have goofed.

The airline captain tells his captive passengers after sitting on the tarmac for five hours, "We're waiting for maintenance to put in a new backup computer. For safety's sake."

Your stockbroker: "The sell order never made it through. The computers were overloaded."

Your bank manager: "I'm sure if you bring in your canceled checks we can find the error in a couple of days and reopen your account. Maybe that's why the ATM ate your card, too."

News magazine subscription clerk: "I'm sorry, but I can't find you anywhere in the computer. Do you spell your name any other way?"

Grocery checkout line after the ice cream already melted: "The scanners aren't working. Give us a few minutes more."

A computerized letter from the IRS: "Tax Lien: Please send $145,376.00 to this office within five days or . . ."

"The number you have dialed is experiencing difficulty, please try again later."

"Sorry, you entered your password with the wrong finger. Please re-enter."

Arguing with a computer is about as useless as teaching Congress how to spell "balanced budget." We've all tried. Even worse are the clerks whose voices merely echo what their computers tell them. The words "But the computer says . . ." really mean, "Read my lips. The computer says so. If you continue to yell in my face, I'll call the police. Next."

Our Binary Schizophrenia is not limited to the business world; it creeps into our psyches everyday. It's what I call "approximation anxiety."

How do you tell time? Are you one of those who respond to the simple inquiry, "Got the time?" with "It's two thirty-seven, seventeen seconds," or do you prefer, "Quarter of three?"

Computers have forced us to speak digital instead of human. Digital interfaces have been subconsciously training us to program our VCRs to the nearest half-minute, prevent us from ruining the dinner in the microwave by an extra ten seconds on high, or drive at exactly sixty-six MPH. You used to buy a pound of meat, and now you receive 1.03 pounds. I don't mean to imply that accuracy is bad—it certainly is a boon. However, as a result of heavy reliance upon digital information, we are losing our ability to discriminate. Can you recognize that if you enter 20 x 26 into your calculator and get an answer of 620, the answer is wrong? You trust your calculator for an extra answer and you can't even approximate an answer in your head, on your own?

For most of us, saying the moon is a quarter million miles away is close enough for discussion but not for science. What about spreadsheets? At one time or another, we have all spent the night working on a long complex budget, or financial analysis, or projections. We hand them in and, to our horror, someone else finds a single column addition error that throws off every other number in all 2,048 rows and XXIV columns. All of that work gone . . . all because most of us don't have the ability to scan a spreadsheet and quickly identify an absurd answer. Far too many of us rely exclusively on what the computer says.

Damn computers.

Humans are essentially fuzzy in their logic. Our eyes don't tell us that the tree is 376.5 yards away. We might say it's ¼ mile or a thousand feet away: both are wrong but useful approximations. Our ears don't tell us that the piano note is 1760 cycles; we hear an A, which we would also hear at 1750 cycles or at 1770 cycles. The computer is exact.

On the other hand, some of us are outwardly pugilistic when computer answers don't match our expectations. Have you ever disagreed with the calculation made by a computer? Of course you have. We all have. "That can't be right," we say. And then we bring out the pocket calculator to double check the results. So what do you trust more in that case? The computer or the calculator. Intriguing dilemma. Enter, enter. If the calculator agrees with the computer you might go, "Oh well, I guess it is right," and shrug off your accusation. On the other hand, if the answer differs what do you do? Accuse the computer of being in error, yet enter the numbers again into the calculator to double check. What confidence! Not many of us can honestly say we bring out a pencil and rely upon our own brains to solve the problem. We have the need to trust computers. If we didn't trust them, at least to a certain extent, we couldn't get much done.

Binary Schizophrenia extends into corporate America's public relations as well. Few companies admit that they have had a computer break-in or were the victims of computer crime. The potential public relations fall-out is just too radical to consider.

Imagine that the Big Bank of Los Angeles (BBLA) has been living a charmed life. Bank of America was hit by hackers, fraudulent ATM cards, and millions of dollars of bad software. Security Pacific supposedly almost lost it all to Information Warriors trying to wire $5 billion overseas via the SWIFT satellite network. But so far, for mythical Big Bank of LA, nothing.

Until, one day, customers receive their monthly statements and their balances are off by varying amounts. Tens of thousands of confused and angry customers find themselves short substantial amounts of money, while others try to figure out how to capitalize on a bank error in their favor. Quick, write checks before the mistake is caught. The bank is inundated with customer calls. Teller lines at the hundred-odd branches snake into the streets. The media gets wind of what's happening and, as the eyes and ears of public concern, start asking questions. Questions the bank doesn't want asked because there are no answers yet. BBLA management has commandeered every computer expert they can find. "What happened? No, don't tell me, just fix it."

By the end of the day, there are still no answers, just problems. A few calls to the right federal agencies and Washington moles descend on the bank within hours. All of the bank's records have been corrupted, going back at least a week. Restoring the computer's memory will require thousands of man-hours to manually recreate accurate records. What will they tell their customers until then? Then, the worst imaginable scenario that any bank can imagine. Customers are demanding their money. In droves. It is a run on the bank, a bank's worst nightmare.

No bank, and no business for that matter, can stomach the

idea of admitting their problems outside of their cozy little boardrooms. Yet, if a bank experienced such problems, you can bet it won't be a well-kept secret for long. It's the equivalent of an electronic meltdown. A private computer Chernobyl. All systems No-Go.

The Information Warrior will count on corporate America's Binary Schizophrenia as a weapon as much as he will use and abuse the technology itself. The Information Warrior knows that stability is an illusion, a perception of reality that may or may not have any true substance. He can take a bank or business or small government that is not shaky in the least, and manipulate its information to his advantage. He can create the perception of instability by using the Global Network and the news services that control the information we see at home on one of our five hundred channels to leak, spread, or alter information garnished from the target. The Information Warrior will massage the new perception into a new reality. Once people hear that a bank just might be shaky, they will take out their money to avoid being victimized. The bank then will actually be shaky, which is exactly what the Information Warrior wanted to achieve.

Digital Addiction

As Thomas Hughes observed, "The price we pay for a cornucopia of goods and services is slavery."[7] That slavery is no more evident than in our addiction to technology.

Nintendo, for example, has addicted an entire generation to interactive video game playing, with riots occurring when insufficient supplies are made available to anxious consumers.[8] Billions of dollars are spent every year so that addicts from preteens to octogenarians can spend endless hours in front of a fourteen-inch computer monitor, trying to find Carmen San Diego, playing with Mario's joystick, or attempting to fit oddly-shaped geometric pieces into compact spaces. Our children spend an average of thirty-five hours per week glued to the television screen inhaling incredible quantities of information of dubious value. Addiction to be sure; Nintendo and Sega are the drugs.

Hackers are similarly addicted to computers. Many live solely for their keyboards and screens, and their meanderings through Cyberspace, across the Global Network into computer systems where they don't belong. In May 1993, a nineteen-year-old British computer hacker, who had admitted breaking into computers and causing hundreds of thousands of dollars in damage, was found not guilty by reason of addiction to computers.[9]

Virtual Reality machines offer an all-immersing plunge into Cyberspace, activating most of our senses with excitement. When body suits offer cybersexual encounters for the price of an arcade ticket, an entirely new addiction—AIDS free—will permeate society. Technology makes it all so easy, and we eat it up with every new gadget and toy that the silicon gurus can muster.

But our addiction far surpasses the entertainment value of Computers Everywhere, transcending age group, ethnicity, and vocation. Once a society gets used to high-speed computers, instant communications, and recreational or professional gratification at the push of a button, it's impossible to wean them of the habit. In 1968, Marshall McLuhan said that emerging information networks are "direct extensions" of our own nervous systems. Losing an ATM machine, according to that reasoning, is the equivalent of a leg or an arm. People panic when their computer goes down.

The financial markets, which make instantaneous decisions on how to handle their trillions, lose millions of dollars an hour if their computers fail. According to Kurtzman, "Today's world is very different from the world of the past. Economic success in this world—especially in the financial sector but increasingly in other sectors as well—is dependent on assimilating large quantities of information very rapidly."[10] We have come to expect computers to work all of the time, exactly when we want; if they fail to perform, our addiction to them forces a virtual shutdown of business—such is the psyche of the modern businessman. The government is probably more addicted to Computers Everywhere than any other segment of society. Who can fight a war without computers? When is the last time you saw a handwritten check from Social Security or the IRS? It won't ever happen, ever again.

The Information Warrior knows and understands our cultural and personal addiction to the tools and toys we have allowed into our homes and businesses. He understands that by causing a computer system or network to malfunction, he will certainly create problems. But he also counts upon the corollary digital addiction to help him in his aims. As we shall see, the Information Warrior will tailor his battle plans to maximize the synergy between the machines and the people who run them. He will count upon our addictive frailties and the resulting human reactions—fear, distrust, and confusion—to exacerbate any crisis he intends.

Information Overload

"Cyberspace, like the earth itself, is becoming polluted. Too much information is filling it. And our brains are just too tiny to sort through it all. Information overload threatens to bring further catastrophe, no matter how well the trading rooms are designed."[11] Kurtzman refers to the overload of technology itself, but the human element faces the same crisis.

We are pushing the systems and networks harder than they were designed to be pushed. The Internet, a major part of the Global Network, moves billions of messages. It's approaching capacity; nonetheless, we demand more from it. Companies are closing their networks, their personal pieces of Cyberspace, to further growth until they can handle the additional overhead. The digital superhighway proposed by then-Senator Albert Gore is an attempt to overcome that limitation, but technical information overload will occur again at some future date as we continue to push the limits of data capacity. The superhighway descendant, the National Information Infrastructure, will virtually guarantee conflicts between man and machine in the coming years.

Information overload is an invitation to disaster for us personally, corporately, and nationally. With five hundred television channels to choose from, what do you watch? You just can't watch the diet channel and the sci-fi channel and "Married With Children" and "I Love Lucy" reruns and the boating channel—and still have a life. Couch potatoes morph into cyberspuds. How do we decide what information we want? That is an unanswered question. Can we make rational, well-informed decisions about which information is truly valuable, or will we inundate ourselves with the inanities of the infomercials and supermarket tabloids, to the exclusion of quality news and information? The Global Network offers literally tens of thousands of choices—seemingly overwhelming freedom of choice—for our edification and growth. How do we make those choices?

Many of us find that TV is our sole source of information about the world around us. Are our politics shaped by Bernard Shaw or Dan Rather? Do our cultural assumptions and beliefs come exclusively from Wile E. Coyote and the Fox Network, or do we allow ourselves a smattering of PBS shows as well? Is Rush Limbaugh the staple diet for the political right, or do John Metzger's anti-black, anti-Semitic white power local cable shows feed our already divided, hate-filled society with more distortions and lies?

More and more, the media has become the central filter by which we view our world, and thus make judgements and decisions about what we will do, how we will respond, and what we will teach our children. The media are filled with people just like you and me, whose personal biases, beliefs, and interests act as the filter for our perceptions. Those of us who read and view only what we already believe, to the exclusion of all else—particularly that which we may find disturbing—do ourselves and our culture a terrible disservice. We allow the media to control our thoughts by feeding us sound bites and quick, tidy synopses of what are in fact world shattering events. Condensing events in Bosnia or China into a three-minute segment to be ingested over salad and dessert is a ratings necessity for the big networks, but we miss out on opposing viewpoints, crucial facts, and in-depth analyses that must be considered before we ourselves can make an informed decision or hold a defensible position. The news—as attractive multimedia stimulation—informs America of highly interconnected global events by reducing them to a form of personal entertainment—an addiction similar to Nintendo—instead of events worthy of thought, interpersonal discussion, and reflection.

The print media offers far better alternatives but *Newsweek* and *US News and World Report*, as do all magazines, have their own editorial slants, opinions, and biases. No reporter, unless he or she is totally devoid of human emotions, can be completely objective. He, by definition, acts as the filter to the news information we receive. The print media has the format to provide in-depth coverage of major issues that face us today. Yet someone who only reads *Time* magazine will get their information filtered through their slant to the exclusion of Bill Buckley's *National Review* or the plethora of left-wing publications.

The New York Times, the *Los Angeles Times*, the *Washington Post*, and the *Wall Street Journal* offer in-depth reporting and intensive editorials, but we cannot be blind to their necessarily human biases. And we have to keep in mind that the likes of the *New York Post* and similar newspapers across the country appeal to sensationalism and headline news with little or no substance. The readers of such news media, who do not partake of more substantial reporting, find themselves at the bottom end of the information filtration process, where the body of their worldly knowledge arrives in 72-point headlines which reduce events to bumper-sticker slogans.

The average American cannot read five newspapers daily as well as a selection of magazines representing the spectrum of political views. Yet, increasingly, we as citizens need more and more information just to keep even. Corporate America faces the same dilemma, as it throws more and more technology at more and more information in hopes that it will be able to make the decisions necessary to survive and compete. Estimations are that the data storage requirements of a large corporation will soon exceed one petabyte or one billion gigabytes. Artificial intelligence systems will have to decide which information is relevant and which is irrelevant: more computers to decide which other computers are worth listening to. Human intervention, even in the decision making process, will no longer be possible. We will have to trust that the cyberpriests develop artificial intelligence machines smart enough—human enough—to make decisions with which we are comfortable.

The talented Information Warrior with a Dale Carnegie course under his belt now has a whole new approach. He no longer needs to go after the underling computers used to sift through the primary sources of information upon which modern society depends. He can talk to the computer that makes the decisions and convince it to see things his way, just as any salesman would do. Who or what can you believe? Is the computer really right, or does the information manager at the World Bank need to question every decision made by the computer itself? Binary Schizophrenia at the highest level.

And so we come full circle. We need to trust the computer that trusts the computer that trusts the computer that trusts the computer. . . .

PsyOps

Winn Schwartau

In military parlance, *PsyOps* stands for "psychological operations." Like dropping thirteen gazillion leaflets over Iraq telling the soldiers and the people how useless their struggle is. Or broadcasting on Radio Free Europe to get the American message through. The point is to shift the paradigm of the target (adversary or not) and his belief systems so they work in your behalf.

Entire divisions of armies worldwide work on this problem and come up with all sorts of novel methods to convince leaders, soldiers, or populations of a particular point of view. But technology proliferation is going to rapidly shift the balance of PsyOps from the conventional centralized command and control structure that the military is familiar with to a decentralized and somewhat anarchistic one.

Take the Net. Someone publishes a piece of "data." Let's say it's not true, but it is intriguing, so it gets passed around a number of communities. You read it and think "how interesting," and then forget it. A few days later you hear about it again, but in another place. And then at a party another person tells you the same thing. The validity of the original data has now grown, and you might just take it more as fact than not.

The Good Times Virus has passed around the Net several times. It makes all sorts of nonsense warnings of impending computer doom unless the reader heeds the message's advice. Problem is, there is no such virus in the physical world that affects both your CPU and real life forms. The Good Times Virus is a so-called meme; the virus is the message itself, and it has shown how rapidly disinformation can spread—just like a conventional virus.

PsyOps was responsible for getting the United States to deploy a peacekeeping mission to Somalia. Pictures of starving children and a country in anarchy where even the UN couldn't get food to the needy. The single image to which our intervention was most often attributed was the hunched over child with the vulture standing behind him. So CNN moves to the beaches of Somalia and waits for the troops and we watch it all live while eating our Wheaties.

Then another indelible image is scorched into our minds: a dead American soldier being dragged through the streets of Mogadishu. The home-front call for a pull-out caused an instant shift in public opinion, and out came the soldiers.

The media is certainly responsible for the filtered contents of what we see and hear on TV, on the radio, and in the papers. And how they perceive the truth is a major factor as to what information is brought to the public. The amount of time or space allotted to a story is a function of how much emphasis the media places on a story, which helps determine how seriously the public takes the story. It might not be fair, but that's the way it is.

A sort of balance in the news has been achieved with the advent of the Net. If you want a lot of informaton about, say, hamsters and duct tape, you won't see it on the six o'clock news but you can probably find it on Usenet. Or if you see a quickie story on Dan Rather's CBS and want more in-depth discussion, there is the *New York Times*—or the Net, where it will undoubtedly be discussed amongst a hundred armchair experts.

And that's part of the point of PsyOps: manipulation of the media. The media are supposed to present a fair, unbiased condensation and filtration of the news that is important to their audiences. That's why local news about local people and local events is often more widely watched than national or international news.

But, back to the proliferation of technology to the masses. We are on the verge of being able to create artificial truth.

I recently saw an awesome demonstration of a technology that will be on our desktops in the next two or three years for less than $1,000. Here was the demo.

1. A fifteen-second video was played. A scene of an office, some guys sitting around. A lady walks from the right side to the left side of the screen.
2. The next clip is the same scene. Except the lady doesn't walk across the screen.

Big deal you say? It is. The lady's virtual optical existence and image on the videotape were electronically erased by a computer, and the background her body obscured while walking across the room was digitally recreated to make the picture look complete.

Oh, you say, that's what they did in *Terminator II* with morphing? Alas, silicon breath—hear this! The technology worked in real time! No delay. What you see in front of your eyes may not be what you get on tape! Artificial truth.

Another of the impressive demos has immediate applications. A video clip of a sports stadium—a baseball game. Around most such events, physical billboards advertise national brands of products like Pennzoil, Wrigley's gum, or any of a hundred different products. As the camera pans the stadium, the billboards are broadcast to millions of homes. The new technology, though, will electronically replace those billboards with new billboards, digitally and in real time. So, when the baserunner runs in front of the electronic sign, it looks as though he is obscuring part of a real sign at the real stadium—but he's not. Get it?

One obvious use of this technology is that the local TV station in

Knoblick, Kentucky can have the local Grain Store or Bootblack or Sausage Barn advertise on what is ostensibly a national event. Or at the Olympics, the myriad billboards along the luge course can be locally and digitally replaced with advertising from a particular country, city, or neighborhood.

Now, let's put on our Information Warrior hats.

Remember back in 1992, when Gennifer Flowers accused presidential contender Bill Clinton of sexual indiscretions. It made news, but fluttered away. What if the accusations had been accompanied with a videotape of the shenanigans? A real-time full motion artificial truth built to create or modify public opinion. Affecting the political process.

Consider the power we are unleashing. The U.S. government releases a video of our political adversary of choice doing nasty things that will hopefully incite his constituency. Without getting graphic here, use your imagination: what kind of real-time, full-motion videos would get your blood going—or influence an entire population the way you want them influenced? That's PsyOps.

And consider this: Political adversary of choice—say someone in Congress—who you and your group really want out of office because she has affronted your particular sensibilities. So you go out and create an artificial truth video of this particular Congressperson taking a big bribe from a lobbyist for an unpopular organization. Then you send the video to the media and the FBI. What happens?

I have asked this question to a lot of law enforcement people and so far, they all come up with the same answer—they have to investigate. They look and they look and they ask and they ask and they eventually come to the Congressperson in the video who is incensed beyond reason that anything like this could have happened. But how can she disprove this? How can she prove it didn't happen? Whoops. And in the meantime, the piece may have run on CNN or some other news show; or maybe the perpetrators sent it to the *National Enquirer* instead. In either case, such an event could mean a career ended, for the videotape is believed first.

Now there are much simpler examples of the tenet "In Cyberspace you are guilty until proven innocent."

Let's say you are driving down the road and your taillight is out. You get pulled over. The cop asks for your license and registration. He enters the info into his keyboard which radios to the local station which connects to the police network which connects to the state database which connects to the national crime database in D.C. In a couple of minutes, he returns to your car, except his gun is unholstered and he asks you to get out of the car and he's not too friendly about it. "You have the right to remain silent. . . ."

Guilty until proven innocent.

So we find a convergence between the PsyOps capabilities that are rapidly descending upon us and the loss of personal identity when people and organizations make decisions and choices about us based upon the contents of a computer or what they see on a videotape and not what we say or maintain about ourselves.

While in many ways technology empowers the individual, at the same time it strips us of our individuality, and our fellow carbon-based humanoids have allowed silicon life forms to determine our fate. This has got to stop.

An Information Warfare SIIOP

Colonel Richard Szafranski, USAF

The views expressed are those of the author and do not necessarily reflect the officially held position of the Department of Defense, the Department of the Air Force, the Air Education and Training Command, the Air University, or the Air War College. This manuscript is UNCLASSIFIED. Not for citation or attribution without author's permission.

The author gratefully acknowledges the contributions to this manuscript of Dr. George Stein; Colonel Miles Baldwin, USAF; Colonel (Dr.) Joseph A. Engelbrecht, Jr., USAF; Lieutenant Colonel Keith Morris, USAF; Lieutenant Colonel Hunter Vardaman, USAF; Major General Peter D. Robinson, USAF; and Lieutenant General Jay W. Kelley, USAF.

"The ability to create, disseminate, access, and manipulate information for one's own ends and to control information available to competitors or adversaries produces a potential for decisive advantage."—Global Presence[1]

"Information operations are no longer a cost of doing business, but presence and warfighting methods in their own right. They substitute for force in some cases, and increasingly serve as a multiplier when force is required."—The Honorable Dr. Sheila A. Widnall, Secretary of the Air Force[2]

Introduction

The post-World War II superpowers, the United States and the Soviet Union, danced an exhausting danse macabre for much of this century. Some far future military or political historian may look back on the era and conclude that throughout the dance each partner took turns leading the other. Stalin, this historian might offer as an example, danced in ways that had the unintended consequence of creating the American Strategic Air Command (SAC) in 1947. The United States, it could be argued, waltzed in a manner that probably unwittingly led to the creation of a robust Soviet Strategic Rocket Forces. Whatever else may be arguable, it cannot be argued that it was Gorbachev who ended the dance. The demise of SAC followed the disintegration of the Soviet Union in 1992. Any post-Gorbachev dance with Russia will be a new dance, since so much has changed on both sides of the Atlantic since 1992. The dance of U.S. and Soviet potential nuclear omnicide[3] indeed may have ended, but somewhere in the background the soft strains of other conflicts made with other kinds of instruments continue. The partners may change, the instruments and music may change, but the United States must be prepared to dance. Taking a leaf from a past relationship suggests that new weapons and emerging capabilities may invite a return to old forms. Organizational entities like SAC and the Joint Strategic Planning Staff, properly modified, may be useful models still.

The Management of "Force"

CONCENTRATING POWER

During its life, SAC existed to pose the credible threat of extinction to the Soviet state and hundreds of millions of its comrade-citizens. It did this by readiness to strike them with large numbers of the most powerful weapons of mass destruction available in its time. Any serious international misbehavior of the Soviet state carried with it the risks of greater death and destruction than Russia experienced in the entire Stalin era, including collectivization, purges, World War II, and the years of the gulag. Noncombatants had little or no sanctuary.[4] We called this threat "deterrence": a form of fire prevention made possible by the credible threat of arson.

The conception of nuclear deterrence spawned the SIOP (Single Integrated Operations Plan).[5] The SIOP was the United States' single and dominant plan for marshalling all of its most powerful weapons—nuclear weapons—to concentrate them, when and if necessary, against the Soviet state, its citizens, and its satraps. Yet the SIOP, supporters and commentators relate, need not have been just an Armageddon plan. The SIOP allowed for tailoring or customization of attacks. Its attacks could be unlimited or limited.[6] The SIOP's advantages were that it was one plan—integrated, synchronized, and carefully maintained.

Nuclear weapons command respectful attention. They remain powerful still, but a greater and more usable power may exist. That is the power of information weapons and Information Warfare, new instruments for a new dance. This essay argues that Information Warfare eventually needs its own SIIOP (a term I will explain) to employ information weapons. Further, the essay inquires into some of the possible features of that SIIOP using the nuclear SIOP as an analogy. The questions raised are, and must be, left unanswered for the present.

Information Power Defined

What is Information Warfare? Information Warfare is warfare waged against the epistemology, the entire structure of knowledge and beliefs, of an adversary. Information war, like execution of the SIOP, could be total war, but need not be. The object of Information Warfare, unlike nuclear warfare, is to subdue hostile will utterly, but without, or with little, physical fighting. (In this regard, if Desert Storm was the first organized information war, then—given such capabilities as described by Winn Schwartau[7] and others—it might have been merely the beta version.) The target sets of Information Warfare are the minds of adversary leaders and adversary citizens: the humans that add the hostile will transforming a state or group into a hostile one. To subdue hostile or noncooperative will, Information Warfare attacks the mind, that complex of protein and synapses and nerve bundles and electrochemical functions that host the will and determine human behavior. Information Warfare is "neocortical warfare."[8]

Attacks against the mind of the adversary, particularly the minds of adversary decision-makers, formerly were prosecuted indirectly or circuitously. That is, to reach and change the mind of the adversary, warfare attacked the "body" of the adversary with physical force. The body's sensory circuits relayed messages to the "will," trusting that the will would yield when the body had been damaged sufficiently. Taken together, this body was any or all of the components of the Clausewitzian trinity: the people, the armed forces, the government.

While Clausewitz concentrated his study on the armed forces, he acknowledged that the aim of fighting between opposed remarkable trinities was political. That is, warfare aimed to force the people-army-government trinity of an adversary state to yield to the will of our state's people-army-government by opposing the adversary's hostile will with physical force. The most effective way to do that in the last century was to vitiate hostile means in physical battle, preferably *Hauptschlacht,* one great decisive battle. The means destroyed, the will would surrender. Yet today one may speculate that information weapons technologies may exist or be emerging that offer the promise of subjugation with less violence. These information weapons and employment schemes theoretically may aim directly at the adversary's mind. This is, excuse the pun, heady stuff.

What are information weapons? Information weapons are any tools intentionally employed to affect the mind of the adversary with minimum physical force and in such a way as to have a high probability of compelling the adversary to do our will. It is critical to understand that Information Warfare is not just command and control warfare. Command and control warfare is a very small and specific form of Information Warfare waged with very unsophisticated weapons. The tools and aims of command and control warfare are modest. Nonetheless, a brief examination of these tools is an instructive introduction into the larger universe of Information Warfare.

The Joint Staff describes these tools as deception, psychological operations, electronic warfare, physical destruction, and operations security. Their orchestrated use aims to affect adversary decision-making and troop control during engagements between hostile military forces or when an engagement is imminent.[9] Command-and-control warfare—like the Information Warfare of which it is a part—appreciates that the decision-making process, as described by John Boyd, requires observations of the external world, some orientation to internally generated or externally sensed phenomena, a decision to act based on these observations and orientation, and action.[10]

Deception aims to corrupt enemy observations. Sensory phenomena are magnified, reduced, hidden, or otherwise changed. The enemy sees or hears things that are not there or does not see or hear the things that are. Exploitable mismatches arise.

Psychological operations affect the adversary's orientation and decision making. They attempt to change the enemy's orientation in both the long and short term, thereby modifying adversary decision-making and affecting enemy actions.

Electronic warfare disables or diminishes the enemy's radio-electronic capability, whether that capability is used for sensing, weapons guidance, or for communications.

Physical destruction can eliminate decision-makers, equipment used for observation or for relaying decisions, or even some of the forces taking action.

Operations security simultaneously protects friendly forces and amplifies the intended effects of deception, electronic warfare, and psychological warfare operations.

Command-and-control warfare is military stuff. Its elements seem to require an acknowledged state of hostilities between belligerents or actual combat. The principal objective of command and control warfare is to enhance the military capabilities of friendly forces while simultaneously reducing the command and control capabilities of the adversary. Thus, no matter how wonderfully done, command and control warfare is fighting done too late and is only capable of achieving tactical effects. Strategic-level Information Warfare would be much less modest in that it could aim for more profound effects. The larger, and I suspect presently unappreciated, aim of strategic Information Warfare requires much more sophisticated weapons than "force-enhancing" command and control warfare. At the zenith in the arsenal are, or would be, undetectable information weapons employed so elegantly that the adversary retains the illusion of choice throughout the force application or "combat."

What is combat? Combat itself requires new conceptions in Information Warfare, the horrified protestations of military historians notwithstanding.[11] Combat in this new view is any interaction wherein the aim of the activity is for the collective national security forces of the United States to change the mind of an adversarial state or group without fighting. Although waging strategic-level Information Warfare would be a seat-of-government decision in the United States, the target need not be another state. The target could be an adversary like a terrorist group. The target could be a competitor economic entity, so the combat could theoretically be a trade war. Strategic-level Information Warfare does not even require a publicly declared state of hostilities; it could be waged as a preventive to more conventional warfare.

Information Warfare, fully exploited, eradicates the demarcation between peace and war, between military and civilian, between combatant and noncombatant. Just as the SIOP planned, if necessary, to take on the entire Soviet state with nuclear weapons, Information Warfare can engage the entire adversary state or group with its weapons. Just as the SIOP could limit its attacks, so too can Information Warfare.

The weapons of Information Warfare are not just those things affected by physical or materiel information systems: computers, software, telephony, telecommunications, electrical power generation, and so forth. Nor is information combat necessarily restricted to information-based systems such as banking, finance, credit, air traffic control, and command and control or troop control apparatus. The weapons of next-generation Information Warfare might include tools designed to enable entering and affecting the brain through sounds, smells, images, tastes, and feelings. They might include drugs. They might include pheromones. They most certainly will include pixels, zeroes and ones, and images.

Because information weapons and Information Warfare can include so much, strategic Information Warfare would seem to require a Single Interagency Information Operations Plan (SIIOP) for its most effective employment. That SIIOP appears to be lacking. Unlike the SIOP, which was a military attack plan produced with some civilian oversight, a SIIOP must be, from the beginning, an interagency plan.[12]

Today, the lack of a SIIOP may not be a serious shortcoming. But if information weapons and Information Warfare have the potential for revolutionizing conflict, the process of orchestration needs to be considered. Orchestration will be difficult. We are not without either historical data or service cultural norms to examine in this regard. *What should we expect from the services, CINCs, and agencies?* If the past is any guide, and as with any discovery of potential new weapons or a potential new warfare, we can expect the armed forces initially to employ the novel to enhance the old and familiar. A special cell or group of experts will arise, as happened in the past—artillerists, Signal Corps, Air Corps, 509th Bomb Group, SAC, Space Command, Information Warfare Center, and so forth. These out-of-the-mainstream experts will be charged with applying the new to improve the old.

Concentration on command and control warfare as a means of force enhancement, for example, is explained by the logic of the model of previous behavior. The original view of nuclear weapons, it should be noted, was that they were nothing more than very powerful conventional bombs. Congressional testimony provided during the 1950s,[13] as well as the nuclear weapons tests conducted using some of our own uniformed (and uninformed) citizens as clinical material, illuminate this view.

As with nuclear weapons or any other new weapons technology, we can count on the services, which are federated (not unified or integrated), to charge off somewhat helter-skelter in a disintegrated way with their own programs and their own new organizations for new weapons technology. Each service can be expected to make its own discoveries regarding weapons and weapons employment schemes. Most often this will be done within the boundaries of "my mission" or "to enhance forces operating in my assigned warfare media." Each service might attempt to hide these discoveries from the other services. Missions are money, and it is money, as Cicero observed, that constitutes the sinews of warfare.[14]

The commanders-in-chief (CINCs) of the unified commands will learn of discoveries from their parent service and attempt to acquire and assimilate these new capabilities in their functional or geographical area of responsibility. (It is a fiction to believe that CINCs are mysteriously transformed into the prodigal sons of their parent service after confirmation as CINCs.) When CINCs acquire a new capability, usually they are insistent that they simultaneously acquire the authority to employ it "should conditions warrant." Other government agencies will follow similar approaches: discovery, development, perhaps even limited deployment. If the CIA makes an Information Warfare discovery, for example, the Agency is not necessarily obligated to share it with the Department of Defense.

The arsenal of such weapons and capabilities could grow in the process, but until marshaled and integrated, will be less effective than it might be. Worse, the commercial sector, especially those segments of it expert in communications, computing machines, entertainment, and the mind, will also discover what could become weapons and weapon employment schemes. Hollywood and Wall Street, for example, had little interest in acquiring nuclear weapons, but information weapons may be different. For instance, there might prove to be scant differences between marketing and propaganda, or between advertising and psychological operations. There also may be scant difference between entertainment and propaganda, or between infomercials and some aspects of Information Warfare.

How and by whom can the resources for strategic Information Warfare be marshaled? Lacking a National Security Decision Memorandum (NSDM), a Presidential Directive (PD), a Presidential Decision Document (PDD), or the contemporary analog of a Gates Commission, a Joint Strategic Target Planning Staff (JSTPS) for Information Warfare cannot be created. Lacking this JSTPS, neither seat-of-government guidance nor the advice and consent of the legislative branch nor the judgments of the judicial branch, nor a database of targets and an integrated plan to attack them will emerge. Lacking an integrated plan, we remain incapable of prosecuting strategic-level information Warfare against hostile, or potentially hostile, states or groups. Worse, we run the risk of being very seriously disadvantaged should we encounter an adversary nation or group that has a strategic information operations plan and its attendant capabilities. The ubiquity of information technology and reliance on it, the apparent growing importance of economic vitality, and the awareness that, at some point, we may approach the limit of the planet's resources and carrying capacity, makes pessimistic forecasts possible, if not quite yet worrisome. Someone out there might be hateful or desperate enough to attack us. Hackers may be the precursor model.

Converting the SIOP Lexicon for the SIIOP

Information technology is ubiquitous and can create asymmetries between opposing forces or groups. An adversary capable of waging information war need not be an easily recognizable great military power. Presuming that such an adversary exists or will emerge (perhaps as the much discussed, much feared "niche" or "peer" competitor of the Revolution in Military Affairs), and presuming an NSDM or PD eventually were forthcoming, what employment doctrine would national leadership espouse through this directive? Would we take a counterforce approach, limiting our offensive operations to retaliation against the adversary's information systems? Would we be directed to take a countervalue perspective and attack the minds of the adversary more directly? Would we aim to deter Information Warfare? Would we opt for mutual assured information destruction? Or should we build our information forces for flexible or selective response? Would it be wise to have some limited Information Warfare response options? Would execution authority reside with the person of the President of the United States, or would the President delegate the authority for some attacks against adversary epistemology to military commanders or even to the commercial sector? Would we be prepared for protracted Information Warfare?

What would the military and nonmilitary force responsible for executing the SIIOP look like? Which service or agency would provide the Director of Strategic Target Planning? How would this force integrate with nonmilitary forces, including the entertainment industry, the press, commercial telecommunications industries, the biomedical industry, and the CIA? Who would prepare the catalog of targeted installations or epistemologies? How would the catalog be modified, updated, or revised? To whom would the SIIOP revision be briefed for approval? What would it look like? How would targets be categorized?

Would forces be on alert? What would these alert forces look like? What would generated forces look like? How does the SIOP notion of range or refueling apply to information operations? Does misinformation extend the range of information, for example? What is an information operations sortie, and how are sorties deconflicted to prevent fratricide? How do notions of positive and negative control apply to strategic-level Information Warfare? Would some Information Warfare weapons require permissive action links (PAL)? What is Information Warfare escalation? What are the escalation control mechanisms? With whom would we

122 Information Warfare

establish an incorruptible communications link similar to MOLINK, and what would it look like?

What does precision mean as it applies to Information Warfare attacks? Are there precision-guided messages (PGM) that could be aimed at single minds? Does the notion of circular error probable become the idea of calculated error probability (CEP) through the statistical technique of Markhov-chaining in Information Warfare?[15] What are the canons of epistemological damage expectancy or probability of damage? What is information collateral damage, and how would it be controlled? What is the information equivalent of fallout, and what would a fallout shelter look like? Is there any civil defense against strategic-level Information Warfare? What science, technology, or arcane art would provide the machine necessary to assure us that truth or validity had not been corrupted? Is there a dosimeter awaiting discovery? Could attacks against some areas or categories of targets be withheld in a globally internetted infosphere? What is Information Warfare termination, and how would it be managed and by whom?

During the heyday of the Cold War dance, a special office of the Joint Staff annually created a Red Integrated Strategic Offensive Plan (RISOP)—essentially a notional Soviet SIOP—to assess the consequences of attacks against the United States. What would be the equivalent of an Information Warfare RIISOP, a "Redoubtable Integrated Information Strategic Offensive Plan"? And who would create the RIISOP? What would an information strategic defense initiative look like? Should we opt for area defenses—banking and finance, our free press—or do point defenses—the National Military Command Center, the *National Enquirer,* the Federal Reserve—seem to make more sense?

In the wake of massive Information Warfare attacks, would some earnest scientists warn of an information winter, a global epistemological condition wherein "truth" is largely destroyed?[16] Would some argue for an information freeze or information-free zones? Would the bishops of one faith group assert that Information Warfare was only moral if it existed to deter?[17] Would another faith group issue a document entitled *In Defense of Truth*?[18] These and many other questions come to mind as the future possibility of strategic-level Information Warfare is contemplated.

Conclusion

We likely have some time to ask and answer these and other questions. If our national security strategy summons us to "engagement," however, we must offer to dance.[19] If we dance, what will our partners do to affect our steps? Information technology engages us everywhere with everyone, and that technology is characterized by tremendous daily "enlargement." How do we know that someone is not already fighting with us? That possibility is to be expected. The question to which we must attend is what organizational structure protects us and allows us to deter or fight back most effectively? Studying the development of nuclear weapons, the creation of the JSTPS, and the old SIOP may provide clues. It would seem to be wiser to have a new SIIOP sooner rather than too late. Or, we might reject the entire notion, trusting that nations and groups are becoming the long-heralded global village.[20] Which course appears to be the wiser one? To not decide yet is, of course, to make a decision. Some decisions, good or bad, are definitive.

Colonel Richard Szafrankski, USAF
Air War College
325 Chennault Circle (AWC/DFN) Suite 154
Maxwell Air Force Base, AL 36112-6427
334-953-2722
Fax: 334-953-4028, 7154
DSN: 493-2722
Fax DSN: 493-4028, 7154
E-mail: rszafranski@max1.au.af.mil

1. U.S. Government, Department of the Air Force, *Global Presence* (Washington, DC: Government Printing Office, 1995), pp. 5-6. The notion of "virtual presence" and the recognition of the potentially decisive power of information power in this Air Force document suggest that another roles, missions, and functions fight may be brewing. The publication of the Air Force's Cornerstones of Information Warfare has been viewed by some as corroboration.
2. The Honorable Dr. Sheila A. Widnall, Secretary of the Air Force, "The State of the Air Force," *Airpower Journal* 9 (1): Spring 1995, p. 13.
3. *Omnicide* is a word used by Grant T. Hammond to describe the mutual and global suicide that would have been a likely consequence of an all-out, unrestricted nuclear war between the United States and the former Soviet Union.
4. Scott D. Sagan, "SIOP-62: The Nuclear War Plan Briefing to President Kennedy," *International Security,* 12 (1): Summer 1987, p. 22; Barbara G. Levi, Frank N. von Hippel, and William H. Daugherty, "Civilian Casualties from 'Limited' Nuclear Attacks on the USSR," *International Security* 13 (3): Winter 1987/1988, p. 169.
5. Widnall and Fogleman, Joint Posture Statement, indicate SIOP stands for "Single Integrated Operating Plan," p. 17. Carter, et al., translate SIOP as "Single Integrated Operational Plan" in managing nuclear operations. See note 12.
6. Desmond Ball, "Development of the SIOP, 1963-1983," in Desmond Ball and Jeffrey Richelson, eds., *Strategic Nuclear Targeting* (Ithaca, NY: Cornell University Press, 1986), pp. 65, 75, 80-81. See also Robert Jervis, *The Meaning of the Nuclear Revolution: Statecraft and the Prospect of Armageddon* (Ithaca, NY: Cornell University Press, 1989).

7. Winn Schwartau, *Information Warfare: Chaos on the Electronic Superhighway* (New York: Thunder's Mouth Press, 1994).

8. Richard Szafranski, "Neocortical Warfare: The Acme of Skill?," *Military Review* 74 (11): November 1994, pp. 41-55. See also Richard Szafranski, "A Theory of Information Warfare: Preparing for 2020," *Airpower Journal* 9: Spring 1995, pp. 56-65.

9. Joint Publication 3-13, Joint Command and Control Warfare (C2W) Operations, First Draft, 15 January 1994. See also: Appendix 4 of the Chairman of the Joint Chiefs of Staff Memorandum of Policy Number 30 (CJCS MOP 30), "Command and Control Warfare," 8 March 1993; Gerald R. Hurst, "Taking Down Telecommunications" (unpublished thesis, School of Advanced Airpower Studies, Air University, Maxwell AFB, AL, 28 May 1993); and Norman B. Hutcherson, *Command and Control Warfare: Putting Another Tool in the War-Fighters Data Base* (Maxwell AFB: Air University Press, 1994).

10. John R. Boyd, "A Discourse on Winning and Losing," August 1987. Boyd's analysis of strategy, tactics, and the operational art led him to the discovery of the now famous "OODA loop." Boyd suggests that the way to win is to operate (that is, to observe, get oriented, decide, and act) more quickly than an adversary. Ways to do this include depriving the adversary of essential information, overloading the adversary with puzzling or difficult-to-interpret information, using the adversary's "genetic heritage" or "cultural tradition" so that the enemy is self-disoriented or self-deceived, frustrating adversary actions, or denying the enemy feedback (or accurate feedback) on the consequences of action taken. All of this is designed to "Generate uncertainty, confusion, disorder, panic, chaos . . ." and to "shatter cohesion, produce paralysis, and bring about collapse."

11. R. L. DiNardo and Daniel J. Hughes, "Some Cautionary Thoughts on Information Warfare," *Airpower Journal* 9 (4): Winter 1995, pp. 69-79. On page 72 they note that this definition "causes problems."

12. Donald C. Latham and John C. Lane, "Management Issues: Planning Acquisition and Oversight," in Ashton B. Carter, John D. Steinbruner, and Charles A. Zraket, eds., Managing Nuclear Operations (Washington, D.C.: The Brookings Institution, 1987), pp. 640-660. This report and the previously cited volume edited by Ball and Richelson are excellent sources for the U.S. nuclear warfare and SIOP lexicon. Note that "Interagency" presumes that the result will be an "integrated" plan.

13. U.S. Congress, Senate, Subcommittee of the Committee on Armed Services, Hearings on Air Power, Part I, 84th Congress, 2d Session, 1956.

14. Service cultures also play a role. See Carl H. Builder, *The Masks of War: American Military Styles in Strategy and Analysis* (Baltimore: Johns Hopkins University Press, 1989).

15. Robert J. Wood, "Information Engineering," An Air War College Research Paper written in fulfillment of the curriculum requirement for graduation from the Air War College (Maxwell AFB, AL: 1995).

16. Dennis M. Drew, *Nuclear Winter and National Security: Implications for Future Policy* (Maxwell AFB, AL: Air University Press, 1986).

17. U.S. National Conference of Catholic Bishops, *The Challenge of Peace: God's Promise and Our Response* (Washington, D.C.: Office of Publishing Services, United States Catholic Congress, 1983). Often referred to as the bishops' "pastoral letter" on the morality of nuclear deterrence and nuclear war.

18. The United Methodist Church's Council of Bishops, *In Defense of Creation: The Nuclear Crisis and a Just Peace* (Nashville: Graded Press, 1986). If there is such a thing as an "information winter," it would be "truth," not "creation," that would need defenders.

19. U.S., The White House, *A National Security Strategy of Engagement and Enlargement* (Washington, D.C.: U.S. Government Printing Office, July 1994).

20. Arthur C. Clarke, *How the World Was One: Beyond the Global Village* (New York: Bantam Books, 1992).

Computer Decency Act

Testimony of Howard Rheingold

I, Howard Rheingold, declare that:

(1) I am a parent of an 11-year-old daughter, Mamie. My wife, Judy, and I recently celebrated our 28th anniversary. I'm an active PTA member, a small business owner, and a voter. My wife and I believe strongly that parents have an obligation to teach our children values, to give them the opportunity to make their own moral choices. We also believe that open communication among citizens, free from fear of government control, is what holds democracies together.

(2) I've written books about technology and its effects on people and institutions for the past 10 years (*Tools for Thought,* 1985; *Virtual Reality,* 1991; *The Virtual Community,* 1993). I write "Tomorrow," a column about the Internet and its effects, syndicated by King Features. I spend hours a day online, and have done so for 10 years. I have a real life with real people around me as much as anyone else,

but much of my business and social communication takes place online. For me, it's a real place, inhabited by real people who can forge deep bonds.

(3) I know from long personal experience that people can build communities from the relationships they grow online with other people who share their interests and concerns. The new medium that connects computers and communications networks transforms every desktop into a printing press and place of assembly, a component of community-building in technological society. An important part of civic life takes place there.

(4) Among the many things left out of the distorted popular image of the Internet are people for whom the Net is a lifeline: the cancer support groups, the disabled people who find a new freedom in this medium, the artists and educators and small businesses who use the Internet as a way for citizens to publish and communicate to other citizens. Experience has taught me that many-to-many communication, used wisely, can magnify the power of individuals to discuss and publish and make possible collaborative thinking among people all over the world.

(5) In my life, the virtual community became my real community. The people I first got to know in open, group conversation online have become my friends in the real world where real things happen to people. I sat with two people when they were dying, spoke at two funerals, danced at two weddings, passed the hat quietly among other virtual community members to help out a member in dire circumstance. The community I know takes place among people who matter to me, and online communication is what enables thousands of geographically dispersed interest groups to build communities. For people who live in remote areas, who share certain special interests, from mathematics to politics to the problems of being an Alzheimer's caregiver to the civic affairs of a small town or large city, virtual communities enable people to form associations that can enrich their lives and often carry over into face-to-face society. In modern society, it is often difficult to find people who share interests and values; the virtual community enables people to find and get to know one another and to establish relationships they might otherwise never have formed, relationships that often carry over into face-to-face friendships.

(6) I grew so fascinated with the nature of online communities that I traveled the world, visiting virtual communities in Japan and Europe, as well as America. I interviewed the people who built the ARPAnet and grew it into the Internet. I interviewed the people who built the Minitel system in France. In both instances, these media for social communication were never intended for people to communicate in new ways. The ARPAnet was a defense-funded experiment in remote computing over telecommunication wires because it was necessary for the scattered ARPA computer researchers to run their

data on each other's computers. The programmers who built the first network started using it for social communication. The early ARPA directors were wise enough to see that a new medium for group communication had emerged, unexpectedly. Minitel was designed as a distributed database, an electronic yellow pages, but people insisted on using it to chat.

(7) The emergence of "social computing" via the Internet is an example of people using a new tool as a means of human-to-human communication, and the medium of many-to-many communication is still in its infancy. People are not only building communities but businesses, and political information and communication associations. We have only begun to see the social and civic uses people will make of the emerging medium. As these examples show, the real virtue of Cyberspace is its ability to permit and even encourage innovation. If strict standards had been set at the beginning, or if planners had insisted on one structure, and by either means prohibited the ARPA or Minitel from carrying e-mail and other messages, one of the most vibrant and important parts of Cyberspace would never have developed.

(8) The topics that people discuss online constitute an enormous variety. Every scientific specialty you could think of has its electronic mailing list, text archive, web site. Support groups for scores of diseases are especially important online. The online breast cancer or AIDS patients in a small town who don't have any other support group, the Alzheimer's caregivers and others who cannot leave the house or hospital, the disabled who find a liberating barrier-free space online, derive vital knowledge, comfort, and human connection for people in need. The nonprofit organizations that set up shelters for battered children and abused spouses. The international networks of medical researchers who collaborate to cure disease. So many people will suffer tremendously if censorious laws shut down Internet providers and unmoderated forums where nobody can guarantee that nobody will say a taboo word at some time. Some of these topics of necessity will involve speech that discusses "sexual or excretory activities or organs." In some cases, the people speaking or the people listening will be minors for whom the information is important and useful. It would be a tragedy if fear of prosecution for failing to police the utterances of every member of a virtual community would lead to the closing of communities that alleviate suffering and help people cope with some of the difficulties of modern life such as life-threatening diseases or domestic violence.

(9) Several months ago, a very bright and articulate young man by the name of Blaine Deatherage sent me an e-mail questionnaire as part of a school project. I started an electronic correspondence. I learned, after I got to know him, that he was born with spina bifida and hydrocephalus, is confined to a wheelchair in near-total paralysis, and has trouble communicating vocally. I didn't know that. All I knew was that he had a lively mind and a way with words. Blaine

and millions of others like him have no other place to go. He's only sixteen. To deprive him of adult conversation in the chess groups he participates in online would be a tragedy. The groups to which he belongs, such as the chess discussions, are likely to choose to exclude all minors rather than risk the consequences should an adult member of the community use a taboo word.

(10) The examples of community I've mentioned are real people to me. When my longtime online friend and sometime online verbal opponent Tom Mandel grew fatally ill, he said goodbye online. The poignance of that experience, and the looks on the faces of Tom's online friends when I stood up for him at his funeral and gave a eulogy, are definitely real to me. When Casey needed an operation, enough of her online conversational partners bought posters from her to finance the medical procedure. When Kathleen Johnson announced that she was dying, dozens of us, including myself, took turns sitting with someone we had only known from the words we had read on a computer screen.

(11) My daughter has used e-mail and the Internet for social communication and for researching her homework since she was eight years old. I told her that she knows to use common sense and be alert when dealing with adult strangers. If someone she doesn't know calls on the telephone, she knows not to answer personal questions. I told her that some people aren't who they pretend to be in real life and in Cyberspace, and just because someone sends her e-mail, it doesn't mean that person is a friend. She knows the importance of nutritious food for her body, so I told her that she has to be careful to put nutritious knowledge into her mind, because the Internet consists of all kinds of mindfood, some of it not very nutritious. I told her that if anyone said anything to her or sent anything to her that made her feel bad or suspicious, that it was okay and a good idea to show it to mommy or daddy.

(12) When I wired up her fifth-grade class to the Internet, on a line donated by a local small Internet service provider, I told her class that they were pioneers. I told them there were wonderful ways to learn and communicate with interesting people on the Internet, and they were going to show the rest of the people in the school, the school district, the county, how to use the Internet as a fun way to learn. I told them that if they were caught doing anything they wouldn't be proud to do in front of their parents, then the experiment would fail, and the other classes and schools would probably think Internet for fifth-graders is a bad idea. But I also told them that I was showing them how to do this because I knew I could count on them to make the right decisions. They didn't fail me.

(13) Many people think Cyberspace is just the World Wide Web and solely involves information retrieval. That is incorrect. As the ARPA and Minitel example illustrate, many if not most people who use Cyberspace find the most important and most used parts to be

those that facilitate many-to-many communication. Thus, I believe the most important parts are newsgroups, chatrooms, mail exploders, and the like. There are many different ways people around the world can use the network to communicate with each other. Many scholarly and scientific groups use an automated service that sends e-mail to everyone in the group of subscribers, who can automatically send their responses to everyone in the group. There is no human moderator who decides which e-mail to send to the group. People who participate in such groups generally regulate their behavior voluntarily. Bulletin board systems and conferences and newsgroups are different ways of organizing public group conversations where nobody is the moderator or editor.

(14) There are moderated groups where an expert in the field acts as editor, deciding which of the submissions are published. Moderators generally do not screen the membership; they only decide what is published.

(15) If the Communications Decency Act is enforced, all unmoderated sites will either have to go out of business or set up prescreening to make sure only adults get access. Most unmoderated sites are nonprofit. They have a volume of both participants and of messages that is too large and too widespread to permit prescreening. In addition, many unmoderated sites were set up long ago and the person who set them up is no longer involved. Thus, there is no one around to do the screening. For these reasons, many of the sites would have to be totally eliminated. I fear that moderated groups won't fare much better. They also have so much volume that no moderator can screen each message and presecreen each subscriber.

(16) Even if a moderator could screen each message, I'm afraid that the standards of the Act are so vague that they won't know what to screen.

(17) I'm concerned about the difficulty of defining a "community standard" for a worldwide network. The way the Internet works, if a geographic standard is applied to everyone in U.S. jurisdiction, it would have to be that of the most conservative place in the country. That would stifle the net, not only domestically, but globally.

(18) I am convinced that screening of sexual and other objectionable material can be accomplished with the kinds of software filtering that all major online services and several commercial companies have offered. I believe the power to determine what goes on or off the prohibited list of knowledge in my household should stay in the household, and shouldn't be seized by the state and used against citizens who don't conform to the moral standards of a small segment of the population.

(19) Probably the most important potential of the Internet is in community-building. People who are able to make contact with others who share interests, to continue conversations with people in other locations, of other races and beliefs and political persuasions,

to get together with fellow citizens locally and nationally, are engaged in activities that are vital to the health of civic life and democracy. I fear that a chilling effect on the use of online forums could damage these important activities.

I declare under penalty of perjury that the foregoing is true and correct.

Executed on March 25, 1996.

4

On The Nature
of Insidious

"Information is the only asset that can be in two places at the same time."

—CHARLES ROBERTELLO
INFORMATION SECURITY EXPERT.

THE INFORMATION WARRIOR is a clever fellow. He knows that out-and-out destruction of buildings or bridges or airplanes will not meet his real goals. The lack of subtlety of the terrorist attacks and attempts in New York City in 1993 make him cringe. "What amateurs," he thinks. The Information Warrior knows there's a better way.

But first, let's take a quick look at what the high-level goals of the Information Warrior really are: Not the details of a particular operation, like which company or trade secret is under attack, but a generalized set of strategic goals for any purpose.

1. Theft of Information

As Robertello states above, information is that unique asset that can be in two places at the same time, and if that information has been purloined competently, only the thief— the Information Warrior—will know that it is in two places. The victim won't have a clue. Regardless of motivation, theft

131

of information is a primary goal for the personal, the corporate, and global Information Warrior.

Stealing corporate secrets can provide competitive advantage. The legal pilfering of our patent offices on a daily basis by organized cadres of Japanese Information Warriors threatens the global competitiveness of American industry. The theft of military secrets and communications codes are relegated to the world of espionage, with many amateur Information Warriors paying the ultimate price for their troubles and receiving only minimal rewards. The nation-state that sponsors such activities still benefits with little or no risk or retaliation on our part.

The theft of credit card numbers, telephone calling card access codes, and other modern "electronic money" devices has a direct pecuniary effect upon the victims. Such purloined information has inherent value that is immediately translatable into goods and services. Stolen access codes for telephone credit cards are sold to dozens of co-conspiring Information Warriors all across the country within minutes of the illegal acquisition. Valuable information will exist in many different locations at the same time, unbeknownst to its legitimate owner, until it comes time to pay the bill.

Then we have blackmail. We all have secrets, skeletons, or even thoughts and ideas that are better kept to ourselves. If they become public, such information can destroy a company, a career, or a life. The Information Warrior, exploiting such techniques as are described in this book, will keep blackmail as one of his options. And you can't have information returned to you and be sure all other copies are gone—ever.

2. Modification of Information

Instead of out-and-out stealing information, the Information Warrior may find that merely altering the information itself suits his particular goals. In the security business, we use the term *integrity* to describe whether or not information has been modified.

The integrity of information is essential in the financial community. We'd all like to be sure that the check for $17.98 we wrote to the drug store doesn't subtract $1,798.00 from our checking account. Banks want to ensure that the wire transfer is for $1,000,000,000.00 and not for $10,000,000,000.00.

But integrity of information—or the lack thereof—can hit home, too. At the personal level, an Information Warrior could make your life miserable if your credit files are mangled beyond recognition, full of falsehoods and distortions. Your mortgage won't be approved, the lease on your new car will be denied, and depending upon your occupation, your future employment opportunities will suffer.

Or if your medical profiles or health records are maliciously modified (in distinction to the ever present accidental errors), you may be denied health insurance or a job. Your status as a medical deadbeat would be easily confirmed to anyone with $50 and the desire to look. The Information Warrior can turn the picture of health into electronic genocide.

Alteration of data is an ideal method for the Information Warrior to instill fear, inflict damage, or embarrass victims with no warning. Imagine a corporate report so filled with errors that SEC investigations and stockholder lawsuits are triggered. Long, complex legal documents with endless minutiae can be intentionally filled with subtle errors that invert the meaning or intent. Errors in spreadsheets are difficult to detect, but compounded faulty calculations can render results meaningless or worse yet, indicting.

3. Destruction of Information

If the Information Warrior has the ability to alter and manipulate information, he also has the ability to destroy it. There have been countless cases of the accidental destruction of information when a computer system simply runs out of steam, or is hit by lightening, by a bomb, or by a flood. But, as we will see, some first-generation Information Warriors have, either out of frustration or pure hostility, simply denied legitimate users or owners access to their own information resources. Phone phreaks have effectively blackmailed some companies by threatening to destroy their PBX systems unless given voice mail boxes for their own use. Companies who don't succumb have lost the use of their entire phone system.

The old adage, "If I can't have it, no one else can, either," is a sophomoric dating game easily applied to Information Warfare. If the goal is to steal information, then an excellent means of covering up the crime is to destroy the access to the very information that was stolen—further complicating the investigative and restorative process. The Information Warrior may destroy data and information as a cover-up. Where have we heard that before . . . uh . . . Watergate, maybe? The courts ruled in 1993 that Government employees may not erase or destroy their own electronic messages, or E-mail, since they are part of the public record of democracy at work. We will see how the Information Warrior will use the destruction of data and information to his advantage when fighting an Information War.

4. Destruction of the Information Infrastructure

We know how critical information networks and communications systems are to the sustenance of companies and to the national economic security of this country. The Information Warrior may well decide that it is within his strategic goals to totally shut down his adversary's ability to process information at all. Inexpensive weapons are available to potential Information Warriors that will accomplish just this. Weapons heretofore exclusively under the domain of governments and military organizations have hit the streets and, properly used, will put any information-processing-based business or entity out of commission.

Insidious Weapons for the Information Warrior

We now need to understand the nature of the weapons used to effect these goals. The Information Warrior has a unique set of needs and his weapons are tailored to the task at hand, just as the military uses task-specific weapons when it wages conventional conflicts. The military may design a fighter plane that provides high speed performance with a small payload. A low altitude bomber has different tasks, thus different requirements from a B-52. Some bombs are designed to explode at a predetermined altitude, others are set to explode only after penetrating a structure or digging themselves into the ground. Some explosive projectiles are designed to be armor piercing; others used for antipersonnel application throw concentrations of skin-piercing shrapnel. They all have a purpose. The Navy patrols the seas armed with a wide range of military options that suit a variety of potential situations: Aircraft carriers, frogmen, big guns, F-15s, depth charges, cruise missiles, ASW. The Army, Air Force, and Marines also deploy a complex mixture of weapon systems each of which is apropos to the circumstances.

In the business world, a company can gain competitive commercial advantage with impressive audio-visual and multimedia demonstrations, better research, and hundreds of other strategies affecting the market. To the "Business Is War" mentality, each of these elements can be thought of as a weapon, to be used judiciously as part of the master plan.

The Information Warrior, however, is less interested in weapons of physical destruction. If all else fails, or as a consequential effect of another act, the Information Warrior might resort to the physical destruction of information systems by conventional explosive means. But such means lack the qualities that the Information Warrior so cherishes. The Information Warrior prefers the elegant approach; he seeks to leverage his advantage of surprise and strengthen it with qualities and characteristics that will synergistically increase the effectiveness of the attack. Familiar criteria are important to the Information Warrior; they correspond to military equivalents.

1. How much damage can be done when the weapon is used? The strength and power of information weaponry can be equated to conventional explosive weapons.
2. From what distance is the weapon effective? The military wants to know and control how far it can shoot its weapons. U.S. battleships stationed off the coast of Beirut can hurl explosive shells over twenty miles into the city. Cruise missiles are effective for several hundred miles regardless of the warhead used. ICBMs can cross the globe and hit their targets within a couple hundred yards. Similarly, the Information Warrior has to gauge the distance versus effectiveness of his weapons, whether they are going to be used against a faraway target in Cyberspace or against a business on the third floor of his office building.
3. Sensitivity is a measure of how weak a signal can be detected by the radio or satellite or other type of listening device. Much of the Information Warrior's arsenal is based upon the ability to eavesdrop invisibly on one's adversary, thereby stealing information.

INVISIBILITY

A secondary set of criteria upon which the Information Warrior evaluates the abilities of his weapons arsenal provides a clearer picture of the nature of Information Warfare. When applied against defenseless businesses and organizations, these criteria will appear to be almost magical. It is these characteristics that make Information Warfare techniques so potentially dangerous to our econotechnical information infrastructure, and ultimately the national security of the United States as a whole.

If the Pentagon could buy invisible tanks, they could park them anywhere they wanted, from the outskirts of Los Angeles in preparation for a riot to the desert fringes of Baghdad. At the first sign of trouble, they would launch a quick surgical strike and then get the heck out of Dodge before anyone knew what hit them. In fact this rationale is the argument for the development of the Stealth bomber. Fly a huge plane carrying a few nukes into enemy territory, drop 'em, and go home. Stealths aren't really invisible, but the enemy's radar systems won't see a reflective signature any larger than that of a basketball—good enough for "spook 'em and nuke 'em."

To the Information Warrior, invisibility is an absolutely crucial quality of his armaments. He does not want to be seen or be in any way identified with his activities, which undoubtedly sit on the wrong side of the law. If you can't be seen, the reasoning goes, then you can't be caught. The first and obvious intent is that he remain physically invisible. However, there is a second and equally important intent: electronic invisibility.

The Information Warrior fights many of his battles in Cyberspace on the digital highways that hold our society together. While physically he may be lounging in a wicker chair by the beach, his terminal is connected to the rest of the Global Network. His power stretches as far as his modem can dial. The Information Warrior needs to insure that his electronic being, the part of him that is projected across networks everywhere, cannot be traced back to the physical him.

Most of the tools that the Information Warrior has at his disposal will provide him with a high degree of invisibility. Of course he has to use his weapons properly, and as time goes by, the Information Warrior will improve his skills. He will get more creative, bolder with his efforts. We could conceptually say that convicted computer hackers forgot one of the Information Warrior's first edicts: Stay Invisible. They didn't. They got caught.

PASSIVITY

The Information Warrior loves passive weapons. They are stunningly elegant, and unless he really screws up, he won't get caught. One of the best examples of passive Information Warfare is the debacle at the U.S. Embassy in Moscow. During the early 1980s, we used Soviet workers to pour concrete and nail sheetrock in the construction process of the new embassy building, a political decision reflecting attempts at brotherly detente. So what did the Soviets do? Out of the kindness of their hearts, they fed thousands upon thousands of electronic diodes into the concrete soup that was poured into columns and floors to support the structure. Using a couple thousand dollars worth of diodes, which cost a penny or two each in quantity, the Soviets confounded our ability to determine if the Embassy was bugged or not, since a diode and a bug look the same to countersurveillance and sweeping equipment. A pretty neat trick, brilliant in its simplicity, to disguise the fact that they might have placed hundreds of real bugs amidst the ersatz ones. The upshot is that over $100 million later, the U.S. is preparing another embassy site. But the elegance of the Soviet trick makes an intelligence agent on either side wink in appreciation, and the Information Warrior nod knowingly.

The Information Warrior places great faith in his passive weapons, the weapons that when used against his victims will leave no scars, no damage, and no one the wiser . . . until the Information Warrior decides that such a course is propitious.

The U.S. government's ability to use passive weaponry against its uninformed citizens causes great concern for constitutional scholars. The passive tools of the Information Warrior have rendered personal and corporate electronic privacy virtually nonexistent. One encouraging thought, though, is that the same passive techniques are available to you, the potential victims.

DRONING

Smart Information Warriors do everything they can to ensure that they don't get caught. Once you're caught, the game's over. So, in order to avoid detection or have his real or electronic face seen, the Information Warrior will use remote control methods when at all possible to effect his strategies.

The most modern and illuminating example of a drone weapon is the Cruise Missile. Guided by computers and sophisticated internal mapping, it can fly hundreds of miles and find its target with pinpoint accuracy. Reminiscent of Hitler's early attempts at technology with the V-1 and V-2 rockets aimed at England, the cruise missile is relatively inexpensive, coming in at less than $1 million each. But more important to the folks here at home, the expendable cruise missile saves American lives: They don't have to be piloted by native sons from Kansas. These remote controlled mechanisms are called drones.

The Information Warrior wants to create deniability—the government loves that word, too. It is amazingly simple to "drone" oneself and one's goals in Cyberspace, and thus droning is a favorite tool of the well-honed Information Warrior. If he can have another person indicted for his deeds by the use of electronic drones, all the better.

FALLOUT

To most of us, the word *fallout* connotes dread, bringing up visions of long-term aftereffects from a nuclear blast. To the Information Warrior, though, fallout is a very desirable characteristic of his weapon. Typically, fallout is the mass effect that a single event caused by an Information Warrior can have on people and organizations other than the primary target. For example, if a computer network, the primary target, is disabled, a large number of people are immediately affected, and then other people who depend upon that network are also affected. The biggest single network is the phone company. In the past few years we have seen just how widespread the effects of a phone computer failure can be. The Information Warrior wants to get the most bang for his buck, and may elect to use weapons which provide plenty of fallout after the initial strike. But he must also keep in mind that the fallout may be indiscriminate, and affect groups it was not intended to, or have little impact upon the intended victims.

A typical bomb goes off once, does its damage, and that's that. But imagine a bomb that goes off, then marches down the street, and goes off again, then moves on to another target, on and on until the bomb is finally disarmed or destroyed. That kind of "bomb" is popular with and available to the Information Warrior. The Information Warrior must design and pick his methods carefully, for too much fallout, too early, might send future plans awry.

INSIDIOUSNESS

When a bomb goes off in an airport terminal, there is no question that an extreme act of violence has occurred. While the placement of the bomb might be insidious, the act itself is overt and will be reported on CNN within minutes. Often the responsible parties will take credit for the act in the furtherance of their own agenda. A bombing at an airport or at a London office building, or a massacre with machine guns, has immediate and usually predictable effects: panic, terror, destabilization, personal trauma, and a military or paramilitary response.

The Information Warrior, though, is not always in search of immediate gratification and headline-grabbing national attention. In many cases he prefers to wait, staging his attack when conditions are optimum. His goals and means are not always as obvious as in the case above. Time is on his side. His victims may not even know that they have been targeted, and the results of his efforts may have unpredictable long-term effects.

We need to remember that the Information Warrior does not want to capture and occupy territory; maintaining financial control or political influence are more likely aims. Being an occupying landlord no longer has the same attractiveness that it once did. The Information Warrior does not want to be bloodied by killing off opponents. Disabling them financially or destabilizing their powerbase is often sufficient. The vengeful Information Warrior will derive greater pleasure from watching his prey wriggle rather than from watching him die. If the target is a well-known company or organization, reading the *Wall Street Journal*'s accounts of its troubles might well bring glee as the tottering company suffers public indignity and its information systems collapse.

In a competitive economic war, the battles are tedious, lengthy, costly, and subject to fluctuating outcomes. Compaq and Apple became powerful economic forces over a period of years, not weeks or months. It took Japan twenty years to gain a thirty-percent share of the U.S. auto market; their early imports were a disaster. Economies tend to move slowly, thus permitting the Information Warrior the luxury of time.

But insidiousness is more than just clever. Investigators found enough pieces of the cassette-player bomb that downed flight Pan Am 103 over Lockerbie, Scotland, to enable them to trace the bomb to its makers and ultimately to the plot's sponsors. Even though the bomb explodes, it leaves traces that, when retrieved, are put to the most rigorous analysis money can buy. The FBI operates the finest criminal forensic laboratories in the world. Their tools are second to none and when applied with vigor, otherwise insignificant evidence can be transformed into case-breaking and courtroom case-making arguments. Microscopic evidence provides the investigator with unique opportunities such as DNA identification, nuclear magnetic resonance, and spectrum analysis. In short, a conventional explosive weapon is traceable.

The Information Warrior would like to eliminate that word from his vocabulary. "Traceable" is just not part of his modus operandi. He wishes to stay deep in the background, plan and plot, quickly and quietly deploy his weapons, and make sure he is a safe, undetectable distance away.

Insidiousness is further exploited by the Information Warrior due to general ignorance on the parts of "computer experts," management, and government policy makers. Most people, unless properly trained, rarely consider that someone

may be out to get them; that data errors and systems malfunctions may be intentional; that they may be purposely attacked
by an Information Warrior whom they have never met.

Thus far we have taken a high-level strategic view of what
qualities the Information Warrior desires in his weapons and
what broad-stroke concepts and philosophies he would consider when choosing a weapon appropriate for a particular
type of strike.

- Theft of Information
- Modification of Information
- Destruction of Information
- Destruction of Information Processing Capability
- Invisibility
- Passivity
- Droning
- Fallout
- Insidiousness

So far we have looked at the big picture, something all too
often not done by those in need of developing a strong
defensive posture. The private sector is nearly blind to the
capabilities of the Information Warrior, and the government is
in much the same sorry state.

In December of 1992, I was invited to speak to about five
hundred U.S. intelligence agents from the CIA, the FBI, Army
Intelligence, the NSA, and every other alphabet soup agency
Washington, D.C., could muster. I asked the promoter of the
Open Source Solutions conference, Robert Steele, "What am I
going to say up there? These guys are on the front lines. They
already understand what this is all about." I was terrified of
boring a highly sophisticated audience.

Robert merely smiled and said, "Do your thing."

The CIA was in the rear, filming the presentation, and I was
flabbergasted to see that the audience followed my descriptions of Information Weaponry with more than merely polite
attention. Afterwards, I was pleasantly surprised to have a

crowd of intelligence agents come forward and ask for more information about Information Warfare. Perplexed but pleased I asked them, "Hey, aren't you guys the ones who are supposed to know about these weapons? Aren't you supposed to know how to fight these battles?"

One voice interrupted my questions with, "We can't talk to each other about what each of us is doing or knows. It's considered classified. We're not supposed to see the big picture. You've put it all together." The government, especially the spooks, spies, and goblins, compartmentalize and restrict information flow so thoroughly that most of what I spoke about was a complete surprise to them. From the government's viewpoint most of it was, and still is, classified.

In the next few pages, you—and they—will begin to see the pieces that make up the big picture.

Hiding in Plain View

Winn Schwartau

Originally published in Network World, *May 1996.*

The perfect military weapon is invisible. Voila Stealth aircraft and silent running submarines. The perfect crime is committed by an invisible perpetrator. Voila La Internet.

And that's exactly how so many criminal hackers take advantage of the global systems upon which businesses increasingly rely. The modern wired organization faces two problems when it comes to individual invisibility, or in net parlance, anonymity.

First, as a network manager you have to deal with anonymous intruders knocking at your electronic front, looking to gain admittance. And second, you need concern yourself with internal employees who want to anonymously navigate outside your internal networks into the aetheric netherworld of the Internet.

So how do they make themselve invisible? You and I have an e-mail address, maybe a Web site, and we trod and slush through the morass of virtual humanity using our designated electronic identity. If, however, we wanted to assume an anonymous persona, what would we do?

One of the most popular ways is to use an anonymous remailer such as anon.penet.fi in Finland. By e-mailing them (info@anon.penet.fi), you too can can acquire a numerical identity which, to the recipient of your mail, has no relation or connection to your real identity. Ostensibly meant to promote free speech, which in some countries can result in persecution or worse, penet.fi can also be a haven for illicit behavior. Of course, from the corporate view, an employee who adapts a penet.fi identity can bypass corporate Internet policies and receive mail from sites that might be otherwise blocked. (Anonymous remailers are popping up all over, many of which are listed at ftp.csua.berkeley.edu/pub/cypherpunks.)

To combat access to or import of offensive materials, some companies block any and all access to penet.fi, do not accept mail from it, and if smarter firewalls are employed, siphon off any suspicious traffic to an information off-ramp for a hands-on inspection of its contents.

A new company, Offshore Information Services, located in the Caribbean tax haven of Antigua, offers anonymous and privacy services over the Internet. According to their promotions, "as a result of recent efforts to censor the Internet in France, Germany, China, and now the U.S.A.," users can adopt a new electronic identity for mail, cryptographic privacy, and Web sites. Check them out at http://online.offshore.com.ai.

Of course, criminal hackers take advantage of the myriad holes around the Internet. According to one well-known hacker, "All you have to do is walk into any university computer lab, logon as guest—they have no concept of physical security—and off you go. It's the easiest thing in the world." He continued to say that if he wanted to send threatening letters to the President (a clear federal infraction) there is no way his true identity could be captured. "Most sites have amazingly poor audit trails, and if you can't see who's coming at you, there's no way you can catch him." Good point.

This suggests that an organization should consider splitting its electronic doors to the Internet into several discreet firewall-protected entryways. Instead of trying to achieve all of your goals with a single server or firewall, distribute the functions with a view toward security.

One door might be for all incoming Internet traffic where outsiders are encouraged to come in, browse, buy, or perhaps, with proper credentials, be permitted to enter the inner sanctums of your networks. In this case, security is the paramount concern, and you should acquire the best firewall/Internet access control device money can buy. You absolutely, without question, want to protect your network resources and ability to cndu. It is your decision, then, to permit or deny access to those without "real" identities.

Another doorway to the Internet might be designated for your company users only—salesmen or even customers—permitting them remote connections to your internal resources. A stronger means of user identification is in order here—certainly stronger than a password; perhaps a software- or hardware-based token such as SecureID cards or LOCKout. In this instance, no token, no access. No one with an anonymous identity need apply.

While many companies place their Web services on their firewall in a money-saving attempt to combine functions on a single logical server, security risks abound. I often suggest to clients that they physically separate their inviting Web sites from their internal network connectivity. "What good reason is there to tie your billboard to your bank statements?" I still wonder.

The playful hacker can, if certain security holes are overlooked, still gain entry, paint a mustache on your female CEO, and in reality, no damage is done. (Just ask United Artists, who suffered similar indignities. The ill-fated movie *Hackers* was so poor it literally begged for the onslaught of electronic grafitti it received.) So, when the anonymous perpetrator comes your way, if it is creative and artful, a good laugh can be had by all and perhaps you'll even find a decent PR hook in there somewhere. In commerce-server applications, Goal #1 is to take the customer's money and deliver a product. Anonymity is almost a non-issue. Either the credit card is accepted by Amex or it's not.

Anonymity can take other forms on the Net as well. Hackers have been known to break into sites (gasp!) using telnet and then move forward in their trek having adopted the identity of the first victim in the chain. From your site, all you see is the last identity adopted; in this case, the hacked telnet site. So from an administrative standpoint, you have a call to make: do you block certain sites or types of sites, such as all .EDUs, to protect yourself, or do you enforce a stronger user identification and authentication mechanism?

Dial-up ports into organizations present similar opportunities to the "bad guys," whoever they may be. If your network permits dial-up and then subsequent Internet access, your site could be assisting the creation of anonymous identities. Once your (password protected, gulp . . .) dial-up site is hacked and then your Internet server is accessed, any behavior carried on thereafter could be traced back to you. Take care, dear administrator, for Internet security is symmetrical. It ain't just one-way access control anymore.

And what about those pesky employees? Does your policy allow them to adopt an anonymous identity from your site? Or is that an understandable no-no? What can you do?

First, you need a smart, strong firewall/access device that will scan the header of all outgoing messages. Do they contain an expected and legitimate address—like yours—or some other return address that might indicate less than honorable intentions? Contents and outgoing header filtering is key to this protection. After all; you don't want to find yourself or your company known as Porn Central because an anonymous user has successfully set up a dirty picture server. Just ask Livermore Labs in California. They lived and breathed it.

Should your corporate policy restrict access to known anonymous remailers, or is a bit of nonbusiness-oriented restriction in order? Should your e-mail come from known "good" sites and ixnay those from "questionable" sources? Either way, you have the ability to limit your exposure from external anonymous threats and from internal users adapting a faux persona from your site. You can make your own choices, but, one bit of advice. Know, or at least be able to identify, the person behind the header. As some old Chinese proverb probably said, "It is far better to know your enemy than to not know one who claims to be your friend."

Anonymously Speaking

Anonymous remailers are growing in popularity around the Net. Most of them are available for free, but sometimes they come and go like other Net phenomenon. If you are so inclined and what to adapt a new electronic identity (for trolling or otherwise), or you want to learn more about how anonymous identities work, here are a few places worth visiting.

    remail@miron.vip.best.comh
    hfinney@shell.portal.com
    hal@alumni.caltech.edu
    nowhere@bsu-cs.bsu.edu
    remail@c2.org

anon@anon.penet.fi
remailer@utopia.hacktic.nl
remailer@flame.alias.net
homer@rahul.net
mixmaster@remail.obscura.com
remailer@bi-node.zerberus.de
mixmaster@vishnu.alias.net
robo@c2.org
remailer@replay.com
remailer@spook.alias.net
remailer@armadillo.com
cpunk@remail.ecafe.org
wmono@valhalla.phoenix.net
remailer@shinobi.alias.net
amnesia@chardos.connix.com
mix@remail.gondolin.org
remailer@tjava.com
pamphlet@idiom.com
alias@alpha.c2.org
alias@nym.gondolin.org
nymrod@nym.alias.net
alias@alias.alias.net
mix@zifi.genetics.utah.edu
remailer@mockingbird.alias.net
remailer@meaning.com
remailer@remailer.nl.com
remailer@vegas.gateway.com
haystack@holy.cow.net
ncognito@gate.net

To learn more about anonymous transactions on the Net, try

http://online.offshore.com.ai (offers for-fee off shore anonymity)
http://www.well.com/user/abacard/remail.html
http://cs.berkeley.edu/
7Eraph/remailer-list.html
http://www.stack.urc.tue.nl galactus/remailers/index.html

Note: As of October 1, 1996, penet.fi closed its doors.

Influenza, Malicious Software, and OOPS!

"Software makes the world go around, the world go around. . . ."

—NOT FROM *CABARET*

"There's always one more bug."

—MURPHY'S SOFTWARE PROGRAMMING LAW

COMPUTERS EVERYWHERE and the Global Network are run by software. When a computer screws up, the problem can only be one of two things: either the hardware or the software, and odds are it's the software. Software tends to fail, especially the complex kind.

When the first F-16 was undergoing flight tests years ago, the computers and backup systems were being shaken-down for accuracy and endurance as much as were the wings and fuselage for stress and life with aerodynamic realities. But when that F-16 crossed the equator and flipped upside down at 750 miles-per-hour, it was software that was at fault.

Software is the brains behind Computers Everywhere. It is the stuff that permits the Global Network to live and breathe throughout Cyberspace. And, software, that intangible stream of 0s and 1s, is a strange beast. Software is less than perfect and thus is one of the most sensitive pieces of a computer system, making it most vulnerable to attack by the Information Warrior.

Software tells the microwave oven to heat the frozen pizza at 450 degrees for six minutes. If the software goes awry, the pizza either remains a pepperoni iceberg or becomes shrunken nuclear waste. Software tells the ATM machine to spit out two twenties when you ask for $40.00 in cash. Not one or ten. Just two.

We think of computers as benign desktop work horses, personal companions, or behemoth disk drives and tapes spinning in climate-controlled rooms processing tens of millions of credit card statements every month. But behind the metal cases, the keyboards, and the photographic-quality screens lie the smarts, the rules by which the computer operates.

Software is a set of human-programmed instructions that tell the computer what to do when it is asked to perform a given task. And what if the software malfunctions? The computer will do something totally unexpected; perhaps innocuous, perhaps life-threatening.

If a computer didn't have software, it would make an excellent reef. It's useless. Software is that necessary invisible companion to you and your computer. Software is what makes your computer behave and look smarter than it is.

A word processor is a software program that tells the computer to accept your keystrokes, display them on the screen, and then save them to disk. Spreadsheet software adds and subtracts and analyzes numbers according to rules you tell the software to execute. A database program sorts information according to your requests. Software can also be a game on floppy disk or a CD-ROM.

A fax machine has built-in software to accept the numbers you dial and it might have a memory for cheap-hours transmission. Your VCR is chock full of software so the kids can tape Barney the dinosaur.

Throughout the growth of the Global Network, we have come to expect software to work correctly, although it all too often does not. We don't even need to consider the Information Warrior to see just how much damage can be caused by software that makes mistakes. On November 21, 1985, the Bank of New York almost crashed and nearly brought down much of the financial system along with it. A faulty software program kept their computers from receiving incoming electronic money, yet was paying all of their bills. At the end of the day, the Bank of New York was short a staggering $23 billion. The only place to raise that kind of cash in a hurry was from the Federal Reserve Bank. Software engineers spent a long sleepless night to find the errors that ultimately cost the Bank of New York $3.1 million in overnight interest.[1]

In August of 1991, an AT&T telephone switch in Manhattan failed. This software- and computer-controlled phone switch not only managed regular telephone services but provided the communication links for air-traffic controllers. That single software failure forced major East Coast airports to shut down, disrupted hundreds of thousands of travelers, and caused worldwide airport chaos for nearly a day.

The Audi 5000 was the target of national news and Department of Transportation investigations for allegedly accelerating when the brake pedal was pushed. The debate is still on, but some experts have suggested that software errors in the computer controlled car were at fault.[2] The Mariner 18 space probe was lost due to a one-line error in its vast coding. Hundreds of millions of dollars and years of work went down the tubes in an instant.[3] The Genini V capsule splashed down one hundred miles off target upon its return to Earth because the NASA programmers forgot to factor the Earth's rotation around the sun into their calculations.[4] During testing of an early F/A-18 jet fighter, it was discovered that its computers were programmed to reject pilot commands deemed too dangerous by the computers. The planes crashed until the software was corrected. A less fatal software error in 1988 cost American Airlines $50 million. It seemed that seats on their normally busy routes were bare because their new whiz-bang Sabre reservations system and its software program had a tendency to say seats were booked when they weren't.

Countless medical devices with errant software have caused death or medical trauma.[5] A software-controlled pacemaker was accidentally reprogrammed by a microwave therapy device, killing the patient. In the mid 1980s, the Canadian-made Therac-25 X-ray machine was found to be overdosing patients with radiation, killing at lease one person and maiming others. A subtle programming error delivered radiation at twenty-five times the lethal dosage. "The tiny error in the software had laid dormant for years, waiting for the particular set of circumstances that would cause it to go berserk."[6]

In 1983, the Bank of America began a design for a huge computer system called MasterNet, a secret project that would have given them an edge over their competitors. When the system was first deployed in 1987 the results were disastrous. Nothing worked properly, causing Bank of America an estimated of $1.5 billion in losses.[7] They gave up the MasterNet experiment in January 1988 after spending over $20 million in development costs alone.

Making software work is expensive. Costs go up like the national debt. One of allstate's software programs for its operations was originally budgeted at $8 million. The final estimates were in the $100 million range.[8]

The examples go on and on, and in most cases, are kept as quiet as possible. No major company is going to willingly announce that they just wasted $50 to $100 million on developing a software program that didn't work.

Software has become incredibly complex, and the likelihood of making it completely reliable is a distant goal. Software for desktop applications like Lotus 1-2-3, Windows, and hundreds of other popular programs has grown to hundreds of thousands of lines of software code, or instructions. Mainframe and large applications run into the millions of lines of codes—entirely too large for any one person to thoroughly understand or make work. It is no surprise that early releases of even the most rigorously tested software are historically "buggy" (containing flaws), often to the point of being unusable. Version 1.0 of any new software is full of problems. Microsoft's DOS 6.0, generally panned by customers, was soon succeeded by DOS 6.2, which corrected the previous version's problems.

Software can be so unreliable that one software company used the following disclaimer to legally protect itself against lawsuits in case their software glitched:

> The Honest We Tested It Thoroughly Software Company does not warrant that the functions contained in the program will meet your requirements or that the operation of the program will be uninterrupted or error-free.
>
> However, Honest We Tested It Thoroughly Software Company warrants the diskettes on which the program is furnished to be of black color and square shape under normal use for a period of ninety (90) days from date of purchase.
>
> We don't claim our Program You Paid For is good for anything—if you think it is, great, but it's up to you to decide. If the Program You Paid For doesn't work: tough. If you lose a million because the Program You Paid For messes up, it's you that's out of the million, not us. If you don't like this disclaimer: tough. We reserve the right to do the absolute minimum provided by law, up to and including nothing.
>
> We didn't really want to include this disclaimer at all, but our lawyers insisted. We tried to ignore them, but they threatened us with the shark attack at which point we relented.

This is a rough translation of a real disclaimer, normally written in intergalactic legalese, that comes with most software. At least this company had the guts to say it so we'd all understand what they were saying.

Future software systems are so complex, and we expect so much of them, that a National Academy of Sciences report says, "Confirmation of software performance in all network modes and conditions may prove unattainable."[10]

Then there's Star Wars. In its heyday, the space-based defense system was estimated to need 100 million lines of code,[11] yet there would be no way to test it except for actual use in a world war.

To get an appreciation of how hard it is to make software work, assume that within the New York City telephone directories, there is one error. Only one. Either a phone number with one wrong digit, an address off by one number, or one name misspelled.

Go find it.

And while you're at it, until that error is found and corrected, the rest of the phone book is no good either. That's what happened to Mariner 18. One error. Assume the possibility, indeed rest assured, that software will have errors: It only requires some simple math. Let's say that a software program is required to make decisions based upon one hundred sets of conditions. That's not a lot in complex systems these days. But the number of possible combination is astronomical, 2^{100} in fact. It turns out that if we tried to test all of the possibilities that the software might encounter, it would require more time than the age of universe, or roughly twenty billion years.

The bottom line is that it's impossible to test software thoroughly enough to make sure it works all of the time. Sooner or later, the software, the computer, the system, will fail. According to a book on computer ethics published in the United Kingdom, "Honest programmers generally admit that for nontrivial software it is impossible to write a program that they guarantee to be bug-free. And this is even truer of sophisticated software such as compliers and operating systems."[12]

The complexity of software, with millions of lines of code, presents fundamental philosophical questions that underscore the problems we have with the reliability of computer systems, from both malicious software and unintentional programming errors. These questions offer us assistance in presaging what kinds of problems will come our way as even more complex systems are required.

At the heart of the matter is an inescapable mathematical theorem set forth by German philosopher Kurt Goedel in 1931. The formal treatment is incomprehensible to anyone but a PhD in mathematical gobbledy-gook. The succinct way of putting Goedel's Incompletness Theorem is as follows: "All consistent axiomatic formulations of number theory include undecidable propositions."[13] That means there's something wrong with our system of calculating. The problem is one of logic, and software is based upon logic. If we interpolate, Goedel implies that software, which is based upon mathematical logic, is inherently flawed because the underpinnings of our system of mathematics are faulty in one of two, if not both, places: consistency and completeness.

Software is a series of carefully crafted instructions, meant to carry out specified tasks in a certain, precise manner. In a short program, the logical flaw is not a problem. But when software is tens of thousands of lines long, the instructions often call up loops, nested loops, routines, subroutines, sub-subroutines: The possibilities are almost endless. It is these loops that are the problem because they tend to be conditional. In a simple conditional case, if the computer receives X signal, it should then perform task A. Or if the computer receives both an X and Y signal, it should then perform task B. But large programs have literally hundreds and thousands of conditions that affect every single decision the computer makes. There is no perfect fix. The Congressional Office of Technology Assessment agrees with Goedel by observation of the results. They say, "Errors in large computer programs are the rules rather than the exception. Errors in the code, and unforeseen and undesired situations, are inevitable."[14]

So what does this condition bode for our increasing reliance upon software and the computers that they control? This inconsistency offers the Information Warrior untold opportunities to ply his trade to the detriment of industry, health, the economy, and the defense of the United States. National Science Foundation scientist Dr. William Wulf said, "Software is a problem of major importance to the entire nation. I do not think that the general population appreciates how important software is to both our economic and military health."[15]

Indeed, most of us don't. The Binary Schizophrenic doesn't sit back and cogitate that an inevitable software error is at fault when his airline reservations send him to Nome instead of Bermuda. He doesn't think twice about reading the riot act to an underpaid Avis employee when the red Jaguar he ordered is nowhere to be found. And I didn't think twice about leaving Fortune Bank in Florida when the ATM machines left me cashless, consistently reporting a balance of zero despite having adequate funds available.

In contrast, the Information Warrior is well aware of the subtleties of software, and he also knows exactly how to exploit the weaknesses that software systems exhibit even without his help.

The most visible example of malicious software is the headline-grabbing computer virus that affects, by and large, IBM-style MS-DOS and Apple computers. The headlines scream, "COMPUTER VIRUS TO CLAIM 5,000,000 VICTIMS," or "MICHELANGELO VIRUS DUE ON HIS BIRTHDAY." Dan Rather, Bernard Shaw, and Tom Brokaw offer us a healthy fix of technonews every few months when the next computer-virus scare comes along: Columbus day, 1989; Michelangelo, March 1992; the 1988 Internet Worm; Friday the 13th; Stoned. Viruses are generally attributed to an untraceable and mythically brilliant virus writer in another country—or just to "the Bulgarians." Computer viruses have cost American industry and government billions of dollars and the end is nowhere in sight.

"Virus" is the one computer-security buzz word that has crept into the lexicon of the general public. Most people may not know exactly what a computer virus is, but they know it's not good. However, the offensive nature and resulting fear of computer viruses fuels Binary Schizophrenia and other tech-nomalaises of the Information Age, not to mention causing increased expenditures that reduce productivity. We see it manifested as viraphobia, the fear of losing a month's work to the effects of a computer virus on the loose. Software doesn't always work as we expect—that's bad enough—and viruses don't help in the least.

During the October 1989 Columbus Day Virus scare, an older family member called and asked me in all seriousness, "This virus I hear about, is it dangerous? Can I catch it? Should I be concerned?" She doesn't even own a computer.

The medical parallel is clear. When you catch the flu, your body has been invaded with a microorganism that makes you ill. The flu bug travels from person to person through personal contact. You can't see it. You can't smell it. You don't feel the effects until you are already infected, and by then it's too late. Similarly, the computer virus is designed to invade your computer. The virus software is carried into your computer when it "contacts" software or when two computers communicate in Cyberspace. Physical contact is not necessary. Viral software is meant to fool other software systems into behaving differently than planned.

A virus is simply a piece of software written like every other piece of software with one key distinction: it has the desire to propagate clones of itself. That is, virus software is designed to make copies of itself, spreading from one computer to another over time. But unlike its biological counterparts, viral software is hermaphroditic in that each generation has only one parent that spawned it. What makes the popularly-known viruses dangerous or virulent are the instructions that the virus writer puts into the program. Conceptually, a computer virus is designed to penetrate or enter a system without the computer user's knowledge. It is offensive in nature. What it does once inside the computer is impossible to predict, except by the person who wrote it. Some popular viruses are known to search out all of the files on your computer and then erase them, perhaps while displaying a message that says, "MEMORY TEST IN PROGRESS. DO NOT REBOOT COMPUTER UNTIL FINISHED." In actuality, that message is giving the virus enough time to finish its instructions and by then it's too late. A viral Trojan horse is a program that accidentally gets put onto your computer because you think it is supposed to do one function but, in Homeric tradition, it really has an ulterior purpose.

A "time bomb" is a computer program that is designed to go off when certain conditions are met. For example, a preset date, such as Friday the 13th, Columbus Day, or Michelangelo's birthday could trigger the logic-bomb component of a virus to detonate and perhaps erase your work over the entire last year. A "logic bomb," related to the time bomb, could be set to go off when a user types in the words "Mickey Mouse" on his keyboard, or the name of a company, or if he answers a question correctly. A Chinese virus, for example, queried the user's political beliefs. The correct answer allowed one to continue unharassed; a politically incorrect response trashed the hard disk and all of its contents.

Some viruses and their malicious codes are suicidal and destroy themselves in the process of activation; others hide themselves only to be reawakened at a later date, just like a Soviet mole from a LeCarré novel. The mutating or polymorphic viruses of 1992 sent chills throughout the computer field. This new batch of viruses are built with a mutation engine, or self-encrypting algorithm. Simply put, every copy that the virus makes of itself is unique. So if we start with one virus that then infects two floppy diskettes, we then have three different viruses to defeat. If each copy makes two copies of itself, we then have six strains of the original. And so it goes, with every virus having unique characteristics.

Advanced viruses look for antiviral software, and if they are detected, will initiate defensive mechanisms to keep themselves alive. Some viruses are hardware-oriented in their designs, but thankfully Information Warriors have had limited success with their distribution. These viruses are designed to physically chatter a hard disk until it dies, cause chips within the computer to overheat and burn, or force a monitor to go up in smoke.

Computer viruses are generally distributed by putting one infected diskette in a desktop computer or by acquiring a piece of software grabbed from somewhere in Cyberspace. Respectable hardware and software firms like Novell, Intel, Adobe Systems, Leading Edge, and others have all been victimized by

viruses that invade their facilities, are duplicated by the
thousands, and then distributed to their customers. In each
case, an honest, proactive response by the company mitigated
major damages in spite of causing major embarrassment in the
press. These incidents forced manufacturers to take the problem of viruses more seriously than they had been, and an
industry has been built around the medical equivalent of
inoculating computer systems against viruses.

A few short years ago, there weren't any wild viruses, but
that changed in 1985. For his PhD thesis, Dr. Fred Cohen wrote
about the nascent concept of self-replication software. Viruses.
The highly technical thesis sought to define what viruses are
in mathematical terms, how they work, and how they bypass
or trick other software. Today, tens of millions of dollars in
antiviral software is sold every year by small companies and
huge industry leaders such as Microsoft, IBM, and Intel.
Virus-fighting has become a "chic" business, with some of the
players becoming quite wealthy in the process.

Virus busters and the virus writers are first generation
Information Warriors. A virus buster designs ways to protect
against what the virus writers conjure up. The virus buster
will write a piece of software that should be able to reliably
detect the presence of a virus or other unwarranted software.
Until, that is, the virus writers come up with another new
virus meant to defeat the last defensive software put out by the
virus busters. And then the virus busters come out with a new
revision, an update that fixes that problem, but the virus
writers are already onto the next one . . . and the cycle
begins again, a game on the chessboard of the Global Network.

In 1987, there were only six viruses; by 1990, virus busters
were combating one thousand viruses; and as of September,
1993, over three thousand computer viruses and strains had
been cataloged.[16] If the current trend continues, some projections estimate that by the end of the decade as many as
100,000 distinct computer viruses may be actively circulating
through Cyberspace.

Viruses capture the popular media's attention, to the chagrin of many virus busters and other computer professionals. The detractors say that media exposure only encourages the virus writers to write more viruses and see if theirs will make the 6 o'clock news. Others maintain that the media exposure creates self-fulfilling prophecies. Virus busters tend to say that the media exposure helps people protect themselves.

The Michelangelo virus has been dubbed the "John McAfee Virus" because of his media prominence during the event and his exaggerated warnings that as many as five million computers could be struck. His company's sales doubled to $6.3 million for the first six months of 1992, venture capital poured into the firm, and plans were made to go public.[17] Estimates suggest that fewer than 25,000 computers were hit by Michelangelo[18] and some virus busters claim that like early warning systems for a hurricane, they were responsible for the minimal damage of the impending virus attack.

Virus busters are susceptible to the same software errors that plague major systems. One of John McAfee's antivirus software products actually made it impossible to use the protected PC, prompting one user to say, "The product is worse than the virus itself."[19]

Antivirus groups look for and collect viruses, catalog them, dissect them, and write antidotes for them. Firms such as the National Computer Security Association bridge the gap between the virus busters who make the products and product claims, and the users who merely want to keep their computers healthy. Magazines and newsletters and on-line bulletin boards services, or BBSs, keep thousands of people informed about new viruses and new virus busting techniques. Indeed, it is a healthy and thriving industry.

Of the thousands of viruses out there, few have admitted authors, underground braggadocio aside. Some semibenevolent virus writers do not advocate the indiscriminate spread of virulent and malevolent viruses, and a small segment of the software programming population believes that virus writing is a good thing. They claim a higher purpose, asserting that their motives are pure science, and the only no-no is releasing viruses into Cyberspace. But one has to wonder. A free software program distributed across the Global Network and BBSs worldwide called the Virus Construction Laboratory is just what its name implies. It automates the process of writing computer viruses; thus, they can be cranked out by the gross. Just for education's sake, of course.

The Little Black Book of Computer Viruses, a how-to manual about writing viruses, contains heavy doses of philosophy. "I am convinced that computer viruses are not evil and that programmers have a right to create them, possess them, and experiment with them."[20] The author, Mark Ludwig, makes a case that viruses are legitimate life forms; an outgrowth from John Von Neumann's early research into automation theory. With references to Karl Marx, the IRS, and the First Amendment, Ludwig devotes considerable time to the defense of viral research as if it were a social service to the computer community.

Ludwig and virus researcher Dr. Fred Cohen both maintain that researching and learning about computer viral behavior will put us in a better position to defend against malicious viral strains in the future. The First Amendment is also thrown in, with virus defenders taking the position that software writing is a form of protected free speech.

"Computer viruses are inherently not dangerous," the book claims.[21] From a purely theoretical standpoint he may be correct, however, in practice I don't know many who agree. Ludwig warns the reader of his book, "This book contains complete source codes for live computer viruses that could be extremely dangerous in the hands of an incompetent person."[22] In pursuit of the perfect virus, the same company began publishing the *Computer Virus Developments Quarterly*, a magazine dedicated to the high art form of writing viruses. Virus busters are besides themselves.

David Stang, PhD, editor of the *Independent Journal of Virus News and Reviews* is virulent in his response to Ludwig and others. "Virus writers belong in jail."[23] He has zero tolerance for any sort of computer virus and he isn't alone. On

June 10, 1993, the National Computer Security Association held Virus Awareness Day on Capitol Hill, in Washington, D.C. Congressman Ed Markey from Massachusetts, along with representatives from Rockwell International and 3M, held hearings on viruses and related computer-crime issues.

Peter Tippitt, a respected virus buster, suggests that laws against viruses be introduced. Defining an illegal virus in an unambiguous way is an exercise in semantics, subject to interpretation. If we get too strict in our definition, we could see prosecutors go after software programmers who make an honest mistake, or the legitimate virus researcher who accidentally releases one into the Global Network could find himself in jail. It's a complex issue, with no immediate social, legal, or moral answers.

Is there such a thing as a good virus? Most professionals do not believe that a virus has any place within the computer field. Ever. The argument is simple: "I don't want anything on my computer that I didn't put there. It's my personal piece of Cyberspace. Stay out unless invited in." But arguments have been made that some good viruses are possible. Their uses are indeed arcane, stretching the imagination a little, but nonetheless intriguing. On January 6, 1994 General Magic, owned partially by AT&T and Apple Computer, announced an adaptable technology called Telescript, an "agent" which behaves like a microorganism. The user tells the agent which instructions to follow, and it meanders through the Global Network executing those commands. For example, the user might tell the agent to find the best rates and scheduling for an airline flight, book the seats, pay for them, and inform the user of any delays or problems. While AT&T and other firms see agents as key market growth items, critics see parallels to virus distribution and are uncomfortable.[24]

One question is often posed by advocates of the military applications of computer viruses: "If you could defeat an enemy by inserting viruses into his computers, would they be considered good viruses?" Dr. Stang immediately interjects an unequivocal "No," but others have to think twice and stammer about such apparently beneficial uses of malicious software. The Iraqi Virus Hoax, as you will read later, claimed that the U.S. used a computer virus to shut down the Iraqi air defense system during the Gulf War.

A common pro-virus argument suggests benign computer viruses could be used to update software revisions on thousands of computers in big companies, saving costly labor expense and valuable time. Technically it's possible, and maybe in the future a modified version of the concept will make sense. But today, people want control. Call it a manifestation of Binary Schizophrenia, but computer operators and business owners are not comfortable with software running around their networks looking for something to do, no matter how well-intentioned the effort.

Network maintenance is also suggested as a possible use for benevolent viruses. Such viruses could run around the company network, testing its computers and switches, and making sure everything is working properly. Should it find something amiss, the virus would call the maintenance man and suggest a timely fix. The same arguments against such use of viruses apply here as well.

Viruses are going to be here awhile. In *Star Trek, the Next Generation,* 400 years in the future, the Starship Enterprise is confounded by a computer virus. And this is where the Information Warrior enters. What can he do with software? Just about anything he wants to do. To the Information Warrior, the software virus is an excellent weapon.

Most virus writers today, those who purposely unleash their creations into the wilds of the Global Network, are young, amateur programmers with few skills. That's one of the reasons that only about three hundred computer viruses have had significant effects. There is a need among this group to feel immediate gratification, to see their names in headlines, and to brag to their compatriots on their private electronic bulletin boards. Virus writers run on ego.

Popular malicious software has largely been relegated to the underground, the province of younger hackers who write surreptitious software designed to steal passwords and shuttle rounded-off pennies to another bank account. The more sophisticated Information Warrior, without the need for notoriety or acknowledgement, uses viruses and malicious software to his advantage. He will exploit the malicious software in a more insidious manner, biding his time, maximizing the desired effect, and never, ever, claiming responsibility. Therein lies the value of malicious software to the Information Warrior and the skill with which he practices his art. He might be well-financed, and have a bevy of able virus writers in his stable. With that premise, the potential for damage is vast.

Consider, for example, that the Information Warrior owned or bought a small software company, perhaps a shareware company that makes quantities of second-tier software programs at super-cheap prices. And let's say that somewhere within the thousands of lines of those programs some malicious command are intentionally placed. Over an extended period of time, a year or two or more, this company's software is widely distributed and has a fine reputation. But because this Information Warrior is in no hurry, he can wait. For you see, his malicious software, a logic bomb maybe, is set to "explode" five years to the day after the fall of the Soviet Union, or perhaps on some arbitrary date years hence. Every computer that runs that program on or after that date would be affected. Maybe it will erase an entire hard disk, bring a computer to a grinding halt, or make the screen wiggle. The more widely distributed the software, the greater the effect. Worse yet would be a big legitimate software company distributing a hugely popular program which had been infected with a virus or other malicious software. If (purely for example's sake) Miscrosoft Windows contained a logic bomb or other malicious code set to go off in 1999, tens of millions of computers would suffer catastrophically and all at once.

The Information Warrior could find other applications for malicious software. At General Dynamics in San Diego, an employee planted malicious software, a logic bomb, into one of the company's weapons-development computers in the hopes he would be hired back to fix the problem he created. Michael Lauffenburger, 31, felt underpaid, so he wrote a program that would not detonate until he was long gone, hoping his involvement would go undetected. It was discovered. Through a plea-bargain, he received a fine of $5,000 and community service.[25]

On a larger scale, the introduction of intentionally defective or destructive software into huge software development projects would potentially have a greater and definitely targeted effect. With U.S. companies spending over $100 billion per year in software development, there is ample opportunity to get inside any number of potential targets.

Do software moles actually roam the hallways and digital highways of corporate America? Does a dedicated Greenpeace advocate work for a logging company as a programmer or in another technical capacity? Would a financial firm hire a mole-programmer to work for a competitor, instructing him to slow things down—software-wise? Would an immigrant or political adversary of the United States be able to work for the Internal Revenue Service or one of their contractors and make sure that appropriate amounts of malicious code was sprinkled through the software? Could a pro-lifer insert malicious software into the computer of an abortion clinic?

It's all a matter of intent and dedication.

Remember, the essential difference between malicious code and a software error is intent, and we know how many "honest" errors get through. So the Information Warrior will exploit this knowledge and situate himself or one of his soldiers to insert the malicious code to act when the time is right. The hit can come sooner or later. The malicious code might look like a legitimate error, or it might erase its own tracks, compounding the problem for the malicious-code police.

Joel Kurtzman addresses that very issue when speaking about the Bank of New York's small $23 billion problem. He suggests that the consequences might have been more dire. What if, he asks, "the problem had been caused deliberately by a virus, by a computer hacker, or a financial terrorist?" Or what if the bank's databases has been destroyed and records no longer existed? Or what if the problem was systemic to the entire FedWire and debts of $1 trillion or more had accumulated? "A disaster that large would take weeks, perhaps even months, to sort out. The costs would have been catastrophic."[26] The possibility exists, and the defensively-postured Information Warrior must guard his econotechnical information infrastructure against that capability.

Kurtzman's financial perspective also provides an insight into what kind of effect well-designed and strategically placed software weapons could have on the national economy. "If VISA's computer went down for just a few hours, it would be enough to show up on the Commerce Department's data on retail sales. If payments were disrupted or cash unavailable on Cirrus during the Christmas shopping season, it could cause riots."[27]

Software errors tend to be subtle, and the subtle Information Warrior can induce errors that, over time, can have significant ramifications. Banks and regulated financial institutions have to account for every penny to their government overseers. It must have caused Chemical Bank in New York great consternation that its ATMs had withdrawn an extra $15 million from over 100,000 checking accounts. The software error doubled every customer's withdrawal—an accident hopefully not to be seen repeated.[28] Malicious software could be written that would offset accounts by mere pennies over a period of months. The cumulative effects would be noticed only during audits, but tracing back the compounded minute errors is like finding the one wrong digit in the phone book. Leonard Lee, in his book, *The Day the Phones Stopped* says, "A University of Minnesota study found that if (a software manufacturer's) software were to completely fail, banks would have to close within two days, retail distributors would be backlogged within four days, and factories and other businesses would have to close by the end of the week."[29] The Information Warrior isn't stupid. He can come up with lot more malicious schemes in a day than you or I could in a year.

The military could easily argue that it has the most acute concern for software reliability—and rightfully so. The Patriot missiles used during the Gulf War are essentially software propelled by a rocket on an intercept-and-destroy mission. The accidental shooting down of an Iranian civilian airliner was partially blamed on the software of an incredibly complex array of electronic systems. To Lee, the sophistication of the new generation of computer controlled aircraft is such that "the major concern with fly-by-wire aircraft is that even if the systems do not fail completely, they could be vulnerable to software errors hidden somewhere in their programming."[30]

As we examine more of the weapons necessary to wage Information Warfare, we will see that many of them are software-based, or indeed use software to control the hardware.

Keep in mind, the difference between a legitimate software error and malicious code is intent.

The Information Warrior's intention isn't honorable.

A Short Discussion on the Plausibility of UNIX Virus Attacks

Peter V. Radatti, President, Cybersoft

Prescript, April 1996. I am still amazed at the number of people who somehow believe that UNIX is immune to software attack. Recently I was the subject of a heckler at a conference in which I was speaking on this subject. It appears that this is a subject that still angers some people so much that they become obnoxious. Days later, a high-level technical manager of a very savvy firewall company made the statement that UNIX viruses don't exist and thereby killed an opportunity to port VFind (a virus scanner that executes on UNIX systems and searches for UNIX, MSDOS, Macintosh, and Amiga attack programs) directly to their firewall. I can only state that those individuals who work hard and diligently at remaining ignorant of the world around them have themselves as their most appropriate punishment.

This paper was first written as a rebuttal to a paper published by a senior scientist within the U.S. government. Dr. Fred Cohen (fc@all.net) also published a rebuttal which, at that time, was distributed with this paper. I will give the scientist who wrote the paper we rebutted credit, because after reading our papers, he retracted his. In fairness, since he retracted his paper, I have removed all references to him and his paper from this document.

This paper is essentially the 1993 paper with sections that have become self-evident eliminated and new updates added to bring it current. In addition, I refer the reader to additional works on the same subject which may be of interest. Two of these papers have been written by me, "Computer Viruses in UNIX Networks—1995, 1996" and "Heterogeneous Computer Viruses in a Networked UNIX Environment—1991, 1996." There are also many excellent papers written by Cohen, Tom Duff, M. Douglas McIlroy, N. Derek Arnold, and Mark Ludwig on this subject. Most of these papers include working examples of UNIX viruses so there is no need to include working examples here. Refer to the References section of this paper for details.

One final note about the applicability of the concepts contained this paper. Since this paper was first published in 1993, the world of operating systems has changed. There are now more operating systems that look like UNIX at the functionality level than existed at that time. I refer the reader specifically to the Linux and Microsoft NT operating systems. Everything contained in this paper that is valid for UNIX will also be valid at the concept level for these newer systems. These systems share more functionality than they are dissimilar.

Magical Immunity

The promotion of the concept of "magical immunity" to computer viral attacks surfaces on a regular basis. This concept, while desirable, is misleading and dangerous since it tends to mask a real threat. The latest paper to surface was published by a respected technical organization of great reputation. This paper asserted that UNIX and Amiga computer systems were immune to viral attacks because they made use of hardware instructions that provide a Supervisor mode of operation. Supervisor mode is a concept that requires access to restricted services in order to perform certain functions. It was implied that this mode imbued the operating system with protection. On the surface, this argument is academically stimulating; however, upon consideration, the argument becomes transparent and fails. The use of Supervisor mode is not necessary for viral infection, therefore the argument is moot. In addition, access to Super User Mode is easily obtainable through the many holes that are common in all operating systems. These facts are supported by the existence of viruses that infect the UNIX and Amiga systems.

ROM-Based Operating Systems Do Not Provide Protection

In the paper "From Little Acorns Mighty Viruses Grow," Alan Glover of Pineapple Software disclosed that the Acorn Archimedes computer, which holds all of its operating system and windowing systems locked in hardware-based read-only memory has been successfully infected by computer viruses. This is an extreme case of hardware-based protection, and yet it failed. As of January 1994, there were 52 virus families totaling 84 viruses affecting the system. Compared to the Acorn computer, UNIX and NT systems have very little chance of magical immunity.

REAL EXAMPLES

Scholarly reports in separate papers by Tom Duff and M. Douglas McIlroy of AT&T Bell Laboratories contained in the USENIX 1989 Volume 2 journal not only attest to the existence of viral code for UNIX, but provide full source code for a few examples. These examples are provided in the Bourne shell script language, and Duff also provided the information necessary for the infection of UNIX system binaries. The existence of these papers in 1989 puts to an end, for all time, the plausibility that UNIX is, or ever has been, immune to viral attack.

Having disproved the immunity of UNIX to virus attacks by referencing known UNIX viruses, I turn the discussion to the virility of these attacks. Past experiments by Dr. Fred Cohen (1984) in which he used a UNIX system user account without privileged access, yielded total security penetration in 30 minutes. Cohen repeated these results on many versions of UNIX, including AT&T Secure UNIX and over 20 commercial implementations. These results have been confirmed by independent researchers.

In McIlroy's paper, he attributes Highland (1988) with the statement, "Most computer programmers, aside from virus researchers, have . . . difficulty in writing the code to make a virus replicate itself and secure itself to another disk." McIlroy then references Thompson (1984): "Despite the claim, programs that reproduce themselves are not hard to make." This has also been my experience.

Operating System Components and Attack Payloads

Those components of an operating system that are deemed necessary for practical use, such as copy, append, change permission settings, and hundreds of other basic functions, are the only necessary building blocks for viral code. Many simple and normal functions that may pass a security screen, when combined implement a virus. A simple example of a virus would be a program that located files, targeted hosts, and then proceeded to infect them. This can be easily accomplished by "find / -type f -exec file{}\; ρep command | sed ---." The options for "sed" were withheld. A virus of this type could potentially carry a payload of "/bin/rm -rf / > /dev/null 2>&1." This payload can be set for a specific activation time and would be both silent and devastating. In fact, the recursive bin remove attack is the most common payload of virus, time bomb, and Trojan Horse attacks in UNIX. Even in systems that are well protected, it is a common practice for users to have their own files unprotected, (permission setting 777 octal). If the remove attack was executed by a standard user account, without privilege, it will remove many of the user data files from the system. I suggest that the reader not experiment with this form of attack.

Script Viruses Are Simple

Many of the examples provided for UNIX viruses have been written in shell script. As proof that a relativity unsophisticated shell language can easily be used for writing virus code, Richard B. Levin published the source code to an MSDOS ".bat" virus in his book *The Computer Virus Handbook* (Osborne, 1990). On page 9 he demonstrated that a .bat virus can be reduced to one line:

```
for %%fin (*.bat) do copy %%f + bfv.bat
```

Virus Technology Is Easily Available

The simplicity of writing virus code is further aided by the existence of virus "cook books." Some of the books provide direction for the design, writing and implementation of computer viruses. One book by Mark Ludwig, *The Little Black Book of Computer Viruses,* contains full source code for sophisticated MSDOS executable viruses. The reader can also obtain the source, hex listings and compiled samples on diskette. A second book by Ludwig, *The Giant Black Book of Computer Viruses,* contains the source code for two UNIX companion viruses written in the C language. The book *UNIX Security: A Practical Tutorial* by N. Derek Arnold dedicated all of Chapter 13 to the explanation of viral activity under UNIX, including a working example in C language source code.

Information of this type is easy to obtain even from sources that do not intend to give it out. *The PC Virus Control Handbook* by Robert V. Jacobson contains enough information about fighting virus infections to write a virus. All of the information, skills, and techniques of virus writing is transferable between operating systems.

Productivity Tools Amplify Ability

Productivity tools that amplify a programmer's ability work equally well on constructive as well as destructive projects. Virus computer-aided design and manufacturing programs V-CAD/CAM programs exist in the MSDOS environment. At least one V-CAD/CAM program is graphically enabled, thereby allowing the user to select virus attributes using a mouse. Automated auditing and penetration testing (attack) programs have existed for many years in the UNIX environment: COPS, Tiger Script, SATAN, Root Kit, and Crack. Since both systems are known to support hostile, it is only a small jump to understand that all V-CAD/CAM ability is portable as a working idea from MSDOS to UNIX.

All of these programs have been available via computer bulletin boards and at least one underground network (Nuke Net) for many years, and they have moved to the Internet with its new widespread popularity and ease of use. It is not hard to locate a library of hacker tools on the Internet using any of the publicly available Internet search engines. (This was predicted in the first printing of this paper: "The advent of Nuke Net will pale in significance once viral authors discover the Internet.")

All of this technology is applicable to UNIX and any other complex operating system such as Microsoft NT. In general, technology and ideas move from simple systems to complex systems. In this case, from MS-DOS to UNIX and Microsoft NT.

Why Not More UNIX Attacks?

In the paper "Computer Virus Awareness for UNIX," I stated that the reason there have not been more UNIX attacks is because virus programmers could not afford the hardware necessary to execute the UNIX system. This is no longer true. UNIX is widely available at universities, offices, and libraries. The cost of used UNIX workstations such as Sun Microsystems Sparc 2 systems are selling at the same price as new PC-based systems. In addition, the advent of Free BSD, BSDI, Linux, and the newer, lower-cost versions of SCO UNIX and SCO Unixware have made full-function UNIX available on low-end PC systems. Due to the new popularity of the Internet, whose backbone and most of the servers are UNIX systems, it is no longer considered unusual to find UNIX systems in people's homes. The availability of UNIX, especially Linux, is now the same as or greater than any other system. Rarity will no longer provide any level of protection for UNIX.

A second reason there have not been more UNIX attacks is that attacks are not reported. Nothing inspires success as well as success, and the lack of publicity UNIX attack programs have received has had a beneficial damping effect. There are two reasons for the minimal publicity: some of the organizations that track these attacks have made it policy not to report them, hoping to not fan the flames; and the media circus surrounding the Internet Worm and Michelangelo attacks has left the press gun shy. (Even the press doesn't want to look foolish by being alarmist, although the nightly television news may convince you otherwise.) In addition, there is no reason to publicize anything but the most spectacular events, such as the Internet Worm. Since then, in 1992 a major European university was infected with a UNIX script virus; in 1993 there were rumors of a virus infection at a major American oil company; in 1995 an international computer network using PC UNIX systems died from the Michelangelo virus, with a repeat performance in 1996. There were also many infections not worthy of special note, and examples of the Typhoid Mary Syndrome that occurred in actual real world operation. None of this was reported to the general public, which while having a desirable and beneficial effect, also left many systems administrators in the dark about the risks they may be facing.

What to Expect

The sophistication of computer viruses and virus programmers are increasing. There is no effective way to turn back the clock, and legal measures will not help. Making the possession of viruses or other attack code illegal may, in fact, make dealing with the problem significantly more complex while removing useful penetration testing tools from the hands of legitimate users.

Complacency caused by a lack of understanding, publicity, and a desire to not acknowledge possible problems in relation to the UNIX system will insure that when the next major incident occurs, it will be of global scale. The interconnection of the world's computer networks via the Internet will insure that no one is spared and that the entire event will occur worldwide before anyone knows that it has happened.

In *Computer Security,* Ralph Roberts and Pamela Kane state that information is today's gold and that "the ultimate responsibility for protection of yourself and your property rests with you." Well said.

*   *   *

Postscript, April 1996. It appears that everyone is from Missouri, the Show Me state. Very few people have bothered to follow the references given in this paper since its release in 1993. Consequently, people are no better educated about or prepared to deal with software-based attacks than they were three years ago.

The reason that I did not give more explicit examples in the original paper was that it was an industry practice to not do so. I don't believe in this practice, but it was intended to fight the rumors that the antivirus industry was creating viruses for it to fight. These rumors were ridiculous and appear to have all but disappeared. No one in the antivirus industry has the time, energy, or money to do so, and no one is willing to take the risk, especially since the problem is already so large. For these reasons and because I believe that "security through obscurity is insecurity" (for philosophical reference, read *Rudimentary Treatise on the Constructions of Locks,* 1853 by Charles Tomlinson), I will now provide a nonfunctional, weak but educational example of code fragments that will allow the reader to understand the actions of a virus attack on a UNIX system. The reader should not make the mistake of believing that this example is the only format that such code may take because examples of code found "in the wild" have included stronger algorithms.

In honor of Tomlinson, whose philosophical treatise has improved my understanding of the world and because it is always convenient to name code fragments for future reference, this example is named the 1853 UNIX Example Virus.

Many parts of the UNIX operating system are written in script languages. It is therefore desirable to write viruses in a script language. An additional benefit of writing the attack in a script language is that script programs are portable between different manufacturers' systems, while executable binaries are not. It is therefore necessary for an attacking script virus to identify other script programs as potential targets. This can be done using this command:

```
find / -type f -exec file { } \; | grep command | awk {print $2} . . .
```

The first line of a program written in script normally controls which script language it executes in. This line appears as a comment if contained anywhere else in the body of the program. It is therefore necessary for an attacking virus to preserve the first line of the target program. This can be done using the "head -1 $target > /tmp/trash" command.

Assuming the virus is the first nine lines of code following the first line of the program, then the virus can be extracted from the attacking host using the following code fragment:

```
head -10 $0 > /tmp/trash
tail -9 /tmp/trash > /tmp/trash2
```

The file "/tmp/trash2" now contains the virus body. To complete the attack and infect a target file, the code fragments may be assembled somewhat like this:

```
head -10 $0 > /tmp/trash
tail -9 /tmp/trash > /tmp/trash2
head -1 $target > /tmp/trash3
cat /tmp/trash3 /tmp/trash2 > /tmp/trash4
cat /tmp/trash4 > $target
/bin/rm -f /tmp/trash*
```

The results of infection will appear as follows:

Original Target Code	*Infected Code*
#!/bin/sh	#!/bin/sh
[body of target program]	[virus body]
	#!/bin/sh
	[body of target program]

Typical payloads such as a recursive bin remove (/bin/rm -rf / > dev/null 2>&1) or the insertion of a back door (cp /bin/sh /tmp/gotu ;chmod 4777 /tmp/gotu) can be carried in the body of the virus.

I hope that this illustration of the mechanical operation of a virus ends the discussion on the plausibility of UNIX viruses. *UNIX viruses can and do exist.* They have been found infecting sites "in the wild" and are not curiosity items.

Reference materials are listed by date of publication. This is not a full or extensive reference but a resource guide for the reader who wishes to continue investigations into this subject.

Tomlinson, Charles. *Rudimentary Treatise on the Construction of Locks,* 1853. Contained in *Firewalls and Internet Security* (see below).

Roberts, Ralph and Pamela Kane. *Computer Security.* Compute! Publications, 1989 (ISBN 88-63151).

Duff, Tom. "Experience with Viruses on UNIX Systems." *USENIX Computing Systems* 2 (2): Spring 1989 (ISBN 0895-6340).

McIlroy, M. Douglas. "Virology 101." *USENIX Computing Systems* 2 (2): Spring 1989 (ISBN 0895-6340).

Cohen, Dr. Frederick B. *A Short Course on Computer Viruses.* ASP Press, 1990 (ISBN 1-878109-01-4). Other papers by Dr. Cohen, multiple dates, are available from HTTP URL:åll.net.

Ludwig, Mark. *The Little Black Book of Computer Viruses.* American Eagle Publications, 1990 (ISBN 0-929408-02-0).

Jacobean, Robert V. *The PC Virus Control Handbook,* 2nd ed. Miller Freedman Publications, 1990 (ISBN 0-87930-194-5).

Radatti, Peter. "Heterogeneous Computer Viruses in a Networked UNIX Environment." Cybersoft, 1991, 1996 (available from HTTP URL:www.cyber.com).

Radatti, Peter. "Computer Virus Awareness for UNIX." *NCSA News* 3 (3): May/June 1992, p. 8.

Arnold, N. Derek. *UNIX Security: A Practical Tutorial.* McGraw-Hill, 1993, paperback (ISBN 0-07-002560-6).

Cheswick, William R. and Steven M. Bellovin. *Firewalls and Internet Security.* Addison-Wesley Professional Computing Series, 1994 (ISBN 0-201-63357-4).

Glover, Alan. "From Little Acorns Mighty Viruses Grow." *Pineapple Software Virus Bulletin* February 1994 (ISSN 0956-9979).

Radatti, Peter. "Computer Viruses in UNIX Networks." Cybersoft, 1995, 1996 (available from HTTP URL:www.cyber.com).

Ludwig, Mark. *The Giant Black Book of Computer Viruses.* American Eagle Publications, 1995 (ISBN 0-929408-10-1).

6

Sniffers and the Switch

"No matter what you do, you can't trust the phone company."

—RAY KAPLAN TELECONFERENCE, NOVEMBER 24, 1992.

SNIFFING THE NETWORKS IS A FAVORITE TECHNIQUE of the Information Warrior. Networks are groups of computers that have been connected to each other with wires or, in some cases, talk to each other over radio signals. Put together enough networks and we end up with the Global Network, populated by Computers Everywhere. A LAN, or local area network, is the easiest to visualize and is found in almost every office. In a LAN, one computer can retrieve information from another computer on the same LAN, or several computers can use the same network-ready software that is shared by everyone. Printers or modems may be shared, and everyone can inundate everyone else on the network with boring E-mail messages, directions to the company picnic, or politically incorrect jokes.

Literally millions of small networks are tied together throughout corporate America, the Government, and small businesses, and it is this massive proliferation of communications connectivity that makes these networks such an inviting target for the Information Warrior. Why? Because during the 1980s, when networks were designed and built, and even

175

today, security has been an afterthought—if considered at all. Networks are essentially wide-open sieves to anyone with minor technical skills and the desire to retrieve other people's information.

The Information Warrior will want to break into a company's network for one of several reasons:

1. To listen to conversations between the computers on the network.
2. To gain illicit entry into the computers and look around for valuable data.
3. To gain illicit entry into the network for the purpose of shutting it down.
4. To learn passwords and access code that will give the Information Warrior unlimited access to the networks any time he chooses.
5. To listen to "private" electronic mail (E-mail) between users on the network.

Given the kinds of private, financially valuable, time-sensitive, and mission-critical information that traverses the Global Network at any given moment, is it any wonder that Information Warriors are constantly on the lookout for means of gaining entry? Of course not. Hundreds of technical articles have been written in the last couple of years describing in great depth just how the Information Warrior gets into networks.

If the Information Warrior is good at his job, his unwanted presence within a company's network will go unnoticed for days, weeks, or months. What can he do during that time period? Pretty much anything he wants, as long as it won't give his activities away.

The Information Warrior may merely be on a hunting expedition, looking for tidbits of value to himself or his superiors. Cliff Stoll's Hanover Hacker in *Cuckoo's Egg* searched around university- and government-sponsored research computers for anything to do with SDI, Star Wars, and a list of similar key words. Or the Information Warrior may have targeted a particular company for very specific information. During the summer of 1991, a U.S. automobile manufacturer estimated it lost $500 million because a hacking Information Warrior broke into their networks and stole designs for future cars. Those plans instantly ended up in the hands of their competitors.[1]

How the Information Warrior breaks into a network offers insight into just how hard it is to protect them. Perhaps the most insidious method is that of "sniffing."

Remember that networks are built with wires connecting the computers together. All of the data run down those wires. How can the Information Warrior get at it? Invisibly. One method is to use a network analyzer. The analyzer is a piece of test equipment meant to diagnose and assist in the repair of the network. It reports who is on the network; how much of the network is being used or is under-used; if the network is operating properly or where it needs fixing; and it divulges secret passwords and access codes. A powerful tool for the network administrator, it is also a fine weapon for the Information Warrior.

Software provides other means of sniffing a network. Commercially available sniffer programs that can run on small desktop or laptop computers are also able to get the information the Information Warrior wants. In some cases, the software is written so that the legitimate network administrator doesn't even know someone is snooping. The manufacturers of such LAN sniffing software aren't attempting to build an arsenal for the Information Warrior, but the capabilities are there nonetheless.

The Cyberspace underground stockpiles a number of software-driven sniffers that function the same way, except that many of them are designed specifically to meet the goals of the Information Warrior. One such program is called "IPX Permissive"; it allows the interloper to read and decipher Novell network packets.[2] According to those familiar with the development of underground software, dozens of similar software programs exist that allow users to listen in on data transmissions undetected.

The employee at a large company who wants to decode other users' passwords might only have to install the correct software on his own computer and let it listen to passwords for days at a time. Once the passwords are in his possession, what he does with them is ultimately at the expense of the company. He might sell them to other Information Warriors, or he might use them to get even more valuable information to which he is not normally given access.

One of the dangers facing a company's networks is the incredible maze of wires that connect the computers. They run down hallways, over doors, under carpets, and through dropped ceilings. The network wiring is functionally invisible and, once installed and working, is generally forgotten— except to the Information Warrior. He could, for example, connect a "sniffer" to the network wire, hiding it in the ceiling of the research and development department and capturing the latest great designs which can then be sold for millions to competitors.

The Information Warrior may elect to use a method known as passive sniffing. Instead of a hard-wired connection, a magnetic inductor, (also known as a current probe or trans- ducer) is strapped around the network wire where it picks up the magnetic fluctuations caused by the electrical data flow, converts them back to an electrical signal, and into the sniffer. The advantages are clear:

1. There is no disruption to the network while the sniffer is installed.
2. Since there is no electrical connection with the net- work, there is no simple way to detect the sniffer's presence.

The Information Warrior would have little trouble install- ing a small passive sniffer in most companies. Often the most protection that the company provides the network, and thus their information, is the receptionist. Consider the following scenario:

At 4:20 PM on Friday, the Secrets for Big Shots Co., Inc., on the thirty-second floor of a Park Avenue high rise in New York, is celebrating the boss's birthday. Everyone is looking forward to the weekend. The elevator bell rings, the door opens, and into the reception area walks a telephone company man. He's dressed in jeans, a Nynex workshirt, a white and blue telephone company hard hat, and his belt is full of tools and phone gear. In his hand is yet another mysterious-looking piece of electronic gear. He says to the receptionist, "Jeeeez, what a day," as he wipes his sweaty forehead. The receptionist barely glances at him, more interested in the revelry behind the glass doors where the cake is being cut.

"Yeah, Thank God it's Friday," she agrees.

"I really hate these last minute emergencies. I was on my way out to the shore for the weekend. . . ."

"What's wrong?" the receptionist asks. If the phones go down, it makes her look bad.

The phone man smiles. "Nothing for you to worry about. Simplex Corp. on the seventeenth floor lost half of their lines, and I've got to fix them before I can get outta here. Where's the phone room?"

"Oh, yeah. Sure." She hands him the keys. "It's over there. And, do me a favor?"

"Sure," the phone man responds. "Whatever."

"If I'm gone when you're through, put the keys back in the top drawer? I'm kind of new and . . ." she hesitates.

"No problem. Most bosses are jerks anyway, and don't know what real work is all about."

"Gee, thanks," she says, smiling a big appreciative smile.

The "phone man" opens the closet, located next to elevators where it was easy to install long wires up and down the height of the building. But, in this phone closet, the Secrets for Big Shots Co., Inc. also put a lot of its network controls. It's a lot easier to run the phone and network wiring at the same time and thus put the control gear in the same place.

He walks into the small phone closet, turns on the lights and, just as expected, a dizzying maze of wires, boxes, power cords, blinking lights, and racks of equipment fill the room. He smiles. This is perfect.

He takes a small donut-shaped piece of metal from his belt, opens it and snaps it tightly around one of the wires. He then plugs a small wire from the metal clamp to the box he carried, and then plugs that into the wall. Power on. Lights on. Good, everything seems to work. He moves a few wires and proceeds to hide the box and the clamp behind a large rack that contains a seemingly endless array of electronic gear. He brings out a walkie-talkie.

"Well?" he asks.

The receiver crackles. "We got it. Not much traffic, but enough to show it works."

"Ten four."

The phone man slaps the walkie-talkie back in his belt, opens the door, turns out the light, and hands the keys back to the receptionist.

"Done already?" she asks.

"Yeah, I was lucky. It was just a dirty connection. Looks like I might beat the traffic yet! Have a great weekend."

"Thanks. You too."

Obviously this wasn't the case of a phone man fixing a faulty line. It was an Information Warrior installing a passive network sniffer which also contained a small radio transmitter. The radio broadcasts all of the data and passwords that the network processes to a remote receiver. Invisible. Passive. Insidious.

Networks are highly vulnerable to the Information Warrior, and he knows of at least fifteen specific Achilles' Heels in the average network. All he needs is the right software or hardware to take advantage of the weakness of the network. In the continuous search for passwords, for example, these vulnerable points are:

1. The user himself.
2. The memory inside the keyboard.
3. The terminal emulator.
4. The LAN, or network driver software.
5. The LAN connection card.
6. The network cabling itself.
7. The network server.
8. The peer, or other user's nodes.
9. The gateway, router, or bridge to other networks.
10. The WAN, or wide area network, interface.
11. The WAN itself.
12. The mainframe front-end processor.
13. The channel to the mainframe.
14. The mainframe itself.
15. The mainframe application.[3]

Many networks are much more complicated than this and have many more points of vulnerability, but the point is clear. To adequately protect the network, the defensive Information Warrior has to secure countless points of possible attack; the offensive Information Warrior only has to find and exploit one weakness. It just doesn't seem fair.

Destruction of the network, thus crippling the company, is another potential goal of the Information Warrior. The Internet WORM of 1988 was just such an event. Robert Morris, Jr., the son of a respected scientist who works for the National Security Agency, single-handedly brought thousands of computers across this country to a grinding halt. His method? He wrote a computer program known as a WORM, which eats up the memory and resources of computers, effectively rendering them useless.

Only when affected users talked to each other did they discover that they all had the same problem. The search was then on for the mysterious piece of software traveling around the Global Network which was turning high speed computers into crawling snails. Releasing a WORM on the Internet, accidental or not, was a major incident, but the same technique is available to any Information Warrior. He might merely choose to aim the WORM at a smaller target; perhaps just one company or one type of computer.

The Internet connects two million host computers and allows access by millions more. Almost every country has at least one Internet connection, and over 100,000 million bytes of data travel across its wires every day.[4] With the volume increasing at fifteen percent per month and doubling every six months, the Internet is getting full. According to David Clark, a researcher at the Massachusetts Institute of Technology's computer science lab, the Internet is an ideal target for terrorists or Information Warriors. "I think we are in deep trouble. . . . What do terrorists like? They like events that cause publicity. Will this be the decade of the cyberterrorist?"[5]

Hackers have been using the Internet as a gateway into thousands of computers for years. One example occurred in mid-1992 when the National Oceanic and Atmospheric Administration found that a hacker had come through its modem pool (a large group of modems connected to the same network) and breached their network in search of a free door to the Internet.[6] Hacker archives, police reports, and the media are full of similar reports, few of which were ever followed up to the point of prosecution. It's just too labor- and time-consuming.

Eugene Shultz, a former security manager at the government-sponsored Lawrence Livermore National Laboratories, agrees that the Internet breeds hackers and their brethren, cyber-punks. "It's very possible to see a hundred or more attacks in a single day."[7]

And Shultz ought to know. In a confidential Livermore internal memo, Shultz speaks about a string of recent break-ins. ". . . one hacker from the Netherlands was bragging that he had been using AUTOVON, the unclassified U.S. military telephone network, to break into systems; subsequently, other sources within the U.S. Army have informed us that they have recently found that AUTOVON has been illegally used for data transfer between computers."[8] The memo further speculates that, according to Livermore sources, the attacks against their networks might be financed by either the German news magazines *Der Spiegel* or *One Magazine* or "countries hostile to the U.S. are supplying the money and funneling it through one of these magazines."[9]

Network break-ins of this type came to a head during the Gulf War. Congress got into the act when it was discovered that Dutch hackers had penetrated at least thirty-four military computer systems by bobbing and weaving through the Internet from April 1990 through May 1991. The Senate Governmental Affairs Subcommittee on Government Information and Regulation held hearings chaired by Senator Herb Kohl (D-Wisc.) who said, "The hackers had access to crucial information regarding military personnel, the type and quantity of equipment being moved, and the development of important weapons systems."[10]

No major U.S. company has gone unaffected by the remote touch of a hacker at his keyboard as was so duly demonstrated in early February of 1994. The Internet experienced security breaches of unprecedented scope when perpetrators unknown cracked into hundreds of computer sites nationwide to steal tens or hundreds of thousands of passwords. Using sophisticated monitoring software, sniffers, and malicious software such as Trojan Horses, the large-scale digital robbery sits in a class by itself for scope, audacity, and potential damage. Their huge collection of purloined access codes would permit illicit entry into government, commercial, financial, and educational computers across the entire Internet.[11] For the first time, countless thousands of Internet users are being forced to change their passwords, which augers future security awareness in Cyberspace. Unfortunately, the sophistication of these Information Warriors will likely precipitate further incidents that will cause extensive damage financially and socially. This time we were lucky.

"The switch" is perhaps the biggest network of them all. The switch generically refers to the networks that carry voice, and now digital, signals to almost every home in America.

The switch is owned and operated by AT&T, Sprint, MCI, and the seven Baby Bells or Regional Bell Operating Companies (RBOCs). It is run by the dozens of small local telephone companies and the cellular phone companies who connect their pieces of the switch to the other pieces of the switch. The data components of the switch are run by such major players as British Telecom, Tymnet, and others who are competing for control of Cyberspace. All of these disparate companies work in a competitive harmony (government regulations and common sense dictate their behavior) to make the switch the largest computer and network in the world, and also the easiest to use. Today the switch and its owners are facing the onslaught of first generation Information Warriors, and their networks face exactly the same challenges as do corporate America.

It is the goal of the Information Warrior to get control of the switch, since he who controls the switch wields immense power. He can listen to and tape conversations, turn a home phone into a pay phone or, as happened to thin-haired security expert Donn Parker of SRI, have all calls to his home number forwarded to the Hair Club for Men. I have called hackers at home only to be forwarded to the White House switchboard. The switch contains billing records, payment histories, addresses, and other pertinent personal data for everyone with a phone. Every call you make, every call you receive, is on record in the telephone companies' computers. They have immense power.

The maintenance circuits for the switch are supposed to be accessible only to telephone company repair people, who can turn phones on or off, reroute them, or give them free billing. But hackers and phone phreaks have taken advantage of the maintenance ports to such an extent that many have had to be shut down in defense. Even unlisted numbers are stored within the switch, and unlisted numbers are still connected with a name and an address—if you know where to look.

Instructions on how to use (and abuse) telephone equipment are allegedly proprietary company information, but many of the secrets have been published in underground journals such as *Hactic, 2600,* and *Phrack.* I have received a number of documents, from various underground sources, that give step-by-step-instructions on exactly how to break into and use Tymnet switches. Once a hacker has access to the switch, he can eavesdrop on any conversation in the U.S.

Companies use their networks to make information and services available to their internal employees; they also want to provide certain information to their regional offices, traveling salespeople, and to some clients and suppliers. The modem is what permits computers to pass information and provide services over conventional telephone lines.

Until quite recently, companies did little if anything to protect the modems that give outsiders access to their networks and information. So, the Information Warrior knows that if he can find the right telephone number of the right modem within the right company, he stands a pretty good chance of breaking through into the network and getting access to the information itself. It happens every day, and major companies admit that they have been the victim of such penetrations, with varying amounts of damage.

The Demon Dialer is a common piece of underground software that scans thousands of phone numbers to determine which ones connect to a telephone and which ones connect to a computer. The software automatically makes a list of the number that have computers at the other end, while other software attempts to break into each computer network by cracking passwords. This information, and the software to obtain it, is then shared by the various types of cyberpunks who populate the computer underground. The hackers and phone phreaks then go after their ultimate target: the computers and networks themselves.

Using Demon Dialers, two young hackers scanned Seattle phone lines, "found a Federal Court computer and gained easy access to it. Once inside they found a list of passwords that were encoded in an unspecified manner. They then allegedly went into Boeing Aircraft's systems and used a super-powerful computer to decode the passwords so they could be used to get into sensitive Federal files, apparently with success. The two gained unrestricted access to Federal Court computers including files from the Grand Jury."[12]

Demon Dialers are typically home-brew devices made from common electronic components for a few dollars, as are a wide array of Colored Boxes that hackers and phone phreaks use to combat the phone system. In the U.S. these "toys" are illegal, but one enterprising Dutch firm, Hack Tic Technologies, makes what hackers call the Ultimate Phreaking Box. One hacker said, "Anything you can imagine doing to a phone or a switch, you can do with this box." According to one hacker, Devil's Advocate, "If you're searching for the phone phreaker's equivalent of an all-terrain vehicle, then you may just want to test drive this rocket."[13] The cost of this magic box designed to defeat billions of dollars worth of communications networks? A mere 350 Dutch Guilders or about $180 U.S. Getting them into the U.S. is easy, since all customs will see is a set of seemingly harmless electronics parts. But place one call to the Netherlands, enter the correct numerical sequence, and un-limited possibilities are opened up. Given the proliferation of such programs and tools within the underground, it is not difficult at all to appreciate the predicament of organizations with large numbers of networks and modems.

Breaking into networks and computers is quite common in the commercial sector, but industry does its best to keep it quiet. Occasionally, they can't. The Masters of Deception, a group of five New York hackers, were indicted on up to eleven charges for invading networks over a period of months in 1991 and 1992.[14] According to the Federal indictment, victims of this series of attacks included Southwestern Bell, British Telecom North America, New York Telephone, Pacific Bell, US West, ITT, Martin Marietta, TRW Information Services, Trans Union Credit, Information America, New York University, and Bank of America, among others.

In May of 1990, the Secret Service culminated a two-year investigation called Operation Sundevil. Arrests were made while forty-two computers and 23,000 disks were confiscated across New York, Chicago, Los Angeles, and ten other cities. The operation was supported by twenty-eight search warrants and 150 agents. The alleged crime ring "may account for losses of over $50 million in fourteen cities," said U.S. Senator Dennis DeConcini (D-Ariz.). Stephen McNamee, a U.S. Attorney in Arizona, said that the illicit use of computers might well become the white collar crime of the 1990s.[15]

For white collar crime, fax machines offer the Information Warrior an almost unlimited supply of information. A conventional phone tap listens in on voice conversations that can be taped, broadcast, and then used as needed. The same is true for fax transmissions. An entire industry is built around devices especially developed to intercept faxes. STG, a company that offers fax interception devices for "sale, lease, or rent," also claims in their brochure. "This fax interception device is so reliable . . . you can take it to court."

It is fairly simple for someone with a modicum of electronics training to build his own fax interception device, but for the Information Warrior who prefers to use off-the-shelf equipment manufacturers such as Burlex International, Mentor Links Inc., Sherwood Communications, El-Tec International, Knox Security Engineering, and others make the task that much easier. Given this widespread capability, one must wonder about how the federal government views the potential for abuse of these products on the part of the bad guys, whoever they might be.

In 1990, President Bush signed National Security Decision Directive 42, which addressed Federal concerns about telecommunications systems within the U.S. This document essentially replaced an earlier version, NSDD-145, signed by President Reagan. Portions of NSDD-42 were declassified on April 1, 1992, due in large part to the efforts of Marc Rotenberg at the D.C.-based Computer Professionals for Social Responsibility.

The opening paragraphs of NSDD-42 are standard boilerplate commentary on the importance of computers; however, the authors admit that the emerging technologies ". . . pose significant security challenges." Further explaining these challenges, NSDD-42 notes, "Telecommunications and information processing systems are highly susceptible to interception, unauthorized access, and related forms of technical exploitation as well as other dimensions of the foreign intelligence threat. The technology to exploit these electronic systems is widespread and is used extensively by foreign nations and can be employed, as well, by terrorist groups and criminal elements."[16]

This fear was realized in several major telephone service outages. In January, 1990, millions of customers were cut off from long distance service for over nine hours when software in an AT&T SS7 switching computer malfunctioned and the contagious failure spread throughout the massive telephone network. A year later in New Jersey, one of AT&T's high capacity fiber cables was accidentally cut. Then on September 17, 1991, telephone service was disrupted in New York when, according to AT&T, "power failures" caused two major switches to fail. Beyond customer inconvenience, the danger of losing telecommunications services became all too clear: The major airports in the New York area rely upon ground-based telephone lines for air traffic control. So, planes couldn't land, planes couldn't take off, and the resulting "stack-em and rack-em," as such a jam is called in air traffic lingo, created aeronautical chaos that spread around the globe for days.

A *Network World* editorial on September 30, 1991 summed up the incident quite succinctly. "The network is the life blood of the U.S. economic system." And so, again, such an obvious commentary was put to the test and proven. (A U.S. Army Intelligence officer told me in August 1990 that there was reason to believe the January 1990 outage may have been the deliberate work of software saboteurs. He claimed, without proof, that some of the hacker bulletin boards his intelligence agency monitored had actually predicted the outage and the sequence of cities to be affected. This allegation has never been proved, but it clearly demonstrates that the U.S. military has some awareness of the vulnerabilities to this country's communications networks.)

On September 29, 1992, as a result of these displays of vulnerability, the Defense Information Systems Agency issued a Statement of Work and followed it up on October 5, 1992 with a solicitation for a contract, Request for Proposal entitled "Public Switched Network Software Vulnerability Collection, Analysis and Modeling." In short, they wanted to find out what can go wrong with the phones. The strategic importance of the phone systems and its apparent vulnerability to the capabilities of the Information Warrior must have been of major interest to the government since DISA, an intelligence agency heavy-weight, was involved, and the winning contractors had to hold a U.S. secret clearance.

From the DISA Statement of Work in the Government's request:

> "The hacker threat may continue to evolve as technology evolves. There is a growing indication that the hacker community is becoming more organized and sophisticated. They have demonstrated the ability to penetrate software systems controlling the switches of the PSN (Public Switched Network, telephone companies). It is critical that the vulnerabilities be identified so that the software systems of the PSN can be modified to effectively lessens the threat to NS/EP (National Security) telecommunications systems."

The proposed contract called for the contractor to find system bugs, errors, and penetrations, and to search BBSs for information about who was likely to attack and by what means. Once the data was collected, the contractor would ". . . perform in-depth analysis to determine potential vulnerabilities within the PSN. The study shall also concentrate on determining trends and patterns that may develop from hacker activities."

The Information Warrior may be able to exploit an even

more subtle weakness within the nation's communications networks. On a recent cross-country trip, I sat next to a senior executive with a major telecommunications company and learned something I didn't know. Of all of the threats to phone switches, the phone company and the switch designers most fear the cutting of a major cable where hundreds and thousands of copper lines connect homes and businesses. Each phone switch is a computer with tens of thousands of phones connected to it, and each telephone unit represents an electrical load to the switch, just as a lightbulb or a refrigerator presents a load to the power company. If tens of thousands were suddenly disconnected from that switch, the load factor would immediately change, to the detriment of the switch and the phone company's other customers.

According to this executive (who wants to remain nameless for obvious reasons), this is what partially caused the domino-like failure of AT&T's network in 1990. One switch went crazy and effectively disconnected itself from other switches, which then had their own electrical temper tantrums. AT&T couldn't publicly admit that they knew they had built-in problems for fear of unleashing a rash of similar attacks. The phone companies fear that someone wanting to strike out at them would discover the location of the huge cables feeding the switch and go snip them. The plane-riding telco executive claims that the switch would essentially implode and be unable to provide service to its customers, whether they were connected to the cut cable or not. The switch itself would simply cease to function.

Why does this condition exist? Because the designers just can't consider every possible worst-case scenario. It is impossible to test for every possible contingency and in some cases the extra cost to protect against the unlikely just doesn't make prudent business sense. Besides, when the current breed of switches were designed, no one gave serious consideration to the idea that the phone company might be a target of an Information Warrior. Here once more, we find the same philosophical and mathematical bottleneck that affects software reliability: Goedel's Theorem strikes again.

Not all of the switch connections are made through and across wires of copper and fiber optics. Communications increasingly use the airwaves, as we see in the proliferation of cellular phones, Motorola's multi-billion dollar Iridium Project, and microwave and satellite transmissions. The electromagnetic ether represents a new battlefield for the Information Warrior.

Cellular phone conversations, for example, are wide open to interception by $179 scanner devices that can be bought from Radio Shack, *Monitoring Times* magazine, or dozens of other sources. Courts have upheld that there is no reasonable expectation of privacy when one is talking on a cellular phone.[17] In fact, the problems are so prevalent that back in 1987, Radio Shack sent out internal memos instructing salespeople not to assist in modification of their scanners, and informing them that future models would not be modifiable for this questionable activity.[18] Cellular phone conversations remain absurdly easy to intercept from a car, a backyard, or an office. Densely populated urban areas with high concentrations of cellular phones are a breeding ground for the Information Warrior.

The political implications of interception of cellular phone calls was brought into the national limelight when two political foes took to Cyberspace to fight their battles. On June 7, 1991, Governor Doug Wilder of Virginia charged that someone had tape recorded his private cellular phone calls and passed them on to his political adversary, Senator Charles Robb.[19] According to *The New York Times*, June 23, 1992, over one thousand cellular phones were used at the Democratic National Convention. Perhaps for reasons best left unsaid, the Republicans banned all cellular phones at their convention later that summer.[20] (What do the Republicans know that the Democrats don't?) And the British tabloids had a field day when transcripts of cellular conversations between Princess Di and her alleged lover were made public.

Cellular fraud is a related weapon of the Information Warrior. The goal is to make "free" phone calls although either you (the victim) get billed or the cellular company does, in which case the rates go up anyway. So you pay or you pay. Here's how it works: when you make a call, each cellular phone also broadcasts its internal electronic serial number or ESN. The ESN is used to legitimize the call by verifying the phone number and billing. The ESN is periodically rebroadcast along with other critical information, making its theft ridiculously simple. The Information Warrior then sucks the subscriber's phone number, the ESN, the station class data, and the manufacturer and dialed number out of the air.

Curtis Electro Devices of Mountain View, California, is one company that makes an ESN reader in a battery-driven, hand-held box, complete with antenna and digital readout. This is a perfectly legal device, ostensibly made for the repair and programming of cellular phones, but in the hands of the Information Warrior it can cost us all a great deal of money. The bad guys only have to reprogram some counterfeit chips, plug them into other cellular phones, and off they go: billing you for their calls to the drug czars in Colombia or Pakistan.

In the major U.S. metropolitan areas, rings work out of limousines focusing on poor immigrant areas, attracting people who cannot afford a phone or who might be here illegally yet still want to phone home. For as little as $5 per quarter hour, phone service is offered to anywhere in the world. Since the limousine is driving around the city, police cannot zero in on it. Income of $10,000 to $50,000 per day in cash, per operation is not unrealistic. The illicit chip may only be good for a few days until the miscreant behavior is discovered, but by then, a new stream of ESNs have been pulled from the air and the Information Warriors are ready to steal from a new set of victims, including the Government. In California, the highways have been outfitted with cellular phone boxes for use by stranded motorists. One phone bill they received was quite a surprise. It included an extra 11,733 calls for 25,875 minutes that cannot be matched with legitimate usage.

If Saddam Hussein had been listening to the microwaves in mid-1993, he might have been able to find out about the impending raid on Baghdad. Secretary of State Warren Christopher was receiving updates and advice from his staff in Washington, D.C., prior to the raid, and the cellular conversations were intercepted by a hacker who was scanning phones.

Maybe listening in isn't what all Information Warriors want to do. Maybe, as we discussed, their aim is more destructive. Truckers use CB radios to steer clear of cops and radar guns, but during the heyday of the 1970s CB rage, a popular game was to increase the power output of the CB to such a level that it would literally cause a passing motorist's CB to smoke. Truckers, of course, had the proper circuitry to handle the massive signal strength their fellow CBers were transmitting.

As satellite communications become the rule, the Information Warrior finds opportunity there, as well. On April 27, 1986, HBO viewers were rudely interrupted during the broadcast of *The Falcon and the Snowman*, when their screens suddenly displayed the message:

> Good evening HBO From Captain Midnight
> $12.95/Month No Way!
> (Showtime/Movie Channel Beware).

HBO's satellite signal had been overridden by a satellite hacker who was displeased with the scrambling of pay-for-view satellite transmissions.[21] The industry instantly convened to discuss the situation. It turned out that a threatening phone call was made prior to the jamming episode by a caller who only identified himself as "Carl." The caller warned, "This is electronic warfare."

Carl alleged that he was associated with the American Technocratic Association, based in Wilmington, Delaware. The group claimed that for a mere $25 million, they could "completely knock every satellite off the globe."[22] Showtime experienced similar interference with their satellite transponders in December of 1985, but not to the same degree.[23]

In an article entitled, "Declaration of Electronic War," author Bill Sullivan cited the concerns of the satellite industry about such threats. After the Captain Midnight interruption, the attendees at the meeting "wanted to keep a low profile and did not want that vulnerability disseminated to the general public . . . because [they] are so vulnerable to jamming." The ATA claimed that they were going to proceed with destructive jamming, by overloading the satellite transponders, and the consensus was that this was possible. John Roberts of United Video said, "I think a knowledgeable person could put together a satellite transmitter inexpensively . . ." and *Radio Electronics* magazine said, "One report stated that the [Captain Midnight] feat required a great deal of technical expertise and about $60,000 worth of equipment."[24] A Federal Communications Commission spokesman, Ron Lepkowski, admitted that, "We've always recognized the possibility."[25]

So, when we add it all up, just how bad is the situation? The SRI, under the leadership of Don Parker, published a report based upon interviews with hackers in the United States and Europe. In an abbreviated version of the paper, "The State of Security in Cyberspace," they concluded that the PSTNs (Public Switched Telephone Networks) are the least vulnerable to interception, PDNs (Public Data Networks) are somewhat more vulnerable, the Internet is "somewhat insecure," and the cellular phone system is the most vulnerable. Highlights of the report state:

- Malicious attacks on most networks . . . cannot be completely prevented now or in the future. . . .
- It is possible individuals or groups could bring down individual systems or related groups of systems on purpose or by accident. . . .
- We found no evidence that the current generation of U.S. hackers is attempting to sabotage entire networks. . . .

- There is some evidence that the newest generation of hackers may be more motivated by personal gain than the traditional ethic of sheer curiosity. . . .
- The four major areas of vulnerability uncovered in our research have little or nothing to do with specific software vulnerabilities per se.[26]

The most comprehensive public study on the actual costs of communications compromises was written under the expert guidance of lawyer John Haugh. In 1992 a two volume reference, *Toll Fraud and Telabuse: A Multibillion Dollar Problem* was published by Telecommunications Advisors. This study, which did not even include the Internet, documented how pervasive a problem telecommunication technology crimes really are. The opening line of the preface quotes an MCI statement from 1991: "There are two kinds of customers; those who have been the victims of toll fraud, and those who will be."

Haugh and his group's research supports that claim, with the statement that "the total cost of toll fraud and teleabuse is more than twice the estimated annual cost of the AIDS epidemic." They can support this statement, too, with detailed analyses. For example:

Stolen Long Distance	$1,800,000,000
800 Toll Fraud	350,000,000
Victim Costs	51,000,000
Carrier and Vendor Fees	32,000,000
Cellular Fraud	700,000,000
Credit Card Toll Fraud	400,000,000
COCOT Fraud	60,000,000
Subscription Fraud	300,000,000
Telabuse	5,200,000,000
Total	$8,893,000,000

That's almost $40 per person per year in the United States alone and, according to Telecommunications Advisors, these are highly conservative figures.

Haugh's group examines why toll fraud has remained a secret. The reasoning is similar to computer crime cover-ups: embarrassment, a tendency to blame the other guy, technological ignorance, and from the vendor standpoint, fear of hindering sales by telling potential customers that they could become victims.

Toll Fraud points out that lawsuits are pending and hundreds more are expected as fraud costs mount. Unless solutions are found, the courts are going to be jammed with fraud cases where ultimately, the perpetrator will not be caught, yet someone will have to pay: either the carrier or the victim. The problem is improving somewhat with Sprint, AT&T, and others offering insurance policies against telabuse. *Toll Fraud* warns companies and individuals who use long distance services that the problem is real and it's getting worse. "We see that the severity of the problem is decreasing; each event causes less financial damage," says Haugh, "but the frequency is dramatically increasing. Ultimately that means greater losses for everyone."

Private phone companies, the PBXs used by American businesses, are also ripped-off by amateur and professional Information Warriors. Just like the switch, a PBX is a small switch serving one company, and it has maintenance ports and a feature called DISA that allows employees to dial in and use the company's data and voice networks. The Information Warrior has found it profitable to break into these private phone companies and steal millions of dollars in services. The victims have to pay the bill or fight the fraudulent charges in court because the perpetrator is long gone.

Voice mail, a popular feature, has also fallen victim to hackers. Some companies have been blackmailed by hackers who have taken over their voice-mail systems. The hackers insist that unless they are permitted to use a portion of the PBX for their own purposes, the entire PBX will be destroyed. One well-known case involved two teenagers who, when they did not receive a promised promotional poster from a company, broke into the offending company's PBX and voice mail, held the company hostage, and eventually caused extensive damage.

But let's take Information Weaponry one step further, and ask ourselves what would happen if the theft of information were effected so discreetly, so invisibly, so insidiously, that there was no way at all to determine the losses? The losses to your organization might be deep, potentially fatal, but you'd never, ever know you'd been a victim of Information Warfare. You might just think that your firm was the victim of bad luck. The Information Warrior relies upon such uncertainty. He really doesn't want us to know what he's up to, and that further complicates our efforts at understanding his real goals and motivations.

Puzzle Palace Conducting Internet Surveillance

Wayne Madsen, Security Analyst

Reprinted with permission of Elsevier Advanced Technology Publications. Copyright Computer Fraud and Security Bulletin, *June 1995.*

According to well-placed sources within the federal government and the Internet service provider industry, the National Security Agency (NSA) is actively sniffing several key Internet router and gateway hosts. The NSA is particularly interested in destination and origination hosts (found within Internet Protocol [IP] packet headers) as well as key words and phrases. The signals intelligence agency has apparently recently contracted with a private company to develop the software code needed to accomplish the capture of Internet data of interest.

With calls for the U.S. intelligence community to become more intimately involved with the surveillance of anti-government Cyberspace groups in the aftermath of the Oklahoma City bombing, the NSA stands in a commanding position to accomplish such monitoring.

The NSA monitoring allegedly takes place primarily at two Internet routers that are controlled by the National Aeronautics and Space Administration (NASA). These are called FIX EAST and FIX WEST and are located at College Park, Maryland and NASA's Ames Research Center in Sunnyvale, California, respectively. One communications industry source has stated that, "NASA is catching traffic for NSA." Other NSA Internet sniffers are reportedly operational at other key Internet routers which, along with the FIX EAST and FIX WEST nodes, handle most or all of the Internet traffic transmitted internationally to and from the United States. Internet service provider sources confirm that the other Internet router nodes under surveillance are known as MAE EAST (an East Coast hub), MAE WEST (a West Coast hub), CIX (reportedly based in San Jose, California), and SWAB (an Internet router located in northern Virginia and operated by Bell Atlantic).

NSA is also apparently monitoring traffic being passed through large Internet gateways. This monitoring is said to be conducted at Network Access Points (NAPs) operated by regional and long-distance service providers. The NAPs allegedly under surveillance are located at gateway facilities in Pennsauken, New Jersey (operated by Sprint), Chicago (operated by AmeriTech and Bell Communications Research) and San Francisco (operated by Pacific Bell).

People familiar with the monitoring claim that the program is one of the NSA's "black projects," but that it is pretty much an open secret in the communications industry. One communications expert claimed that the NSA has "gone overboard" in its funding of the project and that what the NSA gets in return is not worth the money they have already invested in it.

One senior federal government source has reported that NSA has been particularly successful in convincing key members of the U.S. software industry to cooperate with it in producing software that makes Internet messages easier for NSA to intercept, and if they are encrypted, to decode. The knowledgeable government source claims that the NSA has concluded agreements with Microsoft, Lotus, and Netscape to permit the anonymity of Internet electronic mail, the use of cryptographic key-escrow, as well as software industry acceptance of the NSA-developed Digital Signature Standard (DSS).

NSA was almost prosecuted by the U.S. Justice Department during the 1970s when it was discovered that the agency was conducting illegal domestic surveillance of several anti-Vietnam War groups. This was in contravention of its original charter, which limits the communications spy agency to foreign communications intelligence gathering and the development of ciphers to protect U.S. government national security information.

Future Problems With Firewalls

Marcus J. Ranum, Chief Scientist, V-One

The basic problem we're going to encounter with firewalls in the next three to five years of development will revolve around expanding the trust boundaries and defining trust boundaries between firewall networks. Firewalls between networks represent a certain amount of inconvenience, and there's pressure to eliminate firewalls between business partners to make it easier for them to communicate. Many applications require high amounts of connectivity and cause pressure to open the firewall for increased access. We are paying, and will continue to pay, the price for our inability to design network applications with security as a built-in feature rather than as an afterthought.

The kinds of things that we're going to start to see over the next two to three years will be increasing numbers of firewalls that do point-to-point encryption between business partners. Such business partners may not necessarily trust each other but might be doing application-specific (e.g.,

Lotus Notes, SQL) traffic, or providing software updates to systems behind the firewall.

The problem with this type of traffic is that it breaks the firewall
model that everything outside is kept outside. Every time you bring in or
allow in something from the outside, you're increasing the chance that
the thing coming in from the outside is actually a hacker disguised as an
authorized user, or an attack program disguised as authorized data. Encryption is useful for protecting the endpoint connections, but it is not
sufficient to protect the host that the traffic is coming from. As we begin
to see the deployment of secure, wide-area network technologies such as
S-WAN or the IPV6-IPSEC option, we're going to have groups of machines that trust each other such that if you break into one of them you'll
be able to break into the others.

This situation, if you think about it, is not unlike the current situation
where you have a cluster of UNIX workstations where there are ".rhost"
files. If an attacker breaks into one member of that workstation cluster,
he's broken into the entire cluster. From the standpoint of Information
Warfare, attackers who are invading groups of firewalled systems will be
delayed by the firewalls, but firewall administrators will have to carefully manage the domains of trust and the trust relationships between
their systems or successful attacks will proceed extremely rapidly. Administrators must map out their security domains so that somebody who
breaks into one can't parlay that into an attack on another. Three to five
years down the road, the sophisticated hacker who wishes to break into a
target network will no longer simply attack the target network directly.
He will try to break into the target network's business partners with the
intent of stealing a user ID within the target network and then launching
an attack directly from there.

Other issues which firewalls don't address adequately that are going
to be problems in an Information Warfare environment are of course the
problems of insider attacks. Firewalls are implicitly weak against attacks
originating from inside. Therefore, once past the firewall, the successful
attacker can usually exploit the attack and do all sorts of damage within
a relatively unprotected network. One of the problems is going to be
building more flexible firewalls that can have different modes of operations so that if the network administrator determines that the network is
under attack, the firewall may begin to audit more information or may
begin to alert the administrator about certain types of outgoing traffic, etc.
In the future, firewalls and host security systems will need to cooperate
more effectively, with host security systems feeding their audit trail information into intrusion detection engines that might trigger changes in
the security posture of the firewall.

Countering Nonlethal Information Warfare: Lessons Learned on Foiling the Information Superhighwayman of the North American Public Switched Telephone Network

Henry M. Kluepfel, Vice President, SAIC

The United States relies for its very existence—economically, socially, and politically—on an extraordinarily sophisticated and intricate set of long-distance networks for energy distribution, communication, and transportation. Because these networks also rely upon each other, a truly serious disruption in any one will cascade quickly through the others, rending the vital fabric of our nation at its most crucial points. Under these circumstances, the ability to respond to national security crises will at least be severely constrained and may be completely interrupted for some crucial interval. Thus, in addition to their serious vulnerabilities to accidents and nature, these networks present a tempting target to terrorists and to any antagonist contemplating an international move contrary to U.S. interests.[1]—*America's Hidden Vulnerabilities*[2]

While warnings such as this one predict potentially catastrophic consequences, the fragility of today's global networks of computer-based systems, used to re-engineer America's industrial and military infrastructure into lanes on the Information Superhighway, together with concerns over Information Warfare, are taking front-burner attention on the agendas of military and civilian agencies within the United States. A September 1993 Department of Defense report said it best: "if hired by terrorists, hackers could cripple the nation's telephone system, create significant public health and safety problems, and cause serious economic shocks."[3]

This paper will describe and help to further set the stage for the establishment and realization of a defensive Information Warfare security baseline architecture for the National Information Infrastructure (NII) Information Superhighway and its global partners and components throughout their lifecycle, from research and development to deployment and beyond.

The Best Offense Is Often a Good Defense

Pogo said it best: "We have met the enemy, and he is us." Following a rash of intrusion incidents into unclassified but sensitive Department of

Defense computers systems, the DOD is now taking positive defensive Information Warfare steps to assess and correct its potential Information Warfare vulnerabilities.[4] For the past year, hired hackers within various agencies of the DOD have been conducting "sweeps" and vulnerability assessments of agency sites and network systems connected to MILNET/ Internet. According to new reports posted to the SPACE Warfare Website (http:infosec.nosc.mil/infosec.html), the testing consisted of using the same types of tools that hackers use when they penetrate systems connected to the Internet. Although the specific results of such testing are restricted to the affected sites and the Info-Warriors conducting the tests, general findings present a dour state of readiness and response to Information Warfare on the Information Superhighway.

While much has been learned over the last ten years in securing the Information Superhighway's public switched network infrastructure, even greater emphasis must be placed on addressing security in Cyberspace.

Security and information assurance as it applies to telecommunications in defensive Information Warfare may be viewed as a classical quality problem:[5]

- Inconstancy of purpose: There must be a clear goal related to security, privacy, and assurance beyond the immediate and often short term, reactive efforts.
- Emphasis on short-term results: Security is seen as a destination rather than a journey.
- Audits and self-assessment deficiencies: Auditors find and report on troubling exploitable vulnerabilities and inadequacy of controls only to have the reports collect dust waiting for the second and third follow-up report to find exacerbated vulnerabilities. Self-assessments are often inadequate in scope and depth, often tending to tell management what they want to hear. On the contrary, when people in the organization clearly understand corporate objectives, they measure themselves against those objectives.[6] Unfortunately, security objectives for industry or government are not well defined and understood with respect to the robustness issues in a heterogeneous, multi-vendor, multi-carrier/service provider environment of the NII.
- Mobility of management: This does not imbue trust in employees, contractors, and vendors, or offer long-term assurances that the problem is being adequately addressed in emerging technologies.
- Measurements are meaningless: Since less than 5 percent of intrusions are ever detected by systems administrators, and only 5 percent of those detected ever get reported to management, law enforcement, or other incident-tracking systems, striving for zero incidents may realize the narrow focused objective only to leave the infrastructure even more vulnerable to compromise.
- Recovery costs far outweigh prevention: Numerous studies of software quality and physical design have shown that designing it

right the first time is far more cost effective than piecemeal rein-
forcements and recovery efforts.

- Excessive potential liabilities: The potential for product liability
  and negligence often keeps security on the hush for fear of potential consequences if the vulnerabilities become known or inadequate corrective actions are applied.

As the Information Superhighway (national, defense, and global information infrastructures) becomes the metaphor of choice for the potential virtual infrastructure of electronic commerce, many believe that privacy
and security will become the linchpins of this twenty-first-century vision of
an NII.

A new report issued by the Clinton administration[7] summed it up this
way:

> If the NII is to succeed, a structure or a collection of structures—a
> security architecture—must exist to ensure security. The NRC report
> states: "This security architecture must include technical facilities,
> recommended operational procedures, and means for recourse within
> the legal system." This architecture will be based on a variety of public
> and private institutions and policies. Although an architecture will
> define how institutions, policies, and technologies interconnect, a
> sound security architecture will consist not of rigidly prescribed tech-
> nologies or solutions, but must be able to flexibly adapt to change. The
> report also notes that such an architecture will require research and
> development over time.
>
> As the United States as a whole becomes increasingly reliant on
> the NII for communications and information, other key components
> of the U.S. infrastructure will become dependent on it. For example,
> the power grid, transportation systems, financial institutions, and
> economic transaction data will all be dependent on the NII. Security
> weaknesses in the NII can place those infrastructure elements at risk.
> Hence a significant attack on the NII would be a threat to our national
> security in addition to the significant personal and economic harm it
> would cause.[8]

In an international economy and social infrastructure that every day
is growing more dependent on its communications networks, more attention must be placed on the security and integrity of the components and
interfaces of those critical structures by all interconnected service providers, vendors, and users. The old adage that the chain is only as strong
as the weakest link has never been as true as it is today when applied to
the issue of network security and integrity. It is with that tone that this
paper is written to help identify the potential Information Warfare threat
and address the cascading vulnerable infrastructure on which the Information Superhighway is being built.

Information Superhighway Field of Dreams

Over the last 20 years, the number of compromised systems, routers, networks, and development systems supporting the developing Information Superhighway have escalated and may very well approach nearly a quarter of a million nodes.

Dialing for Data in the Public Switched Network

While there is no definite intruder threat profile for the public switched network (PSN), many are adults with previous criminal records for computer-related crimes committed when they were juveniles. In 1987, Herbert Zinn, a 17-year-old hacker who called himself Shadowhawk, electronically broke into logistic support systems of NATO, AT&T #5ESS installation systems for the AUTOVON systems at Robins Air Force Base, and several AT&T Operations Support Systems R&D databases and support systems, stealing source code to 55 programs ranging from development code for installing switching systems to artificial intelligence language. He was detected by AT&T's investigations into allegations of threatening messages left by Shadowhawk on a hacker bulletin board in Texas.

Shadowhawk was later found guilty of violating the Computer Fraud and Abuse Act of 1986 in federal district court in Chicago and sentenced to nine months in prison. In addition, he was ordered to pay a $10,000 fine and serve two-and-a-half years of federal probation when released from prison. That case was a foretelling of the more serious LOD and MOD incidents to follow.[9] While no classified material was obtained, the government viewed the $21,000 in software programs stolen from the NATO computer as "sensitive."

Kevin Lee Poulsen, aka Dark Dante, a 31-year-old man with a history of computer hacking going back to when he was 14, is currently under indictment in California for espionage. He is charged with breaking into computer systems of Pacific Bell and wiretapping the contents of sensitive communications, including Air Force Classified Information on planned targets in the event of war.

Intruders often align themselves into groups of individuals with similar interests and skills, e.g., the Masters of Deception (MOD) who were convicted in federal court in New York City for breaking into some of the nation's most sophisticated computer systems to gain illegal access to the computers of Bank of America, Southwestern Bell, Martin Marietta, TRW Information Services, and New York University, among others. The five were also accused of selling information, such as people's credit reports, that they obtained illegally from the systems. The hackers, an ethnically mixed group from working-class neighborhoods around New York City, defied the stereotype of young computer aficionados as affluent suburbanites. They met through computer bulletin boards, and knew one another by nicknames like "Outlaw," "Corrupt," and "Acid Phreak."

In a written statement submitted to the federal district court, Corrupt admitted to illegal activities as a member of MOD:

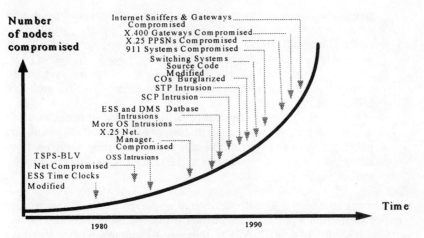

Figure 1. State of the NII security

1. I agreed to possess in excess of fifteen passwords which permitted me to gain access to various computer systems including all systems mentioned in the indictment and others. I did not have authorization to access these systems. I knew at the time that what I did was wrong.

2. I used these access devices and in doing so obtained the value of time I spent within these systems as well as the value of the passwords themselves which I acknowledge was more than $1,000.

3. I intentionally gained access to what I acknowledge are federal interest computers and I acknowledge that work had to be done to improve the security of these systems which was necessitated by my unauthorized access.

4. I was able to monitor data exchange between computer systems and by doing so intentionally obtained more passwords, identifications, and other data transmitted over _____ net and other networks.

5. I acknowledge that I and others planned to share passwords and transmitted information across state boundaries by modem or telephone lines and by doing so obtained the monetary value of the use of the systems I would otherwise have had to pay for.

Among the ways I and others agreed to carry out these acts are the following:

1. I was part of a group called MOD.

2. The members of the group exchanged information including passwords so that we could gain access to computer systems which we were not authorized to access.

3. I got passwords by monitoring _____ net, calling phone com-

pany employees and pretending to be computer technicians, and using computer programs to steal passwords. I participated in installing programs in computer systems that would give the highest level of access to members of MOD who possessed the secret password. I participated in altering telephone computer systems to obtain free calling services such as conference calling and free billing among others.

Finally, I obtained credit reports, telephone numbers and addresses as well as other information about individual people by gaining access to information and credit reporting services. I acknowledge that on November 5, 1991, I obtained passwords by monitoring _____ net.

Corrupt and his MOD colleagues had apparently gained access to a vendor-supported operations, administration, maintenance and provisioning (OAM&P) "debug" port to telephone company's backbone networks. By exploiting the group-based or default password for the diagnostic tool, the intruders then executed the packet monitoring program to read the data traffic at various points in the telcos PPSN—e.g., X.25 multiplexers.

By reading the data on the X.25 nodes and gateways, the intruders were able to capture logins and passwords transiting over or used within the packet network. With the help of the compromised logins and associated passwords, the intruders then attacked the downstream systems and networks.

All five of the defendants subsequently plead guilty and were sentenced to varying degrees of punishment ranging from probation to 14 months in a federal penitentiary followed by three months of home incarceration, followed by two years of probation and up to 600 hours of community service.

In another case, three adults and one juvenile, all members of the hacker group known as the Legion of Doom (LOD), were convicted and sentenced to prison in the fall of 1990 in federal court in Atlanta for their part in compromising the computer systems of BellSouth.

The defendants, who used the handles Leftist, Urvile, Prophet, and Fry Guy, admitted accessing the carrier's internal backbone X.25 packet network to penetrate the carriers OAM&P centers, systems, and databases to affect fraudulent service creation and modification, add call forwarding to customer lines, and monitor customer communications.

In yet another case, a hacker based in Europe claimed to have the ability to shut down a major computer-based financial network located in the United States by affecting environmental support systems such as power, cooling/heating, and ventilation systems. Telco and financial community investigations found a related security risk involving building environmental systems, which allowed potentially vulnerable remote access to heating, air conditioning, humidity, power, and elevator alarms and control settings. Since many of the network nodes supporting the PSN and its customers are designed to operate in controlled environmental conditions,

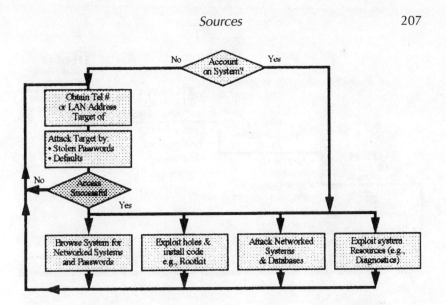

Figure 2. Attack postmortem

a potential vulnerability existed which if exploited by an intruder could cause catastrophic troubles to the network.

Intruders believe that the three easiest ways to penetrate a system are the following:

- Impersonate an authorized employee or vendor agent to affect the disclosure of sensitive access information or allow physical access to a facility housing critical systems
- Take advantage of the defaults shipped with the system and its software
- Fraudulently influence system hot line support personnel to give out information and or affect system changes; e.g., resetting a user's password

Many of the U.S.-based hackers who have been apprehended and prosecuted for their crimes were found to have had indirect electronic association with hackers in Germany, Australia, and Great Britain. The individuals located in Germany are the same espionage operative hackers described by Clifford Stoll in his best-selling book, *The Cuckoo's Egg*.[10] Known objectives for the attacks include financial gain, malicious destruction, and invasion of privacy.

It has become increasingly apparent that, without adequate attention to security, systems and networks are vulnerable to service-quality-impacting intrusions by unauthorized individuals (e.g., hackers) and groups (e.g., the hacker groups known as the Legion of Doom, 8LGM, and Masters of Deception). Such computer crimes always involve unauthorized persons, or persons who exceed their authorization, with adequate

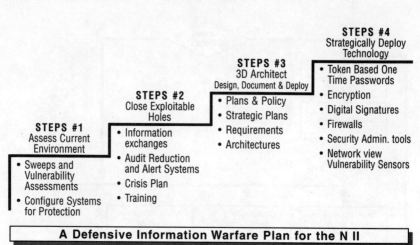

Figure 3. Four STEPS: Strategy to Enhance Protection Smartly

SKAM (Skills, Knowledge, Access, and Motive) acting on exploitable vulnerabilities. Knowledge and access are often afforded the would-be intruders through the compromise of system security bulletins often found in public sources and redistributed by the hackers on their own cites in Cyberspace, such as http://www.8lgm.org/advisories.html.[11]

Intrusion Targets

- Network management systems
- Privileged accounts and passwords
- Dial-in modem access and network PADs
- Data communication network connectivity
- Source and destination addresses
- Trust relationships
- Partitions and firewalls
- New "Security Admin Tools" (e.g., SATAN)
- Electronic commerce and banking

In the past, since it was very often not economically feasible to prevent intrusions, most service providers often focused their efforts on controlling losses through reactive deterrent and control measures.

Accordingly, and in recognition of the significant damage which might occur from such intrusions, a number of telecommunications carriers around the nation have begun to assess the effectiveness of security mechanisms in-place to protect the critical common environments supporting the interconnection of the global public network.[12]

If we assess the current wave of Internet attacks and fraud on the growing volume of electronic commerce transactions, we find surprisingly similar root causes.

Root Causes to NII Intrusions: A Balanced Paradigm

Policy

- No security architecture, critical domain firewalls, or accountability
- Not supported by administrators, users, or vendors

Behavior

- Absence of best practices
- Administrators and users were unaware, untrained, and poorly equipped to detect, counter, and contain threat early enough to succeed in protecting critical assets and resources
- Vendor-supported apathy

Technology

- Authentication mechanisms trailed intruders ability to compromise; e.g., guessable and exploitable passwords
- Maginot Line syndrome
- Overreliance on administrative procedures

It is easy to project that chaos is certain if we as a nation, industry, and government do not clearly define, support, and affect a holistic approach to network and information security focusing on root causes to intrusion to the NII/DII/GII. Technologies such as asychronous transfer mode (ATM) are seen as the platforms of choice for the fast lane of the Information Superhighway. Yet effective solutions and standards have not been developed to address the authentication of the source of OA&M cells which could affect the integrity of network management controls and features such as switched virtual circuits (SVC).

Saying it another way, absent effective security policies, requirements, standards, working agreements for vulnerability closure information-sharing, and penalties for nonconformance, chaos is certain and secure recovery readiness a necessity.

1. *America's Hidden Vulnerabilities: Crisis Management in a Society of Networks.* A Report of the Panel on Crisis Management of the CSIS Science and Technology Committee, Center for Strategic and International Studies, Georgetown University, Washington, D.C., 1984.
2. For 1995, the CSIS has revisited the topic area with its announcement of its Global Organized Crime Study, chaired by the Honor-

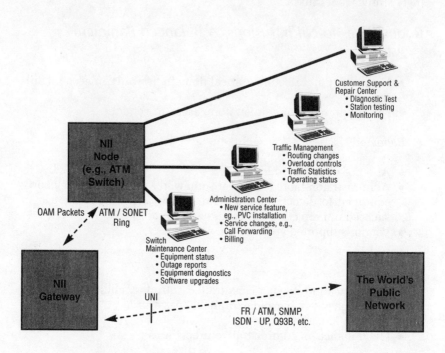

Figure 4. Operations, Administration, and Maintenance: The Achilles heel of security

able Judge William Webster, former head of the FBI and the CIA. The emphasis in the new study is to assess the vulnerability of the information infrastructure as a forensic root cause for criminal exploitation on a global basis.

3. Congressional Record, Senate, June 29, 1995 (legislative day of Monday June 19th), 104th Congress 1st Session. Statement of Senator Kyl introducing the Kyl-Leahy Bill (S.982) The National Information Infrastructure Protection Act of 1995.

4. "Information Warfare is the use of information and information systems as weapons in a conflict where information and information systems are the targets" (NCSA, 1995).

5. A complementary set of paradigms offered by the author to Deming's Seven Deadly Diseases (*From Out of the Crisis*, W. Edwards Deming).

6. Christopher Bartlett and Sumantra Ghosal, "Changing the Role of

Top Management: Beyond Systems to People," *Harvard Business Review,* May-June 1995.

7. *NII Security: The Federal Role,* Office of Management and Budget, 1995.

8. The telecommunications outages of 1990 and 1991 caused considerable concern and attention to be directed at the problem of network integrity, security, and assurance. So great was the potential societal impact of such widescale outages that the U.S. FAA revamped its Telecommunications Strategic Plan to significantly reinforce its reliability and security requirements. Realizing that the security threat to air traffic control has changed in character as computer and telecommunications technologies have grown more powerful, the FAA created a multipoint plan document to address security throughout the lifecycle of its future telecommunications environment.

9. At the time of his arrest, Shadowhawk indicated that he was taking most of his instruction and guidance on system penetration from the Prophet, a member of the Legion of Doom. Although he had never met the Prophet or any other LOD members face-to-face, they communicated over a LOD bulletin board known as PHREAK KLASS 2600 in Lubbock, Texas.

10. "Russian Mobsters Loot US Firms Via Computer; Cyberspace Remains a Lawless Frontier," *Washington Post,* February 6, 1995.

11. The following references, all by the author, are offered for additional information on the threat: "Recipe for Hacker Heartburn," *Security Management,* January 1995; "Securing a Global Village and Its Resources," *IEEE Communications Magazine,* September 1994; "Current Security Issues of Open Networks," *IEEE-ICCST,* October 1990; "In Search of the Cuckoo's Nest: An Auditing Framework for Evaluating the Security of Open Networks," *EDP Auditor Journal* 3: 1991.

12. Reference here is to the plethora of security threat information developed and mitigated by the President's National Security Telecommunications Advisory Committee (NSTAC). Composed of just under 30 senior executives representing the nation's telecommunications, information service providers, equipment manufacturers, and infrastructure-dependent NSEP impacting community members—e.g., national banking concerns—the NSTAC enables the federal government to work in partnership with industry to address a broad range of national security and emergency preparedness (NS/EP) issues. These currently include network security, standards for network infrastructure assurance, priority electric service restoration and refueling of critical telecommunications facilities, enhanced call completion for NS/EP users, the Telecommunications Service Priority (TSP) System, the Government Emergency Telecommunications System

(GETS), Advanced Intelligent Network (AIN) for NS/EP, wireless digital services, potential vulnerabilities of common channel signaling (also known as Signaling System Number 7), and the NS/EP implications of the evolving NII.

Telewar: The Physical Vulnerabilities of a Global Electronic Economy

Ronald S. Eward, President, MarTech Strategies

National concern (and media hype) about information warfare is largely focused on the disruption of computer and communication networks through computer-based attack by hackers, disgruntled employees, industrial spies, and hostile governments. In such scenarios, the attacker normally targets the software which controls a specific level of the system. An attack on a banking network might involve a virus that periodically changes the routing codes on checks, wire transfers, and other time-sensitive financial instruments, resulting in transaction delays and a potentially huge financial loss. An attack on the public telephone network might be carried out by a former employee who, posing as a service technician, loads his own version of control software into a large central office switch—a time bomb set to go off during a peak calling period. Or a foreign agent might break into a miliary supply computer, sending vital equipment to the wrong destination at a critical time.

Although such attacks are very real and potentially very dangerous, there is another, less-glamorous form of attack which can be much more severe and much more difficult to prevent: an attack on the physical network itself.

The global communications network is a marvel of engineering. Undersea cables span the oceans, microwave and satellite systems blanket the earth with radio coverage, and telephone lines are ubiquitous in nearly every town and city. Although designed independently, these various communications facilities have evolved together and have become completely interdependent. This interdependency has resulted in the most complex system the human race has yet created, and also one of the most vulnerable. The hundreds of interconnected networks which make up the global infrastructure were designed to provide a high degree of reliability; however, this reliability is based on the statistical nature of accidental outages, and not on outages caused through hostile intent. This, combined with the simple fact that undersea cables, satellite earth stations, terrestrial lines, and other physical parts of the network are frighteningly simple to disrupt or destroy, creates a dangerous situation and makes the physical structure of the global network a tempting and vulnerable target for the information terrorist. This "telespace," as we call it, underlies Cyberspace and is often taken for granted, overlooked, or underappreciated.

Ironically, the system's complexity has so far protected it from successful attack because an attacker would find it far too difficult to figure out how to disrupt more than a small segment of the network. The proliferation of affordable, high-performance computing power suddenly and frighteningly brings the task of planning a major, controlled disruption into the realm of probability, and it is only a matter of time before a terrorist, a hostile government, or even a powerful and ruthless business interest makes the attempt.

Because certain segments or nodes of the global network are more critical than others, planning a strategically optimal attack requires detailed knowledge of the network's structure and dynamics, including major traffic routes, redundancies, traffic patterns, alternate routing paths, nodal capacity, and numerous other parameters. Much of this information is public; however, it takes a particular set of analytical skills, as well as a well-designed database, to capture this data and use it for destructive ends. Once in hand, both obvious and subtle attacks can be devised, ranging from nearly undetectable delays in financial networks to blatant disruption of military logistic communications during an international crisis. According to the DOD, 95 percent of the U.S. military's data traffic is carried on commercial facilities. Although the percentage of DOD international traffic is not this high, it has reached a critical dependency. The percentage of total traffic migrating to the global commercial infrastructure is rapidly increasing. National policy and U.S. military policy must reevaluate the utilization policies that have led to an overreliance on global commercial paths and nodes. Their predictability alone is a major threat to national security.

Global Electronic Economic Weaknesses

The new global economy is, after all, a global electronic economy; that is, one based on global electronic information networks (GANs). Without continuous and full-period operation of these networks, which require high reliability and availability, these enterprises flat-out lose productivity, lose money, lose knowledge or information advantages, or miss just-in-time delivery dates. Any of these effects can lead to the demise of the enterprise or sufficiently inadequate performance, causing severe losses in market or financial power. This importance to the success of what we call transnational enterprises (TNEs) is raising their consciousness to their dependence on worldwide communications facilities for their transport network (as it is now called in leading user circles) and how to protect their network, as well as the information carried or stored on it. Moreover, governments are becoming increasingly concerned over the damage that can be perpetrated on national economies or individual enterprises or sectors of the global economy.

I have developed and integrated several models, insights, and databases to obtain a unique and dramatic vision of worldwide communications in the early twenty-first century. Importantly, we have discovered and substantiated that the new world economic order (NWEO) and the new world information order (NWIO) have become mirror images. To paraphrase Marshall McLuhan: "The network is the message." It follows that to know one is to know the other. In other words, the collective GANs of the TNEs mirror the production and distribution networks of the global economy. The concentration of global economic activity carried out increasingly on a concentrated global communication plant is dangerously critical.

The year is 2005. Some 2,000 parent corporations operating transnationally control the global economy and largely determine the economic performance of the 200 domestic economies of the world. The TNEs operate principally in and across 105 countries in approximately 500 geographic or metropolitan areas defined by a certain radius or other area network topology. (I have identified six different area topologies).

These new electronics conurbations form metropolitan area networks (MANs) that may evolve into electronic city-states and form worldwide virtual communities. Comprising only 4 percent of the world's land mass, these MANs account for virtually all the world's production of goods and services and control most of the world's capacity for producing and consuming knowledge and information. These MANs are interconnected by a grid of undersea and cross-border terrestrial cable systems and fixed satellite systems via some 3,400 fixed satellite earth stations. The TNE electronic information networks mirror the production and distribution networks of the transnational economy (TE), which is, increasingly, a global electronic economy. This global transport network (GTN) is an integral part of the global information infrastructure and will become the subject of and target for a variety of possible information warfare (IW) or telemanipulation activities or operations. The GTN can be exploited to manipulate, disrupt, or destablize the global economy or selected domestic economies and/or specific sectors or individual enterprises comprising the global economy. In plain talk, knowledge of communication links and activities in relation to the operation of select TNEs can be used to destroy companies; negate sectoral, regional, or national growth; and turn out governments.

Changes in the Global Transport Network

The traditional international gateway/hierarchical switching distribution grid will change dramatically over the next few years.

MAN technology will be implemented throughout the world during the 1990s, establishing a new geographic market segment between local and long distance. The MAN will become a dominant concept in the global market, replacing the individual city as the appropriate planning unit. Each MAN will incorporate many cities and towns. The fiber-optic wired MAN will aggregate and distribute traffic and in many countries offer alternative, competitive distribution options. Emerging wireless technologies and systems will offer alternative and competitive access to businesses and residences. Both cable and satellite systems (teleports) will interconnect MANs around the world and interconnect with both fixed and wireless local distribution systems within each MAN.

New competitive access providers (CAPs) first surfaced in the United States, but are now spreading to other areas of the world such as London, Paris, Munich, Hong Kong, etc. Electric utilities around the world are eyeing telecom opportunities made possible by excess capacity on their optical power ground wire. New global satellite services will emerge to provide selective city-pair—or more appropriately, MAN-pair—connectivities. This presents many new opportunities for satellite-delivered services and should specifically stimulate demand for bandwidth-on-demand (BOD) satellite services.

Whether provided by monopolies or by competing local or metropolitan infrastructures, these new electronic conurbations will create new market aggregation/distribution clusters. This will result in many side effects, including a major transformation of the GTN. Whereas the years 1950-1995 witnessed the emergence of alternative international infrastructure, the years 1995-2005 will produce new or alternative local/metropolitan infrastructure with powerful distributive effects on the evolving worldwide transport network.

The communications industry is becoming an increasingly important aspect of the global community. The information highway is becoming the thread that links economic, political, and demographic societies that, for centuries, have been typically removed from cohabitation. This is a new wave—the information society is here. This is positive or negative, depending on your viewpoint.

The positive perspective is that commerce can benefit from real-time decision-making, banks can transfer money at the speed of light, medical advances in developed societies can stream to the outer reaches of the world to benefit all people, and the expansive knowledge of high-technology societies can reach the third-world nations. These are admirable and noteworthy goals to give guidance and direction to the purveyors of the information superhighway.

There is a dark side to this unfiltered data flow. There are hackers, thieves, terrorists, and generally unfriendly groups who will stop at nothing to get nuclear information to build weapons, to bring down banking industries, and to bring down entire companies and/or countries at the push of a carriage return. The system has vulnerabilities, and they can be exploited by software and hardware attacks. Most research on this subject has focused on the computer side of the network rather than on the transport side. There is a need to educate and train high-level government officials, policy-makers, and miliary planners, as well as telecommunication users and professionals who design and implement global

area networks for intra and inter-enterprise networks, about these vulnerabilities.

The GTN is undergoing a radical transformation that will make it even
more vulnerable. This translates into economic and political concerns for
the United States as well as other countries. As far as users are concerned,
the days of least-cost routing networks will soon be over. We must make
organizations aware of these concerns.

We offer six points to show how telewar acts targeting communications facilities or networks can be used to manipulate economic performance of selected targets and, in turn, manipulate the global economy.

1. The global economy is transitioning to a system of national economies
interconnected by a physical network of submarine cable and satellite information highways. Using these highways, service providers and users
construct logical networks to form wide (worldwide) area electronic information networks and systems for global electronic information transfer.
These networks are becoming the neural systems and connective tissue of
the new global electronic economy.

The global economy is comprised of about 200 domestic economies
plus the transnational economy. This transnational economy is driven
and shaped by the decisions, actions, and operations of some 1,600 parent corporations—TNEs—worldwide today, growing to around 2,000 by
the year 2005. (I call these firms transnational enterprises instead of
multinational enterprises because their behavior is best characterized as
operating transnationally rather than multinationally. The former term
captures the true flavor of operating across borders; the latter term can be
taken to mean operating in multiple countries, suggesting more a multi-
domestic operation rather than transnational operation.)

Research has determined that these relatively few TNEs, along with
associated collateral and derivative effects they spawn, determine the
logical network of global production, distribution, and consumption.
Through various joint ventures and supply-chain management, these
TNEs form inter-enterprise networks and what has also been referred to
as virtual corporations. These TNEs control at least 14 of 16 major sectors
of the transnational economy. The conjoined operation of these 2,000
parents across the 14 sectors creates an array of interconnected knowledge and information networks that mirror the world's production and
distribution networks. The combined operation of these TNEs, because
of their global economic importance, creates a surreal, yet real, virtual
world that is both part of and transcends the collective domestic economies of which they are a part. Telewar will manipulate these electronic
enterprises in a global electronic chess match to destabilize or sanction
specific sectors, enterprises, or governments.

2. In a related area of research, we have concluded that in 2005, over
90 percent of the operations of these TNEs will fall into approximately
500 defined geographic areas of a certain radius or other network topology residing in slightly over 100 countries. These areas will each have
multiple local and, over time, an interconnected MAN. Although some of

these areas are not yet considered metropolitan areas in the major city cluster sense, or they are not yet aware that they will likely become future MANs, MarTech refers to all of the approximate 500 areas as MANs. Each geographic area identified in our global MAN model represents a potential electronic conurbation or logical user or traffic aggregation area that suggests they could take on the characteristics of a future MAN. Whether provided by monopoly entities, municipal authorities, or competitive access providers, it can be predicted that all of the 500 areas will have developed one or more metropolitan area nets by 2005.

3. The global information infrastructure (GII) may be considered the structural or skeletal backbone and frame of this global electronic economy. The author has defined the GII elsewhere*, offering the following formula: $GII = Cn (NII + Ip + TN)$, where GII

= global information infrastructure; Cn

= countries of interest; NII = National Information Infrastructure for Cn; Ip = set of National Information Policies, domestic and international, for n countries; and TN = transport network, domestic and international, for n countries.

The GII is not a static skeletal framework, but a structure constantly undergoing changes, some dramatic and far-reaching, induced by policies (political, economic, industrial), technology, deregulation, and privatization or liberalization initiatives. The GII is formed from an intricate conglomeration of nations, service providers, users, etc., interconnected via an array of traditional and alternative facility options and infrastructures. During the period 1985-1995, we have witnessed the emergence of alternative international communication infrastructure. Likewise, during the period 1995-2005, we will experience the emergence and development of alternative local or metropolitan infrastructure. A danger arises directly with the belief that this infrastructure cannot be sufficiently known and defined to render this an operable domain for acts of telewar.

The combined effect of these developments will be a transformed GTN by the early twenty-first century. MANs will have the highest degree of security with serious vulnerabilities in the local and global area infrastructure.

4. The GTN is composed of domestic and international "highways" that, ultimately, are physical facilities. These facility options (whether nodal points or specific paths—linkages) are susceptible to identification, pinpoint mapping, and selective targeting for acts of telemanipulation or denial of service. Denial of service encompasses a range of actions from quality of service (QOS) to loss of service (LOS). Enterprises can be bankrupted through QOS manipulations. These vulnerabilities are not sufficiently appreciated by the user community.

5. These nodes and paths can be interlinked to providers and users (TNEs) who comprise the transnational economy and the global network of electronic commerce. Moreover, the communication facilities can be interlinked with the MAN areas or cells which, in turn, link the locations of international significance of the TNEs. This linking of economic geog-

raphy with telegeography reveals a new set of societal and worldwide vulnerabilities.

6. The intergration of an appropriate set of key databases and models can be used to interlink critical properties and places with the physical communication plant to assess the damage potential of acts of telewar or information warfare. Thus, the global economy, as well as individual national economies or companies, are highly susceptible and vulnerable to acts of telewar. Specific geographic areas, specific sectors (by SIC codes) of the TE, specific TNEs, specific communications facilities, or all of these combined can be targeted for either active or passive acts of telewar.

The globalization of the economy and deregulation of global communication markets[1] has no doubt increased variety and diversity in the GTN but not necessarily to the degree of density, security, and integrity that many believe is inherent in this new structure.

With the greater expanse of the global economy and new market solutions, an illusion of security has been created. Combined with a serious underappreciation of telespace, as opposed to Cyberspace, a new set of vulnerabilities has emerged centered around denial of service (DOS) possibilities. DOS covers a range of measures and techniques for telemanipulation of the GTN to affect quality of service to, ultimately, loss of service.

The illusion of security means people don't think much about telespace or the telemanipulation possibilities in the transport infrastructure. The latter includes communications network platforms, services, and legal/regulatory issues, as well as the physical media. In part, it is because they are so involved in protecting Cyberspace with encryption, authentification, virus protection, and the like. However, Cyberspace rides on telespace and telespace offers a Gordian knot solution to all the complexities of Cyberspace.

Whereas Cyberspace solutions are aimed at denying access to perpetration into your network, telewarriors will harm you by denying you access to your own network. Current defensive thinking implicitly attributes value to the perpetrator, usually short run or near term financial gain; thereby, the need is to protect network resources rather than telespace. If the perpetrator needs access to your network to attain his goals and values, he or she has no incentive to attack telespace, as this action denies himself access to your network. But what if the perpetrator just wants to do you harm? What if the perpetrator does not want into your network to attain a value for himself? What if the value lies in other values, higher level political or economic goals, that DOS helps attain. Then, attacks on or telemanipulation of telespace enters the realm of possibility.

However, some will argue that even if this is so, that doesn't make it an operable domain. This is the principal argument advanced to me when I raise these concerns. The counterarguments go as follows:

First, it is impossible to know sufficiently all you need to know about telespace to render it an operable domain.

Secondly, even if you had such knowledge and data, the linkages are absent between the complexities and value creations of the global economy and that telespace.

Therefore, it is too theoretical and abstruse to create operable actions that can affect intended parties with intended or desired objectives. Somebody would just be shooting in the dark or tilting at windmills. Besides, they would harm themselves as much as the hoped-for target.

None of these assertions are true, and such ignorance is the source of the most damaging vulnerabilities. As long as these notions are held true and sacrosanct, additional higher layer or higher level vulnerabilities will be built into our networks upon which societal or worldwide infrastructures depend.

The Open Vulnerability Model

Borrowing the framework of open network models, the open vulnerability model is shown in Figure 1. Three broad divisions are shown with a total of ten layers. Each layer has at least ten major sources of vulnerabilities, any of which, or some combination thereof, can be exploited by the telewarrior. The transport layers, as argued above, are often taken for

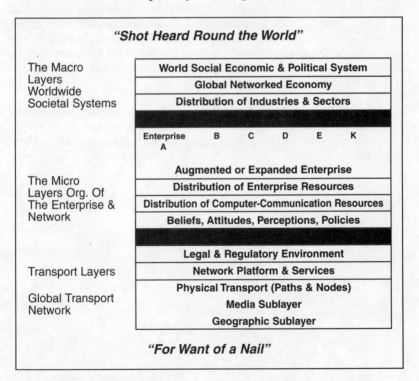

Figure 1. Open vulnerability model

granted and are leading us away from the secure, alternate media infrastructure time we had in the 1970s. Incidentally, this is not the case for all countries, since some (e.g., China, Iran) are putting in place three-dimensional networks consisting of microwave, fiber cable, and satellite trunks that are similar to our physical transport structure of the past. Our rejection of alternative media needs re-examining.

The middle division is made up of many individual decisions of various enterprises or augmented enterprises (virtual corporations). These decisions are based on our trust in the transport layers underneath. Enterprises organize their distributed computer networks as their human knowledge resources around these machine resources. If the transport structure is not as secure as they believe it is, these enterprises then build vulnerabilities on top of vulnerabilities. Nations and governments of the world, in turn, devise and develop macro organizations of worldwide societal systems similarly based on the layers below it and the multitude of micro decisions. The biggest vulnerability at this level is the lack of macro-stabilizers to restabilize by the telewarrior telemanipulating the transport layers.

Ron Eward is President and founder of MarTech Strategies, a consultancy and information service provider operating in international telecommunications. MarTech has designed and developed a number of models and databases that detail critical and sensitive data and information about major users, knowledge and global information technology hubs, facilities used to link them, and Metropolitan Area Networks (MANs)—essentially Schwartau's "maps of Cyberspace," including those of more than 100 national communication infrastructures.

1. Eward, Ronald. *The Competition for Markets in International Telecommunications.* Dedham, MA: ArTech House, 1984; *The Deregulation of International Telecommunication.* Dedham, MA: ArTech House, 1985.

7

The World
of Mr. van Eck

"Who would have thought that a sprinkler system would contain useful information?"

—MORGAN DEATH

OK, so the Information Warrior can tap a phone or a fax machine, royally screw up a computer system by fidgeting with its software, change your home phone into a pay phone, and generally wreak all sorts of havoc. Let's step back for a moment, and review the ideal characteristics of the weapons used by the Information Warrior:

- Invisible
- Passive
- Untraceable
- Readily Available and Inexpensive
- Disposable
- Remote controlled
- Insidious

To varying degrees we have already found that malicious software, network sniffing, and playing with the switch meet many of these ideals. But let's look at another weapon; one that is still considered classified by the government just because it does meet these goals so well.

Electromagnetic Eavesdropping

Any electrical current produces a magnetic field. A television station broadcasts a very small magnetic field from its antenna atop the World Trade Center or in a corn field in Iowa, and a portable TV set in your home can pick up and display *Mr. Ed* reruns or *Murphy Brown* in startling clarity. Let's take this thought one step further. Computers, printers, fax machines, and video monitors are also electrical devices that conduct current and they too emit magnetic fields. Guess what? These magnetic fields can be picked up by a special receiver, too, and can be read in startling clarity, invisibly, passively, and with little fear of detection. Sounds like an ideal tool for the Information Warrior.

A computer is actually a miniature transmitter broadcasting all of its information into the air, where it is ripe for the picking. From an electrical standpoint, the CRT or monitor of a computer is the "loudest" component, meaning that the magnetic field it produces is the strongest. Back in the early days of computers, in the days of Radio Shack TRS-80 ("Trash 80s"), Commodore Pets, and VIC-20s, users often experienced severe interference from their computers on their TV sets.

Many of us set up our computers in the living room so we could spend quality time with our families, watch *M*A*S*H* and play with our latest adult toys. But we also noticed that unless the computers were a safe distance from the TV, the picture was virtually unwatchable. Wavy lines scrolled across and up and down the screen and "noise" filled the picture. If we rotated the computer and sat at a different chair at the dining room table, the interference was less objectionable. If we moved the computer into the bedroom, the interference often went away. To satisfy our desire to watch TV and still peck away at BASIC, we would twiddle for nights on end trying to optimize the picture on the boob tube by minimizing the interference. That might mean finding the only place in the room that would allow us to enjoy both diversions at once, or it might mean using three rolls of properly placed and shaped rolls of Reynolds Wrap around the computer and on the TV aerial. We were trying to shield the television set from the electromagnetic radiation emitted by the computer and its monitor. Little did most of know then that we were experiencing a phenomenon that the National Security Agency had buried deep within their classified Tempest program. The government had known about the national security problems associated with computer-based electromagnetic radiation for years.

Electromagnetic eavesdropping is a formidable weapon to the Information Warrior. Twenty years later the government still shrouds much of the issue in secrecy, and it is only due to the efforts of independent researchers not controlled by the secrecy laws concomitant with government employment that we understand just how much of a risk electromagnetic eavesdropping really is.

Since every computer unintentionally broadcasts information into the air (except those few especially built to tightly-guarded NSA Tempest specifications), the Information Warrior has the means to detect, save, and read every bit of information that passes through a computer and onto a video monitor. And he can do it passively, from some distance, without your ever being the wiser.

Detecting and recovering this data is not possible only for the intelligence community or super-high-tech whiz bangers. The ability to read computer screens from a remote location is available to anyone with a modicum of knowledge of basic electronics. Your television repairman is an ideal candidate for assisting your local Information Warrior. Morgan Death, a former Vice President at Hughes STX, wrote, "Many individuals and corporations have no idea how easy it is to obtain information from electronic radiations. They thought of Tempest protection as a black art that only the intelligence community had to worry about."[1]

In its simplest form, an electromagnetic eavesdropping device consists of no more than a black and white television set and a handful of parts costing less than $5. The interception we experienced with the Trash 80s was the actual video signal (the characters that cross the computer screen) being picked up by the TV antenna. The computer monitor leaks this information at about the same frequencies used by channels two through seven on the TV. All we need to do is tune them in and voila!, we have an echo of what appears on our computer screen. The reason we couldn't read the Trash 80 characters on our TV set was that the detected signals had lost their "sync," or synchronization. The information was there, but it fell apart. The Information Warrior simply puts it back together again.

A television set modified to pick up computer screen emissions needs to have two signals added to those unintentionally leaked by the monitor under surveillance. The first is the vertical sync which, on a TV set, is called vertical hold. The second signal needed is the horizontal sync. If either of these signals is maladjusted, the TV will endlessly "roll" up and down or left to right, as the case may be. (Readers who owned early generation television sets can easily relate to the frustration.) The radiated signals from a computer combined with these two sync signals will produce a perfectly readable copy of whatever appears on the computer with no wires connecting the two. To add more fuel to the fire, the data displayed on the video screen can be detected even when the video monitor itself is turned off.

Many audiences to whom I speak find this simple item alarming and discomforting, thereby leading to a degree of incredulity—until they see the demonstrations. In September of 1991, on Geraldo Rivera's ill-fated TV show, "Now! It Can Be Told," I demonstrated what I believe was the first national broadcast of electromagnetic eavesdropping.[2] Despite the fact that atomic bombs were going off in the background, the demonstration was real.

The publicity surrounding electromagnetic eavesdropping first reached a furor in 1985 when a Dutch scientist, Professor Wim van Eck, published an unclassified paper on the subject.[3] He stated that, based upon his studies, "it seems justified to estimate the maximum reception distance using only a normal TV receiver at around 1km. . . ."[4] As a result of the publication of this document, electromagnetic eavesdropping was popularly dubbed "van Eck radiation." According to Tempest engineers certified by the National Security Agency, the NSA department responsible for the security of the Tempest program went ballistic. They classified the Van Eck report, which included very exacting details and mathematical analysis that they had considered to be exclusively under their domain. Tempest engineers were forbidden, as part of their security agreement with the Government, from speaking about or acknowledging any details of van Eck's work.

But the cat was already out of the bag. The prestigious and scholarly journal *Computers and Security* discussed van Eck in its December 1985 issue, to the continued chagrin of the intelligence community, and in 1988, the British Broadcasting Corporation aired a segment on the phenomenon which is similarly classified in England.[5]

This impressive demonstration was conducted in London, with the detection equipment set up in a van that roamed the streets. The technicians in the unassuming van would lock into "interesting" computer signals, emanating from law offices and brokerage firms located in London high rises, from a distance of several hundred feet. They then recorded the impressively clear computer-screen images on a video tape. When company executives were brought into the van, they viewed a playback of the video tape that demonstrated the capability for remote passive eavesdropping of highly sensitive information. The impact of such capability was evident on their shocked faces and in their commentary. According to Tempest technicians, the NSA classified this tape along with van Eck's publicly available papers.

Swedish television broadcast a similar demonstration on a show called "Aktuellt." These demonstrations provided conclusive evidence that the risk to privacy and the sanctity of information was real. Despite our government's efforts at hiding the potential risk to American businesses, van Eck radiation was becoming widely known everywhere and to everyone else but us.

In 1990, Professor Erhard Möller of Aachen University in Germany published a detailed update to van Eck's work with such eavesdropping. To this date, the NSA still classifies these protective measures in their Tempest program. They allegedly went so far as to classify portions of a university text book written by the legendary expert in electromagnetic control, Don White.[6]

On the home front, Hughes STX (a division of Hughes Aircraft) demonstrated van Eck emissions using a circa-1955 Dumont tube television console set and a small portable black and white unit as receptors. Not only are van Eck radiations broadcast into the air, but water pipes, sprinkler systems, and power lines are excellent conduits, offering ideal tap points for interception. Attaching a wire to a hot water pipe and watching computer screen images appear on a television set is a most disquieting experience, but one that cannot be ignored.

Jim Carter, president of Bank Security in Houston, Texas, has also been publicizing the phenomenon at such events as HoHoCon, the annual hacker's conference, and Jim Ross's Surveillance Expo in Washington, D.C. His experiences with Van Eck were highlighted in 1991 when, in cooperation with Benjamin Franklin Savings and Loan, he demonstrated how to successfully attack a Diebold ATM machine. He says that, using Van Eck radiation, "we got all of the information we needed to reconstruct an ATM card." Carter says that he notified Diebold of the vulnerability to their machines and to their customers. They flew a couple of engineers down "but after two years, we're still waiting for them to get back to us. They really don't give a damn if they fix the problem or not."

Today, if you don't have the expertise to build your own, you can actually buy a van Eck unit, priced from $500 to $2,000, from any number of catalogs. The results range from godawful to darn good. One company, Spy Supply in New Hampshire, no longer sells their unit. According to one of the company's principals, Bob Carp, they were approached by the

NSA and strongly urged to discontinue sales immediately or risk the wrath of the government.[7]

Another company, Consumertronics in Alamogordo, New Mexico, claims to sell a van Eck detection unit for educational purposes only. However, reading their literature and catalog of product offerings suggests other motives.[8] On the high end, sophisticated and expensive test equipment such as that built by Watkins-Johnson of Gaithersberg, Maryland, and an assortment of other U.S. and foreign companies, provide an excellent means to detect a wide range of signals and reconstruct video signals of good quality.

The NSA has gone to extraordinary lengths to maintain the secrecy surrounding van Eck radiation, such as asking Spy Supply to cease and desist and classifying portions of engineering text books that might give too much away. By attempting to bury the issue as completely as possible and allowing discussions of value to occur only under the veil of national security, they have done this country and its industries a great disservice. To the best of my knowledge, they have never openly discussed the realities of van Eck radiation, thus reducing its credibility as a threat in the eyes of corporate America and the protectors of its information. The unfortunate rationale of many security professionals is "if it's not officially acknowledged, then it can't be real."

A few years back, after the initial flare-up of concern about electromagnetic eavesdropping, Chase Manhattan Bank ran some internal test to determine their vulnerability. Based upon their home-brew tests, they determined, "Quite frankly, at the bank, we're not overly concerned about screens being read."[9]

However, in the fall of 1992, Chemical Bank found themselves the apparent target of exactly this type of eavesdropping by unknown Information Warriors. According to Don Delaney of the New York State Police, bank officials were alerted that an antenna was pointed at their midtown New York bank offices, where a large number of ATM machines and credit card processing facilities are located. For reasons that the bank will not discuss, they elected not to pursue the matter although the police offered assistance.[10] From external appearances, it seems that Chemical Bank was the target of what has generically become known as a Tempest attack.

Because van Eck detection is so simple, so insidious, and so passive, the number of reported incidents is bound to be low. In addition, most people aren't even aware of the capability so they wouldn't recognize it if they saw it. A major U.S. chemical company, however, did know that it was the target of industrial espionage using van Eck techniques. The security director of the firm was an ex-CIA employee, well-trained in surveillance techniques. He said that he was alerted by the sight of a Toyota van sitting in the parking lot near one of the company's research and development buildings. What caught his attention was an antenna on the roof of the van, which appeared to be scanning the area and fixing itself on the R&D facility. Although he can't prove his countermeasures solved anything, the van quickly disappeared after he shielded the targeted labs from emitting van Eck radiations.[11]

There are plenty of methods to protect against Information Warriors who want to eavesdrop on screens, keyboards and printers, but a question of legality arises. According to one author, "In the United States, it is illegal for an individual to take effective countermeasures against Tempest surveillance."[12] This statement is ominous if taken at face value. It implies that electromagnetic eavesdropping is commonly practiced in domestic surveillance activities. Could this be one reason why the NSA has been so rigorous in its efforts at downplaying the matter?

Perhaps. The NSA and other government agencies do use these techniques and do have their own surveillance vans, complete with van Eck detection equipment. A specially-constructed chassis is made by Ford Mother Company, so that the eavesdropping van cannot be eavesdropped upon. The vans are then outfitted with the very best surveillance technology that the Pentagon's billions can buy. Who are they listening to? No one I know will say, but their capabilities are most impressive. The NSA recently developed a custom integrated circuit employing specialized Fast Fourier Transforms (FFTs), that will enhance the clarity and range of the van Eck detection equipment substantially, as well as significantly reduce the size of the surveillance equipment.[13]

I assume that by now the problem becomes explicitly clear. The computer screens that we once thought were private are, in fact, veritable radio stations. The keyboard strokes that we enter on our computer are also transmitted into the air and onto conduit pipes and power lines. An A at the keyboard sends out an electromagnetic A into the air or down the sprinkler pipes and any digital oscilloscope, in the hands of a professional, can detect the leaking signals with ease. A keyboard B emits an electromagnetic B, a C at the keyboard sends out its unique signature, and so it goes for the rest of the keyboard. PIN numbers or other potentially sensitive information can be detected, stored, and decoded with the right equipment in the right hands.

Printers, too, betray the privacy of their users; generally unbeknownst to them, but all too well known by the Information Warrior in search of information. The NSA uses a classified technique called digram analysis to assist in eavesdropping on van Eck emanations from printers. Each printer type has its own unique sets of electromagnetic patterns, depending upon how it was designed and built. The NSA will buy one of each, analyze its patterns, and then be more easily able to decode the intercepted information patterns.

As the story goes, during a very intensive security sweep of the American Embassy in Moscow in the early 1980s, a small transmitter was found inside of a classified telex machine. Allegedly, it listened to the electromagnetic patterns generated by the telex machine and retransmitted the raw signals to a secondary listening post where the Soviets performed their own digram analysis to read sensitive U.S. Government messages.

Since there is virtually no way to know that a computer or printer is being "van Ecked", there is no reliable method to determine what losses might actually have been incurred due

to electromagnetic eavesdropping. The possibilities for speculation are endless. Exploitation of van Eck radiation appears to
be responsible, at least in part, for the arrest of senior CIA
intelligence officer Aldrich Hazen Ames on charges of being a
Soviet/Russian mole. According to the affadavit in support of
Arrest Warrant, the FBI used "electronic surveillance of Ames'
personal computer and software within his residence," in
their search for evidence against him. On October 9, 1993, the
FBI "placed an electronic monitor in his (Ames') computer,"[14]
suggesting that a van Eck receiver and transmitter was used to
gather information on a real-time basis. Obviously, then, this is
an ideal tool for criminal investigation—one that apparently
works quiet well.

In 1991, I designed a few scenarios for a defense think tank
in order to define the needs of an urban Information Warrior
who wants to use this approach. The simplest approach
involved a portable van Eck detector with its own transmitter
and receiver, so that it could be remotely tuned into the
computer, printer, or video monitor of choice. Smaller detectors are more expensive but offer advantages to the Information Warrior, who could easily plant a small receiver in the
basement of a building, leave it there unattended, and sit a
comfortable distance away, scanning and listening for the information he wanted.

Consider the following. An Information Warrior who has
profit as his motive uses van Eck detection equipment to listen
in on the computer of a brokerage firm. They are planning to
issue either astoundingly good or astoundingly bad news on
one of their clients, which will soon have a major impact on its
stock price. Now that he knows this "insider information," he
makes the appropriate financial decisions and buys or sells or
shorts a big block of stock with the intent of making a financial
killing. Can the Information Warrior be prosecuted for this?
There is no clear answer at this time.

Perhaps the CEO of a major company is worried about the
outcome of future litigation, and would give anything to know
what the opposing counsel was planning. Electromagnetic

eavesdropping could easily provide him with that information—
and there is hardly any chance that he would ever be caught.
Invisible, passive, and insidious.

Van Eck detection also lends itself nicely to the exploitation of Binary Schizophrenia or other social malaises we
discussed earlier. Imagine that the goal of the Information
Warrior is to exacerbate friction among upper management of
a company. If certain sensitive and supposedly private information were acquired by our insidiously invisible detection
equipment and "accidentally" leaked into the wrong hands,
all members of the management team would suspect one
another of being likely culprits.

Or if a customer's personal financial data were acquired
from a bank's computers and properly leaked to the right
people, the bank would be suspected of and possibly legally
responsible for fiduciary irresponsibility. That it would lose a
customer in the process goes without saying. While the press
might not use such techniques itself, sometimes they don't
know and don't care where and how information is obtained.
Companies are embarrassed enough when stories appear on
activities that aren't meant for public disclosure. Electromagnetic eavesdropping only provides one additional means to
effect breaches of privacy and confidentiality.

According to Mark Baven, an editor at *Government Data
Systems*, "In today's volatile financial market, where inside
information can lead to millions of dollars of profits, a raid on
a corporation's vital data . . . could be extremely worthwhile. The cost of implementing Tempest technology would
be far offset by the potential savings that such security would
provide."

The one thing we can be sure of is that the technology to
listen in on computer leakage will only become better and
better and cheaper and cheaper, just as all technology does. At
one point or another, business is going to have to decide that
its only protection against passive information interception is
an active defense.

8

Cryptography

"The best way to keep a secret between two people is if one of them is dead."

—COMMON SENSE MY MOM TAUGHT ME.

IF YOU TINKER in your garage and come up with a nifty new way to build a nuclear bomb, all of your efforts are automatically classified. Classified at birth, if you will. You can't talk about it and you can't write about it. While this appears to be in violation of our First Amendment rights to freedom of speech and prior restraint, the courts have upheld the government's positions arguing that "thermonuclear annihilation of us all justifies an exception."[1]

And so it almost goes with cryptography. Cryptography is the art and science of scrambling information to keep a message secret. The better the cryptography, the better the secret is kept.

As far as the Department of Defense is concerned, cryptography and nuclear technology are two of the most sensitive areas in science and research since they both represent military strength. The bomb and its power are obvious, but is the cryptoquote puzzle in the daily paper really a threat to national security? No, because that is weak cryptography— call it "crypto" if you want to sound knowledgeable—meant to be solved by Grannie at the kitchen table. The government

232

only cares about the "strong" crypto. The National Security Agency, the country's listening post charged with keeping our secrets and breaking "theirs," is concerned about strong crypto, and expends great effort on its job.

If it weren't for cryptanalysis (the art of breaking codes), World War II could have cost the Allies many more lives and years of war. In order to protect themselves against Allied interception of vital strategic messages, the Axis used secret codes to 'encrypt' their military communications. Only those with the right key could unlock the message to decipher it. The Germans developed a coding or encryption scheme that was so good, the British had to organize a huge analytical apparatus consisting of thousands of men and women just to crack their messages. Ultimately, through serendipity, the British recovered a piece of German naval equipment responsible for building the indecipherable coded messages. That machine was called the Enigma, an invention light years ahead of other cryptosystems of the day. Alan Turing is the intellectual giant often credited with shortening the war by deciphering German messages.

Instead of using advanced technology, the United States employed Native American Navaho to communicate military transmissions in the Pacific Theater, and the Japanese never caught on. The Japanese coding system, on the other hand, proved fairly easy to crack and during much of the war in the Pacific, the U.S. was regularly intercepting and reading Imperial communications. This information remained secret for years.

The use of cryptography to disguise messages is as familiar as the Sunday paper cryptoquote that uses a single level of letter-substitution: For example, an *A* stands for *K* and *L* stands for *C* and so on for all twenty-six letters. Letter substitution was used by Julius Caesar to send secret written messages to his field generals. The key to reading the message was knowing which letter stood for which other letter. Today, the crypto may be such a complex stream of mathematical symbols that an enciphered message would takes the world's most powerful supercomputer years to crack.

Cryptography is all about secrets—keeping them or trying to find out about the other guy's. Cryptography was originally considered a military weapon and, to a great extent, it is still a deeply guarded secret today. The government and the NSA take cryptography so seriously that they tried unsuccessfully to have cryptography placed under the same umbrella as atomic research. That would have put all cryptographic work under the control of the Department of Defense, removed it from the public domain, and established a stranglehold that might still be in place today.

But the Government made some fatal mistakes along the way. Along came computers and the need to protect the information that they contained. In the early days of computers, circa 1970, the biggest private commercial use for computers and thus the demand for cryptography came from the financial community. They recognized that in order to insure an accurate and reliable means of moving money through Cyberspace, their Electronic Funds Transfer (EFT) systems needed protection.

In 1976, the National Bureau of Standards, today known as NIST or the National Institute of Standards and Technology, contracted with IBM to modify their Lucifer encryption algorithms to become the national standard for data protection. (An algorithm is the rule by which the encryption scheme works.) And so was born the Data Encryption Standard, or DES (Pronounced dezz or d-e-s). DES, a strong encryption scheme in its day, was endorsed by the Department of Treasury and has subsequently proven to be an adequate protector of the hundreds of trillions of dollars electronically transferred in the U.S. every year.

The NSA, though, had its concerns, and succeeded in having DES categorized as a weapon system. Therefore, NSA approval is required in order to export DES outside of the United States, in addition to that of the Departments of State and Commerce. DES is controlled by ITAR, the International

Traffic in Arms Regulations, and violators receive harsh penalties. Essentially, the thinking went, the U.S. doesn't want DES to get into unfriendly hands so they can encrypt and disguise their data from our professional eavesdroppers.

But here's where they really screwed up.

Since DES was a national standard, it was entered into the public domain and the DES algorithms were openly published for anyone to see. For the price of a stamp, any American or even a foreign national could, and can, write to NIST and receive a copy of the DES standard. Despite the fact that DES was controlled as a weapon, we published—and gave away free—the instruction manual and parts lists, enabling anyone or any country to build their own. That's like sending a Patriot Missile kit to Libya or Iran with a note saying, "Please don't build this."

The export controls for DES and for products that used it made it nearly impossible for manufacturers of encryption products to sell their wares outside of the United States and Canada. After years of frustration on the part of our friendly allies, they took the obvious route. Since the majority of the commercial sector was unable to legally import DES from the United States, they decided to build it themselves. After all, it is a public domain algorithm.

So what do we find today?

We see American-designed, public-domain DES being manufactured all over the world. The best DES comes from Germany, the cheapest from Taiwan and Hong Kong. Computer stores in Moscow sell Kryptos, a Russian version of the American national encryption standard. According to the Software Publishers Association, of 210 foreign encryption product from at least 33 countries, 129 use DES.[2] So what's the point in restricting the sales of DES? The political gerrymandering surrounding DES is a classic example of inane policy making.

In the mid-1980s, the NSA attempted to have DES decertified as a viable means of protecting financial transactions. That would have meant that vast investments in encryption equipment on the part of the Department of Treasury, the

Federal Reserve Board, and thousands of banks were for
naught. They would have to start from scratch developing
acceptable means of protecting our money. The NSA argued
that DES was no longer considered secure, and that in its
estimation computer technology had sufficiently evolved to
render DES's effectiveness impotent. The Treasury Department dug in its heels and, after protracted fights, NSA acqui-
esced and DES was recertified. The battle will be over in 1997,
by which time a replacement for DES will be in place. In fact
the battle may be over now, because DES is breakable.

At the March 1993 RSA Data Security Conference, Dr.
Martin Hellman presented a theoretical approach to cracking
DES by using parallel processing. On August 20, 1993, Michael
Wiener of Bell-Northern Research in Canada published a
paper "showing how to build an exhaustive DES key search
machine for $1 million that can find a key in 3.5 hours on
average."[3]

With increasingly powerful Computers Everywhere it was
just a matter of time before the key to cracking DES encryption
was out of the bag, and the NSA knew it. They had warned the
Treasury Department almost a decade earlier, but never came
up with enough rationale to force action. The NSA has had
its own DES cracking machines for years, costing between
$50,000 and $100,000 each and using the same techniques that
Hellman and Weiner describe. The Harris Corporation built a
system for the government that can crack DES in less than
fifteen minutes using a very fast, very smart Cray Y/MP
supercomputer.

To the Information Warrior, all of this is good news. To the
Federal Reserve Board and every other financial institution
who relies upon DES to protect their transactions, these
revelations spell a potential disaster. For about $1 million, the
Information Warrior now has the ability to eavesdrop upon
and make modifications to critical financial transactions. If
only the NSA had been more open in sharing their knowledge,
we could have been well on our way to the next generation of
encryption. But in the interest of their limited interpretation of

National Security, they kept their secrets to themselves. The Government (read the NSA and law enforcement) had its own agenda and plans and wouldn't share them—until April 16, 1993, that is.

On that day, President Clinton's press secretary released a statement announcing "a new initiative that will bring the Federal Government together with industry in a voluntary program to improve the security and privacy of telephone communications while meeting the legitimate needs of law enforcement." The needs of the Justice Department spurred the development of a new encryption technique for widespread use. That initiative is called "Clipper." Clipper was announced just after Janet Reno was appointed Attorney General, and might have been announced earlier if Clinton hadn't had trouble with prior designees.

Clipper is a hardware chip based upon the classified "Skipjack" encryption algorithm, common in such government arenas as the Defense Messaging Agency and in unclassified networks such as ARPANET. In theory, it is stronger than DES but because skipjack is classified, it will not be available for the public scrutiny enjoyed by all widely accepted encryption schemes such as DES or the de facto standard RSA public key methods. Without open academic analysis, the encryption strength is subject to question and the success of Clinton's Clipper program is in jeopardy. Clipper was born back when the NSA tried to decertify DES and law enforcement agencies such as the FBI were fearful that criminals would use encryption themselves. Wiretapping is a favorite tool of law enforcement but eavesdropping becomes more difficult if criminals' conversations are encrypted. If drug dealers keep their records on a computer that employs encryption, deciphering the information is an enormous undertaking. Law enforcement understandably wanted action taken so their jobs would not become even more difficult.

In 1991, as a result of in-government lobbying, the Senate Judiciary Committee attempted to add a rider to Senate bill 266, a piece of anticrime legislation: "It is the sense of

Congress that providers of electronic communications services and manufacturers of electronic communications service equipment shall ensure that communications systems permit the government to obtain the plain-text contents of voice, data, and other communications when appropriately authorized by law." The Government wants to be able to decrypt conversations and digital traffic so they can continue their eavesdropping activities. This wording, added two years in advance of the Clipper announcement, was in anticipation of the technology becoming available.

The offensive wording was removed from the bill as a result of vocal objection by the ACLU, CPSR, (Computer Professionals for Social Responsibility), and other privacy advocate groups, but government efforts have not abated. They have pushed ahead with what they call "voluntary compliance" with Clipper for communications and its brethren Capstone, used for computers.

There are several huge problems with the Government's position.

First, unless everyone uses Clipper, the entire effort is futile. In order for everyone to use it, it would have to become a mandate or law, therefore making other forms of encryption illegal. That will never happen in an open society. Second, for Clipper to be accepted, the Government has to be trusted not to abuse their capabilities to decrypt private transmissions without proper court authorization, as is required today.

The proposed method for protecting the average American's privacy is through a complex process of "key escrowing" the means of decypting a Clipper conversation. The Government's plan is to designate "two trusted third parties" who will each hold a piece of the key that could decrypt specific Clipper transmission only. The problem here is that whoever becomes the trusted parties becomes a target for the Information Warrior, because all of the keys to the digital Clipper kingdom would be sitting with two specific groups. The press office of the Attorney General said in April 1993 that they were having trouble finding groups willing to take on that responsibility and risk. Mother Teresa is unavailable.

The third major problem with Clipper is that since no one outside of a select few will be able to examine the internal workings of the Clipper system, we have to take on faith that the Government doesn't have a so-called back-door to bypass the entire escrow system.

Immediately after the announcement, the business community was unexpectedly united in opposition to Clipper. Over thirty-one companies, including IBM, DEC, Apple, Hewlett- Packard, Microsoft, and Lotus have written, in cooperation with the Electronic Frontier Foundation, a letter to the White House and Congress, outlining their concerns about the Clipper plan.

Clipper finds few adherents, and even some NSA, NIST, and other Government officials admit privately that Clipper worries them. One Clipper adherent is Dorothy Denning, an elegant computer scientist from Georgetown University who has taken the unpopular position that Clipper is a reasonable trade-off between personal privacy and the legitimate needs of law enforcement. At one security conference she said, "If Radio Shack sells a cryptophone that the government can't crack, I think we'll have a real crisis on our hands."[4] For her unpopular stand she has suffered undue amounts of "flaming," public ridicule and accusations that she secretly works for the NSA.

Padgett Peterson, Information Security Specialist with Martin Marietta, is a less vocal adherent, but apparently more acquiescent to the Government position. He envisions the day when everyone will be using Clipper, like it or not. "Doctors, lawyers, CPAs, and everyone else will use Clipper," he maintains.

Even the international community is outraged. The French Government isn't about to permit the use of Clipper in France if the U.S. holds the only keys to the kingdom. Other countries voice similar sentiments.

The big question asked by civil libertarians, the ACLU, and

others aware of technology's immense intrusions on our lives and privacy is, "Will the White House drop the other shoe?" The other shoe, of course, is the mandate that Clipper is in and all other encryption is out—by law.

AT&T supported clipper when it was announced, probably due to the fact that the Department of Justice had placed a multimillion dollar order for special encrypted Clipper telephones with them. AT&T even discontinued the DES version of their original secure phone, the Model 3600. But when the Clipper chips were delayed by almost nine months (manufacturing problems yielded a ninety-six percent failure rate), they supported an intermediary encryption technology instead of the original DES version that was already a saleable product. Washington insiders speculate that AT&T was pressured into their actions by the intelligence community with threats of unfavorable Federal contract review.

Perhaps the Government is engaged in a campaign to desensitize the American public, a sophisticated form of Information Warfare. First they attempt to pass a law, then they back off when attacked by privacy advocates and adverse publicity. Next, they make the very technology available that would have been used to implement the proposed law, if it had been passed. Then Clipper is announced and the flak hits the fan, so they back off again. They try to convince the public that Clipper really is OK. Then maybe they'll try to sneak in another law, perhaps in a few months or a year. See what happens. Sooner or later, the reasoning goes, the public will cease to care and Clipper will become the law of the land. It is a scenario that does not take great imagination to conjure. It depends upon who is behind Clipper, the depth of their pockets, their political wherewithal, and their motivation and resolve.

Ultimately I think that the Clipper situation is another misguided effort on the part of the government. Before Clinton's April 16 announcement, not too many Americans were aware of encryption and what it could do. Today front page articles are hitting the general media and awareness of privacy and eavesdropping is at an all-time high. Everyone knows about Clipper. Now the White House says, "While encryption technology can help Americans protect business secrets and the unauthorized release of personal information, it also can be used by terrorists, drug dealers, and other criminals."

That's right. And with Clinton's and Bush's and the NSA's well thought-out plans for Clipper, we can all sleep easier at night knowing that organized crime, the drug cartels, Islamic fundamentalists, and other friendly Information Warriors will sign up for Clipper before plotting their strategies.

To the Information Warrior, cryptography represents the same two-edged sword that our military has had to deal with for decades. The Information Warrior must increase the power of his analytical arsenal to penetrate the secrets we so dearly want to protect with encryption. Is $1 million too much to invest to disrupt the financial transaction between banks?

Crypto works for the Information Warrior. He can, as any of us might decide to do, encrypt all of the voice conversations between the members of his army. He can encrypt cellular calls, telephone calls, computer conversations, and everything on his own computer systems. If he is arrested, or if his equipment is legitimately confiscated in the investigation of a crime, the information will be unreadable and therefore un-available as evidence, presenting an admittedly deep dilemma for law enforcement. Right behind Clipper is the computer-data version called Capstone. It will add more government-approved encryption tools to the suspect Skipjack algorithm and escrow system. Although Clipper is allegedly strong enough to resist attack through the next thirty or forty years of computer advances, the Clinton administration has a long way to go before it is adopted in the private sector.

On Friday, February 4, 1994, the Clinton Administration, after months of study, returned a favorable verdict to adapt Clipper for Government use, and to strongly encourage the private sector to follow suit. The Department of Commerce named the Department of Treasury and NIST (National Insti-tute of Standards and Technology) as the two trusted key-escrow holders despite originally preferring at least one non-Government-trusted third party. The debate certainly isn't over, and Senator Patrick Leahy, Democrat, Vermont said, "The only good aspect of the Clipper Chip program is that it is not mandatory, yet that is exactly why the program is doomed to fail."[5] Wide spread public use is still the law-enforcement officer's idea of the perfect dream: so attractive yet so unreachable.

The government appears to be suffering from its own brand of Binary Schizophrenia regarding cryptography, thus unmasking the internal confusions between agencies. Software engineer Phil Zimmerman designed a scheme he called PGP, or Pretty Good Privacy, that the government thinks is *too* good. PGP has worldwide support and its adherents use it religiously to protect their information transmissions. The government, however, wanted to know whether Zimmerman violated the law by placing PGP on the Internet, thus making it globaly available.

A voice of sanity comes from Congresswoman Maria Cantwell (D-WA) who, on November 22, 1993, proposed a bill that would largely remove export restrictions on DES and other commonly available software encryption schemes. Propelled in part by industry concern over America's competitive disadvantage, the bill attempts to deregulate controls over technology that has already been let out of the bag, so to speak. Although Cantwell's efforts are to be applauded, the bill in its inchoate form still allows arbitrary export restrictions to be imposed by the NSA through the Departments of State and Commerce. Sooner or later, the government will have to realize that they cannot control Cyberspace in the same ways they have controlled aspects of our physical Cold War world.

The Information Warrior knows that cryptography is a powerful tool and he will use it to his best advantage, regardless of what Washington does. Because crypto can be made "strong" with software, and software is not illegal, anyone with the skills can generate strong cryptographic privacy with little trouble. Government and industry must come together and focus on their common interests, not their differences. The ramifications for us as a people and a country are far-reaching.

Is the day coming when, if any of us encrypts our voice or data communications, we will be immediately suspected for a crime? Will the mere fact that we desire privacy suggest we have something to hide?

When the legitimate concerns of national security, corporate protection, and personal privacy suddenly merge, no one answer will keep everyone happy.

Except the Information Warrior. He frankly doesn't care.

The Three Little Pigs and the Big Bad Wolf

Charles L. Smith (softwa19@us.net)

The first Little Pig built his computer security out of straw, 56 bits or less. The Big Bad Wolf huffed and puffed and blew his bits in with a RISC processor. The first Little Pig was eaten by the Big Bad Wolf.

The second Little Pig built his computer security out of escrowed sticks. The Big Bad Wolf huffed and puffed and bought his escrow key from a corrupt official. The second Little Pig was eaten by the Big Bad Wolf.

The last Little Pig built his computer security using bricks of strong (non-escrow) encryption. The Big Bad Wolf huffed and puffed, trying to find a way in but the strong crypto defeated the Big Bad Wolf. The Big Bad Wolf soon starved to death, and the Little Pig lived happily ever after.

The End.

Well . . . almost the end.

The third little pig's encryption was strong, but (choose one): (A) His key management was inadequate, so the NSA got him anyway. (B) His computer security wasn't as good as his crypto-system, and his keys were stolen and used to transfer all his secrets to the enemy. (C) He was arrested for using illegal encryption technology and was never heard of again. (D) His disk crashed and all the king's horses and all the king's men couldn't restore his data again.

The moral of the story: Don't count your crypto-keys before they are batched *or* A key in the escrow is worth two on the disk.

Thank you Info-Sec Heaven at http://all.net/

The Bio-Cyber Future

Dr. Houston T. Hawkins, Los Alamos National Laboratory

The information in this article represents the views of the author and not necessarily those of Los Alamos National Laboratory or the Department of Energy.

244

As we come to rely more and more on silicon-based electronic systems, we should not forget the information processing potential of carbon-based systems. First, by hundreds of orders of magnitude, more information is passed in the fertilization of an egg than we humans have ever chiseled into stone, imprinted into clay, inked on to parchment and paper, or keyboarded to a computer. Second, if neurons equate to processors, the pecan-sized brain of a wild turkey is a more capable and efficient information processing system than the fastest, most powerful computer ever built in silicon. The turkey's brain processes visual, auditory, tactile, and olfactory information, assesses threats, develops defensive strategies, regulates metabolism, directs flight operations, and a thousand other functions while consuming energy at a few calories per minute. By comparison, electronic computers are idiot savants extremely adept at mathematical manipulations of ones and zeros but little else. However, for those of us who depend on numbers, computers—because of their computational speed—are very capable of getting us into serious trouble a lot faster than we could without them. It is this latter aspect that is of most importance to the Information Warrior.

Even aggregates of individual cells are capable of some astonishing calculations. For example, if one were to culture some bacteria, add the powerful disinfectant phenol to the culture, reculture the survivors, and repeat the process about ten times, the final culture would not be affected by adding phenol but likely would require phenol to live. In this example, the cultured cells could be viewed as millions of processors acting in a massively paralleled configuration. They were working singularly as individuals and severally as members of the culture to address this imperative: What changes must be propagated to ensure survival? The correct answer: The changes suggested in the genes of the survivors. One can only guess as to how many supercomputers would be required to answer the same question for the human race. The problem is, how can the incredible information-processing potential of biological systems be coupled with the inherent directability of electronic systems?

Moreover, biological systems have been fighting information wars at the biomolecular level since the genesis cell. Therefore, it is important to understand how biological systems solve problems in information transfer and verification; how they recognize and deal with extraneous or threatening genetic materials; how they employ defenses capable of mutating as the threat mutates; or, offensively, how they penetrate and take over the information systems of host organisms. Applying this understanding to modern information systems will greatly expand and complicate the offensive and defensive dimensions of information warfare. In a sense, neural networks, fuzzy logic, and today's relatively simple computer viruses are the opening forays into this brave new world.

One of the most unique information-processing techniques enjoyed by higher order biological systems—e.g., mammals—is context-dependent information processing. We use this ability to elevate information that would otherwise be background clutter to the foreground. Thus, a bloodhound can track a fugitive by discerning his essence within a universe of essences. The dog's brain relates the target essence in the context of natural ability, training, and reward. For the dog, the essence has meaning. Similarly, we can listen to any speaker we desire within a crowded room full of speakers or hear a baby cry in the next room. We automatically hear the baby's cry, but what we see is a baby in distress. The information has meaning, and giving meaning to information is the heart of context-dependent processing. As simple and pedestrian as these feats seem to us, they cannot be replicated by the best electronic input devices we have today. However, 60 researchers at Los Alamos are working on proximate context-dependent information processing. This latter approach, called adaptive processing, is envisioned as a way to identify and assign value to important bits of data while delegating large volumes of less-germane data to lower status. This approach and others similar to it will be important tools in data mining. By being adaptive (and learning), they will also be useful in identifying anomalies, fraud, and unauthorized access.

Another application in which biotronics might first be employed with specialized detectors. Certain strains of bacteria can detect single molecules of certain materials, such as chemical and biological agents. For example, by splicing the phosphorescent genetic sequence from a firefly into the detector bacteria, it may be possible to electronically record when detection occurs by recording the individual photons emitted by the splice. This approach to detection of airborne or waterborne species could lead to the equivalent of a chemical laboratory on a chip on which generically engineered bacteria—selected for their abilities to detect species of interest—would serve as micro-versions of chemists and their analytical equipment.

In the future, an individual's unique DNA might replace his credit cards, driver's license, passwords, social security number, and other personal identifiers. Already, U.S. service personnel are required to have their DNA on file to assist in casualty identification. The procedures to be used in casualty identification are based on the current polymerase chain reaction (PCR) technique, which takes considerable time to develop an identification. However, devices for cell typing have already been developed for characterizing species released by biological weapons on the battlefield. One such device—called a flow cytometer—has been developed and demonstrated at Los Alamos. The small, rugged device provides rapid analysis of single cells of biological agents. For individual identification, the cytometer could be used to analyze material naturally and continuously exfoliated from individuals. Although today the analysis requires about 15 minutes, in theory the process of collecting and analyzing could be completed in about the same time it takes to process a credit card transaction. The identification in such a system should be absolute. Of course, using this process raises several ethical issues: not only could a person be identified, but predisposition to certain diseases, probable longevity, parentage, etc., could also be determined.

The diversity of organic molecules is phenomenal. The human DNA helix stores the blueprints of our hearts, eyes, brains, and potential. It stores and transmits the athleticism of a Michael Jordan, the genius of an Einstein, and the beauty of a Monroe. Even relatively small organic molecules can be exceedingly complex. Hemoglobin, the organic compound that makes our blood red, is diverse to 10 raised to the power 650. That is, the units comprising hemoglobin could in theory be rearranged in that many different combinations. The potential diversity of the DNA in the "simple" T4 bacteriophage is 10 raised to the power 78,000![1] Only one of those combinations would actually be hemoglobin or a T4 bacteriophage, respectively.

In comparison, the diversity of information in the Library of Congress is on the order of 10 raised to the power 40. Using organic-like matrices, very large amounts of information could be stored with enough variability that unauthorized decryption would be a virtual impossibility. In sum, considering the exponential potential diversities exceeding 78,000 and considering that only 10 to the power 18 seconds have lapsed since the universe began, time itself would be the limiting factor in cracking the code.

While many of the biotronic approaches are on the distant horizon, some are within a few years of being on the market. However, some visionaries believe that these technologies will provide the next leap forward in our quest to acquire and use information to solve the more intractable problems confronting civilization. For sure, they will become part of the panoply of the Information Warrior and defender.

1. David Foster, *The Philosophical Scientists* (New York: Dorset Press, 1985).

The True Story of PGP: An Interview With Kelly Goen

Betty G. O'Hearn, Interpact

A telephone interview with the man who knew it all and now can talk about it!

June 7, 1996
9:30 P.M. EST

Betty: Okay. The tape is on. What is your name for the record?
Kelly: My name is Kelly Goen.
Betty: And where are you residing now?

Kelly: Ah . . . a place around the Central California coast for about 14 years.

Betty: What is your background?

Kelly: My background is in mathematic cryptography, computers, and other stuff I've learned to hack.

Betty: How long have you been hacking?

Kelly: Oh . . . I started hacking back in '68.

Betty: Where did you start?

Kelly: Back in military school. We had the opportunity to get to a PP80, other older IBM equipment, . . . FORTRAN that was laying around.

Betty: What hooked you on it?

Kelly: Well, I got hooked on the circuitry. I was trying to join the ham radio club on campus so I was kind of resurrecting old parts that had been there. Before then, I did not know anything about circuitry. I went to the University of Oklahoma for Nuclear Engineering School, and probably was what you would call a dismal failure, taking the tests and never doing the course work. I wandered into a computer lab and . . . well the rest is history. First security instinct was crashing the IBM 371 58 running 360 50 emulation and they had an IBM facility called Interactive Terminal Facility and they didn't shut off the SYS ADMIN from anybody . . . and it turns out the that the OPRTR account at that time did not have a password. And all you had to do was to send an EOJS which stands for "end of job stream" and the entire system would shut down. A very badly written operating system. A little bit after that is when I got involved in the whole phone freaking angle . . . blue boxing . . .

Betty: What's a blue box?

Kelly: Blue box is a device to generate more frequency tones for a CCIT System 5D signaling, and what this allows you to do is under long distance trunking that allows for more signal supervision or goal frequency supervison, . . . and they normally use a frequency of 2600, that will tell the lineman when it is in use and when it is not in use. You simply blink off the line with 2600 . . . send a message down the line with an appropriate sequence, and you can do pretty much what you want to including direct tapping of government lines, . . . crossing over into the Autoban and Autodin networks at the appropriate control points, if you can get to a switchman in the network like several people did, they set up conference bridges. One of these was known as the Charleston, West Virginia conference bridges—somewhat noteworthy because it is where _____ first latched on to me. And what happened there was I was attending a conference and after a couple of days my true name was mentioned. And a gentleman by the name of _____ who was VP for Security for Southwestern Bell started tracking me. The reason I found out was that I called up his number and listened in. A few days later I turned myself in anonymously. Then I wound up working for South-western Bell to do their security.

Betty: How long were you there?

Kelly: Oh, for about six months till I decided to go into the military and various other organizations. While I was at Southwestern Bell I was hacking into computers and various other things I should not have been hacking into. Where it finally broke was that my brother-in-law involved into military networks, like a U.S. artillery net . . . etc. Nothing much, but it was quite serious to him so he turned me in. He was working for G2 at the time. So after that I entered the U.S. military and was a dismal failure at that, got out very quickly and went to computer school! Since I found out that I loved those during college . . . and that was it. Pretty much its history.

Betty: So what have you been doing in the last couple of years?

Kelly: The last couple of years I have been working in security for a couple interesting clients like _____ and _____. . . . Along about that I was working for _____ at the time and I met a person by the name of John MacAfee who is like pivotal to the whole PGP story. John happened to be the first antiviral pioneer out there.

Betty: Okay, we are talking McAfee, the virus company?

Kelly: Yes; McAfee and Associates at the time. I was his original technical partner. He had a hacker test on a BBS which I took and corrected three errors he had. Then John and I started a number of years' association, basically passing people off to each other businesswise. Along that time I bid on a military project called _____ which was an electric countermeasure computer virus by the DOD Small Business Innovative Research branch. At that point John did not want anything to do with me because I was working on a military virus. Which never got accepted . . . which was fine. But during the whole process of researching viruses we observed a need to be able to ship infectious software mechanisms worldwide without creating danger for present and future customers.

Betty: I see.

Kelly: So at the time I starting using the intelligence that was written by Digital Signature, by a company in Illinois that had shut down by a consent order from Public Key Partners that had been producing a public key system called Cryptmaster from where the original user keys for PGP were taken from and where we formed the model. Jim Bidzos claimed that we used his Mail Safe program as a model, but that is a lie. Neither Phil Zimmerman nor I during the initial development of PGP ever looked at a copy of Mail Safe. I still haven't seen it myself to this day. I was using Cryptmaster as our model.

Betty: So who really developed PGP?

Kelly: Phil Zimmerman.

Betty: Okay.

Kelly: And I tried four other programmers to work on the public key code and finally formed a product that Phil termed PGP, but initially I was trying to go with other people. I didn't meet Phil until . . . let's see, it was 1989. I never met him in person until long after the PGP publication. Ah, basically, Phil was a friend of Charlie Merritt's at the time.

Betty: Charlie Merritts?

Kelly: Charlie Merritt. He is a guy that ran a company in Arkansas who used to sell me RSA code back in '91 for the Osborne 1 called Dedicated 32 which didn't have sufficient key lengths at the time to satisfy me so they were pushing custom key lengths at 512-768 bits at the time. And I also sold 300-baud modems, mobile power supplies, and encryption software to my customers who tended to be techies like me.

Betty: Okay, Kelly. How did PGP get out on the Net?

Kelly: Well, actually neither one of us ever put PGP on the Internet proper because at that time . . .

Betty: When you're talking "neither one of us," are you talking you and Phil?

Kelly: Neither Phil nor myself.

Betty: Okay.

Kelly: You see . . . at that time, the Internet really didn't exist, on June 5, 1991 when I put PGP on the US Usenet.

Betty: You put it out on the US Usenet?

Kelly: Yes. And you see the US Usenet is significant because under UUCP, not NNTP Protocol, its data was stored in a forward network. Now if the distribution line of the publication had worked correctly, it would confide to US-only sites because it checks that before it forwards the same. What actually turned out, the 7th or 8th of June 1991, there was a VMS ESA system in St. Louis, Missouri that had picked up traces of the publication I made, and it looks like either they or a peer site that had connected them had what is known as a Network News Transfer Protocol (NNTP) and basically it zips it off out of the country automatically because they had a misconfigured distribution.

Betty: Okay, explain that again a little slower, Kelly. You are going like a mile a minute here.

Kelly: Basically, what I finally determined might have happened that shipped PGP worldwide is that a misconfigured government computer accidentally shipped it out of the country automatically.

Betty: So this government computer picked it up from US Usenet?

Kelly: Well, they got it from the US Usenet.

Betty: Okay.

Kelly: And I later learned to my dismay that the government had computers on the NFS Net that were forwarding to foreign countries automatically, ignoring distribution.

Betty: The government was what?

Kelly: The government had a few research computers on the network and the people that were working with the NNTP protocol at the time evidently had broken distribution codes.

Betty: I see.

Kelly: And it basically sent it all over the place when it hit this one government site which is kinda funny because they're the ones that later tried to prosecute Phil and myself for supposedly publishing it worldwide which we didn't do.

Betty: How come you were never indicted?

Kelly: Well, actually I was on point all the time for the indictments.

Betty: You were on point for it?

Kelly: Yeah, ya see the the agreement between Phil and I was to divide the labor . . . Phil would design all the code itself, I would develop design, check away the code, and handle all legal publication and ends for Phil. The only thing was, right before publication, I took care to obtain from him verbally basically an irrevocable right to publish. Which means no matter what he said later, the publication would go right on happening.

Betty: Right.

Kelly: Because we were afraid of either legal pressure from private parties, or governmental pressure, okay? And during that time I also took care of shutting off all means of communication to the outside world. You see, if it can't be served, you can't be expected to follow a court order.

Betty: That's right.

Betty: So . . . where did you go?

Kelly: Oh . . . I went to Northern California, up to Washington, Oregon, Nevada, and down into Mexico and then pretty much back home, and I did this in a period of about five days. Dropped off at my brother's places and used their phone line, stopped at pay phones, had a converter in my car and a laptop . . . and a high-speed modem and dial into BBSs and would upload into US BBSs only. And this was supplemental to the original Usenet distribution just to make sure that if they had some way of shutting that down, they could not catch all the copies.

Betty: Right.

Kelly: And then after a five-day cycle, I went home and replaced the hard disk in the machine and shot a number of times through the hard disk and disassembled it and threw the pieces away.

Betty: What do you mean you shot it?

Kelly: I shot it physically.

Betty: With a gun?

Kelly: With a .45. It was a little 60-meg disk in a Canon laptop and it splattered quite nicely with big holes right through the disk head!

Betty: So after you ran around for five days what happened?

Kelly: Well, at this time, in terms of individually uploaded copies, there were about 300 copies as well as copies being uploaded by everyone in the country . . . like a flooding effect. In other words, let's say you arrange a pyramid of matches, and one matchhead touches another matchhead, and you light one matchhead and all of a sudden, you have a pyramid of matches burning.

Betty: Right.

Kelly: So that is basically what happened here. Everybody picked it up and started passing it to every place. Well, even though it was per my insistence because of the fact that I knew about international trafficking and arms regulations from the government _____ project, there was a clear warning all over the code, on the outside of the code, that this was not for export, but for domestic use only. Now, later on foreign citizens did download but that was after accidentally the government computer shipped it all over the world.

Betty: Are you absolutely sure it was government computers that did that? Has it been validated?

Kelly: Well, here is the validation. At the time, I was interviewed by a Customs agent which it turns out my current lawyer said I shouldn't have done, but that was before I fired my original lawyer. When I got my new lawyer, she requested information from the US attorney's office as to what type of evidence they had. Well, it turned out to be a tertiary log off the VMS ESA computer in St. Louis.

Betty: What kind of log?

Kelly: What we call in the security business a tertiary log. These are logs that are not admissible for court evidence. In other words, thirdhand information.

Betty: All right.

Kelly: OK. So anybody who has in the computer security field and tried to worked off of tertiary logs for court prosecution either government or private, is a totally impossible deal. The proper Rules of Evidence are not followed, so therefore, it cannot be used as evidence. So basically they were showing us this, and expecting us to give some admission of guilt or something else. *There was no guilt here.* What we did was a legal act of publication under the First Amendment. It was done to usurp rights that we believed we already had.

Betty: Yes . . .

Kelly: Because you see the whole process of how the law changes is by citizens asserting their rights and literally being taken to court. I have a sister who is an attorney in Oklahoma City. I know exactly how the law gets modified. So I was willing basically to go to court, if necessary to federal court, to extend my right to publish this code.

Betty: Then what?

Kelly: Now one of the things I think that stopped US Customs is, prior to the network publication, there had been a series of 30 copies of both the source and hexed up with the object printed off on paper and these were distributed to various people around the valley—people highly placed enough and willing to come forward in case of my possible prosecution to prove it was a public paper publication and then the network. This was done because the lawyers I had hired felt that we needed a paper publication first. And I think that is the reason why later the government never dared to prosecute me.

Betty: So you were never involved legally at all?

Kelly: Legally, I was the person who would always be charged. There was always doubt if Phil would be charged. And the main reason I took that position was that I was more than sure of my emotional stability to withstand the government onslaught. I am a security person myself. Phil is not.

Betty: Are you still tight with Phil?

Kelly: Actually, no. The past couple of years we haven't been and that is mainly because of the court case. And Phil to me was just another developer. I run projects for security and crypto all the time, so it's not like he was . . . even though he was one of the few that had guts and was libertarian enough to pull it off . . . you have to remember that when I wanted to give PGP away freely, and my one-half of the work involved, and as well as my financial investment which was considerable, he initially objected for a solid month. He did not want to do this. I basically was the one that pushed so heavy to publish all the source freely. It was more of an education project for the public.

Betty: I see. Did it ever get you upset he got all the notoriety, and nobody has really heard too much about you?

Kelly: No. You see I had a former US Attorney, Joe Burton, evoke federal privacy regulations for me subject to grand jury inquiry. I haven't been interested in notoriety working in the computer security business.

Betty: Okay.

Kelly: I do very deep internal security for large clients like _____ and _____ , and basically it would not serve me because I make _____ a year in the professional security business.

Betty: Okay, Kelly, the bottom line. Would you do it again? Exactly what happened. Would you do it again?

Kelly: Given the politics of what was going on at the time, in a heartbeat! I believe my actions were legally correct. I continue to believe they were legally correct. Quite frankly, I was disappointed that the U.S. Attorney did not take my little butt to court. Because this would have been the case that broke ITAR's back. ITAR goes back to the cold war—International Trafficking and Arms Race. It basically regulates crypto as a munition.

Betty: Okay, Kelly. Thank you.

9

Chipping: Silicon-Based Malicious Software

"I'm a dues-paying member of local thirteen, Villains, Thieves, and Scoundrels Union."

—BORIS BADENOV, SPY
"ROCKY AND BULLWINKLE"

OVER THE LAST COUPLE OF YEARS, I have had the opportunity to speak before a number of government groups and present some of the concepts behind what I call "Chipping." In many ways I overestimated the knowledge of my audiences, especially those experts in the intelligence community who claim to know something about computers, software, and technology in general. To my chagrin I found that a fairly small percentage of my Federal audiences had the insight to recognize the yin and yang of that technology. Those dedicated civil servants who do understand the dangers inherent in chipping have become so frustrated with the system (translate: do nothing) that they find it infinitely easier to lay back, get promoted to a G-14 pay grade, and wait until their pension is primed for a profitable retirement buyout.

Unfortunately, the Information Warrior is less laid back. He is on the offensive and has an excellent grasp of the technology. Chipping is just another Information Weapon that can be used against the econotechnical information infrastructure of our society.

At the heart of just about everything electronic sit tiny,

254

sometimes minuscule, components known as integrated circuits. An integrated circuit is the building block upon which toys, cameras, televisions, and computers are made. If you refer to integrated circuits as either ICs or chips, you'll sound like an expert. Chips come in thousands of flavors, but a mere handful dominate the innards of information systems.

We've all heard the term memory chip. A memory chip is an integrated circuit that is designed to act as a storage device for information. A memory chip that can hold 64K of information is called a 64K RAM chip. (RAM stands for Random Access Memory.) We speak of a 256K chip or a one meg or four meg chip, and so on. Designers are now working on RAM chips that can store tens of megabytes (thousands of pages) on a single piece of silicon the size of a thumbnail. Dozens of different kinds of memory chips are used in computers that require high speed storage measured in the megabytes and gigabytes. A gigabyte is a thousand megabytes, and a terrabyte is a million megabytes.

The nomenclature for chips is sometimes incomprehensible to anyone but an engineer—SRAM, NovRAM, 256KDRAM, EEPROM, UVEPROM, FlashRam and so on—but don't let that bother you. RAM is just RAM. Just like a lamp, whose primary purpose is to illuminate a room regardless of its styling and design, a RAM chip is an electronic memory device regardless of the technical intricacies involved. RAM is RAM is RAM.

The most familiar chip in the world might be the CPU, or Central Processing Unit. The CPU is the brains inside the computer or, as Intel says in their ads, "The Computer inside the Computer." CPU chips carrying the Intel trademarks of 286, 386, 486, and Pentium drive the majority of desktop computers today. Apple is a major user of Motorola's 68000 series of CPUs and IBM, Sun, and DEC all have their own CPU chips meant to compete with Intel's virtual monopoly.

Etched onto a small wafer of silicon, with a thickness measured in molecules, is a dizzyingly complex pattern of paths, connections, gates, and millions of switches. The process of CPU design and manufacture is so complex that other computer systems calculate and lay out the digital road maps.

If the CPU is removed, the computer is deader than a door-nail, and arguably no longer even a computer. If the CPU is disabled, the computer system becomes unreliable and fails. The parallel to the human brain is unavoidable; no head, no brain, no life. No CPU, no computer.

Other chips provide the glue to make computers compute, ovens cook, cellular phones call, or airplanes fly. These small logic chips switch signals from on to off to on again, when told to do so by the CPU. Even with the immense power of today's CPUs, unless the so-called glue chips are working properly, the electronic device in question will idly sit on the closet shelf or find its way back to the store for replacement.

Input/output chips let you print on your printer, talk to another computer via modem, or make your television cable-ready. An input chip will listen to the rinse cycle time you enter onto the numeric keypad on the washing machine. An output chip signals that dinner is ready or sends information from a fax machine through Cyberspace across the Global Network. Video chips provide dazzling color and animation on computer monitors. An entire modem is available on a single piece of silicon, or in one chip. Hundreds of manufacturers worldwide offer an unlimited number of chips that perform almost any conceivable function.

Some chips are smarter than others. The RAM chip doesn't have what we might call native intelligence; it doesn't think for itself. The command to write to a RAM chip or read the information stored in it must be made by the CPU. CPU chips are very smart. Built into their microscopic circuits is a set of instructions called microcode. These are a comprehensive set of rules by which the CPU chips live and breathe.

The microcode is a kind of language. Just as a New Yorker might not be able to answer a Russian tourist's request for directions, a CPU chip might sit and do nothing if it is asked to perform a task for which its microcode is not prepared.

Other chips give the impression of being smart, such as

ROM chips. The term ROM Bios describes a set of instructions or rules that tell a particular computer how to function when asked to perform certain clearly defined and prespecified tasks. A ROM chip is really not all that smart, though—no smarter than a library. The information is there but for it to be of any value, you have to know how to access and use it. That is the job of a CPU. The CPU will address the ROM chip and look up the particular information of interest.

More and more chips appear daily. Portable camcorders are possible because of the development of extremely compact and specialized integrated circuits. Color correction circuits keep blue, blue. Gyrostabilizing circuits let you strap a camera to the back of your pet for a dog's view of the world without too much jitter.

Chip specialization is so inexpensive today that it is within the reach of the average electronic hobbyist, not to mention the Information Warrior. For a few dozen dollars, an electronics tinkerer can buy an integrated circuit that he can program himself.

EPROMs (Erasable Programmable Read Only Memory), PALs (Programmable Array Logic) can cost as little as a few dollars, or as much as $100 or more for sophisticated chips with thousands of gates. For more sophisticated engineers, ASIC, or Application Specific Integrated Circuits, can be designed, prototyped, and turned out in large quantity in less than three months for between $10 and $25,000. ASICs are found in almost every electronic device because it reduces manufacturing costs and other waste in the long run if conventional off-the-shelf chips are used.

For big manufacturers who produce millions of copies of the same chip, the use of VLSI, or Very Large Scale Integration, is popular. VLSI techniques permit thousands upon thousands of circuits to be condensed into smaller spaces. The tool-up costs for a custom VLSI chip start at $100,000 and go up from there. However, volume production techniques reduce the per unit cost of each chip, sometimes down to pennies. It's a matter of economy of scale.

Why all of the hubbub about chips? Because, chips are not always what they appear to be. They can neatly provide the insidiousness required by the able and resource intensive Information Warrior. What sort of damage can be caused by Information Warriors using chips or integrated circuits as a weapon? The answer, as you would expect by now, is plenty.

Recall that the essential difference between malicious software and a programming error is intent. The same concept holds true for chips. Occasionally, a chip will fail. A physical imperfection in the manufacturing process will cause the chip to internally break, malfunction, or cease to function altogether. The result? If the chip is a critical component, the device will fail—the television sound just stops, or the readout on the copy machine is blank. A failed chip in a car's electronic ignition will not allow you to start the car and pull out of the driveway. Similarly, if the central processor of a large computer fails, the entire system comes to a grinding halt. A glitch in a single chip is enough to shut down the most extensive electronic system.

Unfortunately, unlike the amateur television repairman of the fifties and sixties, you can't run down to the corner drug store, test the tubes, and replace the one that doesn't glow. Today's circuits are so intricate and intertwined that they need complex test equipment and highly trained technicians to isolate and repair the offending equipment. In the meantime, to the rest of us, it's just broke. Often it doesn't pay to fix the offending chip; the cost of repair is sometimes higher than the cost of replacement. How many of us would consider sending a $19.95 calculator back to the factory for repair? Most of us give the broken one to the baby and buy another at K-Mart.

But what if the chip was meant to fail, or to act differently than it was supposed to? What if the intent of the chip was to fail or malfunction on cue, as if it were following rules that only it knew about? The modification, alteration, design, or use of integrated circuits for purposes other than those originally intended by the designers is called "chipping." And chipping provides the Information Warrior with a bevy of opportunities to wage his war.

A simple example will suffice. In New York and other major metropolitan areas, phone fraud is rampant and costs industry hundreds of millions of dollars yearly. Cellular phones have been particularly hard hit and chipping is at the core of the rip-off. Once the electronic identification number of a cellular phone is in hand, that number must be programmed into chips using a PAL or EEPROM programmer, a tool used by hobbyists and engineers. The newly programmed chip then replaces the original chip that contained the phone's original EIN, in the new modified cellular phone. A phone has been chipped to bill an unsuspecting victim. In this case, the chipping was definitely malicious in both intent and effect, and the act itself runs afoul of quite a few laws.

But let's get imaginative for a moment, and think up other devious chipping activities that might lend themselves to an Information Warrior's agenda. Let's say that our Information Warrior has ample resources and is not looking for immediate gratification. That is, he is content to wait a couple of years before the results of his chipping become apparent. Counterfeit chips would work quite well.

Small chip makers, often from the Pacific Rim, build copies or clones of popular, pricey chips that are widely used and rarely examined. Often the ersatz manufacturer will not have obtained the rights or licenses to legally build the chips, but build them they do. Some are so brazen as to even label the counterfeit chips with the markings and insignias of the legitimate manufacturer. The counterfeiters make a few gazillion chips and sell them illegally, at a discount, as the real McCoy. Deep discounting can be a red flag, but overproduction is often used as an excuse, and raises few eyebrows when there are big profits to be made. The counterfeiters make and sell the chips to manufacturers for use inside VCRs, automobiles, computers, telephone answering machines, even military hardware. To all outside appearances, the chips are legitimate.

Counterfeit chips are generally sold to make quick profits, but they have a more insidious use for the well-armed Information Warrior. What if, in addition to making a counterfeit version of a chip that is in particularly high demand, a few additional functions are added to the chip, functions that would give the original designers a bad case of cardiac arrest?

Let's say that Kumbaya Electronics designs a fancy new chip that combines all of the functions of a clock radio into one component: the tuner, the amplifier, the clock, and its alarm circuits. Works great. Let's say that another company buys one of Kumbaya's chips and reverse-engineers it; takes it apart so thoroughly that they know everything about its inner workings. At a fraction of what it cost Kumbaya to develop the chip, the counterfeiters clone the fancy new chip but, since they are Information Warriors or they are being paid by them, they add extra circuits and instructions not in the original design.

Those instructions might be that at midnight on December 20, 1999, the chip would stop working—period. If the clock radios that used the Kumbaya chip sold well, the clock-radio manufacturer is going to have a lot of returns on his hands. Thousands of dissatisfied customers won't know about each other, but the manufacturer will find out soon enough that he has a problem. In addition to an immediate negative financial impact, whether from extensive returns at Sears and Circuit City or from a bad rash of publicity, the manufacturer faces a potential public relations problem. If the clock-radio manufacturer traces the problem back to the chip, and they undoubtedly will, Kumbaya Electronics will also have a problem. Despite their best efforts, word will get around that their chips are unreliable and shouldn't be used.

Who would want to do such a thing? A competitor is a pretty good place to start the list of suspects if the motivation is an economic battle between companies. Such sabotage is very effective and hard to detect and prove. The clock radio example is a pretty simple one, without earthshaking effects, but the same chipping technique can be used with devastating results.

Imagine that the battle between Japan and the U.S. for the automobile market becomes more heated than ever. U.S. trade restrictions have hurt Toyota, Nissan, Honda, and the rest. Detroit has gotten its act together, and sales of Rising Sun cars to aging baby boomers and the younger generation are way down. Since the Japanese economic system, *keiretsu*, is based upon interlocked relationships between thousands of smaller companies and their seven huge parent companies, the economic impact is felt throughout the small island nation. As a matter of international pride, Japan does not wish to lose face in the economic battle for motor vehicle superiority. Something must be done about the resurgence of the American automobile industry. This is a matter of Japanese Economic National Security.

Several Japanese companies now supply chips to American car companies; they provide the brains for electronic ignitions and braking systems as well as other chips for less mission-critical functions. Whether unofficially sanctioned with a wink on a national level, or as a knee-jerk reaction at the industrial level, a simple plan is hatched. Sell the Americans the chips they want, except there will be a little "surprise" waiting for drivers of certain American cars. The chips will look and function the same as ever and pass the necessary tests to be qualified for use, just as they always have. But, at some time in the future, according to a set of rules inserted into the chip by its designers, the chip will fail.

Maybe the windshield wipers will go haywire every day at 6:30, but only when the car is traveling at fifty-five MPH. Or the left blinker and the right blinker will intermittently cross their wires, further maddening the victim when he can't reproduce the symptom to his mechanic. Depending upon the desired results, the victim cars could become a joke as a result of their peculiarities, or gain an impossible-to-shake reputation for being deadly, such as happened to the Audi 5000. The results could be fatal—not only to passengers but to the car company.

Tens of billions of dollars could be lost if the Ford Taurus were subject to a rash of sudden uncontrollable failures when operating at a high-speed, or certain maneuvers resulted in accidents and deaths. The resultant publicity could be devastating—all because a chip was told to fail.

Chipping is the Trojan horse of microelectronics. Like the Greek gift to their Homeric enemy, the chip allows the electronic terrorist to slip his devastation in undetected. The more common the chip, the easier it is to counterfeit and distribute. What if, however, the Information Warrior did not want to destroy his target? What if his Trojan Horse had a different purpose, perhaps one of tracking or surveillance? The chipper might add, for example, a circuit that electromagnetically broadcasts a distinctive signal or pattern as a tracking device, like those often used in Hollywood's great car chase scenes.

Electromagnetic eavesdropping, or van Eck detection, is a useful tool for gathering information in a clandestine manner, but the state of the art has a way to go and chipping is one way to get there. While the chip performs its expected tasks, our silicon Trojan Horse will perform two unexpected functions. One, it will be tuned to listen for a specific type of Van Eck radiation. Two, it will transmit that information, to make distant reception easier. Conceptually, this is the equivalent of a phone bug, except that it is a computer being tapped.

There is immense value in knowing the channel on which every computer in foreign consulates broadcasts; it makes interception all the easier. The signal is cleaner, less data reconstruction is required, and the cost of surveillance is reduced. The only hitch? Getting the bug into the computer. In Gordon Liddy parlance, that requires a "bag job," or physical entry into the target. Replacing or adding a chip to a computer or printer is not too difficult for a repairman or computer dealer. Or, as the CIA supposedly did, you can sell the printer with the chip to the guy who's gonna sell it to the guy who's gonna ship it to the guy who's gonna buy it. Or you can fill the sales pipeline and listen in on everybody.

Some military planners recognize the power of chipping in

the furtherance of their goals. These are not the types of projects that one will routinely hear about in the *Washington Post* or in a Congressional hearing. Chipping is a carefully guarded technique that the NSA, the CIA, and their brethren whisper about in shielded windowless rooms. The funding is "black," meaning that R&D efforts into chipping are not line items in a general ledger. Accountability for chipping lies within the intelligence agencies, not within the Congress that funds it. Compared with the high cost of B-2 bombers, submarines, and satellites, chipping is chump change. Perhaps that is why it is so carefully protected. The powers that be don't want the other side's Information Warriors to do unto them what they are doing unto others.

The arms industry is an ideal market for government-sponsored chipping. The international dealers either sell indiscriminately to the highest bidder, or they are sponsored by governments in the pursuit of their political agenda. The U.S. is no exception in its sale of weapons systems to political allies and foes alike. Modern armaments are highly sophisticated electronic devices, the Patriot missile perhaps claiming first place in name recognition.

Let's assume for a moment that CIA and Pentagon Information Warriors want to play a trick on the customers who buy American weapons. A few of the electronic goodies inside the weapon system have been chipped; they have been modified perhaps to fail in three months time, or to shoot off course by three degrees, or to blow themselves up after two shots. Or maybe they have a radio beacon installed in them that identifies their exact location to overhead satellites. If the U.S. had built Iraq's Scuds and chipped them, it would have been a far sight easier to take them all out on day one. Imagine if North Korea's IBM 360 mainframe computers which control their missiles contained a "back door" to which only the U.S. military had access. Some close to the Department of Defense maintain this is exactly the case.

Chips have no sense of right or wrong, no morals or conscience. The chip only does what it is designed to do, and the intent and purpose of the chip is imbued in silicon by its designers. It is no more difficult to design a malevolent chip than to design one that works flawlessly for years. The cost to make the chips is the same, and only a little extra effort is required to maintain invisibility and insidiousness. Other than that, the distinction between a good chip and a bad chip is in the eyes of the beholder—or of its victims.

From the Information Warrior's viewpoint, chipping takes advantage of unexploited vulnerabilities that exist in virtually every electronic system. Chipping offers a wide range of capabilities and is usually a reasonably priced tool. When gigadollars are involved, chipping is an insignificant cost in the equation. Due to the insidiousness of the technique, it ranks as a highly effective weapon for the Information Warrior.

Denial of Service

Winn Schwartau

In the world of information security ("infosec"), there are three basic tenets upon which much of the field was founded.

Confidentiality. Keeping secrets a secret: In the electronic netherworld of Cyberspace, or in storage within a network or a personal computer, to insure confidentiality one must employ an encryption scheme of some sort.

Integrity. Maintaining accuracy of data: If you don't want data intentionally or accidentally modified either in transmission or in storage, one must employ an integrity checking mechanism which can vary from super simple (parity checkers) to complex encryption-based coding.

Availability. Making sure systems and data are available for use.

For all intents and purposes, technologically we have solved the first two of these criteria. We have had the technology publicly available for 20 years to protect against confidentiality and integrity breaches. When DES was introduced in 1976, it offered (and still offers) a strong deterrence against eavesdroppers and would-be modifiers of data.

Today, with advanced technques like PGP, PKE of various flavors, and "wrapping" messages with electronic signatures, protection is offered against all but the most intense nation-state effort at penetrating electronic shields, and then only at great expense. But technology alone does not solve the problem. Encryption is only as strong as the key-management system used, and if that collapses, so does the encryption. Add the complexity of scaling such a system up to the corporate level of thousands of users, and the administrative problem is magnified. But the bottom line is we do have the technology to solve the problems associated with confidentiality and integrity. (Other facets of infosec have emerged, including strong user identification and authentication, repudiation, etc. But the use of encryption addresses these, too.)

However, problems of availability are not so easily handled. If I, as the bad guy, can make your computers, networks, and data unavailable to you, I have waged a Denial of Service (DOS) attack. A few examples will suffice.

In mid-1995, a New Jersey construction worker jack-hammered through the pavement into an electrical conduit, and somehow survived cutting through the primary power feed to Newark Airport. Power went down. Switch to backup power. But the backup power was run in the same conduit. It had been cut, too. Denial of Service.

In April and May 1995, air traffic to Kennedy and LaGuardia airports was suspended because the controllers couldn't communicate. In three separate events within a seven-week period, communications and power failures cascaded into Denial of Service events at these New York airports. These incidents were part of the reason that 1995 was the year when antiquated air traffic control systems around the United States became the subject of media scrutiny and derision.

Chicago suffered airport computer failures three times during one week in early summer 1995. The archaic system is still working—sort of—even though the main system is now 30 years old.

The Airport Surveillance Radar 9 systems (ASR9) deployed at more than 101 airports are supposed to be reliable. Miami International Airport and Fort Lauderdale-Hollywood International Airport experienced failures 13 times between May 24 and June 26, 1995, and six times in the week of July 17 alone. A break in a telephone line could prevent the radar screen from displaying data essential for tracking planes.

The *Cleveland Plain Dealer* reported that the Huntsville airport (which uses the ASR9) sustained 42 outages totaling 130 hours of downtime between January 1990 and December 1993. But the worst string of outages during that period, according to the *Plain Dealer*, occurred at the Tri-Cities Airport in Pasco, Washington, where the ASR9 was down a total of 3,545 hours, or an average of 1,181 hours (49 days) a year.

David Dietz of the *San Francisco Chronicle* reported that on August 9, 1995, the Oakland air-traffic control center was down for over an hour, having lost all radar and radio contact with planes in the 18,000,000-square mile vicinity of Oakland. He also noted that computers failed 20 times at the ATC centers in Chicago, Washington, D.C., Dallas-Fort Worth, Cleveland, and New York in the prior four months. Denial of Service.

The *San Francisco Chronicle* reported that on Saturday, August 12, 1995, lighting knocked out both the main power and the backup for almost 1.5 hours at the Miami-area ATC radar center. The Miami center tracks 400,000 square miles of air space over Florida, the Atlantic, and the Gulf of Mexico.

And these are just the ones we have heard about. The FAA understandably wants to maintain customer confidence in the system. But after the ValuJet crash in May 1996, such confidence in the FAA's ability to maintain control and safety has been waning under intense scrutiny. But Denial of Service affects more than just transportation systems.

The World Trade Center bombing was a Denial-of-Service event that, when combined with the effects of the Great No Name Storm of 1993, created the Double Whammy effect: millions of customers had no access to ATM machines from Maine to Chicago for up to a month. Denial of Service.

No matter the means, the effect is what counts with Denial of Service. Bad software causes a production facility to close for an hour? DOS. A virus gets into a defense contractor's computer networks? DOS.

Now, the banking industry is talking about getting rid of 50 percent of its retail presence and shifting its emphasis to electronic banking on the

Internet. Wonderful. But, with Denial of Service attacks so easy to launch on the Net, specific banks could be targeted as victims. When an organization counts on electronic services for revenues and profits, it must, for its own good, remain acutely aware of how the bad guys can affect it.

So, occasionally one must think way "outside the box" to get a handle on what can happen.

In late 1995, Melbourne, Australia air traffic control received complaints from pilots that one or more of their communications channels was picking up so much interference as to be unusable. Investigators tried to identify the intermittent jamming effects (a different form of DOS). One opinion was that rogue hacker/pranksters were responsible, and such reports were released to the media, possibly in an attempt to shut down the offending person. The search continued, finally zeroing in on a VCR in a house directly under the flight path to the airport. Authorities bought the owner a new VCR, took the old one, and all seemed to go well thereafter.

In May 1996, alleged proponents of the Church of Scientology launched DOS attacks against alt.religion.scientology. Thousands of postings were repeatedly sent to a.r.s. in an apparent attempt to silence criticism of the church. The mail-storm is indicative of the capabilities that individual netizens really do have. In September 1996, PANIX, a New York Internet service provider, was shut down for days by a DOS attack.

So, we have essentially solved confidentiality and integrity. We can send secret e-mail and store messages privately, and we can make sure that the right amount of money is properly transferred to the right account number in the right country; that's integrity. But this Denial of Service is a mess. We have no fundamental conceptual solutions—yet.

Let's look at the Internet issue. Can Denial of Service attacks be thwarted? As a domain on the Net with the right firewall, with the latest tools, I can detect that I am under a broadcast storm DOS attack. But I can really do only a couple of things: (1) shut down, which means the DOS attack has been successful; (2) detect the source of the attack by address and other heuristics, and then shunt the incoming traffic to another location, which takes a ton of bandwidth and CPU time.

We need another approach to Net-based DOS attacks that involve the cooperation of the victim and the providers. There are two views to be taken.

From the firewall standpoint, let's assume that my detection software detects that I am under a DOS attack and sends an immediate message to my primary ISP advising its software to cut off all traffic from a certain address or that is behaving in certain ways (such as repeated messages of X length repeated every Y time periods). To keep the site alive and well, the traffic has to be cut off. It might prove vindictively humorous to return the incoming messages from whence they came, but given the typical anonymity of the perpetrators, this retort might merely serve to annoy others downstream.

We have to get the ISPs of all sizes involved in protection against DOS attacks on the Net. The scheme, very roughly outlined, would be to employ a heuristic agent which looks for anomalous behavior in the traffic. For example, any ISP or carrier in the chain should look for a long series of small messages from one particular address or site. My ISP, at the end of the chain, should look for high-density mail coming my way that meets particular characteristics.

The software used for this purpose at the ISP (and carriers) must have a back channel for communications, so that all will be in sync on what is happening and what actions to take if one or more of the distriibuted DOS detection agents determines that a DOS attack is under way. The appropriate actions to take would include the following:

- Filtering the source and putting it in the electronic trash
- Collecting the messages for later forensic use
- Identifying the source and taking social/legal action
- Putting up a data mirror back to the source (ethically questionable)

The point is that if we decide we care about DOS on the Internet, we can find workable solutions where the anarchy of freedom of speech remains intact but the offensive anarchy of actions is restricted.

Now, Denial of Service is nothing new to the military: bomb the target, take it out with whatever weapon is necessary, and move on. But with the concept of nonlethal warfare coming into favor, Denial of Service takes on new meaning. How can the military effect its mission and inflict minimal physical damage and loss of life? Certainly one technique is to take apart as much of the target's infrastructure as possible. I have worked on what I call ECO-D scenarios: Economic Deactivation of Opposition Infrastructures. The premise is that launching DOS attacks against a target nation-state prior to conventional conflict will make the whole affair cleaner and somehow more palatable.

But the military has been and is acutely aware of the need for DOS capability in C4I (Command, Control, Communications, Computers, and Intelligence). This is the system which allows generals to run a war. It's how soldiers receive instructions, field commanders report back to headquarters, and intelligence distributes information. Of course it's all a lot more complicated than that, but C4I is the backbone of the modern war. In Toffleresque thinking, it's the backbone of a third-wave military.

The object from a DOS standpoint is to make your enemy blind and deaf. Cut off his ability to see you, deny him access to the information necessary to fight a war, and isolate command from the troops.

Some, but not all, forms of DOS are "fixable." As we pay attention to the issues from a civilian view as much as from a military view, we will find that many adversarial efforts will be thwarted.

However, this discussion brings up a very special area of DOS, one for which the private sector is generally naive, for which there are few widely available solutions, and which the military prefers to keep secret. As discussed in the next chapter, these are the nuclear weapons of the Information Age.

10

HERF Guns
and EMP/T Bombs

"Lock phasers."

—CAPTAIN JAMES T. KIRK, *STAR TREK*

THE AZURE SEA GLISTENED 10,000 feet beneath the U.S. Navy P-3 patrol plane. Rays of light streamed from the sunset crimson skies in the west, creating mosaics of color that shimmered across the surface of the warm Caribbean waters. But the pilot and the two drug enforcement agents in the cockpit had little time to appreciate the beckoning views.

They were too busy concentrating on the video screens, digital readouts, and communications equipment that filled the forward section of the highly-customized airplane. The interior of the specially outfitted craft was darkened to facilitate use of the racks of sophisticated electronic equipment.

A conflict was brewing.

"Bogey heading twenty degrees-seventeen miles due north. No ID," the voice crackled over the cryptographically secure communications line. Everyone in the plane listened to all comm.

"Roger that, Blazer. Casa One in pursuit," the P-3's pilot answered immediately, as he sharply banked the plane to the right.

"Make it clean, Casa One," the invisible voice retorted.

"Always have been, Blazer. We're batting a thousand." Knowing glances were passed around the cockpit.

The P-3 began a rapid descent; the motors roared as the plane flew through the thicker air.

The DEA agent in charge spoke into his mouthpiece. "Are we ready?"

The other agent scanned the wall of displays and pressed a couple of switches. "114%, nominal. Charge rate 1.7 seconds. What's the target?"

"Let you know when we know."

The plane descended to 2,000 feet on the same heading as the Bogey. "Eight clicks upwind," the P-3 captain said, pointing at the full color radar screen sitting between his and the copilot's seat.

The radar screen was filled with a number of small symbols, geometric figures with numbers attached to each one. The numbers indicated the call, the sign, and other identifying information on each aircraft in the area. Except one. A single symbol, flashing bright red, reading: UNIDENTIFIED.

"Got a broken transponder, y'think?" the DEA agent in the rear of the cockpit asked.

"I sincerely hope so, for his sake," said the bearded senior DEA agent. There wasn't any trace of humor in his words.

"Four clicks. Got a visual," the pilot said casually. Both DEA agents looked out the front of the plane and the pilot instinctively pointed.

"He see us?"

"Not yet. I got in silent."

"What is it?"

The pilot leaned forward, as though a few extra inches would improve his view of a plane over two miles away. "DC-3. Couldn't outrun my grandmother's Vespa."

"Yes!" shouted the second, younger DEA man. "They leak like a sieve. I need less than a mile." He proceeded to make a few adjustments to an oscilloscope, mumbling to himself. "Point nine six five gig . . . four millisecond. . . ."

"OK, Ace, bring us in. I'd like to ask a few questions."

The P-3 lurched forward and the old DC-3 rapidly got closer and closer. "Wave him?"

"Go for it." The wings of the P-3 appeared to flap, trying to attract the attention of the target DC-3. No response. The DC-3 flew straight. "Again." No response. "The book says three, do it again." Nothing.

"OK, let's see if he's got his ears on." The head DEA man was in charge, absolutely professional. He adjusted his radio. "Ah . . . the DC-3 without markings . . . yeah, you. Please identify yourself." He looked over at the plane, now only a few hundred yards to his right. "I repeat, please identify yourself." Nothing.

He spoke to the pilot. "Get me in visual, Ace." The plane inched toward the DC-3 until the outline of the other pilot's face was visible. "Flare him." The other DEA man adjusted a dial and pushed a button secured by a hinged plastic Molly-cover.

"Flare deployed," he said casually as a large flare traced its way on a near-interception course with the cockpit of the DC-3.

"That'll get his attention." By now the DEA chase plane was so close that the DC-3 pilot's reaction, one of near terror, caused the head DEA man and his pilot to guffaw. When the flare shot past the front of the DC-3, the pilot's fear turned to anger, eliciting an unfriendly hand gesture in response.

"Well, I do believe that he's not on his way to Disney World with the family. Wouldn't you agree?" Nods all around, and the tension was somewhat abated. In these cases, you have to make sure that Ozzie and Harriet aren't out for a spin or you are in real trouble.

"He knows damn well we can't shoot him down."

"Maybe he'll listen to reason now."

"Think so?"

"No, but it's worth a try."

"Ah . . . you in the DC-3 . . . this is the Drug Enforcement Administration. We are operating under the authority of a multinational enforcement group and within the laws and powers granted us. We'd like to have a word with you if you don't mind. There's a little island about forty miles ahead where you can land. Please indicate your willingness to comply by responding immediately."

The senior DEA man gazed over at the DC-3 pilot. Nothing. Par for the course.

"Hey dirtball. Drop the load, now." Nothing.

"OK, here's the deal," he said calmly. "I will give you fifteen seconds to respond. If you do not respond in a positive way, expect the following to occur. First, your radio systems will fail. You will notice that because the static will disappear and no reception will be possible. Not even from us. Got it?"

They looked for some response and got none.

"I will give you one minute after your communications fail to give us the sign that you will comply. At the end of one minute, you will then find that your avionics will fail, all electrical systems will fail, your engines will stop, and your plane will sink into the water beneath you at a high rate of speed. If my memory serves me right, the laws of physics say you will not survive the crash. Do I make myself clear?" No response.

"Hey, Señor Stupid in the DC-3. Your fifteen seconds begins . . . Now!" He clicked off the radio and said to the pilot, "Take us out about a half mile. Is that good for you?" he asked the other DEA man at the equipment.

"Who could ask for anything more," he responded in the singsong voice of an old Toyota commercial.

The plane slowly glided away from the DC-3.

"Five seconds." Silence in the cockpit.

"Got it fixed on target."

"Two . . . one . . . fire."

The technical DEA man again raised a hinged panel and pushed a large red button. "Full power . . . front antenna struck . . . 4.5 megawatts. A poodle in a microwave would have fared better." There was no sound, no bullets, no missiles. Just an invisible beam of energy shot at the misbehaving DC-3. "Charge complete. Again?"

"For good luck." Again the red button was depressed and the DEA man repeated his report of an invisible bullseye.

"Let's see if he comes around to seeing things our way," the head DEA man said, relaxing back in his chair. The DC-3 turned suddenly to the right and accelerated. "I guess he wasn't convinced. Stay with him, Ace."

"No problem," the pilot said, following the DC-3 in a steep turn.

"Thirty seconds. Get in front of him." The Navy P-3 airplane accelerated and it soon seemed that they were the ones being chased; they were in front of the DC-3. "Avionics next."

The other DEA man said, "Power up to 180%, directionality .083, 1.21 gig. Ready when you are."

"Ten seconds."

The more maneuverable P-3 matched every move of the old lumbering DC-3, and maintained a forward position. "Five . . . four . . . three . . . oh, screw it . . . fire." Again, the red button was pressed.

"Shouldn't be long now," said the head DEA man.

They watched for several seconds, until the starboard propeller began to sputter and decelerate. The plane dipped to the left and they then saw the port propeller turn more slowly and the poor DC-3 twisted in the opposite direction. In many ways, this was the sad part of every operation for all three in the chase plane. Their target had no chance, none at all, but he just wouldn't listen. It would be over in a few seconds.

The DC-3 propellers were coming to a stop and the plane was plummeting rapidly. A plane of that size falling into the water makes a substantial splash.

"Call it in, Ace."

The pilot flipped a switch on the secure communications panel. "Blazer, this is Casa One."

"Copy you, Casa One," the static voice answered.

"Bogey fell into the drink, Blazer. Apparently a total systems failure."

"Copy that, Casa One. Survivors?"

"Not likely."

"Well, that's a darn shame. C'mon home Casa One. Good work."

Fiction? A true story? Maybe. Maybe not.

Even though the antidrug effort has cost tens of billions of dollars and the Pentagon spends some $1.2 billion annually to support such endeavors, America's War on Drugs has been less than successful.[1] One of the rules of the war is that we don't use bombs, bullets, or missiles to shoot down airplanes in international airspace. Unless of course they shoot first.

But where does it say that it's illegal for a drug courier's plane to go haywire and crash?

The beauty of the scenario above is that there is no obvious trace of foul play. There are no bullet holes or missing fuselage. The plane is largely intact, and when and if it is found, a close physical inspection will show the plane to be in pristine physical condition.

If the electronics packages are removed and subjected to intensive testing, all that will be found are components that failed without an obvious cause. Drug barons will not likely perform rescue and surveillance operations, at least not initially. The cost of such a flight is comparatively modest: $500,000 for the drugs, $1.5 million for the plane, $400,000 for the pilot, all for an ultimate $12.5 million-per-plane load payoff.[2] Losing planes, pilots, and drugs are part of the cost of doing business.

In our scenario, though, the DEA, the DoD, and antidrug forces have access to a weapon that is ideally suited to waging Narco Warfare. It is powerful, it is remote, and it is invisible. And ultimately, it is deniable—a government favorite. And there's not a whole lot the drug guys can do about it.

HERF Guns

Equipment such as that described in this tale is in use today and has become part of the arsenal of the U.S. military and other law enforcement agencies.

When I first presented the concept of High Energy Radio Frequency (or HERF) Guns as an Information Weapon to a Congressional Committee, their initial reaction provided pure comic relief to an otherwise dull Government hearing. On June 27, 1991, the day following a widespread telephone outage in the Northeast, Congressman Dan Glickman's and Tim Valentine's Technology and Competitiveness Subcommittee held hearings on the effectiveness of the Computer Security Act of 1987. This Act is designed to force all government agencies to develop information security policies for their respective operations, submit them for approval, and then implement them. The CSA-1987 has no impact on or authority over commercial and private computer systems. Serendipitously, the timing of the telephone outage heightened anticipation of the hearings.

Congressman Glickman, a Democrat from Kansas, opened the session with a statement that showed his true concern for the security, integrity, and sanctity of computer systems in both the public and private sectors. The events of the day before, and the prior system crashes, framed his remarks. He established the tone of the session, and then it was my turn.

Taking his words to heart, I pointed out and described how a magnetic gun could be harmful, if not deadly, to computer systems. I called them HERF Guns. I have dubbed the really big HERF guns with greater range and greater power EMP/T (pronounced 'empty') Bombs.

One of the first questions asked was, as you might expect, about HERF Guns. Congressman Glickman asked, "Do you think we ought to consider banning these kinds of devices?" I replied, "If you did you would be banning the microwave and communications industries from existence." Laughter rippled for some time and certainly lightened the load for the rest of the hearing.

If I may put on my Congress-bashing hat to offer an aside, I would like to see a greater number of engineering types elected to office instead of the infinite stream of pork barrel lawyers we get today. Very few people are aware of the fact that guns and bombs can be built that target only computers, communications, and other electronic systems. The situation sort of reminds me of Jimmy Carter's neutron bomb—kill all the people but leave the buildings standing.

A lesson in HERF: HERF stands for High Energy Radio Frequency. It's an easy acronym that's even fun to say. A HERF Gun is a very powerful weapon in the Information Warrior's arsenal, and it can come in all sorts of different configurations to meet one's needs. At a very basic level, a HERF Gun shoots a high power radio signal at an electronic target and puts it out of commission.

Electronic circuits are sensitive to interference from external magnetic fields. We have all experienced interference in radios, televisions, or portable phones. When the radio crackles, that's electromagnetic interference. When the television aerial gets twisted every which way, or a lightening bolt strikes nearby, or a cellular phone call is cut off when the car crosses a bridge or enters a tunnel, that's interference. Or, as mentioned earlier, the earliest models of computers could cause substantial interference to our television reception.

But electronic circuits can also be overloaded and forced to malfunction. If you take the 110 volts from the wall and plug it into a VCR's video input, your VCR will cease to be a working VCR. It might even exhibit the telltale sign of the ultimate electronic failure: smoke. When jump-starting a car, we all make sure that plus is connected to plus and minus to minus, because of the dire warnings on the battery. Similarly, lightening and cable television systems do not get along well at all. Power strips have surge protection circuits to keep sensitive electronic equipment from being blasted into silicon heaven when the power company glitches or lightening strikes the pole transformer on the corner.

Electronic circuits are more vulnerable to overload than most people realize, and that weakness is exploited by a HERF Gun. A HERF Gun is nothing more than a radio transmitter, conceptually similar to the real tall ones with blinking red lights on top to keep planes from hitting them. Your portable CB or your cellular phone are also radio transmitters, with different purposes, working at different power levels. The HERF Gun shoots enough energy at its target to disable it, at least temporarily. A HERF Gun can shut down a computer, cause an entire computer network to crash, or send a telephone switch into electronic orbit. The circuitry within modern computer and communications equipment is designed for low-level signals; nice and quiet 1s and 0s which operate within normal limits. The HERF Gun is designed to overload this electronic circuitry so that the information system under attack will become, at least temporarily, a meaningless string of babbling bytes.

For the Information Warrior, a HERF Gun need only meet a couple of criteria to be effective. First, the HERF Gun should put out as much energy as possible—the more energy it puts out, the more damage it can cause. Secondly, a HERF Gun should have some directionality or control over where its magnetic bullets are going. Some HERF Guns are like shotguns, spreading out their radiation in all directions; others are highly focussed like a precision rifle. A HERF Gun can be a remarkably simple device or a complex one that takes up truckloads full of equipment, but they all have the same basic pieces: a source of energy, a method of storing the energy until the gun is discharged, and an output device or an antenna. Everything else is up for grabs.

In 1991, I put on a briefing for a defense contractor which covered various approaches and uses for HERF Guns. In conventional military-think, the following objectives can be met with electromagnetic weaponry:

- Personnel and Transportation Interdiction
- Harassment of Opposition
- Communications Disruption
- Destruction of ADP Capability
- Interruption of Transportation Services
- Sabotage
- Terrorism/Anti-Terrorism
- Air/Land Defense
- Military Offensive
- Enemy Ordinance Activation
- Communications Interference
- Electronic Component Destruction

If a HERF Gun is too small to bring about the damage the Information Warrior wants to inflict, he might find himself interested in the ElectroMagnetic Pulse Transformer, or EMP/T Bomb. The EMP/T Bomb is essentially the same as a HERF Gun, but a thousand or more times more powerful.

The electromagnetic pulse or signal, catapulted at the speed of light from an EMP/T Bomb, is so incredibly strong that any computer in its path will likely be rendered useless forever. Its internal organs, the chips, will be electrically melted beyond repair. But there is more. With an electromagnetic signal of that strength, all floppy diskettes, hard disks, tapes, and tape backups will be thoroughly erased. *All* the data will be gone—forever. An EMP/T Bomb is a powerfully insidious weapon in the hands of a dedicated Information Warrior, and, as in so many cases, these advanced technical weapons are created by the denizens of the Pentagon.

The military has for nearly two decades been interested in what is euphemistically called Nonlethal Weapons; that is, weapons whose primary function is not to kill a human adversary, but to disable their ability to wage war. In a January 4, 1993, *Wall Street Journal* article, Colonel Jamie Gough explained that "without killing people, such weaponry would disrupt telephones, radars, computers, and other communications and targeting equipment." Other defense officials say the damage would be inflicted by "a new electromagnetic pulse generator that disables equipment without hurting people."[3]

It turns out that during the Gulf War, the United States did indeed use such Information Weapons. The April 15, 1992, issue of *Defense Week* stated that "The U.S. Navy used a new class of highly secret, nonnuclear electromagnetic warheads during the opening hours of the Persian Gulf War to disrupt and destroy Iraqi electronics systems, including air-defense weapons and command and control centers, military and industry sources say."[4] The experimental weapons were supposedly mounted on a few of the Navy's Tomahawk cruise missiles.

For the record, officials from the program deny any such warheads exist. However, in a private conversation, a Defense Department official told me that such weapons had indeed been used. In order to get our cruise missiles and planes into Baghdad without warning Hussein, we needed to shut down the Iraqi air defense systems that ringed the country. So, as a test of the technology under actual battlefield conditions as well as a real weapons systems deployment, the Navy targeted two main air defense stations on the southern border of Iraq. The magnetic-tipped EMP/T bomb cruise missiles exploded near the defense stations and immediately the lights went out, radar screens went blank, electrical lines went down, communications to Baghdad were cut, and Iraqi soldiers went searching for the circuit breakers. By the time they realized what had happened, it was too late. The real cruise missiles were making right turns at the El Rashid Hotel and our F-117s were strafing armaments factories.

As a result of these successes,

"The U.S. Central Command, the unified command for the Middle East that formerly was headed by General Norman Schwarzkopf, has told the Joint Chiefs of Staff that it wants a wide-area-pulse capability—that is, the ability to fry enemy electronics by detonating a warhead outside the atmosphere. The Central Command's statement didn't expressly say so, but only a nuclear explosion would be powerful enough to do the job. 'You're probably talking about a few tens of kilotons,' says Earl Rubright, science adviser to the General Command."[5]

The Navy seems to be ahead of the pack in the development of such weapons. They realize that the warfare of the future may be much less dependent on traditional bombs and bullets than on nonlethal electronic- and information-based weapons. After all, transportation, communications, and finances are largely reliant upon the correct operation of computer and communications systems. Thus, if those systems are knocked out, the opposition will feel the immense effects of the systemic collapse of its infrastructure.

In response to the fact that antagonists of the United States already have the capability to wage limited forms of such warfare, the Office of Chief of Naval Operations published in April of 1992, an internal draft of a document entitled "Space and Electronic Warfare: A Navy Policy Paper on a New Warfare Area."

The internal Navy document is less than thirty pages long, but the table of contents alone is enlightening. Sections are entitled "Navy SEW Policy" (SEW stands for Space and Electronic Warfare), "SEW Disciplines," "SEW Technology," "The Surveillance Grid Concept," "The Communications Grid," "SEW Battle Space Modeling," "EW Techniques," "Electronic Combat Subsystems," and more.[6] Obviously, the Navy had begun some serious efforts under Admiral Tuttle's command to restructure Navy conflict goals and techniques. The Navy, in fact, has been the victim of HERF, as has been the Air Force, albeit accidentally.

In the early fall of 1992, a U.S. naval ship entering the Panama Canal Zone forgot to turn off its radar systems, which operate on the same principle as HERF, but in the form of HPM, or high power microwaves. In this case the Canal Zone computer systems got zapped! The radar hits were so strong that nearby computers were fried and had to be replaced.[7]

Earlier we discussed the software-intensive fly-by-wire aircraft that the military, and even civilians, are increasingly using. The maze of wiring that runs the planes is susceptible to HERF damage. In the 1980s, the Army's UH-60 Blackhawk helicopter was the victim of a series of crashes and mishaps. "Critics charge electromagnetic interference with software-driven controls may have been responsible for five Blackhawk crashes that killed twenty-two servicemen. In fact, tests found that radio waves could trigger a complete hydraulic failure which could lead to loss of control of the aircraft. . . . In all, forty out of the Blackhawk's forty-two systems were susceptible to electromagnetic interference from radio and radar transmissions."[8]

Air Force planes are routinely fitted with EEDs (electro-explosive devices) that are used to trigger ejection seats, release bombs, and the like. A sophisticated Air Force radar system, known as PAVE PAWS, can detect a baseball from a thousands miles away and also has the capability to blow one of our own planes from the sky. PAVE PAWS is so powerful that it can accidentally detonate an EED with potentially disastrous results.[9] The B1 Bomber's radar system was so clumsy that it even interfered with itself![10]

So guess what HERF and EMP/T, designed for the express purpose of doing damage, can do to a computer or a computer network, not to mention a telephone system, a cash register, a bank's ATM network, or a communications system? If the military, who is supposed to be prepared for such contingencies, is having trouble with interference, how well would the myriad computers on Wall Street fare under a HERF attack?

Don White, one of the premier experts on electromagnetic shielding, is an extraordinary man. Short and in his mid-fifties, with willowy white hair, Don exudes the enthusiasm of a man half his age. White has written several widely-used text books on the subject, which are openly available in engineering libraries. But some chapters of his books, used for government training are actually given classified status by the National Security Agency.

White feels that HERF represents a real challenge for the commercial sector, especially if used by terrorists. He agrees that HERF, since it is both invisible and insidious, is a much-overlooked threat. In one editorial he wrote,

So, if there is an adversary whose operation is located inside a building you want to disrupt, merely drive your radar van and park it within a quarter mile (even the lay are accustomed to seeing dish antennas). Erect the stored parabolic dish on top of the van and point it at the target building. And presto! You did them in. Better yet, to make it less conspicuous, place the dish inside the van and use plastic sides in the van rather than metal.

Of course, you could be much more subtle about it and cause your adversary to have EMI intermittents. That way, he would economically suffer without being shot down, which might otherwise precipitate greater investigation.

With a radar van temporarily parked on an overpass, a field strength in excess of 1000 V/m could be laid down on Brand X automobiles passing thereunder. Think of the resulting adverse publicity about Brand X cars, which have problems with antiskid braking microprocessors.

The opportunities become mind-boggling, especially if done in "good taste." However, in the hands of terrorists, (industrial as well as political), the whole subject becomes outright scary.[11]

Maxwell Laboratories, a defense contractor specializing in high energy weapons, published an arcane paper in 1992 entitled, "Utilization of High Power Microwaves Sources in Electronic Sabotage and Terrorism." The authors describe the history of HERF-style weapons, beginning in the early 1970s.

High power microwaves sources have been under investigation for several years as potential weapons for a variety of sabotage, terrorism, counter-security and combat applications. However, in recent years, there has been an increasing awareness of HPM (a form of HERF) as a tool for commercial sabotage and civil terrorism.

Several similar papers have been written which describe the techniques that make such Information Weapons possible. The language used by Defense Department contractors is highly technical, describing detonation methods such as slug-tuning, magnetrons, klysterons, gyrotrons, vircators, and magnetically insulated oscillator tubes. The scary part is the detachment with which these papers are written.

It is expected that for all civil attacks, with the possible exception of sophisticated terrorists, electronic sources (of power) . . . will be used. For short ranges and directional attacks, submegawatt levels can be used. For longer ranges or omnidirectional radiation, higher, but still achievable, powers will be achieved.[12]

Even though "due to classifications restrictions, details of this work are relatively unknown outside of the military community and its contractors,"[13] advanced technology is extremely hard to contain, especially since many other countries are paralleling the U.S.'s classified work on HERF. "In many instances, if the military has it, it will rapidly find its way into terrorist hands."[14] In a draft document, high-energy expert E.R. Van Keuren further fans the flames by stating that "when discussing terrorism and sabotage . . . our adversaries are much less reluctant to make their weapons available to terrorist nations than the United States."[15]

HERF Guns and EMP/T Bombs meet the Information Warrior's criteria as the ultimate weapon. What are his potential targets? James Rawles writes for *Defense Electronics*,

Likely terrorist targets are key financial centers such as Wall Street in New York, the City district in London, or the Paradeplatz in Zurich. This would cause incalculable damage to computer hardware and software associated with stock and commodities markets, banking, international currency exchanges, and pension funds. Rebuilding computer systems and restoring software databases from paper records would doubtless take many months.[16]

HERF Guns are portable and can sit inside a van, making them virtually invisible to passersby. Who pays any attention to a small truck with an antenna, and television or film crew markings on the side? But what about at the end of a runway? Or even on a commercial airliner itself? With terrorists beginning to arrive on our shores thanks to their state-sponsored travel agents, we have to consider all of the possibilities. When HERF Guns can be carried in a suitcase or a backpack, our cause for alarm rises to critical levels.

Companies near airports have known for a long time that radar systems can cause computer systems to crash for no apparent reason. Poof! They're just down. The FAA has known as well, but hasn't been very public with its knowledge. According to sources, the FAA is replacing the glass in its control towers and offices in and around airports, investing millions of dollars to protect itself from the nasty side effects of radar signals so that their computers and navigation and guidance systems stay "up" at all times.[17] The only problem is they're not telling much to anyone else, and therein lies the danger to John Q. Frequent Flyer, who careens coast-to-coast unaware of any possible danger.

On a recent series of commercial airline flights, I heard a new spiel from a flight attendant. "We're descending below 10,000 feet for our approach into (safe major metropolitan airport). Please turn off all laptop computers, CD, and cassette players. Thank you for flying US Air."

In the July 26, 1993 issue of *Newsweek*, the following appeared.

On an uneventful flight over the southern Pacific last February, the 747–400 pilot stared wide-eyed as his navigational displays suddenly flared and crackled. The data made no sense. But a flight attendant was already whisking a passenger's laptop computer up to the flight deck. When the crew turned it on, the navigation displays went crazy. They returned to normal when the crew switched off the laptop. The plane reached its destination safely. Investigating the incident, Boeing engineers bought the same model laptop and tried to replicate the glitch in another 747. They couldn't.

. . . In a holding pattern 13,000 feet somewhere above the southeastern United States, the pilot saw the guidance computers and controls that maintain the craft's lateral stability shut down. A passenger in row one—directly above the flight computers and near the navigation antennas—was using a radio transmitter and receiver, a flight attendant said. The first officer hurried back and the told the man to shut it off; the systems blinked back on. Five years later, no one can explain how, or even if, the radio zapped the computers.[18]

So what's happening here, HERF? A CD player is certainly not a HERF Gun, but to a poorly shielded avionics package in a fly-by-wire airplane, with the 145 miles of wires and cables that are in the latest Boeing 747–400s, it could all be the same.

While the FAA and most airlines deny any safety concerns, malfunctions of avionics systems do bring up serious public-safety issues. Since 1990 the FAA has compiled almost one hundred reports of such occurrences with a six-fold increase this year alone.[19] Why? Very possibly because fly-by-wire airplanes are indeed affected by computers and digital music systems. It's no wonder that the engineers at Boeing, NASA, and Apple are having such a time trying to figure out what's happening: we live in an electromagnetic sewer. God knows we shouldn't be saying "let's not worry about it" with computers flying planes at 37,000 feet.

The FAA knows better, and I would hazard to guess, wants to do everything within its power to avoid a panic, or loss of public faith in the airline industry. Imagine some nut who brings a specially modified laptop onto an airplane. Airport security in the United States is so dismal that anyone can get just about any electronic device through it with no trouble. But this laptop is modified to emit very high levels of radiation, either automatically or upon command. A real fanatic who is totally committed to his cause might be willing to go down with the plane; more than a few people meet that criteria. Or, if his survival is important, he might check his luggage through with a HERF device, timed to go off at some point during the flight—without him on board, of course. Luggage scanning can't tell the difference between a good electronic device and a malicious one. If the FAA has cause to worry, this certainly qualifies.

In a scenario described by the FBI during a CPSR meeting in Washington, D.C. on June 7, 1993, agents revealed a case in which a rocket launcher was nearly placed at the end of the O'Hare runway in Chicago, ready to shoot down commercial airliners. Let's replace that weapon with an even more powerful HERF Gun. Situated in a van, powered by a V-8 and an alternator, the HERF energy could have a devastating effect on planes taking off and landing.

Acquiring HERF Guns is pretty simple. You can go out and build one: I have seen home-brewed versions capable of firing twelve megawatt blasts. Electronic hobbyist magazines occasionally provide construction details of high voltage-high current power generators. It's an exercise in Electronics 101. Or you can buy one. Where? Kits are available from catalogs, or you can construct one courtesy of the U.S. government: a military surplus high-power radar system can be modified by someone familiar with electronics. Don White offers a four-day course called "HERF and Electromagnetic Terrorism," which teaches how to protect against electromagnetic weaponry.[20]

Cyberspace has indeed come of age, and modern airplanes are as much a part of it as computer networks.

So there you have it—the basic Information Weapons for

the well-armed Information Warrior. From malicious software to EMP/T Bombs, with dozens of tricks in the middle, even the least technically astute reader gets a pretty fair idea of what the Global Network and Computers Everywhere will be facing in the coming years. It doesn't take a rocket scientist to make or use Information Weapons, just a little knowledge and resourcefulness, the kind that is taught in high school and college science classes all across this country. There is no magic required, just a fundamental working knowledge of electronics and software, and a target. Anyone with the motivation has access to these technologies.

Thus far, we have concentrated on capabilities instead of intention. So now, let's take the next step in our exploration of Information Warfare and take a look at what kind of enemies and adversaries we will be coming up against in the Battle for Cyberspace.

What we want to know now is—who are the Information Warriors?

More About HERF and Then Some

Winn Schwartau

When I coined the term HERF in 1990 (or was it 1989?), I had no idea it would fall into the general lexicon nor that it would be as widely accepted as it has been. When I had first publicly presented the concepts in 1990, many audiences didn't quite laugh, but were convinced that my presentation was more Star Wars than reality.

My critics have been silenced.

In fact, today, I regularly receive mail and phone calls and requests for interviews about HERF and EMP/T bombs and the like. Since the military considers the offensive nature of the subject Code Word Classified (above Top Secret), there aren't too many places to go for information. Since the first version of this book came out, I have learned a great deal.

In April 1994, a scant two days after the first edition of this book appeared in the United States, I received a call from a gentleman who represented a British subsidiary of the American defense contractor Arthur D. Little.

"Your work has upset some people," he said. "In fact, there's even talk of banning your book from sale over here." Which didn't happen, but the thought was there. It seemed that the Brits were quite concerned about this area of research. There had been talk about attacks against financial institutions using sophisticated techniques (maybe even magnetic weapons systems) and they wanted to follow-up that line to see what was real and what was fantasy. I, of course, offered to help.

They were particularly interested in what I called "electronic pipe bombs." My main interest was not what the U.S. or Russian or British government could or could not do on the battlefield with whatever secret backpack versions of some new whiz-bang weapons they may have developed. (Although we now know a lot more about such endeavors.) I wanted to know, and prove, what could be done on the cheap by a smart guy or group with a little money, and how much damage they could cause.

Over the next several months, the representatives from these companies kept badgering me for more information, and I recognized that they were attempting to suck my brain. At one point, I called a halt and said, "Gentlemen, this is how I make my living." They got the point.

Nonetheless, my British contacts were pushing me more into the realm of the super-sophisticated military-level systems. We mutually developed contractual mechanisms by which they could get a full road map of the systems capabilities from the terrorist level on up, all from open unclassified sources. During my visits overseas they were particularly insistent that I guarantee in writing that I did not cross any lines of secrecy or break any laws. (This premise would soon bite them back.)

In September 1994, right after returning from a lecture series in the U.K. and France, I received a call from GCHQ—Government Communications Headquarters, the British equivalent of our NSA. I won't use his name, but he was adamant.

"I, ah, we feel, Mr. Schwartau, that . . . ah," he stammered, "that quite frankly we'd like you to be quiet about all of this. You know, the subject we've been discussing." I was stunned. First of all, the topic was obviously of more concern than they had ever let on, and they had just told me so. Spooks and spies don't really keep secrets all that well.

But more importantly, I told him, "We have two problems here. One, I am an American citizen, and I do not believe that I am subject to the British Official Secrets Act. And two, I do offer my clients high degrees of confidentiality, but as of now, you are not a client." He, too, got the point.

At one point during the subsequent negotiations, the contractors asked about DOS attacks against satellites and such. Could I help them out? I readily offered them a demonstration as part of our pending agreement. "How about we take the BBC off the air," I suggested. "It would make quite a show." We talked about price and how the demonstrations would work, until I asked that as part of any deal, GCHQ or not, I wanted a get-out-of-jail-free card signed by Prime Minister John Major. "I am not going to take down the BBC without formal written approval from the highest levels of government. I hope you understand." That sort of put that deal in the toilet, for whatever reason. I was never told.

Nonetheless, I was more than intrigued and continued discussions with my contacts about the attacks on financial institutions. I kept hearing that the numbers increased, the perpetrators got more bold, and vast sums of money were involved at every demand. Extortion, pure and simple; high-tech, but still extortion.

Over two-and-a-half years, quite a large set of files were developed. Lots of details, some speculations, astounding conclusions. Similar events taking place in London, Paris, Germany, the United States, Australia, and so on. Disturbing similarities with apparent but unsubstantiated connections.

Then, during the week of May 20, 1996, I was the co-sponsor of the fourth international InfoWarCon conference in Brussels. The *London Times* attended and told of a story they were going to run about how four renegade bands of "cyber-terrorists" were threatening financial institutions with "electronic meltdown" if payments of huge sums of money weren't made. I was stunned. They had the support and backup and officials on the record! In my view, this was the first set of significant events (outside of the military community) that could be regarded as Class III Information Warfare.

The June 2, 1996 *Sunday Times* front-page headline read "City Surrenders to £400 Million Gangs."

The first attack mentioned was in my files, dated January 6, 1993. A trading house in London was blackmailed into paying £10 million to unknown extortionists who demonstrated they could crash the company's computers at will. The next incident in the *Times* article was also in my files: January 14, 1993, when similar demonstrations and demands were made, this time for £12.5 million. So was the next—January 29, 1993, another £10 million siphoned off by the bad guys. According to my figures and those in the *Times* article, hundreds of millions of pounds have been paid ransom in what is clearly an example of Class III Information Warfare.

According to officials cited by the article in Washington, Whitehall, London, City of London Police, the NSA, Kroll Associates, Bank of England, and elsewhere, the threats are credible. The attackers have the clear ability to bring trading and financial operations to a halt exactly when they say they will. "Banks, brokerage firms, and investment houses in America have also secretly paid ransom to prevent costly computer meltdowns and a collapse in the confidence among their customers," sources said in the article.

The article discussed the advanced Information Warfare techniques used by the perpetrators. "According to the American National Security Agency (NSA), they have penetrated computer systems using logic bombs' (coded devices that can be remotely detonated), electromagnetic pulses and 'high emission radio frequency guns' which blow a devastating electronic 'wind' through the computer systems."

The perpetrators have also left encrypted messages, apparently bypassing the highest security levels of the systems, leaving messages such as, "Now do you believe we can destroy your computers?" The NSA and other officials believe that four gangs are involved; probably one from the United States and probably one from Russia. But because the crimes are international, investigation is more difficult. Investigations and official inquiries had been in progress for some time, according to the article.

In subsequent months, abject denials and accusations have blown both ways across the Atlantic. To date, I have confirmation of four software-based attacks and lots of speculation from three continents.

A Bank of England official said of the incidents, "it is not the biggest issue in the banking market." If the criminal theft and extortion of hundreds of millions of dollars is not a big issue, then what is?

Some of the Technical Stuff About HERF

I've followed HERF and related areas and come to learn more and respect the capabilities of the military. We did use such weapons in the Gulf, and we have been building up arsenals, as we should be doing. Since then, the U.S. military has taken great strides in the area it calls directed energy weapons (DEW). On June 14-15, 1995, a secret U.S.-only conference was held in the suburbs of Washington, D.C. for a "Detailed Review of Directed Energy Warfare Today and for the Future."

This conference brought together players from the Joint Chiefs at the Pentagon, Kirkland Air Force Base (where research is being conducted in the field), Boeing, Mitre Corporation, TRW, Rockwell, Hughes, and a host of similarly minded government officials and contractors who develop the weapons. The Air Force, Army, Navy, and Marines all have their own DEW programs and they fall into a broad range of categories which were all presented at the conference: lasers, ground-based and satellite-based; particle beam weapons; and high-power RF (HERF) and related technologies.

Part and parcel of the discussions were not only the effects of the weapons' use on equipment in-theater combat, but on the corollary biological effects of HERF and magnetic fields on the human body. The potential of HERF-style weapons is increasing with time. Consider the potential for use of DEW against the soldier or citizen and not the computer:

- Exposure to UHF radiation could have effects upon humans. In one experiment, a five-minute exposure to 100,000 microwatts of UHF reduced the swimming endurance of rats by a factor of 10.
- Pulsed microwave beams have been shown to increase the permeability of the blood-brain barrier. Such a technique could enhance the effects of chemical or biological weapons.
- Pulsed microwaves of 300-3,000 mhz can cause even deaf people to "hear." Enhanced DEW capability suggests that "voices" can be induced into people or troops from a fair distance. Considering the highly religious nature of many of America's potential adversaries, such a technique is certainly alluring.
- Driving someone crazy with invisible voices is part of the urban lore from ex-CIA agents who claim to be victims of rogue experimentation.
- Tests have shown that it is possible to slow down, speed up, or stop the heart of frogs using microwaves of particular frequencies. The research suggests that inducing heart attacks from afar may not be science fiction.
- Substantial research has been done on inducing specific behavior in target animals: causing a cat to lick the bars of a cage instead of its fur; causing a monkey to continuously perform a complex series of unnatural tasks; inducing smiles. As one researcher said, "The animals looked like electronic toys." (This research, as documented in *The Body Electric* by Dr. Robert Becker, is indicative not of paranoia or conspiracy, but of capability.)

The connection of the body and computers is getting closer. Using super sensitive SQUID (superconducting quantum interference devices), the magnetic neural activity of the brain can be measured. The magnetic impulses from the brain are on the order of one-billionth the strength of the Earth's magnetic field. The purpose is to provide mapping of the brain noninvasively; good medical purposes. So now we have a reasonable method of measuring the direct effects of external electromagnetic stimulus on the human body.

Ultimately, with a military mindset, offensive applications to undermine the enemy are critical to minimize lethality and inflict our will on the adversary and perhaps his population. But we have to recognize that protection and defense are critical elements of survivability, and part of the goal of making so much of this public is to get the government to assent that protecting the private sector is as much a national concern as is protecting the military.

But at the same time, the general knowledge of magnetic weapons has increased more broadly, throughout the Internet and electronic hobbyist community. No, Joe Six Pack cannot make the full-fledged offensive magnetic weapons that the military can, but nonetheless, the miniature home brew weapons do have significant power.

Consider, just for fun, that a guy at home builds a small—maybe no more than 20-30 megawatts—magnetic weapon; a dirty device with random timing pulses, untuned frequency components and harmonics, but one that shoots out a pretty good-sized pulse. Imagine tucking one of these babies into a briefcase and walking into a video arcade filled with an infinite number of teenagers. BLAM! What does 20 megawatts do to the video game fun? Or take a similar device to a Las Vegas casino and BLAM! What happens to the ethernet backbone and electronic counters of the digitial slot machines, not to mention the overhead security systems. Ocean's Eleven revisited. (Now there's a movie.)

So given the limited space in this second edition, I'll merely outline some of the more interesting data that we have found since the last edition.

The HERF/EMP effects of a nuclear detonation provide interesting reflection. According to a brilliant young lieutenant at the Naval Post Graduate School in Monterey, California, "I have confirmed that the entire United States, from D.C. to L.A., can be targeted with a single relatively low-order nuclear detonation at an altitude of 300 km. The average electric field strength will exceed 10,000 volts/meter with peak values exceeding 50,000 volts/meter. The transient time is on the order of 10E-8 seconds and associated frequency approaching 1 GHZ. This type of effect requires an altitude greater than approximately 90 km. The target area can be controlled be locating the detonation closer to the ionosphere but the area is still rather large, we are after all speaking of nuclear exoatmospheric detonations!" [To put things in perspective, effects from 50 - 400 volts/meter are sufficient to put most unshielded electronic devices out of commission.]

In a proprietary document I recently received, the title says it all: "Terrorist Use of EMP Against U.S. Facilities." Since the first version of *Information Warfare* appeared, I have had the opportunity to present white papers and proposals for evealuating the risk to the U.S. from terrorist-level HERF/EMP attack. This paper echoed those sentiments: "classes of targets to be identified which if attacked could represent a significant threat to the public health and safety of American citizens. Key installations of possible interest include but are not limited to nuclear power plants, commerecial power supply and distribution systems, communications systems, air traffic control systems, aids to navigation, and facilities utilizing solid state devices for purposes of handling and/or disposing of toxic materials."

There has been a legitimate concern that intense EMP or HERF may have a biological effect, and recently acquired documents show that the government has made efforts to protect humans while testing the effects of EMP on systems. Since it is highly unfeasible to set off a nuke every time it is necessary to test the survivability of a new military system, researchers resorted to creating so-called EMP simulators.

The AURORA Flash X-Ray Facility at the U.S. Army Electronics Research and Development Command in Adelphi, Maryland was the premier Source Region EMP (SREMP) facility for some time, but it had limitations. The EMP produced was not considered a true model of the EMP of a nuke. According to critiques of AURORA, the test cells were too small, the metallic walls of the test chamber effectively shorted out the electic fields generated, and the rise time of the pulses was too long. New approaches were needed to more accurately simulate a true nuclear EMP. One of the early U.S. approaches was devised by George Merkel and William Scharf in their invention called "Source-Region Electromagnetic Pulse Simulator." The highly technical document offers solutions to the problems with the AURORA designs.

The Russians were also working along similar lines, with EMP and high-power microwave generators like the IMA2-150D, IMA2-150E and the MIRA-2D. In a machine-translated document, a G. A. Mesyats outlined several areas of Russian/Soviet research in "New Types of Electron Beam Devices With Explosive Emission." Their work in high power and pulsed microwaves shows progress with pulsed beam high power outputs: voltages of 150-220 kv or more, current up to 2,500 amps, controlled pulse widths from 100 nsec down to fractions of a nanosecond, and highly focused beam patterns. From a weapons standpoint (HERF or HPM), such capabilities in the wrong hands represents a serious threat.

Later U.S. versions got bigger and bigger as the power output increased. The Army MPS II C-Band HPM Demonstrator is a fairly large unit, employs large 20-stage Marx generators, superconducting magnets, and an A6 magnetron. The output antenna is a 10-foot-diameter dish which couples to the high power microwave source.

This is a strong generator with a timed output pulse of about 265,000 volts and 3,500 amperes. The military applications seem obvious, and from the Information Warrior's standpoint can offer a tremendous opportunity to deactivate adversary infrastructures, vehicles, or possibly aircraft.

The effects of such a weapon on a civilian high technology target soon become obvious. According to the operations and maintenance manual for the MPS-II, a published Zone of Denied Occupancy is defined, which extends a full 800 meters in front of the device in a beam 24 degrees wide. During testing and use of the device, people with pacemakers are denied access. But the manual and the suggested signage says that it "erases credit cards and magnetic recording media." What company wants their hard disks or tape library on the receiving end of such a pulse?

This also brings up the possible effects on humans. The ARES test facility is a wideband transmitter which simulates the very short duration EMP radiated from some nuclear bursts. In a 1995 memo, concerns were raised by the MILSTAR HEMP Test Working Group about the possible effects of the tests of high power on the workers at the ARES site. According to the memo, the ARES pulses of less than 500 nanoseconds created electric forces of about 60 kv/meter repeated every 10 minutes or so. The operators were shielded from the effects of each test detonation inside a MILSTAR Mobile Constellation Control Station (MMCCS), which offers heavy shielding to the workers.

On the smaller side, the military has been working on portable DEW systems that can be carried by a soldier; so-called backpack weapons which might prove useful for infiltration operations. I have heard from people within the military, contractors, researchers, and civilians who indicate a wide spectrum of development and capabilities. Some early prototype systems from the late 1980s had less than magnificent performance. But later backpack versions of HERF guns and EMP cannons reportedly can stop automobiles and interfere with power transmissions. (A CBS broadcast showed how high power microwaves can actually stop a modern car engine.)

Forget the details, but the concern over short duration exposure to very high intensity megnetic and electric fields is real and has been seriously addressed by the military. The ARES operators work well within the prescribed DOD limits for exposure to wide band pulses. However, we cannot forget that direct targeting of a person (or a dog) by a high power microwave signal can overheat the internal organs and . . . well, you know. But the debate over long term exposure to low levels of magnetic and electric fields is not so clear-cut, as we have seen from the controversy over the impact of cellular phones on the human brain.

This all brings up the effects of low-level radiation on the econotechnical infrastructure around us. While not specifically EMP or HERF in nature, we are soon going to see a rash of events involving EMI—electromagnetic interference of very low signal strengths. While a nuke and military weapons puts out gigawatt and terawatt levels, the effects of interference from signals on the micro- and milliwatt level are already newsworthy. We are talking about a difference in signal strength of between 12 and 18 orders of magnitude! Huge, almost incomprehensible differences which have similar, unpredictable results.

We've seen events like Sony TV remote controls turning Apple Performas on and off. Connie Chung aired a fascinating report in 1995 on the unanticipated effects of low level electromagnetic interference:

- Cellular phones controlling the movements of electronic wheelchairs
- Mobile radios causing respirators in a neonatal unit to totally fail.
- Airplanes being deflected off course while onboard computers and electronic games are in use.
- Total loss of avionics caused by a passenger's electronic device
- Life-saving defibrillators failing to operate correctly in ambulances

We live in an electromagnetic sewer—in cities more so than in the countryside—and as we further pollute the electromagnetic spectrum with new frequencies for personal digitial assistants and radio-based local area networks and more computers and video games and interactivity, the results will be chaotic and totally unpredictable. We do not have enough understanding of electromagnetics to either predict or prevent ita and the Information Warrior knows this. He knows that causing seemingly unrelated events to unfold under his auspices of directed energy control adds confusion to systems already capable of failure and error on their own. We will see even more of these apparent EMC problems that are in fact induced intentionally.

One of the more interesting and confounding stories to come out in the last year or so is about a government project up in Alaska called HAARP. At the core of it is 50 high-power antennas, synchronized in an array that is capable of putting out sustained transmissions in excess of 2.8 billion watts. In pulse form, this would be on the order 3,000 terawatts, if you can think that high!

So what do you do with a facility that has to warn off airplanes for a 500-mile diameter when you turn it on? Theories abound. Facts are slim. Here's what's being said (by folks of not necessarily impeccable credentials, but which have been reported in *Popular Science* and across the Web.)

- HAARP is an experimental facility to develop ELF communications with submarines.
- It is a huge alien intelligence monitoring facility. Hmmm.
- According to U.S. patent #4,686,605 (August 11, 1987) by focusing an intense beam of electromagnetic energy into the ionosphere, a phenomenon called "the mirror force" occurs. According to the inventor, "you can virtually lift off part of the upper atmosphere. You can make it move, do things to it." Disrupt global communications? Good, if the "good guys" have a backup system that remains unaffected. Create high altitude "drag" that might heat and deflect enemy missiles or by the created plasma field, cause the missile to detonate in mid-trajectory?

- HAARP puts out an intense beam of energy, which is deflected from the ionosphere to the earth, where it can "look" underground and see what other countries are doing. Underground orbiting surveillance. Satellites would pick up the reflections which would then be retransmitted down to earth for analysis.
- Weather modification to screw up the enemy in time of conflict. "Triggering ionospheric processes that potentially could be exploited for DOD purposes."
- Atmsopheric research.
- And the conspiratorial coup de grace: HAARP's intense energy fields from the 50 antennas can be configured to build an electromagnetic stealth tunnel from the earth to lower space, so that alien space ships can commute unnoticed.

Do a WWW search on HAARP. It's quite a trip.

Carlo Kopp's paper, which follows, provides even more insight into this fascinating area that bodes ill for the nearly naked technical foundation of late second- and early third-wave societies.

The E-Bomb—A Weapon of Electrical Mass Destruction

Carlo Kopp, Computer Science Dept., Monash University

carlo@cs.monash.edu.au; http://www.cs.monash.edu.au/carlo/

High Power Electromagnetic Pulse generation techniques and High Power Microwave technology have matured to the point where practical E-bombs (Electromagnetic bombs) are becoming technically feasible, with new applications in both strategic and tactical Information Warfare. The development of conventional E-bomb devices allows their use in non-nuclear confrontations. This paper discusses aspects of the technology base and weapon delivery techniques, and proposes a doctrinal foundation for the use of such devices in warhead and bomb applications.

Introduction

The prosecution of a successful Information Warfare (IW) campaign against an industrialized or post-industrial opponent will require a suitable set of tools. As demonstrated in the Desert Storm air campaign, air power has proven to be a most effective means of inhibiting the functions of an opponent's vital information processing infrastructure. This is because air power allows concurrent or parallel engagement of a large number of targets over geographically significant areas (Szafranski, 1995).

While Desert Storm demonstrated that the application of air power was the most practical means of crushing an opponent's information processing and transmission nodes, the need to physically destroy these with guided munitions absorbed a substantial proportion of available air assets in the early phase of the air campaign. Indeed, the aircraft capable of delivering laser-guided bombs were largely occupied with this very target set during the first nights of the air battle.

The efficient execution of an IW campaign against a modern industrial or post-industrial opponent will require the use of specialized tools designed to destroy information systems. Electromagnetic bombs built for this purpose can provide, where delivered by suitable means, a very effective tool for this purpose.

The EMP Effect

The electromagnetic pulse (EMP) effect was first observed during the early testing of high altitude airburst nuclear weapons (Glasstone, 1964). The effect is characterized by the production of a very short (hundreds of nanoseconds) but intense electromagnetic pulse, which propagates away from its source with ever-diminishing intensity, governed by the theory of electromagnetism. The electromagnetic pulse is in effect an electromagnetic shock wave.

(Electromagnetic pulse, or EMP device, is a generic term applied to any device, nuclear or conventional, which is capable of generating a very intense but short electromagnetic field transient. For weapons applications, this transient must be sufficiently intense to produce electromagnetic power densities which are lethal to electronic and electrical equipment. Electromagnetic weapons are electromagnetic devices specifically designed as weapons. While the terms *conventional EMP weapon* and *high power microwave [HPM] weapon* have been used interchangeably in trade journals [see Fulghum, 1993], this paper will distinguish between microwave band and low frequency weapons. The term *electromagnetic bomb* or E-bomb will be used to describe both microwave and low frequency nonnuclear bombs. This paper will not address the use of nuclear EMP, or alternate uses of HPM technology. HPM technology has a broad range of potential applications in EW, radar and directed energy weapons (DEW). The general conclusions of this paper in the areas of infrastructure vulnerability and hardening are also true for microwave-directed energy weapons. This paper extends the scope of earlier work by the author on this subject [Kopp, 1993].)

This pulse of energy produces a powerful electromagnetic field, particularly within the vicinity of the weapon burst. The field can be sufficiently strong to produce short-lived transient voltages of thousands of volts on exposed electrical conductors, such as wires, or conductive tracks on printed circuit boards, where exposed.

It is this aspect of the EMP effect which is of military significance, as it can result in irreversible damage to a wide range of electrical and electronic equipment, particularly computers and radio or radar receivers. Subject to the electromagnetic hardness of the electronics, a measure of the equipment's resilience to this effect, and the intensity of the field produced by the weapon, the equipment can be irreversibly damaged or in effect electrically destroyed. The damage inflicted is not unlike that experienced through exposure to close proximity lightning strikes, and may require complete replacement of the equipment or at least substantial portions thereof.

Commercial computer equipment is particularly vulnerable to EMP effects, as it is largely built up of high-density metal oxide semiconductor (MOS) devices, which are very sensitive to exposure to high-voltage transients. What is significant about MOS devices is that very little energy is required to permanently wound or destroy them: typically, any voltage in excess of tens of volts can produce an effect called "gate breakdown," which effectively destroys the device. Even if the pulse is not powerful enough to produce thermal damage, the power supply in the equipment will provides enough energy to complete the destruction. Wounded devices may still function, but their reliability will be seriously impaired. Shielding electronics by equipment chassis provides only limited protection, as any cables running in and out of the equipment will behave very much like antennae—guiding the high voltage transients into the equipment.

Computers used in data processing systems, communications systems, displays, industrial control applications, including road and rail signalling, and those embedded in military equipment, such as signal processors, electronic flight controls and digital engine control systems, are all potentially vulnerable to the EMP effect.

Other electronic devices and electrical equipment may also be destroyed by the EMP effect. Telecommunications equipment can be highly vulnerable, due to the presence of lengthy copper cables between devices. Receivers of all varieties are particularly sensitive to EMP, as the highly sensitive miniature high frequency transistors and diodes in such equipment are easily destroyed by exposure to high voltage electrical transients. Therefore, radar and electronic warfare equipment, satellite, microwave, UHF, VHF, HF, and low band communications equipment and television equipment are all potentially vulnerable to the EMP effect.

It is significant that modern military platforms are densely packed with electronic equipment, and unless these platforms are well hardened, an EMP device can substantially reduce their function or render them unusable.

Technology Base for Conventional Electromagnetic Bombs

The technology base which may be applied to the design of electromagnetic bombs is both diverse and, in many areas, quite mature. Key technologies which are extant in the area are explosively pumped flux compression generators (FCG), explosive or propellant driven magneto-hydrodynamic (MHD) generators, and a range of HPM devices, the foremost of which is the virtual cathode oscillator or Vircator. A wide range of experimental designs have been tested in these technology areas, and a considerable volume of work has been published in unclassified literature.

This paper will review the basic principles and attributes of these technologies in relation to bomb and warhead applications. This treatment is not exhaustive, and is only intended to illustrate how the technology base can be adapted to an operationally deployable capability.

EXPLOSIVELY PUMPED FLUX COMPRESSION GENERATORS

The explosively pumped FCG is the most mature technology applicable to bomb designs. The FCG was first demonstrated by Clarence Fowler at Los Alamos National Laboratories (LANL) in the late 1950s (Fowler, 1960). Since that time a wide range of FCG configurations has been built and tested in the United States, the USSR, and more recently in the CIS.

The FCG is a device capable of producing electrical energies of tens of megajoules in tens to hundreds of microseconds, in a relatively compact package. With peak power levels of the order of terawatts to tens of terawatts, FCGs may be used directly or as one-shot pulse power supplies for microwave tubes. To place this in perspective, the current produced by a large FCG is between ten to a thousand times greater than that produced by a typical lightning stroke (White, 1978).

The central idea behind the construction of FCGs is that of using a fast explosive to rapidly compress a magnetic field, transferring much energy from the explosive into the magnetic field.

The initial magnetic field in the FCG prior to explosive initiation is produced by a start current. The start current is supplied by an external source, such as a high voltage capacitor bank (Marx bank), a smaller FCG, or an MHD device. In principle, any device capable of producing a pulse of electrical current of the order of tens of kiloamperes to mega-amperes will be suitable.

A number of geometrical configurations for FCGs have been published (see Reinovsky, 1985; Caird, 1985; Fowler, 1989). The most commonly used arrangement is that of the coaxial FCG. The coaxial arrangement is of particular interest in this context, as its essentially cylindrical form lends itself to packaging into munitions.

In a typical coaxial FCG, a cylindrical copper tube forms the armature. This tube is filled with a fast high energy explosive. A number of explosive types have been used, ranging from B- and C-type compositions to machined blocks of PBX-9501. The armature is surrounded by a helical coil of heavy wire, typically copper, which forms the FCG stator. The stator winding is in some designs split into segments, with wires bifur-

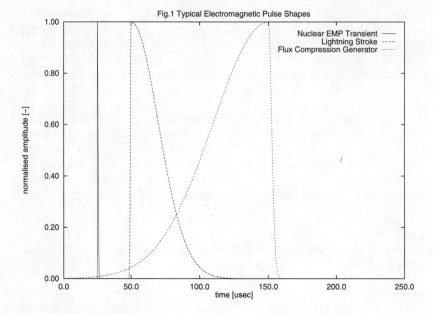

Figure 1. Typical Electromagnetic Pulse Shapes

cating at the boundaries of the segments, to optimize the electromagnetic inductance of the armature coil.

The intense magnetic forces produced during the operation of the FCG could cause the device to disintegrate prematurely if not dealt with. This is typically accomplished by the addition of a structural jacket of nonmagnetic material. Materials such as concrete or fiberglass in an epoxy matrix have been used. In principle, any material with suitable electrical and mechanical properties could be used. In applications where weight is an issue, such as air-delivered bombs or missile warheads, a glass or Kevlar epoxy composite would be a viable candidate.

Typically, the explosive is initiated when the start current peaks. This is usually accomplished with an explosive lense plane wave generator which produces a uniform plane wave burn (or detonation) front in the explosive. Once initiated, the front propagates through the explosive in the armature, distorting it into a conical shape (typically 12 to 14 degrees of arc). Where the armature has expanded to the full diameter of the stator, it forms a short circuit between the ends of the stator coil, shorting and thus isolating the start current source and trapping the current within the device. The propagating short has the effect of compressing the magnetic field while reducing the inductance of the stator winding. The result is that such generators produce a ramping current pulse, which peaks before the final disintegration of the device. Published results suggest ramp times of tens to hundreds of microseconds, specific to the

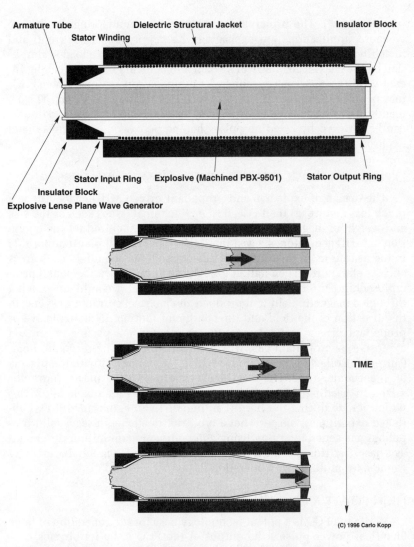

Armature Tube Dielectric Structural Jacket Insulator Block
Stator Winding

Stator Input Ring Explosive (Machined PBX-9501) Stator Output Ring
Insulator Block
Explosive Lense Plane Wave Generator

TIME

(C) 1996 Carlo Kopp

Figure 2. Explosively pumped coaxial flux compression generator

characteristics of the device, for peak currents of tens of mega-amperes
and peak energies of tens of megajoules. The current multiplication (i.e.,
ratio of output current to start current) achieved varies with designs, but
numbers as high as 60 have been demonstrated.

In a munitions application, where space and weight are at a premium,
the smallest possible start current source is desirable. These applications
can exploit cascading FCGs, where a small FCG is used to prime a larger
FCG with a start current. Experiments conducted by LANL and AFWL
have demonstrated the viability of this technique (Kirtland, 1994; Re-

inovsky, 1985). The principal technical issues in adapting the FCG to weapons applications are packaging, the supply of start current, and matching the device to the intended load. Interfacing to a load is simplified by the coaxial geometry of coaxial and conical FCG designs. Significantly, this geometry is convenient for weapons applications, where FCGs may be stacked axially with devices such as microwave Vircators. The demands of a load such as a Vircator, in terms of waveform shape and timing, can be satisfied by inserting pulse shaping networks, transformers, and explosive high current switches.

EXPLOSIVE AND PROPELLANT DRIVEN MHD GENERATORS

The design of explosive and propellant driven MHD generators is a much less mature art than FCG design. Technical issues such as the size and weight of magnetic field generating devices required for the operation of MHD generators suggest that MHD devices will play a minor role in the near term. In the context of this paper, their potential lies in areas such as start current generation for FCG devices. The fundamental principle behind the design of MHD devices is that a conductor moving through a magnetic field will produce an electrical current transverse to the direction of the field and the conductor motion. In an explosive or propellant driven MHD device, the conductor is a plasma of ionized explosive or propellant gas, which travels through the magnetic field. Current is collected by electrodes which are in contact with the plasma jet (Fanthome, 1989).The electrical properties of the plasma are optimized by seeding the explosive or propellant with suitable additives, which ionize during the burn (Fanthome, 1989; Flanagan, 1981). Published experiments suggest that a typical arrangement uses a solid propellant gas generator, often using conventional ammunition propellant as a base. Cartridges of such propellant can be loaded much like artillery rounds, for multiple shot operation.

HIGH POWER MICROWAVE SOURCES: VIRCATOR

While the FCG is a potent technology base for the generation of large electrical power pulses, the output of the FCG is by its physics constrained to the frequency band below 1 mHz. Many target sets are difficult to attack even with very high power levels at such frequencies; moreover, focusing the energy output from such a device will be problematic. An HPM device overcomes both of these problems, as its output power may be tightly focused and it has a much better ability to couple energy into many target types. A wide range of HPM devices exist: relativistic klystrons, magnetrons, slow wave devices, reflex triodes, and Vircators are all examples of the available technology base (Granatstein, 1987; Hoeberling, 1992). From the perspective of a bomb or warhead designer, the device of choice at this time is the Vircator—a one shot device capable of producing a very powerful single pulse of radiation that is mechanically simple, small and robust, and can operate over a relatively broad band of microwave frequencies.

The physics of the Vircator tube are substantially more complex than those of the preceding devices. The fundamental idea behind the Vircator is that of accelerating a high current electron beam against a mesh (or foil) anode. Many electrons will pass through the anode, forming a bubble of space charge behind the anode. Under the proper conditions, this space charge region will oscillate at microwave frequencies. If the space charge region is placed into a resonant cavity which is appropriately tuned, very high peak powers may be achieved. Conventional microwave engineering techniques may then be used to extract microwave power from the resonant cavity. Because the frequency of oscillation is dependent upon the electron beam parameters, Vircators may be tuned or chirped in frequency, where the microwave cavity will support appropriate modes. Power levels achieved in Vircator experiments range from 170 kilowatts to 40 gigawatts over frequencies spanning the decimetric and centimetric bands (Thode, 1987).

The two most commonly described configurations for the Vircator are the axial Vircator (AV) (Figure 3) and the transverse Vircator (TV). The Axial Vircator is the simplest by design, and has generally produced the best power output in experiments. It is typically built into a cylindrical waveguide structure. Power is most often extracted by transitioning the waveguide into a conical horn structure, which functions as an antenna. AVs typically oscillate in transverse magnetic (TM) modes. The Transverse Vircator injects cathode current from the side of the cavity and will typically oscillate in a transverse electric (TE) mode.

Technical issues in Vircator design are output pulse duration, which is typically of the order of a microsecond and is limited by anode melting; stability of oscillation frequency, often compromised by cavity mode hopping; conversion efficiency; and total power output. Coupling power efficiently from the Vircator cavity in modes suitable for a chosen antenna type may also be an issue, given the high power levels involved and thus the potential for electrical breakdown in insulators.

The Lethality of Electromagnetic Warheads

The issue of electromagnetic weapon lethality is complex. Unlike the technology base for weapon construction, which has been widely published in the open literature, lethality related issues have been published much less frequently. While the calculation of electromagnetic field strengths achievable at a given radius for a given device design is a straightforward task, determining a kill probability for a given class of target under such conditions is not.This is for good reasons. The first is that target types are very diverse in their electromagnetic hardness, or ability to resist damage. Equipment which has been intentionally shielded and hardened against electromagnetic attack will withstand orders of magnitude greater field strengths than standard commercially rated equipment. Moreover,

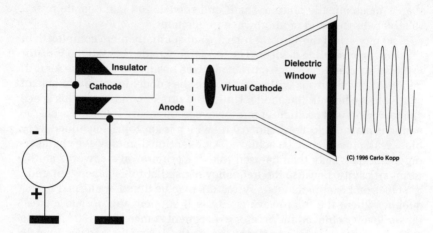

Figure 3. Axial virtual cathode oscillator

various manufacturer's implementations of like types of equipment may vary significantly in hardness due to the idiosyncrasies of specific electrical designs, cabling schemes, and chassis/shielding designs used. The second major problem in determining lethality is that of coupling efficiency, which is a measure of how much power is transferred from the field produced by the weapon into the target. Only power coupled into the target can cause useful damage.

COUPLING MODES

In assessing how power is coupled into targets, two principal coupling modes are recognized in the literature. *Front door coupling* occurs typically when power from an electromagnetic weapon is coupled into an antenna associated with radar or communications equipment. The antenna subsystem is designed to couple power in and out of the equipment, and thus provides an efficient path for the power flow from the electromagnetic weapon to enter the equipment and cause damage. *Back door coupling* occurs when the electromagnetic field from a weapon produces large transient currents called spikes (when produced by a low frequency weapon) or electrical standing waves (when produced by an HPM weapon) on fixed electrical wiring and cables interconnecting equipment or providing connections to main power or the telephone network (Taylor, 1992; White, 1978). Equipment connected to exposed cables or wiring will experience either high voltage transient spikes or standing waves, which can damage unhardened power supplies and communications interfaces. Moreover, should the transient penetrate into the equipment, damage can be done to other devices inside. A low frequency weapon will couple well into a typical wiring infrastructure, as most telephone lines, networking cables, and power lines follow streets, building risers, and corridors. In most instances any particular cable run will comprise multiple linear segments joined at approximately right angles. Whatever the relative orientation of the weapons field, more than one linear segment of the cable run is likely to be oriented such that a good coupling efficiency can be achieved.

It is worth noting the safe operating envelopes of some typical types of semiconductor devices. Manufacturers' guaranteed breakdown voltage ratings for silicon high frequency bipolar transistors, widely used in communications equipment, typically vary between 15 V and 65 V. Gallium arsenide field effect transistors are usually rated at about 10 V. High density dynamic random access memories (DRAM), an essential part of any computer, are usually rated to 7 V against earth. Generic CMOS logic is rated between 7 V and 15 V, and microprocessors running off 3.3 V or 5 V power supplies are usually rated very closely to that voltage. While many modern devices are equipped with additional protection circuits at each pin, to sink electrostatic discharges, sustained or repeated application of a high voltage will often defeat these (Motorola, 1983; Micron, 1992; National Semiconductor, 1986). Communications interfaces and power supplies must typically meet electrical safety requirements imposed by regulators. Such interfaces are usually protected by isolation transformers with ratings from hundreds of volts to about 2-3 kV (NPI, 1993). It is clearly evident that once the defense provided by a transformer, cable pulse arrestor, or shielding is breached, voltages as low as 50 V can inflict substantial damage upon computer and communications equipment. The author has seen a number of equipment items (computers, consumer electronics) exposed to low frequency high voltage spikes (near lightning strikes, electrical power transients), and in every instance the damage was extensive, often requiring replacement of most semiconductors in the equipment.

(One bizzare instance of lightning strike electrical damage was described to the author by an eyewitness technician, tasked with assessing the damage on the site. A lightning bolt impacted in the close vicinity of a transmitter shed. RF and power cables ran from the transmitter shed to a transmission tower through a rectangular, metal shielded tunnel. The effect of the lightning strike was to produce an electromagnetic standing wave in the tunnel, much like in a microwave waveguide. All cables within the tunnel were burned through at regular spacings along the tunnel, corresponding precisely to the half wavelength of the standing wave in the tunnel.)

HPM weapons operating in the centimetric and millimetric bands offer an additional coupling mechanism to back door coupling: the ability to directly couple into equipment through ventilation holes, gaps between panels, and poorly shielded interfaces. Under these conditions, any aperture into the equipment behaves much like a slot in a microwave cavity, allowing microwave radiation to directly excite or enter the cavity. The microwave radiation will form a spatial standing wave pattern within the equipment. Components situated within the anti-nodes within the standing wave pattern will be exposed to potentially high electromagnetic fields.

Because microwave weapons can couple more readily than low frequency weapons, and can in many instances bypass protection devices designed to stop low frequency coupling, they have the potential to be significantly more lethal than low frequency weapons. The research done in this area illustrates the difficulty of producing workable models for predicting equipment vulnerability. It does, however, provide a solid basis for shielding strategies and hardening of equipment. The diversity of likely target types and the unknown geometrical layout and electrical characteristics of the wiring and cabling infrastructure surrounding a target makes the exact prediction of lethality impossible.

A general approach to dealing with wiring and cabling related back door coupling is to determine a known lethal voltage level and then use this to find the required field strength to generate this voltage. Once the field strength is known, the lethal radius for a given weapon configuration can be calculated. A trivial example is that of a 10 gW 5 gHz HPM device illuminating a footprint of 400-500 meters diameter from a distance of several hundred meters. This will result in field strengths of several kV per meter within the device footprint, in turn capable of producing voltages of hundreds of volts to kilovolts on exposed wires or cables (Kraus, 1988; Taylor, 1992). This suggests lethal radii on the order of hundreds of meters, subject to weapon performance and target set electrical hardness.

MAXIMIZING ELECTROMAGNETIC BOMB LETHALITY

To maximize the lethality of an electromagnetic bomb it is necessary to maximize the power coupled into the target set. The first step in maximizing bomb lethality is is to maximize the peak power and duration of the radiation of the weapon. For a given bomb size, this is accomplished by using the most powerful flux compression generator (Vircator in an HPM bomb) which will fit the weapon size, and by maximizing the efficiency of internal power transfers in the weapon. Energy which is not emitted is energy wasted at the expense of lethality.

The second step is to maximize the coupling efficiency into the target set. A good strategy for dealing with a complex and diverse target set is to exploit every coupling opportunity available within the bandwidth of the weapon.

A low frequency bomb built around an FCG will require a large antenna to provide good coupling of power from the weapon into the surrounding environment. While weapons built this way are inherently wide band, as most of the power produced lies in the frequency band below 1 mHz, compact antennas are not an option. One possible scheme is for a bomb approaching its programmed firing altitude to deploy five linear antenna elements. These are produced by firing off cable spools which unwind several hundred meters of cable. Four radial antenna

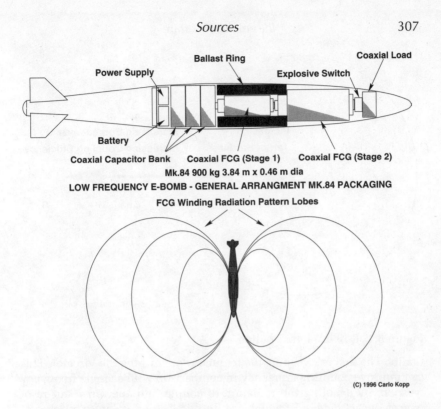

Figure 4. Low frequency E-Bomb warhead (mk.i84 form factor)

elements form a "virtual" earth plane around the bomb, while an axial antenna element is used to radiate the power from the FCG. The choice of element lengths would need to be carefully matched to the frequency characteristics of the weapon, to produce the desired field strength. A high power coupling pulse transformer is used to match the low imped-ance FCG output to the much higher impedance of the antenna, and ensure that the current pulse does not vaporize the cable prematurely.

Other alternatives are possible. One is to simply guide the bomb very close to the target, and rely upon the near field produced by the FCG winding, which is in effect a loop antenna of very small diameter relative to the wavelength. While coupling efficiency is inherently poor, the use of a guided bomb would allow the warhead to be positioned accurately within meters of a target. An area worth further investigation in this context is the use of low frequency bombs to damage or destroy magnetic tape libraries.

Microwave bombs have a broader range of coupling modes, and given their small wavelength in comparison with bomb dimensions, can be readily focused against targets with a compact antenna assembly. Assum-ing that the antenna provides the required weapon footprint, there are at least two mechanisms which can be employed to further maximise le-

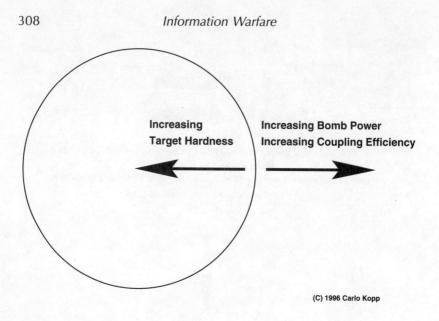

Increasing
Target Hardness

Increasing Bomb Power
Increasing Coupling Efficiency

(C) 1996 Carlo Kopp

Figure 5.1. E-Bomb lethal radius

thality. The first is sweeping the frequency or chirping the Vircator. This can improve coupling efficiency in comparison with a single frequency weapon, by enabling the radiation to couple into apertures and resonances over a range of frequencies. In this fashion, a larger number of coupling opportunities are exploited. The second mechanism is the polarization of the weapon's emission. If we assume that the orientations of possible coupling apertures and resonances in the target set are random in relation to the weapon's antenna orientation, a linearly polarized emission will only exploit half of the opportunities available. A circularly polarized emission will exploit all coupling opportunities.

The practical constraint is that it may be difficult to produce an effi-

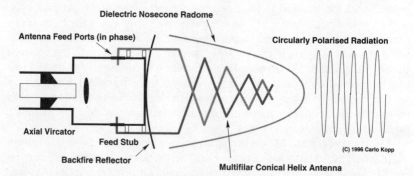

Dielectric Nosecone Radome

Antenna Feed Ports (in phase)

Circularly Polarised Radiation

Axial Vircator

Feed Stub

Backfire Reflector

(C) 1996 Carlo Kopp

Multifilar Conical Helix Antenna

Figure 5.2. Example of vircator/antenna assembly

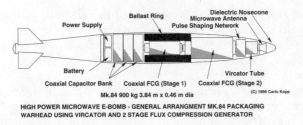

Figure 6. HPM E-Bomb Warhead (Mk.84 form factor)

cient high power circularly polarized antenna design which is compact and performs over a wide band. Some work therefore needs to be done on tapered helix or conical spiral type antennas capable of handling high power levels, and a suitable interface to a Vircator with multiple extraction ports must devised. A possible implementation is depicted in Figure 5. In this arrangement, power is coupled from the tube by stubs which directly feed a multi-filar conical helix antenna. An implementation of this scheme would need to address the specific requirements of bandwidth, beamwidth, efficiency of coupling from the tube, while delivering circularly polarised radiation.

Another aspect of electromagnetic bomb lethality is its detonation altitude. By varying the detonation altitude, a tradeoff may be achieved

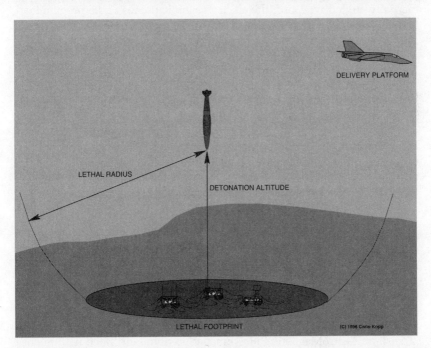

Figure 7. Lethal footprint of low frequency E-Bomb in relation to altitude

between the size of the lethal footprint and the intensity of the electromagnetic field in that footprint. This provides the option of sacrificing
weapon coverage to achieve kills against targets of greater electromagnetic hardness, for a given bomb size (Figures 7 and 8). This is not unlike
the use of airburst explosive devices.

In summary, lethality is maximized by maximizing power output and
the efficiency of energy transfer from the weapon to the target set. Microwave weapons offer the ability to focus nearly all of their energy output
into the lethal footprint, and offer the ability to exploit a wider range of
coupling modes. Therefore, microwave bombs are the preferred choice.

Targeting Electromagnetic Bombs

The task of identifying targets for attack with electromagnetic bombs
can be complex. Certain categories of target will be very easy to identify
and engage. Buildings housing government offices and thus computer
equipment, production facilities, military bases and known radar sites
and communications nodes are all targets which can be readily identified
through conventional photographic, satellite, imaging radar, electronic
reconnaissance and humint operations. These targets are typically geographically fixed and thus may be attacked providing that the aircraft can
penetrate to weapon release range. With the accuracy inherent in GPS/
inertially guided weapons, the electromagnetic bomb can be programmed
to detonate at the optimal position to inflict a maximum of electrical damage.

Mobile and camouflaged targets which radiate overtly can also be
readily engaged. Mobile and relocatable air defense equipment, mobile
communications nodes and naval vessels are all good examples of this
category of target. While radiating, their positions can be precisely tracked
with suitable electronic support measures (ESM) and emitter locating
systems (ELS) carried either by the launch platform or a remote surveillance platform. In the latter instance target coordinates can be continuously datalinked to the launch platform. As most such targets move
relatively slowly, they are unlikely to escape the footprint of the electromagnetic bomb during the weapon's flight time.

Mobile or hidden targets which do not overtly radiate may present a
problem, particularly should conventional means of targeting be employed. A technical solution to this problem does however exist for many
types of target. This solution is the detection and tracking of unintentional emission (UE) (Herskowitz, 1996). UE has attracted most attention
in the context of TEMPEST surveillance, where transient emanations
leaking out from equipment due to poor shielding can be detected and in
many instances demodulated to recover useful intelligence. (The NAC-
SIM 5100A standard specifies acceptable emission levels for TEMPEST
[Transient ElectroMagnetic Pulse Emanation Standard] rated equipment.)
Termed Van Eck radiation (Van Eck, 1985), such emissions can only be

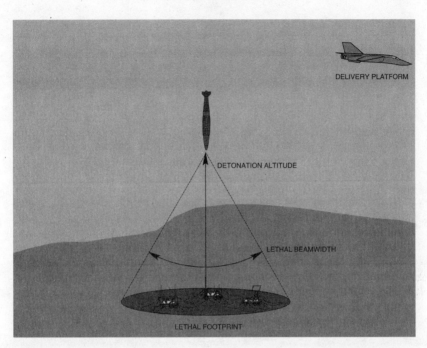

Figure 8. Lethal footprint of a hpm E-Bomb in relation to altitude

suppressed by rigorous shielding and emission control techniques, such as are employed in TEMPEST rated equipment.

While the demodulation of UE can be a technically difficult task to perform well, in the context of targeting electromagnetic bombs this problem does not arise. To target such an emitter for attack requires only the ability to identify the type of emission and thus target type, and to isolate its position with sufficient accuracy to deliver the bomb. Because the emissions from computer monitors, peripherals, processor equipment, switchmode power supplies, electrical motors, internal combustion engine ignition systems, variable duty cycle electrical power controllers (thyristor or triac based), superheterodyne receiver local oscillators and computer networking cables are all distinct in their frequencies and modulations, a suitable ELS can be designed to detect, identify, and track such sources of emission.

A good precedent for this targeting paradigm exists. During the SEA (Vietnam) conflict, the United States Air Force (USAF) operated a number of night interdiction gunships which used direction finding receivers to track the emissions from vehicle ignition systems. Once a truck was identified and tracked, the gunship would engage it. (The Northrop/Lockheed ASD-5 Black Crow DF receiver was fitted to the AC-130A Pave Pronto gunships, rebuilt from obsoleted C-130 transports [International Countermeasures Handbook, 10th ed.].)

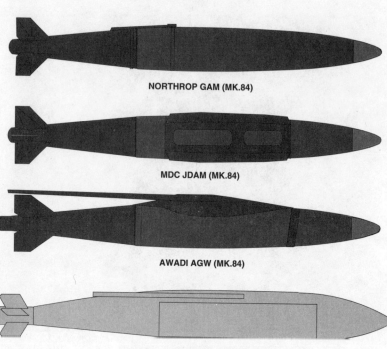

NORTHROP GAM (MK.84)

MDC JDAM (MK.84)

AWADI AGW (MK.84)

TI AGM-154C JSOW (800 lb/360 kg)

(C) 1996 Carlo Kopp

Figure 9. GPS guided bomb/glidebomb kits

Because UE occurs at relatively low power levels, the use of this detection method prior to the outbreak of hostilities can be difficult, as it may be necessary to overfly hostile territory to find signals of usable intensity. (A noteworthy technical issue in this context is that even equipment not rated to TEMPEST standards will radiate energy at very low power levels, in comparison with intentional transmissions by radar or communications equipment. A receiver designed to detect, identify and locate sources of UE radiation will either need to be highly sensitive, or deployed very close to the emitter. UE from computer monitors and networks exhibit known regular patterns, and correlation techniques could be used to significantly improve receiver sensitivity [Dixon, 1984].) The use of stealthy reconnaissance aircraft or long range, stealthy unmanned aerial vehicles (UAV) may be required. The latter also raises the possibility of autonomous electromagnetic warhead armed expendable UAVs, fitted with appropriate homing receivers. These would be programmed to loiter in a target area until a suitable emitter is detected, upon which the UAV would home in and expend itself against the target.

The Delivery of Conventional Electromagnetic Bombs

As with explosive warheads, electromagnetic warheads will occupy a volume of physical space and will also have some given mass (weight) determined by the density of the internal hardware. Like explosive warheads, electromagnetic warheads may be fitted to a range of delivery vehicles.

Known existing applications (see Fulghum, 1993) involve fitting an electromagnetic warhead to a cruise missile airframe. The choice of a cruise missile airframe will restrict the weight of the weapon to about 340 kg (750 lb), although some sacrifice in airframe fuel capacity could see this size increased. A limitation in all such applications is the need to carry an electrical energy storage device, e.g. a battery, to provide the current used to charge the capacitors used to prime the FCG prior to its discharge. Therefore the available payload capacity will be split between the electrical storage and the weapon itself. (Fulghum's article indicates that the U.S. has progressed significantly with its development work on electromagnetic warhead technology. An electromagnetic warhead was fitted to the USAF AGM-86 Air Launched Cruise Missile airframe, involving both structural and guidance system modifications. The description in this report suggests the use of an explosive pumped flux generator feeding a device such as a Vircator. References to magnetic coils almost certainly relate to the flux compression generator hardware.)

In wholly autonomous weapons such as cruise missiles, the size of the priming current source and its battery may well impose important limitations on weapon capability. Air delivered bombs, which have a flight time between tens of seconds to minutes, could be built to exploit the launch aircraft's power systems. In such a bomb design, the bomb's capacitor bank can be charged by the launch aircraft en route to target, and after release a much smaller onboard power supply could be used to maintain the charge in the priming source prior to weapon initiation.

An electromagnetic bomb delivered by a conventional aircraft (see *Journal of Electronic Defence,* 1996) can offer a much better ratio of electromagnetic device mass to total bomb mass, as most of the bomb mass can be dedicated to the electromagnetic device installation itself. It follows therefore, that for a given technology an electromagnetic bomb of identical mass to a electromagnetic warhead equipped missile can have a much greater lethality, assuming equal accuracy of delivery and technologically similar electromagnetic device design. (The Journal of Electronic Defence article reported on the USAF Phillips Laboratory at Kirtland awarding a $6.6 million HPM SEAD weapon technology demonstration program contract to Hughes Missile Systems Co. This contract will see Hughes conduct design studies in order to define design goals, and then fabricate brassboard demonstration hardware using government developed technology. The journal speculated that the weapon will be an FCG driven microwave tube, which is most likely the case given the USAF's prior research activities in this area [Reinovsky, 1985]. A 1995 report in the same journal indicated the existence of a related program which addresses command and control warfare and counter-air capabilities. In any event, the devices produced by these programs are likely to become the first operationally fielded HPM electromagnetic bombs for delivery by combat aircraft.)

A missile borne electromagnetic warhead installation will comprise the electromagnetic device, an electrical energy converter, and an onboard storage device such as a battery. As the weapon is pumped, the battery is drained. The electromagnetic device will be detonated by the missile's onboard fusing system. In a cruise missile, this will be tied to the navigation system; in an anti-shipping missile the radar seeker; and in an air-to-air missile, the proximity fusing system. The warhead fraction (ratio of total payload [warhead] mass to launch mass of the weapon) will be between 15 percent and 30 percent. (This may be readily determined by calculating the ratio of warhead mass to total weapon launch mass, for representative missile types. Taking the AGM-78 Standard as a lower limit yields 15.9 percent, whereas taking the AGM/BGM-109 Tomahawk as an upper limit yields about 28 percent. Figures are derived from manufacturers' brochures and reference publications; e.g., *Jane's Air-Launched Weapons.*

An electromagnetic bomb warhead will comprise an electromagnetic device, an electrical energy converter, and an energy storage device to pump and sustain the electromagnetic device charge after separation from the delivery platform. Fusing could be provided by a radar altimeter fuse to airburst the bomb, a barometric fuse, or in GPS/inertially guided bombs, the navigation system. The warhead fraction could be as high as 85 percent, with most of the usable mass occupied by the electromagnetic device and its supporting hardware.

Due to the potentially large lethal radius of an electromagnetic device, compared to an explosive device of similar mass, standoff delivery would be prudent. While this is an inherent characteristic of weapons such as cruise missiles, potential applications of these devices to glide-bombs, anti-shipping missiles, and air-to-air missiles would dictate fire and forget guidance of the appropriate variety to allow the launching aircraft to gain adequate separation of several miles before warhead detonation.

The recent advent of GPS satellite navigation guidance kits for conventional bombs and glidebombs has provided the optimal means for cheaply delivering such weapons. While GPS guided weapons without differential GPS enhancements may lack the pinpoint accuracy of laser or television guided munitions, they are still quite accurate (CEP approximately 40 ft) and importantly, cheap, autonomous all-weather weapons.

The USAF has recently deployed the Northrop GAM (GPS Aided Munition) on the B-2 bomber (Northrop, 1995), and will by the end of the decade deploy the GPS/inertially guided GBU-29/30 JDAM (Joint Direct Attack Munition)(McDonnell Douglas, 1995) and the AGM-154 JSOW (Joint Stand Off Weapon) (Pergler, 1994) glidebomb. Other countries are also developing this technology, the Australian BAeA AGW (Agile Glide

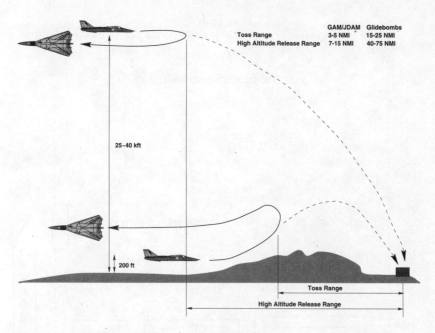

Figure 10. Delivery profiles for GPS/inertial guided weapons

Weapon) glidebomb achieves a glide range of about 140 km (75 nmi) when launched from altitude (Kopp, 1996).

The importance of glidebombs as delivery means for HPM warheads is threefold. First, the glidebomb can be released from outside effective radius of target air defenses, therefore minimizing the risk to the launch aircraft. Second, the large standoff range means that the aircraft can remain well clear of the bomb's effects. Third, the bomb's autopilot may be programmed to shape the terminal trajectory of the weapon, such that a target may be engaged from the most suitable altitude and aspect.

A major advantage of using electromagnetic bombs is that they may be delivered by any tactical aircraft with a nav-attack system capable of delivering GPS guided munitions. As we can expect GPS guided munitions to be become the standard weapon in use by Western air forces by the end of this decade, every aircraft capable of delivering a standard guided munition also becomes a potential delivery vehicle for an electromagnetic bomb. Should weapon ballistic properties be identical to the standard weapon, no software changes to the aircraft would be required.

Because of the simplicity of electromagnetic bombs in comparison with weapons such as Anti Radiation Missiles (ARM), it is not unreasonable to expect that these should be both cheaper to manufacture and easier to support in the field, thus allowing for more substantial weapon stocks. In turn this makes saturation attacks a much more viable proposition.

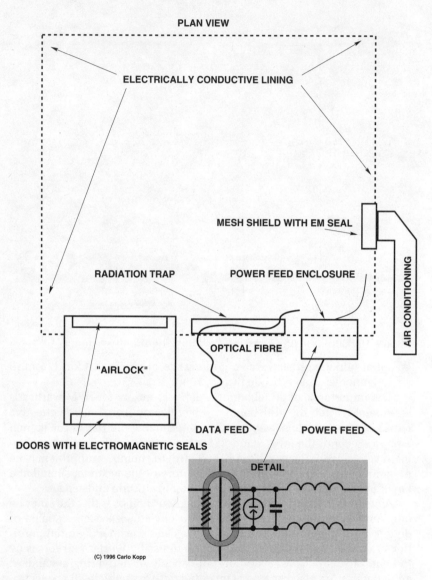

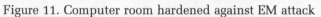

Figure 11. Computer room hardened against EM attack

Defense Against Electromagnetic Bombs

The most effective defense against electromagnetic bombs is to prevent their delivery by destroying the launch platform or delivery vehicle, as is the case with nuclear weapons. This may not always be possible, and therefore systems which can be expected to suffer exposure to the electromagnetic weapons effects must be electromagnetically hardened.

The most effective method is to wholly contain the equipment in an electrically conductive enclosure—a Faraday cage—which prevents the electromagnetic field from gaining access to the protected equipment. However, most such equipment must communicate with and be fed by power from the outside world, and this can provide points via which electrical transients may enter the enclosure and effect damage. While optical fibers address this requirement for transferring data in and out, electrical power feeds remain an ongoing vulnerability.

Where an electrically conductive channel must enter the enclosure, electromagnetic arresting devices must be fitted. A range of devices exist; however, care must be taken in determining their parameters to ensure that they can deal with the rise time and strength of electrical transients produced by electromagnetic devices. Reports from the U.S. (Staines, 1993; Fulghum, 1993) indicate that hardening measures attuned to the behavior of nuclear EMP bombs do not perform well when dealing with some conventional microwave electromagnetic device designs. (This is entirely consistent with theoretical expectations, as the different spectral characteristics of microwave electromagnetic warheads, compared to nuclear electromagnetic weapons, will significantly affect the effectiveness of protective filters. What is important from an electrical engineering viewpoint is that a filter designed to stop signals in the lower frequency bands may perform very poorly at microwave frequencies.)

It is significant that hardening of systems must be carried out at a system level, as electromagnetic damage to any single element of a complex system could inhibit the function of the whole system. Hardening newly built equipment and systems will add a substantial cost burden. Older equipment and systems may be impossible to harden properly and may require complete replacement. In simple terms, hardening by design is significantly easier than attempting to harden existing equipment.

An interesting aspect of electrical damage to targets is the possibility of wounding semiconductor devices, thereby causing equipment to suffer repetitive intermittent faults rather than complete failures. Such faults would tie down considerable maintenance resources while also diminishing the confidence of the operators in the equipment's reliability. Intermittent faults may not be possible to repair economically, thereby causing equipment in this state to be removed from service permanently, with considerable loss in maintenance hours during damage diagnosis. This factor must also be considered when assessing the hardness of equipment against electromagnetic attack, as partial or incomplete hardening may in this fashion cause more difficulties than it would solve. Indeed, shielding which is incomplete may resonate when excited by radiation and thus contribute to damage inflicted upon the equipment contained within it.

Other than hardening against attack, facilities which are concealed should not radiate readily detectable emissions. Where radio frequency communications must be used, low probability of intercept (i.e., spread spectrum) techniques should be employed exclusively to preclude the

318 *Information Warfare*

use of site emissions for electromagnetic targeting purposes (Dixon 1984). Appropriate suppression of UE is also mandatory.

Communications networks for voice, data, and services should employ topologies with sufficient redundancy and failover mechanisms to allow operation with multiple nodes and links inoperative. This will deny a user of electromagnetic bombs the option of disabling large portions if not the whole of the network by taking down one or more key nodes or links with a single or small number of attacks.

Limitations of Electromagnetic Bombs

The limitations of electromagnetic weapons are determined by weapon implementation and means of delivery. Weapon implementation will determine the electromagnetic field strength achievable at a given radius, and its spectral distribution. Means of delivery will constrain the accuracy with which the weapon can be positioned in relation to the intended target. Both constrain lethality.

In the context of targeting military equipment, it must be noted that thermionic technology (vacuum tube equipment) is substantially more resilient to electromagnetic weapons effects than is solid state (transistor) technology. Therefore, a weapon optimized to destroy solid state computers and receivers may cause little or no damage to a thermionic technology device—for instance early 1960s Soviet military equipment. Therefore, a hard electrical kill may not be achieved against such targets unless a suitable weapon is used.

This underscores another limitation of electromagnetic weapons— the difficulty in kill assessment. Radiating targets such as radars or communications equipment may continue to radiate after an attack even though their receivers and data processing systems have been damaged or destroyed. This means that equipment which has been successfully attacked may still appear to operate. Conversely, an opponent may shut down an emitter if attack is imminent and the absence of emissions means that the success or failure of the attack may not be immediately apparent.

Assessing whether an attack on a nonradiating emitter has been successful is more problematic. A good case can be made for developing tools specifically for the purpose of analyzing unintended emissions, not only for targeting purposes, but also for kill assessment.

An important factor in assessing the lethal coverage of an electromagnetic weapon is atmospheric propagation. While the relationship between electromagnetic field strength and distance from the weapon is one of an inverse square law in free space, the decay in lethal effect with increasing distance within the atmosphere will be greater due to quantum physical absorption effects. (See International Countermeasures Handbook, 14th ed., page 104.) This is particularly so at higher frequencies, and significant absorption peaks due to water vapor and oxygen exist at frequencies above 20 gHz. These will therefore contain the effect of HPM weapons to shorter radii than are ideally achievable in the K and L frequency bands.

Means of delivery will limit the lethality of an electromagnetic bomb by introducing limits to the weapon's size and the accuracy of its delivery. Should the delivery error be of the order of the weapon's lethal radius for a given detonation altitude, lethality will be significantly diminished. This is of particular importance when assessing the lethality of unguided electromagnetic bombs, as delivery errors will be more substantial than those experienced with guided weapons such as GPS guided bombs.

Therefore, accuracy of delivery and achievable lethal radius must be considered against the allowable collateral damage for the chosen target. Where collateral electrical damage is a consideration, accuracy of delivery and lethal radius are key parameters. An inaccurately delivered weapon of large lethal radius may be unusable against a target should the likely collateral electrical damage be beyond acceptable limits. This can be a major issue for users constrained by treaty provisions on collateral damage (AAP1003).

The Proliferation of Electromagnetic Bomb

At the time of writing, the United States and the CIS are the only two nations with the established technology base and the depth of specific experience to design weapons based upon this technology. However, the relative simplicity of the FCG and the Vircator suggests that any nation with even a 1940s technology base, once in possession of engineering drawings and specifications for such weapons, could manufacture them. As an example, the fabrication of an effective FCG can be accomplished with basic electrical materials, common plastic explosives such as C-4 or Semtex, and readily available machine tools such as lathes and suitable mandrels for forming coils. Disregarding the overheads of design, which do not apply in this context, a two stage FCG could be fabricated for as low as $1,000-$2,000 at Western labor rates (Reinovsky, 1985). This cost could be even lower in a Third World or newly industrialized economy.

While the relative simplicity and low cost of such weapons can be considered of benefit to First World nations intending to build viable war stocks or maintain production in wartime, the possibility of less developed nations mass producing such weapons is alarming. The dependence of modern economies upon their information technology infrastructure makes them highly vulnerable to attack with such weapons, providing that these can be delivered to their targets. Of major concern is the vulnerability resulting from increasing use of communications and data communications schemes based upon copper cable media. If the copper medium were to be replaced en masse with optical fiber in order to achieve higher bandwidths, the communications infrastructure would become significantly more robust against electromagnetic attack. However, the current trend is to exploit existing distribution media such as cable TV and telephone wiring to provide multiple megabits data distribution (e.g., cable modems, ADSL/HDSL/VDSL) to premises. Moreover, the gradual replacement of coaxial Ethernet networking with 10-Base-T twisted pair equipment has further increased the vulnerability of wiring systems inside buildings. It is not unreasonable to assume that the data and services communications infrastructure in the West will remain a "soft" electromagnetic target in the foreseeable future.

At this time, no counter-proliferation regimes exist. Should treaties be agreed to limit the proliferation of electromagnetic weapons, they would be virtually impossible to enforce given the common availability of suitable materials and tools. With the former CIS suffering significant economic difficulties, the possibility of CIS-designed microwave and pulse power technology leaking out to Third World nations or terrorist organizations should not be discounted. The threat of electromagnetic bomb proliferation is very real.

A Doctrine for Use of Conventional Electromagnetic Bombs

A fundamental tenet of IW is that complex organizational systems such as governments, industries, and military forces cannot function without the flow of information through their structures. Information flows within these structures in several directions, under typical conditions of function. A trivial model for this function would see commands and directives flowing outward from a central decisionmaking element, with information about the state of the system flowing in the opposite direction. Real systems are substantially more complex.

This is of military significance because stopping this flow of information will severely debilitate the function of any such system. Stopping the outward flow of information produces paralysis, as commands cannot reach the elements which are to execute them. Stopping the inward flow of information isolates the decisionmaking element from reality, and thus severely inhibits its capacity to make rational decisions which are sensitive to the currency of information at hand.

The recent evolution of strategic (air) warfare indicates a growing trend toward targeting strategies which exploit this most fundamental vulnerability of any large and organized system. (Waters, 1992. Chapter 16 of this reference provides a good discussion of both the rationale and implementation of this strategy.) The Desert Storm air war of 1991 is a good instance, with a substantial effort expended against such targets. Indeed, the model used for modern strategic air attack places leadership and its supporting communications in the position of highest targeting priority (Warden, 1995). No less importantly, modern electronic combat concentrates upon the disruption and destruction of communications and information gathering sensors used to support military operations. Again, the Desert Storm air war provides a good illustration of the application of this method. A strategy which stresses attack upon the information processing and communications elements of the systems which it is targeting offers a very high payoff, as it will introduce an increasing level of paralysis and disorientation within its target. Electromagnetic bombs are a powerful tool in the implementation of such a strategy.

ELECTRONIC COMBAT OPERATIONS USING ELECTROMAGNETIC BOMBS

The central objective of electronic combat (EC) operations is the command of the electromagnetic spectrum, achieved by soft and hard kill means against the opponent's electronic assets. (Soft kill means will inhibit or degrade the function of a target system during their application, leaving the target system electrically and physically intact upon the cessation of their application. Hard kill means will damage or destroy the target system, and are thus a means of inflicting attrition.) The underlying objective of commanding the electromagnetic spectrum is to interrupt or substantially reduce the flow of information through the opponent's air defense system, air operations environment, and between functional elements of weapon systems. In this context the ability of electromagnetic bombs to achieve kills against a wide range of target types allows their general application to the task of inflicting attrition upon an opponent's electronic assets, be they specialized air defense assets or more general Command-Control-Communications (C3) and other military assets.

Electromagnetic bombs can be a means of both soft and hard electrical kill, subject to the lethality of the weapon and the hardness of its target. A hard electrical kill by means of an electromagnetic device will be achieved in those instances where such severe electrical damage is achieved against a target so as to require the replacement of most if not all of its internal electronics.

Electronic combat operations using electromagnetic devices involve the use of these to attack radar, C3, and air defense weapon systems. These should always be attacked initially with an electromagnetic weapon to achieve soft or hard electrical kills, followed up by attack with conventional munitions to preclude possible repair of disabled assets at a later time. As with conventional SEAD operations, the greatest payoff will be achieved by using electromagnetic weapons against systems of strategic importance first, followed in turn by those of operational and tactical importance (Kopp, 1992).

In comparison with an anti-radiation missile (ARM—a missile which homes on the emissions from a threat radar), the established and specialized tool in the conduct of SEAD operations, an electromagnetic bomb can achieve kills against multiple targets of diverse types within its lethal footprint. In this respect an electromagnetic device may be described as a weapon of electrical mass destruction (WEMD). Therefore, electromagnetic weapons are a significant force multiplier in electronic combat operations.

A conventional electronic combat campaign, or intensive electronic combat operations, will initially concentrate on saturating the opponent's electronic defenses, denying information and inflicting maximum attrition upon electronic assets. The force multiplication offered by electromagnetic weapons vastly reduces the number of air assets required to inflict substantial attrition, and where proper electronic reconnaissance has been carried out beforehand, also reduces the need for specialized assets such as ARM firing aircraft equipped with costly ELS.

The massed application of electromagnetic bombs in the opening phase of an electronic battle will allow much faster attainment of command of the electromagnetic spectrum, as it will inflict attrition upon electronic assets at a much faster rate than possible with conventional means. While the immaturity of conventional electromagnetic weapons precludes an exact analysis of the scale of force multiplication achievable, it is evident that a single aircraft carrying an electromagnetic bomb capable of concurrently disabling a SAM site with its co-located acquisition radar and supporting radar directed AAA weapons, will have the potency of several ARM firing and support jamming aircraft required to accomplish the same result by conventional means. This and the ability of multirole tactical aircraft to perform this task allows for a much greater concentration of force in the opening phase of the battle, for a given force size.

In summary, the massed application of electromagnetic weapons to EC operations will provide for a much faster rate of attrition against hostile electronic assets, achievable with a significantly reduced number of specialized and multirole air assets. (This is also the stated intent of the USAF HPM SEAD technology demonstration program. The fact that the first application of an HPM bomb is electronic combat underscores the tactical, operational, and strategic importance of first defeating an air defense system when prosecuting a strategic air war.) This will allow even a modestly sized force to apply overwhelming pressure in the initial phase of an electronic battle, and therefore achieve command of the electromagnetic spectrum in a significantly shorter time than by conventional means.

STRATEGIC AIR ATTACK OPERATIONS USING ELECTROMAGNETIC BOMBS

The modern approach to strategic air warfare reflects in many respects aspects of the IW model, in that much effort is expended in disabling an opponent's fundamental information processing infrastructure. Since we are yet to see a systematic IW doctrine which has been tested in combat, this paper will approach the subject from a more conservative viewpoint and use established strategic doctrine.

Modern strategic air attack theory is based upon Warden's Five Rings model (Warden, 1995), which identifies five centers of gravity in a nation's warfighting capability. In descending order of importance, these are the nation's leadership and supporting C3 system, its essential economic infrastructure, its transportation network, its population, and its fielded military forces. Electromagnetic weapons may be productively used against all elements in this model, and provide a particularly high payoff when applied against a highly industrialized and geographically concentrated opponent. Of particular importance in the context of stra-

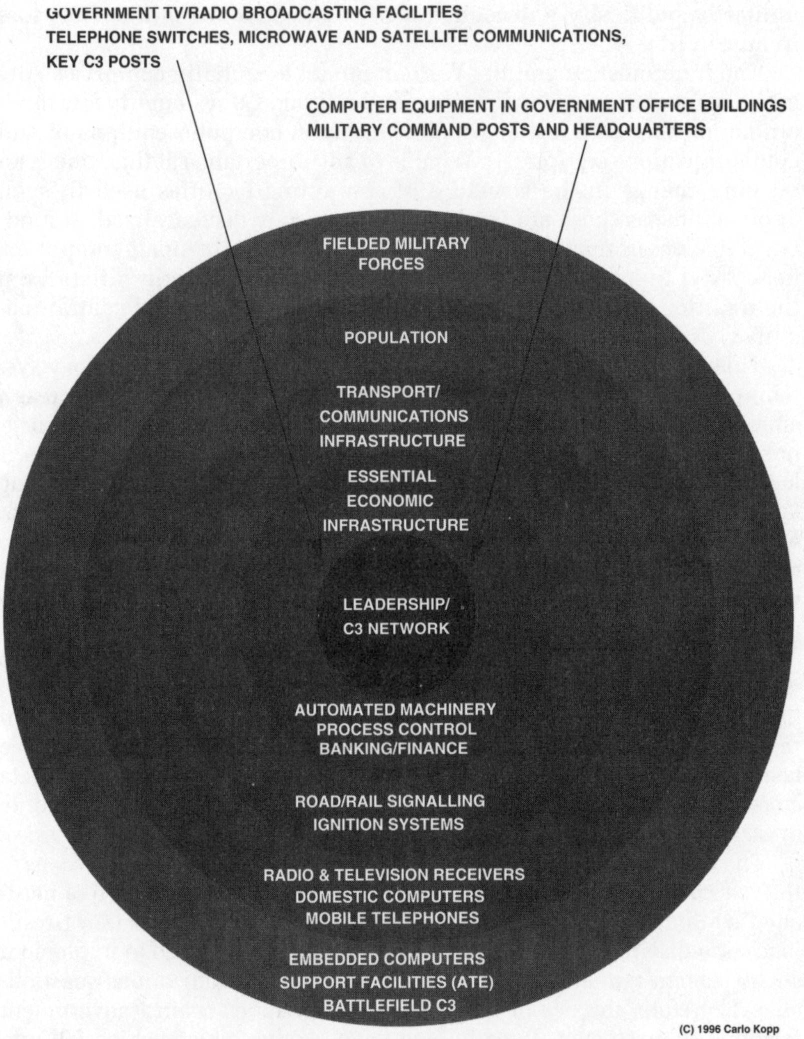

GOVERNMENT TV/RADIO BROADCASTING FACILITIES
TELEPHONE SWITCHES, MICROWAVE AND SATELLITE COMMUNICATIONS,
KEY C3 POSTS

COMPUTER EQUIPMENT IN GOVERNMENT OFFICE BUILDINGS
MILITARY COMMAND POSTS AND HEADQUARTERS

FIELDED MILITARY
FORCES

POPULATION

TRANSPORT/
COMMUNICATIONS
INFRASTRUCTURE

ESSENTIAL
ECONOMIC
INFRASTRUCTURE

LEADERSHIP/
C3 NETWORK

AUTOMATED MACHINERY
PROCESS CONTROL
BANKING/FINANCE

ROAD/RAIL SIGNALLING
IGNITION SYSTEMS

RADIO & TELEVISION RECEIVERS
DOMESTIC COMPUTERS
MOBILE TELEPHONES

EMBEDDED COMPUTERS
SUPPORT FACILITIES (ATE)
BATTLEFIELD C3

(C) 1996 Carlo Kopp

Figure 12. Wardens' "Five Rings" strategic air attack model
in the context of electromagnetically vulnerable target sets

tegic air attack is that while electromagnetic weapons are lethal to electronics, they have little if any effect on humans. This is a characteristic which is not shared with established conventional and nuclear weapons.

This selectivity in lethal effect makes electromagnetic weapons far more readily applicable to a strategic air attack campaign, and reduces the internal political pressure experienced by the leadership of any democracy which must commit to warfare. An opponent may be rendered militarily, politically, and economically ineffective with little if any loss in human life.

The innermost ring in the Warden model essentially comprises government bureaucracies and civilian and military C3 systems. In any modern nation these are heavily dependent upon computer equipment and communications equipment. What is of key importance at this time is an ongoing change in the structure of computing facilities used in such applications, as these are becoming increasingly decentralized. A modern office environment relies upon a large number of small computers, networked to interchange information, in which respect it differs from the traditional model of using a small number of powerful central machines.

This decentralization and networking of information technology systems produces a major vulnerability to electromagnetic attack. Whereas a small number of larger computers could be defended against electromagnetic attack by the use of electromagnetic-hardened computer rooms, a large distributed network cannot. Moreover, unless optical fiber networking is used, the networking cables are themselves a medium via which electromagnetic effects can be efficiently propagated throughout the network to destroy machines. While the use of distributed computer networks reduces vulnerability to attack by conventional munitions, it increases vulnerability to attack by electromagnetic weapons.

Selective targeting of government buildings with electromagnetic weapons will result in a substantial reduction in a government's ability to handle and process information. The damage inflicted upon information records may be permanent, should inappropriate backup strategies have been used to protect stored data. It is reasonable to expect most data stored on machines which are affected will perish with the host machine, or become extremely difficult to recover from damaged storage devices.

The cost of hardening existing computer networks is prohibitive, as is the cost of replacement with hardened equipment. While the use of hardened equipment for critical tasks would provide some measure of resilience, the discipline in the handling of information required to implement such a scheme renders its utility outside of military organizations questionable. Therefore, the use of electromagnetic weapons against government facilities offers an exceptionally high payoff. Other targets which fall into the innermost ring may also be profitably attacked. Satellite link and importantly control facilities are vital means of communication as well as the primary interface to military and commercial reconnaissance satellites. Television and radio broadcasting stations, one of the most powerful tools of any government, are also vulnerable to electromagnetic attack due to the very high concentration of electronic equipment in such sites. Telephone exchanges, particularly later generation digital switching systems, are also highly vulnerable to appropriate electromagnetic attack.

In summary, the use of electromagnetic weapons against leadership and C3 targets is highly profitable, in that a modest number of weapons appropriately used can introduce the sought-after state of strategic paralysis without the substantial costs incurred by the use of conventional munitions.

Essential economic infrastructure is also vulnerable to electromagnetic attack. The finance industry and stock markets are almost wholly dependent upon computers and their supporting communications. Manufacturing, chemical, petroleum product industries, and metallurgical industries rely heavily upon automation, which is almost universally implemented with electronic PLC (Programmable Logic Controller) systems or digital computers. Furthermore, most sensors and telemetry devices used are electrical or electronic. Attacking such economic targets with electromagnetic weapons will halt operations for the time required to either repair the destroyed equipment or to reconfigure for manual operation. Some production processes, however, require automated operation, either because hazardous conditions prevent human intervention or the complexity of the control process required cannot be carried out by a human operator in real time. A good instance are larger chemical, petrochemical, and oil/gas production facilities. Destroying automated control facilities will therefore result in substantial loss of production, causing shortages of these vital materials.

Manufacturing industries which rely heavily upon robotic and semi-automatic machinery, such as the electronics, computer, and electrical industry, precision machine industry, and aerospace industries, are all key assets in supporting a military capability. They are all highly vulnerable to electromagnetic attack. While material processing industries may in some instances be capable of function with manual process control, the manufacturing industries are almost wholly dependent upon their automated machines to achieve any useful production output.

Historical experience suggests that manufacturing industries are highly resilient to air attack as production machinery is inherently mechanically robust; thus, a very high blast overpressure is required to destroy it. (The classical argument here centers upon Allied experience in bombing Germany during World War II, where even repeated raids on industrial targets were unable to wholly stop production, and in many instances only served to reduce the rate of increase in production. What must not be overlooked is that both the accuracy and lethality of weapons in this period bore little comparison to what is available today, and automation of production facilities was almost nonexistent.) The proliferation of electronic and computer controlled machinery has produced a major vulnerability, for which historical precedent does not exist. Therefore it will be necessary to reevaluate this orthodoxy in targeting strategy.

The finance industry and stock markets are a special case in this context, as the destruction of their electronic infrastructure can yield, unlike with manufacturing industries, much faster economic dislocation. This can in turn produce large systemic effects across a whole economy, including elements which are not vulnerable to direct electromagnetic attack. This may be of particular relevance when dealing with an opponent which does not have a large and thus vulnerable manufacturing economy. Nations which rely on agriculture, mining, or trade for a large proportion of their gross domestic product are prime candidates for electromagnetic attack on their finance industry and stock markets. Since the latter are usually geographically concentrated and typically electromagnetically "soft" targets, they are highly vulnerable.

In summary, there is a large payoff in striking at economic essentials with electromagnetic weapons, particularly in the opening phase of a strategic air attack campaign, as economic activity may be halted or reduced with modest expenditure of the attacker's resources. An important caveat is that centers of gravity within the target economy must be properly identified and prioritized for strikes to ensure that maximum effect is achieved as quickly as possible.

Transport infrastructure is the third ring in the Warden model, and also offers some useful opportunities for the application of electromagnetic weapons. Unlike the innermost rings, the concentration of electronic and computer equipment is typically much lower, and therefore considerable care must be taken in the selection of targets. Railway and road signaling systems, where automated, are most vulnerable to electromagnetic attack on their control centers. This could be used to produce traffic congestion by preventing the proper scheduling of rail traffic and disabling road traffic signaling, although the latter may not yield particularly useful results. Significantly, most modern automobiles and trucks use electronic ignition systems which are known to be vulnerable to electromagnetic weapons effects, although opportunities to find such concentrations so as to allow the profitable use of an electromagnetic bomb may be scarce.

The population of the target nation is the fourth ring in the Warden model, and its morale is the object of attack. The morale of the population will be affected significantly by the quality and quantity of the government propaganda it is subjected to, as will it be affected by living conditions. Using electromagnetic weapons against urban areas provides the opportunity to prevent government propaganda from reaching the population via mass media, through the damaging or destruction of all television and radio receivers within the footprint of the weapon. Whether this is necessary, given that broadcast facilities may have already been destroyed, is open to discussion. Arguably it may be counterproductive, as it will prevent the target population from being subjected to friendly means of psychological warfare such as propaganda broadcasts. The use of electromagnetic weapons against a target population is therefore an area which requires careful consideration in the context of the overall IW campaign strategy. If useful objectives can be achieved by isolating the population from government propaganda, then the population is a valid target for electromagnetic attack. Forces constrained by treaty obligations will have to reconcile this against the applicable regulations relating to denial of services to noncombatants (AAP1003).

The outermost and last ring in the Warden model includes the fielded military forces. These are by all means a target vulnerable to electromagnetic attack, and C3 nodes, fixed support bases, and deployed forces should be attacked with electromagnetic devices. Fixed support bases which carry out depot-level maintenance on military equipment offer a substantial payoff, as the concentration of computers in both automatic test equipment and administrative and logistic support functions offers a good return per expended weapon. Any site where more complex military equipment is concentrated should be attacked with electromagnetic weapons to render the equipment unserviceable and hence reduce fighting capability, and where possible also mobility of the targeted force. As discussed earlier in the context of EC, the ability of an electromagnetic weapon to achieve hard electrical kills against any nonhardened targets within its lethal footprint suggests that some target sites may require electromagnetic attack only to render them both undefended and nonoperational. Whether to expend conventional munitions on targets in this state would depend on the immediate military situation.

In summary, the use of electromagnetic weapons in strategic air attack campaign offers a potentially high payoff, particularly when applied to leadership, C3, and vital economic targets, all of which may be deprived of much of their function for substantial periods of time. The massed application of electromagnetic weapons in the opening phase of the campaign would introduce paralysis within the government, deprived of much of its information processing infrastructure, as well as paralysis in most vital industries. This would greatly reduce the capability of the target nation to conduct military operations of any substantial intensity.

Because conventional electromagnetic weapons produce negligible collateral damage in comparison with conventional explosive munitions, they allow the conduct of an effective and high tempo campaign without the loss of life which is typical of conventional campaigns. This will make the option of a strategic bombing campaign more attractive to a Western democracy, where mass media coverage of the results of conventional strategic strike operations will adversely affect domestic civilian morale. The long term effects of a sustained and concentrated strategic bombing campaign using a combination of conventional and electromagnetic weapons will be important. The cost of computer and communications infrastructure is substantial, and its massed destruction would be a major economic burden for any industrialized nation. In addition, it is likely that poor protection of stored data will add to further economic losses, as much data will be lost with the destroyed machines.

From the perspective of conducting an IW campaign, this method of attack achieves many of the central objectives sought. Importantly, the massed application of electromagnetic weapons would inflict attrition on an opponent's information processing infrastructure very rapidly, and this would arguably add a further psychological dimension to the potency of the attack. Unlike the classical IW model of Gibsonian CyberWar, in which the opponent can arguably isolate his infrastructure from hostile penetration, parallel or hyperwar style massed attack with electromagnetic bombs will be be extremely difficult to defend against.

OFFENSIVE COUNTER AIR (OCA) OPERATIONS USING ELECTROMAGNETIC BOMBSS

Electromagnetic bombs may be usefully applied to OCA operations. Modern aircraft are densely packed with electronics, and unless properly hardened, are highly vulnerable targets for electromagnetic weapons. The cost of the onboard electronics represents a substantial fraction of the total cost of a modern military aircraft, and therefore stock levels of spares will in most instances be limited to what is deemed necessary to cover operational usage at some nominal sortie rate. Therefore, electromagnetic damage could render aircraft unusable for substantial periods of time.

Attacking airfields with electromagnetic weapons will disable communications, air traffic control facilities, navigational aids, and operational support equipment, if these items are not suitably electromagnetic hardened. Conventional blast hardening measures will not be effective, as electrical power and fixed communications cabling will carry electromagnetic induced transients into most buildings. Hardened aircraft shelters may provide some measure of protection due to electrically conductive reinforcement embedded in the concrete, but conventional revetments will not. Therefore, OCA operations against airfields and aircraft on the ground should include the use of electromagnetic weapons as they offer the potential to substantially reduce hostile sortie rates.

MARITIME AIR OPERATIONS USING ELECTROMAGNETIC BOMBS

As with modern military aircraft, naval surface combatants are fitted with a substantial volume of electronic equipment, performing similar functions in detecting and engaging targets and warning of attack. As such they are vulnerable to electromagnetic attack, if not suitably hardened. Should they be hardened, volumetric, weight and cost penalties will be incurred.

Conventional methods for attacking surface combatants involve the use of saturation attacks by anti-ship missiles or coordinated attacks using a combination of ARMs and anti-ship missiles. The latter instance is where disabling the target electronically by stripping its antennae precedes lethal attack with specialized anti-ship weapons. An electromagnetic warhead detonated within lethal radius of a surface combatant will render its air defense system inoperable, as well as damaging other electronic equipment such as electronic countermeasures, electronic support measures and communications. This leaves the vessel undefended until these systems can be restored, which may or may not be possible on the high seas. Therefore launching an electromagnetic glidebomb onto a surface combatant, and then reducing it with laser- or television-guided weapons is an alternate strategy for dealing with such targets.

BATTLEFIELD AIR INTERDICTION OPERATIONS USING ELECTROMAGNETIC BOMBS

Modern land warfare doctrine emphasizes mobility, and maneuver warfare methods are typical for contemporary land warfare. Coordination and control are essential to the successful conduct of maneuver operations, and this provides another opportunity to apply electromagnetic weapons. Communications and command sites are key elements in the structure of such a land army, and these concentrate communications and computer equipment. Therefore they should be attacked with electromagnetic weapons, to disrupt the command and control of land operations. Should concentrations of armoured vehicles be found, these are also profitable targets for electromagnetic attack, as their communications and fire control systems may be substantially damaged or disabled as a result. A useful tactic would be initial attack with electromagnetic weapons to create a maximum of confusion, followed by attack with conventional weapons to take advantage of the immediate situation.

A STRATEGY OF GRADUATED RESPONSE

The introduction of non-nuclear electromagnetic bombs into the arsenal of a modern air force considerably broadens the options for conducting strategic campaigns. Clearly such weapons are potent force multipliers in conducting a conventional war, particularly when applied to EC, OCA, and strategic air attack operations. The massed use of such weapons would provide a decisive advantage to any nation with the capability to effectively target and deliver them. The qualitative advantage in capability so gained would provide a significant advantage even against a much stronger opponent not in the possession of this capability.

Electromagnetic weapons, however, open up less-conventional alternatives for the conduct of a strategic campaign, which derive from their ability to inflict significant material damage without inflicting visible collateral damage and loss of life. Western governments have been traditionally reluctant to commit to strategic campaigns, as the expectation of a lengthy and costly battle, with mass media coverage of its highly visible results, will quickly produce domestic political pressure to cease the conflict. An alternative is a strategy of graduated response (SGR). In this strategy, an opponent who threatens escalation to a full-scale war is preemptively attacked with electromagnetic weapons, to gain command of the electromagnetic spectrum and of the air. Selective attacks with electromagnetic weapons may then be applied against chosen strategic targets to force concession. Should these fail to produce results, more targets may be disabled by electromagnetic attack. Escalation would be sustained and graduated to produce steadily increasing pressure to concede the dispute. Air and sea blockade are complementary means via which pressure may be applied.

Because electromagnetic weapons can cause damage on a large scale very quickly, the rate at which damage can be inflicted can be very rapid, in which respect such a campaign will differ from the conventional, where the rate at which damage is inflicted is limited by the usable sortie rate of strategic air attack capable assets. (This constraint primarily results from limitations in numbers. Strategic air attack requires precision delivery of substantial payloads, and is thus most effectively performed with specialized bomber assets, such as the B-52, B-1, B-2, F-111, F-15E, F-117A, Tornado, or Su-24. These are typically more maintenance-intensive than less-complex multirole fighters, and this will become a constraint to the sortie rate achievable with a finite number of aircraft, assuming the availability of aircrew. While multirole fighters may be applied to strategic air attack, their typically lesser payload radius performance and lesser accuracy will reduce their effectiveness. In the doctrinal context, this can be directly related to existing USAF aerospace doctrine [AFM1-1] in several areas.)

Should blockade and the total disabling of vital economic assets fail to yield results, these may then be systematically reduced by conventional weapons, to further escalate the pressure. Finally, a full-scale conventional strategic air attack campaign would follow, to wholly destroy the hostile nation's warfighting capability.

Another situation where electromagnetic bombs may find useful application is in dealing with governments which actively implement a policy of state-sponsored terrorism or info-terrorism, or alternately choose to conduct a sustained low-intensity land warfare campaign. Again the SGR, using electromagnetic bombs in the initial phases, would place the government under significant pressure to concede. As a punitive weapon, electromagnetic devices are attractive for dealing with belligerent governments. Substantial economic, military, and political damage may be inflicted with a modest commitment of resources by their users, and without politically damaging loss of life.

Conclusions

Electromagnetic bombs are weapons of electrical mass destruction with applications across a broad spectrum of targets, spanning both the strategic and tactical. As such their use offers a very high payoff in attacking the fundamental information processing and communication facilities of a target system. The massed application of these weapons will produce substantial paralysis in any target system, thus providing a decisive advantage in the conduct of EC, OCA, and strategic air attack.

Because E-bombs can cause hard electrical kills over larger areas than conventional explosive weapons of similar mass, they offer substantial economies in force size for a given level of inflicted damage, and are thus a potent force multiplier for appropriate target sets.

The nonlethal nature of electromagnetic weapons makes their use far less politically damaging than that of conventional munitions, and therefore broadens the range of military options available.

This paper has included a discussion of the technical, operational, and targeting aspects of using such weapons, as no historical experience exists as yet upon which to build a doctrinal model. The immaturity of this weapons technology limits the scope of this discussion, and many potential areas of application have intentionally not been discussed. The ongoing technological evolution of this family of weapons will clarify the relationship between weapon size and lethality, thus producing further applications and areas for study.

E-bombs can be an affordable force multiplier for military forces which are under post-Cold War pressures to reduce force sizes, increasing both their combat potential and political utility in resolving disputes. Given the potentially high payoff deriving from the use of these devices, it is incumbent upon such military forces to appreciate both the offensive and defensive implications of this technology. It is also incumbent upon governments and private industry to consider the implications of the proliferation of this technology, and to take measures to safeguard their vital assets from possible future attack. Those who choose not to may become losers in any future wars.

Thanks to Dr. D. H. Steven for his insightful comment on microwave coupling and propagation; and to Professor C. S. Wallace, Dr. Ronald Pose, and Dr. Peter Leigh-Jones for their most helpful critique of the drafts. Thanks also to the RAAF Air Power Studies Centre and its then Director, Group Captain Gary Waters, for encouraging the author to investigate this subject in 1993.

Carlo Kopp is one of Australia's foremost proponents of Information Warfare. Born in Perth, Western Australia, he graduated with first class honors in Electrical Engineering in 1984 from the University of Western Australia. In 1996 he completed an M.S. in Computer Science and is currently working on a Ph.D. in the same discipline, at Monash University in Melbourne, Australia. He has over a decade of diverse industry experience, including the design of high-speed communications equipment, optical fiber receivers and transmitters, and communications equipment including embedded code, Unix computer workstation motherboards, graphics adaptors and chassis. More recently, he has consulted in Unix systems programming, performance engineering, and system administration. Actively publishing as a defense analyst in Australia's leading aviation trade journal, Australian Aviation, since 1980, he has become a locally recognized authority on the application of modern military technology to operations and strategy. His work on electronic combat doctrine, electromagnetic weapons doctrine, laser remote sensing, and signature reduction has been published by the Royal Australian Air Force since 1992.

AAP1000, *The Air Power Manual* (2nd ed.). RAAF APSC, Canberra, 1994.
    AAP1003, *The Law of Aerial Targeting, Operations Law for RAAF Commanders* (1st ed.). RAAF APSC, Canberra, 1994, chap. 8.
Basic Aerospace Doctrine of the United States Air Force, Air Force Manual
    1-1, vol. 1, March 1992.

Caird, R. S. et al. "Tests of an Explosive Driven Coaxial Generator." *Digest of Technical Papers, 5th IEEE Pulsed Power Conference.* New York: IEEE, 1985, p. 220.

Dixon, R. C. *Spread Spectrum Systems.* New York: John Wiley & Sons, 1984.

Fanthome, B. A. "MHD Pulsed Power Generation." *Digest of Technical Papers, 7th IEEE Pulsed Power Conference.* New York: IEEE, 1989, p. 483.

Flanagan, J. High-Performance MHD Solid Gas Generator, Naval Research Lab, Patent Application 4269637, May 1981.

Fowler, C. M., Garn, W. B., and Caird, R. S. 'Production of Very High Magnetic Fields by Implosion." *Journal of Applied Physics* 31 (3): 588-594, March 1960.

Fowler, C. M., Caird, R. S. "The Mark IX Generator." *Digest of Technical Papers, Seventh IEEE Pulsed Power Conference.* New York: IEEE, 1989, p. 475.

Fulghum, D. A. "ALCMs Given Non-Lethal Role." *Aviation Week & Space Technology,* February 22, 1993.

Glasstone, S. (ed.). *The Effects of Nuclear Weapons.* US AEC, April 1962 (rev. ed. February 1964).

Goforth, J. H., et al. "Experiments With Explosively Formed Fuse Opening Switches in Higher Efficiency Circuits." *Digest of Technical Papers, 7th IEEE Pulsed Power Conference.* New York: IEEE, 1989, p. 479.

Granatstein, V. L., Alexeff, I. *High Power Microwave Sources.* Boston: Artech House, 1987.

Herskowitz, D. "The Other SIGINT/ELINT." *Journal of Electronic Defence* April 1996.

Heoberling, R. F., Fazio, M. V. "Advances in Virtual Cathode Microwave Sources." *IEEE Transactions on Electromagnetic Compatibility* 34 (3): 252, August 1992.

International Countermeasures Handbook, 10th ed. "EW Systems: AN/Designated Hardware." Colorado: Cardiff Publishing, 1985, p. 86.

International Countermeasures Handbook, 14th ed. Colorado: Cardiff Publishing, 1989.

"USAF Looks for HPM SEAD Solution." *Journal of Electronic Defence,* September 1995, p. 36.

"Hughes to Build HPM SEAD Demonstrator," Journal of Electronic Defence, February 1996, p. 29.

Kirtland AFB, Phillips Laboratory. "High Energy Microwave Laboratory, Fact Sheet." USAF AFMC, 1994.

Kopp, C. "Command of the Electromagnetic Spectrum—An Electronic Combat Doctrine for the RAAF." Working Paper No. 8. Air Power Studies Centre, Royal Australian Air Force, Canberra, November 1992.

Kopp, C. "A Doctrine for the Use of Electromagnetic Pulse Bombs." Working Paper No. 15. Air Power Studies Centre, Royal Australian Air Force, Canberra, July 1993.

Kopp, C. "Australia's Kerkanya Based Agile Gliding Weapon," *Australian Aviation.* Canberra: Aerospace Publications, June 1996, p. 28.

Kraus, J. D. *Antennas,* 2nd ed. New York: McGraw-Hill, 1988.

McDonnell Douglas Corporation. Joint Direct Attack Munition (JDAM), unclassified briefing, 1995 (unpublished).

Micron Technology, Inc. *Micron DRAM Data Book,* 1992.

Motorola Semiconductor Products, Inc. "Motorola RF Device Data," 1983.

National Semiconductor Corporation. *CMOS Databook,* 1978.

Northrop-Grumman Corporation. B-2 Precision Weapons, unclassified briefing, September 1995 (unpublished).

Nano Pulse Industries. *NPI Local Area Network Products, SMD Transformers,* 1993.

Pergler, R. Joint Standoff Weapon System (JSOW), unclassified briefing, Texas Instruments, Inc., December 1994 (unpublished).

Ramo, S., et al. *Fields and Waves in Communications Electronics.* New York: John Wiley & Sons, 1965.

Reinovsky, R. E., Levi, P. S., and Welby, J. M. "An Economical, 2 Stage Flux Compression Generator System." *Digest of Technical Papers, 5th IEEE Pulsed Power Conference.* New York: IEEE, 1985, p. 216.

Sander, K. F., Reed, G. A. L. *Transmission and Propagation of Electromagnetic Waves.* Cambridge: Cambridge University Press, 1986.

Staines, G. W. "High Power Microwave Technology—Part IV: Military Applications of High Power Microwaves." Salisbury, DSTO ERL, EWD, 1993, draft paper.

Szafranski, R., "Parallel War and Hyperwar," in Schneider, B. R, Grinter L. E., *Battlefield of the Future, 21st Century Warfare Issues.* Maxwell AFB: Air University Press, September 1995, chap. 5.

Taylor, C. D., Harrison, C. W. "On the Coupling of Microwave Radiation to Wire Structures." *IEEE Transactions on Electromagnetic Compatibility* 34 (3): 183, August 1992.

Thode, L. E. "Virtual-Cathode Microwave Device Research: Experiment and Simulation," in Granatstein, V. L., Alexeff, I. *High Power Microwave Sources.* Boston: Artech House, 1987, chap. 14.

Van Eck, W. "Electromagnetic Radiation from Video Display Units: An Eavesdropping Risk." *Computers and Security,* 1985, p. 269.

Warden, J. A. III. "Air Theory for the Twenty-first Century," in Schneider, B. R., Grinter, L. E., *Battlefield of the Future, 21st Century Warfare Issues.* Maxwell AFB: Air University Press, September 1995, chap. 4.

Waters Gary. *Gulf Lesson One.* Canberra: Air Power Studies Centre, 1992.

White Consultants. "The EMP—A Triangular Impulse," No. 2.29 in *A Handbook Series on Electromagnetic Interference and Compatibility.* Maryland: Don White Consultants, 1978.

11

Hackers: The First
Information Warriors
in Cyberspace

THE BEST EXAMPLE of how computer crime can be waged through social engineering was provided by an ex-hacker whom I will call Jesse James. One afternoon in Newport Beach, California, he put on a demonstration to show how easy it was to rob a bank.

Jesse took his audience to a trash bin behind Pacific Bell, the Southern California Baby Bell service provider. Dumpster diving proved to be an effective means of social engineering because within minutes, an internal telephone company employee list was dredged out of the garbage. On it, predictably, were hand-written notes with computer passwords.

In the neighborhood was a bank, which shall go nameless. After some more dumpster diving, financial and personal profiles of wealthy bank customers surfaced. That was all Jesse said he needed to commit the crime.

At a nearby phone booth, Jesse used a portable computer with an acoustic modem to dial into the telephone company's computer. Jesse knew a lot about the telephone company's computers, so he made a few changes. He gave the pay phone a new number; that of one of the wealthy clients about whom he now knew almost everything. He also turned off the victim's phone with that same number. Jesse then called the bank and identified himself as Mr. Rich, an alias.

"How can we help you, Mr. Rich?"

"I would like to transfer $100,000 to this bank account number."

"I will need certain information."

"Of course."

"What is your balance?"

"About ____," he supplied the number accurately.

"What is your address?"

Jesse gave the address.

"Are you at home, Mr. Rich?"

"Yes."

"We'll need to call you back for positive identification."

"I understand. Thank you for providing such good security."

In less than a minute the phone rang.

"Hello. Rich here."

The money was transferred, then transferred back to Mr. Rich's account again, to the surprise and embarrassment of the bank. The money was returned and the point was made.

Other than the governments of the world, hackers can arguably be given the unenviable title of the first Information Warriors. Hackers seem to get blamed for just about everything these days. The phones go down—it's a hacker. There's a new computer virus—it's a hacker. Dan Quayle's credit report shows up on TV—it's a hacker.

According to most hackers, the media gets it all wrong. Lay people are still too grounded in snail-mail and big business; the Feds are still embroiled in paper-based bureaucracies. Even hackers themselves can't agree on the proper terminology to describe themselves.

Today, the nom-de-guerre "hacker" takes on a somewhat sinister connotation. Most people, when asked, say something like, "Isn't a hacker someone who breaks into computers?" Right or wrong, that's the image. Locked into the modern lexicon by popular usage, the term "hacker" may well be forever doomed to suffer such pejorative overtones. Hackers are often blamed for credit-card fraud and other more conventional crimes, in which the use of computers were merely incidental. As one would imagine, hackers are not happy about such misperceptions, blaming what they term "clueless Feds and the idiot police" for destroying the original ethos of hacking.

To begin with, the term hacker is derived from the word "hackney," which means drudgery, "hackneyed" means "worn out from overuse; trite." A writer who knocks out lackluster words for pay is a hack. An old, worn out horse is a hack. A taxi driver is a hack who drives a hack. How about the golf hack who can't score below 100 even with two Mulligans a side and an occasional foot wedge?

Anyone can be a hack and the connotations aren't always negative. Most of us are hackers in one way or another. The car enthusiast who tinkers and tunes his car every weekend is a hack. He constantly wants to improve his knowledge and techniques, sharing them with others at car meets or races. He relentlessly pursues the perfect engine, or transmission, or whatever else makes a car tick. A hacker, regardless of area of interest, is curious by nature. Rop Gonggrijp, a well-known ex-hacker and editor of *Hacktic*, a Dutch computer hacker magazine, said it this way.

Pretend you're walking down the street, the same street you have always walked down. One day, you see a big wooden or metal box with wires coming out of it sitting on the sidewalk where there had been none.

Many people won't even notice. Others might say, "Oh, a box on the street." A few might wonder what it is and what it does and then move on. The hacker, the true hacker, will see the box, stop, examine it, wonder about it, and spend mental time trying to figure it out. Given the proper circumstances, he might come back later to look closely at the wiring or even be so bold as to open the box. Not maliciously, just out of curiosity.

The hacker wants to know how things work[1].

And that is exactly what pure hackers say. They only want to know more about computers: the ins and the outs, the undocumented features, how can they push the system to its outer envelope and make it do things the original designers never envisioned. Hackers try to cram ten megabytes onto a 1.4 megabyte disk.

The original generation of computer hackers could be said to include John Von Neumann (the acknowledged father of the digital computer), Alan Turing, and Grace Hopper, among other computable notables. These pioneers pushed the limits of computer science. However, most hackers envolved out of academia in the 1960s and 1970s, when terminals were connected to distant huge computers that filled rooms with vacuum tubes, core memories, and immense power supplies.

The undisputed catalyst for mass-market hacking was the introduction of the microprocessor by Intel, and the subsequent development of the personal desktop computer. Millions of PCs and Apples were bought by businesses, students, and former and future hackers during the incubation phases of the Global Network and Computers Everywhere. The nascent personal computer field was a petri dish full of ripe agar solution encouraging unbounded creativity, learning . . . and hacking. But then the money motive kicked in, which according to Rop meant the loss of true hacking creativity. Some hackers soon became budding millionaires, motivated only by the search for the Almighty Buck.

Over the years, new technology and the Global Network allowed a new breed of hackers to emerge. For the hacking phenomenon to increase logarithmically, one last piece of the equation was needed and was already well on its way to market: Infinite Connectivity. How do we get all of these computers to talk to each other? Novell took care of that with the proliferation of inexpensive Local Area Networks, or LANs, for PCs in the office. Modems allowed simple computer-to-computer conversations, as well as the creation of thousands of database and bulletin boards accessible by anyone with inexpensive equipment. Wide area networks (WANs) began to connect through the phone companies and the switch, entwining the globe in a spider's web of communications based upon systems with such uninviting names as X.25, ISDN, TCP/IP, OSI, T1, and 10 Base T. Such interconnectedness now gives anyone who wants it access to the Global Network via an incomprehensively complex matrix of digital highways. The hacker-purist, however, would likely prefer the word *free*way.

Hackers, long confined to their lone desktop PC and its limited communications capabilities, knew there was a world to explore out there—and explore they did. They traveled throughout Cyberspace and the growing Global Network, and found that the computers at the other end of the line were indeed fascinating targets of investigation. Every imaginable type of computer system was no more than a phone call away and there were thousands of others willing to help you on your way to conquering the next system. You could talk to a VAX over at the hospital, a 3090 over at the IRS, or the Tandems running the credit card division over at American Express. That euphoria, that sense of power, had been given to anyone with a couple of hundred dollars.

Billsf, a thirty-six-year-old post-Woodstock American expatriate and self-described phone phreak who now calls Amsterdam home, speaks for many from the first generation of hackers. He says the thrill is in getting into the system and doing what "they" say can't be done. For him voyeurism is not part of the equation. Of breaking into a computer he says, "The first time it's a hack. The second time it's a crime." In his mind that legitimizes and proves the innocence of the hunt. He continues to defend hackers who enter computers without permission. "If there is unused computing power out there, it should be free. If I have the smarts to get it, I should be able to use it." He uses the same argument to justify phone phreaking, where the aim is to figure out how the phone systems work and then make calls for free. "If there's an open phone line, I should be able to use it for free. Otherwise it's going to waste."

Victims and potential victims of computer hackers are not so generous. The most common accusation is that hackers are nothing more than glorified criminals. The debate often goes like this:

"It's like my house. If I don't invite you in, don't come in or it's called breaking and entering and I'll call the police."

"It's not the same thing. What if I went into your house, ate an apple, and watched some TV. Then I make two phone calls and went to the bathroom. Before I left, I put $2.14 on the counter to cover the cost of the apple and the phone calls and water. I was just looking around. That should not be illegal."

"Yes it should! And is. The same laws should apply for you coming into my computers uninvited."

"What if my presence kept your house from being robbed? Would that make a difference?"

"You still invaded my privacy. I would feel violated. My house belongs to me and so does my computer. Please stay out."

"My entering or not entering your computers is a matter of ethics—not the law. It is up to my sense of responsibility to keep a clean house when I'm in your computer."

Breaking into a computer system, cracking its password scheme, or learning how to beat down the front door, is often referred to as "cracking" in distinction to "hacking." This is far from a universal definition, as there are many dissident hacker factions, but I'm going to use it anyway. Hackers, like any other group, come in many flavors but despite their claims to the contrary, they can be accurately described by category. Let's examine a few of them.

Amateur Hacking

I know that term will offend some, but amateur hacking is a part-time effort and does not provide income. The term amateur hacker, or perhaps semi-professional hacker, is not a derogatory one nor does it belittle their skills. It merely distinguishes them from professional hackers who utilize the same techniques and tools to make a living, either legally or illegally.

Consider the following profile of a typical hacker as offered by some of their own. Hackers are

- mostly males between twelve and twenty-eight
- smart but did lousy in school
- misfits and misunderstood
- from dysfunctional families
- and of course, they can't get a date

I know a lot of hackers, and in many cases, they tend to work and play on the edges of society. Some hackers—apparently too many—"consume their own body weight in controlled pharmaceutical substances," according to one underground member who himself imbibes in same.

According to Dr. Mich Kabay, Director of Education for the National Computer Security Association, some hackers could be suffering from a clinical narcissist personality disorder. He suggests that the classic hacker personality is anathemetic to society, characterized by such traits as:

- a grandiose sense of self-importance
- preoccupation with fantasies of unlimited success
- need for constant attention and admiration
- strong negative responses to threats to self-esteem
- feelings of entitlement
- interpersonal exploitiveness
- alternating feelings of overidealization and devaluation
- a lack of empathy

No, not all hackers are nuts nor do they universally suffer from clinical personality disorders. They are a varied group but they do tend to think and live "on the edge." According to Dr. Percy Black, Professor of Psychology at Pace University in New York, "they're just kids," no matter what their age. He explains that malicious hacking may come from "inadequate endogenous stimulation." Simply put, either their home life, diet, or social life is such that their brains don't secrete enough "get-excited-feel-good" chemicals to create an internal feeling of satisfaction in any other way.

Some say that Ian Murphy, a 36-year-old former hacker with the nom-de-hack Captain Zap, is the perfect example of such a chemo-social imbalance. His claims to fame include federal prosecution for, among other things, electronically "stealing" computers and breaking into White House computers. His stories stretch the imagination. Murphy was featured in a 1992 *People* magazine profile and is, to say the very least, a loud, personable character. He has graced the cover of *Information Week*, a popular trade magazine, and claims to make over $500,000 a year as a hacker-advisor to corporate America.

As one probes the history and behavior of hackers, we see that a gang mentality quickly envolved. A subculture of people with common interests gathered in their favorite electronic watering hole to "hang out." BBSs and the Global Network provided the tools to allow anyone to organize a database, add a modem, and start a digital party. The term "virtual community" has come into vogue, referring to a common electronic location in Cyberspace where kindred spirits can meet. As Cyberspace developed, cliques evolved and cybernetic hierarchies formed. The teenage 414 Gang earned their rep—and national attention—for their penetrations of the Sloan-Kettering Cancer Center and Los Alamos military computers in 1982.

Competition among teenagers being what it is, whether on skateboards or with the opposite sex, it is only enhanced in Cyberspace. On hacker group might feel challenged by another's claim, so they would then have to go out and better it.

Membership in a particular group quickly becomes a status symbol, one that has to be earned. Ostracism from a group is considered a major embarrassment in the Global Network. So competing hacking groups popped up all over the country, and indeed the world. Sherwood Forest, Anarchy Inc., Bad Ass MF, Chaos Computer Club, Damage Inc., Circle of Death, The Punk Mafia, Lords of Chaos, Phreaks Against Geeks, Phreaks against Phreaks Against Geeks, Elite Hackers Guild, and Feds R Us were but a few of the estimated thirty thousand private BBSs operating in 1990.[2]

As competition in Cyberspace grew, the country's networks and computers became the playground for all genres of hackers and cybernauts. Occasionally the competition got out of hand, as it did in the case of the Legion of Doom versus the Masters of Destruction. From 1989 through the end of 1991, a so-called Hacker War was waged on the battle field of corporate America's information infrastructure.

On July 8, 1992, five New York hackers who belonged to the MoD, an organized hacking group, were indicted in Federal Court on eleven separate serious charges. (Depending upon who you listen to, MoD stands for Masters of Destruction, Deceit, or Deception.) What adds intrigue to this story is the claim that other hackers were responsible for turning the MoD in to the authorities. The Federal indictment said that the five defendants, who pleaded not guilty at their July 16, 1992 arraignment, conspired to commit a range of computer crimes, including

- Eavesdropping on phone conversations from public switch networks
- Eavesdropping on data transmissions
- Intercepting data transmissions
- Owning computer cracking hardware and software equipment
- Reprogramming phone company computer switches
- Stealing passwords
- Selling passwords

- Stealing credit profiles
- Selling credit profiles
- Destroying computer systems
- Causing losses of $370,000[3]

One of the defendants was quoted as saying the group could "destroy people's lives or make them look like saints." All told there were eleven counts with up to fifty-five years in prison and $2.75 million in fines if the defendants were found guilty. All five have since pled guilty or lost their court cases. Their jail sentences are intended to be an example to other would-be hackers.

The Defendants named were

- Phiber Optik (aka Mark Abene)
- Outlaw (aka Julio Fernandez)
- Corrupt (aka John Lee)
- Acid Phreak (aka Elias Ladopoulos) and
- Scorpion (aka Paul Stira)

Aged eighteen to twenty-two, they all come from lower to lower-middle class neighborhoods in Brooklyn, the Bronx, and Queens in New York City.

"That's absurd," a defensive Mark Abene (aka Phiber Optik) told me. "There is no group in New York and there is no computer underground. I have never been a member of any organized group." Phiber vehemently denied his involvement. However, Abene, after pleading guilty to reduced charges, was sentenced on November 3, 1993 to a year and a day for his escapades. Emmanual Goldstein, editor of *2600*, called it a "dark day for hackers."

Chris Goggans (aka Eric Bloodaxe) and Scott Chasin (aka Doc Holiday) disagree. They are ex-members of a rival hacker group, the Legion of Doom. Although other members of the LoD have periodically vacationed at government expense, neither of these two have ever been prosecuted. In mid-1991, they disavowed their hacking days and started a security

consulting company, Comsec Data, which survived less than a
year. Business was bad. Corporate America could not bring
itself to hire ex-hackers to work on their security problems,
and the security community loudly ostracized them. The
founders were young and inexperienced in business, and the
press was generally negative.

But during the demise of their company, the Comsec Data
boys were busy. Very busy. They were collecting evidence
against their underground adversaries, the Masters of Destruction and especially Phiber Optic. Evidence, they claim, that
they turned in to the authorities.

According to Chris Goggans, twenty-three, his first contact
with Phiber was back in early 1989, when he heard that Phiber
Optik was claiming to be a member of the Legion of Doom.
After recommendations from another member of LoD, Phiber
was able to prove his technical knowledge and worth and was
permitted into the group. Soon thereafter, Phiber and Goggans
agreed to share some information: Goggans knew how to
access the Nynex switches, bypassing all security and authentication. Phiber knew the syntax and knew his way around the
host mainframe computers themselves. A deal was struck to
trade information.

Goggans says Phiber never lived up to his end of the
bargain—a big no-no in underground cyberspace. "He told us
to go to hell." As a result, the LoD threw Phiber Optic out in
mid-1989. Phiber denies much of this account, saying he
wasn't a member of LoD, just an occasional acquaintance. But
according to Goggans, Phiber Optic began an electronic smear
campaign against him, Chasin, and others connected with the
LoD as a result of the public embarrassment. The sophomoric
pranksterism included such antics as placing menacing messages and commentary on BBSs.

Enter Corrupt.

A new BBS called the 5th Amendment, or 5A, was created
by Micron (an anonymous hacker) and Chasin in December

1989, with access limited to the "cream of the crop of hackers." Phiber was not invited. In February 1990, Corrupt was admitted to 5A because of his knowledge of holes in VMS systems and security. In April 1990, a number of 5A and ex-LoD hackers were illegally using a telephone voice conference bridge owned by a local Texas oil company. Anyone with the right phone number can dial in and participate in a conferenced conversation—a very common way to rip off big companies.

Alfredo de la Fe, eighteen, who was convicted on June 19, 1992, for trafficking in stolen PBX codes, agrees with other hackers who were in on that conversation that someone broke into the conference and said, "Yo! This is Dope Fiend. MoD," with a thick ethnic accent. Apparently someone responded with, "Hang up, you stupid nigger." The caller was Corrupt, who happens to be black, and who took great offense. He had been "dissed" in public and revenge was necessary. However, it may be that Corrupt misunderstood, because another member of the group, who actually is white, had been dubbed SuperNigger.

The wording distinction is important, because Phiber Optik insists that his future problems with Goggans, Chasin, and their Texas Legion of Doom friends were racially motivated. "They're just a bunch of racist rednecks," Phiber told me in a four-hour telephone interview that his lawyer advised against.

Goggans bristles at the suggestion. "We never even knew that Corrupt was black." Other hackers present on the call maintain that the racial epithet was only a "friendly" insult. Nothing racial, just kidding, if you will. Others say that the New York-based Masters of Destruction took the comment as fighting words.

Corrupt apparently sought revenge.

Shortly after the conference call, the LoD, their cohorts, and their neighbors began receiving harassing calls. Goggans says, "They (the MoD) were pulling our phone records, finding our friends, and then their friends." LoD's underground reputation grew, apparently in part because the growing MoD population (fourteen on August 1, 1990, according to the written History of the MoD) were attacking computers and leaving messages that laid blame on the Legion of doom. Phiber swears that the name MoD was an insult aimed at the LoD, intended to make fun of them. "Goggans is a strangely deluded kid from Texas. Besides, he's an asshole."

The animosity, Phiber says, came from the LoD's racial slurs against MoD members, only one of whom does not belong to a minority. Plus, "they weren't very good and bragged and took credit for anything and everything. Just rednecks who should keep out of our way." Goggans says the attacks increased in early 1991 because of the escalating tensions between the two groups. Insults were hurled at each other over BBSs, E-mail, and voice-mail circuits.

Goggans further charges that the MoD changed his long distance carrier from Sprint to AT&T, to make access to his billing records easier. Goggans says MoD bragged about the hack and claimed, "We rule MicroLink!" (Microlink is a subnet of Southwestern Bell's network.) The 1992 Federal indictment specifically charges MoD with tampering with Houston-based phone switches, and Southwestern Bell alleges $370,000 in damages. The indictment says the MoD "altered calling features, installed back door programs, and made other modifications." (This should sound familiar: malicious software being put into a switch.)

Credit reports were the next weapon allegedly used by the MoD against the Texans. Chasin, his mother, her friends, and neighbors were all victimized by MoD's access to credit databases. TRW admits that its computers were penetrated and that credit reports were improperly taken. The Federal indictment includes details surrounding 176 separate credit reports that the MoD had in their possession, not to mention database access codes. Goggans says that during this phase of the conflict, "they would call us and admit what they had done. . . . It had gotten totally out of hand. The MoD were hurting innocent people and we had to do something about it. No one else could have."

According to Chasin, "They are electronic terrorists."

Corrupt's own words seem to explain the hacker paranoia that inflamed this incident. "It's not just winning the game that counts, but making sure that everyone else loses," he wrote into the MoDNet computers.

De la Fe, an acquaintance of Corrupt, claims, "MoD was listening to the Feds and their computers. They were planning to wreck government computers." Morton Rosenburg, eighteen, was sentenced to eight months in prison for purchasing passwords to TRW computers from MoD's Corrupt and Outlaw and using them to illegally access credit reports. He says that the MoD was highly organized in its efforts. "The MoD had printed up price lists for passwords." Conflict, another hacker, adds, "Knowledgewise they were incredible—but with a bad attitude. They harassed hackers everywhere." Chasin says, "They were into 'outing' hackers."

Phiber says about Goggans, "He's a pain in the ass. This is none of his damn business. He should stay out of other people's lives."

As a result of the harassment they felt they were receiving from the MoD, Goggans and Chasin documented the Mod's electronic activities—in effect, snooping on the snoopers in Cyberspace. They turned this information over to security officers at the regional Bell Operating Companies (RBOCs), and the Secret Service and FBI were brought in to investigate. Tymnet (a notoriously weak communications network, according to hackers) was also notified by Goggans, as were a number of other companies who were allegedly the victims of Phiber and crew.

"We gave the Feds everything," Goggans claims. "We had all of the files, the dates, the times, the logs. We could have responded electronically but we decided to play by the rules. We called the authorities." The FBI will only admit they began their case in May 1991, the same time that Southwestern Bell and Goggans called them.

Goggans claims that in order to find out more about the MoD, he penetrated the weak security of a supposedly impenetrable MoD computer. He gave the FBI, Tymnet, and the Computer Emergency Response Team (CERT) MoD's lists of Tymnet passwords and IDs for Goddard Space Center, Trans Union Credit, CBI-Equifax (another major credit database), MIT, and a host of other targets.

According to the Federal indictment handed down in New York, many of the passwords found in the possession of the defendants were collected by "sniffing the switch" or monitoring data communications circuits on Tymnet. Since the defendants allegedly had access to the Tymnet computers, they were able to eavesdrop on the Tymnet network and record packets of information, including the passwords and access codes of thousands of users.

After cooperating with federal investigators, Goggans was on the receiving end of what he considers bodily threats. On Sept. 7, 1991, Phiber sent E-mail to Goggans saying, "You need to get the shit beat out of you. Count on it," and "Never know when someone will plant a bat in your skull." Other threats allegedly included a promise to give Goggans a trip home from a computer conference in a body bag. Phiber admits making the threats, but says in his defense, "he sent me an ad for an LoD T-shirt and I went totally crazy. It was just a joke." Some joke.

The so-called LoD-MoD hacker war was over. Rosenberg was put away even though he once claimed, "I stay out of jail because I do too much LSD. They're afraid to lock me up." Phiber Optik claimed innocence even though his codefendant Corrupt pled guilty to many of the eleven indictments. I received a copy of Corrupt's handwritten confession, which further showed how much control some hackers have had over the phone networks and computers. He admits:

I agreed to possess in excess of fifteen passwords, which permitted me to gain access to various computer systems, including all systems mentioned in the indictment and others. I did not have authorization to access these systems. I knew at the time that what I did was wrong.

I intentionally gained access to what I acknowledge are Federal-interest computers and I acknowledge that work had to be done, to improve the security of these systems, which was necessitated by my unauthorized access.

I was able to monitor data exchange between computer systems and by doing so intentionally obtained more passwords, identifications, and other data transmitted over Tymnet and other networks.

I was part of a group called MoD.

The members of the group exchanged information, including passwords, so that we could gain access to computer systems which we were not authorized to access.

I got passwords by monitoring Tymnet, calling phone company employees and pretending to be a computer technician, and using computer programs to steal passwords.

I participated in installing programs in computer systems that would give the highest level of access to members of MoD who possessed the secret password.

I participated in altering telephone computer systems to obtain free calling services, such as conference calling and free billing, among others.

Finally, I obtained credit reports, telephone numbers, and addresses, as well as other information about individual people, by gaining access to information and credit reporting services. I acknowledge that on November 5, 1991, I obtained passwords by monitoring Tymnet.[4]

One of the saddest comments to come from this entire affair was made by MoD member Outlaw, who said, "It was only a game. Not a war."

Inner-City Hacking

Inner cities are truly a study in disaster. This disaster, though, is no longer the exclusive province of any particular racial or ethnic group. Our inner cities have become melting pots, where the populace—regardless of race, color, or creed—behaves as if all hope is gone. When a ten-year-old boy carries a gun to defend his drug-dealing turf and sees little chance of survival past his teens, he has lost the ability to function in society. He sees himself as the victim of a government and a culture that have abandoned him. Why should he care about anything?

Now imagine the same angry inner-city kid, armed with a computer instead of a gun. The inner-city hacker, unlike his middle-class brethren, is angry over his social condition, intensely dislikes "the system," and has generally been powerless over his station in life—until now. For the first time he has the power and ability to affect people and events by remote control. The power of Cyberspace is in his hands.

The inner-city hacker has the same knowledge and power as his technoprecedents, regardless of the poor state of education in his neighborhood. He has little or no social conscience and the specter of jail is hardly a deterrent. It might even be an improvement over his current situation. I have had conversations with these hackers and their sense of arrogance, disdain, and alienation echoes that of the social dissidents of the 1960s. However, many radicals in the sixties were middle-class kids rebelling against the comfortable lifestyle of their parents. If things got tough, they could always go back to their well-manicured ranch-style house. Inner-city hackers have nowhere else to go. So, Cyberspace is an ideal destination. It gives them a new place to live and a turf of their own. It is the only place where they have power and can make the rules.

Eurohacking

Eurohackers offer a unique perspective. From my interactions with them, I find them to be more worldly, and enlightened than their American counterparts. This observation is consistent with most Americans' image of the sophisticated European. Eurohackers are generally motivated much more by philosophical or political concerns than by the American hacker's desire for profit or simple revenge. Cliff Stoll's Hanover Hacker in *Cuckoo's Egg* was linked to the East German Stasi and the KGB. The world's best computer hackers are supposed to be in Amsterdam, Holland. I went to find out if that was true.

I was introduced to a hacker group portrayed on a late-1991 Geraldo Rivera show.[5] Rop lived, with a couple of other hackers, in a reasonably-sized apartment overlooking Balmar, a suburb of Amsterdam. Computers, phones, wires, and shelves full of three-ring binders dominated one wall of the large living room. Attached to the phones were various electronic contraptions which, I would learn, allowed me to phone home for free—on whose dime I do not know.

The wallful of books, as it turned out, were chronicles of their activities: logs, schematics, accumulated information on computer and phone systems worldwide, just about anything you'd need to break into any computer anywhere. I certainly did not expect this level of organization. As it turns out, though, Rop and his small group of friends are not part of any large, coordinated hacking effort. They speak to and share information with hackers around the world, but they basically work alone.

Rop—an ex-hacker—is the philosopher of the group, spry-small in stature but big in the ideas and ethos departments. His sandy-blond shoulder-length hair was the only sign of antiestablishmentarianism. "I don't drink, I don't smoke anything, and I don't do drugs," he boasted.

Rop and I ended up with strongly diverging viewpoints throughout our discussions. For instance, he strenuously argued that hacking is a way of life and not a crime. In his view, society has got it all wrong. Despite our differing views, I found Rop to be a most likable person, with a tremendous body of knowledge. He was the promoter behind the "Hacking at the End of the Universe" convention in August 1993, which was attended by several hundred hackers from around the world. They camped in a field at eighteen feet below sea level to discuss the latest and greatest, the law, the philosophy of Cyberspace, and anything else that popped up.

One of the other hackers present was a tall, thin, pale American expatriate from Berkeley. Billsf is and has been a phone phreak since the 1960s, when he was twelve. He looked and acted the part of an extra from a Love-In, with long black hair and an attitude that reflected the naive altruism of a free Haight-Ashbury concert. He told me that his middle-class father was politically to the right of Attila the Hun and that he prefers the freer lifestyle in Holland to that of his homeland.

If I had to peg Billsf with a political label, it would be that of the anarchist. But basically, he is what I would call lost: the Great American Dream was never right for him. There had to be bigger, better, and greener pastures out there and he went in search of them. From all appearances, he found what he was looking for in Europe and Cyberspace.

Billsf, Rop, and the other hackers present were as congenial as could be. On many occasions we simply agreed to disagree and then moved on. The Euroview of hacking is much richer and more complex than that of their American counterparts. Indeed, in many cases, they view American hacking with varying degrees of disdain.

My questions about "good" (nondestructive)-hacking versus "bad" (malicious)-hacking struck a dissonant chord to Rop, for whom there is no substantial difference. "First of all," Rop said, "you must know that hacking is value-free. When you speak of good and bad, it really doesn't mean anything within the context of true hacking. Hacking is beating technology. The Germans have a phrase for it: 'Treating technology without respect.' . . . It's a system of laws as flaws," Rop said cryptically. "Breaking into a computer should not be a crime! No one gets hurt and we all learn something. But hurting people with the data or hurting the computer should be illegal. Having a negative impact should be illegal."

"You have a lot of benign people going to jail," Rop said, obviously displeased. "They're not real criminals. They are explorers who are being persecuted for thinking." These political overtones became increasingly clear as we talked further. Rop and Billsf and their comrades live by a code of ethics that is self-restrained, occasionally inconsistent, and generally difficult to pinpoint. They continuously refer to individual responsibility and the need for each person to determine what is right and what is wrong, and to act upon those beliefs. To these Eurohackers, the system is self-balancing. Anarchy can well be tolerated in Cyberspace because most people act responsibly.

According to Rop, the U.S. establishment has an antihacker attitude that borders on paranoia, which makes hacking on U.S. systems all the more attractive. Just like the school bully who always picks on the whiniest kid in class, Eurohackers "pick" on U.S. computers because, instead of just doing something about the problem, in their eyes we constantly whine about it.

The phone companies are a good example, they maintain. The U.S. phone system is the biggest and best, and therefore the most fun to hack-phreak. Although AT&T, Tymnet, and the other public carriers get real annoyed when their piece of Cyberspace is invaded, the hackers say they are just using empty wires not filled with either voice or data. It's not like the phone companies are losing money.

Sometimes, hackers go into systems for kicks, just because they know it is annoying. An avid Eurohacker described to me how he likes to go into military computers and use key words that trigger intelligence agents. "Bothering the military is loads of fun. It really seem to get to them. For example, if you get into a classified computer, make it look like you know more than you really do. Use some secret phrases, or talk about the

President or Star Wars or something like that. If you do it right, you'll trip their listening devices and then you can just laugh at them."

In an almost total turnaround the hackers denied any misdeeds on their part. "They treat us like some kind of national security threat."

As the hours passed, I learned that not only were the social mores of the Eurohackers more worldly than those of American hackers but that they were more politically aware, committed to using their talents as a powerful tool in creating change. A modern version of the sixties ethos was dominant, as was the fervent belief that the "system" needs a major overhaul. The biggest surprise of all was that they believed it was okay, in many cases, to interfere with computer and communications systems with which they disagreed politically.

One hacker told me, "I would love to get a group together and crash the entire Justice Department. I see nothing wrong with trashing the U.S. government's computers so the U.S. has to start over again." Another said, "It would be great fun to shave a couple of hundred points off of the Dow and see what happens." He then curled up in a ball in his chair and amused himself with imagining the outcome. So, are Eurohackers a national security threat? Do they work for anyone? Are they benign, or are they causing trouble far beyond what is reported in the general press?

Eurohacker politics could be viewed as libertarian, even anarchistic. "Why should I follow a law that, when broken, doesn't hurt anyone else?" is a foundation of Rop's philosophy. I believe that he believes what he says, but I also see a slight twinkle in his eye that might suggest he carries his point to an extreme for effect. I think he may even see a little bit of the antihacker's side—just a little.

"Everyone hacks TRW. It's a big game." Rop sat back and laughed a mocking laugh; he just can't believe how poor the security is. "We all know that credit records in the U.S. are totally worthless because of hackers." The Dutch hackers maintain that the lax security policies of credit databases make them ideal targets for criminal hackers. "We got into one database and we found a list of credit cards that were assigned to people who were part of the witness protection program. It was all there. Names, addresses, aliases. The government got so freaked they pulled it all and changed databases."

So breaking in shouldn't be illegal? "Who cares if it's legal? The Mafia can do the same thing. And you think they care if it's illegal? The bad guys are going to do it anyway." They have a point. The Eurohackers seem to be warning us about how their skills can be used by truly motivated and dangerous Information Warriors with specific criminal goals.

But couldn't hackers do the same thing, just for "fun"? "Sure we could and maybe we should. It would wake a lot of people up," Rop said, adding that this was his opinion alone. "There are many instances where breaking into a computer is almost a necessity. And then once you're in, there are many good reasons to do a lot of illegal things. . . . There are a lot of bad companies. Companies that make things bad for people and for the planet." Rop focused on what might be called the military-industrial complex for his examples of bad companies. "Chemical companies that make poison gases for warfare; I see no reason not to take down their computers."

Nowhere did Rop suggest that he has, is now, or is planning to implement his concepts. There wasn't even an indication of a threat to carry any of them out. To him it is pure intellectual speculation, and Rop does not appear to be the kind of person bent on vengeance, malice, or misguided high jinx. According to him, he is merely an ex-hacker with a system of beliefs that are contrary to many laws.

The motives of Eurohackers seem to be purer than those of their American counterparts who sell and buy credit card numbers. "I don't get my jollies by harassing people," said one of Rop's group. "That's not the kick. Breaking in and looking around; that's the object." Rop cynically added, "There are some machines much more interesting than people to talk to."

On the other hand, Rop warns that "there are a lot of

mercenaries out there, people who live by the credo "hacking for dollars." (The Masters of Destruction appear to fit into that category.) He added, "I am sure I could find a team of people to do specific things to computers. They could target the military computers, the draft computers, anybody's. . . . Putting a team together can be done." Rop would not say how such a group would be organized or who might be a candidate for membership. However, he and his friends did say that if they were approached by the right person with the right goals and with the right sense of right and wrong, then maybe it might be a group worth joining.

Another hacker with strong sociopolitical beliefs smiled broadly. "I could see a real nice virus whose only purpose in life is to waste military computers." He smiled even further. "Yeah . . . that would be great."

The Eurohackers to whom I spoke did not have anyone else's agenda in mind. They did not have mastery over an enemy as a goal, nor were they power hungry. Instead, they feel that if they or others were to so choose, they could dramatically disrupt the social fabric of Western society. The hackers said it would be great fun to sit back and watch the resulting chaos, how people and society coped. Then, they say, society would be better off for the experience.

"You see," said on of the more radical ones, "computers are to be used as a tool for revolution. It is up to us to stir up the social system. It's not working. We have to make the waves."

We discussed a few hypothetical situations. In one, the computerized food distribution system is forced down, as is transportation. Food is not getting into major urban areas and Los Angeles, for example, is teeming.

"It's a great social experiment. After a few days the farmers will bring in their trucks and set up on the streets, real farmer's markets. In a few weeks everyone will get used to the new way of shopping for food." But can we reasonably expect such a rational social response to such inconvience, if not deprivation? I think not. Our altruistic hackers are being naive.

In another instance, it was suggested that the heavily-computerized broadcast industry might be a viable target for social revolutionaries. They agreed, partially. "Take out the television. The radio can stay. It's not as harmful." NBC-TV in New York, for example, uses a massive Novell network for scheduling. No schedule means no ads, which would hit GE's pocketbook. Throwing the system out of whack might just be considered great fun. Get to the antennas . . . or the satellites. . . .

It's hard for me to imagine getting many of the drug-crazed American hackers I know to organize cogent arguments, much less put forth a minority political platform, but Rop did successfully apply some Boolean logic to define himself.

"I am a computer revolutionary. If a revolutionary is a terrorist, then a computer revolutionary is a computer terrorist and therefore I am a computer terrorist."

Professional Hacking

Why have I spent so much time on hackers? Because as bad as some hackers have been, and as bad as hackers can be, I believe hackers are merely endemic of the real problems that our economic and technical infrastructure face today. Hackers have shown the chinks in the electronic armor. Their pioneering activities have defined Cyberspace as much as have the billions of dollars worth of fiber networks which comprise the Global Network. They have penetrated the establishment's technocastle and crossed the moat with little resistance. They have shown that the walls that protect our resources are not as solid as the managers of the information would have us believe. As we will see, threats to the fabric of Western society come from places that we might not have known about without the hackers. This is not a defense of hacking activities, but one could certainly make a case that hackers have made us aware of issues about which we otherwise might still be blithely ignorant.

No, the issue is not hackers, but hacking.

Hacking is one of the tools which the Information Warrior will use against his targets. We should be concerned with their capabilities, the skills and techniques used by hackers in the pursuance of their particular interests, whatever they may be—criminal or political, educational or for-profit, malicious or benign. Bruce Sterling ended *The Hacker Crackdown* with seven words that cannot be more explicit: "It is the end of the amateurs."[6]

Simply put: if a bunch of kids have the ability to cause the kinds of damage they have, how much damage can dedicated, well-financed—perhaps mercenary—professionals cause at their master's bequest? You will soon discover the disquieting answer to that question.

Declaring War on France

Winn Schwartau

Late one night in early 1995 I got a call from a drunk hacker or two or three.

"We want your help," they said.

"Doing what?" I asked while clicking on the Ace of Spades.

"We want a lot of press. Cameras. Can you bring CNN?"

I'm used to the occasional rants of hackers so I remained nonplussed. "That depends. What are you going to do?"

"Declare war on France."

Now they had my attention. In retribution for endless spying against the U.S., and because the "spineless pukes in Washington won't do anything about it," they felt that as patriotic Americans, it was their job to get back at the French.

"You're kidding," I tried to convince them.

"No, no, no," they countered. "We've already established beachheads in their computers." They explained that they had already hacked into pharmaceutical companies, aircraft companies, computer firms, government sites, and could get back in any time they wanted. "We want to do it on national television."

National TV, I thought. Good choice. "Listen," I responded, "I don't know if what you're planning is against the law or not; I'll find out. But, you might care about the repercussions." They didn't want to hear about them, but I insisted.

"The FBI won't do anything," they declared. "They have no jurisdiction over France." Drunk can make you a little less than coherent.

"That's not really the point," I countered. "Forget the FBI. You should be so lucky they arrest you and save you."

"From whom?"

"The French intelligence services. They won't arrest you, they'll kill you."

That stopped them for a moment. "You serious?"

"Damn right I am." I proceeded to call some FBI friends who said that, against the law or not, they would arrest the offending hackers if they pulled such a stunt—and could think of a dozen or so laws to throw at them. But, ultimately, it would be to protect them against international retribution.

So, war was averted. The U.S. hackers never invaded France, but it was interesting while it lasted.

Social Engineering

Hackers of Planet Earth 1994 Convention, New York City

Panelist #1. Hi. This is Social Engineering. Who does not know what social engineering is? If you don't know it is nothing to be ashamed of.

Engineering is when you take a wrench and a bolt and turn it and something happens. Social engineering is when you pick up a telephone and get someone as dumb as a bolt on the other end, and turn it.

I should not be on this panel. I have complained because I don't do it half as well as I've seen some people do true social engineering. John Draper, the infamous Captain Crunch. [Crowd applauds.] Yes, let's clap for Captain Crunch. John could pick up a telephone and call a central office switch at 10 or 11 at night. He would get some dumb switchman who was tired or bored. John understands because he would be the *other* poor dumb switchman over across town and he would know how dull and boring it is. Of course he knew all the buzz words across. In a short time he'd have the guy believing that he is truly who he says he is. He'd talk about the #5 switch we were on, and this and that. He'd say to the other guy, "Hey I threw this command into the main console the other day." The other guy would respond, "Hey man, you forgot to do it this way, etc. You need to put the semicolon here. . . ."

That is social engineering. John will take it to extremes. He would throw body english into the thing. I remember I was down in Homestead as a ham operator after the hurricane and supplies were not getting through and I would throw panic into my voice and speak to the other end. The guys in the van with me would have a weird look when I got off the phone. I would put so much into it with body english, speaking with panic in my voice, etc., how the supplies needed to be done, how we needed them NOW.

And that is social engineering. Making them believe that you are the one to receive the information, whatever that information is. One of the ways you can do this is of course to have information that you can share with them. You know, spreading of knowledge. I do it pretty readily. I used to hack around on the Mariset . . . Mariset Communications Satellite, which is tied into the telephone systems, which is very dumb of them. TWIX, the NYC entire network was on TWIX. They never told anyone that this back door was there. In fact I finally realized it was not a back door to the TWIX network, the back wall was on a hinge. The entire network was that open and certainly not locked. But nobody ever played with Model 33 teletypes and modems. I would just take a Model 33, or ADM 3, Lear Zeigler dumb terminal, dial 690, enter the last 4 digits of the TWIX number, wait for the tone, and put it in the acoustic coupler at 110 baud half duplex and the damn thing thought I was a TWIX machine. I show up on a ship at sea . . . "Hi, this is _____ computer hacker, NYC," and ask the ship radio operator if anyone wanted to chat. Of course there were people there who wanted to chat on someone else's nickel!

I have reached ship radio operators hundreds of miles at sea. I get these guys out there and we'd chat and they would say, "Gee, RCA Globe Comm gave me these here unicodes so I could get back to my home office" . . . of course I'm reading this off my screen . . . "and I can't figure out how to use them."

"MOM please," which is the telex abbreviation for "moment, please." I reach for my publicly available stack of literature for TWIX teletype operators. "Take your carrier ID thumbwheel and turn it to 2 for RCA and then follow the one plus instructions and it will get you right back to your home office." And so you share information like this. Here I was doing some salesman's job explaining how this stuff works to these poor guys on ships who never had access to computerized kind of stuff before. I was a computer hacker, right, so I shared knowledge. So it worked out.

Panelist #2. We all have had some experiences with social engineering dealing with the phone company trying to get information that we have a right to. You call and speak to an operator and get one piece of information and then call back and speak to another operator giving one piece of information, getting more information, etc. It is like computer hacking. Except the people on the other end are not quite as intelligent as computers. [Crowd laughs.] I could really tell you some war stories but I won't. [Crowd claps and asks for a story.]

Recently we got a phone line installed and we asked them please not to send the bill to the address because the mail delivery is not reliable. Send it to this PO box in this town over here. Well, a month later we got a bill that was sent to the wrong PO box in the wrong town. Somehow it got to us. We even got a calling card we did not ask for, and we got it in the mail to the right PO box in a handwritten envelope. Imagine they sent an unsolicited calling card, it came back opened, they resent it . . .

We have been trying to get phone lines installed to 2600 and I don't know what they are doing. Are they doing something else that takes their time, etc. Look at the outside phone booths. They are in horrible shape. They don't get fixed. The same with residential. Anybody who has a business . . . everybody has problems. It is awful what they do to people.

Panelist #1. I remember when I worked in New York I worked for a large firm and every few months I had to call the Western Union rep to talk about the TWIX and TELEX lines. I always had a new rep. I kind of suspected the reasons. I had to sit down with the guys and try to teach them what their job was about and explain to the reps how the network worked. I sounded like one of their trainers.

Panelist #2. Phone company mentality is kind of weird. Has anybody worked with a phone company? They don't last long. They don't want you to ask questions. A good example—a phone man came to my house and he tried to find out what the line code was to my house, and he was dialing 958 . . . 958 . . . and I finally said, "You can dial 158." He kept dialing 958.

Before deregulation, they owned the long distance, all the local area, a total monopoly. They were a big enemy. Now we have lots of enemies. We need some competition. The only company we have here is the Nine-X. We want competition to lower prices, etc. As far as social engineering, I cannot think of a phone company that is not stupid. I once called Cable and Wireless and asked them for my code. They asked me for my phone number, gave me my code, no verification whatsoever. Another time . . . how many of you have MCI Friends and Family? You have an 800 number, you call up, enter your phone number, and then as security enter your zip code. They will tell you all ten people that are in your circle. Not only that, they tell you how those people are related to you, like your a brother at _____ with their phone numbers, some of which are not listed. Well they changed that because we broadcasted that over the radio here, live, and now you have to get part of your account number. So phone companies don't handle security too well and you can easily find information. Almost any entity will give out information. We even get social engineering here on 9600. Someone will call up and ask "What address do you have for my account number?" I ask them for their code. Don't help anyone without the code. But phone companies will give out anything.

Panelist #3. You said that social engineers don't last long within the phone company. In Amsterdam, we had four different phone contracts for about ninety lines with about four feeds coming in. Nobody kept the records straight at all those phone companies. After three weeks of messing with it, they all just lost track. The only people who had the correct information were us. We would tell the techs what to do and about the history when they came. I had all the numbers coming out of the box, the IDs, everything. We had to give it to them. Then when all else failed, they sent someone out to get it straightened out. So they send someone, a social engineer from their own company to hack to get the information and get it working. If all else fails after three or four weeks, they send out a social engineer.

Panelist #1. So social engineering is not only limited to telephone companies. One story I told last year was about trying to get a dial-up number. We were at a university and all we wanted to know what was the dial-up number for the mainframe. They would not tell us that—that was information for the "computer elitist." So we called the computer center and they would not give us any information: "We are not going to give you that information," and hung up on us. We were all kinda bummed out about it so about a half hour later we called the computer center again and said we were from administration. We told them we just heard that someone was calling them for information. So we said, "Well, what kind of information were they trying to get?" [Crowd laughs.] "Our computer number." "What number would that be?" They got the number! "THANK YOU . . ."

Panelist #4. I am sure you know how phone companies are helpful when they wanna be. The thing about phone companies are that they are a service-based organization and try to be helpful. If you call them and ask them for help and are nice, they can be very helpful, maybe not doing things, but in giving out information.

Does anyone know what a CNA is? It's a Customer Name and Address— the reverse way to look up a phone number. You provide them the phone number, and they provide you with the name and address.

There is CNA #313-424-0900; an automated one . . . pretty much public knowledge. According to the phone company policy, they should not give them out. That one has been around for a little less than ten years.

So I am going to show you . . . I am going to procure a phone number using that number I just gave out. The training employees get on this really sucks. Does anyone have legitimate Sprint calling cards? [Some in the audience do.] Well, I don't know, I would, ah, think about that. [Crowd laughs.]

Panelist #1. How about those Voice Sprint Cards in airports? Aren't those great? Not only do you have to speak out loud, but your social security number is your ID code.

Panelist #4. Everyone keep the noise down. [Continues with demonstration.] I am not used to doing this in front of crowds, so I will ask for three tries. [Dials number.]

Automated Attendant. "Thank you for calling Sprint."

Panelist #4. [Punches in zero.]

Automated Attendant. "One moment and a customer representative will be right with you."

Sprint Customer Service Representative Kathy Osmond. "Can I have your number please?"

"Hi, how ya doing? This is Bob Dywer over at Sprint Social Engineering."

"How ya doing?"

"Fine, and you?"

"Great."

"Hey, is your CIS [Customer Information System] up over there? Someone gave me the number for the CNA for area code 313 from here as a 518 . . . No, that would not be in the CIS would it? Do you have the number for the CNA for 313?"

"And your name is Bob Dryer?"

"No. Bob Dwyer."

"And you can't look it up?"

"Our computers are down, that is why I am calling you."

"Oh, okay. Hold on please."

Panelist #4. [Hangs up.] Well, that obviously didn't work. When they put you on hold, it doesn't work. They are going to check with a supervisor. Don't even try it.

From audience. ANI (Automated Number Information) on those lines? No, they do not have that on their lines. AT&T does.

Where do you get the CNA list?

They have 'em.

Do you sell them?

Hey, I don't make a dime off of this! Okay, if there is not Sprint, there is always MCI. [Dials Sprint again.]

"Sprint Customer Service Representative Debra Brown. Can I help you, please?

"Hey, this is Bob Dwyer over at Sprint Social Engineering. How ya doing, Debra?"

"Fine, and yourself?"

"Pretty good. It's one of those days. Would you have the number for CNA in area code 313 . . . I think its Michigan?"

"Sure, I think so. Just a moment."

"Thanks. You guys been busy today?"

"Really busy."

"I know what that is like!"

"Okay . . . 313-424-0900. Do you need the PIN?"

"No. I think I got that. We don't need it. Is it a five-digit?"

"Yes. It sure is."

"Hey, Debra! Is your CIS up over there? We have been having a problem with CIS data loss to the switch. It's not processing the TCs too well."

"Yeah, I'm up."

"What is the last account you processed?"

"Last account?"

"Yeah."

"Okay. It's 180 . . ."

"No, wait. Never mind. CIS just came up online for us. Thanks, Debra, for your help. You have a good day."

"All right. Bye."

All right. That's the fun with CNAs.

Now, is everyone familiar with how 800 routing works? Lots of times 800 numbers just go to regular potts lines, which is just like area code and phone number. Sometimes its real interesting to know the regular area code and phone number that the 800 number goes to. There are several ways to find that out too. For example, here is a regular number to a syndicated talk show: 800-282-2882. That number is pretty much public knowledge, but it also goes to a number here in 212 which I don't have off the top of my head. So I want to find out. [Dials phone.]

"This is Mike at Sprint Customer Service."

"Hi, Mike. This is Bob Dwyer over at NSAC. How you doing over there?"

"I'm doing fine, and you?"

"Okay, just chilling. Hey, you busy over there?"

"No."

"Is your NSS up over there?"

"Yes."

"Try an 800 number. I need to see if there is a potts number associated with that."

"Okay."

"Its 800-282-2882."

"Hang on . . . I have a number for a basic radio line. AT&T. WABC."

"Show the potts number?"

"What is that name again?"

"WABC."

"That sounds right."

[Operator laughs.] "212-268-8080"

"Do you show what band is it on?"

"It's not there."

"What do you mean it's not there?"

"It's not saying what band."

"Do you show a contact name? Oh, that wouldn't show up in NSS."

"Yeah."

"Okay. Thank you for your help."

"Bye."

Panelist #1. The basic technician that you heard was being friendly and personal. Respond with a "how are you?" Show you care. Commiserate. Schmooz 'em. Anger works, too, but you have to have a justifiable reason for your anger. You get them to take pity on you. People want to help. It's Sunday at 3 P.M., so the boss is not around. They can afford to be nice and chit chat. If you are nice, they will be nice. If you're aggressive, it starts on both sides. It all depends on how things are going down.

Panelist #3. Sometimes if you talk with a thick accent, pretend you're foreign, they will tell you what you want just to get rid of you. Try being as annoying as possible.

You become the authority figure to them in social engineering. With Nine-X, I can call and get a number assigned that will be used only if I want to access my records. So if I do that before the real person, I am at the advantage.

You call up with a phone bill or document, you become the person in their eyes. You can have the number disconnected, change the number, change the features.

Panelist #2. If you know nothing, act dumb. They will feel sorry for you. "My training session is next week. How am I going to get through this? Can you help me out."

Panelist #1. Sometimes it is hard to keep an operator on the phone. They are judged on how many calls they handle. But I remember that during the crisis with Iran, we were calling the embassy over there. We were placing the calls person-to-person to a hostage. That operator stayed with us 45 minutes. I don't know if you could get someone to do that these days. But we thought then if we ever got through it would be worth the price of the calls.

The best way to have an unlisted number is to get the number under someone else's name. That way you don't have to pay for it, which is one of the most ridiculous things they do to you.

We are always compared to being the big bad wolf. It is not computer security. It is information security. Years ago it was kept in file cabinets. A lot of the phone companies are still like that. They go in the drawer and pull out the file for information. At the computer security shows, I see hardware, software, firmware, detection devices. But the most important thing I see are the videos.

You need to wake up employees that it is INFORMATION SECURITY.

Hackers as a National Resource

Matthew G. Devost, Systems Analyst

The following is an extract from my thesis National Security in the Information Age. *Copies of the thesis are available upon request. The opinions and conclusions contained herein are solely those of the author, and do not necessarily reflect policy, institutional opinion, or proprietary information of my employer or of any organization I might represent. They are provided to provoke discourse in this area.*

The digital underground should be viewed as an asset to the United States. Its members use illegal means to satisfy their curiosity about the workings of computer technology because the system has denied them other means of accessing the digital realm they love. Harvard Law professor Laurence H. Tribe even suggests that access to technology may be a required goal of democratic society. He states:

> It's true that certain technologies may become socially indispensable—
> so that equal or at least minimal access to basic computer power, for
> example, might be as significant a constitutional goal as equal or mini-
> mal access to the franchise, or to dispute resolution through the judicial
> system, or to elementary and secondary education. But all this means
> (or should mean) is that the Constitution's constraints on government
> must at times take the form of imposing "affirmative duties": to assure
> access rather than merely enforcing "negative prohibitions" against
> designated sorts of invasion or intrusion.[1]

Some hackers are loyal to the ideals of their nation. For example, when news of Stoll's German hacker selling U.S. secrets to the KGB hit the underground, many hackers responded with hatred toward the guy who had associated their movement with national espionage and threats to national security. They were willing to use their abilities to combat this problem, and were even willing to target Soviet computers for the CIA.

One case of a hacker making a contribution to society is the story of Michael Synergy and his quest for presidential credit information. Synergy decided one day that it would be interesting to look at the credit history of President Ronald Reagan. He easily found the information he was looking for and noticed that 63 other people had requested the same information that day. In his explorations, he also noticed that a group of about 700 Americans all appeared to hold one credit card, even though they had no personal credit history. Synergy soon realized that he had stumbled upon the names and addresses of people in the federal Witness Protection Program. Being a good citizen, he informed the FBI of his discoveries and the breach of security in the Witness Protection Program.[2]

One of the basic benefits to U.S. national security is the lack of a coherent movement among the members of the digital underground. Hackers are by nature individualistic. They lack a common bond that allows them to focus their energies on one specific target. If there is a common target among hackers, it is corporate America in general, especially the telephone companies. These corporations have become targets because hackers rely on their service to access Cyberspace, which can be a very expensive proposition. The U.S. government has a vested interest in not providing hackers with another target, especially if that target is the government itself. The United States should utilize hackers, and give them recognition in exchange for the service they provide by finding security holes in computer systems.

The U.S. government does not have to trust hackers, because no trust is necessary. The government is not offering the hackers anything that they don't already have, except recognition for their ability to discover security flaws. Hackers will remain on the networks regardless of what policy the United States follows concerning their activity. It is simply a matter of giving them the forum they need to meet people with similar interests on a legitimate basis, rather than a secret one. Robert Steele argues, "If someone gets into a system, that is not a violation of law, it is poor engineering. When we catch a hacker, rather than learn from him, we kick him in the teeth. When the Israelis catch a hacker, they give him a job working for the Mossad."[3]

Many U.S. corporations already allow hackers to identify security weaknesses in their computer systems. The Legion of Doom, the most notorious group of American hackers, briefly entered the computer security business as Comsec Security. Bruce Sterling reported, "The Legion boys are now digital guns for hire. If you're a well-heeled company, and you can cough up enough per diem and airfare, the most notorious computer hackers in America will show up right on your doorstep and put your digital house in order—guaranteed."[4] Some argue that this is simply extortion, but individuals are not saying "pay up or else we will enter your system." They are offering their skills to secure vulnerable computer systems from possible electronic intrusion.

Hackers can be used to secure the United States' digital interests. Every effort should be made to accept them as part of the newly emerging digital infrastructure. In the same Congressional hearing where his publication was branded a manual for computer crime, Emmanuel Goldstein made the following remarks about access to technology and computer crime:

> This represents a fundamental change in our society's outlook. Technology as a way of life, not just another way to make money. After all, we encourage people to read books even if they can't pay for them because to our society literacy is a very important goal. I believe technological literacy is becoming increasingly important. But you cannot have literacy of any kind without having access. . . . If we continue to make access to technology difficult, bureaucratic, and illogical, then there will also be more computer crime. The reason being that if you treat someone like a criminal they will begin to act like one.[5]

It is ridiculous to assume that the entire hacker subculture is motivated by criminal intentions. Hackers, like all other groups or subcultures, contain a diverse array of individuals. Every group has a criminal element and the hackersÆ criminal element is no different than the criminal element that exists within the law enforcement community. A General Accounting Office report on threats to the National Crime Information Center found that the greatest threat to this centralized criminal database was not from outside hackers but from corrupt insiders.[6]

Most hackers are still young and have not formulated complete ideologies regarding right and wrong behavior. Bob Stratton, a former hacker who now works as a highly trusted security expert, argues that "These people (hackers) haven't decided in some cases to be good or evil yet, and it is up to us to decide which way we want to point them."[7] Mr. Stratton argues that we can mentor these individuals and thereby utilize their technological skills.

Mitch Kapor, founder of one of America's most successful software companies, notes that "the image of hackers as malevolent is purchased at the price of ignoring the underlying reality—the typical teenage hacker is simply tempted by the prospect of exploring forbidden territory. . . . A system in which an exploratory hacker receives more time in jail than a defendant convicted of assault violates our sense of justice."[8]

There does seem to be a trend in the past year to utilize hacker capabilities, both in the public and private sectors. This needs to increase, and perhaps some evaluation of our own laws might be necessary if we wish to continue learning where the holes in America's information infrastructure are.

1. Laurence H. Tribe, "The Constitution in Cyberspace." Paper presented at the First Annual Conference on Computers, Freedom and Privacy Conference, Burlingame, CA. 1991.

2. Paul Mungo and Bryan Clough, *Approaching Zero: The Extraordinary Underworld of Hackers, Phreakers, Virus Writers & Keyboard Criminals.* New York: Random House, 1992, p. 57.
3. Robert D. Steele, "Hackers and Crackers: Using and Abusing the Networks." Presentation at the Fourth Annual Conference on Computers, Freedom and Privacy, Chicago, March 1994.
4. Bruce Sterling, "Cyberview." *Phrack* 3(33): phile 10, 1991.
5. Emmanuel Goldstein, Testimony before House Subcommittee on Telecommunications and Finance. Washington, D.C., June 9, 1993; "Congress Takes a Holiday." *2600: The Hacker Quarterly* 10(3), Autumn 1993, pp. 14-15.
6. General Accounting Office. *NCIC Criminal Misuse.* Washington, D.C.: GPO, 1993.
7. Robert Stratton, "Hackers and Crackers: Using and Abusing the Networks." Presentation at the Fourth Annual Conferene on Computers, Freedom and Privacy, Chicago, March 1994.
8. Mitchell Kapor, "Civil Liberties in Cyberspace." *Scientific American* Special Issue, 1995, pp. 174-178.

12

Who Are The
Information Warriors?

"There's a war out there, and it's about who controls the information. It's all about the information."

—COSMO IN *SNEAKERS*[1]

"We're in the information business. Then we put it on the table and analyze it."

—JIM KALLSTROM, SPECIAL AGENT, FBI[2]

Yes, hackers can be called the original Information Warriors, and many of us consider this relatively benign group the end-all and be-all of potential dangers to our information infrastructure.

Unfortunately, this is simply not the case.

As we examine who the Information Warriors are—or could be—several surprises will crop up. We will find that many of them are blue-suited, starched-shirt executives who, since they are working within the framework of the law, see nothing dangerous or insidious about what they are doing.

The military has spent millions of dollars playing war games against real, potential, or imagined enemies and fighting them on real, electronic, and virtual battlefields in order to fine-tune its capacity to win a war. The Pentagon deals with capabilities, possibilities, probabilities, plausibilities, and of course deniability. Cold War scenarios largely concentrated on the threat of Soviet expansionism. It was only a question of where we were going to fight the Russkies (In Eastern Europe? On the Autobahn? In Paris? Under the polar ice cap?) and who we could count on as an ally.

370

A few short years ago, only a handful of even the most insightful intelligence analysts considered the possibility that the world would peacefully evolve into a unipolar military structure, in which our principal adversary would all but disappear. In decades hence, we may well look back on the Cold War as the good old days of "us" against "them." The concept of mutual assured destruction provided a nervous, but reasonably solid, reason for the two world powers to keep their fingers off of the Button. It also kept 140 other countries in line. If they supported Iran, we supported Iraq. If we supported Israel, they supported an Israeli foe. If nothing else, such common-sense-defying logic kept the peace.

But look what we got in exchange for an end to the threat of thermonuclear conflagration! There is a rash of ethnic, cultural, and national regional uprisings on every continent. Our attention is now spread across the globe, as each new conflict competes for our intervention, benevolence, or leadership. Our priorities are no longer as simple as scanning the Arctic Circle for incoming missiles. As we have learned already, our national interests have taken on a decidedly global nature focused on economic influence, with immediate and long-term sociopolitical ramifications. Today we not only have to compete actively with first- and second-world nations for leverage and position; third-world nations are growing at staggering rates and they, too, will be our competitors in the next century.

Today, a major military attack aimed directly against the U.S. is a statistical improbability, conventional terrorism notwithstanding. However, that does not mean an attack against the national security or economic interests of the United States is equally unlikely. In fact, the odds of such assaults have increased.

Information Warfare is still warfare, whether it is waged as a politically acceptable alternative to bombs and bullets, or if it is waged against companies or organizations that represent the power or money of the United States, or if it is waged against individuals. Not every potential Information Warrior will have the same motivations, the same resources, or the same manpower or organizational abilities. But they all have or can develop the capability. As we explore the roster of potential Information Warriors, we will now shift our attention to motivation; capability is a given.

We can identify people, organizations, and ecopolitical groups with the motivation and capability to wage Information Warfare, but we cannot predict who will or who won't become an active adversary. With that in mind, let's examine candidates who might resort to Information Warfare as a means of executing their agenda.

Corporate Employees

Employees hold the keys to a company's success or failure. A company counts on its employees for trust and allegiance in exchange for a paycheck, but that is no longer enough. The recession of the early 1990s found employees cast aside after decades of faithful service, while upper management gave themselves seven-figure bonuses. The prospect of a secure future for the loyal, so common during the 1950s and 1960s in corporate America, was traded for a pink slip—with not even a word of thanks. Some employees felt they had been royally screwed, despite having played by the rules of the game for so long.

Other employees feel underpaid, underappreciated, or want to make a little money on the side. They may have grudges against their bosses, and depending upon their positions within their firms, they can still cause damage if properly motivated. Stressed-out post office employees are getting a reputation for murder and mayhem. Why shouldn't they screw up the computers instead? They are less likely to get caught, there's less jail time if convicted, and it is far more devastating to the reputation of snail mail. A few cases in point:

Thomas Ferguson was convicted of aggravated assault in

1988 and received three years probation. The following year, he was convicted of violating probation and sentenced to three years of prison and another year of probation. Despite this less-than-glorious background, Time Customer Service, a division of Time, Inc., hired Ferguson as a computer analyst in its Tampa data processing office. On June 26, 1992, Ferguson was arrested for attempting to sell computer disks containing credit card information on three thousand Time, Inc. subscribers to undercover detectives. He was selling names, credit card numbers, expiration dates, and other information needed to make purchases. His asking price? One dollar each. The going price on the streets is $20 per credit card number, but according to police, Ferguson wasn't a very sophisticated criminal. Upon further examination of Ferguson's apartment, additional credit card data was found on computer disks, compromising the privacy and security of eighty thousand more people who had entrusted their information to Time. Also found were tape cartridges with a mailing list containing eight million names and addresses.[3]

Technicians in the London offices of AT&T manipulated computers to funnel money into their own pockets by setting up a 900 number to incur charges to the calling party. They then had the main AT&T computers call their 900 number. The British Computer Misuse Law of 1990 is stiff, yet the perpetrators were never prosecuted due to legal technicalities.[4]

In 1979 Mark Rifkin, a Security Pacific Bank consultant, transferred small amounts of money to a New York account until it totaled $10.2 million. If not for his amateurish boasting, he would have gotten away with transferring it all to a Swiss account.[5]

A Pinkerton Security employee was given high level access to company computers and permitted to override her manager's approval codes. She used those codes to transmit money to bogus company accounts. Since she was also the person who reconciled the company's accounts, the scheme went undetected for two years.[6]

At the Charles Schwab brokerage firm, employees used computers to buy and sell cocaine.[7]

Then there's the story about the married couple who worked for competing companies. "While her husband slept, she used her laptop to log onto his mainframe at his company and download confidential sales data and profiles of current and prospective customers." The husband lost his job; she didn't.[8]

Money seems to be a key ingredient in turning a normally trustworthy employee into an enemy of his employer. On December 24, 1987, Frans Noe, a Lloyds bank employee in Amsterdam, attempted transfers of $8.4 million and $6.7 million from the Lloyds bank in New York to an account he had opened in Zurich at the Swiss Bank Corporation using the SWIFT network. Unknown to anyone, though, the software contained an error that halted the transfer of the $6.7 million. That is the only reason Herr Noe was caught and finally sentenced to eighteen months in jail.[9]

Even small companies are vulnerable. At Southeastern Color Lithographers in Athens, Georgia, the company lost hundreds of thousands of dollars in sales. Their accounting records were regularly blitzkrieged by invisible forces, causing a number of employees to quit. They couldn't handle the pressure of computers that just wouldn't work. The employee behind these antics was eventually caught and is now serving five years in prison.[10]

Benjamin Francois, a personnel supervisor at Jeweler's Financial Services in Clearwater, Florida, had access to thousands of East Coast customer records. He altered the customer files, listing credit cards as lost or stolen. His accomplice, John Wise, would then go to expensive stores, armed with the right names and social security numbers, and walk off with thousands of dollars in jewelry.[11]

Kind of gives you a warm and fuzzy feeling about the people you trust with your name, rank, and credit card, doesn't it? If you are doing the hiring, it makes you wonder what's behind the smiling face across the desk.

Sun Microsystems got the chance to review *its* hiring policies when twenty-seven-year-old Kevin Poulson, a computer programmer, was arrested for "conspiring to break into Pacific Bell Telephone Company computers, stealing and trafficking in telephone access codes, obtaining unlisted phone numbers for the Soviet Consulate in San Francisco, and wiretapping conversations of Pacific Bell officials who were investigating them."[12] Despite the fact that he had been prosecuted for a youthful history of hacking, Sun hired Paulson to work on the Air Force Caber Dragon 88 computer system, used to conduct war exercises at Fort Bragg, New Jersey. He penetrated Air Force computers and allegedly retrieved a classified Air Force Tasking Order which specified real-life military targets in case of conflict.

Stories abound about employees getting even. In 1988, a disgruntled employee was found guilty of planting a computer virus that destroyed $168,000 in sales commission records. In another case, a jealous engineer modified another employee's files in the hopes his rival would receive a bad performance review.

At a certain point we must ask, "Are our hiring policies designed to protect our corporate interests?" When companies such as IBM, Apple, Xerox, and dozens of high-tech firms release hundreds of thousands of skilled technical workers into the realm of the unemployed, social blacklash must be considered a very real possibility. What sort of information do they take with them? Did they, and do they still, have access to sensitive company information and computers?

In order to wage more successful attacks, company insiders are a desirable and accessible asset for the Information Warrior. Money talks, blackmail works, and the company suffers. But we also find a huge army of capable ex-employees who, if properly frustrated or antagonized, could easily join the ranks of the Information Warrior. Revenge is sweet, and in this case, a fairly safe means of retribution.

Vendors and Contractors

If you hire an outside organization to perform services, they, too, can wage Information Warfare against you. Revlon, the giant cosmetics firm, was the victim of a software developer who felt mistreated. The supplier, Logisticon, figured it had only one recourse: to shut the Revlon computer systems down. Revlon was effectively out of business for a full day.

The Florida State Department of Health Rehabilitative Services claims that Electronic Data Systems, a division of General Motors, intentionally sabotaged its computer system. EDS's contract with the state was to end on May 31, 1992. In a series of internal audits, it was found that the computers had high failure rates. According to Inspector General Bobby Brochin, HRS employees said that "program bugs by EDS" caused the problems and when the contract period was over, EDS "left it (the computer) with mistakes in it." HRS employees Viann Hardy and others suspected deliberate mischief by EDS, but Jack Pridgen of EDS flatly calls the allegations "preposterous and not true."[13] (EDS subsequently won back the contract.)

A technical vendor can hold a tight grip over computer systems; he has access to most of a company's operation and is often responsible for insuring that all systems are "go." Contractual and payment disputes can become decidedly ugly if the vendor turns to Information Warfare as an alternative means of forcing settlement or compliance. The concept of outsourcing information processing services may no longer be attractive if the vendor can literally shut down an entire organization's operation when and if the business relationship turns sour.

Government Employees

Government employees are supposed to be the backbone of the civil services that keep society on an even keel. A life of civil service was once held in high esteem: the pay was OK, the benefits excellent, and life tenure was expected. When one went into government employ, part of the reward was a sense of gratification in knowing one was working for the common good of society. In the past we tended to trust our civil servants. They have access to an awful lot of sensitive information—our medical records, our tax records, our employment histories, our military service, just about every aspect of our life. But is that trust still warranted?

Without even considering the possibility of international espionage and spying for the "other side" (whichever side that is today), we find that low-level Government employees occasionally act the part of the Information Warrior, ultimately at the expense of our personal privacy.

The Social Security Administration needs to have faith and trust in their employees. Its computers process over fifteen million transactions a day—five hundred per second—including such confidential data as earnings histories, criminal records, addresses, family relationships, and so on. A breach of trust would be devastating, which it was. In December of 1991, eighteen people, including six employees, were indicted for buying and selling confidential data from SSA computers. The SSA employees were based in New York, Maryland, and Phoenix—indicating a broad-based operation—and were allegedly selling confidential information to private investigators.[14] What makes this case even more disturbing is the fact that a Chicago police officer and an employee of the Fulton County, Georgia, sheriff's office were also involved in the operation.

Unfortunately for us, the Social Security Administration feels that it can do little about such security violations. Since some employees legitimately need access to sensitive files and information in the course of doing their job, it becomes a matter of trust. Are the employees acting within the law or outside of it? According to Renato DiPentima, assistant commissioner in charge of the Office of Systems Design and Development, "Admittedly, it would be very difficult to tell, in that situation, when a person got an occasional query, that one of them was not legitimate."[15]

The same argument applies to the IRS or any other federal agency that holds private data on us, the American people. Bill Clinton's White House and the State Department were accused of illegally tapping the phone of former Assistant Secretary of State Elizabeth Tamposi for her alleged investigation into Clinton's passport history.[16]

Even the limited number of reported cases of information abuse makes the hair on one's neck stand on end. According to author Ronald Kessler, members of the IRS Intelligence staff used their position to help friends and associates in law enforcement. They were "willing to provide copies of income tax forms, the same ones the government promised were absolutely privileged and would not be shown to anyone outside the IRS, to help them. Returns led straight to deals, properties, investments, a whole wealth of confidential data." Cops apparently operate by their own set of rules, and their form of Information Warfare belies the trust we place in them and in Washington. "It didn't take much coaxing to get the IRS just to audit the son of a bitch if he was guilty, say, of contempt of cop. IRS cops understood the rules. They were universal."[17]

The Department of Treasury's Financial Crimes Enforcement Network, known as FinCEN, was launched in 1990 and has the privacy community understandably outraged. Although originally conceived as a means of tracking drug barons, terrorists, and money launderers, FinCEN's power grows daily. Users of the network can access very sensitive personal and commercial financial information from several national databases, including the Currency and Banking Database (the CBDB) and the massive federal Financial Database (FDB). They search hundreds of millions of records, looking for banking transactions that smell of illegal activities.

Most disturbing, however, is the proposed Deposit Tracking System (or DTS), which would be able to invade the privacy of 388 million bank account holders in the United States. According to Diane Casey, executive director of the

Independent Bankers Association, "Our open and democratic society would be changed profoundly if any agency of the government maintained the scope of information on private citizens in this proposal. It raises questions about our democracy that would have to be addressed by the highest policy-making levels of government."[18]

Coupled with FinCEN's planned Artificial Intelligence/ Massive Parallel Processing program (AI/MPP), the government could examine any financial transaction on a real time basis. We have to ask, "Can we trust the keepers of the secrets?"

The problem apparently runs deep, within a culture that imbues power without accountability to our civil servants. In many ways, control over our personal privacy is the only sense of power some IRS employees will ever get. "An internal IRS survey . . . found that of every hundred credit reports accessed by IRS workers, five are illegally obtained."[19] Since 1990, despite laws prohibiting it, criminal investigators at the IRS regularly eavesdrop on the cordless and cellular phone conversations of suspected tax dodgers.[20]

The Resolution Trust Company (the RTC), supposed to get the United States out of $500 billion in losses, may have also acted the part of an Information Warrior. According to the Associated Press, Barbara Shangraw, a top RTC legal eagle, received orders from RTC's D.C. office to look into the files of employee Bruce Pederson. Apparently, during Congressional testimony in the summer of 1992, he criticized management policies—and management was none too happy. Barbara E-mailed a request to computer technician John Waechter: "I have been requested by D.C. to get into Bruce Pederson's Word Perfect. Please copy into a directory for me what Bruce has in his Word Perfect." This smells like a direct violation of antiwiretapping law, expanded in 1986 to include computers and electronic mailboxes. She got caught.[21]

To make matters worse, the White House allegedly ordered the IRS to illegally investigate tax records for political purposes.[22] At the height of such executive abuses, former Attorneys General Edwin Meese III and Richard Thornburgh were accused by the Congressional report of covering up allegations that the Department of Justice had stolen millions of dollars in software from Inslaw, Inc. The House Judiciary Committee report came to the conclusion that not only did the Justice Department steal software, but that Meese and Thornburgh lied as to their knowledge of the case.

Civil servants are given power—immense power—and that power will only increase as bigger and faster systems connect more of our digital essences into what has often been referred to as a national database. (Clinton's proposed health care system would put medical records into a single repository, a fine target if ever there was one.) Abuses of this power are symbolic of the social sicknesses that permeate society as a whole. There is no reason to expect government employees to be immune.

Law Enforcement

Even some law enforcement officials, the people who are supposed to protect us, are Information Warriors in their own right. Mike Peros, an expert in electronics countermeasures, runs Privacy Electronics in St. Petersburg, Florida. He performs "sweeps" to find out if someone is bugging you, tapping your lines, or otherwise electronically intruding on your privacy. When hired, he regularly finds taps—some obvious, some better disguised. One day in 1991 he was hired by a Tampa, based firm to search for bugs. Apparently the owners were concerned about their competition. Peros went in and quickly found one crude bug. "It was pretty shoddy work," he said. After he left the firm, he found himself being pursued. The Florida Department of Law Enforcement (FDLE), wanted to know what happened to their bug. When Peros wanted to know if it was a legal intercept, the agents got particularly nervous; apparently, the bug had been placed without proper court approval. When Peros suggested that a court reporter transcribe their conversation, the police said, "We don't want the media involved." The FDLE quickly backed off.

Peros says he's seen plenty of wiretaps and bugs planted illegally by law enforcement, and he expects to see more. According to him, "When the police or the Fed can't get a warrant, sometimes they decide to get creative . . . and bug the place anyway. They collect enough evidence, attribute it to unnamed informants, and then use the illegal evidence to get a judge to sign an order for a legitimate wiretap. It's done all the time."

I hear similar stories from private investigators; moonlighting police; on-duty police; federal, state, and local law enforcement agencies; and professional surveillance and countersurveillance folks. The FBI was issued fewer than three hundred legal, court authorized Federal phone taps in 1991, but according to countersurveillance people, the real count of taps—illegal and legal—is staggeringly high.

Private investigators claim that this type of behavior is par for the course for police trying to build a case, and that it is indeed necessary to prosecute criminal activities. Some police officials I have spoken with deny it, but not convincingly so. After all, they have the power, so why not use it? It's all in the name of serving the public good.

But sometimes the strategy can blow up in their faces. The celebrated Key Bank scandal in Florida resulted in multiple prosecutions, but because the wiretaps used in the case were issued based upon "stale and often uncorroborated information," the evidence obtained through 65,000 intercepted calls was tossed out of court. Hillsborough County, Florida, can brag that due to the overzealousness of State Attorneys Lee Atkinson and Harry Cole (and their habit of "judge shopping" to expedite wiretap orders), they have placed more wiretaps than forty-seven other *states*—not counties—combined. "I've got everyone on tape," said Atkinson in a newspaper interview. To make matters worse, Coe has refused to comply with federal law by suppling Washington with the files on his wiretapping habits.[23]

When law enforcement abuses its power, trust of authority disintegrates. As a result, some people are openly antagonistic toward the government and consider themselves technological survivalists—small, ingenious Davids up against the Big Brother Goliath.

At the heart of the country's criminal investigation labyrinth is the FBI's National Crime Information Center. Think of it as a huge computer database with millions upon millions of records on millions of criminals and their modus operandi. The NCIC databases also contain massive records on people who have never been charged with a crime, but may have been investigated or thought to be of interest to law enforcement. Civil libertarians decry the potential for abuse when mere allegations and hearsay are filed away as evidence, in the event one of us might commit a crime. In addition, the NCIC computers can tie into the vast number of computer systems and databases around the country. Agents can look for missing persons, track large cash transactions, correlate driving records from all fifty states—or find out which hotels you frequent and what your travel itineraries are. Such power in the hands of too many people is an obvious danger, tempting even the most virtuous person to give Information Warfare a try.

In July 1993, the General Accounting Office testified before a congressional subcommittee that the NCIC databases have been the subject of regular abuse by law enforcement workers and their associates nationwide. The NCIC databases are legally accessed by 19,000 law enforcement groups within the United States and Canada, using 97,000 terminals and personal computers. However, security mechanisms at the terminals, other than those directly controlled by the FBI itself, is dismal or nonexistent. The federal government is unable to mandate controls on a local level.

So what happens when just about anybody can ask a computer to find out who's done what to whom?

- A former law enforcement officer in Arizona used NCIC to track down his ex-girlfriend. He later killed her.
- A terminal operator in Pennsylvania used the system to aid her drug dealer boyfriend, by checking to see if his customers were undercover agents.
- A dispatcher in Rhode Island used NCIC for background checks on her fiancé's political opponents.[24]

This is not the behavior we expect, nor wish to pay for with our tax dollars.

On another front, the National Security Agency uses its own collection of toys for domestic surveillance. The data it collects is shared with cooperating agencies such as the CIA and the FBI. The NSA monitors fifty-three thousand communications signals in the U.S. every day. Then, acres and acres of super-supercomputers dedicated to the fine old art of eavesdropping and code breaking automatically look for meaningful information amongst the hurricane of data that enters Fort Meade, Maryland. The NSA can listen for and detect key words in phone conversations. Let's say you're talking to a close personal friend in Libya and he asks you, "Were you able to get that nuclear fuel from the Iraqis for me?" NSA computers will trigger alarms and in seconds a platoon of experts will be dissecting the recorded conversation, perhaps in preparation for a friendly visit to your home or office.

Remember those Toyota vans used to electromagnetically eavesdrop on the chemical company in Northern California? According to NSA employees, the Agency has its own listening vans, which can only be described as highly sophisticated electronic eavesdropping laboratories-on-wheels. From inside one of the NSA vans, you can talk to anyone, anywhere, anytime, or listen in on just about any communication system known to man.

Listening in on a computer using van Eck techniques has been raised to a pure applied science at the NSA. The technology developed by and available to the FBI is startling,

and in many cases undetectable by almost any means. FinCEN
eavesdrops on legitimate banking transactions without justification. In other words, we are all suspects, and all of our
supposedly private business dealings are undergoing government scrutiny without our knowledge or permission.[25]

When we see the police—those dedicated to protect and
serve—violate our trust, we have reason for deep concern. The
epitome of such abuse of trust may lie with the Los Angeles
Police Department. By any and all standards, the LAPD and,
most assuredly, ex-LAPD Police Chief Daryl Gates, qualify as
Information Warriors. The organization spent over fifty years
violating the law and mocking the integrity of every dedicated
and honest law enforcement officer in the country.

It started in the 1930s, during the Hoover era, when files
began to be kept on those suspected of having gangster ties. By
1957, when the Organized Crime Intelligence Division (OCID)
was founded, the files were immense, and growing by leaps
and bounds. Dossiers were kept on all the movers and shakers.
"Using an elaborate intelligence network of informants, surveillance, and devices to intercept phone calls, OCID operatives
monitored all kinds of celebrities—politicians, union leaders,
Hollywood stars, professional athletes, team owners, TV and
print journalists."[26]

The OCID evolved into a project that was Stalinesque in its
nature and scope. "OCID's goal was not to protect the public,
it was information."[27] One case with enormous implications
was the surveillance of Governor Edmund G. "Pat" Brown.
Years later the file on his son, presidential hopeful Jerry
brown, involved higher technology such as illegal phone taps
and intensive electronic surveillance.

For decades, the LAPD's crime unit ran wild, its surveillance employing state-of-the-art technology. "Bugging became
almost a way of life at the OCID."[28] Their offices contained the
latest and greatest in miniaturized electronic spy gear, enough
to make the KGB proud.

Over 50,000 of the private records were to have been
destroyed in 1983, but some people within the LAPD felt they

didn't have to follow the rules and the files were subsequently found in a cop's home. (Once an Information Warrior, always an Information Warrior.) The essential characteristics of the LAPD's secret police remained the same, with newer and better technotoys being added to the arsenal at least through 1988, shortly before an explosive book, *The L.A. Secret Police*, was published.

In Los Angeles, one man was labeled and convicted as a sex offender based upon testimony of the LAPD. In a conversation between two officers, the truth came out.

"Do you remember that social worker I popped for lewd conduct?"

"Yes?"

"I lied. The guy didn't actually do anything."[29]

An innocent man's life was totally destroyed by a crooked Los Angeles cop who swore, in a court of law, to the veracity of information he knew was false.

In Los Angeles, the OCID had support from the highest levels. Amazingly, Daryl Gates, ex-LAPD chief and ex-captain of OCID, admitted that bugs and other Information Warrior tricks of the trade were used "for our own edification."[30] Gates and the LAPD were Information Warriors. What is the most disturbing though, is that the attitude that created such abuses has reared its head in countless communities across this country. How many of the nearly 20,000 law enforcement agencies are engaged in Information Warfare? It is a question that must be asked, and more important, answered.

Unchecked power brings tyranny and vigilantism. The police have vast capability to wage Information Warfare against real or imagined enemies, completely innocent citizens, or suspects they have presumed to be guilty. They have the capability to construct an electronic case by manipulation of computerized profiles; such power, if misused, places the police in the position of being the judge and jury as well. One must ask whether a desperate law enforcement agency would contrive a case by compiling an indicting and incriminating digital profile of a suspect. Most of us would say that this is an unacceptable extension of the law, but few of us have any answers on how to curtail it.

Narcoterrorists

The leaders of the world's drug cartels are among the most ruthless people on the planet. They mete out brutal punishments for even the slightest hint of disloyalty, kill scores of innocents every year, and wage a literal war against their own governments with their own well-armed militia. Protecting their multi-billion dollar turf with torture and murder is their normal means of doing business. Is there any reason to think they don't have the motivation or the means to wage Information Warfare against anyone who stands in their way?

The first I heard about narcoterrorists becoming involved in Information Warfare was in 1990, during a conversation with a Drug Enforcement Administration agent based in Miami.

"We finally figured it out," my contact said.

"What's that?"

"Why we haven't been able to catch them. The drug runners."

"I thought you were catching them," I said naively.

"Yeah, right. We get about one percent of what's coming in. They've been way ahead of us."

"How's that?"

"You know that speech you just gave," he said to me. "Where you described how you can listen in on computers by a radio, van Eck?"

"Yeah?"

"Well, they were doing it to us!" he claimed.

"You're putting me on," I said in genuine shock.

"No, they've been listening to our computers. They always know where we are, who's assigned where, and if there's going to be a bust. They always knew, and now we know how."

"But I thought you guys used Tempest computers?"

"On our budget we're lucky to get bullets. But things are

going to be different. We just got budgeted for a ton of Tempest computers, and we think that's going to make a difference."

I'd had no idea that operations as sensitive as those of the DEA could function without a high degree of security, especially with as worthy an adversary as the drug cartels. The bad guys have a ton of money. They can buy the best equipment, pay for the best brains, and launch their own attacks at will. Pick a weapon from our list of Information Weapons, place it in the hands of the drug syndicates, and see what can happen.

Small Time Criminals and Organized Crime

Criminal elements have not lost sight of the opportunities that technology brings them, even without the assistance of government masters. Young foreign nationals have been focusing on credit card and other types of fraud while making their mark as Information Warriors. Arab, Chinese, Japanese, and African groups have gained the attention of the Secret Service while "using confidential data as a weapon," said David Leroy, chief of domestic intelligence for the Drug Enforcement Administration.[31]

According to New York postal inspector Martin Biegelman, organized credit card scam artists "obtain security guard positions that are generally low paying and hard to fill. Then, when they're assigned to a building at night, these individuals are given free reign to patrol the offices and the computers located there. They go through personnel files and even employees' desks to obtain names, job titles, Social Security numbers, home addresses, and whatever other personal information is available."[32] Usually, one group of criminals specializes in acquiring the information, another specializes in distributing the stolen information on their own network, and another sells it on the streets to unsuspecting immigrants in the form of fake but usable credit cards.

ATMs have been favorite targets of these criminals. At any

given time, there sits between $4 and $8 billion in cash in the thousands of cash machines that are scattered across the country, ripe for the picking. In May 1993, a creative Information Warrior made national news by putting a fake ATM machine is a Connecticut mall. The modified machine gave out no cash, but captured and saved account information and PIN numbers from everyone who tried to use it.

While some thieves prefer to rip the ATMs from their moorings with a bulldozer, true Information Warriors take the elegant approach. "Shoulder surfers" look at the numbers punched into the ATM and then, with the help of insiders, walk off with the victim's cash. In 1987, ATM repairman Robert Post walked off with $86,000 using this method.

In 1988 Security Pacific National bank was hit for $237,000 from three hundred accounts using a forged MasterCard. Also in 1988, Mark Koenig and friends forged seven thousand ATM cards as part of a plan to rip off Bank of America for $14 million. An insider tip-off put an end to the scheme.[33] Another criminal, from New Zealand, faked an ATM card out of cardboard and transferred NZ $1 million to his account. He turned himself in out of guilt.

Banks are logical targets for criminals who operate as Information Warriors: Go where the money is. And it's surprisingly safe to rob a bank electronically. If you get away with it, the bank will probably not call in law enforcement because they don't want the publicity. In 1989, six City of London banks and brokerage houses allegedly signed agreements offering amnesty and money to criminals in return for their silence and the secrets of their trade.[34]

Bank officials privately admit that they lose millions of dollars yearly to both internal and external thefts, but they consider it a cost of doing business. I can accept the loss of a few candy bars from a K-Mart to be a cost of doing business, but not the loss of my money. The banks say it's their money—and their profits—but that is a difficult argument to defend. If the bank loses, ultimately so do its customers and stockholders. A bank official in Atlanta told me, "We fudge the books to keep the Feds away. If they ever found out the truth, they could shut us down." A security official from one of the nation's largest banks claimed they experienced losses in excess of $100 million in 1993 alone, but because they are so large they can bury the losses in bad debt accounts. Great way to run a business.

The problem is, of course, that their silence only encourages more daring escapades by other criminals, and invites more professionals and organized groups to join in the profit-sharing. Organized crime likes information because it helps them establish control, through extortion and blackmail, over their victims. Since murder and torture are their historical modus operandi, Information Warfare seems benign by comparison. Acquiring the technical skills is a simple matter of money or motivation. Unfortunately their intentions are just as clear.

There is a balance between the Cyber Police State and anarchy, suggests Bob Lesnick, a private investigator from West Paterson, New Jersey. "People are afraid of a police state emerging from the use of computers by the authorities. But they should be concerned about the flip side; an uncontrollable computer dominated crime wave led by dangerous criminals. That will be much more invasive."[35]

Direct Mailers and Telemarketers

They want to know exactly who you are. They want to know, before they invest a dime in a phone call to you, that you love camping, or you have a penchant for travel, or you just had a baby and your first child is entering first grade. They want to know everything they can know about you before they call to interrupt your dinner and offer a wonderful opportunity to move money from your pocket to theirs. They want to know that you are health oriented and own both a Nordic Track and a set of weights from Sears. They want to know your zip code—which side of the tracks do you live on? Do you lease or own a car? Is your house big enough to handle the newest family member, or does your house need an addition? They want to know whether you are a decent demographic target, and worth their time. But most important, they want to know that your credit cards have enough room on them to purchase whatever they're selling you. In order to get that kind of information, the sales company has to rent a list of names and phone numbers based upon their criteria, which spell out in detail exactly who their ideal customer is: income, family size, buying habits. For a fee, a list is then compiled to meet those specifications.

We all get junk mail. If you buy one kid's toy from one catalog, you will receive a dozen similar catalogs three months prior to Christmas. If you travel more than 20,000 miles per year, upscale travel brochures, resorts, and magazines will solicit your business. If you subscribe to *Time*, bet your bottom dollar that *Newsweek, U.S. News and World Report* and *People* will be on your doorstep with deals for pennies an issue.

Once they have your name, you're on the List forever. Your name and address, buying habits, and credit-worthiness are moved from computer to computer, from store to store, from catalog to catalog, all in the hopes that soliciting you will enrich their pockets.

If you've ever declared bankruptcy Citibank won't offer you a credit card, but other firms who offer overpriced products with their own credit card will be on your doorstep. If you spend $5,000 a month with American Express, they will provide your name to a list broker and you'll receive sales pitches from the crème de la crème. However, if you pay for everything with cash, you get probably no junk mail. They can't trace you and your buying propensities, and therefore you are nearly worthless to them. An entirely new kind of discrimination results when one pays cash because, for all intents and purposes, you don't exist. Bad junk mail. Now that's redundant.

I can't wait for that one to go to court. A class action lawsuit on behalf of the lower economic classes, not even given the opportunity to turn down a sales pitch. Now that's discrimination against what Jeffrey Rothfeder calls the "data-disenfranchised." While many of us receive nasty sneers from mailmen trying to force oversized catalogs into undersized mail boxes, a large percentage of the population sits in an information void, never even aware of the staggering possibilities.

Doctors, Hospitals, and Insurance Companies

Arkansas Republican Tommy Robinson wanted a shot at then-Governor Bill Clinton's job. Tommy had spent six good years in Congress, but his chances for political advancement disappeared when one newspaper article claimed he drank a pint of bourbon a day. His medical file had been leaked to the media, and unfortunately for Robinson, the file was wrong.[36]

This is only one example of the untold grief experienced by honest, law-abiding citizens every day. There are no laws governing how, when, and to whom private medical records are to be handled. With the right sequence of keystrokes, a career or a life can be shattered. A medical record is perhaps the most revealing portion of our digital selves. In addition to the usual identification information at the top of the forms, how much we drink or smoke is included, our family history, with social and medical characteristics, is detailed. Complaints, diagnoses, treatments, drugs prescribed and in what quantities—all this paints a picture that is supposed to be confidential between patient and doctor.

The Medical Information Bureau contains files on millions of Americans, and just as with the credit bureaus, the errors are momentous. If a doctor says you have AIDS, it is entered into the MIB database to remain there forever, even if the data is wrong.

When a low-paid data entry clerk types in a medical code as part of a patient's record, one transposed digit can make the difference between the picture of health and a hemophiliac or drug addict with AIDS. Or, maybe the data clerk had a fight with his or her spouse and decides to make a few errors on purpose. Or, it could be a sort of revenge against society, striking out indiscriminately. As of today, there is no recourse, and Congress really doesn't give a damn.

If you have a dispute with your doctor, he could download an inaccurate medical profile onto a database like the MIB. Instead of suing you, he labels you as a sociomedical misfit and ruins your chances of acquiring insurance or getting a promotion. Quite a bit of power within the hands of the medical community, wouldn't you say?

Hospitals, too, maintain extensive medical records and their computers talk to the government's medical computers and the insurance companies' computers, all in the name of business expediency. But the sinister side of the Information Warrior constantly looms. Imagine a night nurse, so fed up with an irritable patient, that she alters his records enough to make the insurance company refuse to pay the bill. Maybe she turns him into a drug addict instead of a patient with a broken leg; insurance companies love that. Or, as in the medical terror thrillers of fiction author Robin Cook, perhaps the records of a patient's allergies are altered so that a doctor's drug prescription will trigger a fatal response.

Private Investigators

"Get the information. However you have to, and I don't want to know about it." A CEO might utter these words to his aide, who in turn hires an investigator to get the goods. The private investigator is an Information Warrior in every sense of the word. PIs will acquire the information they need to satisfy their clients and pick up their check.

The aggressive PI, not content only to work within the limits of the law, will exploit the same technology and capabilities we have previously described. After all, they meet his needs, insidiousness and invisibility being at the head of the list. The good PI will have a network of databankers on whom he can count to get legally attainable, but presumably private, information on individuals; he will have a contact at the police department who, for a bottle of Black Label or tickets to the Jets game, will delve into the theoretically sacrosanct world of law enforcement databases. Bob Lesnick says that a computer is "the most modern weapon we have. Few people, even criminals, can evade a databank."[37] Or, he will get hired as a security guard and have free reign for an evening in the building of his client's competitor. Illegal bugs and taps? Sure, why not, say many PIs. He will even sink as low as "dumpster diving," the refined art of poring through a target's garbage in the search of either valuable or incriminating information.

Ex-FBI agents, ex-cops, ex-anybodies with the skills and a shingle over the door will, for a price, act as your personal Information Warrior.

Security Professionals

Cops treat cops differently from the way they treat you and me; we're not part of the fraternity. Ex-cops are still cops, always part of the brotherhood, and they can count upon each other for favors. Big companies who hire ex-cops and ex-intelligence agents as heads of security unwittingly aid and abet the Information Warrior.

Law enforcement folks will help each other, even at the expense of our privacy or in violation of the law. One ex-cop working for a bank might willingly give access codes to another security pal—no questions asked. Once into one bank's private network, the Information Warrior can navigate into most other banking systems, including ATM networks.

Joseph Van Winkle, a former FBI agent working for a New York bank, doesn't like what he sees. "Every time we build another computer network, private information is compromised even more; dozens of new lines of data communications are opened up. I don't like it, but I don't know what to do about it."[38]

The Information Warrior with that kind of access can do a lot more than print out bank statements for a friend: loans can be paid off, bank balances increased, credit limits raised. On the other hand, foreclosure proceedings could be instituted against the bank's most creditworthy customer. It's all a matter of motivation. Or, if the bank itself is the target, all banking operations could come to a halt with a handful of keystrokes.

It all depends on capability, motivation, and intention.

Supermarkets

One Midwest grocery chain appears to have joined the ranks of the Information Warrior. Dominick's sent a letter to customers that ominously warned: "We have been confidentially recording the purchases you make when you pay by check and use your Dominick's Check Cashing Card at the register. We are studying this data and will soon make a decision on how to use it."[39]

Soon, you may have no choice but to shop and pay through Cyberspace. In the coming months and years, the debit card and the electronic check cashing card will become the norm in stores from coast to coast. Somewhere in a computer at Grand Union, Vons, Food Lion, or any other chain store in America, you will leave behind a trail that says you buy low-fat everything, wear a size sixty-two shirt, or you're a size eighteen female. Guess what kind of solicitations you'll then be getting? Stuff for fat people.

Each and every one of your individual purchases will be monitored, recorded, stored, compared, and analyzed by a hundred different computers. The results will be sold to direct marketing firms that have a customized catalog, just for you. Pretty soon the supermarket will be capable of delivering your groceries to your door before you even knew you needed them.

Imagine who will get your name and address if you buy condoms from any national drug chain and pay by debit card. Now that's privacy.

Proctor and Gamble, the consumer goods conglomerate based in Cincinnati, Ohio, was publicly humiliated when they were caught engaging in this type of Information Warfare. Their management was convinced that an employee was leaking confidential company information to a newspaper reporter. They recruited a local police department fraud detective to use his tax-payer paid power and law enforcement influence to get the cooperation of the phone company to perform an exhaustive search of over one million telephone numbers and forty million toll calls. (How many Information Warriors are involved here?) Despite this extraordinary effort, and the involvement of those who should have known better, no one ever found the leak, if there was one, and the company eventually had to face the embarrassment of admitting they had randomly invaded the privacy of so many people in an ill-conceived operation.

Politicians

Politics has the reputation of being dirty and unscrupulous; anything is fair game as long as your candidate wins. The Robb-Wilder cellular telephone incident discussed earlier is only a more sophisticated form of Information Warfare as pioneered by the attack on Democratic National Headquarters that spawned the downfall of President Nixon. Watergate was Information Warfare at its best, run by the best operatives around. And today, with the commonly available weapons of the Information Warrior as tools, political adjutants will have little reluctance to use them where they best see fit.

Southern Bell, one of the regional telephone companies, has been actively lobbying the Public Service Commission about a pending rate case. Commissioner Tom Beard, under investigation to determine his relationships with key Southern Bell

employees, resigned under the scrutiny, but not before someone contributed substantial evidence to support the suspicions.
In mid-1993, a floppy disk was provided to investigators that
contained logs of telephone calls to and from the homes and
offices of commission members and lobbyists with an interest
in the case, including the Governor's son, Bud Chiles, a
lobbyist for Southern Bell. Either the records were provided
illegally from an inside source, or phones were tapped. In the
process, Assistant Florida State Attorney General Mike Twomey
also resigned, refusing to disclose the source of the mysterious
disk that apparently contained damning information.[40]

No, the political process will not be immune from Information Warfare; I think that it will assume an even more acute
form of what's been practiced for decades. Only the technology is new and improved. Perhaps with the advent of safe sex,
we can imagine a high-tech Congressional scandal involving
ménage-à-trois E-mail.

Political Action Groups

Radical environmental groups such as Earth First! have
resorted to "spiking" trees in forests they think worth preserving. Such acts could be called violent, since loggers have been
badly hurt when their chain saws met up with these spikes.
The abortion debate has also sparked violence—even murder.
The antiabortionists have said that since abortion is killing a
fetus, they will resort to nearly any tactic to protect the life of
the unborn. Environmentalists believe that *all* human life
could end because we have so disrupted the ecological balance that Mother Nature provided: Ergo saving whales and the
rain forest are attempts to save mankind.

Any of these groups is a candidate for waging Information
Warfare against their real or perceived adversaries. Given the
power of information and the tools available, it would be folly
to pretend that politically motivated organizations won't avail
themselves of the capabilities of the Information Warrior. The

domestic infighting we experience right here in America, and the international factionalism spurred by the New World Order, will only create more and more splinter groups who want to forge their own agendas. It is these groups, many of them heretofore considered benign, who may use their ability to attack information systems as a modern means of civil disobedience.

Far-right Neo-Nazi and White Supremist groups have become well-known for their brutality, base behavior, and social pathology. As disgusted as we may be by their political agenda, we must not underestimate their ability to wage Information Warfare. It is a tool they apparently are already using. When Peter Lake penetrated the Aryan Nation on behalf of CBS News in Los Angeles, he was asked by convicted killer David Lane to assist in what is certainly a form of Information Warfare. Lane asked the reporter, "What do you know about telephone installations? I want to knock out the telephone system in a major Western city for one hour to silence the bank alarms."[41]

Mercenaries, Freelancers, and Ex-Soviet and Eastern Bloc Experts

If you think *we* have an unemployment problem, just look behind what used to be the Iron Curtain. Hundreds of thousands of people, whose job for years was to listen to and interpret information, are now out of work. The information they gained during the heydays of the Cold War was gathered in any way possible, ranging from pure threat and intimidation to high tech surveillance. No one ever accused the Soviets of being stupid when it came to intelligence gathering—so much of the Eastern Bloc's economic power was placed in the military and intelligence gathering, it's no wonder they were good. And now what are these unemployed Cold Warriors going to do to feed their families?

Terrorists

The rules have changed and Americans are feeling the effects of terrorism on our shores for the first time. Aside from bombings, terrorist groups have the capabilities to acquire and use Information Weapons. The results promise to be as devastating as those seen in New York at the bombing of the World Trade Center.

Walter Friedman of IVI Travel in Chicago thinks that huge databases are invaluable to terrorists. "With this kind of data automatically spread to hundreds of thousands of computers world-wide literally as the bookings are made, the thought of how easy it would be for terrorists to get their hands on it and use to plan kidnappings or worse makes one shudder."[42] Terrorists are not generally known for their subtlety, but with government support and the influx of vast amounts of funds, extremist political and religious groups who use terrorism as a means to their ends can now bring the necessary technical sophistication to bear on their activities.

Alvin Toffler says in his book *War and Anti-War*, "Whatever the terms, it is now possible for a Hindu fanatic in Hyderabad or a Muslim fanatic in Madras or a deranged nerd in Denver to cause immense damage to people, countries, or, even with some difficulty, to armies 10,000 miles away."[43]

We will further examine these unnerving possibilities shortly.

Business Competitors: Domestic

Competitive Information Warfare between firms is difficult to identify, much less prove. Publicly at least, American businesses claim that spying on one another only hurts our national competitiveness in the long run, but skillful use of Information Weapons makes identification of the culprits next to impossible. All too many companies are lax in their security against such attacks, thereby increasing their vulnerability and decreasing the chances of satisfactory recourse.

However, some cases have been publicized. Assistant News Director Michael Shapiro and News Director Terry Cole of ABC affiliate WTSP-TV in Tampa were charged with fourteen felony counts for breaking into a competitor's computer system. According to the *St. Petersburg Times* and *Computerworld*, Shapiro broke into WTVT-TV's computers to steal sensitive competitive news information. Shapiro had once worked for WTVT as the administrator for the station's computers, and police found computer disks and software guides from the rival station's computers at his home.

Domestically, industrial espionage as we think of it is rare; most Americans don't play that way. But it still occurs. Borland International, Inc. and Symantec are rival software companies in California. Both would love to know the other's new design specs, product plans, sales data, and contract bid information. According to a grand jury indictment in March 1993, Borland executive Eugene Wang sent E-mail to Symantec CEO Gordon Banks containing just such valuable competitive information. Why? He was getting ready to jump ship and move to Symantec.[44]

General Motors accused former purchasing executive Jose Lopez of taking crates of proprietary company information with him to rival Volkswagon.[45] Even Macy's found itself in a tussle when one of its key executives who "knew too much" moved to a rival retailer. Thus far in this country, espionage seems to be concentrated on what one knows and how much value it is to a new boss.

In a more celebrated case, Virgin Atlantic Airways accused British Airways of hacking into its reservations systems in an attempt to steal passengers. Airline reservation systems are fairly open; a lot of information is shared between competing airlines so that carriers can better assist their customers, but the names and phone numbers of passengers are supposed to be kept secret. A former British Airways employee, Sadig Khalifia, said that he and other employees were shown how to tap into the BA booking system computer that Virgin rented. Once they had the names and phone numbers of the Virgin customers, British Airways employees called and tried to convince passengers to switch airlines. The case never went to court, but British Airways had to pay Virgin Atlantic almost $4 million in damages and costs.[46]

Finding the real dollar amounts lost by businesses to domestic competitive espionage—or perhaps one might call it creative intelligence—is just not going to happen today. Big business is plainly too paranoid to admit they have a problem, much less the extent of it. According to Charles Cresson Woods, a security consultant in Sausalito, California, we don't hear a lot about these type of industrial espionage cases because "a lot of people don't know they're being wiretapped. These taps can go on for years before—or if—they are ever discovered."[47]

From the examples in this book, the informed reader now can assume capability, add to it motivation and intent, and then estimate probability. Does Chase spy on Chemical Bank for lists of their very best customers? Does 3M have insiders working at Monsanto in the hopes of discovering the next generation of chemicals at a fraction of the time and investment? Ultimately, I believe the answer to these and similar questions is, "Of course. They'd be stupid not to."

Business Competitors: International

Airbus can find out an awful lot about Boeing if it has access to an airline's database and plots out where its executives are traveling. It turns out they have access to even better information than that. Industrial espionage is today the stuff of James Bond. Industrial espionage is much more than company fighting company for the latest whiz-bang electro-static micro-metro pink filistoid distiller, or the recipe to Oreos or Coke.

In the international information marketplace, where industrial espionage is a day-to-day expense, the differentiation between foreign business and foreign government has become distinctly hazy. The success of a particular company may be deemed by that country's government to be of strategic value to national economic security. In such cases where corporate and national interests merge, the United States finds itself at a costly, embarrassing, and distinct competitive disadvantage. I hope this point hits home, because it is critical that we understand our shortcomings in this area. *Any* U.S. company, be it small and innovative or of global reach and impact, may find itself battling for survival against the combined forces of not only another corporation but one supported by the resources of its entire parent government. When it comes to waging Information Warfare, our international competitors vastly outclass even the largest U.S. corporations. Some might complain that we're not playing on a level playing field. But those are the rules in a tripolar, aggressively competitive global economy.

Consider the recent revelations of global spy networks within the oil industry. The vast sums of money involved have invited data brokers to acquire information through any means, and offer it for sale to competing organizations worldwide. These spy networks have penetrated Mobil Oil, USX, British Petroleum, and others through the use of clandestine moles and employees paid off in quick bucks in a Swiss account. The oil industry spy brokers from Boston to Hong Kong, Houston to Singapore, London to Libya trade in illegally obtained information and, in mercenary style, sell it to the highest bidder.[48]

The French have openly admitted to attacks against U.S. business interests. The Japanese have refined Information Warfare into an art. Even our old allies, the Israelies, have been caught as well. Just about every major economic power or wannabe economic power is using Information Warfare in the pursuit of its particular national agendas.

And then, who could forget those Russians? Since the demise of World War II, we've been spying on them and they've been spying on us. In that game, I think they won. How else could their ill-fated supersonic passenger plane be named

Concordski and look exactly like the sleek British Airways original? Why do you think that their space shuttle is remarkably similar to ours? Is that a coincidence or did they hire ex-NASA designers to work in Kazikistan for twenty years? I think not. They stole it, and today they even admit it.

Who Else?

How much money could someone make if they knew what government futures prices were going to be, even if only a few hours ahead of time? Should the person in a firm who consistently makes staggering investment profits be considered a brilliant market analyst, or should he be viewed as a likely Information Warrior? And how do you catch him, anyway? The money to be made with insider knowledge is phenomenal; it's like knowing the winning lottery numbers before they're picked. Some of Wall Street's famous power brokers from the 1980s were sent to prison as a result of their illegal profit-taking enterprises. Doesn't the Information Warfare have a similar motive—windfall profits—with substantially less risk? When billions of dollars and lives are at stake, is any quasilegal act or deniable source of information off limits?

Is our society so sick that an unhappy customer would resort to putting the offending company's computers out of commission? Hackers have already done it; causing millions of dollars in damage because they didn't receive their free poster. Considering that we have seen murder and kidnapping in such cases, perhaps Information Warfare is a welcome alternative.

And what about those serial-killers who indiscriminately kill young girls for the thrill of being chased by police? Will any of the emotionally devastated types who got blasted in the recession turn to Information Warfare as a means of extracting revenge from a cruel society? Or maybe it will just be cyberpunks with attitude, who want to raise hell in Cyberspace.

They're well-trained, experienced, and dangerous. Then there's pure harassment by mean people out to cause trouble, who find that the Global Network gives them the ability and the protection all at once.

These are the Information Warriors.

Cyber-Civil Disobedience

Winn Schwartau

During the question-and-answer period after a speech to 800 raving New York hackers in the summer of 1994, I made what I considered at the time to be an innocuous comment. "If my generation had had the technical toys you guys have, the 1980s never would have happened." The house came down as the crowd pondered the implications.

Twenty-five and thirty years ago, millions of Americans shouted their convictions and antiwar sentiments by marching in the streets and engaging in variously creative forms of civil disobedience. Antinuclear activists and environmentalists have maintained the tradition over the years while repeat offender antiabortionists seemingly wear the badge of both misdemeanor and murder arrests with pride. But the visceral images of huge traffic-jamming Vietnam era protests broadcast live on the evening news will be the ones indelibly etched in our minds and history books.

Twenty-five years later, due to ever unpopular White House stances on the National Information Infrastructure, the Clinton administration similarly invites demonstrable outcries, but with the modern twist of technology-driven protest.

In April 1993 the White House announced the Clipper Chip: perhaps the most loathed invention the government has ever sprung upon the American public. Ostensibly designed to protect telephone conversations from interception with government-quality encryption, the NSA-designed Clipper is outfitted with a "back door" to allow law enforcement agents to listen in on the encoded signals when approved by the courts. Outside of a small handful of vocal adherents, Clipper is viewed by its critics (darn close to 100 percent of the population) as anything from silly and stupid to technically flawed to evidence of the totalitarian tendencies of government.

Despite the continuing outpouring of hatred for the ill-conceived and unworkable Clipper, the White House has reaffirmed its support for this "voluntary" initiative. The IRS reportedly considered that electronically filed tax returns would have to be Clippered, and that sounds like anything but voluntary. The U.S. Postal Service wants to get into the electronic mail business, and there is legitimate concern that in order to provide the general public with security and privacy, a Clipper derivative, such as Capstone, may be the requisite technical solution. The word *voluntary* apparently takes on new meaning in Washington.

White House support for the Justice Department's efforts at successfully passing the Digital Telephony Bill further exacerbated an already disgruntled cyberpublic. Law enforcement wanted to continue its court-authorized surveillance activities despite, critics say, no proven need for expensive and possibly invasive antiprivacy technology and legislation. In general, the administration's handling of Cyberspace has been severely questioned and criticized from the board room to the university to millions of online users. And President Clinton's conceptual endorsement of an electronic national ID card may prove to be the needed fodder to create an explosive critical mass of popular dissatisfaction.

So what is a disgruntled citizenry to do? Cyber-civil disobedience is timely, poignant, and potentially highly effective.

Twenty-five years ago, youthful and academic demographics flavored the antiwar movement: predictable-looking people predictably demonstrating against their government's policies while always aware the TV cameras were rolling. Today, administration policies are loathed by a cross section of America that traverses most social, economic, and age barriers.

Twenty-five years ago, a demonstration or protest required organization and the congregation of huge numbers of people, all within the limits of the necessary police permit. Signs and slogans and chants prefaced the occasional Mayor Daley-like headline-grabbing overreactions. Today, the nether world of Cyberspace offers an unrestricted, unregulated, and certainly unorganized refuse as a 1990s alternative to conventional assembly. Cyberspace provides the ideal mechanism for cyber-civil disobedience, the protest means of choice for the information age. Cyber-civil disobedience is waged by remote control, over vast distances, yet the effects can be highly focused against selected targets.

And, best yet, there isn't a police officer guarding each and every portal to the Information Superhighway waiting to haul a civil disobedient off to the slammer.

Phil Zimmerman would probably disagree. He was under investigation for violating U.S. export control laws governing encryption schemes, and was facing the potential of years in prison. Someone, in an apparent act of cyber-civil disobedience, placed an electronic copy of Phil's PGP (Pretty Good Privacy) software encryption program on the Internet, resulting now in near universal availability of a virtually uncrackable coding method. Governments, notably ours, aren't happy and want to put a stop to copycat "crimes." My recent book, *The Complete Internet Business Toolkit* (VNR, 1996) is banned from export from the United States because it contains dozens of cryptographic programs. Forty-two or more months in the slammer for taking my book on a trans-Atlantic flight.

One widely discussed act of mass civil disobedience would be the intentional violation of encryption export laws by tens or hundreds of thousands of people, rendering attempted export policy enforcement virtually impotent. All that protestors have to do is make a copy of their favorite encryption scheme and place it on the Net, electronically mail it to their buddies overseas, or just post it on a domestic BBS. All of these acts are, depending upon your interpretation, against the law. Precedent-setting cyber-civil disobedience on this scale gives the government the unenviable and unpopular choice of either selective enforcement or policy revision.

Cyber-civil disobedience is easily disguised. If, for example, the electronic mailboxes of selected, presumably offensive government services are overloaded with lengthy, unnecessary garbage-laden messages, they will literally collapse under the weight of popular opinion. Such widespread shrapneling of targeted systems by millions of cyber-civil disobedients could effectively shut down noncritical electronic government services whose demise would act as highly visible media-magnets. Cyber-events are news and news spreads the word: the protesters need the publicity for enlistment of more sympathizers.

Rotary dial telephones that once used to ring in one's opinion are today replaced with millions of home PCs connected to millions of modems. Using a little piece of software known as an auto-dialer, it would take only a few thousand distant and invisible confederates to shut down a company's or agency's PBX, or even president@whitehouse.gov, and thus their ability to communicate. With a larger "demonstration" of cyber-civil disobedience, entire telephone exchanges would be capable of responding to would-be callers only with, "All circuits are busy."

With an electronic U.S. population of an estimated 30-40 million, a high percentage of which are cyber-aware, the capability for cyber-civil disobedience is within the realm of short term possibility, if not probability. Network systems have limited bandwidth; an obvious weak point that a cyber-civil disobedient can easily exploit to the detriment of the service provider and its customers.

Whether it's Right-to-Lifers shutting down an abortion clinic's ability to communicate, or extreme environmentalists striking in Cyberspace instead of in the woods, or an angry public venting electronic frustration at its government, the capability for cyber-civil disobedience is real, and within the power of millions of people.

The 1990 movie *Flashback* concludes with captured '60s radical-activist-hippie Dennis Hopper warning FBI agent Keifer Sutherland, "Kid, the '90s are going to make the '60s look like the '50s."

The Clinton administration should keep in mind that for an information age population to aggressively voice its discontent, America doesn't have to take to the streets.

An edited version of this was published in *Information Week* in March 1995. I wrote it as a speculative piece, in no way trying to incite or encourage immediate action. However, people must be listening.

In November and December 1995, protesting French and Italian citizens targeted their respective government's Internet presence to voice their dissatisfaction with official actions and policies. Here is a posting from the Internet which describes what happened. (No corrections to the English have been made.)

NET STRIKE ECHO

The first international Internet's strike has been developed in a good result!

It is not possible to know how many Internet's users were on-line but as there were many www french government servers listed in our strike's msg we think several thousands of Internet users have participated to the strike!
Strike effects were the above reported:
5.45 p.m. Quick access to fr [French] servers;
6.00 p.m. first difficulties to access to fr servers;
6.15 p.m. it is not possible to access to the Health and to the Educational Ministers' www servers;
6.30 p.m. Also the servers of the Nuclear Agency, of the French Government and of the Indusrial Ministry decline the access;
6.45 p.m. The access to the servers of the National Education and of the Health Ministers is denied while the link with other fr servers meets several difficulties;
7.00 p.m. Only the link with the servers of the Educational and Health servers is denied while the functioning of the other servers is on standard level.
Apart from the "on-line" partecipation we have recorded the arrive of several msg of approval to the demonstration from all over the world. The comrades of the French ECN have translated our msg and spread all over France while several well known fellows such as Bruce Sterling has joint the strike. [This assertion was subsequently contested and determined to be in error.]

The Italian press has shown attention to this kind of strike by publishing several articles *La Nazione, Unita', Repubblica* while the left-wing newspaper *Manifesto*- has not published any note on this demonstration!)

The strike has been "transmitted" by several Italian "radio" such as Controradio and Radio Popolare and other kinds of local and national information networks has spread news about the strike.

Our protest msg developed on 14.12.95 has been spread all over the world after few days showing:
the interest of many people to counteract the French current policy on nuclear and social items;
the willing to be involved in a NET'STRIKE;
the existence of a world-wide movement able to counteract world-wide injustice;
the capacity to develop a such kind of movement in a short time.

Finally we outline that: several users have not set browser preferences in such a way to really link with the server each time (cache memory at 0) and not with its own PC;

it could be possible (for the next time) to build up software oriented to the specific goal to make an "electronic demonstration" at the internal of a www server.

As a result of this first net'strike's test we are sure that a strike organized at the internal of internet (with more days to organize the strike, specific software, specific instructions) can be a powerful media to counteract international injustice.

We are happy to see how the inter-activity offered by Internet has offered the opportunity to many people to stand-up on the electronic frontier not for business or for show goals but for social global demonstration!

On February 29, 1996 the White House was to be the target of an immense "broadcast storm" of e-mail, each containing the Bill of Rights. The goal was to shut down part of whitehouse.gov and alert President Clinton that much of the Internet community was fearful that administration cyberpolicies were inconsistent with the Constitution. The results, however, were ineffective; apparently not enough people participated.

Then in March 1996, Mexicans called for Internet strikes similar to those in Europe. In May 1996, someone or some group blasted broadcast storms to the alt.religion.scientology Usenet news group in an apparent attempt to stifle critics of the Church of Scientology through a denial of service attack.

I was certainly surprised that cyber-civil disobedient acts occurred so soon after I published, but in my mind it only presages what is likely to be more of a regular occurrence.

Should Spies Be Cops?

Stewart A. Baker, Esq., Steptoe and Johnson

Reprinted with permission from Foreign Policy *97 (Winter 1994-1995). Copyright 1994 by the Carnegie Endowment for International Peace.*

Like generals ready to fight the last war, bureaucrats excel at avoiding last year's scandal. Usually that does no harm. But every once in a while avoiding last year's scandal means sowing the seeds for next year's.

That is what is happening today in a strenuous but largely hidden struggle among the federal agencies that operate at the intersection of law enforcement and intelligence gathering. The struggle has come to a head as a result of the BNL affair. Also known as Iraqgate, the BNL affair centered on charges that the Justice Department and the CIA had covered up the Bush administration's channeling of prewar military assistance to Iraq through the Atlanta branch of Banca Nazionale del Lavoro, or BNL.

Though driven by recent headlines, the struggle has its roots in the late 1940s, when the American peacetime intelligence "community" was created to help fight the Cold War. American intelligence agencies were shaped by individuals who understood the mechanics of totalitarianism and wanted none of it here. They knew that the Gestapo and the Soviet KGB had in common a sweeping authority to conduct internal and external security and intelligence gathering. Determined not to become what they were fighting, the drafters of the 1947 National Security Act declared that the newly created CIA "shall have no police, subpoena [sic], or law enforcement powers or internal security functions." The CIA's role was to deal with America's foreign enemies, not its domestic wrongdoers.

The drafters of that language were only being prudent. Combining domestic and foreign intelligence functions creates the possibility that domestic law enforcement will be infected by the secrecy, deception, and ruthlessness that international espionage requires. Dividing the responsibilities among different agencies reduces that risk. It also creates a tension between agencies that is itself a safeguard against abuse. It is surely no accident that the Russian democrats who helped break up the Soviet Union also stripped the KGB of its internal security duties— adopting, in essence, an American system of divided responsibility.

The irony, of course, is that the end of the Cold War has pushed U.S. policymakers in the opposite direction. A strict separation of intelligence from law enforcement proved workable enough while the Cold War continued. Apart from counterespionage work, there was little overlap between the two. The intelligence agencies had a desperate job to do abroad, but they faced a threat that was almost exclusively foreign. Law enforcement, by contrast, had few international dimensions and almost no way to address international criminal activity.

By the 1990s much had changed. Because the Soviet Union was no longer a threat, some of the resources devoted to extracting its secrets could be turned to other tasks, to other foreign targets. But some of those foreign targets had a domestic tinge. As topics like international narcotics trafficking, terrorism, alien smuggling, and Russian organized crime rose in priority for the intelligence community, it became harder to distinguish between targets of law enforcement and those of national security.

Intelligence agencies were not alone in expanding their traditional beat. The Justice Department had gradually extended its reach into foreign affairs. If foreign heads of state could be indicted in the United States for acts committed while in office (as Manuel Noriega and Ferdinand Marcos were in the 1980s), almost any foreign policy problem could wind up as a criminal matter.

These were the practical responses of law enforcement and intelligence officials to changing times. As the 1980s wore on, the same practical officials began to see the admonition of the 1947 act as more a technicality than a guiding principle. Surely, the pragmatists argued, the two communities should coordinate their efforts to understand common problems, should pool resources to avoid unnecessary duplication, should share what they know. What was wrong with that? As intelligence "centers" focusing on joint concerns like terrorism and narcotics trade proliferated, the Justice Department became a major consumer (or at least recipient) of intelligence reports.

All that was done like border trading between vast, self-sufficient empires—at the margin, and when it suited both communities. Neither community intended to change its fundamental way of doing business. Few foresaw any danger in nibbling a bit at the principle that intelligence and law enforcement must remain separate undertakings.

The BNL Affair

Then came the BNL affair, with its charges of a massive coverup at Justice and the CIA. Two years later, such claims seem overwrought. At least three separate investigations have turned up no support for them, and no intelligence or law enforcement official has been indicted—or apparently even disciplined—as a result of BNL. Even the Clinton administration, which had no reason to soft-pedal its probe, seems now to have quietly concluded that no wrongdoing occurred in either community.

At the time, however, press coverage of the affair had a strident breathlessness that brought to mind coverage of Watergate and Iran-contra. When it turned out that both the CIA and the Justice Department had failed to identify all of the intelligence reports on BNL in their files, respected career professionals in both agencies found themselves attacked as co-conspirators in a coverup.

Thus did these agencies learn the hidden cost of their practical accommodations in years past. Their critics were simply carrying the concept of "coordination" to its logical conclusion. If intelligence gathering has been harnessed to the cause of catching and prosecuting criminals, the outsiders said, then intelligence agencies should live by the rules that govern criminal investigators. The critics assumed that the intelligence community was obliged to search its files for any information that might help the defendant's case. So when the CIA produced arguably exculpatory documents that the Justice Department had never shown the defendant or the judge, it looked like dereliction of duty or worse.

Later, a postmortem would show that some of the intelligence reports had been sent to Justice, where they were lost or forgotten; that others were simply overlooked when the CIA first searched its own records; and that some were informal reports that had never been formalized for fear of exposing sensitive intelligence sources and methods in a criminal investigation. Gallingly, even the agencies' defenders found themselves arguing that the agencies were not corrupt, just incompetent.

That, it turned out, was also the conclusion reached in the investigation that followed. The staff of the Senate Select Intelligence Committee wrote a detailed report criticizing the government's failure to use intelligence assets to get to the bottom of the BNL affair, calling for more and better coordination between the communities and for more and better access to intelligence files. The attorney general's independent counsel, Judge Frederick Lacey, found no criminal wrongdoing at Justice or the CIA but criticized the CIA's procedures for disseminating information as well as the lack of systematic intelligence recordkeeping and processing at Justice.

In the wake of the investigations, a task force dominated by career officials was formed to recommend ways to improve the relationship between Justice and the intelligence community. The career officials, perhaps predictably, proposed to do more of what they had been doing— only better this time. The career officials' report has not yet been adopted by the administration, but its thrust is clear: The law enforcement and intelligence communities will continue to converge; and there are no problems in their converging relationship that cannot be solved with more staff, more computers, and more high-level coordination. It is an eminently practical conclusion.

The Risk to Civil Liberties

But on this issue the forces of practicality are simply wrong. Putting intelligence resources increasingly at the disposal of prosecutors poses much the same threat today as it did in 1947. Intelligence gathering tolerates a degree of intrusiveness, harshness, and deceit that Americans do not want applied against themselves.

Today the risk to civil liberties is largely theoretical. Among the more surprising discoveries I made when I joined the National Security Agency was the depth of the agency's commitment to obeying the legal limits on gathering intelligence relating to American citizens. The intelligence scandals and institutional reforms of the 1970s remain living lessons in the secret world.

However theoretical the risks to civil liberties may be, they cannot be ignored. The intelligence community serves a constituency of several hundred officials. If top military and civilian policymakers are pleased with what the community produces, it glows with success. When President Bill Clinton cancels his intelligence briefing four or five times in a week, as he did early in his term, the entire community trembles. No other part of the government has so narrow an audience—or responds so enthusiastically to guidance from above.

One of my office's jobs at the agency was to review requests for intelligence from drug enforcement agencies. In some cases, we suspected they were trying to shortcut constitutional or statutory limits, and their requests were denied. But I have no illusions that our objections would have prevailed if a different message had been coming from the leaders of the agency and the government.

As a counterweight to the risk of shortcuts, the reforms of the 1970s brought the rule of law explicitly to intelligence activities. For security reasons, that has meant attorney general review more often than judicial review. And for 20 years, it has worked well: The Justice Department has served as an effective check on the intelligence community. The department could credibly act as a surrogate judge in that period because it did not owe the intelligence agencies anything. But should it come to depend on the intelligence agencies to help it enforce the law, the department will be less credible, and perhaps less vigilant, as a guardian of civil liberties.

The difference between the legal regimes governing law enforcement and intelligence can perhaps best be seen by looking at the way each conducts wiretaps, or electronic surveillance. Police taps are governed by Title III of the Omnibus Crime Control and Safe Streets Act of 1968, which imposes elaborate controls. Police must have probable cause to believe that the target is engaged in a crime, the crime must be one identified by Congress as particularly serious, the police must have no way other than a tap to collect the evidence they seek, they must persuade a judge to issue a warrant for it, and they must report to the judge every few weeks to show that it is still yielding valuable information.

Taps performed for foreign intelligence purposes were not regulated until 1978, when Congress enacted the Foreign Intelligence Surveillance Act. That act governs national security wiretaps, providing protections against surveillance of Americans and requiring the government to obtain a warrant for national security wiretaps within the United States. But the warrants can last for up to a year, and the standards for granting a warrant depend not on behavior but on status. If the target is a foreign power or agent of a foreign power, surveillance will be authorized.

The standards for intelligence taps are—and must be—looser, for obvious reasons. For one, the stakes are higher. Foreign powers like the old Soviet Union certainly pose a greater threat to this country than any conceivable criminal organization. For another, the targets are more elusive. Intelligence agencies spend years intercepting anodyne conversations, waiting for the one moment when discipline breaks down and a crucial fact slips out. For a third, relations between the United States and foreign governments are governed not by the social contract underlying American democracy, but by the rules of international relations, in which espionage is hallowed by tradition.

But what happens when the distinction between law enforcement and foreign intelligence wiretaps begins to fade? The most obvious consequence is that law enforcement officials hoping to conduct a wiretap are tempted to redefine their criminal investigations in foreign intelligence terms. That saves them much of the hassle of meeting Title III standards for the wiretap. The bigger the role assigned to law enforcement in defining the country's foreign intelligence requirements, the easier that becomes. It may all be done in good faith by pragmatic men and women. But it will gradually erode some of the protections that Title III was designed to confer.

The other threat is also real though less obvious. It is that the courts will respond to the growing convergence by forcing intelligence agencies to live by the rules that govern law enforcement. The Supreme Court was careful to separate national security from criminal investigative taps in 1967 when it first declared wiretaps to be "searches" subject to the Fourth Amendment, and both Congress and the lower courts have agreed that foreign intelligence taps are judged by a different standard under the U.S. Constitution.

But courts are quick to spot a risk of abuse. In 1972, for example, the Supreme Court struck down a Nixon administration claim that the calls of domestic dissidents could be intercepted without warrants under the rubric of national security. If the distinction between intelligence and law enforcement grows too artificial, the judiciary could cripple intelligence surveillance by demanding that it conform to the same standards as law enforcement.

In fact, the consequences would be worse than that. If the courts were to determine that just one intelligence wiretap has in fact crossed the line into law enforcement's territory (and that would be easy to do, given the vagueness of the line and the growing convergence of investigative targets), a series of statutory traps would be sprung. The target would be entitled to notice of the tap. Those who approved and carried out would be subject to prosecution for committing a felony. The sources and methods used to conduct the tap would be at risk, if not fatally blown.

A similar problem arises in deciding how and when to share intelligence with law enforcement agencies. That field is less sexy than intelligence collection but no less crucial. From Pearl Harbor to BNL, the intelligence failures that hurt the worst have not been those of collection but rather those of dissemination.

Investigative Dissemination

Dissemination to law enforcement falls into two categories: investigative and exculpatory. Investigative dissemination in many respects resembles ordinary intelligence dissemination. If, say, the Drug Enforcement Administration (DEA) is concerned about Central Asian drugs smuggled by the Russian mob, it will want to know more about both Central Asian drugs and organized crime in Russia. In preparing analyses and transmitting intelligence on these topics, the intelligence agencies are acting in an entirely traditional fashion. Over the years, law enforcement agencies and the Justice Department have expressed interest in a wide range of such topics, with the result that a torrent of intelligence has been transmitted to that department on many issues. But, as was embarrassingly clear in the aftermath of the investigations into the

BNL affair, much of the intelligence that Justice gets is desultorily skimmed and discarded—if it is read at all.

Why? General information on law enforcement topics has limited value for investigators and prosecutors. What they care about, for the most part, are individual investigations leading to individual convictions. Their narrow focus shapes their view of intelligence. Intelligence that is vital while an investigation is underway suddenly becomes irrelevant once the jury has spoken. Law enforcement respects secrecy and confidential sources—but only for a time. Intelligence that cannot ultimately be introduced as evidence at trial borders on worthless.

So if intelligence is to be valuable to Justice Department prosecutors, it must be focused on what they care about—individual investigations. That is the inevitable direction in which closer coordination with Justice will push the intelligence agencies. Not only is that what prosecutors want, but that is what the intelligence community was criticized for not doing in BNL. Critics found it incredible that the CIA did not know what defense the accused was likely to make in the BNL prosecution and that it had not sent reports relevant to that defense to the right lawyers.

Any dissemination system that seeks to move all intelligence relevant to all Justice prosecutions into the hands of prosecutors is doomed to fail. The self-preservation instincts of government officials would make coordination resemble a game of hearts: Everyone knows that, sooner or later, the game will end—that some arguably relevant piece of intelligence will not be delivered to a federal prosecutor in, say, the Southern District of Florida. When that happens, no one wants to be holding the queen of spades. Thus, the Justice Department will be increasingly inclined to issue sweeping demands for "all relevant intelligence" in any case with an international flavor. And the intelligence community will be increasingly inclined to send masses of intelligence indiscriminately to the Justice Department and let Justice figure out where it might be relevant. By implicitly offering tighter coordination as a way to avoid future BNLs, the task force is writing a check that no dissemination system can cash.

That is a recipe for failure—and a colossal waste of resources. But the cost of success would be equally high. If intelligence agencies succeed in providing the kind of case-oriented "tactical" intelligence that law enforcement values most, the distinction between intelligence and law enforcement will erode even more, with the consequences described above: a long-term risk to civil liberties or an invitation for the courts to impose law-enforcement procedures on intelligence agencies.

Exculpatory Dissemination

The other sort of dissemination to law enforcement is exculpatory. A good example of the kind of procedures that the courts could impose is found in *Brady v. Maryland* (1963). In that case, the U.S. Supreme Court held that prosecutors may not withhold from a criminal defendant information that is material and favorable to the defense. That and related rulings have left prosecutors with a clear obligation to review their files and those of investigating agencies for information that could help the defendant.

The more closely intelligence agencies work with investigators, the more often this obligation will fall on them. The long-term consequences will be worse than the pragmatists suppose. For law enforcement agencies, Brady searches are a pain in the neck. But for intelligence agencies, they are a nightmare.

Law enforcement agencies have learned to live with Brady. When the FBI opens a case, it knows that a successful investigation will end only in one place—in court. The entire investigative recordkeeping system used by the FBI is designed with that end in mind. Records likely to be relevant to a later prosecution are identified and stored so as to make later criminal discovery searches easy. And reports are prepared with the trial in mind—every agent who writes a report on a case does so in the knowledge that what he writes will be read by a defense attorney at the end of the day.

Not so for intelligence agencies. The uses of their information are more diverse, the process more fluid. Intelligence agencies gather information for policymakers. An error that creeps into intelligence reporting may go uncorrected—may even be repeated—if having that fact exactly right is irrelevant to the policy issues of the day. And intelligence does not have a predetermined goal. The information does not have to be made public. So intelligence agency files are more likely than law enforcement files to contain casual speculation or fragments of data that could be construed as exculpatory. The prospect of releasing those files is thus more likely to come as a painful surprise.

That is what happened in BNL. And given the structural barriers to thorough Brady searches of intelligence files, we can be certain that that particular queen of spades will turn up again and again, though perhaps not in quite so charged an atmosphere.

Nor are intelligence agencies' problems finished once they find and review all the relevant documents. The Justice Department will want its prosecutors to decide which reports are relevant to their case. The prosecutors will want to be briefed on the sources and methods that produced each report. And even if they conclude that a piece of intelligence is probably not exculpatory, they will want to discuss any piece of intelligence that could conceivably assist the defendant with the judge in the case. So the judge will have to be briefed as well. Then, if any of the information is deemed materially exculpatory, it will have to be revealed in some form to the defendant and his lawyers. Under the Classified Information Procedures Act, to avoid a risk to intelligence sources and methods, the government is allowed to propose a sanitized substitute for classified data; but the substitute must be just as good as the original for the defendant's purposes. If it is not, the government must reveal its secrets or drop the prosecution.

It is bad security to describe highly sensitive sources and methods to a steady stream of prosecutors—many of them young lawyers who will soon be making a career out of representing criminal defendants. Even worse, when a court says classified information is relevant to the defense, intelligence agencies will find themselves locked in battle with prosecutors who would rather reveal classified information than give up their prosecution. Of course, defense counsel will have every incentive to exploit the opportunity for graymail. They will strain to find ways of including classified information in their defenses, all in the hope of forcing the government to drop the case rather than reveal its secrets.

What does this add up to? In an effort to give law enforcement more information that it does not want very badly and does not use very well, government officials may be about to stretch the rules that preserve civil liberties, flirt with harsh new judicial limits on how intelligence is gathered, impose unworkable new search and recordkeeping duties on intelligence agencies, spread the knowledge of intelligence sources and methods much more widely, routinize conflict between prosecutors seeking convictions and agents keeping secrets, and encourage defense lawyers to exploit each of those problems to the hilt in the hope of forcing the government to abandon the prosecution of their clients.

Why are we doing this? The practical men and women in law enforcement and intelligence tell us we have no choice. They say that all those problems will arise to some degree no matter what we do; that we cannot go back to the days when intelligence and law enforcement were sealed off from each other; and that proper coordination and good will on all sides can minimize the damage.

Maybe so, but given the stakes perhaps we should try an alternative approach first—one that preserves, perhaps even raises, the wall between the two communities. We should begin by shedding illusions. The first and most dangerous is the illusion that intelligence agencies or the Justice Department itself should be expected to identify and disseminate every piece of intelligence that might be relevant to every investigation conducted by federal law enforcement agencies. No one knows enough about the thousands of pending investigations to route intelligence reports efficiently to every interested prosecutor and investigator. To accept responsibility for doing so is like starting every game with the queen of spades in your hand. Instead of establishing mechanisms that purport to carry out that task, we should frankly declare that it cannot be done. Indeed it should not be done; such all-encompassing distribution would align law enforcement and intelligence to a degree that should appall any student of twentieth-century history.

Instead, we should construct a dissemination system that makes sense. That means distinguishing between top Justice Department officials, who need intelligence to help them make wise policy choices, and other law enforcement officials, who want intelligence to help them make their cases.

Top law enforcement officials—the ones who allocate resources and set strategy—need the same kind of "strategic" intelligence that other policymakers do. If Chinese gangs are planning massive alien smuggling drives, or if the Russian mob has turned Central Asian collective farms into opium factories, the attorney general and the heads of the FBI and DEA need to know. But such information can and should be fairly tightly controlled. There is not much reason for it to go below the level of deputy assistant attorney general.

Individual Justice Department attorneys, and generalists like the U.S. attorneys around the country, are unlikely to need such strategic intelligence, at least in detail. To the extent that such intelligence requires analysis, the function could be centralized in a Justice Department (or investigating agency) intelligence unit. Under such a system, Justice would not get thousands of documents of doubtful relevance. And what it did get would be controlled and analyzed in a way that would make for greater accountability.

It should go without saying that such information would be gathered only if it has foreign intelligence—and not simply international law enforcement—significance. Decisions about what intelligence to gather must remain the province of the director of central intelligence and the national security apparatus. But there is no reason to insist that the Justice Department be treated differently from, say, the Defense Department in the dissemination of such "strategic" intelligence.

That is not the case for "tactical" intelligence—information about particular shipments, particular schemes, particular individuals. Here the wall of separation between intelligence and law enforcement should largely be maintained. Intelligence agencies should not be asked routinely to use their intelligence-gathering authority to help law enforcement agencies bust criminals.

What about cases where both communities have a legitimate interest in gathering information about the same person or group? Surely there are both law enforcement and intelligence reasons to seek information about the man who shot several CIA employees outside CIA headquarters and then fled the country. Must the FBI and CIA work separately to track him down? No, but the investigations should be coordinated under strict controls. Most important, intelligence agencies should know in advance that they are entering into a coordinated investigation. Then they can keep records in a way that makes it easier to search for exculpatory information—and they can use sources and methods that could, in a pinch, be made public if that is the only way to bring to justice a particularly dangerous offender.

Similarly, a conscious decision to coordinate law enforcement and intelligence activities for an investigation could be preceded by an analysis of whether law enforcement is the predominant interest. If it is, intelligence should be gathered only under law enforcement authority, subject to law enforcement limits and supervision. In such cases, intelligence agencies will know from the start that they are working for—not with—law enforcement.

A system in which tactical intelligence is shared only rarely and only after careful thought will go a long way toward preserving the spirit of the

1947 act. It will protect the current legal distinction between how information may be gathered for law enforcement and national security purposes. And, with luck, it will help address the thorny question of criminal discovery.

The cases requiring that prosecutors turn over exculpatory evidence can be read as applying broadly or narrowly. Read narrowly, the obligation applies to information in the hands of the prosecutors themselves and to the investigators who developed the case. Read broadly, the obligation covers any information in any government file. In my view, the better reading of the cases is that the government ordinarily must search only those records available to the prosecutor and those aligned with the prosecutor. On that reading, intelligence records would be subject to discovery whenever the two communities engaged in a coordinated investigation—although probably only the information gathered in that coordinated effort should be open to discovery.

If there is no coordinated investigation but the defendant believes that his other activities are likely to have been of interest to intelligence agencies, no searches should be ordered—at least in the absence of strong indications that particular intelligence records will produce exculpatory evidence. The burden and risks of searching intelligence files are simply too great. Such cases will be rare. Perhaps the best example is a defendant who claims to have been violating U.S. law because he was hired by the CIA to do so; in that event, checking the CIA's employment records might be an appropriate search, but checking every operational file in the agency would not.

Ironically, the loudest objections to restricting discovery in this way will come not from judges and defendants but from prosecutors who do not want to surrender their chance to review intelligence files. The reasons for the resistance are many. Turning over exculpatory evidence is seen as a prosecutor's ethical obligation. It is difficult to delegate that obligation to another, particularly someone who does not know the case as well as the prosecutor. And, some prosecutors say, the intelligence agencies have not proven reliable when they conduct Brady searches on their own. Some in the intelligence community, on the other hand, suspect that while prosecutors talk about having to search for exculpatory information, they never really abandon the hope that their search will turn up something inculpatory. Finally, prosecutors are heavily influenced by the expectations of district court judges, who tend to want broad discovery in order to forestall postconviction appeals. Prosecutors would much rather inconvenience intelligence agencies than annoy the local judges they deal with (and depend on) every day.

The only way out of that box is to elevate the issue beyond the reach of individual prosecutors' preferences and district courts' jawboning. That will happen only if the highest levels of the Justice Department decide that discovery of intelligence agency files should be resisted strongly. The department and the intelligence community need to agree on when a search is necessary and when it is not. At a minimum, that standard should be written into the prosecutors' manual; a statutory standard would be even better.

Either way, to maximize the chances of prevailing against the inevitable constitutional challenge, access limits should apply to prosecutors as well as defendants. As a practical matter, judges are more likely to order that documents be turned over if they come from files the prosecutor has already searched. And the briefing of sources and methods that accompanies prosecutorial searches is at least as great a strain on security as debating the relevance of a few arguably exculpatory documents before a federal judge.

When I was at the National Security Agency, we used to joke about the predictable stages traversed by prosecutors who sought intelligence reports in connection with big investigations. The first reaction was open-mouthed wonder at what the intelligence agencies were able to collect. That was followed by an enthusiastic assumption that vast quantities of useful data must lie in our files. Next came the grinding review of individual documents and the growing realization that the reports were prepared for other purposes and so were unlikely to contain much of relevance to the investigator's specific concerns. Last came ennui, and a gritted-teethed plod through the reports, mostly to avoid a later charge that the examination was incomplete.

The lesson of that progression is one that must be conveyed more widely. Intelligence agencies have great capabilities, but they only produce useful intelligence if they are asked the right questions. Reviewing intelligence collected for one purpose in the hopes that it will shed light on some related issue is almost always a fool's errand. Except for employment files and the like, the only intelligence files likely to contain information genuinely relevant to a criminal case are those assembled as part of a coordinated law enforcement/intelligence investigation. In short, prosecutors and defendants lose little or nothing if searches are restricted to such files.

Implementing that alternative approach will take courage and persistence. It may well seem impractical, at least in the short run. The advantages of coordination and convergence can be realized here and now: New roles are created for intelligence officials; new worlds are opened to law enforcement; the echoes of the BNL affair are stilled. The risks that come with more coordination and convergence—risks to sources and intelligence-gathering techniques—all lie in the future. But the advantages of convergence are so fleeting, and the risks so palpable, that we cannot afford to settle for practicality.

Assassination Politics

Jim Bell

Society has a problem. Actually, it has many problems, but chief among them are wars, political tyranny, and crime. And the odd thing is, these problems are actually the product of the systems (governments) that we select to solve them. Such an assertion will certainly be a surprise to the various people ostensibly in charge of solving those problems: the military, the politicians, and the police. Just ask them! They'll tell you that they do their best to protect us from these scourges. But that simply isn't true. The problem is, anybody who supplies a service has a subtle motivation to ensure that the people to whom he provides that service never escape from this need. To be sure, some don't have enough control to make their desires stick, and some are simply to scrupulously honest to control us, but it's always a tempting goal to make your customer your slave. There is always a tendency, in fact, to induce your customer to purchase more of your "solution" than he really needs.

And that is what has happened to us as a society. We have soldiers who are supposed to protect us, but we have had more and bloodier wars this century than we've ever had before. We have politicians who are supposed to protect our freedoms, but the reality is that politicians are the worst thieves of freedom there are. They steal half our incomes (in some countries far more) in taxes, and oppress us with voluminous and occasionally illogical laws. Most countries in this world are not free by the standards of the people in this room, and in the opinion of some of us (libertarians), no country on the face of the earth is really free. We have police to protect us from crime, but they push to fill our jails and prisons with nonviolent drug offenders, crowding out the space and leading to early release of truly violent criminals. All this completes the cycle: more crime and more misguided public clamor for more prisons and convictions. All at public expense.

In short, we live in a terribly mixed-up, screwed-up world, one that has seen the deaths of tens of millions because a few crazy dictators got control of their little portions of society. And even when wars don't occur, freedom is lacking.

Sounds pretty pessimistic, right? Well, no. I'm going to make a claim that will strike many of you as being at the very least implausible, and more likely fantastic, and for some of you totally unbelievable. I assert that there is an answer. The solution to wars, nuclear weapons, militaries, politicians, tyrannies, dictators, holocausts, governments, taxes, and at the very least a substantial fraction of crime. The fix. The cure. The complete and total repair job. The last correction. That's the good news.

420

The bad news is that it's going to be a roller-coaster ride on the way there. And some of you will fall out if you resist the ride.

The following ten notes are the current progress on my essay, which I term "Assassination Politics" or "AP." This improbably named musing was written between June 1995 and early 1996, and is a continuing work. It's not really a paper; it's more like a forecast. A manifesto. A warning. A promise. To many of you it will seem quite extreme, and understandably so: anybody who has a stake in the status quo will not enjoy the prospect of a quick and truly revolutionary change in society, especially one that changes just about everything we're used to. And the worst part to such people (the best part to the rest of us) is that if I'm right, this is not a change we can choose to forgo: The word *inevitable* was practically invented for it.

I started publishing this essay on an Internet mailing list called Digitaliberty, continued on a number of areas on a different computer network called FIDOnet, and continued on yet other Internet mailing lists—Cypherpunks@toad.com as well as nwlibertarians@teleport.com.

I will not try to cover all the possible changes that AP will engender; that would take up far too much space and time. Since this is for the "Information Warfare Conference," I will focus primarily on the military-defense aspects. First, I should point out that it would be misleading and incorrect to speak of "national defense" or "national security" in the context of AP. The way I view it, there is nothing fundamentally different between defending yourself from your neighbor, the crook who lives across town, the village over the next hill, the region over the next mountain, or the continent over the next ocean. This position alone will be extraordinarily disconcerting to those people who hold jobs supposedly to "protect the country" or "protect the citizens." AP will allow ordinary citizens to defend themselves not only against threatening foreigners, but also against fellow citizens who want them to pay taxes to support a bloated military and political and judicial structure.

Defending your country for pennies on the dollar . . . or even less.

America spends around $250 billion per year on what is called "defense." Does this make sense? It does not, in view of AP. Conventional military defense assumes that during peacetime you must maintain whatever level of military is necessary to fight a war. To provide an analogy, if you have a castle, it's like making the walls of the castle as high and strong as is necessary to protect yourself against the most powerful adversary you may ever encounter in decades or centuries. This is vastly inefficient, because maintaining military forces doesn't cost dramatically less in peacetime than during war, and we're all paying the bills. Any country which does this is at a serious disadvantage against those that can demilitarize, as Japan did after WWII. I contend that any country which adopts AP as a military strategy automatically benefits from a huge reduction in defense costs.

Suppose your hypothetical castle had crank-up walls, ones that could be dynamically changed from short chain-link fences in peacetime to tall wooden walls when minor threats appear to high stone walls topped with razor wire under more serious conditions, etc. Further, suppose you only had to pay for the level of protection you needed at any particular time. This alone would be a dramatic reduction in cost over the current system. And suppose all your soldiers were rented "just in time" as they say. Suppose you didn't have to pay them overtime, or a pension, or give them medical benefits, or even provide them weapons or housing. Suppose, in fact, you hired your soldiers from the ranks of the "enemy," the people who are in the best position to do damage to those who threaten you. In short, suppose you bought only the defense you needed, attacking exactly where it's needed, and only when it's needed, and chose only the highest-efficiency attacks. How much more economical could you get your defense?

AP postulates that if there is a warring country out there, controlled by an abusive hostile government, it should be possible to defeat it simply by targeting the leaders—and all its government hierarchy, as necessary—and whoever replaces them, for as many and as long as it takes. Its own citizens, as well as any other people it threatens, should be able to pick off the leaders one by one, in effect bribing anyone to eliminate that leadership anonymously. The presumption is that, faced with a series of such eliminations, the remaining leaders will either resign or will adopt friendlier policies toward the nation's citizens as well as foreign regions.

It is well known how useful a spy, turncoat, or saboteur can be during wartime, if he's on your side. AP turns all people (including those who might normally be called "the enemy") into potential allies, even if their identities are not known, and even if they didn't know until yesterday that they would be an ally. They would not, in fact, know with whom they are allied! And you wouldn't know who they are, nor would you need to. Furthermore, the number of such potential allies is essentially unlimited: The reward is based on the completion of a task, which means that even a relatively limited reward can affect the behavior of thousands of people. It can also easily destabilize a foreign government, even if the reward is not yet collected, because it makes the people in those systems unable to trust each other, putting an enormous financial wedge between all relations. A foreign general won't be able to trust the people under his command, a dictator won't be able to trust his cronies, and that these rewards can be collected anonymously means that nobody has to risk exposure to collect, which makes the danger to your enemies even more palpable.

The biggest advantage to AP, however, is the fact that it will have the same effect on the political and military system of "the other guy" as it does on us. To whatever extent another region or country represents a threat to us, it does so primarily because the leadership in that country has managed to seize control of the political system and direct it in a hostile fashion toward "us." It does this in ways which will be as undesirable for the average citizen of his country as military adventure is to our country. It can therefore be expected that any militarily hostile country would dissolve, with its government going the way of Eastern Europe in 1989 and the former Soviet Union a few years after. As we learned, the average citizen of these countries had no reason to be hostile to the average citizen of America, or any other western country, so the elimination of the hostile government eliminated the threat.

All this said, it is somewhat difficult to estimate how inexpensive such defense should be. It was pointed out during the Gulf War that the larger the number of people available to participate on one side of a military operation, the fewer the casualties would be. Ironically, in a similar fashion, the more money that's available to defend a group of people, the less that group may eventually end up spending.

The overall cost of such an operation is probably inversely dependent on the likelihood that it will succeed. This sounds odd, but consider yourself in the position of one of that doomed leadership. If it is essentially certain that you will die if you don't resign, it is hard to remain enthusiastic about staying in your current job, no matter how much prestige you've had in the past. If the people you are threatening have far more than enough money to buy your death and those of a few hundred of your fellow leaders, you will have to accept the fact that you're getting out of your current job, and resignation will appear to be the most attractive outcome.

The more certain your doom, however, the more likely that you won't wait to stop a bullet. That's one less target for those you're threatening to aim for, increasing the danger for your ex-associates. You might even choose to target them yourself, since you presumably have access for a while. You might do this, because you know that they might also target you!

For a first shot at a ballpark estimate, however, let's assume that security from large-scale, external threats for the people inside a region currently called "America" requires financing the deaths of 1,000 people each in 150 different regions corresponding to 150 current countries. Assuming each such death was purchased for $50,000, which is probably an overestimate, that works out to $7.5 billion. Even such an estimate is closer to a one-time investment, because once hostile people are eliminated from positions of leadership, it will be difficult for others to return and carry out threats. They will not be inclined to seek such an office, and the public in their country will not want to pay for such threats. Most of them, in fact, will resign, which makes the remaining ones even more at risk, because the rewards will tend to build up if they are not used.

Someone will probably object that these countries contain far more than 1,000 people each, and "if you kill 1,000 another 1,000 will pop up in their place." Well, not really. We're not talking about the ordinary citizen. We're talking about the leaders, the upper-level managers, the cadres, the decisionmakers. The more certain the deaths of those who represent a threat to "us," the less likely anybody with such a bent is going to want to occupy an office. After the deaths of the first few hundred tinpot-dictator wannabes, the rest will discover that it is far more profitable being a friendly, nice country. We'll learn the same lesson, by the way. Their ordinary citizens will be able to do the same to us, or more specifically to our political and military leaders. The citizens of this country won't object; in fact, they'll appreciate having their tyrants eliminated. Don't believe me? Wait and see!

Another potential objection: "Won't those people object to having 'their' people killed by us?" The answer is nobody will know who is killing whom. It's all anonymous, and AP will work internal to their country as it does here. When a politician or military leader dies there, there will be no way for anybody to know who actually financed it, and if the person who did the killing isn't caught, there will be no way for anybody to know who carried it out. No resentment will accrue to the enemy, whoever he might be, because everyone's aware that "a friend" might have done it. And any large-scale attempt to exact revenge will fail, because conventional military won't work, and threatening another country for a false reason will simply induce more danger from other countries.

And, of course, "they" will have the same power over us, which would probably give the U.S. government hierarchy the willies. Not only will the average American not want to finance hundreds of billions of dollars in defense, especially once he finds out there is no reason to, but there will be no government to collect the taxes to accomplish this, and any so-called enemies that remain will be similarly disarmed.

Dismantling the Nukes?

One of the most useful and fascinating consequences of AP will be the effect on the world's stockpile of nuclear weapons. For decades, it has been assumed that "the nuclear genie is out of the bottle" and it would never be possible to return to a bomb-free world. However, I believe that AP will provide not only an easy solution, but a trivial one. Because the only purpose of a nuclear bomb (other than attacking the enemy's bomb silos) is to threaten a large number of people, any large number of people will consider themselves threatened, implicitly, by the presence of a nuclear bomb anywhere on the earth. Thus, they will be interested in donating money to fund the deaths of anybody or any group of people possessing such weapons. Since such deaths can be financed secretly and the assassins paid anonymously, it will be impossible to maintain such weapons in secret.

If, say, a billion people live in cities and suburbs that might potentially be at risk due to nuclear bombs, an average donation of only $1 per person constitutes a reward fund of $1 billion, which would be a major danger to the few people likely to be in control of those bombs. If 10,000 bombs exist, that would be $100,000 per bomb, against anyone who might be inclined to want to keep it. And assuming that 99 percent of the bombs are openly dismantled, the reward fund grows to $10 million per bomb. Considering the fact that the reward can be collected anonymously, conspiracies toward the keeping of such a bomb would be downright suicidal.

I predict, therefore, that any organizations still possessing such weapons will hold "bomb dismantling parties," in which they prove to the world that they are eliminating all their bombs. The results will be transmitted by television and other media, and groups from around the world would attend, perhaps by proxy, to establish that the bombs are disassembled. Secretly saving a bomb would be impractical, because word couldn't help but escape, and anybody associated with the operation or any friend or acquaintance could reveal the truth to the public anonymously, making it impossible to keep the secret for long.

Besides, there would be no reason to keep a bomb. Anybody who justifiably felt the need to use any weapon against his enemies could just use AP instead. It would be quicker, easier, cheaper, and far more specific. Bombs would be hopelessly useless, extraordinarily unspecific, and (still) extremely expensive. You couldn't threaten anybody with them, because those threatened would simply assume that the bomb really existed, and would target you with AP. Anyone even nearby those threatened would, themselves, feel equally threatened, for obvious reasons. It goes even further than that: Anyone nearby a person claiming to own the bomb would feel threatened, and would feel obliged to "help" dismantle it, or its owner, by force if necessary.

Crime, Politics, and Social Implications

While the margins of this paper are far too small to contain the details, I also predict that AP will result in the elimination of at least 90 percent of the crime in America, first and foremost by eliminating laws against victimless crimes and eliminating the laws which keep various drugs illegal and at high prices, but also by giving ordinary citizens a strong motivation to detect and fight crime, and giving them the tools to do so.

In addition, AP will essentially eliminate politics, because a stable anarchy doesn't need to be managed.

As for social implications, I'm still working on it. Many people will find the prospect of AP to be rather scary because of the vast social changes it will cause. We'll no longer be led by a single, hierarchical political structure, which may leave a few of the "followers" among us adrift. I think they'll get over it.

Which leaves one last thing: Inevitability.

One of the most astonishing things about AP didn't occur to me for a while. It turns out that this system is basically inevitable. Once the triad of digital cash, good encryption, and worldwide networking exist and are readily used, systems such as this can spring up literally anywhere. And if they can operate anywhere, they can operate everywhere the Internet goes, and a few places besides. At that point its effects would inexorably sweep the globe, erasing governments and militaries as it goes.

Which is why some of you won't like it.

13

The
Military Perspective

"U.S. Satellites carry twenty sorts of sensors, including electronic eavesdropping equipment that can pick up virtually any individual on-the-ground conversation."

—CIA DIRECTOR R. JAMES WOOLSEY[1]

ON FRIDAY, JANUARY 10, 1992, ABC's "Nightline" reported a story that I thought was a joke. According to *U.S. News and World Report*, the Allies, in preparation for the Gulf War, attacked and disabled Iraqi military computer systems with a computer virus developed by the Pentagon.

That's right. We took out the Iraqis with a computer virus.

According to the tale, the super-secret National Security Agency built a custom integrated circuit or chip that, in addition to performing its normal function, contained a computer virus. Viruses can be placed in hardware by chipping, as we have shown, but the technical and logistical problems of getting the right chip to the right printer to the right Iraqi . . . well, it's not a terribly efficient way to go about it. The chip was allegedly installed in a dot matrix printer in France that was destined for Iraq via Amman, Jordan.

The infected chip was reported to have shut down portions of the Iraqi defensive radar systems. This had to be a put on, a joke. But, no, not Ted Koppel! Something was wrong here. I was deeply troubled that "Nightline" could air a story that was so obviously in error.

I spent the early morning hours looking back over my archives and found an old article in which I spoke of airborne viruses and their offensive military applications.[2] In 1990, I had given a speech on mechanisms that the military could use to inject malicious software into enemy computers from thousands of miles away. Still, the back of my brain itched; the story Ted Koppel told just didn't make sense. Although I didn't know what I was looking for I knew I would recognize it if I saw it, so I kept up the frenetic search. About 3 AM, I found what I was looking for.

In the April 1, 1991, issue of *Infoworld*, John Gantz's weekly column was titled "Meta-Virus Set to Unleash Plague on Windows 3.0 Users."[3] Gantz said he had heard that the NSA had written a computer virus dubbed AF/91 that was to "attack the software in printer and display controllers." The column went further, stating "each machine makes the virus a little stronger." I remembered reading this column and thinking, "How absurd!" It continued to allege that the CIA had inserted the virus into an Iraqi-bound printer, and that by January 8, 1991, half of the Iraqi defense network was dead and gone—thanks to the efficiency of the AF/91 virus. "The NSA now believes that any Windowing technology is doomed," Mr. Gantz wrote.

The *Infoworld* article concluded, as many a computer column does, "And now for the final secret. The meaning of the AF/91 designation: 91 is the Julian date for April Fool's Day."[4] Alternately, AF/91 can mean April Fool, 1991; here was the joke!

Ted Koppel and "Nightline" were the victims of mis- or dis-information given to them by *U.S. News and World Report*, who in turn were first duped by their sources. Associated Press subscribers also had the opportunity to read the same "news" as if it were fact. The story went nationwide, and to this day, wherever I lecture, this story is still remembered as fact. Once I demonstrate the absurdity of it all, the audience rolls with laughter.

On Jan. 13, 1992, when faced with the evidence that the
story was really just a year-old April Fool's joke rehashed
through the military grapevine, or perhaps a plagiaristic
attempt at spreading disinformation, *U.S. News* still stood by
the accuracy of its story and the credibility of the two senior
level intelligence officers who confirmed it. The writer, Brian
Duffy, did admit, though, that there were some "disturbing
similarities" between the two tales. (No kidding.) I've included a point-by-point comparison of the original *Infoworld*
April Fool's story and the one put out by ABC and *U.S. News
and World Report.*[5]

InfoWorld	*U.S. News and World Report*
1. By January 8, Allies had confirmation that half the displays and printers . . . were out of commission	1. Several weeks before the air campaign of Desert Storm . . .
2. Virus targeted against Iraq's air defense	2. Virus targeted against Iraq's air defense
3. Designed by the NSA	3. Designed by the NSA
4. Virus built into printer	4. Virus built into a chip in a printer
5. The CIA inserted the virus	5. U.S. intelligence agents insert the virus
6. Printer went through Jordan on its way to Iraq	6. Printer went through Jordan on its way to Iraq
7. Peripherals not protected by electronic fortress	7. Able to circumvent electronic security measures through peripherals
8. Disables real-time computer systems (Mainframes)	8. Virus inserted into (their) large computers. Disables mainframe computers
9. "the NSA wizards"	9. "Cunningly designed . . ."
10. "It eats Windows."	10. " . . . each time (he)
11. Source: Old ADP navy buddy	
12. "So, it worked."	

13. NSA believes that any Windowing technology is doomed: There doesn't seem to be an antidote.
14. It could be four years before users start seeing their Windows blur. Maybe the NSA can discover a cure by then.

opened a window . . . the contents of the screen simply vanished."
11. Two senior U.S. officials
12. "It worked."

Government Information

April Fool's Joke.

Myth, fantasy, hoax, or just plain disinformation? Decide for yourself if Duffy was duped by the Air Force intelligence contacts he used for the story, if his Air Force contacts were also victims, or if the whole story was a prank by someone who read Gantz's article. No matter how you look at it, Information Warfare is a part of the picture.

Desert Storm computer stories abound, perhaps because it was the first high-tech war: You could turn on CNN, watch the action, then flip to "Roseanne" during lulls in the fighting.

Prior to the onset of hostilities, a British officer returned from the Gulf for a briefing at 10 Downing Street. Plans and contingencies for the Allied effort were stored on a laptop computer. Unfortunately, the laptop, along with its military secrets, was stolen from the officer in question. What made it even worse was that the information on the computer was not encrypted.

The British tabloids caught wind of the story and by evening everyone in the U.K. knew what happened. That much has been pretty well established but from here on, the various tales diverge. According to the most entertaining one, a common, third-rate West London petty thief, no tidier than a chimney sweep, appeared at a local police station the next morning with a laptop computer in hand. He politely suggested to the desk constable that this might be what they were looking for. The police were incredulous that the computer, containing the country's most secret intelligence information, had been returned, much less by the crook himself. They wanted to know why.

Mustering the best of British pride, still upper lip and all, the man replied, "I'm a thief, not a bloody traitor."

Rumor has it that the thief was released. In any event, the British officer was demoted and court martialed for his dereliction.

The American military was the target of a less benevolent intrusion during the same period. U.S. and European hackers broke into Pentagon computers by fooling the system into thinking they were Dan Quayle. Unclassified files about domestic antiterrorist efforts were accessed, but what made the event even more disconcerting to the military is that the break-in was broadcast nationally on U.S. television.[6]

The Navy makes an unexpectedly honest self-assessment of how well-protected our computers were in the Gulf War: "While Desert Storm appeared to the public to be a high-technology war in all aspects, many systems were several generations behind available commercial technology, and were in fact, vulnerable."[7] That astute, understated observation reminds us that technology does indeed march on, and that the equipment available to the military may not be of the same quality or caliber as that used by everyone else.

The Navy's SEW, or Space and Electronic Warfare, policy is coincident with that of a class-two corporate Information Warfare effort: "Destroy, deny, degrade, confuse, or deceive the enemy's capabilities to communicate, sense, reconnoiter, classify, target, and direct an attack.[8] And just how is the military going to achieve that aim? With the same tools that other Information Warriors use.

In the fall of 1990, a military contract was awarded to study how airborne computer viruses could be inserted into enemy computers. Not by hand, not by person, not by diskette, not by dial-up, but by air. The $500,000 year-long study may have provided the impetus behind the almost laughable Iraqi Virus Hoax.

In a follow up 1993 contract called Statement of Work (SOW) for the Malicious Code Security Model Development Program, the U.S. Army wanted to study the vulnerability of its Army Tactical Command and Control System (ATCCS) that serves as the technical core of battlefield operations. The army is concerned that Information Warriors on the other side could penetrate their systems with malicious software.

Through computerized simulations,

> These (malicious) codes are representative simulations of potential network intruders (hackers) who could disrupt the ATCCS networks.
>
> The contractor shall research and develop a computer model that simulates potential malicious codes that could disrupt or delay any sort of ATCCS information (e.g. programs, software, etc.) These codes simulate how would-be network intrudes actions could disrupt the ATCCS's command and control.
>
> The contractor shall easily introduce simulated malicious code into the ATCCS type internetwork in order to see the effects on ATCCS.[9]

The military, for all of its security and paranoia, suffers from the very same problems as corporate America. Duane Andrews, a former Assistant Secretary of Defense for C3I, (Command, Control, Communications, and Intelligence), said in late 1992, "Our information security is atrocious, our operational (security) is atrocious, our communications security is atrocious."[10]

A few years ago, a senior level Air Force officer I'll call Bob was in charge of a Tiger Team that was supposed to test the physical and electronic defenses of a facility such as a classified office building or an embassy. In an attack mode, the Tiger Team is to do everything within its power to break in and compromise its defensive posture. In this case, Bob's goal was to determine how well the information within a Texas air force base was protected.

A meeting was scheduled a few hours before the simulated attack just to make sure everything was in place. Bob showed his ID at the facility checkpoint and was admitted. But instead of attending the meeting, he left the facility a few minutes later. When leaving, he was subjected to another search. His briefcase was opened, the Sergeant poked around looking for something, then finally said with a crisp salute, "Thank you sir. Have a nice day."

"Excuse me, sergeant."

"Yessir."

"Could you tell me what you're looking for?"

"Yessir. Calculators, sir. We've been having a lot of them stolen recently."

"Thank you, sergeant. Carry on."

Bob walked to his car and called into the meeting.

"Where the hell are you? You're late."

"There's no need for the meeting. I've already cracked security."

Angry silence on the other end of the phone. "Get in here, now!"

Back inside the facility, Bob went to the meeting and was asked to explain. After gaining access to the facility the first time, he had walked up and down a few corridors and into a few offices, slipping floppy disks into his pockets and his briefcase. The guard who checked his briefcase when he left saw the diskettes, but he was too preoccupied with missing calculators.

"I have here," Bob said, spilling the contents of his briefcase on the conference table, "one hundred and forty classified diskettes full of military information. I respectfully submit, sir, that your facility has no security. This Air Force Base fails."

"But you cheated," a higher-up officer stutteringly complained.

"And the bad guys won't? You expect them to announce their visits the way you wanted mine announced?"

"But the procedures, the rules . . ."
"I lied. You still fail."

In all sincerity I hope it's not that bad throughout the government, but I fear the worst.

The military worries about a lot of things, and one of them is the terrorist threat. Our own list of culprits is long enough, and undoubtedly theirs is longer. We know what terrorist groups are capable of if properly motivated, and we know that the battlefield could likely be the networks and computers of corporate America, our communications infrastructure, transportation support systems, or portions of government Cyberspace.

But questions arise. If such a assault were made, what would our reaction be? Would the military step in? Should they? Is a debilitating attack against General Electric by an overseas Green group considered worthy of a national response? If narcoterrorists from an immense drug cartel successfully shut down U.S. border radar systems, what is the appropriate reaction? How do we politically and militarily deal with a remote controlled foreign incursion into U.S. Cyberspace? How do we deal with a situation where the victims are unquestionably on American soil, but the invaders are physically located thousands of miles away?

International law is even more confused than U.S. computer crime law. Extradition for hackers? Prosecutorial reciprocity? It's hard enough with hijackers and war criminals. Can we reasonably expect a lengthy legal process to be the only recourse in the case of a substantial attack by Information Warriors?

Answers to these questions are either deeply buried in the bowels of the Pentagon, or more likely, we haven't made preparations for such eventualities. We are deft with electronic countermeasures (ECM) in guarding air space and the electromagnetic spectra in a hot war zone, but government-business coordination to protect civilian U.S.-based electronic systems for extreme eventualities is barely on the drawing board. The Government's Software Vulnerability Analysis contract to evaluate the vulnerability of the public-switched networks is a healthy step forward in the right direction.

As the role of the U.S. military evolves into that of good Samaritan and humanitarian as well as soldier, we need a frank and open discussion of the role the military would play in such extreme scenarios. Outside of conventional military countermeasures, electronic warfare, and sophisticated secretive intelligence gathering, military assistance in the protection of the commercial technoeconomic infrastructure will never occur unless and until we implement and enforce a National Information Policy.

Iraqi Virus Hoax Update

Winn Schwartau

US News & World Report never came to grips with it; DataPro Research wrote an interesting albeit inconclusive article. I consider the following e-mail message to set the record straight. Thank you, John.

Winn,

Don Ulsch of Dataquest bought me a copy of your book, *Information Warfare,* in which you discuss my *Infoworld* April Fool's article in Chapter 13.

Your analysis that the whole thing started as an April Fool's joke is right on. When USN&WR ran the story—about the same time as that Ted Koppel interview—I contacted Brian Duffy to find out how they got it. Apparently, my column had been translated into Japanese for *Infoworld Japan,* and the meaning of "April Fool's" was lost on the average Japanese reader. In the dragnet for information for the book and USN&WR article "Secrets of the Gulf War," the information on this miraculous computer virus was actually unearthed by the magazine's Tokyo Bureau, which got it from the *Infoworld Japan* piece. And thus was fact created out of fiction.

I was chagrined that USN&WR, which I called and to which I wrote letters, never owned up to the error, even after that dialog with Duffy. I am also chagrined that (according to Duffy) at least two sources in the government claimed the story was accurate, but I understand why they might. It makes them seem "in the know" and their employer look smarter than it probably is.

Keep up the good work.

John Gantz

Sometimes the Dragon Wins: A Perspective on Information Age Warfare

Colonel Charles J. Dunlap, Jr., USAF

Introduction

I want to take this opportunity to thank the sponsors of this conference for providing me the opportunity to share my views with such a distinguished audience of international experts.

I must caution you that I use the phrase "my views" literally. Everything that I say is my opinion alone and does not necessarily represent the views or opinions of the United States government, the U.S. Department of Defense, or any of its components, including U.S. Strategic Command.

My presentation this afternoon will center on an article I wrote last January for the *Weekly Standard* entitled "How We Lost the High-Tech War of 2007: A Warning from the Future." In writing it, I was influenced by my experiences serving in Africa during our relief efforts in Somalia. I was struck by the resourcefulness, cleverness, and fierceness of the Somalis in confronting us. With that experience as a starting point, I theorized about the broader issue of what impact information-age technologies might have on the less-developed world, especially as the cost of extremely capable and easy-to-use information systems continues to fall. I wondered to what extent cheaper technology might affect the combat capability of societies we had considered too resource-poor to challenge us.

Those of you who may have read my article will realize that it is not a technical document. Rather, it is an imagined tale wherein the leader of a mythical non-Western nation delivers an "after action" report to his colleagues in his country's "Supreme War Council." In his speech, the unnamed chieftain explains how he engineered the defeat of the United States in a conflict set in the year 2007.

The scenario I set out is deliberately vague, but it does imply that this mythical nation has invaded a weak neighboring state. America, together with other members of the international community, endeavors to expel the aggressors.

What I tried to do is put myself in the position of a potential adversary some ten years in the future and postulate how war might be waged against a high-tech power. In setting the scene for my fictional war I made a number of assumptions:

1. That Western nations, and particularly the United States, would develop and deploy sophisticated information-based weaponry (e.g., F-22 fighters), and would organize their forces and develop doctrine accordingly.
2. That these same nations would develop and deploy information-based methodologies that could defend their most vital civilian and military facilities not only from hackers and other forms of cyberassault, but also from Oklahoma City-style physical attacks.

Many of you may properly think that such assumptions are overly optimistic. Nevertheless, what I wanted to do is to hypothesize a best-case scenario for the United States and the West.

Despite this background, my fictional enemy nevertheless master-minded the defeat of the United States by waging not limited war, but a new kind of conflict that I call "neo-absolutist war." This is a vicious form of confrontation that extends across the spectrum of warfare. It differs from more traditional total war by, among other things, the propensity of the aggressor to focus on shattering the opponent's will by openly and unapologizingly employing brutality against combatants and noncombatants alike. In a sense, such warfare has existed throughout history, but information-age technology modernizes it (hence "neo-absolutist") and vastly expands its potential.

In order to explain the theories that "High-Tech War of 2007" was meant to illustrate, I've extracted a number of propositions:

Proposition #1. Our most likely future adversaries will be unlike ourselves.

The adversary I invented for "High-Tech War of 2007" is not a first world nation and perhaps not even a nation-state in the traditional sense. Instead, it is more a grouping of peoples who are profoundly unlike ourselves in several critical respects. My analysis causes me to disagree with those—including some information-warfare gurus—who too often seem to assume that our future opponents will be Westernized, technology-dependent societies whose armed forces are built more or less along the lines of the U.S. armed forces. Likewise, I believe that many information-warfare enthusiasts mistakenly suppose that our future opponents will have cultural mores and values similar enough to ours so that a "rational" (in a Western sense) cost-benefit analysis would drive decisions of peace and war.

I do not entirely discount any possibility. Given the history of the twentieth century, it's theoretically possible that a high-tech Western European nation might wage war against the United States in the future. Furthermore, I recognize that we in the West are finding groups of rather bizarre extremists who might someday pose more than the mere law enforcement threat that they do today. But I still think the much more likely scenario is what Samuel Huntington called in his 1993 *Foreign Affairs* article of the same name, a "clash of civilizations."

What would be the nature of such civilizations with whom we might clash? In a fascinating piece in the summer 1994 issue of *Parameters,* Ralph Peters, then a U.S. Army major, described what he called the rise of "The New Warrior Class," a multitude which he contends already numbers in the millions. Peters says that in the future America "will face [warriors] who have acquired a taste for killing, who do not behave rationally according to our definition of rationality, who are capable of atrocities that challenge the descriptive powers of language, and who will sacrifice their own kind in order to survive."

In a similar vein, eminent British military historian John Keegan maintains that we are seeing the re-emergence of not just a warrior class, but warrior-peoples who are psychologically distinct from the West. These are societies, he says, where the young are "brought up to fight, think fighting honorable and think killing in warfare glorious." A warrior in such societies, Keegan has written, "prefers death to dishonor and kills without pity when he gets the chance."

A civilization so composed, perhaps organized around some powerful social or cultural force, will be a most dangerous foe because of the uncompromising zealotry and ferocity with which it can wage war. In my scenario, the aggressor nation's motivating psychological force is an unspecified religion that completely dominates its culture. I might add that the driving force could have just as easily been an ethnic identification, political ideology, or even some kind of as yet unknown cult.

If one is looking for a prototype of the kind of adversary and type of conflict that I foresee, I would suggest studying the war in Chechnya. Despite the application of tremendous military power, savage fighting persists. I submit that a lesson of that conflict, and one that I'll talk more about later, is that such peoples are hardly the type to capitulate solely as a result of the bloodless Information Warfare techniques touted by so many as the future of war following the purported "revolution in military affairs."

These warrior societies (or "streetfighter nations" as one commentator aptly described them) actually enjoy certain warfighting advantages over the United States and the West. Their populations are usually much more disciplined, casualty-tolerant, and able to endure deprivation than we are. Their troops are unfazed by orthodox calculations of what is militarily "doable," and quite often have much more austere logistical and support requirements.

For most of the nineteenth and twentieth century, however, these warrior societies and streetfighter nations infrequently succeeded—in a purely military sense—against the technologically superior forces of the West, especially when the Western power put its full resources into the effort. Indeed, a common critique of my article is that no adversary like the one I invented could possibly conduct the global military and para-military operations necessary to achieve the victory I describe. However, I assert that new developments in cyberscience have the potential to prove my detractors wrong.

Proposition #2. Information technology will facilitate and hasten the consolidation of potential opponents, including warrior societies.

I believe that new, simplified, but enormously effective methods of communication will allow the consolidation of national and transnational warrior societies (as well as radical elements of streetfighter nations) to a degree hardly dreamt of today. Specialized satellite television networks, comsats, Internet gateways, faxes, cell phones, and all the other attributes of the global communications revolution may enable the formation of "cybertribes." These could unite what now might be a diaspora of like-minded peoples hostile to U.S. interests. We already know, for instance, that neo-Nazi groups use the Internet to maintain contact with each other.

Enhanced communications can also be a catalyst that releases potent but presently inchoate psychological energy. That venting can produce violent results: one observer insists, for example, that the Milosevic regime "fanned the fires of pan-Serbism by taking over the national television system and using it to magnify semi-dormant hatreds."

Where once the word *communications* conjured up expensive networks of telephone lines, microwave towers, repeater stations, and so forth, a defining mark of the information age is the radical decline in the cost of all forms of communications. New hardware such as direct broadcast satellites eliminates the need for expensive cable or fiber-optic distribution systems while making it possible to reach audiences numbering into the billions. A similar result is produced by the growing use of cellular phones. I once visited the Khyber Pass which, as you know, is in a desolate region of Pakistan near the Afghanistan border. To my great surprise I saw people who were living much as Rudyard Kipling must have found them, but who were, nevertheless, using cellular phones to maintain communications, often with the help of satellites.

Please note, however, that in the future it may not even be necessary for a less-developed nation to spend the huge sums necessary to launch satellites. The *L.A. Times* reported last month that the U.S. Marines were experimenting with communication "satellites" that are actually held aloft by high-altitude balloons as a less costly alternative to space-based systems. Obviously, a potential adversary could do likewise.

I am convinced that the employment of new and increasingly inexpensive means of communications can tremendously influence and mobilize significant populations against U.S. and Western interests. The leadership of the warrior cybertribes can use cheap communications to not only unite their followers, but also to exercise effective command and control over groups that might be widely separated yet whose aggregate capabilities create genuine military concerns.

Along this line I should note that a phenomena of warrior societies and extremist streetfighter nations is that they tend to produce charismatic leaders. Modern communications systems will enable telegenic leaders to leverage their personal aura to reach huge numbers of peoples. Even wholly illiterate people will be able to see and hear their leader via telepresence. What's more, coming holographic imagery will project the leader's charisma in an enormously convincing way for audiences at multiple locations. Perhaps more importantly, a variety of emerging information and communication technologies will also leverage the streetfighter nation's military capabilities.

Proposition #3. Most analysts dangerously underestimate how significantly emerging technologies will empower warrior peoples.

As I mentioned, a common critique of my article is that no such warrior society could ever carry out the sort of worldwide attacks that happen in the scenario. Such attitudes dangerously underrate potential enemies, and reflect an arrogance that has had unfortunate consequences for the United States and the West throughout history. In conflicts ranging from Vietnam to Somalia to the Balkans, we have repeatedly seen how crafty opponents can offset high-tech hubris. Frankly, I think my critics misread the true implications of the information revolution on military affairs.

One key implication is that our potential adversaries will be technology-enfranchised in ways which will obviate many of the advantages first-world militaries enjoy today. The United States and the West seem to believe that they can safely downsize their forces so long as they maintain relatively small numbers of well-educated troops supplied with high-tech equipment. But I question how much longer we can expect to maintain a monopoly on the world's best-trained troops. Realistic new combat simulators and self-paced computerized teaching technologies will make sophisticated training available to the masses in the less-developed world. Furthermore, this kind of technology does not depend upon the presence of foreign military trainers who might otherwise be able to influence and moderate warrior societies' actions.

In any event, I'm not at all sure how much technical training the average combatant will need in the future—my guess is that most will need very little. My article predicts that extremely user-friendly software will empower poorly trained or even illiterate fighters to operate what is today considered complicated weaponry. Furthermore, some adversaries may abandon whole classes of weapons that require highly trained operators (e.g., manned fighter aircraft) in favor of fully automated, easy-to-use systems (e.g., antiaircraft missiles).

With the help of artificial intelligence systems incorporated into personal information devices, raw but determined conscripts might be able to use complex weapons in a strategically and tactically effective manner. The wisdom of the West Points, the Sandhursts, and the St. Cyrs of the world could be available—in the local language—to anyone who can wear a headset and push an "on" button. A step in this direction has already been taken by a company called Intervision with its "computer-on-a-hip."

Because new technology can implant expertise into a military organization in so many ways, it may not be necessary to educate the force as a whole. I disagree, therefore, with those strategists who contend that success in future conflicts will depend upon the technical knowledge of individual soldiers. By using technology to replace the intellectual achievement that could previously be obtained only through laborious and time-consuming courses of study, the combatants on future battlefields will become much more equal than has historically been the case. Moreover, given the innate martial qualities of warrior societies, the diminishing importance of the educational credentials cannot favor today's high-tech nations.

Besides eroding the training and education advantage that the U.S. and the West are counting upon to maintain their military edge, I also believe that technology itself will be much more level on future battlefields than most people think. This coming parity can be largely ascribed to the fundamental difference in what Alvin and Heidi Toffler would call "Second Wave" and "Third Wave" weaponry.

Second Wave weaponry are the planes, tanks, and ships produced by industrialized countries. Nations without sufficient heavy industry to allow at least some degree of weapons' autarky had little hope of prevailing militarily in all-out struggles against countries so equipped.

Likewise, for most of the twentieth century, the invention of revolutionary new weaponry usually occurred in those nations able to sustain a rather specialized and militarily unique research and development base. In large measure, this was the industrialized West and, accordingly, the West could monopolize and control the creation and production of the most advanced armaments.

That, in my opinion, will not be the case much longer. The key to Third Wave warfare does not lie in producing traditional weapons platforms; rather, if the experts are to be believed, the critical element will be the new information technologies that are largely computer-sourced. For this reason I do not believe that tomorrow's information-based weaponry will be produced by another resource-intensive Manhattan Project or Skunk Works. Obviously, it does not take a huge dedication of assets to turn out, for example, a piece of devastatingly effective software weaponry. Low-cost personal computers available in retail stores worldwide will more than suffice.

But a more fundamental reason the United States and the West will not have the high-tech advantage that they now possess is the simple fact that there are too many commercial applications of the new information technologies for the defense establishment of the United States or any other country to monopolize and control them. Businesses all over the globe are racing to invent new information-oriented software and hardware products. Accordingly, our future opponents (without investing anything in indigenous R & D infrastructures) can leverage the whole world's research and development capacity as they look for information technologies with possible military uses.

There are additional reasons that the most up-to-date technology will be readily available to our potential opponents. Producing computers is a much less taxing enterprise than building aircraft carriers, so there will be far more sources, perhaps even the streetfighter/warrior nation itself. After all, the manufacture of some systems may favor countries—unlike the United States and those in Western Europe—with low-cost labor pools. In addition, notwithstanding the potential military applications of information technologies, third-party financing and economic assistance is much more likely to be available to a less-developed nation for this kind of venture than for a traditional arms industry. The inherent versatility of cyberscience means that a country can build an information infrastructure with military capabilities while simultaneously serving the needs of economic development and not necessarily arousing the world's suspicions. Our potential adversaries will not have to choose between guns and butter in building information-age warfighting capabilities.

Yet another reason that the battlefield will become more technologically level lies in the growing dependence of American and other armed forces on commercial off-the-shelf (COTS) technology. This means we have to expect that sooner or later our enemies will make similar purchases in the retail market. Like the decline in communication costs, the astonishing reduction in the price of computer power brings extraordinarily versatile systems within the range of even the poorest potential foes. Because of the ready availability of cybertechnologies and the continuing decline in costs, I contend that the era when the first world could produce and control the latest weapons is over, at least to the extent that information technology is the linchpin to the most sought-after arms.

Nondemocratic opponents may well have another significant advantage over us; specifically, their acquisition policies are not necessarily as fettered by Byzantine rules and regulations as are ours. We all know that information technology can become outmoded in a matter of months, and that's much too fast for our current procurement process to react very well. Thus, a totalitarian regime may well be able to get inside our acquisition loop and procure and field advanced information-based weaponry before we can. In short, I am not confident that our existing contracting laws are dynamic enough to accommodate the information-age's environment of rapid technological change.

Proposition #4. The age of mass warfare may not be over!

As I've indicated, most first-world militaries—including ours—are counting upon an advantage in high-tech weaponry and superior training to allow dramatic downsizing of forces. If our adversaries will have much the same technology as we have, and information technology can neutralize the technical expertise and training that gives first-world forces so much of an advantage today, then the difference between victory and defeat might well revert to a question of the sheer numbers of combatants deployed. A future Napoleon might rightly echo the words of the original: "Victory goes to the big battalions."

In my estimation those in the United States who think that the Vietnam-era draft protests are little more than historical curiosities may be in for a shock. In the future we could find it necessary to conscript huge numbers of people to battle civilizations willing to place millions of technology-empowered citizens under arms. Even if the fashionable view prevails, i.e., that future armies will be populated by highly educated cybersoldiers, I am not so sure that an all-volunteer force will be able to attract enough such specialists in the coming years to permanently rule out conscription. Media reports of anti-draft demonstrations may again fill our television screens.

Proposition #5. The impact of information-age technology on the global media will be the most immediate and powerful influence on information-age warfare.

It amazes me how little discussion there is about this in the reams of literature concerning the alleged revolution in military affairs. What discussion exists is, in my view, incredibly naive and underdeveloped.

We already know that the media can project powerful images. What is new is the explosive growth in the media's ability to find and report these images from areas of armed conflict. Historically, governments with a mind to do so have been able to exercise considerable control over reporters' access to war zones as well as the dispatch of stories from battlefields. The press was often forced to depend upon the benevolence of the armed forces for transportation and communication in combat theaters.

That will seldom be the case in the future. As I predict in my article, news organizations will own surveillance satellites and self-contained communication systems that will allow them to function almost autonomously. Indeed, one firm, Aerobureau of McLean, Virginia, run by Chuck de Caro, can already deploy a self-sustaining flying newsroom. The airplane is equipped not only with multiple video, audio, and data links, but also gyro-stabilized cameras, side- and forward-looking radars, and its own pair of camera-equipped remotely piloted vehicles. In addition to being able to land on short unimproved runways, the aircraft can also dispatch satellite uplink-equipped reporters by parachute! Clearly, the media will be physically able to report the news, live from the battlefield, totally independent of military support or, even more importantly, the military's permission.

While we might be able to prevail upon the ethics or patriotism of individual correspondents who are our own nationals, the growing globalization of the news will always leave foreign journalists willing to report and broadcast such intensely newsworthy events as armed conflicts, especially those involving U.S. or other first-world forces. I am convinced that information technologies will empower the media to such a degree that virtually no observable detail of any consequence will escape their view. Furthermore, huge interconnected databases will add tremendously to their news sources. Advanced software will enable them to fuse the raw inputs into useful real-time or near real-time reportage. Such developments, in my opinion, will profoundly affect the conduct of future war.

The media revolution is but another example of how the information age will diminish the first-world militaries' current superiority. The press will become the poor man's intelligence service, and this will help warrior societies and streetfighter nations to wage war on the cheap. With immense quantities of information available from global news groups, what need will there be for our future enemies to spend enormous amounts of money building Western-style intelligence infrastructures?

None of this should really surprise us. We already see decisionmakers of many nations relying upon information from media sources like CNN. Some might say that if the media serves as a de facto intelligence service for a hostile force, then they should be treated accordingly. I doubt, however, that Western democracies can muster the political will to forcefully block reporters' activities, especially those of nonbelligerent countries.

The media revolution will have another important effect on military operations: the increasing obsolescence of operational security (along with deception and psyops) as useful military concepts. The rise of aggressive, technology-infused global news organizations will fill the air with colossal amounts of data. Every military move, or seeming military move, will be scrutinized and analyzed by the press and the expert consultants they hire. In that context, few military courses of action can remain concealed for very long.

I might add that it is not only the media that is responsible for this evolution. The proliferating numbers of personal cell phones, e-mail-capable laptop computers, fax machines, and so forth that troops themselves carry with them will also contribute to the avalanche of information available about military operations. I think that commanders will find these devices nearly impossible to monitor and censor. While our adversaries will have a similar problem, I think it will be more pronounced for the militaries of Western-style democracies because of the open nature of our societies.

Indeed, we are already experiencing an inkling of what's coming. I invite your attention to a recent report that 90 percent of Israeli recruits arriving for service brought along their own personal cell phones. Some used them to call their parents and others to complain about various aspects of their military duties. As *Newsweek* predicted over five years ago, "if soldiers can phone mom or the local newspaper from the middle of the battlefield, what are the implications for maintaining military discipline or secrecy?" I think the obvious answer is that both will suffer.

Proposition #6. The technology-empowered media and the proliferation of personal information/communication devices will have the effect of limiting the practical ability of casualty-averse democracies to engage in combat for much more than 30 days.

I maintain that the synergistic effect of the media revolution combined with a proliferation of personal information devices will make it politically unfeasible for most democracies to wage intense combat operations for much more than a month or so. During the Gulf War we saw how gruesome photos of the so-called "highway of death" undermined support for continuing the war—and those were pictures of the destruction of brutal enemy invaders. What should we expect when the bodies are those of our friends and relatives?

In the future, the type of real-time reportage of death and mutilation of our own soldiers that the new technology makes possible will likely create unsolvable political problems. Tomorrow's communication capabilities may allow commercial news services to furnish soldiers' families with customized coverage of their loved one's units, and perhaps even of specific individuals. This kind of coverage supplementing personal communications from the troops' own information/data devices will enable the soldiers' families to establish a virtual presence with them on the battlefield. When such telepresence begins to communicate the horrific shrieks and terrifying sights of death and mutilation as they happen to a loved one in combat, the political pressure to terminate hostilities at almost any price may become inexorable.

To accommodate this approaching reality, I think that the United States and other Western democracies may need to retain larger standing forces than are presently contemplated. We must be able to react swiftly to fight time-sensitive come-as-you-are wars. Because there will be only a short period before the enhanced communication of the horrors of war makes continuing the war not politically viable, there will not be enough time, for example, to prepare and deploy those reserves who require refresher training prior to combat. Rethinking the size and composition of reserve forces may therefore be in order. Similarly, if political demands dictate that fighting must be brief, then sustainment and reconstitution may be less important than many militaries think. In short, if a military solution cannot be achieved quickly, political exigencies may make it unachievable, notwithstanding the gravity of the interest at stake.

Planners for information-age conflicts ought to consider training and equipping forces for extremely intense, hyper- or blitzkrieg-style warfare. Regrettably, pressure for quick resolutions may compel military commanders to forego time-consuming tactics even though they might limit casualties on all sides in the long run. Once fighting has begun, I don't think that the public will have the stomach or patience for methodical approaches even if they promise less bloodshed over time. Accordingly, it will be imperative to develop stratagems that maximize the application of combat power before public support and political will evaporate.

Proposition #7. Seeking information dominance on tomorrow's battlefield is unrealistic and quixotic; instead, the United States should focus on developing doctrine and strategies for operating in an environment of information equality or information transparency.

Among the stratagems, that should *not* be counted upon for achieving rapid military success is gaining information dominance. For all the reasons I've mentioned—the likely technological parity of future belligerents, the stupendous multiplication of personal information devices, and most importantly, the explosive growth of the technology-empowered media—it will be nearly impossible for any belligerent to dominate the information dimension. What we should do now is not chase an unrealistic and quixotic strategy of information dominance, but rather think about how forces will fight in an environment of information equality or a totally transparent information environment where each side knows everything about the other.

As already described, the nature of the information age will likely find ourselves with equipment at best equivalent, and very possibly inferior, to that of our enemy. Even if we were able to deploy somewhat superior devices, I still think that achieving true "dominance" in anything more than a transient, tactical sense will be frustrated by our inability to degrade enemy systems. Information technology, and particularly communication systems, will become too inexpensive, too compact, and too redundant for military action or cyberaction to neutralize all of them.

I can foresee a time when the communication capabilities that today require entire units will be found in the personal information devices I've mentioned. There will no longer be any key communication nodes upon which to focus an attack—ultramodern information technologies will turn individual soldiers into self-contained communication centers. In fact, the *L.A. Times* article I referenced previously reports that the Marines are experimenting with small three-man groups linked to units by computers as a substitute for personnel-heavy command structures. Taking out all of the new-style C3I nodes will mean, literally, having to destroy every combatant on the battlefield. And, when confronting warrior peoples and streetfighter nations, such bloody business may be exactly what information-age warfare requires.

Proposition #8. Information-age warfare will not become the almost bloodless electronic exchange that some predict; rather, it will be as savage, and likely more savage, than ever.

One of the principal reasons I wrote "High-Tech War of 2007" was to attack what is becoming conventional wisdom in the United States and many Western nations: that information technologies will allow wars to be waged virtually bloodlessly. In a scenario depicted in *Time* magazine last summer, a U.S. Army officer conjured up a future crisis where someone like himself ensconced at a computer terminal in the United States could derail a potential aggressor without firing a shot. He visualized the foe's phone system brought down by a computer virus, logic bombs ravaging the transportation network, false orders confusing the adversary's military, television broadcasts jammed with propaganda messages, and the enemy leader's bank account electronically zeroed out. All of this is expected to cause an opponent to capitulate without fighting.

I don't really know if what he implied is technologically possible. I do think, however, that he failed to anticipate a point I've tried to emphasize: that future information technology may become so inexpensive that aggressive-minded nations—even relatively impoverished ones—will be able to afford redundancies that will make it difficult or impossible to accomplish what he suggests. Consider that the Internet, access to which requires only an inexpensive computer, originated in a system meant to survive nuclear attack by exploiting redundancies in modern communication processes. Surely critical communications and information technologies based on this or similar systems will be very difficult to defeat.

It seems that the ability of foes to devise low-tech ways to circumvent high-tech capabilities is being underestimated. Should we not anticipate that our future adversaries will plan workarounds for precisely this kind of cyberassault? Even assuming the colonel's plan is technologically feasible, and assuming the profound legal, ethical, and policy issues that his storyline raises can be resolved, I still maintain that it reflects a fundamental misunderstanding as to the character and temperament of our most likely future opponents. Warrior societies and streetfighter nations are just not as vulnerable to technology loss as is the United States and the industrialized West.

To me the Army colonel's scheme also mistakenly assumes that future foes would plan to fight in the same high-tech way as we would, and that they would engage in the kind of cost-benefit approach to conflict that the United States and the West do. It may be that we in the West in the late twentieth century might be ready to abandon military effort if our phone and electrical systems were disrupted or if our bank accounts were emptied. But it is a peculiarly Western notion to presume that every enemy in a future conflict would back down for like reasons. I would not count on such discomfiture deterring a warrior society acting in pursuit of a powerful cultural imperative and under the spell of a charismatic leader.

In any event, I doubt that a warrior society or streetfighter nation would try to defeat us by assaulting our domestic information infrastructure. I believe they would conclude—as the potentate in my article does—that to do so is too difficult for a less-developed nation with limited resources. I anticipate that they would determine that the center of gravity in conflicts with first-world democracies is not the information infrastructure per se, but the will of the people in a Clausewitzean sense. They will concentrate not so much on destroying our things as on smashing our spirit. In doing so, they may well decide that preserving our information infrastructure would facilitate their strategy, helping them to graphically communicate their willingness to do anything, however despicable, for victory.

Streetfighter nations like the one in my scenario will feel no compunction about waging war—particularly against the West—completely outside the norms of international law. Indeed, in my story their strategy is to deliberately wage war in the most inhumane and public way possible as a means of intimidating us and undermining our will to win. I think emerging information technologies will enable them to do that in quite innovative ways. This further explains what I mean by neo-absolutist war: Total war ruthlessly waged by unconstrained enemies enfranchised by technology.

That said, I should note that while a few of our future enemies will no doubt be sociopathic, I do not mean to suggest that their whole society would be similarly affected. I think that some groups may be able to form a moral, political, or cultural construct that leaves those outside of it unworthy of humane treatment. Aiding and abetting such a *weltanschauung* might be real or perceived affronts occasioned by American or Western actions, perhaps of relatively ancient origin. An adversary's population might somehow be able to rationalize abominable behavior in a war with a high-tech power.

Accordingly, I believe that a future opponent will not hesitate to use brutality to exploit the growing aversion to casualties that more and more shapes the political and military decisions of the United States and other first-world countries. Consistent with neo-absolutist war, atrocities will be brazenly displayed, not hidden. Our enemies will seek to manipulate us through barbarism, and enhanced information age technologies will help them do just that.

Why would they choose this strategy? For the simple reason that they might believe, rightly or wrongly, that it has worked in the past. I invite your attention to another criticism of my essay: an adversary who conducted himself as the one in my story does would so incite the United States that America would never abandon its military effort until the enemy was fully prostrate. I hope that would be true, but I wonder. That did not occur when Somalis dragged the body of a U.S. soldier through the streets of Mogadishu. There was no public demand to crush the perpetrators.

Although there were many reasons for the subsequent U.S. withdrawal from Somalia, I worry that our future enemies might conclude that the atrocious behavior the Somalis displayed helped undermine U.S. public support for the whole operation. If that is so, then the perceived failure to make those responsible pay a terrible price for such barbarism might encourage even greater viciousness in future information-age conflicts.

I fear that one target of their strategy will be prisoners of war. POWs became an important bargaining chip for the Communists during the Vietnam War and they were often used for propaganda purposes. In my scenario, female POWs would be particularly victimized by an enemy hoping to capitalize on our domestic debate concerning the extent to which women should be involved in combat. That victimization would not be done in secret; rather, the enemy would use modern communications to broadcast live the torture of the POWs to their families at home. Clearly, this would be designed to demoralize us and erode our will—a classic example of neo-absolutist war.

A few might wonder who could commit such terrible crimes. Apart from the fact that the twentieth century has witnessed more than its share of such deeds, last August *Newsweek* magazine reported a disturbing trend: several third-world countries are recruiting young teenagers and even preteens into their armies. Among the reasons for doing so, *Newsweek* concluded, was that boys will do things grown men can't stomach. A UNICEF worker observed that kids make more brutal fighters because they haven't developed a sense of judgment. You may recall that most of the Somalis mugging for the camera with the body of the U.S. soldier were youths. Because a basic tenet of neo-absolutist war is brutality, we might expect that young fighters will become a staple of our adversaries' soldiery.

The inexpensive but powerful communication capabilities we've discussed will allow a future opponent to offset other aspects of our current military superiority, especially when aided by willingness to ignore fundamental precepts of humanity and the law of war. For instance, our opponents will be able to maintain command and control while at the same time dispersing their forces in such a way as to be extremely difficult to find and destroy. I foresee virtual armies composed of small numbers of people, even individuals, remaining widely dispersed until immediately prior to an assault. In carrying out this tactic, I believe that our enemies will present ethical quandaries for first-world nations by purposely dispersing themselves among noncombatant civilians. Every attempt to strike them will risk noncombatant casualties.

Some might believe that information-age precision-guided munitions are the solution. But I think that underestimates the ingenuity of an enemy prepared to wage neo-absolutist war. In my story, for instance, the adversary counters the American advantage in high-tech airpower and precision-guided munitions by building VIP shelters, supply depots, and other vital facilities beneath hospitals, apartment houses, churches, and even POW camps. The clear aim of the enemy would be to create the same kind of dilemma as did the bombing of the Al Firdos bunker during the Gulf War. What was thought to be a command bunker apparently housed Iraqi civilians, many of whom were killed in a strike by the precision munitions delivered by F-117 stealth bombers. Because of the political furor that ensued, attacks on Baghdad were sharply curtailed.

In a way, information age technology and its success in the Gulf War have produced a problem for the United States and the other Western nations. The repeated television displays of smart weapons scrupulously hitting strictly military targets has created the public perception that war can be waged very discretely and relatively cleanly. In fact, however, over 90 percent of the munitions dropped in the Gulf War were dumb bombs with predictable inaccuracy.

If we need to rely on such weapons in future conflicts, as will probably be the case, our opponents can propagandize the inevitable collateral damage, particularly if they widely disperse their forces among noncombatants as I imagine they will. In large measure, we will have no one to blame but ourselves because we have, as I say, oversold the salutary potential of precision munitions on modern war. Furthermore, as the United States and the West pour billions of scarce procurement dollars into expensive smart bombs in the hopes of limiting casualties, an adversary intent upon waging neo-absolutist war can rely upon cheap dumb munitions. Ironically, the propensity of such weapons to cause collateral damage may even serve the enemy's interests by inflicting terror on noncombatants.

In yet another manifestation of neo-absolutist war, I think that future opponents will make hostage-taking an integral part of their warmaking strategy, because it can further offset technological advantages. In my story, hostages are taken and chained to all kinds of potential targets, including tanks, vehicles, and aircraft, the idea being to present Western forces with the terrible moral and political conundrum of having to kill civilians or even their own comrades in order to attack critical objectives. Hostage-taking seems to work. This is what the Serbs did in the Balkans. The Chechens successfully used hostages in several operations and I expect they will continue to do so. Nothing succeeds like success.

I also think that hostages will be taken not only from among our people, but also from the nationals of other countries in order to pressure key nations into denying us logistical bases necessary to support forward deployed troops. In addition, since so many important communication satellites are consortium-owned, an enemy may try to use hostage-taking to blackmail member countries, including neutrals. By taking hostages from third countries, our adversary will seek to assault us employing an indirect approach.

Proposition #9. Future adversaries will seek asymmetries in confronting technologically superior opponents like the United States and may do so by embracing an indirect approach.

Our future opponents, and particularly those technologically weaker than us, will almost certainly seek asymmetries in waging war against us. Being freed of what we would consider legal and moral restraints, will look for them in places that may not be immediately apparent to us. In my article, the enemy does so by applying B. H. Lidell Hart's indirect approach, though in a somewhat different manner than he perhaps contemplated. To avoid U.S. strengths, they chose to attack another, weaker country (or the nationals of that country) with a view toward influencing U.S. actions. These third countries become proxy or surrogate belligerents in a conflict in which they have few, if any, interests and are not otherwise involved. Tragically, they are attacked mainly because they can be attacked. The expectation was that their ill fortune could adversely impact the United States in some way.

In my fictional piece, one such proxy target was Mexico. The warrior-chieftain orders cyberassaults on Mexico's computer systems on the theory that they might be less protected than U.S. systems. In addition, information-age document technologies are used to print billions in counterfeit pesos to undermine the Mexican economy. Finally, insurgency groups are encouraged to renew their activities. The collective effect of all this causes the Mexican government and economy to collapse. In turn, millions of refugees flee across the border into the United States, creating a crisis there. The strategy is to divert U.S. resources and effort away from an overseas conflict while at the same time causing U.S. domestic upheaval.

I've already indicated that the nationals of minor, militarily weak nations are used as hostages in my scenario. One lesson of my essay might be that even in the information age, small nations still need to maintain an authentic national defense capability. This capability should include some means to project at least a deterrent force beyond its borders. Otherwise, they and their expatriate citizens are susceptible to becoming pawns in conflicts if for no other reason than they are vulnerable to attack. If victimizing small, defenseless countries helps bring pressure on the United States or other powers, then I think that the streetfighter nations will not hesitate to do so.

But the indirect approach can be applied not only to nations but to domestic targets as well. If critical centers of government and business are secure against cyberassault and more conventional terror attacks, then the enemy—as in my story—will seek asymmetries by striking more exposed targets. Unrestrained ethically or legally, my notional adversary chose to strike America's growing population of politically powerful elderly. Bombs were placed in parks and elder care facilities—again to divert resources and generate political difficulties.

The enemy leader in my tale engages in other nasty and appalling conduct. For example, he openly wages environmental war by sinking oil tankers to pollute our coasts, and scatters AIDS-infected needles on bathing beaches to create hysteria. He attacks U.S. agriculture for much the same reason that he attacks the vulnerable proxy countries: because it is within his means to do so.

In each instance the warrior/streetfighter nation does not seek to hide its culpability. To the contrary, it is a precept of neo-absolutist war to use the technology-enhanced media to broadcast to the world the extreme methods that they are willing to use to achieve their ends. The enemy's fanaticism extends to sacrificing their own people in a completely unexpected way.

Proposition #10: Information-age warfare will likely see both new techno-weapons and more traditional arms used in innovative and unexpected ways.

One of the more startling aspects of my article was the way in which the potentate used nuclear weapons. In my story, his nation had managed to assemble a few crude nuclear devices but had no reliable way of delivering them in the face of high-tech U.S. weaponry. Accordingly, a plan was developed where an American attack is induced on the warrior-nation's Military City by building a genuine biological warfare lab there. The attack is carried out during a live TV news broadcast, and just as the F-117s are dropping their precision munitions, the nuclear weapon is detonated.

Of course, it appears that it was an American weapon that was detonated, and there was a predictably hostile world reaction. The Japanese withdraw their support and begin to sell U.S. securities, panicking American financial markets. The rest of the world turns against the U.S., despite vehement protestations of innocence. The streetfighter nation then presents itself as a victim state and gains world sympathy.

I got the idea for this part of the scenario from the discussions concerning the bombing of Hiroshima and Nagasaki during the World War II anniversary last year. Personally, I was amazed that the propriety of the weapons' use during that conflict was so intensely questioned and that there was—and is—so little discussion of the savagery of the Japanese aggression that was responsible for the war in the first place. This persuaded me that nuclear weapons could be used in such a way as to undermine the U.S. war effort while providing an excuse of sorts for barbaric behavior on the part of an enemy.

At the same time I wanted to suggest that although a strategy like this might be unthinkable to us, it isn't necessarily beyond the ken of other societies. Every culture does not value self-preservation above all else. We find examples throughout history—the Jews at Masada, kamikazes during World War II, the Revolutionary Guards during the Iran-Iraq War—where surely suicidal actions were more or less willingly undertaken. During the Vietnam War Buddhist monks publicly immolated themselves as a symbolic statement to advance their cause.

Conclusions and Observations

A fundamental lesson that I hope my nightmare scenario presents is the importance of preparing for innovative uses not only of the new information technology but of existing weapons. Potential opponents may integrate both into an information-age warfighting doctrine that may be significantly different than what is popularly supposed today. Admiral Charles Turner Joy warned more than 40 years ago that "we cannot expect the enemy to oblige by planning his wars to suit our weapons; we must plan our weapons to fight war where, when, and how the enemy chooses." In this regard we cannot allow our fascination with electronic gadgetry to blind us to the fact that warfighting is a holistic endeavor that has many different elements of which information technology is but one aspect, and not necessarily the most important at that.

Lest anyone misread my intentions, it is my hope that by graphically discussing these issues, viable counters and defenses will be developed. That's the reason, incidentally, that the *Weekly Standard* piece was subtitled "A Warning from the Future." Someone who read my article complained that I was giving potential adversaries ideas. I find it comical that anyone would think that a lawyer sitting in his study in Papillion, Nebraska, could possibly think up strategies that our crafty potential foes would overlook. This is another example of profoundly underestimating our likely enemies.

Such naivete is exactly what I want to confront. As we study the implications of emerging information technologies, I urge you to evaluate these new scientific achievements from other than the Western point of view. Additionally, I recommend that you seek the views of the nontechnocrat. As with anything, one's own expertise can make the forest indistinguishable from the trees. I hope that as a nontechnocrat I've been able to offer some insights that are, as I like to say, out-of-the-box.

At the conclusion of my article, I indicated that the United States needed to confront barbarity and cruelty promptly and unequivocally when it arises. One writer insists that the only way to deal with the emerging warrior class is to hunt them down and kill them in summary fashion. In addition to the ethical and legal problems that presents, I do not think that such a policy is practical. While I agree with the theory that warrior societies (and particularly their leaders) must suffer ignominious defeat in order to be subdued, the spectacle of summary executions presented via information-age technologies would likely sap public support for the war effort very quickly.

So I am certainly not downplaying the importance of political and diplomatic actions as some of my critics suggest. I believe, for example, that the international war crimes tribunal now sitting in the Hague is an important step toward holding accountable those who engage in barbaric behavior. I am merely saying that such behavior must be confronted in an effective way; otherwise there are too many who will perceive us as weak and see nefarious opportunity in such assumed weakness. Make no mistake about it, opposing savagery will often require unambiguous force of arms, to include, as Bevin Alexander predicts in *The Future of War,* the murderous business of soldiers physically "moving into enemy territory and taking charge." As Plato said, "Only the dead have seen the end of war."

Finally, as we consider the impact of new information-based technology on future warfare, I want to emphasize again that we must not deceive ourselves with the notion that war can somehow be made antiseptic and bloodless. This is an extremely dangerous proposition that in its worst extrapolation could even encourage conflict by deluding decisionmakers that the horror of war can be electronically avoided. As my article tried to show, even in the information age, war will remain a gory business, full of unthinkable cruelty and relentless misery. We must not forget the deadly warning of the warrior-chieftain of "High-Tech War of 2007": "No computer wages war with the exquisite finality of a simple bayonet thrust." And there will always be those willing to thrust bayonets to achieve their aims. Thank you for your kind attention.

Excerpts from Worldwide Threat Assessment Brief to the Senate Select Committee on Intelligence, February 22, 1996

John M. Deutch, Director of Central Intelligence

I am here today to outline the threats to the United States and its interests now and into the next century.

We still call this the post-Cold War world. Among the opportunities and challenges of our time, there is not yet one dominant enough to

define the era on its own terms and give it a name. Looking beyond our
borders, we see much that is uncertain:

- The stability of many regions of the world is threatened by ethnic
  turmoil and humanitarian crises.
- Two great powers, Russia and China, are in the process of metamor-
  phosis and their final shape is still very much in question.
- Free nations of the world are threatened by rogue nations—Iran,
  Iraq, North Korea, and Libya—that have built up significant military forces and seek to acquire weapons of mass destruction.
- The world community is under assault from those who deal in
  proliferation of weapons of mass destruction, terrorism, drugs, and
  crime.
- And the interdependence of the world economy has made us more
  vulnerable to economic shocks beyond our borders.

The strategic threat to our continent is reduced, but the potential for
surprise is greater than it was in the days when we could focus our
energies on the well-recognized instruments of Soviet power.

No one challenge today is yet as formidable as the threat from the
former Soviet Union. If nurtured by neglect on our part, these new challenges could expand to threaten the growth of democracy and free markets. All the tools of national security—diplomacy, the military, and
intelligence—must remain sharp.

It is the task of the intelligence community to provide policymakers
and military commanders with early warning of emerging problems—
warning that can allow us to avoid crisis or military conflict. We must
continuously monitor and assess the threats so that our leaders can manage them wisely. It is also our responsibility, as the nation's first line of
defense, to help counter emerging threats so that the next generation does
not confront them in a vastly more dangerous and intractable form. The
mission of intelligence is clear.

Transnational Issues

Now I would like to turn to the transnational challenges that we face.
Terrorists, organized criminals, and traffickers in drugs and weapons
cross easily over international borders and blur the lines that once divided domestic and international threats. To meet these new challenges,
we must find the most effective way to harmonize the unique talents and
resources of law enforcement and intelligence. The law enforcement
community has tremendous investigative skills and techniques. The intelligence community has a vast foreign collection effort that includes
advanced technical systems and human sources of intelligence. By em-
phasizing cooperation and coordination of efforts, we can bring all of our
skills to bear against transnational threats and minimize costly and time-
consuming duplication of effort. Effective, extensive, and routine coop-

eration between intelligence and law enforcement will profoundly improve our nation's security in the post-Cold War world. Recent experience has proven that when intelligence and law enforcement cooperate effectively, we can be spectacularly successful.

Proliferation. Of the transnational issues, the proliferation of weapons of mass destruction and advanced conventional weapons systems pose the gravest threat to national security and to world stability. At least 20 countries have or may be developing nuclear, chemical, and biological weapons and ballistic missile systems to deliver them.

The nuclear weapons programs of several countries cause us great concern. For example, Iran is now developing its nuclear infrastructure and the means to hide nuclear weapons development. Cooperation with Russia and China—even carried out legally under international safeguards—could substantially aid Iran's nuclear weapons efforts. Iran remains years away from producing a nuclear weapon, but extensive foreign assistance could shorten the timeframe. We are also monitoring a potential nuclear arms race in South Asia. India appears to be planning an underground nuclear test. Last month it test-fired an improved short-range ballistic missile. Prime Minister Bhutto has hinted that Pakistan might conduct a nuclear test in response to an Indian test.

Chemical weapons programs are active in 18 countries, including most major states of the Middle East. Libya, for example, is now building the world's largest underground chemical weapons plant in a mountain near Tarhunnah. Chemical weapons countries are also developing more and longer-range delivery systems, including ballistic and cruise missiles and UAVs.

Biological weapons, often called the "poor man's atomic bombs," are also on the rise. Small, less-developed countries are often eager to acquire such weapons to compensate on the cheap for shortcomings in conventional arms. Small quantities of precursors, available on the open market, can produce a deadly chemical or biological weapon.

Ballistic missile systems that can deliver nuclear, chemical, or biological warheads are available to more countries. China, North Korea, the industrialized states in Europe and South America, several Third World countries, and private consortiums supply ballistic missile technology—and in some cases entire missile systems—to developing countries around the world. North Korea, for example, has sold its SCUD Bs and Cs—with a range of 300 and 500 km, respectively—to Iran, Libya, Syria, and other countries. Pyongyang is now developing a 1,000-km No Dong missile that could be deployed in the near future. A Taepo Dong missile, which could reach as far as Alaska, is in development and could be operational after the turn of the century.

Advanced conventional weapons and technologies such as stealth, propulsion, and sensors are allowing countries such as North Korea and Iran to accelerate their military modernization. Such weapons could inflict significant casualties on U.S. forces or regional allies in future conflicts.

All of these programs are aided through the illegal export of controlled equipment, technology, and materials, including dual-use items, and through indigenous research and development.

In confronting proliferation, the first task of intelligence is to discover the hidden plans and intentions of countries of concern well before we have to confront the devastating power of the weapons themselves. The intelligence community, for example, was instrumental in uncovering North Korea's nuclear ambitions, its violation of safeguards, and its production of enough plutonium for at least one and possibly two nuclear weapons. We are now monitoring North Korea's compliance with the October 1994 US-DPRK Agreed Framework, freezing Pyongyang's nuclear program. Fifteen months after the agreement, North Korea has not refueled its 5-Mwe reactor at Yongbyon or operated its reprocessing plant and it has halted construction on two larger reactors.

Once weapons of mass destruction programs have come to light, then it is the task of intelligence to support arms control negotiations, to monitor compliance with treaties and control regimes, including the Nuclear Nonproliferation treaty and the Chemical Weapons Convention, and to uncover violations of sanctions. For example, sanctions imposed by the UN have done much to contain Saddam and steadily weaken his regime. The intelligence community has been very active in the effort to assure that these sanctions continue to be effective. Without an effective, long-term monitoring program by the UN, however, Baghdad could use its large pool of scientific expertise, as well as hidden materials and components, to reconstitute its nuclear, chemical, and biological weapons programs.

The intelligence community has been aggressive in its efforts to uncover hidden supply lines and stop key materials and technologies from reaching countries of proliferation concern. The U.S. government, in cooperation with other governments, has been able to halt the transfer of a large amount of equipment that could be used in developing nuclear weapons programs, including mass spectrometers, custom-made cable equipment, graphite materials, aluminum melting furnaces, arc-welding equipment, and a gas jet atomizer. Now is the time to prevent countries of proliferation concern from obtaining the materials and technology they need to advance their weapons of mass destruction programs. We must prevent North Korea, for example, from obtaining the guidance and control technology that could make its long-range missiles accurate as well as deadly. We must keep Iran from obtaining the foreign assistance it needs to complete a nuclear weapon. We have to keep Iraq from obtaining equipment and materials that would enhance its nuclear, chemical, and biological weapons programs. We cannot relax our efforts.

Terrorism. Let me move on now to the problem of terrorism. In the post-Cold War era, terrorists have become increasingly capable, lethal, and wide-ranging. Their operating methods and technical expertise—in bomb-making and other skills—are more sophisticated. The U.S. government recorded 440 international terrorism incidents in 1995, the highest total since 1991.

Terrorist attacks today are more deadly than in the past. Where once terrorists undertook relatively small operations aimed at attaining specific political objectives, today they are more likely to inflict mass casualties as a form of punishment or revenge. The bombing of the World Trade Center is an example.

We are concerned that terrorists will push this trend to its most awful extreme by employing weapons of mass destruction. Indeed, the prospects for chemical and biological terrorism will increase with the spread of dual-use technologies and expertise. Many of the technologies and materials associated with these programs have legitimate civilian or military applications. Trade in such materials cannot be banned. For example, chemicals used to make nerve agents are also used to make plastics and process foodstuffs. And any modern pharmaceutical facility can produce biological warfare agents as easily as vaccines or antibiotics. The Japanese cult Aum Shinrikyo was able to legally obtain all components needed to build the massive chemical infrastructure that produced the poison gas released in the Tokyo subway. The use of nuclear materials is less likely, but in December we saw terrorists employ radioactive material for the first time, when Chechen rebels planted radioactive material in a public park in Moscow.

The most active terrorist groups have greatly expanded the geographic scope of their operations over the last two years. Organizations such as Lebanese Hezbollah and the Egyptian group al-Gamaat al-Islamiyya have developed transnational infrastructures that they use for fundraising, logistical support, and cooperation with other terrorist groups. These operations enable them to strike when and where they choose. For example, Egyptian extremists, who until recently had confined their major activities to Egypt, have over the past eight months attempted to assassinate President Mubarak in Ethiopia, set off a car bomb in Croatia, and bombed the Egyptian embassy in Pakistan.

In the Philippines, radical Muslim insurgents, including Abu Sayyaf Group and the larger Moro Islamic Liberation Front, have threatened to disrupt APEC meetings. These elements may be cultivating ties with foreign terrorists, who in January 1995 attempted to bomb U.S. air carriers flying through Manila and elsewhere in East Asia.

In Turkey, terrorism and drugs combine to pose a major threat to the security and territorial integrity of this key ally. Through front organizations and drug trafficking, the Kurdistan Workers' Party (PKK) receives help for its terrorist and counterinsurgency activities from rogue states, other terrorist groups, and historical Turkish rivals.

State sponsorship remains an important part of the international terrorist threat and Iran is by far the most active and capable sponsor. Tehran appears to consider terrorism a legitimate instrument of statecraft, whether practiced by Iranian state agents or by heavily supported surrogates such as Hezbollah.

We have made a concerted effort to apply human and technical intelligence to the problem of terrorism. In cooperation with friendly security services, we have had success in breaking up some terrorist cells overseas and exploiting these opportunities to learn more about the methods and techniques being used by today's terrorists. The intelligence community also works closely with the FBI and other law enforcement agencies to support their efforts to investigate and prosecute terrorist crimes. We use our overseas resources to develop and follow up investigatory leads, and to help locate and facilitate the apprehension of individual terrorists. There have been several notable successes of this type over the past year, including the arrest of Ramzi Yousef, the alleged mastermind of the World Trade Center bombing.

Organized Crime. Transnational organized criminal activities are growing rapidly in every region of the world, undermining political and economic development in many countries. In Russia, organized crime is a challenge for the national leadership. Criminal groups have significant influence in strategic sectors of the economy—including the banking sector—and have high-level political connections. The increasing power of organized crime threatens political stability, undermines popular confidence in government at all levels, and encourages support for hard-line politicians. The increasing sophistication, flexibility, and worldwide connections of organized crime groups help them to expand their activities and thwart law enforcement.

Intelligence is aiding law enforcement in the fight against other transnational criminal threats. U.S. intelligence, for example, contributed to the arrest of Gloria Canales, who headed a major alien-smuggling network in Latin America.

Economic Security. Earlier I spoke of the interdependence of the world economy. Economic security has become an integral part of our national security. Accordingly, we increasingly focus economic intelligence efforts on warning of key risks to American economic interests. We monitor threats to international financial stability and U.S. interests. We alert policymakers when foreign firms use questionable business practices, such as bribery, to disadvantage U.S. firms. Economic intelligence reporting helps us expose activities that may support terrorism, narcotics trafficking, proliferation, and gray arms dealing. Finally, as I mentioned earlier, we also monitor compliance with economic sanctions. In all of these areas, there is a tremendous demand from senior policymakers for the information we provide.

Security of Information Systems. Allow me to turn now to a transnational threat that is, at present, difficult to measure—the threat of attack against our information systems and information-based infrastructures. Hackers, criminal groups, and foreign intelligence services consider these systems lucrative targets, as evidenced by the growing number of intrusions into corporate and financial information systems. While intelligence sources have only identified a handful of countries that have instituted formal Information Warfare programs, I am concerned that the threat to our information systems will grow in coming years as the en-

abling technologies to attack these systems proliferate and more countries and groups develop new strategies that incorporate such attacks.

Our efforts to identify and characterize the threat are continuing. I am
encouraged by our progress over the past year. We are developing cooperative efforts within the community, and establishing valuable links
with other agencies outside the Community and outside government. We
have a lot more to do, however. We must identify sufficient resources to
work on this problem and work through many of the legal and regulatory
obstacles to collecting needed intelligence.

Conclusion

What I have just given you is an abbreviated list of the threats to our
national security today. I would like to conclude by saying that intelligence
is an integral part of an effective national security structure. It does not and
should not work in isolation. In recent years, the intelligence community
has strongly emphasized the need to know our intelligence consumers better so that we can provide information that makes a difference to policy, to
diplomacy, to the conduct of military operations, and, ultimately, to the
security of the American people. I believe that intelligence is especially
critical now. Policymakers, dealing with a shifting menu of international
crises, need fast and reliable information on current conflicts, and advance
warning of emerging problems. A smaller U.S. military, required to take on
new challenges in remote and unfamiliar areas of the world, needs detailed
and accurate intelligence on the ground and at the highest levels of
decision-making. Law enforcement, which must increasingly deal with
foreign-based threats to American cities, needs our analytical and collection
support more than ever. Mr. Chairman, the intelligence community is determined to meet these needs and to earn and keep the trust of the Congress
and the American people. Thank you.

Nonlethal Weapons—
Let's Make Them Happen

General John J. Sheehan, USMC

*Speech given at the Nonlethal Defense Conference II, Washington,
D.C., March 7, 1996.*

For the last few years, we have been debating the concept of nonlethal
weapons and capabilities. The theory is that technology will bring new
concepts to the battlefield that will make the soldier's job safer and potentially reduce the loss of life and property.

This promise of broadening the commander's options, and thus allowing for a graduated response capability has long been the aim of our research and technology centers. Unfortunately, as is often the case, expectations far outstrip reality and we have to wait for a catastrophic event to really stimulate the process.

Nonlethal weapons are in danger of falling into that category of "tomorrow's weapon." They may very well always be a weapon of the future if we do not do something about this concept.

Over the past two days, many people from diverse backgrounds and organizations have talked about moving nonlethal weapons from the laboratory into the operational arena, but are hamstrung by institutional inertia and bureaucratic red tape.

We must change the perception that "Nonlethal is the stuff that never happens." This is a riot baton. It has a place in history. Once you use it, you are engaged for good or bad. "Why do our troops and law enforcement people just have two choices?" "Why do we continue to put our young men and women in situations where they must decide between using deadly force or risk possible injury and death?"

Most of the post-Cold War missions our forces face today fall in the "other-than-war" category on the conflict spectrum. Whether it's U.S. forces in Somalia, Implementation Force (IFOR) troops in Bosnia, QRF in Panama or either Haiti or Guantanamo Bay, Cuba, we have all faced operational situations where nonlethal weapons and capabilities were needed but unavailable.

The requirement for nonlethal weapons and capability is well-known. Congress gave us $38 million to invest in nonlethal development, and now Dr. Kaminski is conducting a program review to ensure DoD gets its money's worth.

I know that the services have been bringing nonlethal concepts through their respective research, development, and acquisition (RDA) activities for several years. You have heard and seen some of the indications of that work over the past two days.

Yet our existing weapons' development, procurement, training, and equipping policies have not kept pace with the emerging needs for non- and less-lethal weapons. We must move on to the next step of either creating or empowering the sponsors of this technology. This nation should no longer tolerate dedicated, professional troops equipped with the wrong tools for new, more complex missions.

In the CNN era, an individual's decision to use or not use deadly force is no longer merely a tactical decision. The implications of the decision will be immediately broadcast to every capital in the world. It therefore has a strategic dimension.

Today, the NATO and non-NATO troops in Bosnia that make up the IFOR are in a very difficult situation. They obviously have sufficient power to counter any armed adversary. But what about the unarmed demonstrator? What are the implications for the IFOR mission if they are forced to use deadly force to break through a threatening demonstration or roadblock?

The same holds true for a noncombatant evacuation. The ability of our forces to control a situation without prematurely resorting to deadly force could mean the difference between a permissive and a nonpermissive situation. Nonlethal weapons provide that capability.

Readiness

All Geographic CINCs want the capability/flexibility that nonlethal weapons provide—but they are still limited by the TO & E of the units provided to them.

In Haiti, we used a tiger-team approach with the RDA activities of a particular service to address requirements for nonlethal capabilities. We were able to accomplish safety and legal screening, acquire the nonlethal devices, and train the troops before deploying them with these capabilities. When these units were about to complete their tour in Haiti, we wanted to leave their nonlethal capability in place and transfer it to the units replacing them.

The mission had not changed, but the service carrying out the mission had. Working through the roadblocks to transfer those devices across service boundaries was time-consuming and should not have been necessary.

As a supported CINC, and a force provider of most of the combat forces in CONUS, I want to know that the units I'm getting or sending forward have similar capabilities. It makes no sense to break OPTEMPO or PERSTEMPO goals of specific units, for example an MP company, when either a Marine company or an Air Force Security Flight could provide the same capability with the proper equipment and training.

That also goes for active and reserve forces. In today's active-reserve integrated force structure, a supported CINC shouldn't have to settle for a reduced capability when getting a reserve force.

When one considers that National Guard forces are often the first DoD forces called on to respond to civil disturbance in this country, it makes no sense for them not to have the latest nonlethal technology as part of their standard equipment.

The Challenge

My challenge to all in this room, and the organizations you represent, is to respond to these new requirements.

It is time for these various service programs to be pulled out of the lab and put into the operational arena to be tested against actual requirements and priorities and realistic scenarios.

The S&T laboratories need to explore the best that science and technology has to offer. Bring us your best ideas. Transfer your mature ideas to industry.

Let's move beyond the close-quarters technology and explore innovative ways in which our troops can control situations and disable suspect vehicles, go-fast boats, and aircraft on the ground without placing themselves in danger or allowing the smugglers or perpetrators to go free.

Industry has a great opportunity to invest in nonlethal weapons. The requirements, and therefore the market, are already there.

The services have the mission and resources to develop concepts, doctrine, training, and logistics to get nonlethal weapons out of the laboratories and into the hands of the troops who need them. You have been bringing these ideas along through the RDA systems. But the ultimate "users" of nonlethal weapons and capabilities—the Combatant CINCs— need to better articulate their "joint" requirements for these weapons.

I noticed that no other Geographic CINC has clearly stated the requirement for less- or nonlethal weapons in their Integrated Priority Lists. We need to revisit this requirement and focus more on capabilities rather than on specific platforms.

USACOM is currently in discussion with OSD and JCS to develop and sponsor nonlethal weapons as a separate ACTD for FY97 if not sooner. Such an ACTD will give us the proper level of focus on the whole area of nonlethal weapons and concepts.

The ACTD process is an appropriate vehicle to bring together the joint warfighter requirements and the technologies that hold the most promise.

It is time to accept the challenge to meet the changing realities before us. Nonlethal weapons must be part of today's tool kit.

Ethical Conundra of Information Warfare

Winn Schwartau

Sources were private and confidential conversations with members of the intelligence community, the military, and a journalist from a major news magazine. All of them spoke on the condition of anonymity. Originally published in Alan Campen, Douglas Dearth, and R. Thomas Goodden (eds.), Cyberwar: Security, Strategy and Conflict in the Information Age *(AFCEA Press, 1996).*

At first blush it sounds so clean, so nonviolent, so intangible. Then you get to thinking about it: Information Warfare.

In the late 1980s, the American military began to think about a new kind of warfare. Apart from the operational considerations, there was also concern for a strategic approach which would insure American popular support for military deployment. A new and better kind of warfare; more palatable for the dinner-eating, news-watching family of four. Vietnam-era pictures on the six o'clock news graphically showed dead soldiers—ours and theirs—and children—theirs—burning from napalm strikes. These images did not fit neatly with the desired American self-image. As a country, we are not comfortable with viewing ourselves as purveyors of random violence.

The media has had a tremendous effect on how we view war, and with the advent of "anywhere, anytime" instant remote communications, our soldiers are no longer thousands of miles away fighting for American national interests. Today, they fight in real-time, in our living rooms, where not only we, but the entire world, watch and judge their actions.

Consider the involvement of U.S. troops in Somalia. Media broadcasts of horrendous conditions, medieval chaos, and civilian tragedies created a swell of support for America to "do something" to assist a helpless population. So we landed on East African shores for a peacekeeping mission; but, oddly enough, the media beat the troops to the scene. Entrenched on the hot beachheads with their cameras and boom microphones, the media filled the airwaves with live broadcasts of arriving SEALs and Marines. And then the troops went to work, attempting to bring some sort of order to a country in dire straits.

Our exit from Somalia was as cathartic as our entry. Full-color videos of Somalian rebels dragging a dead U.S. soldier through the streets was too much for most Americans to stomach. Nearly instantly, support for U.S. intervention waned, and we pulled out.

Based upon conversations with, and getting to know, hundreds of military folks over the last five years, I believe that a new breed of soldier—a post-World War II soldier—is coming to the fore. We are being served by military leaders who are charged with defending our country, but who are also keenly aware that we do indeed live in a new world. They thoroughly understand that the typical war-fighting projection of power must be handled in ways that not only make military sense, but do not violate the political, social, and ethical consciences of those who must support them.

I believe that the U.S. military genuinely wants to be a "kinder and gentler" fighting force. Inherently, we have attained what might be referred to as an "enhanced consciousness." We have a fundamental desire to whip the bad guy, but we want to do it honestly, quickly, efficiently, and with a minimum of bloodshed. From what I have seen and learned, every effort is being made to develop ways for America to fight a "clean war."

As part of the way to achieve that goal, the military has been developing an array of technologies which fit into the "nonlethal" category. Sticky-foam which, when shot out of a hand-held "cannon," binds the enemy in a spiderweb of inescapable gluey substances. Sonic guns which incapacitate adversarial forces. Nerve-shattering electromagnetic emanations which effectively paralyze the enemy's ability to function. Electromagnetic pulse cannons, EMP bombs, and HERF guns which debilitate or destroy the electronics of computers, communications, satellites, or power systems.

Of all the "nonlethal" methods developed, none have attracted as much attention as Information Warfare.

The definition I first proposed for Information Warfare back in 1993 was a conflict in which "information and information systems act as both the weapons and the targets." At that time, the working military definitions of InfoWar were classified, but some versions were close to the one I offered. Today, the Pentagon's working definition of InfoWar has been expanded to include the concepts "deny, destroy, or intercept adversary computer, network, or communications, while protecting one's own."

The other criteria I have used when describing Information Warfare is "the total absence of bombs, bullets, or other conventional tools of physical destruction." Thinking in this focused manner, concentrating exclusively within the virtual domain, or fourth dimension of warfare, hones the process of problem-solving and generates new paradigms of thought.

Within this model of (pure) Information Warfare, many options become apparent that are not so readily available for conventional conflict.

Simply put, if we (or anyone else, for that matter) fly a plane into the airspace of a sovereign state and drop a load of bombs, there is a reasonable chance that such an act would be considered an act of war. However, we must note that the United States has not "officially" been at war with anyone since the end of World War II, which further complicates the lines of war/no-war. (I say this with full recognition and respect for the soldiers and families who suffered during the last half century of conflict in undeclared "wars.")

Consider that in the last decade or so, several international—allegedly unprovoked—"shoot-downs" did not trigger war: the Soviet downing of KAL 007; the American missiles that destroyed a civilian Iranian jet-liner; the recent Cuban fatal interception of Cessnas in the Caribbean. Then consider that in 1986, American warplanes ravaged downtown Tripoli, and there was no military response.

The bottom line we have come to accept, perhaps in too cavalier a fashion, is that we are the king of the hill militarily: don't challenge us if you know what's good for you. As a result, one could argue, we have seen an increase in terrorist-type, State-side events by foreign elements. They can't beat us in a "fair" fight, so they resort to terrorism.

Now, with the advent of Information Warfare as an increasingly viable option to conventional armed conflict, we should inwardly examine those issues which—eventually—we must openly face, come to terms with, and if I have my say-so, clearly announce our policy and intentions to the world.

Pure Information Warfare takes many forms, and I will concern myself with only Class II and Class III InfoWar as detailed elsewhere in this book.

Offensive Capabilities

Forgetting about defensive aspects for a moment, what do we have in our arsenal that would permit the United States to wage InfoWar against an adversary, whether by the military or by other official, government-sanctioned organizations? Briefly, they include the following:

1. Offensive software: viruses, Trojan horses, embedded exported systems, or other malicious software
2. Sniffing the communications of foreign (domestic) civilian and military networks and communications
3. Tempest-style eavesdropping upon electronic devices with characteristic emissions
4. Chipping: hardware-based malicious software embedded surreptitiously in systems
5. Directed energy weapons which disable or destroy electronic systems
6. A full range of PsyOp capabilities

Used in various combinations, deployed by a politically willing and ably armed force, these "weapons" have the potential to enhance much of our military's conventional means of conflict.

But should we use them other than in times of "war" (i.e., Gulf Conflict) or as an adjunct to conventional conflict? Can the weapons of Information Warfare stand alone as means to project force? The ethical conundra before us display many faces and beget a wide range of cultural and national introspective questions that must be honestly addressed and answered.

Is it ethically correct for the United States to defend its economic national security interests by resorting to those same tactics that are used against us?

It goes without saying that the United States is a highly visible and rich target for the theft of intellectual property from the private sector, and to a lesser degree from the military sector. We have the most sophisticated spying apparatus in the world, to the tune of nearly $30 billion per year; but, to date, these immense capabilities have been relegated to Cold War tactics and military protectionism.

Should we redirect our "eyes and ears" to the industrial and economic treasures of our friends and adversaries alike, not with the prime intention of military advantage, but rather of global economic supremacy? We know full well that in less than two decades, unless radical steps are taken, the United States will become second or third in national economic might. Should we not use the same tactics and techniques as our competition? Or is second-rank status our chosen destiny? A 200-year-long national experiment that fails for lack of will?

Do we find it ethically displeasing to "read other peoples' mail"? Why not? They do it to us. On the other hand, what choice do we have?

Is there a middle ground such that, while we may choose to listen to our competitors, we will do nothing overt or active to disrupt their operations or interfere with those transmissions? Is that an ethical line that we should not cross? Or do we find ourselves in the position that we must use clandestine and covert methods (resorting to any necessary tactics) to maintain an "even playing field" of global competitiveness? Perhaps we should employ technical mercenaries, in no way officially affiliated with the U.S. government, who will remotely, invisibly, and with deniability effect our will.

The capability distinctly exists. Some corporations allegedly are already engaged in such missions for their own interests. If they are caught, will the United States prosecute those persons and organizations that are operating—ultimately—in the best interests of our country?

How we respond to these ethical considerations and the decisions we make will set the tone for America for generations to come.

Another option we face, one which also creates an ethical dilemma, is whether we should use export controls as means of proactive defensive Information Warfare.

The United States has the capability to export technology, ostensibly for the good of the buyer and the seller. However, using advanced software and hardware techniques, we can also export goods that can effectively be used as "weapons" if the need arises. In the early 1970s, according to sources, when AT&T sold a national telephone switch to Poland (then a Warsaw Pact country), the company was asked to include "bits and pieces" that would allow the United States to remotely shut down that country's communications infrastructure. The idea was that, in the event of a Soviet attack, we could slow down and perhaps thwart hostile activities. It has been claimed by other confidential sources that we have developed similar capabilities against North Korean military 360/370 and AS-400 computers.

The question becomes, though, should we, as a matter of policy, exploit this capability by using "infected" or malicious software, or by installing modified silicon chips whose payload can be activated by the United States when deemed appropriate? In a world of global competition, and as military, national economic, and civilian interests converge, how do we draw a line between those actions that should be taken, and those from which we should refrain?

Collateral Damage

I pose this hypothetical situation for your consideration: The United States is involved in an armed conflict with a recognized adversary, and we have the support of our significant allies and the majority of our population. CNN and the world's news services have access at least as open as that in the Gulf War. In order to achieve some very specific tactical goals, the field commanders are faced with a choice.

1. They can pick a sophisticated smart bomb (conventional explosive), which will almost assuredly strike the exact designated target, and will almost certainly kill a dozen innocent civilians—whose death will be broadcast to the world in near real-time.
2. They can choose to use a nonlethal weapon (of whatever sort), which will have the same tactical effect as the first option. How-

ever, there will be no civilian deaths to record on videotape. Instead, planners project 100-200 collateral civilian deaths within two weeks as a result of the nonlethal attack.

What do they do?

This is the crux of the ethical conundrum that we face, for the use of nonlethal weapons in no way means that deaths will not occur. "Nonlethal" generally refers to the immediate casualties caused by the weapon's use.

Further complicating the issue is the fact that Information Warfare offers additional opportunities other than in strict conflict, war or not. The techniques and offensive capabilities of InfoWar weapons can be considered part of our arsenal for operations other than war, as a prelude to conflict, as an alternative to conflict, for sanctions, and as a middle ground between diplomacy and war (conflict). A couple of hypothetical examples should suffice.

Country A is misbehaving, and the international community agrees that steps must be taken to bring it into line. One of the options available is to deny the country access to international communications and financial commerce. Through the use of jamming, denial of service attacks, or assorted other methods, Country A is electronically isolated from the rest of the world. As a result, the internal economy suffers and a range of social effects are felt, perhaps including starvation, inability to care for sick people, etc. If the only other alternative is conventional conflict, with gauaranteed high-profile civilian carnage, is IW an acceptable route for us and our allies to take? I have had the opportunity to design (for the good guys) a range of ECO-D (economic deactivation) scenarios which analyze such options. The ramifications can be staggering, but not obvious.

We then have to consider if the "attacks" against Country A are all conducted from outside of its physical sovereign boundaries, or are some waged from within the physical boundaries? Does this make a ethical (or legal) difference as to whether or not we take such actions?

Denial of service attacks offer a great deal of power to the IW-enabled nation-state. The targets for such attacks in today's integrated information society (given an appropriately vulnerable target) blur the lines between the military and civilian, as convergence between them increases.

Therefore, is an InfoWar attack against a power plant which services a military target acceptable, if we know that the same power source is the lifeline to a civilian population as well? Or is it politically and socially acceptable to avoid the headline- grabbing visuals that a military strike might cause, preferring instead to permit invisible collateral damage (perhaps greater in terms of long-term fatalities).

Military and political planners will have to come to terms with these fundamental issues as we move into the fourth dimension of war—cyber or pure Information Warfare—but we must also remain acutely aware of the political, social, and ethical fallout of such actions.

Let us assume that the United States does initiate a sanctions-based, offensive denial of service (financial or otherwise) assault against a target nation-state. Or fraught with even more complexity, we launch an InfoWar offensive against a non-state entity, whose physical location happens to lie within the physical boundaries of a nation-state.

Even though U.S. policy is still unclear as to what constitutes an act of war against us, we must consider how the target—and the international community—will view such offensive actions on our part. Perception is the name of the game; especially with a worldwide audience watching. Will the target react as though the United States had, in fact, declared war, absence of military action notwithstanding? Will the target react offensively against U.S. interests, using conventional, unconventional, or InfoWar weapons? And then what is our response to be?

This issue begs the question: Is Information Warfare a potential step which can cause escalation to a military conflict that was meant to be avoided in the first place? Or does Information Warfare present merely ethical questions, since no country with sane leadership would assault us militarily?

The definition of war in this new age of global networks, transnational commerce, and increasingly fuzzy borders is arguable at best—and the search for a definition generates an essential debate for the future of peace. At the core of any nation-state's view of war should be a National Information Policy which clearly delineates intangible values, ethical positions, national security, and the thresholds over which another nation-state may not cross. But additionally, such a policy must include options for dealing with renegades, terrorists, corporations, or individuals who provoke the international community outside of the control of their physical nation-state hosts.

Can we or should we respond to a transnational corporate attack against critical U.S. interests by taking action against that entity—even though it physically resides within another sovereign state? Or can we respond with pure InfoWar tactics, in the hope of avoiding an unpleasant international situation? And then, how do we avoid the domino effects that an attack upon a civilian infrastructure will likely create?

Many would maintain that an act of war implicitly involves fatalities. I no longer believe that to be the case, and thus the ethical conundrum of exactly what is an act of war comes to the fore. What is a measured response to an act of "cyber-aggression" against our interests? If the United States is hit with a nonlethal or InfoWar weapon, how should we respond? Our options are wide open today, and they will increase as our arsenals grow in sophistication and complexity. Further, as third-world nations get wired to the global information infrastructure, they too will find a demonstrable vulnerability that they currently do not have—and they will become a more viable target for U.S. response.

If, for example, "bad guy of choice" bombed the Statue of Liberty to the bottom of New York Harbor, I think it's a safe bet we'd bomb the living bejeezus out of him and his country. If, however, a sports stadium is bombed with little or no loss of life, our national will and thus our response might not be so acute. But now, if the bad guy somehow drains Citibank of it's entire asset base, some $300 billion, do we do anything? Hmmmm. Our ethical dilemma is not put on the defensive, and we as a nation have to decide if our economy and the civilian wealth-producing sector is a national security asset worthy of protection.

There are no immediate answers that are right or wrong, but the questions and conundra beget more questions and dilemmas as we look into the future of warfare. It is my sincere hope that this type of thinking and pondering will allow us all, as a nation and as a planet, to evolve our thinking past bombs and bullets, past military superiority, and find a common strength and unity amongst ourselves.

The alternative is not pleasant, for we find—each of us as we leap forward into the future—that our greatest assets are, indeed, also our greatest vulnerability. The ethical balance that we choose to follow in the coming decades will define us as a species.

Let's make the right choices.

The Fourth Force

Winn Schwartau

The military and intelligence services have been very good to me since the first edition of this book came out in 1994. I feel sort of adopted by them with their support of my work. They also know that I have no particular bias toward any one of the forces or services: I do not favor the Army over the Air Force or the Navy over the Marines or the CIA or NSA over the FBI or FEMA. They are all part and parcel of the system which provides defense for this country. So with this discussion, I do not intend to offend any one of them: I merely want to put forward some thoughts on how to further both the offensive and defensive strengths of this country.

With the advent of Information Warfare (as distinct from information in warfare) as a bombs-and-bullets-free theater (perhaps in support of conventional operations), I have seen a terrific amount of in-fighting between the services. Much of it is for budgetary survival. Thus, the info-in-warfare model has captured much of the media's attention since we are talking about billions of dollars in annual expenditures. Understandably, each of the services wants to remain well funded.

But when it comes to pure Information Warfare, I find that the budgetary paradigms of info-in-warfare muddy the waters. Each of the services has an IW element. The intelligence agencies also have or are developing IW capabilities of various flavors. And now the Pentagon at the highest levels is similarly appending some of its C4I capabilities and goals with an IW component. The Air Force, as of May 1996, stood up its first IW element, and we can expect similar cyber-corps from the other services to be activated as well. The NSA is standing up its 1,000-man IW army, and the CIA is getting into the business too.

This is good. The awareness level of IW capabilities has has been raised immeasurably in the last two years as much of the contents of the subject has come into the open source arena. But I have to question the means by which we are developing our cyber-fighting capabilities. Each service competitively argues that its own IW efforts are superior to those of the others. (Historically, the services have maintained a generally good- natured banter amongst themselves about who is best.) The words are well-intentioned; the goals are pro-America and pro-information dominance. However, when it comes to actively defending the United States, or offensively promoting our interests, I think that until we find a more centralized command and control authority over IW interests, we are going to fall behind the curve at a time when we need cohesion the most.

If we look back to the post-World War II era, the Air Force made a successful break from its parent, the Army, which had managed the Air Corps (and its various incarnations) since World War I. The Air Force came into its own as an independent fighting force, with an equal footing in the new Department of Defense.

The Army fought on the ground; the Navy fought at sea. That was fine for thousands of years, until the introduction of the airplane as a weapon changed the face of conflict during World War I. A new dimension—some call it a third dimension—had been added. It was unrealistic for the Army to develop doctrine and policy for both land and air campaigns. And besides, during World War II, the Air Corps did develop an autonomous attitude which carried over into peacetime.

Today, we find ourselves in a similar position. With all of the physical dimensions of conflict managed by the three traditional forces (no offense to the Marines), the battle for control of the cyber-battlespace (and dollars) rages. I find the comparison tempting and compelling. Cyberspace isn't in a "place"; the Air Force can't bomb it, the Army can't shoot at it, and the Navy can't sink it. But it can be influenced, taken away, or distorted. The methods are different because the medium is so vastly different. No ground, sea, or air—just the quantum hopes that the bits and bytes will all come out right at the other end. So should any of the existing forces dominate the defense and offense of Cyberspace? I think not.

Cyberspace is indeed a fourth dimension, and conflict there operates with different rules. Yet the fundamentals of military doctrine and policy must hold for it to become a viable battlefield:

- When to turn off the adversary's power
- When to take over the media transmission capability

- When to HERF the communications centers
- When to inject malicious software into the foreign banking system

What I call Force-4 should become a technical and policy center of excellence for the entire U.S. military. Information Warfare is not merely an enhancement of bombs and bullets efficiency, but is a coordinated myriad of operations, many of which do not take place or have an effect in the physical plane.

Our thinking needs to get out of the box and consider this question: "If we had no bombs, no soldiers, and no bayonets, how would we get the job done?" There is no perfect answer, but the mental exercise is valuable to avoid a particular service's bias toward itself and its own methods.

Hypothetically, let's say we have a small imminent conflict; maybe a Panama- or Grenada-sized operation. The Secretary of Defense wants options, plans, and more options. If the IW tool kits are developed independently by the services, their potential for use is filtered through the eyes of each service, whose first allegiance is to its own survival. Therefore, it is easy to imagine (again, no offense here guys) that a service might well opt for a physically impressive conventional operation that makes great headlines (and future budgeting easier) and filter out the IW possibilities.

However, let's say there is a Force-4 that has a high-profile presence within the DOD/Pentagon structure, and that same conflict is coming our way. Each of the traditional services will offer it's capabilities into a coordinated plan of action and create the options for the SecDef. But in this case, Force-4 will offer its options with the others, thus permitting the leadership to make decisions with a more balanced weighting.

With a Force-4 center of excellence, other law enforcement and civilian agencies will be able to have one-stop IW shopping. Today, dozens of organizations claim domestic IW superiority, and who knows which one is good, bad, or great? (I don't think they know either because of the compartmentalization in the classified world even among the good guys.) So where does the FBI or FEMA go for help? The answer to that question is a tome unto itself.

With a Force-4 acting as a center of excellence, a central repository of capabilities becomes available for all those who need and are authorized to have such information. Whether it's for offense in conflict or defense for the American military or business, Force-4 will be the place to go. Now this does not mean that AFIWC and other IW-oriented facilities need to go away. On the contrary, with a Force-4 command and presence at the senior level, IW groups will garner additional recognition, legitimacy, and funding to expand their efforts and further integrate their unique skill sets into the overall C4I structure.

Of course, IW will have to be further defined, carved up into pieces, and divvied up amongst the many players involved in national defense. And a lot of questions will have to be answered within the new paradigm. Does electronic warfare (EW) fit within the new model? Who handles

PsyOps? Because the use of some of the weapons herein have ramifications reaching well beyond the battlefield (right into the private sector and civilian populations), should their use be a mere subset of conventional forces, or dealt with more suitably in the new dimensions they represent?

I do not suggest that the transition to an IW center of excellence is easy; nor do I think, based upon what I have learned about the military in three short years, that the creation of an additional force is going to be accomplished without a major uphill battle. But it is a battle that must be fought for us all to come to grips with the new realities of warfare, whether in the desert or jungle or the tethers of Cyberspace.

I have no doubt there are dozens of good reasons that a dozen generals a lot smarter than me can devise as to why the creation of a Force-4 is not a good idea. However, all I ask is that we examine the concept by getting out of the box, and forget many of the mentalities in which we have been constrained during fifty years of Cold War experience. It is indeed a new world and we need new solutions to new problems and to new forms of war.

14

Class 1: Personal Information Warfare

"The Cold War is over, a lot of people are out of work, but it's hard to break old habits. A former CIA agent was working as a waiter. He took my order and then ate it."

—CONAN O'BRIAN.

THERE ARE THREE FUNDAMENTAL AXIOMS that must be remembered to appreciate the potential effects of Class 1 Information Warfare.

1. There is no such thing as electronic privacy.
2. In Cyberspace, you are guilty until proven innocent.
3. Information is a weapon.

Class 1 Information Warfare is an attack against an individual's electronic privacy: his digital records, files, or other portions of a person's electronic essence. The digital you is composed of far-strewn bits and bytes, each of which, when assembled, contributes to building an electronic picture of each of us. The average American has absolutely no control over his electronic privacy and Congress has chosen to ignore that fact in favor of PAC monies and special interest lobbying groups that today seem to control our elected representatives more effectively than we do. It seems that Congress will not or cannot address an issue that is snowballing, at breakneck speeds, towards a technological future so precarious that we as a society may lose control over our personal freedom.

Most of us Americans believe that we have an inherent right to privacy; however, the nature and extent of that right is only today becoming a front-page debate. According to a *USA Today* poll, 78% of us are concerned or very concerned about the loss of our privacy. That figure was only around 30% in 1970, but rose precipitously after the introduction of personal computers in 1977.[1] At the center of our concern is not only the issue of electronic privacy and the protection of the vast repositories of information across the Global Network, but the accuracy of that information. Credit records, for example, are notoriously inaccurate. I spent the better part of a year proving the electronic claims against me were false.

The premise of assumed guilt in Cyberspace causes many of us to shudder with anxiety, exacerbates Binary Schizophrenia, and is in one hundred percent violation of the foundation of the legal system. Yet Congress won't touch it. Computers contain a seemingly infinite stream of data on us, yet we have no control over its content, its accuracy, its dissemination, or its use. This is a sad, sad state of affairs and our nation's lawmakers should be ashamed of themselves.

Class 1 Information Warfare rains digital fallout upon the innocent electronic bystander whose only sin is to be a name stored in a computer database somewhere. This is the area of Information Warfare that most resembles terrorism. But the genesis of modern Information Warfare is based on simple, time-proven techniques. When we think of electronic snooping, most people I speak with come up with a few of the classic methods.

1. Install a hidden microphone.
2. Install a miniature camera.
3. Tap phone lines.

Not exactly a complete list, but enough to make the point.

With technology's great march forward, the means to bug adversaries is more widely available, less expensive, and more reliable than just a couple of years ago. Miniature cameras are so small that the lens is the size of a head of a pin, and fiber optic wire is almost as thin as a human hair. All this makes detection difficult, to say the least.

Countersurveillance is based upon the recognition that the "bad guys" know how to tap phones, place hidden transmitters, and take pictures discreetly. Countersurveillance teams perform sweeps of a client's residence or office looking for telltale signs that a surveillance is underway. Since today's technology is available to both sides, a gamesmanship mentality prevails, with the surveillance and countersurveillance teams jockeying for technical superiority over the target or suspect. Phone tapping is at the point now where, if a professional is behind it, there is little chance of ever discovering it.

Invading our electronic privacy (if we ever had any) is as simple as reaching for the Yellow Pages to call a data banker, a private investigator, or a hacker, or reading relevant newsletters and magazines. Take a look at the kinds of information available from only one issue of *Full Disclosure*, a proprivacy tabloid. Their banner reads "For Truth, Justice, and the American Way," and their editorial slant is "providing in-depth, inside information on electronic surveillance technology."[2]

- How To Get Anything on Anybody
- How to Investigate By Computer
- How To Find Anyone Anywhere
- Cellular Telephone Modification Handbook
- Eavesdrop on PCs
- How To Determine Undisclosed Financial Assets
- A Practical Guide to Photographic Intelligence
- The Latest In Cellular Monitoring Equipment
- Business Intelligence Investigations
- Don't Bug Me: The Latest High-Tech Spy Methods
- Fax Interception
- The Psychological Subversion of Information Systems
- Super Picking (locks that is)
- Don't Expose Yourself When You Use Your Phone

- Privacy Poachers (What 'they' do with information on you)
- Video Surveillance Recorders
- Finder's Fee: The Skip Tracer's Text
- SpyCam—A miniature ⅓" CCD camera

And let's not forget the half-page ad for Spy World, a surveillance and countersurveillance retail and mail order operation, which bills itself as "New York's Leading Supplier of Professional Spy Equipment."

All the tools needed to wage Class 1 Information War on individuals are available from catalogs, magazines, and books. Consumertronics, a group in New Mexico, publishes techniques for ripping off credit card companies, cracking into ATM machines, beating the phone company, and just about any other scheme you could imagine. For example, one of their publications details how to cheat the electric companies by slowing down power meters. All of their publications are labeled "For Educational Purposes Only," because they don't want to be accused of encouraging illegal behavior. Next time you're at the supermarket, check out an issue of *Soldier of Fortune* magazine. The small classified ads in the back offer everything from weapons that would make any small country's army proud, to survivalism supplies, to ideas on how to protect yourself from the WOG (World Government) and the Communism that dominates the hills of Washington, D.C. The point is, of course, that almost any kind of information on just about anything is available, and the tools to get it are a phone call away. The amazing thing is that most of this is legal, and in some circles, encouraged as a legitimate means of investigation—privacy be damned.

Joe Apter is president of Telephonic Info, Inc., a databanker based in St. Petersburg, Florida which finds information on people and their assets. Telephonic Info offers a shopping list detailing the company's services. Looking for bad debtors or deadbeat husbands? Need to prescreen a possible employee, check out a possible mate or business partner, or find out if someone is a good credit risk? Joe's firm will do it all, and he does it totally within the law. But Joe's company is not alone; there are dozens if not hundreds of databanking firms around the country who offer similar services, but who might not be quite as ethical as Joe.

Imagine that someone wanted to put together a dossier on you, your spouse, or your parents. Here is what Telephonic Info or other data bankers can legally dig up: Address and length of residence; phone number (even if unpublished); social security number; date of birth; names of household members; maiden name; married name; previous marriages, divorces, dates, final decrees; age at death and amount of death benefits; creditors, credit inquiries, and credit reports. They can find out about your driving record, including any infractions and restrictions; real property owned, including sales prices, taxes, and property descriptions; IRS or contractor liens; mortgages; judgments; bankruptcies; equity value of assets. They can get info on your current employer, length of employment, wages, previous employers, and previous earnings history; your banking affiliations, bank account numbers, and balances; uniform commercial code filings; recorded financial transactions such as loans; your medical history, including hospitalizations, emergency room services, and doctors, treatment facilities, dates of service, description of medical care; and any past lawsuits, criminal offenses, misdemeanors, felonies, arrests, and convictions. Federal court, Superior Court, District Court, worker's compensation claims, payments, disputes, hearings; corporate affiliations, business type, names of corporate officers. All these—and more—are legal to obtain.[3]

How many of us would honestly want all of that information printed in the newspaper, open to inspection by our family, friends, and business associates? But the worst part of this is not so much that the records are spread all across the Global Network, but that the information may be wrong, and no one takes responsibility for the accuracy or the integrity of it. You can spend a lifetime and a fortune attempting to repaint the correct digital picture with no assurance of success.

Now, if we want to reach out to less scrupulous databankers, we can get an even more complete picture of our target. We can find, for a price, social security account balances, tax records, military records, video rentals, hotel stays, past and pending air and rail reservations, car rentals, passport number, immigration files, Medicare and Medicaid files, psychiatric records, prescription drug use, drug or alcohol rehabilitation, credit card balances, credit card statements, credit applications, education, grades, youthful offenses, telephone bills, current police investigations, allegations, law enforcement surveillance, insinuating affiliations, NCIC records, Department of Justice files, and just about any other bit of private information that you have generated during your life.

Such a complete electronic picture of an individual gives the Information Warrior unbelievable power over his victim, especially when the composite information is edited to paint an unflattering image. Despite the frightening potential for abuse, Congress has thus far done little to promise personal electronic privacy. But I would guess that if an enterprising databank customer had the wherewithal to assemble a complete data record of every member of Congress, we might see some action.

The Government Accounting Office has urged Congress to criminalize the abuse of medical records, at least. With Clinton's universal health plan coming to reality, the problem of abuse of NCIC and credit databases becomes even clearer. As Congressman Gary A. Condit said, "How will we be able to protect health records in a computerized environment if we can't adequately protect criminal history records or credit records?"[4]

The American people agree. In a 1992 Harris poll, 89% of those surveyed agreed that "computers have made it much easier for someone to obtain confidential personal information about individuals."[5] We should all be concerned because the Information Warrior, as usual, is way ahead of the good guys. The Class 1 Information Warrior armed with a complete profile of an individual with a skeleton in his closet, has the leverage to induce his victim to do his bidding by means no more subtle than pure extortion or blackmail.

Once armed with a complete picture of the digital you, the Class 1 Information Warrior can do a lot.

1. He can edit the information to paint the picture he wishes to paint. Selective truth is as good as a lie, and trying to repair a damaged reputation is often futile. Suppose someone accused you of renting adult videos, but didn't mention that of the 176 tapes you rented, only two were adult in nature. The picture is skewed in favor of accuser. (This intense, unfair investigation into one's personal life is sometimes known as getting Borked, after Congress's treatment of Supreme Court nominee Robert Bork.)

2. The Information Warrior can find your Achilles' Heel and exploit it to his advantage. Your position or access to further information might make you of value to him; in exchange for his silence, you might be persuaded to assist him in future endeavors rather than suffer embarrassment, family strife, financial loss, or criminal prosecution.

3. The Class 1 Information Warrior can send your dossier to people whom you would rather not have it. For example, if you committed a minor legal transgression in the past and omitted it from a job application, your job might be history. If your digital picture is different than the one you provided to get life insurance, Poof! you could lose it all. If you lied on a credit application and the Information Warrior finds the discrepancies, you could lose your assets and face Federal criminal mail fraud charges.

Yes, the Information Warrior can do a lot when he has your picture. But I find another capability of the Class 1 Information Warrior a thousand-fold more disturbing than the mere accumulation of a floppy disk full of data on an individual. What if the Information Warrior intentionally modifies or alters the digital picture of his victim? Let's put the pieces together.

- Thousands of databases hold together the digital pieces of our lives.
- Computers constantly trade information about each of us.
- Low-paid data clerks enter that information into the computers.
- Getting erroneous information corrected is a painstakingly difficult challenge.

I will paint a few scenarios, and let you consider the ramifications:

- An envious coworker with a friend who works for the local police arranges to have you listed as a car thief wanted in three states. You are stopped for a missing taillight.
- An insurance company clerk has been given two weeks notice. In a misguided attempt to strike back at her employer, she alters hundreds of random records, including yours, with a code saying you've died. Your social security checks stop coming, the public records confirm your death, and your obituary is printed. Try proving you're alive.
- The credit card receipts of a dozen Congressmen are given to the *Washington Post*. The receipts say they all had dinner at La Vielle Femme, which is actually a cover for a call girl agency. A reporter calls the agency to confirm Congressional "dining" preferences. What do they say?
- Racist right wingers alter the medical records of all state politicians who support minority causes to reflect a serious history of alcoholism. Then they tip off the media.

- Right-to-Lifers arrange to include child abuse charges in the police records of doctors who perform abortions.

Moreover, an Information Warrior will not rely upon only *one* method to strike out at his targets, especially with so many available to him. He may use a series of electronic weapons to achieve his goals or to be more assured of success.

In an astounding case of alleged Class 1 Information Warfare, Gilles Guilbault of Montreal claims that the Canadian government has waged an Information War against him for over a decade. In a letter dated September 20, 1993, he claims that his University credentials were erased, his career was shattered, he was forced into bankruptcy, and his life was all but destroyed by the government because he himself had too much information. M. Guilbault alleges that when he was an upper-echelon stockbroker and a member of several elite and exclusive private clubs, he learned of a sophisticated conspiracy to commit high level financial fraud. The plot, which included a kidnapping and the political assassination of Quebec minister Pierre Laporte, occurred during the Trudeau reign. He says that this case is the Canadian equivalent of the Kennedy assassination, and full disclosure would implicate many people in power. He further alleges that a number of prominent figures conspired to turn him into an electronic nonentity, so discredited that he would never be believed.[6]

Remember our very important businessman who got bumped off his flight to Vegas? What if a company vying for a huge contract needed to get its primary business competitor, our very important friend, out of the way for a few days? What could that company do if it had the services of an Information Warrior at its disposal?

You are the only person can pull this deal off. The *only* one. The whole deal rests on your ability to convince the brass that your company is the right one for the job. Your company is depending upon you but you're prepared. You arrive at the counter to pick up your first class tickets to D.C., the last flight that will get you there on time for the morning meeting.

"Excuse me, sir, there doesn't seem to be a reservation in your name. Could it be under another name?" Pretty smile.

"No, no, I made it myself. It has to be there."

"I'm sorry, sir, but it's not here. Would you like a seat?"

"Of course I would. That's why I made the reservation in the first place." Indignant.

"Yessir." The smile is gone. "That'll be $1,252. How will you be paying for that?"

You throw out the Platinum American Express card, looking at the clock. The boarding has already begun.

"Excuse me, sir. There seems to be a problem with your credit card."

"What problem?" you demand.

"It refused the charge." What she didn't tell you is that the little readout on the credit card machine said "STOLEN CARD: CALL POLICE."

"That's impossible . . . oh, all right, use this one." You hand over a VISA card which is also refused by the computer for the same reason, but as per her training, the ticket agent proceeds as if nothing is wrong, waiting for the police to arrive.

You suddenly feel a strong arm grasp yours. "Would you mind stepping over this way, sir?" You turn and two policemen—*not* the airport rent-a-cop types—are giving you the once-over.

"What's the problem, officers?"

"Would you mind stepping over this way, sir," the really big one repeats while not so gently pushing you to the side of the ticketing area. You have no choice, but panic sets in. "Do you have any identification, sir?"

"Of course I do. What the hell is the problem?"

"Your identification, please."

You make a sudden move to your inside breast pocket and both officers react as they were trained. The unholstered guns cause you to stop. You smile sheepishly. "My wallet . . . it's in here. . . .

"Slowly, please, sir."

You give them your driver's license. One cop takes it, steps away about ten yards, and speaks into his cellular phone. The other one just watches you. As the crackle of the speaker echoes through the hall you hear a couple of disconcerting words: wanted . . . Colorado . . . armed robbery. . . .

The cop returns. "You have the right to remain silent. . . ."

In less severe circumstances, harassment might be sufficient. One week, they might delete all funds from your checking account. The next week, they might add 114 calls to Zimbabwe to your phone bill. The next week your name is added to every X-rated mailing list in the country, and the next week your life insurance is cancelled. Good luck getting your life back.

One last technique that the Information Warrior might use in an assault against an individual is "spoofing," which takes many forms. Spoofing, or the intentional electronic masquerading of oneself as another person or electronic entity, is a powerful way to infect a victim's electronic life with misery.

Millions of people communicate across the Internet every day, discussing thousands of subjects in as many forums. One area of hot activity are the myriad sex boards, where people of kindred spirit from across the globe meet, trade stories, talk dirty, and exchange X-rated and pornographic materials. The following message appeared on a sex board in August 1993. (Names have been changed.)

FROM:tim@bigcompany.com
TO: everyone

Hey, does anybody know where I can get some good kiddy porn? I love little boys and little girls.

Thanks

Within minutes, "tim" was derided from every corner of Cyberspace and his name sent to the police. Even within the anarchistic culture of the Internet sex-forums, there are self-imposed limits. The messages were explicit in their response. "You freak! You should be castrated . . . ," "The police are on their way . . . ," "We got a bunch of us coming over to beat the shit out of you. . . ." Those were the mild ones. Unfortunately, it wasn't "tim" who sent the message. A friend of his got his account and his passwords and thought it would be funny to play a little practical joke. If the boards can be believed, the "friend" quickly took a trip to the hospital.

As bad as Class 1 Information Warfare is, there are some goofballs out there in Cyberspace who think it's a big giggle. The demon dialer that hackers use to identify computers sitting on phone lines can also be used as a weapon of harassment. A demon dialer can be set to call a phone number every minute on the minute, or every ten minutes, ring once or twice, and then hang up. (Imagine being on the receiving end of that.) In one case, every time someone dialed a particular church, they were connected to a Dial-A-Porn 900 number. In juvenile days past, I was guilty of calling the local meat market, asking if they had pig's feet, and responding to an affirmative answer with "wear shoes and no one will notice." I fear that with profoundly sophisticated technology in the hands of the disenfranchised, the bored, the latch-key kids, and the downright malicious, our younger generations will learn the tricks of the Information Warriors without any help from us.

Class 1 might appear to be the kindergarten of Information Warfare, consisting only of isolated incidents and causing comparatively minor harm. Relatively speaking, that may in fact be true. But in more aggressive hands, Class 1 Information Warfare is employed as a means to an end, a preliminary tool, a diversion from the real task at hand. Let's not fool ourselves into thinking, "Ah, it's just a bunch of kids letting off some steam. Or maybe a few adults who never grew up, or would break the law no matter what the technology. That's nothing to worry about." Conventional wisdom forgets that the international cumulative effects of Class 1 Information Warfare, if properly organized, can lead to far more sinister acts, with far reaching consequences. Conventional wisdom has suggested that once the hackers are gone, all of our problems are over. Nothing could be farther from the truth. Because, sooner or later, we all graduate from kindergarten, and move on to learn and apply our knowledge with greater and greater skill.

No Privacy

Elizabeth Weise, Associated Press Cyberspace Writer

John Kaufman didn't know he was being followed. No dark sedans tailed his car, no mysterious clicks interrupted his phone calls. But every word he typed in the deepest corners of the Internet was being downloaded by an obsessive stalker.

Kaufman was well aware that his posts and ruminations were considered public on Usenet, a global bulletin board made up of more than 15,000 separate discussion groups on every topic imaginable. He meant to reach a worldwide audience, after all.

But what surprised him was the ease with which someone who'd taken such an overwhelming interest in his life was able to track down everything he'd ever said online.

It's a realization many people are having, now that the rules of the game have changed. In the last year, a new and powerful generation of search programs have begun to systematically index the entire Internet, making it possible for the first time to find just about anything if a request is sufficiently precise.

The story Kaufman relates started innocently enough: He had posted a note on a local computer bulletin board in December about a program he wanted to sell. A woman e-mailed that she was interested, they agreed on a price and, a few days later, she stopped by his apartment to pick it up.

Everything seemed normal, he said, until the next day. "She sent me e-mail saying she'd conducted a search of Usenet, looking at the posts I'd made, and she was very interested in me and the things I'd done," Kaufman said.

A San Francisco-based writer, Kaufman's words have appeared in numerous national magazines. They also appear in far-flung corners of the Internet, where he takes part in many of the free-floating conversations on Usenet.

It was those words that came back to haunt him when his admirer began sending him daily e-mail messages, often commenting on things he'd posted in newsgroups on topics ranging from Latin American politics to the weather in the Shetland Islands.

Finally, in January, she sent a message that shook him badly, a three-page letter that basically was a dossier of his entire life. "She's pieced together the puzzle of my life from Usenet. She knows my mother was a concert pianist. She knows what I wanted to be when I was growing up, all because of Usenet, from postings and discussions I've had there," said Kaufman, who is gay—a fact also known to the woman.

"When this thing flashed on the screen, my mouth dropped open," he said. "Here was a total stranger who knew my cat's name." The problem with the Internet had always been that while the wisdom of the world might be contained within it, there was no way to figure out exactly what was there. It was like the Library of Congress without a card catalog.

Where once it would have been almost impossible to read through the millions of messages posted daily to the various newsgroups to find one by a particular person, services such as Deja News now sift through that 580 megabytes of data in seconds and supply an "Author Profile" of any given person.

These profiles list the number of original posts an author has made, called "articles" on Usenet, their percentage of follow-up posts, and a complete listing of every newsgroup they've taken part in. Simply clicking on a listing brings their original post to your screen.

"I think this is a situation where there has been a great step forward in technology, but how we absorb it into society and use it responsibly hasn't quite been defined yet," said Lori Fena, director of the Electronic Frontier Foundation, a San Francisco-based online rights organization.

"The rules have changed, but people's actions haven't changed. Before," she said of posting, "it was a public act in a private room. These new search engines are going back into those private rooms, listening to the recordings, and making everything said there available to everyone else."

Legally, there doesn't appear to be a problem with these new search tools and archives. Someone writing a letter to the editor of a newspaper gives an implied license that it be published. Someone posting to the most assuredly public forum of Usenet would have every reason to believe his or her words would be resent around the globe.

"The courts will probably find some kind of implied license. As you posted it for thousands of people to read, it would be hard to convince the court that it was private," said Eugene Volokh, a law professor specializing in online issues at the University of California at Los Angeles. However, different services take different stands on just how public those old posts were.

Usenet began in 1979, but the services that index it started up only in the last year or so. Digital Equipment Corp.'s Alta Vista search program keeps only the last month or so of Usenet live online. "We think Usenet is like a conversation. It's not something that should be kept forever to haunt you. Say some student posts something about Microsoft being the big evil empire and then, two years later in a suit and a tie, they're applying for a job there," said Louis Monier, lead scientist of the Alta Vista project, based in Palo Alto, California.

But down in Austin, Texas, Deja News is trying hard to be the memory of Usenet. Since May 1995, the tiny start-up company has been offering an ever-growing full text index of Usenet. If you said something about iguanas in 1986 in the rec.pets newsgroup, they want the rest of the world to be able to find it. Deja News plans on having a complete index going back to 1979 by the end of this year.

Normally, Usenet postings last only a few days or weeks, depending on how busy a particular newsgroup is. As new messages come in, old ones are purged from the system. It used to be that if you didn't read a message when it first was posted, you were out of luck. Back-up tapes on computer systems around the country contain older chunks of Usenet, however, just like stacks of newspaper sitting in someone's basement. By piecing together various back-ups, Deja News plans to have an archive of every newsgroup since its inception.

That can come as something of a shock to people who thought their words were gone forever. "I've certainly gotten some irate mail," said George D. Nicas, the service's user liaison. To deal with the problem, Deja News will delete the contents of old posts at the request of the person who wrote them. In addition, the service is putting together a feature that will allow Usenet users to keep their messages out of the index by including the words "no-archive" in the addressing information at the beginning of their post.

Nicas said the service also plans to do a mass posting to all 15,000 newsgroups, telling people their words are being archived and how to use the no-archive header if they don't want to be a part of the index. "Even if we didn't index it, 30 million people could read it, but we're instituting this feature anyway," he said.

But in the end, according to Volokh, the only true privacy is silence. "If you don't want something to be known," he said, "don't put it in a medium where thousands of strangers can see it." As for John Kaufman, after he sent his stalker strongly worded e-mail, weeks went by without any response. But he knows she's still out there, and that his words on the Internet are an open book.

"In the back of my mind as I'm writing, I'm thinking, 'This woman is going to be reading this,'" he said. "But there's no hesitation to push the send key, because I have nothing to hide."

Personal Information Warfare: The Individual Perspective

Mark Aldrich, GRCI

Introduction

It is surprising the factors that influence our ideas of precisely what Information Warfare really is. Beyond the Schwartau categorizations, there seem many subcategories and specializations, some which blend with one another and ultimately confound our efforts at categorization. When we look at infowar from a personal or individual perspective, we've all read the reports and the prophesies about the hackers. The "cyber-cowboy" redefining notions of the rugged individualist, surviving by his or her wits, and, if not a total criminal, then certainly a member of one of the fringe groups that our society permits to exist. Drawing from that, we can summon foreboding auspices of the information terrorists, information gangs, and organized information criminals, all preying upon the hapless and ill-informed civilians who cannot survive without accurate digital medical records, correct credit reports, and faultless government records.

Somehow, the issues of personal infowar concerns seem (hopefully temporarily) trapped in the feud that surrounds personal cryptography. It's almost as if many people believe that if we only had untappable encrypted telephone lines and Internet connections, that threats against individuals, particularly those that might be government-sponsored, would be mitigated. Hopefully, we're outgrowing this notion and are realizing that cryptography is merely one quirky mathematical tool that we have, while the real problem is rooted less in science than in the framework of our society and how we choose to treat one another. Rather than dwell upon the horrific omens of fourteen-year-olds usurping our cell phone ID codes and VISA numbers, I'm going to look at some of the societal phenomena, particularly from an anthropological view, that's led us here and some ideas about where we can expect to be going.

The Self-Named Naked Ape

We differentiate ourselves from other forms of life in many ways, but one of the most frequently cited is our ability to form and use language. Language offers an interesting reflection of a group's values, objectives, and belief systems, because ultimately those things shape and define the language that those individuals use. Some languages have 50 different words for "whale blubber" while others offer a hundred different variations on the verb *to dream*. Of all the lexicons I have been able to access, of both dead and living languages, all of them contain notions of "same" and "other." All of them permit the expression of the idea of "us" and the idea of "them."

In our language, we seem to have spent an inordinate amount of time coining and refining terms based upon this notion. "Them" can, it seems, be almost anything. We identify "them" as clubs, clans, groups, factions, gangs, consortiums, syndicates, blocs, cartels, coalitions, combines, conglomerates, trusts, associations, unions, federations, and leagues. We call "them" a nation, or nation-state, or government, or the Republicans or

Democrats. We can peg one another with an associative label that tells us what we want to know about each other: Whether it be our race, our faith, our political ideals, our profession, our gender, our sexual preferences, or our social beliefs.

These expressions all have one thing in common: They permit us to segregate the parties of conflict. They delineate the lines between friend and foe. Any act of war must always have an "us" and a "them." For many, it is convenient to rely upon these abstractions. It does, however, make it easy to forget a fundamental concept of war: it is fought between individuals, not by "us" or by "them." Every act of war is an act carried out by individuals. In actuality, there is no such thing as Information Warfare at the international level. *Nation* is just another one of those words we use for "us" or "them." There is no infowar fought by corporations; there is no infowar fought by government. War is waged by individuals, who seek to bend others to their will.

Information as a Source of War

We concoct many notions of why we wage war, infowar certainly not being an exception. It is, partially, through our arrogance and romanticism that we justify our actions against one another: We hold up ideas we call "God" or "Country" or "Clan" or "our way of life" or, perhaps most interesting, "peace." In doing so, the utter irony of what we do is disguised: Since the beginning of history, time and time again, we have been told by our leaders, our priests, our philosophers, our prophets, our gods, and our messiahs, if only we would stop fighting each other, everything would be fine.

But we don't stop. Why?

The answer is information.

But war, you might say, is an act of survival—either ensuring your own or denying it to another. What does that have to do with information? It has a lot to do with it if we look at how we fit into the larger scheme of things and see ourselves as applications running on the platform of life. We see, in living things, an intense competition for survival. We are not the only species to try to kill those who would take our territory and, along with it, the natural resources we need in order to survive. Everything, it seems, has rooted at its core a fundamentally powerful impulse to continue to survive. To survive and to reproduce.

Evolutionary biologists, like Dawkins, Thompkins, and even Darwin, are quick to point out an obvious fact that most of us overlook: Every living thing on earth, each person alive today, in fact every person hearing these words has a simple, but remarkable, common heritage: We can proudly state that every single one of our ancestors lived long enough to have children. Every last one of them avoided being killed by the plague, falling off a cliff, getting fatally slashed up in a bar fight, or being trounced upon by an enemy before they brought at least one child into this world. Without a single exception, we come from an unbroken line of successful ancestors. We live, compete, die, and wage war in a world that is full of organisms who have what it takes to become ancestors.

Deoxyribonucleic Acid and Addiction

Dawkins, for example, has proposed that we, our bodies, our five fingers, two eyes, and our incredible mammalian brains are nothing but the corporeal weapons being used by our DNA to ensure its own survival. Consequently, our society, our minds, and our language are symptoms of our brain's ability to assist in the survival of the genome that created it. To ensure that its pattern, its "program," is reproduced, we are, in effect, compelled to act out the primal dictates of our genome. The human genome is hell-bent on survival, and it will go to any lengths, pay any price, including encasing itself in a body of bone, muscle, neurons, water, tissues, organs, systems, and ultimately "organism," in order to procreate itself. DNA is, however, ultimately a program—a base-four encoding, using only adenine and thymine or cytosine and guanine. It has two amazing programming primitives: it can self-replicate and it can make RNA. From a purely evolutionary viewpoint, everything else it does, and everything we do, is just icing on the cake, a by-product of basic survival.

That is, until now. It used to be that what it took to be a successful ancestor was 46 chromosomes and some luck. Now it takes a lot more. A little glitch snuck into our programs, it seems. We are one of four species of great apes alive on this planet. All of these species share well over 95 percent of the same genetic sequences, and all of us are tool builders. But tool building doesn't work if you have to keep discovering and inventing the same tools again and again. A species that can preserve tool-making skills, from one generation to another, will tend to excel at survival. In order to ensure that environmental manipulation, and the inherent benefits thereof, continue to be lavished upon the genome, some incentive has to come into play that encourages such behavior. This incentive is called "addiction."

We quickly become addicted to any tool that enters widespread use within our civilization. We can't ever "forget" how to make these tools, nor can we return to life without them. This is not a matter of social conditioning, nor of insurmountable laziness. These tools are now as instrumental to the survival of our DNA as are our bodies. It is no wonder, then, that we are willing to fight others for control of these things.

The tools we build are amplifiers. We build telescopes and microscopes so that we can see more than is possible with our eyes. We build telephones so that we can hear and speak over distances too great to permit the use of our vocal chords and our ears. We build planes, trains, and automobiles so that we can travel faster and farther than our muscles and skeletons can accommodate without such amplifiers. Perhaps most significant of all, however, is the brain amplifier: the electronic digital computer. Using this, the genome is able to off-load memory and survival information management functions to a durable and exceedingly fast augmentation to the mammalian brain. The basic functions of our bodies are amplifiers for the genome and, as such, the tools we build are amplifiers for our bodies. The objective, however, remains the same: Survival at any cost.

The Evolution of Information Systems and Genome Amplifiers

It is not by accident that the first computers were isolated, self-sufficient, stand-alone machines that remind us of single-celled organisms. If you look at what we did with our information-processing capabilities, we see startling parallels with our own biological ancestry: single cells that begin to colonize together and then begin to differentiate and then to specialize. We now have computers so specialized in function that they can no longer serve any function autonomously. They must be connected, they must communicate and share the total goal of the collective, in order to be of any use. Layer upon layer of information-processing protocols, discovered by chance, like some accelerated sequence of genetic mutation, is stacked one upon another: the reptilian brain, the mammalian brain, the simian brain, the human brain, each representative of how we artificially evolved our information-processing capabilities. This is not by chance. This is how we know to evolve. We model and mimic the functions we see in all those generations of successful ancestors. The program must be a very good one, because it's been running a very, very long time.

The information revolution is the next step in genome amplification. The genome remembers, it learns, and it communicates, but it takes so incredibly long for it to affect each of these functions. Having a large, complex, language-capable brain can help, but we've reached the point where even that is not enough. We must accelerate the process and amplify the base functions of the genome. The life of the tool makers undergoes a paradigm shift.

The Genome Is Making the Hackers

Has anyone wondered why we have hackers—what Schwartau calls the first Infowarriors? Haven't you ever wondered why this whole phenomenon came about? Do you ever wonder about why other industries don't have hackers? We don't have 13-year-olds breaking into hospitals in the middle of the night to do a little amateur surgery. We don't see kids spending 18 hours a day studying fashion design. We have no groups of young people investing their own time, buying their own supplies, recklessly breaking laws, and risking potential punishment to study the commodities markets. If you go into a shopping mall food court, you might run across a 2600 meeting. You won't, however, find a juvenile equivalent of the plumbers union swapping secrets on how to unstop a plugged toilet. You won't find a bunch of kids who want to be firemen when they grow up. Hacking, for whatever reason, is exclusively information technology-related. It is the computers and telecommunications systems that draw our children into this strange subculture, hidden in plain view from us. No other technology or career field has experienced this phenomenon. Why?

Programming and telecommunication technologies strike a deep, resonant chord with many people. These people are compelled and driven to learn and manipulate the systems with which we manage information. They do with these amplifiers what their genomes do with DNA. Sequencing, programming, routing, switching, Boolean logic, conditional execution: all of these are from the language of genetics as well as that of the information sciences. As well they should be. The genome is nothing more than information itself. Information is, and always will be, the ultimate commodity.

We like to think of ourselves as having reached the point where we are shifting from a commodities-based market economy to an information-based market economy. This is, in fact, an indicator of us having come full circle in terms of identifying the ultimate commodity. Before any other commodity, there was information. Although we were not aware of it, it's always been there. It was not until 1953 that Crick and Watson revealed the truth to us: Molecular biology is digital. Buried in almost every cell of our bodies is the program that is "us." Information is at the root of the quest for survival in the form of our genetic code. Before we fought any war for God or country, for land or resources, we fought for information. Information warfare is the only kind of warfare we have ever fought.

To answer the question posed to the panel, "Your applications versus the Infowarriors, who's going to win?" I can only say: nobody. To win, of course, means to end the game. Stop the competition. Declare a victor. But we can't do that. We can't quit because to do so would mean stopping the program. With all of our technology, however, with all our scientific powers of understanding, we cannot build a human brain. We can't stop the program because we rely upon it, those 46 tiny little clumps of amino acids, to make each one of those brains, each one of us. While we can bring to bear technology so powerful that it will wipe all life from this planet, ironically we must rely upon a genetic sequence we don't even understand to bring about that life in the first place.

What we must do is stop our fascination with "us" and "them" and fight our urge to rationalize war as something waged only by "the government" or "the enemy" or "the competition" or "that other nation over there." War is about individuals. Seeking to deal with Information Warfare, which is ultimately the most personal form of battle in which we will ever engage, through government oversight, law enforcement, legislation, social reforms, or any other "us" and "them" mechanism, is to miss the point. If individuals are powerless to defend themselves, powerless to understand what drives the battle, incapable of safeguarding the genome they carry within their bodies as well as the external data it needs to survive, we're fools to think that the Department of Defense is going to deal with that for us, or that Congress can fix it, or that widespread Information Warfare defense forces can somehow protect us. The DoD is people—it's individuals. The Congress is flesh and blood, simply a collection of individuals. There is no magic "they" as in, "I'm sure they will take care of that for us." We are all individuals, each of us responsible for ourselves, and we will wage war for our children just like we always have. Let us hope that we are the best ancestors we can possibly be.

Information Warfare: The Personal Front

Beth Givens, Privacy Rights Clearinghouse

Each year, staff members of the Privacy Rights Clearinghouse talk to thousands of Californians who call our hotline seeking information on ways to safeguard their privacy. We have been alarmed in recent years by the marked increase in calls regarding "identity theft." This is a form of Class 1 information warfare, defined by Schwartau as an "attack against an individual's electronic privacy: his digital records, files, or other portions of a person's electronic essence."

Using a variety of methods, criminals steal credit card numbers, driver's license numbers, Social Security numbers, ATM cards, telephone calling cards, and/or other key pieces of individuals' identities. They use this information to impersonate the victims, spending as much money as they can in as short a time as possible before moving on to someone else's name and account information. Under federal law, credit and banking fraud victims are liable for only the first $50 of their losses, and most financial institutions will waive this amount. However, even though victims of identity theft are not saddled with paying their imposters' bills, they are usually left with a bad credit report, and must spend months and sometimes years regaining their financial health. In the meantime, they have difficulty writing checks, obtaining loans, renting apartments, and even getting hired.

To make matters worse, victims of identity theft get almost no help from the authorities as they attempt to untangle the web of deception that has allowed another person to impersonate them. Nearly every victim who contacted the hotline had a variation of the same lament:

> I couldn't get the Department of Motor Vehicles to change my driver's license number, even though someone was still using it to write bad checks.

The Social Security Administration said there's nothing they can do. They wouldn't even allow me to get a new SSN.

The police were no help. They said they didn't have sufficient time or staff to investigate my case. I had to plead to even get them to write a police report so I could give it to the credit card company to prove my innocence.

I called the credit bureaus [TRW, Equifax, Trans Union] and had them put a "fraud alert" on my records. But that didn't seem to stop the imposter. Whoever it was could still get new credit cards in my name and continue to ring up large unpaid bills.

Victims complain that it is far too easy for criminals to perpetrate identity thefts. While employees in the credit granting industry had the opportunity to verify the identity of the credit applicant, many did not. While DMV officials might have questioned why someone was ordering a new driver's license and having it sent to a new address, they often did not. While retailers might have asked for other pieces of identification before replacing the "lost" credit card, there were many instances when they did not. And while credit reporting bureaus might have contacted the individual when someone requested that the credit report be sent to a "new" address, they did not always do so.

Another factor that facilitates the crime of identity theft is simple carelessness in handling personal information. For instance, the auto dealer who does not shred loan applications before depositing them in the trash receptacle puts his customers at risk because of the ease in which dumpster divers and even dishonest employees can retrieve them and use the detailed information to impersonate loan applicants.

Clearly, negligent practices across the board are contributing to the skyrocketing incidence of identity theft in the United States. And businesses' interest in providing an easy-credit environment for consumers has spawned the unwelcome side effect of fraud. Is it any wonder that substantially more money is stolen via identity theft than through armed robbery?

Here are just a few examples from the Clearinghouse hotline showing the plight of victims of this form of information warfare. They depict both the ease with which imposters can take on someone else's identity as well as the difficulty victims have in getting help from government and industry officials in recovering from their losses and pursuing the criminals.

First, Martha's purse was stolen, and then her mail. An imposter filed a change of address with the Post Office which caused her mail to be sent to someone else's residence. Martha filed a report with the Postal Service, but after six months has not heard from them. The imposter ordered merchandise from a mail order company. When a company representative called Martha to confirm the order, Martha told her about the stolen identity and asked that the merchandise not be sent.

The catalog company ignored her request, mailed the merchandise and billed her.

John was the victim of identity theft as a result of filling out an automobile loan application. An employee of the auto dealership used information from the loan application to open several credit card accounts. He even leased an apartment in John's name. John thinks the imposter called John's home several times to listen to his telephone answering machine in order to copy his speech patterns. John had difficulty getting the police department to take an interest in his case. He finally hired a private investigator who had once worked for the police department. The PI not only was able to uncover information about the imposter, he convinced an acquaintance in the police department to take on the case. The imposter has since been arrested.

Belinda's ex-roommate Nancy fraudulently obtained a driver's license under Belinda's name. When Belinda contacted the Department of Motor Vehicles about it, they told her not to worry. Soon thereafter Belinda got a new job. After one month on the job, she was fired. Her employer learned that Belinda had committed a felony, even though it was her ex-roommate Nancy who had committed the crime while in possession of Belinda's driver's license. Belinda called the DMV again and was told they would not be able to "flag" her driver's license record. The Clearinghouse called the DMV on her behalf and found someone who would help Belinda.

The Clearinghouse does not see the problem of identity theft abating in the near future. Significant changes must be made by the credit and banking industries in the way individuals' financial information is compiled, accessed, and used. As the above cases illustrate, it is far too easy for imposters to gain access to credit and bank account information and other identifying information such as driver's license numbers.

The societal costs of identity fraud are enormous. Consumers are paying significantly more for goods and services because of the billions of dollars in losses incurred by financial institutions. The productivity of thousands of individuals is substantially lowered because of the amount of time needed to resolve the problems associated with identity theft.

There is even a psychological price to be paid. Many victims use the analogy of rape to describe their experiences. They tell of the long process they must go through as they deal with feelings of vulnerability, powerlessness, and anger. They find out that the burden is placed entirely on victims' shoulders and that they are largely alone in remedying the problems caused by identity theft.

Solutions to the problem lie in the adoption of tighter verification procedures and more stringent access requirements by the credit and banking industries. In addition, fraud awareness programs must be implemented for all individuals who handle identification documentation, whether they are in the private or public sector. More must be done via society-wide training to instill a "culture of confidentiality" in all who handle personal information. And law enforcement must be funded adequately to handle the growing amount of identity theft.

One of the purposes of the Privacy Rights Clearinghouse is to shed light on privacy problems. While the Clearinghouse can suggest solutions, a problem as massive as identity theft requires a concerted effort by representatives of all the institutions which are party to this type of fraud.

Clearly, consumers are paying the full price of this type of information warfare—both in increased cost of goods and services needed to cover business losses due to fraud and in scarred psyches and lost productivity borne by victims. It's time for industry interests to come to terms with the problem of identity theft and seek solutions that take the burden off consumers' shoulders.

How to Beat Goliath: Why Strong Privacy Protection Is the Best Defense Against Information Warfare

Simon Davies, Director, Privacy International

When Winn Schwartau first asked me to write on the subject of "privacy and Information Warfare," my initial reaction was to run for cover. Privacy is a controversial notion at any time, but its unruliness knows no bounds in the context of a conference such as this.

As soon as the subject of privacy is raised, many people react instinctively. Some are hostile to the idea. Some see it as being the province of selfishness. Others regard privacy as unruly, unnecessary, or just plain self-indulgent. When I speak to government or commercial representatives, most will chant privacy like a mantra in public, while doing all in their power in the backroom to undermine it. They see privacy as a selfish and overstated notion that gets in the way of the "bigger" agenda.

I am hoping for a different response. My own view is that from a defense perspective in Information Warfare, a population's insistence on privacy is potentially the greatest asset we possess.

All the same, I can see why some of you may find privacy distasteful. It can be a loose cannon on an otherwise well-ordered deck. Privacy is a politically charged topic that brings into focus the balance of power between the individual and the many large organizations in a modern society. As a consequence it is often hoisted as a defense for individual rights.

(When I use the word *hoisted* I am referring to the situation in the

United States. In most European countries, I'd use the word *exhumed*. More on that later.)

My intention here today is threefold. First, I want to take a brief stab at defining privacy. We need to have some basic tools to work with. Second, I want to explain why privacy is crucial to both hemispheres of Information Warfare. Finally, I intend to present the case for a strong, unwavering, and passionate pursuit of privacy. And by that I do not mean to suggest that the mere passage of legislation will be the sole answer. In fact, legislation has universally failed to protect or promote privacy. My own view is that privacy must be a privately held passion as well as a set of legal conditions. Ideally, they would form a symbiotic relationship. One is lame without the other.

I should also say something to ensure that you are in no doubt about my own views on the nature of privacy and the power of the state.

I have come to believe that most countries are heading rapidly toward being surveillance societies dominated by powerful information-based entities. I believe privacy is being engineered into extinction. I deeply fear that the individual is being stripped of crucial and ancient rights. And I believe these are dangerous trends. My job as a privacy advocate is to slow—and preferably to reverse—these developments. My own view is that more and more people will come across to my way of thinking; that is, privacy is one of the pillars of a free society, and its defense is justified under virtually any circumstance. And by that I also mean ethical sabotage, civil resistance, civilian espionage, and luddism.

Having come out of the closet on that, let me attempt to define privacy.

Privacy is a little like freedom: the less you have of it, the easier it is to recognize. And like the concept of freedom (and for that matter, Information Warfare), privacy has many wildly different definitions. Even after decades of academic interest in the subject, the world's leading experts have been unable to agree on a single definition. One pioneer in the field described privacy as "part philosophy, some semantics, and much pure passion."[1] At least on that point, everyone agrees.

Some countries—France for example—see the concept of privacy as a form of liberty. Others, including Britain, view privacy as being preservation of a space around us. Some European countries interpret privacy as the protection of our personal information. One popular definition is expressed in the Oxford dictionary, which explains privacy as "being withdrawn from society or public interest."

One school of thought argues that privacy protection is one way of drawing the line at how far society can intrude into your affairs. In that context, privacy is a question of power—yours, the government's, the corporations'. "The bedrock of civil liberties," social justice campaigner Patricia Hewitt once observed, "is the setting of limits on the power of the state to interfere in the private life of its citizens." Privacy can be viewed as a measure of how much surveillance and control can be established over our lives. It is a measure of how much we should become subjects of the expanding technological empire. Privacy can even be a benchmark to indicate how much autonomy a nation should have in the emerging international order.

A hundred years ago, the prominent U.S. judge (later Supreme Court Justice) Louis Brandeis articulated a concept of privacy that urged that it was the individual's "right to be left alone." Brandeis argued that privacy was the most cherished of freedoms in a democracy, and he was deeply concerned that it was not specifically protected by the U.S. Constitution. A century later, the Constitution still gives only limited protection for privacy. In my own country, Britain, privacy is given even less weight.

In 1975, the California Supreme Court ruled, "The right of privacy is the right to be left alone. It is a fundamental and compelling interest. It protects our homes, our families, our thoughts, our emotions, our expressions, our personalities, our freedom of communion, and our freedom to associate with whom we choose. It prevents government and business interests from collecting and stockpiling unnecessary information about us, and from misusing information gathered for one purpose in order to serve other purposes or embarrass us."[2]

In Britain, as in most countries, there exists no Bill of Rights to enshrine privacy, and there are minimal specific privacy laws. The Data Protection Acts in two dozen countries establish some rudimentary rules about the handling of information, but set up few barriers to the establishment of intrusive computer systems.

One of the pioneers of privacy, Alan Westin, defined privacy as the desire of people to choose freely under what circumstances and to what extent they will expose themselves, their attitude, and their behavior to others.[3] Arnold Simmel argues, "the right to privacy asserts the sacredness of the person." He believes a violation of a person's privacy is a violation of the person's dignity, individualism, and freedom.[4]

Part of the problem of developing a broadly accepted definition is that privacy is being portrayed more and more by governments and the corporate sector as being equivalent to selfishness or secrecy. Anyone standing in the way of government information strategies must have something to hide. The surrender of personal information has become a routine and automatic process. We scarcely give it a thought.

From my own perspective, the definition has to be at least as potent as the forces that oppose privacy. So the definition of my own choosing (and my own making) is:

> The right to privacy is the right to protect ourselves against intrusion by the outside world. It is the measure we use to set limits on the demands made by organizations and people. It is the right we invoke to defend our personal freedom, our autonomy and our identity. It is the basis upon which we assess the balance of power between ourselves, and the world around us.

Now, as I mentioned earlier, there are many more definitions. In Europe, privacy was long ago defined in legalistic terms, and was given the rather uninspiring pseudonym "data protection." My own view is that over the next few years the population at large will come to recognize that data protection is something of a hoax. It's certainly true that outside the United States we are enjoying a mild epidemic of privacy activity around the planet. We can celebrate more codes, conventions, and legislation than ever before. And yet, more data are being collected by more powerful systems on more people and for more purposes than ever before. The traditional power struggle that once defined privacy has been neutralized.

Even where Privacy Acts are governed by a dedicated and forceful regulator (rare indeed), the opposing forces are now so overwhelming that it is often impossible to stand in the way of the most sophisticated data practices. David Flaherty, Privacy Commissioner of British Columbia and without doubt one of the most thoughtful people in the field, says, "There is a real risk that data protection of today will be looked back on as a rather quaint, failed effort to cope with an overpowering technological tide."[5]

Given these shortcomings, is it any wonder that privacy is likely to be viewed in similar ways to environmental protection? It's appropriate we should be talking warfare here, because privacy advocates have expressed the belief for a while now that a privacy battleground is being formed. On one side are forces that seek total disclosure in a framework of uniformity. On the other side are people who believe in privacy through informational chaos. They oppose the unification of standards and the trend to regulation and registration.

In the context of Information Warfare, however, the antagonists should in fact be on the same side. As the world moves toward one compatible, integrated data canopy, the vulnerability of the economic systems will increase.[6] As the vulnerability increases, opportunities for terrorism will also become more apparent. Yielding to the demands of privacy advocates would in fact be a smart move for defense authorities.

Governments appear to be moving in the opposite direction. Instead of allowing chaos within information systems, and permitting people to strongly defend their privacy, they are increasingly attempting to pass legislation to allow routine and mass surveillance of computer communication, partly in an attempt to monitor information that may threaten computer networks.[7]

To minimize the possibility of terrorist attack or sabotage, government is demanding more and more access to our personal computers and our communications. It is feasible that national biometric identity cards would be used to access computer systems. In this scenario, everybody who wanted to access computer networks would have to use cards which verify (through fingerprints or voice recognition) that they were who they say they are. This would make it easier for the authorities to track down any malicious action. As more and more people need to access these networks, a compulsory national or international biometric smart card is quite feasible. This is the wrong way to deal with the threat.

From the defensive point of view, a kaleidoscopic information matrix would prove difficult for an enemy to infiltrate and destroy. Widespread, unregulated cryptographic systems and strong security would decrease the chances even further. Functional separation of systems would improve the situation still further.

And yet none of these aims are being pursued. Instead, government wants to have its cake and eat it, too. In the end, we may all be losers on the battlefield.

1. Alan F. Westin, *Privacy and Freedom* (New York: Atheneum, 1967), p. x.
2. California Supreme Court, *White v. Davis* (13 Cal. 3d., 757, 1975).
3. Westin, *Privacy and Freedom,* p. 7
4. Arnold Simmel, "Privacy," *International Encyclopedia of the Social Sciences* 12 (1968): 480, 482, 485
5. David H. Flaherty, *Protecting Privacy in Surveillance Societies* (University of North Carolina Press, 1989).
6. The development of Open Systems planning means that computers in many different environments will have the capacity to fully communicate.
7. Bill S-266 of 1991 specified that people encrypting (encoding) their communications through the computer networks had to tell the government how to unscramble the code.

Church and Statutes

Mike Godwin, Internet World

Reprinted with permission from Internet World, *April 1996. Copyright 1996.*

It is important to understand the copyright and trade secret laws the Church of Scientology has been using to prosecute its critics.

I've been dreading writing in this space about the legal war going on between the Church of Scientology and the Internet. It's not because I fear reprisal. Rather, it's because the legal dimension of the Scientology cases involves what for many people is one of the driest and least engaging areas of the law—the law of intellectual property.

But the nature of the Net is such that we're all going to be thinking hard about intellectual property issues over the next few years. So the issues raised by the Scientology cases may serve a useful purpose by giving us an opportunity to review the outlines of copyright and trade secret law and to consider the policies that underlie these two branches of the law. Once we've done that, we can better evaluate the Church's legal claims.

The Church of Scientology's legal conflicts basically involve its prosecution of former members and critics who have posted Church documents on the Internet that the Church claims are copyrighted trade secrets. So far, the defendants have fallen primarily into two basic groups: publishers/posters and online service providers. In the first group are people like Dennis Erlich, a former minister of Scientology who is now an outspoken critic of the Church; Arnold Lerma, who has published controversial court documents concerning one of the many cases in which the Church—a famously litigious organization—has been involved; and Lawrence Wollersheim, who runs a BBS called FactNet. Also in the first group is "Scamizdat," an anonymous Usenet poster who has distributed dozens of Scientology documents. Arguably, the *Washington Post* also belongs in this group. The newspaper was sued by the Church over materials it received (some of which it published) as part of its coverage of the Lerma case.

In the second group you find major Internet service providers Netcom and Digital Gateway Systems, as well as support.com, a BBS run by Tom Klemesrud. These three services have been sued by the Church on the grounds that it is their legal duty to act as intellectual property policemen (at least where the Church's intellectual property is concerned). A different sort of online service provider, anon.penet.fi—an anonymous remailer operated in Finland by Johan Helsingius—also has been targeted by the Church. Helsingius was legally compelled in 1995 to surrender the identity of one of his anonymous users whom the Church believed was circulating secret documents.

(For a more detailed report on the facts surrounding the Scientology cases, see Mark Fearer's "Scientology's Secrets" in the December 1995 issue of *Internet World* and Wendy Grossman's "alt.scientology.war" which appeared in the December 1995 issue of *Wired.*)

At the core of all the legal conflicts collectively (and unofficially) referred to online as "Scientology vs. the Net" are two questions. First, to what extent can individuals post Church of Scientology documents and other information about the Church? Second, are online service providers responsible for policing their systems for infringement of the Church's intellectual property? We'll be dealing mostly with the first question here.

The documents in question are mostly the writings of the late L. Ron Hubbard, the former pulp science-fiction writer who founded the Church of Scientology in 1954. Hubbard's writings recount the Church's mythology—including practices for dealing with "thetans" (entities that can cause humans mental or physical problems)—and describe the Church's internal problems. Church officials refer to these documents as "sacred scriptures."

Although the Church has relied on other legal theories in the course of its conflicts with Net critics—including trademark law and First Amendment freedom-of-religion provisions—its primary rationale for its legal actions has involved two rather distinct areas of the law of intellectual property: U.S. copyright and trade secret law. Let's consider each of these in turn.

U.S. Copyright Law

Modern copyright law in the United States is laid out in Title 17 of the United States Code. The last major revision of the Copyright Act took place in 1976, but the fundamental approach of the copyright law in this county can be found in a passage from the legislative report on the Copyright Act of 1909:

> In enacting a copyright law Congress must consider . . . two questions: First, how much will the legislation stimulate the producer and so benefit the public, and, second, how much will the monopoly granted be detrimental to the public? The granting of such exclusive rights, under the proper terms and conditions, confers a benefit upon the public that outweighs the evils of the temporary monopoly.

In short, the idea behind copyright law is to encourage creators to generate expressive works because they benefit society. The types of works that can be protected by copyright law are listed in Section 102 of the Copyright Act, and include:

- Literary works
- Musical works, including any accompanying words
- Dramatic works, including any accompanying music
- Pantomimes and choreographic works
- Pictorial, graphic, and sculptural works
- Motion pictures and other audiovisual works
- Sound recordings
- Architectural works

To be protected by copyright law, works have to have been fixed at some point in a tangible medium, and they have to be original. The copyright law protects the particular expression of an idea, but not the idea itself. For example, you can copyright the movie *Before Sunrise,* but you can't copyright the idea "boy meets girl."

For the most part, the Copyright Act addresses, appropriately enough, the right to make a copy. If you make copies of a copyrighted work without a license granted by the copyright holder and you can't avail yourself of any defense, such as "fair use" (discussed below), you are a copyright infringer.

Section 503 of the Act describes legal action for possible infringement that has been used dramatically against several of the publisher defendants in the Scientology cases:

At any time while an action under this title is pending, the court may order the impounding, on such terms as it may deem reasonable, of all copies or phonorecords claimed to have been made or used in violation of the copyright owner's exclusive rights and of all plates, molds, matrices, masters, tapes, film negatives, or other articles by means of which such copies or phonorecords may be reproduced.

In other words, the plaintiffs in a copyright case can conduct a search and seizure at the alleged infringer's premises, ostensibly to prevent further infringement. In the Scientology cases, this has meant that Scientology lawyers have gone to defendants' homes with law enforcement agents in tow to seize defendants' computers and other possessions. It's the kind of utterly disconcerting, frightening event that few people— even vociferous critics of a controversial and litigious church—really expect, given that this kind of seizure can take place before an infringement case goes to court, or even before the defendant's lawyer has had a chance to talk to the judge. It's a tactic that was designed to handle commercial infringers, but it's one that the Church of Scientology has adapted to its own purposes—a sort of *in terrorem* tactic aimed at certain critics of the Church.

Even though folks like Erlich and Lerma are being treated as presumptive infringers, are they in fact infringers? They claim that even if they are making unlicensed copies of copyright-protected Scientology works, their copying is protected by the principle of "fair use." Under Section 107 of the Act, an otherwise infringing use of a copyrighted work can qualify as fair use. It all depends on how a court weighs factors such as "the purpose and character of the use" and "the amount and substantially of the portion used in relation to the copyrighted work as a whole."

There's no easy test to determine what is fair use. Sometimes use of the entire work can qualify, and sometimes use of only a small part of a work is too much. But given that the Church's critics claimed to be using Scientology materials to engage in public education and criticism of the Church's activities, it seems likely that some of the defendants' uses of the materials qualify as fair use.

The fair use doctrine, together with the fact that copyright law does not protect ideas or facts—only particular expressions of ideas or facts— creates a problem for the Church. Even though the Copyright Act's impoundment provisions give the Church a tool for silencing critics over the short run, the Act's careful balancing of authorial rights with the public's rights (that's what "fair use" is about, really) means the Church can never totally control its documents through copyright. Similarly, the distinction between an idea and its expression in the Copyright Act means the law can't be used to stop critics from paraphrasing material in Church documents. The Act protects only the actual words used, not the information the words convey. This is why the Church chose to characterize its materials as trade secrets as well as copyrighted works.

Trade Secrets

But what exactly is a trade secret, and how does trade secret law work? While copyright law is created by federal statute, there is no corresponding federal law governing trade secrets, although there have been federal cases—including Supreme Court cases—that discuss the legal concept. For the most part, trade secrets are defined by state law. Thus, the definition of what constitutes a trade secret varies from state to state.

Still, most trade secrets definitions have certain elements in common, which is one reason federal courts can talk sensibly about the concept. The U.S. Supreme Court defined the term in *Kewanee Oil Co. V. Bicron Corp.,* 416 U.S. 470 (1974): "[A] trade secret may consist of any formula, pattern, device, or compilation of information which is used in one's business and which gives one an opportunity to obtain an advantage over competitors who do not know or use it. It may be a formula for a chemical compound, a process of manufacturing, treating or preserving materials, a pattern for a machine or other device, or a list of customers." This isn't the sort of material one normally associates with a religion, but let's look further.

In *Kewanee Oil,* the Supreme Court listed the particular attributes of a trade secret, which included the following:

- The information must, in fact, be secret—"not of public knowledge or of general knowledge in the trade or business."
- A trade secret keeps its status as a trade secret if it is revealed in confidence to someone who is under a contractual or other duty not to reveal it.
- A trade secret is protected against those who acquire it through "improper means"—for example, by violating a contractual duty or by inducing someone else to violate his or her duty not to disclose it.
- A trade secret is not protected if someone discovers it independently, or if the trade secret holder doesn't take adequate precautions to keep it a secret.

In some respects, trade secret law seems made to order for the Church in its efforts to silence its critics. For example, most of the material in question really is secret (or, at least, it was until it was posted on the Net). Normally, a member of the Church would have to be a member for a long time—and would have to have paid a lot of money—before the Church would disclose the material to the person voluntarily. And Church members can be routinely required to sign confidentiality agreements that ensure that any "trade secrets" retain their legal status if a disgruntled former member like Erlich should choose to reveal them.

What's more, there's no "fair use" exception when it comes to trade secrets (although anyone who discovers a trade secret without violating a confidentiality agreement can disseminate it freely). And trade secret law protects the information itself, not merely its particular expression. Trade secret law, unlike copyright, can protect ideas and facts directly.

But does the material in question really qualify as "trade secrets"? Among the material the Church has been trying to suppress is what might be called a "genesis myth of Scientology": a story about a galactic despot named Xenu who decided 75 million years ago to kill a group of people by chaining them to volcanoes and dropping nuclear bombs on them.

Remember that part of the definition of "trade secret" in the *Kewanee Oil* case is that it "gives one an opportunity to obtain an advantage over competitors who do not know or use it." Does a church normally have competitors in the trade secret sense? If the Catholics get hold of the full facts about Xenu, does this mean they'll get more market share?

It seems likely, given what we know about the case now, that even a combination of copyright and trade secret law prosecution won't accomplish what the Church would like to accomplish—namely, the total suppression of any dissemination of Church documents or doctrines. But the fact that the Church is unlikely to gain any complete legal victories in its cases doesn't mean it won't litigate. It's disputable that the mere threat of litigation, or the costs of actual litigation, may accomplish what the legal theories alone do not: the effective silencing of many critics of the Church.

That this is the real goal of the litigation is apparent to federal Judge Leonie Brinkema, who dismissed the Church's lawsuit against the *Washington Post.*

"The court finds the motivation of plaintiff in filing this lawsuit against the *Post* is reprehensible," she states in her opinion. "Although the [Church, through its secular arm, the Religious Technology Center (RTC)] brought the complaint under traditional secular concepts of copyright and trade secret law, it has become clear that a much broader motivation prevailed—the stifling of criticism and dissent of the religious practice of Scientology and the destruction of its opponents."

In a subsequent order in which she addressed a Free Exercise of Religion argument that the Church had newly raised, Judge Brinkema tied together the intellectual property threads that have been the focus of most of the Scientology cases:

> We recognize that the RTC has installed extraordinary measures to maintain the secrecy of its OT [Operating Thetan] documents and that they have zealously pursued any reported leaks of information. However, it is a quantum leap to claim that Scientology's endeavors to enforce the secrecy of these documents thereby prohibits secular organizations from undertaking legally permissible criticism of Scientology, including quotes from these documents as long as possession of the documents was achieved lawfully. In their effort to enjoin the *Post,* the RTC is essentially urging that we permit their religious belief in the secrecy of the OT documents to "trump" significant conflicting constitutional rights. In particular, they ask us to dismiss the equally valid First Amendment protections of freedom of the

press. Furthermore, RTC asks that we allow the Free Exercise Clause to deflate the doctrine of fair use as embodied in the copyright stat-ute, one of the very status laws upon which the RTC has based this lawsuit.

In short, the ruling that the *Post*'s "possession of the documents was achieved lawfully" defeats any trade secret claim, and the *Post*'s limited quotation of the documents is allowed under the Copyright Act's "fair use" provisions.

Like the case against the *Washington Post,* most Scientology vs. the Net cases seem to be moving toward eventual victory for the defendants who have followed the rule of fair use. (Judge Brinkema recently found Lerma guilty of infringement because he posted Church documents with-out commentary.) None of the legal theories advanced by the Church seems adequate to stop the hemorrhaging of Scientology's secrets on the Net.

The problem for the Church is that in Cyberspace, nobody is isolated. Once the Church seizes upon a defendant and attempts to suppress him through litigation, it creates a backlash in the online community, which generally is zealous in its regard for freedom of speech—including Sci-entology's critics. Countless individuals who never would have given the Church a second thought have been moved by its heavy-handed legal tactics to take part in an organized effort to frustrate the Church's efforts to keep its secrets. (Although there have been people who have voiced support for the idea of seeking to protect copyrighted material.)

The sheer power of the Net as a mass medium, together with its decentralized character, make the backlash against the Church nearly impossible to stop.

Privacy in the Workplace: A Call to Action

Professor David F. Linowes, University of Illinois

This call to action was issued by Professor Linowes when he released his research survey on privacy in the workplace at the National Press Club, Washington, D.C. on April 22, 1996.

"Eternal vigilance is the price of liberty," Thomas Jefferson warned his fellow citizens of their newly formed nation. This "Call to Action" is a part of that vigilance.

Nearly twenty years after the U.S. Privacy Protection Commission submitted its recommendations urging businesses to voluntarily adopt privacy safeguards for their employment-related records, too many of the nation's largest industrial corporations still do not have adequate policies to protect sensitive confidential employee data from possible abuse. This was revealed by a survey recently completed at the University of Illinois for Professor David F. Linowes, former chairman of the U.S. Privacy Protection Commission.

At the behest of many leading business executives, when we presented our report to the President and Congress on July 12, 1977, we indicated that mandatory privacy protection through private sector legislation might have been premature, and could have caused unnecessary hardships. Therefore, we recommended that business executives be given the opportunity to act on their own now that the needs were being clearly and creditably established. The President and Congress endorsed that recommendation. Although some progress has been made, in view of our present findings, new steps for action should now be considered by this President and Congress.

A basic fair information practice is for employers to examine periodically and systematically their employment and personnel recordkeeping practices. Only by such a systematic examination can executives determine the extent of vulnerability to abuse of their employment records. Yet, in response to the question, "Does your organization have a policy for conducting periodic evaluations of its personnel recordkeeping system?" more than 2 of 5 corporations (42 percent) responded that they still do not have such a policy.

Also, more than 2 of 5 corporations (42 percent) still have not designated an executive-level person to be responsible for maintaining privacy safeguards in employment recordkeeping practices.

Government's ever-increasing intrusion into the information privacy rights of the average citizen has been an ongoing concern for business executives and civil libertarians alike. An important source of confidential personal data about individuals is the files and databanks of employers— large and small alike. To attempt to place some control over the easy access of employment records by overzealous administrators of the many branches of government, it is necessary for employers to have a policy concerning which records will be routinely disclosed to inquiries from government agencies. Yet, in response to the query whether corporations had such a policy, 3 out of 10 (30 percent) said they do not. When no such policy exists, the person in charge—whether executive or record clerk—decides for himself or herself what and when sensitive personal information is routinely released to any government agency representative, whether that person is entitled to have it or not.

When it comes to nongovernment inquirers for personal information, 70 percent of the companies disclose such information to credit grantors.

The fact that over two-thirds of the companies disclose information to credit grantors apparently is a reflection of our credit-hungry society, in which extenders of credit are increasingly hard-pressed to evaluate creditworthiness. However, if this kind of liberal cooperation with credit grantors is to prevail, the subject individual should be informed. Forty-seven percent gave information to landlords, and 19 percent to charitable organizations.

In response to the question, "Does your organization have a policy to inform personnel of the organization's routine disclosure practices to nongovernmental inquirers?" only 49 percent indicated that they had such a policy.

Fair employment practice calls for employers to allow employees to see and copy their personnel records, and to make corrections when appropriate. The survey revealed that 8 percent of the companies still do not give employees access to personnel records. For supervisors' records, 72 percent do not allow access. Twenty-four percent of the companies do not permit employees to place corrections in their personnel records.

In response to the question, "Does your organization have a policy to forward corrections to anyone who received incorrect information within the past two years?" almost 1 out of 4 (23 percent) said they did not take such action. With information being transmitted across the country and abroad at the speed of light, an error in one record can be propagated a hundredfold instantaneously. If no effort is made to forward a correction, decisions are made based on incorrect information, to the detriment of both the recipient organization and the individual.

Apparently, many employees still are not being told much about their own records. Of the companies responding, 38 percent do not inform their personnel of the types of records maintained on them; 44 percent do not inform personnel how they are used; 58 percent do not inform about disclosure practices to government; and 51 percent do not inform personnel about nongovernment disclosure practices. Almost 1 of 5 (18 percent) do not tell their personnel to which records they have access.

Seventy-five percent of the companies verify or supplement background information collected directly from their personnel, but only 42 percent of these companies let the individual see this information. Fair information practices would considerably open communications between the corporate recordkeeper and the individual.

Largely because medical information can be misunderstood by an uninformed layman, medical records should not be used for an employment decision. Nevertheless, 35 percent of the companies surveyed do use such medical records in making employment-related decisions.

The foregoing sampling of survey findings indicates much remains to be done to achieve fair information practices by employers in their employment relationships.

In view of the slow progress by too many companies during the past 20 years, it is apparent that adequate universal information privacy safeguards can be achieved only by the enactment of public policy legislation by the Congress and the President. Such legislation would require that in dealings between an organization and an individual: (1) there should be minimum intrusiveness into the personal affairs of a person, thereby eliminating the collection of data that is irrelevant to the decision at hand; (2) fairness should be emphasized, thereby permitting the individual to see the data about himself or herself upon which a decision is based; (3) there should be a means for enforcing confidentiality when information privacy is expected, by allowing for punitive damages (capped at $10,000) for violations.

Such legislation would point the direction for all the fair information practices recommended by the U.S. Privacy Protection Commission, and help bring our nation up to the standards already adopted by most of the other industrialized nations.

Recommendations of the U.S. Privacy Protection Commission

Disclosures of Personal Employment Data. An employer should limit external disclosures of information in records kept on individual employees, former employees, and applicants; it should also limit the internal use of such records.

Individual Access. An employer should permit individual employees, former employees, and applicants to see, copy, correct, or amend the records maintained about them, except highly restricted security records, where necessary.

An employer should assure that the personnel and payroll records it maintains are available internally only to authorized users and on a need-to-know basis.

Informing the Individual. An employer, prior to collecting the type of information generally collected about an applicant, employees, or other individual in connection with an employment decision, should notify him/her as to (1) the types of information expected to be collected; (2) the techniques that may be used to collect such information; (3) the types of sources that are expected to be asked; (4) the types of parties to whom and circumstances under which information about the individual may be disclosed without his authorization, and the types of information that may be disclosed; (5) the procedures established by statute by which the individual may gain access to any resulting record about himself; (6) the procedures whereby the individual may correct, amend, or dispute any resulting records about himself.

An employer should clearly inform all its applicants upon request, and all employees automatically, of the types of disclosures it may make of information in the records it maintains on them, including disclosures of directory information, and of its procedures for involving the individual in particular disclosures.

Authorizing Personal Data Collection. No employer should ask, require, or otherwise induce an applicant or employee to sign any statement authorizing any individual or institution to disclose information about him, or about any other individual, unless the statement is (1) in plain language; (2) dated; (3) specific as to the individuals and institutions he is authorizing to disclose information about him; (4) specific as to the nature of the information he is authorizing to be disclosed; (5) specific as to the individuals or institutions to whom he is authorizing information to be disclosed; (6) specific as to the purpose(s) for which the information may be used; (7) specific as to its expiration date, which should be for a reasonable period of time not to exceed one year.

Medical Records. An employer that maintains an employment-related medical record about an individual should assure that no diagnostic or treatment information in any such record is made available for use in any employment decision. However, in certain limited circumstances, special medical information might be so used after informing the employee.

Upon request, an individual who is the subject of a medical record maintained by an employer, or another responsible person designated by the individual, should be allowed to have access to that medical record, including an opportunity to see and copy it. The employer may charge a reasonable fee for preparing and copying the record.

An employer should establish a procedure whereby an individual who is the subject of a medical record maintained by the employer can request correction or amendment of the record.

Use of Investigative Firms. Each employer and agent of an employer should exercise reasonable care in the selection and use of investigative organizations, so as to assure that the collection, maintenance, use, and disclosure practices of such organizations fully protect the rights of the subject being investigated.

Arrest, Conviction, and Security Records. When an arrest record is lawfully sought or used by an employer to make a specific decision about an applicant or employee, the employer should not maintain the records for a period longer than specifically required by law, if any, or unless there is an outstanding indictment.

Unless otherwise required by law, an employer should seek or use a conviction record pertaining to an individual applicant or employee only when the record is directly relevant to a specific employment decision affecting the individual.

Except as specifically required by federal or state statute or regulation, or by municipal ordinance or regulation, an employer should not seek or use a record of arrest pertaining to an individual applicant or employee.

Where conviction information is collected, it should be maintained separately from other individually identifiable employment records so that it will not be available to persons who have no need of it.

An employer should maintain security records apart from other records.

General Practices. An employer should periodically and systematically examine its employment and personnel recordkeeping practices, including a review of (1) the number and types of records it maintains on individual employees, former employees, and applicants; (2) the items of information contained in each type of employment record it maintains; (3) the uses made of the items of information in each type of record; (4) the uses made of such records within the employing organization; (5) the disclosures made of such records to parties outside the employing organization; (6) the extent to which individual employees, former employees, and applicants are both aware and systematically informed of the uses and disclosures that are made of information in the records kept about them.

15

Class 2: Corporate Information Warfare

"Business is War."

—JAPANESE ADAGE

"All's fair in love and war."

—CERVANTES, *DON QUIXOTE*

WE ARE AT WAR.

Michael Sekora of Technology Strategic Planning in Stewart, Florida, agrees with former President Richard Nixon that we are involved in World War III. Ex-master spy Count de Marenches calls it World War IV.

Whatever conflict number we assign Information Warfare, the New World Order is filled with tens of thousands of ex-spies, well practiced in the art of espionage, who are looking for work to feed their families. The world is filled with countries and economic interests that are no longer siding with either of the two erstwhile superpowers. The Haves want to keep their piece of the pie and expand it; the Have Nots want a piece of the pie they never had. And everyone is fending for himself and his future survival in the evolving global economy.

The words *industrial espionage* are spoken every day from the halls of Washington to the boardrooms of corporate America, and *global economic competitiveness* is now becoming as potent a national security buzz word as Reagan's *Evil Empire* once was. The theory behind industrial espionage is simple to the point of absurdity. If you invest five years and $1 billion in a new invention, either a product or process, you hope to make a profit on that investment. If, however, I can steal the knowledge to make that product, say for $10 million, I can sell the same item for substantially less and bring it to market in months instead of years. You invest the time and money, I steal the results, then we compete. Who's got the advantage?

While the United States was busily preparing to survive Armageddon by outspending the Soviets on military hardware, we ignored the fact that our entire industrial base was being raped and pillaged by economic competitors from around the world. We of course expected the Russians to do it; that was their job. Many of the educational attachés and trade delegations they sent to the United States were in reality KGB or intelligence operatives, with a mission to seek out our technology and our strategic plans for a possible military conflict. The FBI's CI-3 division on Half Street in Washington chased them hither and yon, trying to keep them honest, winning some and losing more. Today, the Russians still spy, but less for militaristic reasons. William Sessions, former director of the FBI, told a House subcommittee, "Russians do not have the currency to pay for advanced systems and designs, so they will steal them or obtain them through other illegitimate means."[1] They of course want to keep up, and they use the best means they have available to do so.

The Russian conundrum is simple: they have a minimal industrial base, a withering economy, no distribution system, a shaky political structure, and a couple of hundred thousand ex-spies. What is their best chance for moving into the world economy?

As we chased the Soviets and the Poles and the Czechs and the Bulgarians, our "allies" took us to the cleaners. In his 1993 book, *Friendly Spies,* Peter Schweizer examines in detail how our global allies pinched cookies from the American cookie jar while we protected them from the big bad Red Bear. The French, the Germans, the Israelis, the Koreans, the Japanese, the British, and the Canadians have all targeted the American industrial base and stolen as much as they could while our backs were turned. It just doesn't seem fair, yet we have only ourselves to blame. Foreigners see stealing information as a short cut to making costly and time consuming investments. If caught, the penalties are so low that most companies consider it a cost of doing business.

The U.S. Department of State can be surprisingly honest at times, as they were in a recent publication:

> Each day America becomes driven more and more by information. Proprietary information is our chief competitive asset, vital to both our industry and our society. Our livelihood and, indeed, our national strength depend on our ability to protect industrial and economic data.
>
> The struggle between capitalism and communism was decided essentially over two issues—the desire of humanity for freedom and the relative effectiveness of each system's economic competitiveness. While of utmost importance during the period of the Cold War, the need to protect economic information looms even larger in the coming years.
>
> Recent revelations in the media indicate strenuous efforts on the part of some foreign intelligence agencies to benefit their national industries. These efforts have included eavesdropping, hotel room burglaries, and introduction of "moles," as well as other sophisticated intelligence techniques. Our foreign competitor's interest in our information has never been more intense.[2]

Foreign companies have always recognized that the majority of the world's technology has come from the United States, and that since World War II we have been the technological king of the hill. So what were they to do? Thomas Hughes wrote in *American Genesis*, "Modern technology was made in America. Even the Germans who developed it so well acknowledged the United States as the prime source."[3] Not wanting to be overshadowed by America's commercial and military superiority, many countries went to extraordinary effort to steal our technology. More often than not, these foreign corporations in search of American intelligence or technology have received assistance from their cooperative governments. Spying is just another way of doing business in most parts of the world and we haven't been smart enough to realize that our secrets are worth protecting.

There is little suggestion that a paradigm shift of any appreciable size is on the horizon, but fortunately, a few voices have spoken up about the problem. Senator David Boren said, "An increasing share of espionage directed against the United States comes from spying by foreign governments against private American companies aimed at stealing commercial secrets to gain a national competitive advantage."[4] He warns that as we enter the next century, "it's going to really increase."[5]

During Congressional testimony on April 29, 1992, CIA Director Robert Gates said that foreign espionage is "assuming even greater importance than previously," and "is likely to assume . . . greater importance . . . in the future." Without giving away too many of the top spook shop's secrets, he went on to discuss the extent of industrial espionage that the U.S. is officially now acknowledging. As Gates points out, "There has been a proliferation of commercially available intelligence technology. . . . Some fifty Third World countries [are] now able to operate [espionage activities] and . . . there are large numbers of unemployed intelligence operatives from former Communist countries." So now not only do we have to worry about our allies, but the less highly developed nations who can also easily afford the technology and the staff to spy as well.

In 1989, Wayne Madson of Information Security Engineering published a list, entitled "Computer Communication Espionage Activities," that defined each of the world's countries' capabilities. He rated countries like Nepal and Yemen as "poor." Those countries with an "excellent" computer espionage capability included the U.S., Switzerland, the U.K., Taiwan,

South Africa, Sweden, Norway, the Netherlands, New Zealand, Israel, Japan, Finland, France, Germany, Canada, and Australia. As one peruses the list, with hundreds of security and intelligence agencies listed, the sheer number who are "above average" or "improving" should lend credence to the assumption that the battle for Cyberspace is only now beginning.

The stakes are huge in Class 2 Information Warfare, as seen in the oil industry's immense global spy ring. In 1988, the University of Illinois published "A Study of Trade Secrets in High Technology Industries" and found that 48 percent of all companies surveyed admitted to being the victim of industrial espionage. In a real global economy of $26 trillion, properly serving only twenty-five percent of the planet's population, the motivation to open up new markets is too compelling to resist. Around the world, industrial spying is a national pastime.

Japanese spying against the United States is supported and coordinated by the national trade organization, MITI. MITI sets goals on behalf of hundreds of interlocking *keiretsu*, and determines which trade secrets to steal. The Japanese sponsor thousands upon thousands of students to come to the U.S. to study in our universities, but a little moonlighting is requested. Students are told where to keep their ears and eyes open, and they report information back to MITI on a regular basis. Nothing unscrupulous, just taking a few photos of technical facilities and noting seemingly innocuous off-handed comments. With MITI support, according to Herb Meyer, an intelligence expert, "the Mitsubishi intelligence staff takes up two entire floors of a Manhattan skyscraper."[6] I lay odds Americans don't have an equivalent operation in Tokyo, Paris, London, or Seoul.

According to author Peter Schweitzer, "IBM alone, according to internal company documents, was targeted twenty-five known times by foreign entities between 1975-1984. Japanese espionage in Silicon Valley nearly devastated the U.S. computer industry."[7] Hitachi, for instance, ponied up a reported $300 million in a settlement agreement after spying on a new generation of IBM computer equipment. The Hitachi plan was successful and the estimated losses to IBM could be in the billions. Not a bad investment on Hitachi's part.

Kodak lost a fortune when Fuji stole their top-secret plans to build disposable cameras. In response, Kodak hired their own Information Warriors, ex-CIA operatives, and beat Fuji to market with a new camera.[8] Nippon Telephone regularly records calls made by Japan-based U.S. companies and the Government requires that all encryption keys be given to them for safekeeping.

But we cannot accuse the Japanese alone. The French have come out of the closet and made their position clear: "militarily we're allies, but economically, we're competitors." And they have proved that over the years. Count de Marenches, whose tenure as head of French Intelligence lasted over a decade, hobnobbed with international powerbrokers from Churchill to Gorbachev to Reagan. He had unlimited control over the French intelligence community, and ultimately went public with the details of his cadre of hundreds of professional agents' espionage against the United States in the interest of French international competitiveness.

The airline industry has been of keen interest to the French for decades. Since industry and government are almost synonymous in France, it should come as no surprise that their cooperation could spell problems for our airline industry. To help out Airbus in 1988, French intelligence targeted Boeing—specifically a new generation of plane, the 747-400. In order to learn what Boeing was doing, the intelligence folks used communications receivers designed to pick up test flight data beamed down from the planes to Boeing technicians. The data was simply transmitted over radio, and the signals were unencrypted. All that the French needed was a portable dish, a receiver and two computers. The very same information that Boeing would never voluntarily give to an American competitor was being broadcast right into French hands.[9] One would hope that Boeing learned its lesson, but apparently not.

According to an official who left the company in 1993, Boeing is practically giving its new design secrets to the French on a silver platter.

Designing airplanes today is a long, expensive, and incredibly technical process. To save costs in building and testing a series of prototype planes, highly specialized software is used to electronically simulate how the plane will fly. This automated process makes it easier to build the plane and cuts the time from drawing board to runway by months or years, which can mean substantial profits for the company. Boeing uses such software, a million dollar program named Catia, supplied by IBM. However, IBM didn't design Catia. They acquired the U.S. marketing rights from Dassault Systems, the U.S. arm of French-based Dassault Aviation, a major supplier of aircraft to the French military. Dassault has offices in Los Angeles, Chicago, and Detroit which serve other aerospace and automotive customers, but the development of Catia software is done outside of Paris and so, unfortunately, is the customer support and product upgrades.[10]

The ex-Boeing expert claims that Dassault engineers are inside Boeing's facility on a regular basis—without security or supervision. He fears that Boeing's latest and greatest designs for the planned 777 airplane are Fed-Ex'd straight over to France on a regular basis. Is Boeing permitting itself to be a victim of Class 2 Information Warfare by inviting a known foreign competitor into their labs? Is it in fact providing costly design and research information to Aero-Spatiale and the European Airbus Consortium? Boeing's only response to these charges was that they were "comfortable" with the security of their 777 development program.

The French are notorious for national economic espionage endeavors, such as breaking into hotel rooms, rifling briefcases, stealing laptop computers, eavesdropping on international business telephone calls, and intercepting faxes and telexes. And if that isn't enough, they even use Air France stewardesses to listen in on the conversations of first class travelers.[11] They stole U.S. trade negotiation position papers from Undersecretary of State George Ball in 1964,[12] and had a bug put into H.R. Haldeman's overcoat during President Nixon's first trip to France.[13] Service-Seven of the French intelligence agencies bounced laser beams off President Reagan's hotel room windows to eavesdrop on sensitive conversations.[14] These French efforts come from the top of their government; in October 1981, a special department was created within French intelligence to increase the yield of industrial and economic secrets.[15]

One tried and true method for getting close to industrial secrets is the use of company moles, who are actually loyal to or in the pay of another country. During his confirmation hearing in the fall of 1991, Robert Gates said, "We know that foreign intelligence services plant moles in our high tech companies."[16]

Technological Information Weapons will be used more and more when physical access to the targets of Class 2 Information Warfare becomes difficult, and as employers screen out potential moles and spies with greater efficiency. But again, we may have to look in the mirror for a scapegoat. "The intelligence agencies of Germany, Japan, South Korea, and France, for example, were all developed with the assistance of the U.S. intelligence community. Their methods, even their eavesdropping equipment, came from the United States. Many of these assets are now being used against the United States in the name of economic competitiveness."[17]

While the U.S. media and law enforcement decried the activities of our homegrown hackers, the Germans have been using theirs to spy on other countries. One of the goals of the German federal intelligence service, the *Bundesnachrichtendienst* (BND), was the monitoring of foreign technological developments. In addition to performing "regular eavesdrops on transatlantic business conversation with the full cooperation of the German national telephone company,"[18] and conventional spying techniques, computer hacking was a full time occupation.

On the outskirts of Frankfurt, writes Schweizer, "approximately thirty-six computer specialists and senior intelligence officials are working on a top secret project to bring computer hacking into the realm of spying and intelligence. They hope that through the use of sophisticated computers and specially trained personnel, German intelligence agents will be able to enter computer databases of corporations and foreign governments around the world, and the access could be achieved while agents remained thousands of miles away."[19] The idea, called Project Rahab, was conceived in 1985 and formalized in 1988. Since only the West had any appreciable number of computers—there were next to none in Russia—the targets were obvious.

Success was theirs, according to CIA officials. In typically fastidious Germanic fashion, Rahab hackers plotted out the roadways and network connections across the Global Network to those computers and systems of interest. "In March 1991, Rahab employees hacked their way into . . . SWIFT . . . in order to establish a roadway to ensure easy access for when such access is deemed necessary." BND will be able, at will, to monitor or interfere with global financial transactions.

Computer viruses were also of great interest to the BND folks working on Project Rahab. A German hacker, Bernard Fix, created a virus that was particularly powerful, and in April 1989, Rahab began a duplication effort. "It was capable of destroying all the information in a large mainframe computer in a matter of minutes. If widely used, it could render national computer systems useless in the course of a few hours."[20]

Thanking the young American hacker for illuminating foreign capabilities may be a bit much for some people, but the lesson should be heeded. Schweizer sums up the publicized German Rahab activities thusly: ". . . In all likelihood [Rahab-styled techniques] will augur an era in which state-sponsored computer hacking becomes every bit the intelligence tool that spy satellites have been for the past thirty years. It offers the benefit of an agent on the inside without the costs inherent in his potential unmasking. German intelligence has seen the future, and it lies with Rahab."[21] We can no longer assume that the Germans are alone in their awareness that hacking is a tool of immense competitive value.

Class 2 Information Warfare is more than just industrial espionage. It can also involve economic espionage, the study and analysis of financial trends which are often available from nonclassified, open sources such as newspapers and television. Count de Marenches maintains that the French knew for a fact America would devalue the dollar in 1971—before it was announced. That move was of intense interest to our allies, and such knowledge can be turned into enormous profits if used correctly on the currency exchange markets.

Economic espionage is typically focused on large economic spheres instead of on a single company or technology. Advance knowledge of a quarter- or half-point change on the part of the Federal Reserve System is worth a fortune. If a major currency trader is preparing to shift his holdings, there is immense value in that data.

How many people became stinking filthy rich in the '80s? A lot. Of course a lot lost their shirts as result of fiscal overindulgence, but boats full of money were made—more than at any time in history. When we look back on many of the extraordinarily profitable ventures that were launched in those heady days, some of us may experience twenty-twenty hindsight envy. If only we had known about that computer deal, we would have made millions. Or if we had known They were going to build That Contraption, we would have bought in early. None of us can deny wishing, at least once, that we had been in on The Big One. At one time or another every one of us has said, "If only I was a fly on the wall. . . ."

Tens of billions of dollars went through the hands of KKR, the merger-maniacal New York investment firm who put together the RJR Nabisco deal immortalized in the book and movie *Barbarians At The Gate*. When companies merge or are targets of a takeover bid, their stock price is likely to rise appreciably in a small amount of time. The merger of Time Inc. and Warner Bros., the AT&T-McCaw cellular deal—think of any of the big headling-grabbing deals and we wistfully regret that we didn't know about it in advance.

In the Eddie Murphy movie *Trading Places*, advance knowledge of the price of orange juice futures made insiders a fortune in minutes. Advance insider information is time-sensitive; it only has value prior to the time when it becomes public knowledge. Once everyone knows it, the information's value plummets to about zero. The government publishes numbers every day, and some of those numbers can make or break fortunes by depressing or increasing the value of industries, stocks, and Treasury bonds. Many investors consider Federally-released employment statistics to be the most important monthly statistics. Advance knowledge of that information and ability to interpret it is worth a fortune, if acted upon prior to its general release.

Apparently this happened at least once. On October 8, 1993, the price of Treasury bonds surged about one-half point, just moments before the monthly employment numbers were announced. To make the bond prices move that much requires substantial capital, and the profits made are enormous. The Labor Department and the Chicago Board of Trade consider leaks as the likely culprit.[22]

But the Information Warrior, with the right tools and weapons at his disposal, will always be able to know which way the market is going. If he is clever, he can regularly make impressive profits without alerting the official overseers of the markets that he is trading with illegally-acquired insider information.

On a global scale, a big move by any major economy will create ripples throughout the world's markets in microseconds as automatic trading programs takeover. In *The Death of Money*, Joel Kurtzman says, "Today's world is very different from the world of the past. Economic success in this world, especially in the financial sector but increasingly in other sectors as well, is dependent on assimilating large quantities of information very rapidly."[23]

The increased amount of information and need to make

rapid decisions to exploit a particular opportunity or stay out of trouble often means that decisions are made on the fly. There is no time for reasoned thought.[24] The more time that one has to study the information and make a decision, the better off he is. The financial manager and his traders are the air traffic controllers of cybermoney; the pressures are enormous and mistakes can be unimaginably costly. There is strong motivation to go to extreme lengths to acquire economic information before it's officially announced.

Class 2 Information Warfare, however, is about more than the acquisition of information; it's also about the use of information—real or ersatz. Imagine the fallout if the following article appeared in the Paris dailies. "According to well-placed officials, the French government has launched a secret study that will definitively prove that the American drug Fix-It-All, manufactured by Drugco, Inc., causes severe liver damage. Sources say that the results of the study will be published in the next few months, but in the meantime, doctors are advised not to prescribe Fix-It-All to any of their patients." The study could be a fake, the findings totally manufactured as part of a well-constructed campaign of disinformation, but the results will be just the same. Drugco, Inc., won't sell much Fix-It-All and the company's image will suffer. Drugco, Inc. will have to go into defensive mode and expend considerable time and resources in damage control. Disinformation is as dangerous a weapon in the hands of an Information Warrior as it was in the hands of the Soviets.

The uncontrolled release of even legitimate information from a company can be just as devastating. Perhaps an Information Warrior is not profit oriented; he just wants to damage the reputation of the company in question. He could, for example, intercept the company's E-mail and identify any incriminating documents—or, if need be, create and disseminate them to the media, competitors, and the public.

Sowing distrust electronically has the appearance of authority and integrity. A bank could be hurt by having its customers' records suddenly distributed on street corners or plastered up as posters on construction sites. The mere appearance of impropriety could easily devastate a financial institution, despite their claims of being victimized themselves by the activities of an Information Warrior.

An investment house's strategies and formulas are among their most valued assets. Their open publication on Wall Street would not only be an embarrassment and a PR disaster, but a sure way to empty the company of customers. Knowing a competitor's exact investment methods would cause the most staid investment banker to shout in glee.

Politically, the power of information has been and will continue to be used as a weapon. The Bonn government was given a list of two thousand West Germans who spied for the notorious East German state police, the Stasi, during the Cold War. In 1974, West German Chancellor Willy Brandt resigned over the identification of just one spy in his government's midst.[25] What could happen if the names of two thousand more traitors are suddenly made public? Or more important, what careers are made and broken to keep the list secret?

Car magazines pay husky prices for photos of new car models months prior to their release. Computer-aided design terminals display three-dimensional pictures of these car designs years before they are made. An Information Warrior armed with quality van Eck detection equipment can keep car magazines happy for years. Imagine that Ford, GM, and Chrysler all are hit and their plans are published, years before release, in glowing color for millions of hungry eyes.

Make a valuable secret public, and all of a sudden it becomes next to worthless. The U.S. pharmaceutical industry loses about $5 billion per year, and the U.S. chemical industry between $3-6 billion, to overseas counterfeiters.[26] If the formulas and techniques for these and other industries were openly disseminated instead of stolen for profit, the losses could be much greater. The companies affected would see nothing in return for their multi-billion dollar investment.

Again, the Information Warrior has options, depending upon his motives.

Class 2 Information Warfare can also mean putting a company's information systems out of commission. In security parlance we call this "denial of service." What it means is that an Information Warrior may not elect to steal your secrets, or even seek to discredit you; he may merely want to see you suffer or go out of business. Accomplishing this requires some investment of time, money, and manpower (Motivation) but American business is so reliant upon their Computers Everywhere and their pieces of the Global Network that it is possible (Capability).

First of all the Information Warrior needs to pick his victim. It should be one that relies heavily upon computers and communications to carry on its day to day business activities. Without its computers, it would essentially be out of business, or so impacted that its customer base immediately defects to other companies. In either case, the results are the same. Obvious candidates for such an assault might be a small airline, a bank, an automated distributor, a private courier like Federal Express, an accounting firm, a payroll company, or any of thousands of other organizations. Even a hospital would come to a halt without computers these days. Although they wouldn't "go out of business," portions of local, state, or federal government operations would come to a grinding halt without their information systems.

Information Weapons will be chosen based upon the desired aim, but first things first: we must scout out and learn about our target. From publicly available sources we can learn about its finances, its products, and its market position. Find out its strengths and its weaknesses. Competitors will emphasize the weaknesses of our target from their perspective; for a few hundred dollars we can begin to construct a mosaic of the company's alliances, business relationships, its history, failures, and successes. In a large conglomerate, it might be necessary to first identify each of the smaller operating divisions to weigh the various importance of each to the whole before picking a specific target. Which division is the most profitable? Where can the most damage be done? It will not take long to draw a complete picture of our target and figure out where he is most vulnerable.

(Thus far, the Information Warrior can work entirely within the law. He can employ a competitive intelligence organization to learn everything about a company that it doesn't want made public—open secrets that are buried, but not dead.)

Then there is the element of timing. When is the best time for the Information Warrior to strike? What about tax time— would a systems collapse create trouble with the IRS? Is there a big deal pending? Would a massive system failure jeopardize a public offering, a bond issue, or a billion dollar merger? Timing is everything; just like the military landing on Normandy beach, or sending cruise missiles into Iraq, all of the elements of the assault force must be in place and prepared to strike in a coordinated manner. It is no different with Class 2 Information Warfare aimed at disabling any company or organization.

If the goal is to stop a big deal, the enemy must be engaged at the most propitious point, i.e., not after the fact but not so early that damage control can be implemented. Take the case of Gennifer Flowers. If her accusations against Bill Clinton had been made the day before the Democratic National Convention instead of months earlier, history might well have been different. The Information Warrior must be astutely aware that timing is absolutely crucial to the success of his endeavors.

Depending upon his target and his aims, the Information Warrior may elect to break into a computer system in order to get in information about a company now, or to have a future entry point when desired. Any and all information is of value, as is a surreptitious means of accessing the computers at will. But the Information Warrior may want closer contact; a means of physical access to his target. One way is to get one of his people hired at the company as an insider, another is to find a friend of a friend with access who is not above taking a bribe, and another is to compromise a current worker.

Poking through internal computer systems is one method of identifying potential accomplices, as is dumpster diving for lists of employees and their phone extensions. Finding a likely candidate for compromise, bribery, or blackmail is no more difficult than running names through the same databankers who profiled the company in the first place. Does a certain employee owe too much money? Have an extra apartment on the side? Is there an incriminating file in their college records? What skeletons do they have that may prove embarrassing to the target and therefore valuable to the Information Warrior? Getting the cooperation of unwilling participants is not all that difficult, as recent history has shown.

So how will the Information Warrior achieve his aims? The most efficient way is through what might be called the double whammy. Companies prepare for "single-event" disasters if they prepare for them at all. *The* flood, *the* power outage, even *the* hacker. But what about if more than one disaster strikes at once? Early 1993 showed us what happens. The World Trade Center bombing forced computer-reliant companies into emergency action, and for those firms with foresightedness, into their Hot Sites. Many firms though handicapped, were able to continue functioning by moving the critical portions of their operations into these bunker-like facilities across the Hudson River in New Jersey. Hot Sites are operated as a business by companies who offer an effective insurance policy to keep backup telecommunications lines and computer facilities running in the event of disaster.

But right after the bombing, the Great No-Name Storm of 1993 knocked out banking and ATM networks throughout the Northeast. Hot Sites, already overburdened by Trade Center customers, had no more room; some companies found they had to relocate essential services anywhere in the country they could. As a result, millions of banking customers were without ATM service for as long as a month. The Information Warrior is probably going to use the double whammy as a tactic against a major target just because it is so effective. The double whammy could actually be three or more congruent attacks, all centrally coordinated for maximum effect.

Let's hypothesize for the moment that an Information Warrior wants to totally disrupt the operations of a financial institution. Maybe he wants it out of business because they have the wrong political affiliations, or there is a perceived wrong to be avenged. Maybe our warrior is an international competitor who seeks to embarrass the bank out of business, or maybe he's just a complete nut-case running amok in Cyberspace. Through the assistance of an accomplice who works inside the bank, a piece of malicious software will be released into the central computers on, say, a Monday morning. By day's end, the accounts won't balance, error-filled customer account statements will be issued, or maybe the bank's credit card division will find an extraordinary number of deadbeats who aren't paying their monthly obligations.

If the Information Warrior has associates who are especially skilled with bank's software, he may elect to have one piece of malicious code detonate on Monday, and then another on Wednesday, but never on a Friday—that would give the bank plenty of time for damage control and repair. Banking computer software is complicated, so each and every error intentionally introduced into the system will have to be methodically sought out and repaired. Maybe the same error is reproduced several times in the code, so that when they think they have found the problem, an identical incident will crop up in a day or a week. Customers become very unhappy in the process.

If the software errors are reported to the media, or creep up day after day, the reputation of the institution will immediately begin to suffer. Who wants to have his money in a bank whose computers can't add two and two?

But the Information Warrior is only using malicious software as a ruse, a decoy for his real attack with the real Information Weapon he chose to debilitate the bank. The primary Information Weapon will be a portable HERF Gun, mounted in a bland, unmarked van. The planned assault is a simple one. After several days or weeks of constantly failing software, system collapses, miscounted money, federal investigations, media scrutiny, and customers abandoning the ship in droves, tensions will be extremely high throughout the entire organization. Employees *expect* the computers to fail. All trust in the system is gone. Are the print-outs right or wrong? Does every one of millions of daily calculations have to be rechecked by hand or by abacus to insure accuracy? Binary Schizophrenia is running at full tilt.

At 9:00 AM, the van will drive in front of the bank computer facilities, located and identified by the insider-accomplice. When the bank opens it's business as usual, despite mass defections of employees and customers. Inside the van, the HERF Gun (a modified radar system), is powered by a souped-up generator; one Information Warrior has his finger on the button. At the right moment, he pushes "shoot" and several megawatts of high frequency power enter into the bank's computers for a few milliseconds. The van turns the corner and drives off. Inside the bank, computer circuits are overloaded; network wiring carries a massive energy surge to the gateways, bridges, routers, and communications links that connect hundreds of branches and terminals; and the system crashes. If the bank has other computer centers, maybe HERF Guns will be used there as well.

The system is down, and what is the culprit? The software of course. Dozens of technicians spring into action, fearful that management will put their heads on the chopping block. In several minutes the system is back up and everything seems to be working, but still, why did the system crash? When they were repairing the software glitches they found, they had to make changes that might have caused other problems. But at least the system is up.

Until the van comes around the corner again at 9:24 AM and lets loose with another volley of electromagnetic disruption— blam!—and the systems go down again. The repair process is repeated, and ATMs and tellers are at work again in minutes.

Until 10:06 AM, when the van drives down the street and—ready-aim-shoot—it bombards the computers with another round of digital death. The engineers feel that there's hope, though, and they tell the bank president and the media that because the problem is occurring more often, they should be able to isolate it more quickly. 10:29 AM, 11:00 AM, 11:46 AM, High Noon, and so on throughout the day until 3:00 PM, when the bank closes. Thank heavens. Throughout the rest of the day, into the evening, and for the entire night, hoards of technicians attempt to duplicate every condition that the system experienced. They think they have found a couple more lines of code that might be responsible. They hesitantly reassure management.

Tuesday morning, the bank opens again, and at 9:15 AM, the van comes wheeling down the street and. . . .

The question is, how long can our fictitious bank survive such an onslaught? If the bank's security officers have read this book or come to my sessions, they might suspect early on that some fool rigged up a HERF Gun, but then there's still the matter of figuring out which car or truck or van is the culprit. And by then, the Information Warrior will have won the battle. A big bank or Fortune 500 Company has its own army of technicians, and sooner or later, someone will remember reading or hearing about HERF Guns and begin the complex and tedious process of triangulating the source. Small companies do not have the same deep pockets to keep themselves in business.

For small battles against smaller adversaries, the Information Warrior will probably not be able to get inside the target; he might have to rely on other methods to create a diversionary distraction. Small companies can be hacked into with amazing ease, and malicious software might be inserted from afar. Creating dissension within the ranks works well in smaller companies. The theft of proprietary information can be selectively leaked to the right people within the company, as an indictment of others. Stir up the Binary Schizophrenia by making sure that the right people are already suspected as "industrial traitors." Then, when tensions are high, blast 'em with a dose of HERF.

Small accounting firms will come to a halt instantly if their PCs die. Local area network-reliant operations will come to a halt with the proper prescription of HERF. NBC headquarters in New York uses LANs for its on-air programming, and staff has been so cut back that a return to the old way of working by-hand would be a scramble at best. Sales and distribution operations must have computers up at all times, as must hospitals, power companies, manufacturers, and the local K-Mart—and none of them are in a position to recognize or react to such an assault. In many ways it would be easier for them to have a murderer walk in the front door with a semiautomatic and spray bullets at the workers—they can then get back to business—than it would be for them to deal with constant computer and communications failures that they do not fully understand.

Class 2 Information Warfare is creative, relatively inexpensive, and if well-planned, terribly effective. The myriad of double whammy scenarios is endless, yet most companies don't plan for one, much less two, disasters at a time. And that is a mistake.

The Information Warrior is not as rare as a flood, or as benign as an ice storm. The Information Warrior is not a natural catastrophe, an act of God, or Mother Nature getting even with man. The Information Warrior creates well-planned man-made disasters with all contingencies considered, all alternatives explored, and all escape plans evaluated.

Class 2 Information Warfare is more than just industrial or economic espionage; it's more than stealing secrets, eavesdropping on faxes, or reading computer screens via a sewer pipe. It's more than a HERF Gun in a back pack or bad code with a purpose. It's *all* of these things.

And with all that knowledge, power, and capability, a few Information Warriors will develop the means to wage Class 3 Information Warfare.

Corporate Civil Defense: Defensive Class II Information Warfare

Winn Schwartau

Originally published in Network World, *1996.*

"It'll never happen to me."

I sat in the corporate offices of a huge multinational company, surrounded by lawyers and financial types and vice presidents and managers. They had never even thought about it. Not the question that I asked, and still that was their response. "It'll never happen to me."

Not so unusual actually; lying somewhere between apathy and arrogance, this company typifies the corporate preference to deal with situations that they can wrap their arms around and ignore those that create internal dissent.

My question was simple.

"I see you guys have a well-formulated policy to handle the effects of hurricanes. You can recover quickly from a flood and a tornado. Your West Coast office can relocate services if an earthquake strikes. Fires? No problem." They took the compliments well, applauding themselves for a job well done. Their self-congratulations were appropriate for disaster recovery, natural disasters: the so-called acts of God.

"But," I broke through their reverie, "what is your policy if your company is intentionally targeted and attacked? Do you have a corporate civil defense policy that will handle the effects of the acts of man?"

Eyes darted around the room nervously, each person afraid to be the first to speak.

I repeated the question. "It's obvious you have the acts of God thing down; you're well prepared. What about the acts of man?" I pressed the point, which caused the attorneys to caucus and the managers to huddle. Amazing what reactions you can get from a simple question.

Someone finally spoke up. "It'll never happen to us," the timid voice said sheepishly. Others looked his way, their raised eyebrows questioning the sanity of that statement.

"Do you really believe that?" I queried suspiciously. I wasn't accusing; I was merely trying to get the speaker to think through his response. No one came to his defense and he shrank into his seat all alone with his delusions. How could he possibly say it would never happen to them? I had just presented a two-hour lesson on exactly what has happened to the Other Guy.

Someone else piped up. "No. We have no plans," he said forcefully, challenging the policymakers. The roomful of 50 or so people rumbled, many showing agreement by the pained looks on their faces.

Another voice with ridicule and dissention: "Don't be silly," he chided. "Of course we have plans. We've installed a dozen of the best firewalls on the planet. We use hardware-based tokens for user identification and authentication. The hackers will have a real hard time getting in here at all." Some of the attendees—probably those responsible for those efforts—nodded in assent. Others remained skeptical.

"That's the problem," I countered, raising my finger high in the air. "Class II Information Warfare attacks against your company have little or nothing to do with hackers. The real problem is what dedicated adversaries with financial and manpower resources can do." The audience sat up; they hadn't heard it put like this before. "Are you prepared for them?"

No response, but many glazed eyes.

"To get a feel for what I'm talking about," I said, "Let's examine the three classic triads of information security for a moment. Confidentiality is keeping secrets a secret." A few nods of comprehension.

"How much of your internal network traffic, external network traffic, and storage is encrypted—using any algorithm and any key management system?" By the time the argument was through, most of the attendees agreed that less than 10 percent of the company's communications were protected from eavesdropping on the Net, although they used the Net heavily for global conversations. Passwords were encrypted for remote logons, the occasional sensitive e-mail was PGP'd, and a few other cases of isolated concern were permitted the luxury of cryptographic protection. Nothing else.

"Okay, let's look at the second leg of the classic infosec triad," I suggested as I wrote on the whiteboard at the head of the room. "Integrity. You want to make sure that data is not intentionally or accidentally modified in transit or during storage. So how much integrity modeling do you use?"

One of the corporate finance types said they used public key encryption for financial transactions with their banks and throughout their global networks, but without data encryption. Another bean counter said they used DES-based MAC (message authentication codes) for a handful of financial transactions to make sure the right amount of money was moved to the right account. That was it. "So you guys have no real way of knowing if the information that appears on your desktop or sits on your servers or resides within your mainframe is accurate. Is that right?"

That thought shook 'em up, but they were forced to agree. "We haven't had any problems . . . ," one person suggested.

"That we know about!" a voice shouted from the back of the room. Someone was getting the idea.

"And so you wait to fix the problem until it occurs, right?" I asked. "Reactive management instead of proactive defensive posturing."

"Sure, why not?" I thought I recognized this arrogant voice as the one who said "It won't happen to us." Hrrmmph.

"Do you take that same attitude with your contingency or disaster planning? Has your data center ever been hit by a tornado?"

"No."

"Ever burnt down?"

"No."

"Ever been flooded?"

"Ah, no . . ."

"Then why plan for the statistical improbability of an earthquake striking downtown Kansas City?"

No answer.

"Why treat the value of your company, its information resources, with any less concern?" The debate heated up with the attendees forming two oppposing factions. Good. They were thinking.

I raised my arms to calm them down so I could stir them up even further. "We've only dealt with the first two triads so far, not the third triad of infosec: availability."

The murmurs abated and I continued. "Availability intends to make sure that your systems are up and flying, working, when you need them to conduct business. That your phones are operational; that the databases are accessible to service your millions of clients; that your data center can bill customers; that your remote users have remote access to the services for which they pay. If any of these go down, or become unavailable, that is called denial of service, or DOS." A few giggles. "No, not that kind of DOS," I joked. "A new kind of DOS, infinitely more unpleasant than the kind that sits on our desktops." More giggles.

"Okay. Let's say that I, as the bad guy, decide that you have really annoyed me. Maybe I'm an environmentalist, and you just poisoned the water with an oil spill or you dump toxic waste into lakes and streams. Or let's say I am from another country and we are competing for a huge job worth billions, and I'd like to see you out of the picture. Our culture operates by different values and rules and messing up the competition is considered fair play. Or perhaps I'm an ex-employee and I feel like you screwed me out of what I think I deserve. Or make up any scenario you want. Be creative. The question you need to ask yourselves is: 'Is my company adequately prepared to defend against a concerted denial of service attack?'" The room gasped a slight gasp and I knew what the answer would be.

"This," I exclaimed, "is Class II Information Warfare, where the company is the victim, or perhaps two adversarial organizations battle it out over some issue that isn't terribly germane to us at the moment. How can you defend yourself against the acts of man without a policy, a procedure, and a means of execution?"

"What sort of attacks might we see?" one very astute attendee asked.

"Good question. For example, if you migrate a percentage of your customer service programs to the Internet, or choose to conduct a wide range of electronic commerce on the Net, do you have a back-up method if your network connections are intentionally disabled? Maybe through a broadcast storm of some sort which ties up all of the available bandwidth to your site? How do you get back into business?" Scrunched-up noses, furrowed foreheads. They were really thinking now.

"Or if I am really a bad guy, I might choose to physically cut your telephone connections *and* launch a broadcast storm. These two methods alone can cause your communications links to suffer unless there is an appropriate contingency for acts of man."

Eyes widened and attendees mumbled to each other: "I never thought about that." "Do we have a plan for this?"

"Denial of service can get more egregious the nastier I am. I could cut power lines in addition to the above and then you really find yourselves in an electronic black hole." A few laughs to ward off a complete case of the heebie-jeebies.

"Or, with a little more sophistication I might inject high-intensity-frequency noise down your power lines, which for many companies can cause havoc with their computers unless proper filtering is in place." A couple of ladies in the front row shuddered.

"There is no limit to what the bad guys can do if they really want to. And don't forget that historically, the majority of crimes are committed from inside the company, by those you trust and to whom you have given access. They can be the most offensive, and work from right inside your own shop." Eyes suspiciously peered at one another.

"So, again, you have to ask yourselves what levels of protection are appropriate. Do you have systems that you *must* have working at all times? Without them you are out of business? And for how long? You've figured it out for acts of God. This is just a different way of looking at the same problem."

"So where do you recommend we start?" a flighty lawyer cackled.

Perfect. Paradigm shift. I had done my job. "You have to think like the bad guys. You have to become information warriors in your own right. You have to be honest with yourselves and truly look at your vulnerabilities. Examine how much energy, time, manpower, and resources it takes to exploit one or more of them. How robust they are—honestly. Don't take anything for granted. A real introspective look-see. Remember that the dedicated information warrior will take advantage of all of your weaknesses—it's in his best interest to do so.

"And also remember, the game is not fair; it's skewed in the info warrior's favor. You have to protect every hole in your infrastructure—he just has to find one."

I paused, and my audience took a breath for the first time in 14 minutes. A huge exhale engulfed the room, followed by a nervous titter.

I had one more point to make. "This is the same problem that we as a country face: deciding what is important enough to protect. Should we as a nation choose to defend an attack against the National Information Infrastructure as we would foreign submarines putt-putting up the Potomac? Should the civil sector, the critical life-giving systems which keep the engine of our country going, be defended with vigor and measured response?" A lot of heads were nodding in cadence.

"We as a country have to decide whether the economy of this country is a national security asset worthy of protection against a new, capable distributed threat. Or maybe we don't care, and prefer to ignore the threats. That choice will decide the future of our country.

"For you and your company, the issues are the same—it's merely an issue of scale. You have the same choice to make: to defend yourself against the Class II information warrior or not. To protect your interests, and those of your stockholders, and those of your employees against attack and exploitation by those who do not have your best interests at heart."

One sole voice made my day. "Where do I sign up?"

They got it.

Diary of an Industrial Spy

Ira Winkler, Director of Technology, NCSA

The following case study was performed at the request of the targeted company by the author to identify needed security countermeasures.

I was hired to get all possible information from Tech Enterprises, a multi-billion dollar high-tech firm. I started by finding out general information about the company, their products, and their people. The Internet provided me dozens of library resources, as did the company. A quick call to the company got me a copy of their corporate newsletter and annual report. These sources provided me a shopping list of the company's top product, which was worth billions of dollars, as per financial analysts. I also had the names of the lead people working on the projects.

I then got a job in the company as a temporary technical employee. Prior to arriving onsite, I got a Tech Enterprises business card out of a fishbowl at a local restaurant that has people put their business card into the bowl for the possibility of winning a free meal. I took the business card to a local print shop that created an apparently real Tech Enterprises business card, with my name and the stated title of Information Security Supervisor.

Upon arriving at the company, I report to Human Resources to fill out paperwork and get an access card. I fill in inaccurate information that is not verified by the HR person. I get my access badge, and am shown my office. Within a minute, I am on the phone to the lead researcher of the company's top product. I state that I was just hired into the Information Security Department, and that I have the broad responsibility of protecting all sensitive information. I therefore need to know what information is sensitive and where it is stored. The researcher says the Team Leader is the best person to talk to.

I contact the Team Leader, and meet with him a few minutes later. Again claiming to be the new Supervisor for Information Security, I ask for the types of information that are sensitive and ask where the information is stored. After establishing a rapport with the Team Leader, I am given copies of all project meeting minutes. I am also added to the distribution list for the minutes. The minutes contain a variety of critical product information, including test results, schedules, and various manufacturing details. I then ask if there is a single place where the most sensitive information is stored. I am told that the company Government Affairs Office (GAO) and Business Managers compile all project information.

At the recommendation of the Team Leader, I contact the GAO representative and a Business Manager to make an appointment. I meet with the GAO representative, who tells me about specific documents that go to the government for licensing purposes. These documents contain complete manufacturing data. After meeting with the GAO, I review the meeting minutes that I got from the Team Leader. While it contains a variety of very sensitive information, there is a single paragraph that tells the location of a draft document going to the government available for review. The access password for the document is included in the meeting minutes. I access the document, and have the manufacturing instructions for the company's emerging multibillion dollar product.

A review of the directory also produces similar documents for two other products. I could now manufacture three of the company's top products. So much for the first day of the task.

After dinner that evening, I go back to Tech Enterprises and start going through sensitive areas of the company. All I need is my access badge to get in the building. Starting in the Legal Department, I go through desks, offices, and computers that are not locked. Within 30 minutes, I have the product licensing strategies for several products, a complete patent application that is not filed, the company's bargaining position on a multimillion dollar lawsuit, etc. I then move on to the Research and Development area. I get a wide variety of extremely sensitive information, including the manufacturing instructions for five more products.

On Day 2, I have an early morning meeting with the Business Manager. I use the same ruse with him that I used with everyone else. Throughout the meeting, I learn about the importance of Management Reports, which are provided to senior executives to keep them abreast of all developments. I ask him to show me the location of the computer directory where all of the reports are stored. I observe him type in his user ID, but cannot see his password as he accesses the directory. After the meeting, I walk back to my desk. I try common passwords, and discover that he uses his user ID as his password. I now have access to all of his files. It turns out that he is the business manager for several projects. I also find that all business managers store their files in the same directory. I have access to sensitive information on all of the company's emerging developments.

It's 10:30 A.M. on the second day, and I have everything that an industrial spy could want.

Prologue. Weeks later, nobody has reported anything strange to security. Technical people did not notice massive downloads of data. Senior employees did not report the sudden appearance and disappearance of the Supervisor for Information Security. Nobody knows that their top products have been compromised to the extent that any competitor could possibly beat them to market.

16

Class 3: Global Information Warfare

> *"History does not teach that better technology necessarily leads to victory. Rather victory goes to the commander who uses technology better, or who can deny the enemy his technology."*
>
> —OFFICE OF THE CHIEF OF NAVAL OPERATIONS.[1]

CLASS 3 INFORMATION WARFARE IS WAGED AGAINST INDUSTRIES, political spheres of influence, global economic forces, or even against entire countries. It is the use of technology against technology; it is about secrets and the theft of secrets; it is about turning information against its owners; it is about denying an enemy the ability to use both his technology and his information. Class 3 Information Warfare is the ultimate form of conflict in Cyberspace, waged across the Global Network by Computers Everywhere against Computers Everywhere. Class 3 Information Warfare is *very* bad news.

It is an invisible but very real war, where Information Weapons of mass destruction are let loose, either in a focused way, to achieve specific results, or indiscriminately, to have the widest possible impact. The victims are not only the targeted computers, companies, or economies, but the tens of millions of people who depend upon those information systems for their very survival. Take the power of Class 1 and Class 2 Information Warfare, multiply it tenfold, and you will begin to get a sense of the kind of damage that can be done. Class 3 Information Warfare creates chaos.

By now the reader should have a clear idea of the havoc that can be raised in Cyberspace by anyone—a preteen, a vengeful mother-in-law, a military man, a madman, or a terrorist. We know that anyone with the desire can acquire the same power that a mere two decades ago was only in the hands of the information elite. We also understand what sort of motivations might drive a person or group to take advantage of those capabilities.

Class 3 Information Warfare is bigger, and more widespread than the capability of even a hundred hackers. It is bigger than the FBI or the LAPD. It is bigger than the biggest company willing to spend a few million dollars for their competitor's secrets. Not everyone has the wherewithal to wage Information Warfare at this intensity, but there are powerful and rich individuals and institutions in the world who have, or will soon have, the capability and the motivation.

When teaching about Class 3 Information Warfare, I have found it useful to reinforce one thought: From both a competitive and combative perspective, it would be stupid for a well-financed and motivated group *not* to attack the technical infrastructure of an adversary. The vulnerabilities are clear, the risk so low, and the rewards so great. In fact, if someone wants to take on a technologically sophisticated society, the real question we should ask is not "why would they attack the computers?" but "why wouldn't they?"

Along this line of reasoning, it is evident that portions of the U.S. econotechnical infrastructure would be inviting objectives. In fact, we are already being targeted, but thus far, thankfully, in limited doses. We have not yet had to face the all-out devastation that Class 3 intensity brings with it. But that means we haven't had the opportunity to prepare for an inevitable assault in Cyberspace. We can, and must, begin to heed the warnings. The military understands their enemies; they plan for all eventualities in conflict. So we should understand what a Class 3 conflict might entail, and how we will react.

All of the stops are pulled out when one wages Information

Warfare at the Class 3 level. This level is waged by only the most elite of the Information Warriors, those very few individuals or groups who meet a number of select criteria.

Class 3 Information Warriors must have

- extensive financial resources
- sufficient motivation
- the ability to organize and control a large number of people
- a target with substantial reliance upon information processing capability
- a technical target
- patience

1. The Information Warriors must be well funded to be effective on the scale envisioned. The United States spends about $250 billion per year for bombs, bullets, and invisible airplanes. About $30 billion of that is spent on intelligence organizations (such as the NSA) for our own militarily focused Information Warfare. That annual investment makes America militarily impervious to attack, localized terrorist attacks notwithstanding. But our computers are another story, as we have learned.

   Even if the Information Warrior only spends millions of dollars (as opposed to billions) to launch an attack, say $100 million or so over two to three years, the results would be unimaginable. When compared to the cost and effectiveness of a well-armed militia, that means that almost anyone can play. When we think that drug cartels spend billions of dollars annually to protect themselves, an additional investment in an offensive information strategy would be a relatively minor expense. And that's scary.

2. The motivation of the Information Warriors must be strong. On a Class 3 level, the hope of becoming wealthy beyond imagination, richer even than Microsoft founder Bill Gates, might be enough. With money comes power, and megalomania is a millennia-old motivation. Re-

venge for real or imagined wrongs is also a pretty good motivator, too, and Information Warfare offers a fine way to extract retribution. Class 3 Information Warfare offers those nation-states unfriendly to the U.S. an alternative to conventional warfare. Iran, Iraq, Libya, Islamic fanatics, drug cartels, old-regime Stalinists, and Red Brigade-style terrorists head the long list of those antagonistic towards the U.S. It also offers the Have Not nation-states a means of becoming competitive quickly at our expense. Any list of candidates would be incomplete without mentioning the isolated fanatic or lunatic whose motivations are well beyond sound rationale. It is not inconceivable for small groups of individuals in positions of power, as suggested by Oliver Stone in his film *JFK*, to have the ability and motivation to finance such an invasion.

3. Manpower must be available. Waging Class 3 Information Warfare is not a one-man show. It will necessarily involve hundreds of people, probably located all over the globe, each with little knowledge of the ultimate purpose of their task, and with even less knowledge of their fellow warriors. These rank-and-file Information Warriors must be willing to work without questioning superiors. There are copious and willing populations worldwide from which to recruit assistance. In 1992 when presidential also-ran Pat Buchanan spoke critically about American immigration policies, he emphasized that with millions of foreigners in the United States, not all of them will have the best interests of this country at heart.

   As Count de Marenches points out, taxi drivers would make ideal operatives in an Information War. The majority of Washington, D.C., taxi drivers are immigrants who, de Marenches claims, could represent a security threat. The Count told ex-FBI director William Webster in March 1987, "A cab is quite simply an automobile with a big trunk that can transport people, papers, ideas, explosives, weapons—plus it has a radio. It's perfect. If I had to organize terrorists in Washington, I'd recruit a couple of cabbies. They're terrific. They're everywhere. And totally invisible."[2]

The Information Army must be disciplined. In a conventional military conflict, generals expect 100 percent compliance with orders, but a nation's military has certain powers that a private army doesn't have. Fear of the brig, treason charges, and court martial keep most soldiers in line. Likewise, in an Information Army, discipline must be maintained, even though the Warriors function in Cyberspace. Fear of death by murder is a pretty good start. The Mafia has historically maintained excellent discipline employing just such methods. Drug barons have little fear of reprisal for torturing and killing their own who are, or appear to be, disloyal. Radical political and religious factions use didactics or spiritual teaching to rationalize such extreme measures.

Information Warriors occasionally have to act ruthlessly. They should be willing and able to quickly and quietly eliminate those individuals within their own organization who may jeopardize their overall plans. Similarly, it may be necessary to eliminate innocent civilians who accidentally occasion upon illicit activities. On the other hand, the leaders might choose to sacrifice members of their Information Army as pawns in order to create a sense of discipline or push their plans forward.

4. The target must be an advanced post-industrial technical society. Shooting HERF Guns at sub-Saharan fruit vendors is not the way to disrupt a barter-based economy. If communications are accomplished with smoke signals, drums, or tin cans connected by strings, you can forget about malicious software as a viable weapon. Attacking a neolithic community with twenty-first century weapons is beyond useless; it's downright crazy.

But the Information Warrior who is planning to wage a Class 3 conflict in Cyberspace already knows that.

The target must heavily rely upon his technical infrastructure for its continued good health. Even a primarily industrial society such as Eastern Europe is not an ideal target. If the Information Warrior's target can continue to thrive without its information infrastructure intact, it does not become an attractive prey.

5. Patience is absolutely necessary to wage effective Information Warfare. Sure, we'll see the occasional goofball who attacks Cyberspace with an impulsive vengeance, only to effect limited and isolated damage. Like the Hinkleys of the world, he's just an amateur. The professional Information Warrior is willing to commit the funds, the personnel, and the energy to a Class 3 assault; he will bide his time, plan out every detail, develop contingencies, design redundancies, have backsups and backups of backups, spy on his own troops, and rehearse as many of the field operations as possible before the actual attack commences. He will make sure that only a small handful of his Army knows the big picture, with everyone else working on a need-to-know basis. With the right warriors at the head of the Information Army, patience becomes another effective weapon. Timing and patience go hand in hand. Strike too soon or too late, and all is lost.

The Information Army

For a Class 3 operation to work, an organization must be developed and in place prior to an effective assault. Everyone should know his or her job, where to be, and how to communicate. There are countless small operations to carry out beforehand, and they must be done efficiently and professionally.

For a cyberconflict of this magnitude, the money must be in

place, free to be drawn upon without first having to wade through a cumbersome vertical bureaucracy. For purposes of this discussion, we are assuming that the financial resources behind our imaginary Information Army are substantial, and that it has the means to distribute the monies and the influence to keep a large group happy and loyal for the duration. Financial experts who know how to manipulate large amounts of money undetected are available around the world. (The amount of cash that is laundered within the U.S. every year, $100 billion or more, is a thousand times more than the monies to be spent by our hypothetical Information Warriors.)

For the sake of secrecy, our Information Army will be a horizontal organization; unlike in most big companies or in the military, most of the divisions or groups will report to the top. Middle management won't cut it in the Information Army since the extra layers cut down on effective and timely communications, allow for power bases independent of the leader, and create opportunities for security leaks. The organization of the Information Army will be simple. Think of it as having one president, about a dozen vice presidents, each with his own specialty, and then several dozen terrorist-like cells reporting directly to each vice president. Our Information Army will not be so unlike a large multinational conglomerate, except that it will be run more militaristically.

C3I

At the pinnacle of the Information Army is what the military calls C3I—Command, Control, Communications, and Intelligence (some military planners now call it C4I, adding computers into the equation)—and what business calls the board of directors. This is where strategic plans are made and directives for tactical support are calculated. C3I motivates and finances the Information Army; it is its raison d'être. Decisions are made here. All monies come through C3I. The power over life and death sits with these very few individuals who will ultimately exert extraordinary influence over the lives of millions.

There may only be a couple of generals in the Information Army who can see the whole picture. Terrorist groups are often organized in this way. Thus, if one member is captured, he can't tell what he doesn't know, regardless of the interrogation methods used. A leader, very possibly the financial sponsor, will be the single voice guiding the entire effort. A trustworthy technical general will sit at his side, to design and oversee the technical operations. He will need to know the big picture, and will actively contribute to the planning. An internal security chief will set the policies and guidelines for loyalty. Financial management will have to know almost everything, and internal legal counsel will have to know as little as possible, yet still be able to serve the client. The more ruthless the leadership, the greater the allegiance.

C3I will be as small as possible since publicity and fame are the last things the Information Army wants, at least at this point. The smaller the core group, the better the secret. It would also make sense for the leaders of the Information Army to headquarter themselves somewhere other than in the United States. There is no compelling need to be here physically and if they are positioned on our shores, the potential legal problems are vast.

The Information Army reporting to C3I will consist of divisions, each of which has a specialty necessary to the overall goal.

COMMUNICATIONS GROUP

One of the most critical tasks is the creation of a system to fill the many communications needs of the Information Army. While planning will be required, there is nothing new to invent here. Run by the Communications Group, or "C Group," most communications can be done over the Global Network itself. Using the public phone networks for voice, fax, and data communications is inexpensive, reliable, and portable. The Information Warriors will supply the security and privacy with strong encryption and key management schemes available from tens of security products manufacturers. They may even build some of their own products to maintain as low a profile as possible.

The Information Warriors can even use the Global Network to achieve anonymity and privacy. They will be able to communicate just as tens of millions do every day, but with encrypted messages. Unless encryption is made illegal, such messaging techniques will be invisible. The use of secure private bulletin boards scattered among different locations will provide yet another method for communications, and will not raise anyone's suspicions.

Redundancy will be necessary; multiple communications routes will be made available in the event one is compromised or lost due to systems failures. Ham radio offers a portable means of backup communications in the event that the phones or the Global Network itself are the ultimate targets or if there is reason to suspect a security compromise. Headquarters will always need to be able to communicate with its troops. By the time the operation commences, the Information Army will have built its own virtual network, perhaps even using its target's communication systems as the initial underpinnings. C-Group will take advantage of Global Positioning Satellites (GPS) to track the locations and activities of the Information Warriors as a means of further control.

C-Group is intrinsically involved with the strategic planning that occurs within C3I Headquarters. Almost all members of C-Group must be trusted beyond reproach, as they must have a degree of understanding of the scope of their activities. To make interception and traffic analysis of their activities much more difficult, convoluted routing of communications paths all over the country and the world will require C-Group to be multinational. From the Information Warrior's standpoint, it's worth the extra effort: better safe than sorry.

MAPPERS

I call the mappers the navigators of Cyberspace. They will calculate and draw pictures of the Global Network to show how things are connected, graphically depicting how the telephone systems connect to each other and to the cellular networks and the satellite links. Some members will concentrate on how banks move money—the Federal Reserve System, the SWIFT network, the ATM networks. Other mappers will concentrate on the hundreds and hundreds of civilian and military networks that permit government to function. The mappers will organize a Rand McNally of Cyberspace, including insets and details, with the capability for zooming into areas of particular interest. They will map out how the Global Network connects to hospitals, doctors, insurance companies, and pharmacies through the medical databases. They will map out how Corporate America communicates with itself and with the rest of the world by navigating through the internal private networks of the country's biggest companies.

One of the mappers' most important functions is to designate, by location and type, the entrances and exits of each digital highway system. Not only will the mappers need to provide directions to a particular electronic neighborhood for other Information Warriors, but they will point out exactly where the doors are and where the escape routes lie. It's like having a street map with the addresses of each house, the names of each resident, and the kind of lock that each house uses to protect its assets.

Much of the information needed to build these maps will come from open source materials available to anyone for the asking. The telephone companies publish entirely too much private information for anyone's own good. The government, to support competition, openly publishes the designs for future networks. A mapper's job is never done.

CRACKERS

Once the mappers provide the addresses of the target, these guys will be responsible for breaking the locks on the electronic doors. The crackers will use a set of software tools for deciphering passwords, breaching operating system security, and building trap doors for future use. This group will not officially know that the mappers exist, but will rely upon their directions for Global Network navigation. They are to be as quiet and invisible as possible.

Once they gain entry into a system, they will want to install a door via a Trojan Horse program so that they can have access in the future, as occurred in the 1994 Internet security breaches. This is to be done as quickly as possible as the crackers want to raise no suspicion at all—if they do, the doors will be closed. In some cases, they may be given passwords or access codes to certain addresses, but they will not know that they came from their highly organized brethren, the sniffers.

SNIFFERS

Sniffers working in the Information Army will be broken into three groups. One group will concentrate on "sniffing the switch," looking for passwords, access methods, and security-related information that can then be provided to the crackers. They will gain access into the phone systems using information provided by the mappers and the crackers, then eavesdrop upon data traffic in search of even more access information.

The second group of sniffers will, from their terminals located anywhere in the world, travel the Global Network and capture as much sensitive and proprietary information as they can. Following the directions of the mappers and using the tools the cracker left behind, the sniffers will search for any information of value. They will sniff away on the LANs, WANs, MANs and every other network they can penetrate. They will capture and store satellite or microwave communications containing hundreds of conversations. They will accumulate, categorize, and store vast amounts of information that they themselves will probably never look at, much less analyze. That is left to another group altogether.

The third set of sniffers will function more like a military or paramilitary unit. They may need to install physical taps or eavesdropping equipment on selected targets where electronic access is insufficient. They may need to tap a phone or a fax, or use laser beams to read the vibrations on a window pane from a mile away. In conventional parlance, these guys would be regarded as the "black bag" sniffers, used where physical access to the targets is required.

READERS

The readers have a most interesting task. Their job is to listen to the emanations coming from computers and computer screens. Using the best van Eck detection equipment available, including real-time fast Fourier transform hardware chips, they will target businesses and industries in search of secrets. Since most people don't know their computers are transmitting information through the air, they are ripe to be plucked by the readers. Readers will also search powerlines and water lines for information that is proprietary, sensitive, and valuable.

SOFTWARE DEVELOPMENT GROUP

This team of engineers could come from former Iron Curtain countries, since there are plenty from whom to choose, and they could telecommute from home. Wherever they are based in the world, their task is to develop the software tools that the mappers and crackers use and that make the lives of the readers and the sniffers easier.

Some engineers will be experts in mainframes, some in minis, some in PCs, and others in communications. Their labs will be equipped with everything they need to get the job done. They will be able to duplicate a field condition as reported by the mapper or cracker, develop a reliable means to compromise it, and then deploy that software to their comrades. One group of engineers will develop malicious software—the

Trojan horses and worms and spoofing software that will be used by other divisions of the Information Army. A "virus factory" will develop self-replicating viral software. Others will develop software that can crash systems almost undetectably. This group's only goal will be to efficiently turn software-based technology against its owners.

MOLES

During the Cold War, the Russians placed their moles in England and the U.S., while we had our moles inside of Russian organizations. Industrial spies place moles within target companies. And so the Information Warrior will use moles as key agents in his master plan.

Moles are the inside agents of the Information Warrior. As insiders, they can deploy malicious software, garner confidential information from the target, or provide invaluable inside information in time of conflict to C3I. Some moles may only be security guards or delivery men who are given physical access to their bosses' confidential information. Moles are occasionally expandable, but in a well-run operation, they disappear at the right moment.

ANALYSTS

With endless streams of information pouring into headquarters, the top Information Warriors are going to need to have a method of organizing it into a useful form. As in any intelligence operation, the collected data is essentially useless until it is cataloged and cross-referenced. This is the analyst's job.

Information of immediate value—security information of worth to the crackers or the sniffers—will need to be quickly processed and distributed. Information to be used later, as a weapon, will need to be easily located and retrieved. The Information Warriors will want to have all this data at their fingertips.

The analysts will constantly massage the databases they create, probably using heuristic artificial intelligence techniques, and allow their team and C3I to examine it from different perspectives. They may identify the data by location, industry, or financial benefit. The information they analyze may force changes in the overall plans of the assault, but that is to be expected. None of the Information Warrior's plans are in concrete for Cyberspace is a breathing, dynamic place. Thus, they will make constant adjustments to meet their overall goals.

MANUFACTURING GROUP

The Information Warriors will need to build some of their own equipment in addition to buying what is available from retail sources. Quality van Eck radiation detectors will be manufactured in-house, to avoid raising suspicion by purchasing too many on the open market. Illegal cracker tools, if unattainable by scrounging through hacker bulletin boards, will also be built from scratch. If the plan calls for custom integrated chips built, they will be designed by chippers, in cooperation with the software development group. Chip manufacturing can be done by a silicon foundry in the Far East, where few questions are asked when cash is on the table.

SOFTWARE DISTRIBUTION GROUP

If C3I decides that massive PC and LAN failures are required, this can be accomplished by wide-spread distribution of malicious software. The Information Army will have sufficient resources to buy a legitimate software company with a reasonable market penetration for its products. Given the patience of the Information Warrior, he could take the time to build up the company by offering quality products at a low price and selling as many copies of the software as possible. Alternatively or in combination, a shareware company might be organized or purchased that would extensively distribute software through an apparently legitimate operation. What customers will not know, however, is that the software upon which they have come to rely has a ticking time bomb inside.

SHOOTERS

Shooters are the infantrymen of the Information Army. They are the ones who will use the HERF Guns to disable their adversary's systems. (Or, if the technology becomes more widely available, they may strategically place EMP/T Bombs for even greater damage.) Vans carrying HERF Guns can be rendered invisible with proper urban and suburban camouflage: people will not notice a repair truck that happens to have an antenna on its roof. The shooters will also have additional gear in their vehicle, perhaps legitimate broadcast or repair equipment in case of a casual look-see by law enforcement if stopped for a traffic violation. Since HERF Guns often look like a normal transmission setup, identification of their purpose would be most difficult. EMP/T bombs will be a bit more difficult to position but as the technology improves in quality and shrinks in size, a good sized canister of electronic equipment is pretty innocuous in appearance.

The shooters might use the same electromagnetic weapons against satellite communications systems, which would require more power and larger facilities, but the transmitting equipment could be located anywhere from the desert of the American West to the jungles of South America to tiny islands in the Caribbean.

Depending upon the ruthlessness of those at C3I, the shooters may or may not be told of the potential for collateral biological damage; a dose of electromagnetic energy might take out the shooter as well as his victim's information processing systems. The EMP/T bomb might be built to physically destroy itself with a conventional explosive after its initial detonation. The explosive is assumed to be the sole source of damage until the real effects are discovered. Forensics is a well-developed science and sooner or later the FBI will find out the bomb's real function, but the shooters will be long gone by then.

PUBLIC RELATIONS GROUP

I use this term loosely, for the Information Warriors do not have the best interests of the public at heart. For example, one PR effort might be to "turn" key employees at selected companies or agencies. If they need a mole or an insider, they may use embarrassing information as a weapon to accomplish that task. The fear of disclosure to one's company or family, to law enforcement, or even to the general public is plenty of motivation for an otherwise innocent individual to assist the Information Warriors. A cash incentive can be used if blackmail fails.

The disclosure of supposedly confidential information to the public is a very effective weapon for the Class 3 Information Warrior. If the private financial records of a high roller at an investment firm or bank is given to the *National Enquirer* or the *Wall Street Journal*, his entire company will certainly suffer. Imagine the effects of such a leak if used as a component of Class 3 Information Warfare. Alan Greenspan has stated that the private meetings of the Federal Reserve Board should not be made public; such disclosure could severely hurt the economy. That is just the sort of information that the Class 3 Information Warrior would like to use.

The PR crew will feed information to the press on a selective basis. After a few serious cyberevents, our experts might decide they should make an announcement to the media that our computers are being targeted and there's nothing we can do in defense. The widespread dissemination of such threats is a useful tool for the Information Warrior, especially if he can back up his claims with solid evidence or predictions of future events.

Public pronouncements will be tightly controlled by the Information Warriors. Perhaps they want to sway opinion against the banks, the government, or an entire industry. They will disseminate half-truths and distortions throughout the business world to further their goals. The Information Warriors will have collected substantial information, some of it very negative. If that data is released on company or agency letterhead, it will carry extra weight. Since they will be working by remote control over secured communications channels, detection will be most difficult, and the threats near anonymous. If the blackmail operation is carried out against a hundred or more private groups simultaneously, the Information Warrior might well succeed in tying up law enforcement resources for a very long time. There are only so many agents to go around and sooner or later they will be unable to address, much less solve, so many cases. The results might be considered humorous by the top dog Information Warriors at C3I. Law enforcement will have to pick and choose those cases for which they have the manpower, and ignore the others.

This is exactly the situation faced by the police in New York city when it comes to street crime. Mugged in Central Park? Fill out this form, but don't count on us finding the guy. Robbed of $100 at gunpoint? It's a waste of time, but here's the complaint form. The FBI does take blackmail and computer crime seriously, but in Cyberspace there will be little they can do to fight them if carried out on a wholesale level. For most victimized organizations, they will probably face the embarrassing likelihood of disclosure and have to live with the consequences, especially if the motives are not profit driven.

We have hypothesized an organization whose sole aim is to act as malevolently as possible towards its adversaries. In the case of Class 3 Information Warfare, the biggest adversary that they can come up against is the United States itself, by attacking our econotechnical information infrastructure.

At one point or another, the Information Warrior is going to have to land on the so-called beaches of Cyberspace and attack. When he attacks and in what manner is, of course, decided by C3I. Since we are addressing the vulnerability of the American econotechnical information infrastructure, let's take a bird's eye view of the possibilities. Remember, we are looking at the Big Picture.

DAY ONE

Day One will been preceded by lengthy planning and coordination. The moles will be in place. Substantial information will have been collected, organized, and distributed. The clandestine software will have been designed and distributed; the front companies will be in place and operational; the tools and weapons designed, built, tested, and deployed. The military goes through this exercise daily, and large companies adhere to a similarly well-thought out business plan. Class 3 Information Warriors are no different.

To have the greatest impact on the American economy and society, very specific targets will have been selected and their vulnerabilities found.

The three biggest financial targets in the United States are the Federal Reserve System, the Internal Revenue Service, and Wall Street. If any one of them suffers substantial damage, the effects will be felt in milliseconds, nationally and internationally. Individually, each of these could represent a computer Chernobyl. If all three are severely disrupted, the effects would be unlike any disaster we have never seen.

If *only* these institutions are hit, the impact would have immediate repercussions on our populace, and cause an instant decline in confidence in the financial underpinnings of our society. A run on the banks? Maybe. Will our international loans be called in? What will happen to interest rates? What about the International Monetary Fund?

For maximum effect, the Information Warrior will want to use the double (or triple) whammy. The moles will unleash the malicious software; the shooters will fire HERF Guns. The more widely the attack is distributed, against multiple locations, the more effective the results. The same double whammy will be applied to the other quarry of the Information Warriors. Our communications systems are so intertwined that bringing them all down at once is not likely, but strategic communications systems failures associated with the primary targets will further confuse any efforts at disaster control and recovery. By this time, every news network will have broken into the afternoon soap operas with a report and CNN will be covering events live. All we will know for sure is that something is terribly, terribly, wrong.

If the chippers have been able, for example, to place defective chips in late-model Chryslers, programming them to fail upon the reception of a specific radio frequencies, the electronic ignitions of hundreds of thousands of cars could all fail in a matter of hours. To add insult to injury, moles within the traffic control departments of major cities could instigate a major system-wide failure, turning every light green at the same time. Airports connected by ground-based communications systems would be crippled, in any case, the computer reservation systems for the big airlines would also be set to fail.

At this point, panic is spreading and Binary Schizophrenia is raging. The Information Warriors have struck the money, the communications, and the transportation industries. What's left of Wall Street is reeling, and the London and Tokyo markets have no idea how to react. Computers are failing everywhere. What next?

Bringing down the power companies' computers would further the Information Warrior's goal of fueling public panic and further shrouding his identity in mystery. If a nuclear plant were disrupted, our natural paranoia would be heightened, contributing to the feeling of helplessness. The broadcast networks who have been covering these events then find their feeds cut, their satellites jammed or non-functional. The "man in the street" loses his source of news, the comfort of being informed, the sense of community he gains from sitting in front of his global village hearth. Sitting in a veritable electronic black-out, he looks for those radio and cable stations that still can transmit.

Among the confusion, less noticeable victims are also under attack but with potentially deadly results. A few local hospitals lose power and computer controlled life-support systems fail. Software-driven 911 emergency systems are overloaded by an invisible enemy.

The experts are baffled and shaken, no one seems to know what to do, so survivalist adrenalin kicks in, tempers flare, and the fear of the unknown dominates the collective psyche. Stores are emptied as families stock up on the necessities for an emergency of unknown origin and indeterminate duration. It's every man for himself, except in New York where the bars are full of revelers remembering the last blackout or trying to relive Saint Patrick's Day.

Then comes the announcement.

The Information Warriors break into the communications networks that are still functioning. They spread their message all across the Global Network, via fax, and E-mail to every cybernaut in the world. They provide the media, the White House, and the Pentagon with their statement.

They announce that this is an attack against the United States of America—for reasons to be enunciated at their convenience—and this is only the beginning. They warn us that from now on, our computers are under attack. They can never again be trusted to work as expected. Baby Boomers will recall the television show "The Outer Limits:" "Your television is under our control. Do not attempt to adjust the dial. . . ."

From locations far away from the chaos, the Information Warriors will spell out what America can expect in the next week, month, or year. "Forget life as you know it. Things are going to be different for a while. We are in control." Their message will be clear and unmistakable. They are not going to let up their assault. They will continue until a) their demands are met, b) they feel like stopping, or c) every last one of them is dead. Not the kind of warm and fuzzy message we Americans want to hear.

When we repair the damage in one area, they will have

already struck somewhere else, and then they'll return to the first and strike again. They'll make perfectly clear that no person, no company, no government function is off limits. They'll tell us that we'll never know where or when or how the next victim will be hit, but rest assured it will happen. And, with appropriate arrogance, they'll deny that they can ever be caught. After all, they are hiding within the infinitely complex fabric of Cyberspace.

The big question will be, how do we respond?

Information Warfare: Time for Some Constructive Skepticism?

Col. John Rothrock (Ret.), USAF

Except as otherwise noted, the views presented in this article are those of the author. They do not represent a position of SRI International or of any element of the U.S. government.

Future historians might well cite the years 1993-1995 as the period during which the U.S. military and the rest of the American national security community committed themselves to Information Warfare as a conceptual vehicle for transitioning from the precepts of the Cold War to the new relaities of the Inofrmation Age. Now widely accepted (at least as a general concept) within U.S. policy, strategy, and planning circles, Information Warfare is more and more often cited as a rationale for reorganization initiatives and resource demands throughout the Department of Defense and associated national security institutions.

It seems that every week, more military and other national security organizations announce Information Warfare to be a key element of their mission responsibilities. Many other organizations have been explicitly created or substantially revamped to pursue and advance the concept. Simultaneously, hefty sums and extremely complex projects are being programmed to provide new databases, network architectures, advanced software, and other sophisticated capabilities, all under the rubric of Information Warfare.

Also by now, most military and intelligence organizations have specially selected some of their best minds to help them define and address the new intellectual, organizational, programmatic, and technological challenges that the concept presents. Similarly, defense industry has quickly and heavily come on board, seeing the concept to present a legitimate need and therefore also a business opportunity for bringing new, innovative mixes of its expertise to bearn on post-Cold War problems. Throughout the national security community, belief in and enthusiasm for the concept seem to grow by the day as a key to coping with the ever-accelerating changes that have continued to beset it since the fall of the Berlin Wall.

The following extended quote from the Secretary of Defense's 1994 report to the President and the Congress summarizes the compelling logic which undergirds this enthusiasm while also testifying to the broad acceptance which the concept seems to enjoy at the highest policy levels.

561

Information Warfare is a means to not only better integrate C4I (Command, Control, Communications, Computers, and Intelligence), but also to address the comparative effectiveness of a potential adversary's C4I. It consists of the actions taken to preserve the integrity off one's own information systems from exploitation, corruption, or destruction while at the same time exploiting, corrupting, or destroying an adversary's information system and, in the process, achieving information advantage in the application of force. Thus, Information Warfare is an aggregation of and better integration of C4, C4 countermeasures, information systems security and security countermeasures, and intelligence.

Information Warfare provides a method of better organizing and coordinating efforts to ensure an optimized information system responsive to the very demanding information requirements inherent in a smaller force structure, a rapid response capability, and advancing military technologies such as deep strike and precision guided weapons and enhanced mobility of forces. Information Warfare is an integrating strategy that makes better ouse of resources to provide for a better informed force—a force that can act more decisively increasing the likelihood of success while minimizing casualties and collateral effects.[1]

Certainly, if the first milestone for achieving a U.S. Information Warfare capacity suitable for the early decades of the coming century must be development of policy and resource support for the concept throughout the breadth and depth of the national security establishment, that objective now seems to be farily well secured. The concept's impressive acceptance within the national security community has accelerated to the point where most briefings and discussions of the concept now acknowledge Information Warfare to constitute a new medium of conflict even beyond the military dimesion to include new modes of global economic, political, and even cultural competition.

Issues of Thrust *Versus* Vector *and* Means *Versus* Objectives

But, what *is* Information Warfare, beyond the nondiscriminating generalities of the DOD Annual Report and claims that it is a new form of global competition for the Information Age? The Information Warfare concept's institutional and resources *thrust* seems to be farily well established. Now the challenge is to address the intellectually even more difficult issues of its policy and strategic *vector*.

Thus far, the specifics of the concept's achieved thrust have focused primarily upon organization, process, and resources issues—i.e., essentially the *means* of Information Warfare. But beyond the generalities of the DOD Annual Report and claims of the concept's relevance as a new ubiquitous form of Information Age competition and now well-established military objectives of countering enemy command and control while protecting your own, the *objectives* of Information Warfare remain largely undefined. And, with the concept's objectives lacking definition, its potential *implications* also suffer from underdefinition and therefore still lack rigorous examination.

Much of this tendency to shy away from difficult, comprehensive definitions of conceptual objectives has to do with the traditional American intellectual style which is one of pronounced pragmatism. American institutions generally—and the American military particularly—are decidedly more comfortable with process than with theory, with action more than reflection, with efficiences more than effectiveness (there is often a difference), with specific performance than with general coherence. In sum, it is a style of thought that is weighted decidedly more toward particular rather than holistic definitions and address of issues and problems.

The U.S. military is thus readily inclinded to reduce general propositions such as Information Warfare as quickly as possible to specific issues concerned with "means"—i.e., essentially those of resources, organization, and process. More general concerns associated with the concept's fundamental objectives and implications (e.g., doctrine) and the integrated, more coherent address that such concerns logically demande enjoy substantially less advocacy and focus.

Recent nominal reforms notwithstanding, traditional American resource management tools (most notably the DOD's venerable Planning, Programming, and Budgeting System) have long reflected and reinforced these tendencies. Ideas and issues which lack explicit association with one or more management "programs" and are therefore not readily definable in dollar amounts in conjunction with specific "program line items" have always generally warranted less attention and expenditure of bureaucratic energy than have those which could be so defined.

While this American style of thinking and organizaition has proven its practical mettle time and again in dealing effectively with specific problems, it has definite weaknesses in its capacity to treat several problems at once in contect with each other. Unfortunately, it is exactly this sort of integrated and coherent contextual address that an idea as complex and far-reaching as Information Warfare demands. Today, it is still far from certain that the structure of institutional relationships and processes through which the U.S. government manages the country's global security affairs—the Five Year Defense Program (FYDP), service department and joint service doctrinal and ogranizational relationships, the functional junctures of military and civil infrastructures, to name just a few—can cope conceptually with Information Warfare in all of the dimensions and manifestations that the concept's logic demands.

Some Challenging Questions

Today, when one reads about Information Warfare and hears about the concept in presentations, it remains very difficult to determine if there is anything that Information Warfare is *not*. A skeptical mind is soon prompted to ask, "If Information Warfare is everything, can it be anything?"

Several other questions logically follow. For example: Is the concept primarily of a bureaucratic and resources thrust toward specific means with little intellectual vector toward specific objectives, as some of its harsher critics suspect? Is it truly a trend or merely "trend surfing"? Might not the concept be fundamentally flawed intellectually in constituting, as it does, an attempt to *explicitly* address phenomena (those of information) which are *implicit* to all human endeavor, including warfighting? Is there a risk that Information Warfare could become a convenient lip-service response for all of the difficult issues of post-Cold War relevance that confront a national security structure and military whose general froms and culture remain rooted in Cold War precepts—"Sure, we're relevant in the new era—we subscribe to Information Warfare. (Now stop bothering us and let us get back to our traditional considerations of force structure.)"

And more specifically: If Information Warfare holds that all or most information is valuable and targetable but that it also must be accessible and readily fungible, what are the implications for traditional concepts of information security and classification? Can classified, heavily compartmented approaches—running as the do essentially against the grain of the Information Age's defining characteristic, information proliferation—be effective in pursuing a military concept supposedly suited specifically to the character of that age? Where do the military's purview and responsibilities concerning Information Warfare and information security begin? Where do they end?

And some even larger questions: Are American society and its military, as the most information-dependent in the world, really wise in advocating Information Warfare as our preferred new style of conflict? If, as is increasingly espoused, Information Warfare is more than just a military proposition, must the society as a whole be capable of pursuing—and defending against—it if the military is to be able to do its part effectively? If the society has problems in meeting IW's challenges (especially in mustering the national will that the concept's defensive imperative presume), does the military have an appropriate role in helping society deal with such nonmilitary requirements and implications? If so, what is that role?

These are hard but fair questions which the quickly forming Information Warfare community should be prepared to answer. At a minimum, their rigorous consideration should provide the concept with an intellectual vector appropriate to its thrust. Serious address of these questions should ferret out if Information Warfare is more than merely the post-Cold War resources rationale that some skeptics still suspect it to be. They would also force close examination of whether or not our national security structure is capable of recasting itself adequately to effectively implement such a comprehensive and complex idea.

A Suggested Prism Through Which to Consider Information Warfare

How are such questions most effectively considere? Is there perhaps a particulary suitable intellectual prism through which to coniser Information Warfare with the necessary regor appropriate to the importance that the concept's advocates claim for it? How best to explicitly examine a spectrum of issues as implicit to so many other considerations as those comprising Information Warfare?

The accompanying graphic, the "Information Warfare Arrow," attempts to protray the primary components of Information Warfare as it is currently commonly referred to—including dimensions that go well beyond the traditional military perspectives of attacking the enemy's intelligence and command and control capabilities while protecting your own. (If Information Warfare is, in fact, no more than the latter, what else is new? Our success in nullifying Iraqi military Command and Control during the Gulf War was the result of American conceptual and technological sophistication in "Counter Command and Control" that has been evolving at least since the 1970s.)

The graphic is an attempt to portray explicitly a concept which has implicit to it many subtle components and which also is itself implicit to many other societal, governmental, economic, legal, and cultural perspectives.

THE "INFORMATION WARFARE ARROW"

The head of the Information Warfare Arrow is comprised of *intellectual effectiveness* of a highly complex sort. Probably more so than any other form of global security competition, Information Warfare will require exceptional intellectual mastery of the important but subtle hierarchical relationships between *policy, strategy, operations* ("campaigns"), and *tactics*. It wil equally demand a sophisticated apprection of the relationships of all of these perspectives to *technology*. Without such mastery of these relationships, Information Warfare carries with it great risks.

The best technology, even when employed with the greatest of tactical effectiveness, can be counterproductive if the technology and its employment are not orchestrated against a set of well-conceived, hierarchically consistent operational, strategic, and policy objectives. While this observation is true regarding any military or quasi-military undertaking, it is especially important regarding Information Warfare, which is first and foremost an intellectual rather than a technological or physical undertaking. Information Warfare carries with it especially heavy risks of winning battles but losing wars. The best of technology and tactics cannot protect against these risks int he face of poor policy, strategy, and operational concepts and the unprecedented degree of conceptual, doctrinal, structural, procedural, and technological integration—i.e., far beyond "jointness"—that effective Information Warfare is certain to demand.

The arcane (and now largely irrelevant) policy and strategic machinations of the Cold War excepted, post-World War II U.S. military thinking has been generally at its best at the levels of tactics (i.e., the specifics of employment) and technology. True, the 1970s saw a renewed appreciation of the "operational art" perspective (also known as the "campaign level") of military employment, and the Gulf War demonstrated that since then we have made great strides in organizing ourselves at that level. However, most observers agree that the operational level still does not constitute our military's longest suit. Yet, excellence at the operational level is vital to success in Information Warfare for it is the conceptual bridge between higher-level objectives and the means for achieving them.

Beyond these concerns, our system of government necessarily places considerable ethical and political burdens upon those charged with developing policy, strategic, and higher-level operational objectives—burdens that are rooted in a logic borne of tradition and culture that goes far beyond the exigencies of any particular set of global security considerations. The net result is a national security and military structure that is much more comfortable in addressing the technological and resource *means* of conflict than it is in considering the higher policy and strategic objectives of conflict.

For this much greater proficiency regarding means as opposed to objectives not to constitute a potentially fatal flaw in the United States' pursuit of Information Warfare—certainly if the concep tis carried to its ultimate logic—will require fundamental changes in how we understand conflict and the appropriate responses of our society to it. In fact, the changes that might be required could be so great as to raise a legitimate issue of not only whether we can but even of whether we *should* make them, the challenges of Information Warfare notwithstanding. Does our society want to be the sort that is adept at the degree and types of control of information that some of the more enthusiastic advocates of Information Warfare seem to presume?

This brings us to the arrow's *shaft*—national will. Advocates of Information Warfare must discipline themselves to assure that the overal concept—or any particular aspects of it, even those under cover of heavy security classification—do not conflict with or exceed the imperatives of the national will and the crucial bond of trust between people and their government. The loss of this trust would obviously be the greatest Information Warfare disaster that can be imagined.

An Information Warfare concept that depends upon an unrealisticor warped perception of the national will, while possibly still maintaining its means thurst, will certainly lack appropriate vector, possibly even to the point of coming back to victimize those employing it. In judging how and to what degree specifics of Information Warfare employment are or are not commensurate with national will, it will alway sbe instructive to look at the factors portrayed in the graphic as the arrow's guiding *feathers*—culture, politics, economics, law, and infrastructure (all as perceived, assumed and subscribed to by society). If a concept runs against the reality or, as importantly, the society's perception of any of these determine factors, it must be regarded as highly risky. Again, overreliance upon heavy security classification (or, for that matter, name changes such as the now increasingly heard reference to "Information Dominance") to protect a concept from the extent to which it might run against the social grain can only exacerbate the possibility and potential consequences of its failure.

THE ARROW'S IMPLICATIONS

Those who are currently responsible for Information Warfare initiatives and also those who are advocating particular ideas within the concept might do well to consider how their initiatives and ideas play to this graphic. Is the arrow's head conceptually sound? Does it coherently reflect perspectives from the lowest to the highest intellectual level of conflict? Does the shaft reflect a national will adequate to support the concept? (For example, what legal accommodations of Information Warfare might the society need to be prepared to accept?) Do the feathers sufficiently reflect reality and also societal perceptions for the idea to proceed on its intended trajectory? If not, might the concept turn on its perpetrators? If so, how?

Information Warfare and Employment Doctrine

Even if fairly conservatively applied, the Information Warfare concept will require highly integrated, holistic employment throughout the policy>strategy>campaign>tactics/technology spectrum of perspectives which must exceed anything our current military culture and structure has ever demonstrated to date. (Again, if, as is implied in the narrower articulations of the conept, Information Warfare remains confined to the tactical level and middle/lower rungs of the operational perspective— such as during the Gulf War—one might ask what is to differentiate Information Warfare from what are now more or less conventionally held Counter Command and Control concepts.[2]) Without such a high degree of conceptual integration, the concept is certain to founder in its practical employment for lack of coherence.

As with all forms of military employment, the key to coherence in Information Warfare will be effective *doctrine.* In addition to the several interdependent perspectives portrayed by the arrow, this doctrine—and the structures and procedures it implies—will have to acknowledge Information Warfare also to include three highly interdependent spheres of competition with adversaries of the United States. These are (1) the capacity for offensive action against an opponent's (or opponents') decision-making structures and processes; (2) protection of our own capabilities to make and effect decisions; and, perhaps less obvious, (3) the capacity to create and use information for our own purposes more effectively than adversaries can create and use information for their purposes. In regard to the latter, there will often be substantial situationally and culturally dictated differences between the ways and degrees in and to which the adversary depends upon information and the pattern of our own dependence on it.

Underlying all of these relationships, and adding to their maddeningly subtle complexities is a curious but unavoidable irony that is implicit to the Information Warfare concept: i.e., that the United States must develop very sophisticated and complex means for attacking adversaries' typically far less developed information/decision structures while still further having to protect our own highly developed infrastructure from relatively simple—but potentially grievous—threats.

THE OFFENSIVE SPHERE

Of the three competitive spheres, the heavy preponderance of attention currently given Information Warfare seems certainly to focus on the concept's offensive potentials. Not only does this reflect the U.S. military's traditional affinity for the offense, it also probably reflects the fact that offensive concepts are less fettered by limitations of established U.S. information practice, infrastructure, and process.

An already observable feature of this is the tendency for Information Warfare responsibilities—even seemingly operational ones—to migrate into organizations that are part of—or which are at least heavily involved with—the intelligence community (especially its SIGINT components). These are organizations that, at least in theory, are most suited to assessing targets for Information Warfare.

How these intelligence-focused organizations will handle the inherent tension between the natural intelligence inclidnation to exploit enemy information for its intelligence potential and the operators' natural inclination to destroy or disrupt enemy information sources and flows is likely to become a major doctrinal (as well as a bureaucratic political) issue. (A cynic from outside the intelligence community might see something here akin to the intelligence fox being put in charge of the Information Warfare henhouse.) However that issue might eventually play out, the necessary doctrinal responsibility and authority to assure that offensive applications accord with all levels of conflict perspective—technological and tactical up through the policy level—are sure to be demanding ones and to require concepts of organization and process for which there is little precedent.

THE PROTECTIVE SPHERE

The protective (i.e., defensive) aspects of the Information Warfare concept are even more difficult to handle—doctrinally, structurally, and procedurally. This is because convenience and operational efficacy in the handling of information usually imply vulnerabilities in the information and decision-making processes which can be fairly readily assessed and exploited/interfered with by an adversary.

Strong doctrinal guidance will be required to direct the IW concept through the maze of "either/or" issues that this tension between general security and immediate operational efficacy must inevitably raise. Once again, whether a community which is heavily imbued with an intelligence and security perspective can adequately define, let alone resolve, such operational issues remains an important question. It promises to present a perpetual revisit of issues directly akin to the old Vietnam-era contention between operators and intelligence regarding whether enemy ground control intercept (GCI) sites were best knocked out ("killed") or preserved for intelligence monitoring.

THE COMPETITIVE-USE-OF-INFORMATION SPHERE

As complex as these first two competitive spheres of the Information War concept are, they pale in difficulty in comparison to the third—that of the relative effectiveness of our own information handling and decision-making structures and processes.[3] This is where sublt asymmetries between our own objectives, capabilities, and information dependencies and those of our adversaries, if not readily recognized and taken into account, can wreak havoc.

It might be useful to characterize the situation as follows: We must alway sbe prepared to see ourselves as highly sophisticated "cyber-warriors" who might eventually need to be able to attack and defend against enemies much of our own kind. But we need more immediately the capacity to attack and defend against the equivalent of clever Information Age "neanderthals" who are less dependent upon sophisticated information means than are we, but who had adequate sophistication to understand and means to exploit that fact.

Even without considering direct attacks against each other's information/decision capacities notwithstanding, the effective use of information to make timely appropriate decisions is a highly complex proposition. Again, it is a challenge primarily of intellect. It is only secondarily one of technology.

Viewed in this sense, the Command and Control process must be seen as one too profound to be left to those who are merely expert in its technical means—i.e., "communicators," computer specialists, experts in the technologies of information, and the like who in our military culture are most closely identified with the means and processes of Command and Control. To relegate the C2 information/decision-making process to the technical perspectives of these specialists would be uncomfortably analogous to having the telephone company install a telephone and then expecting them to tell you what to say on it. The best of C2 technology and technology architectures cannot substitute for the conceptual and intellectual quality of the decisions they support. Similarly, mere sophistication in specific technical endeavors cannot substitute for the ability needed by Information Warfare decision-makers to achieve great degrees of situation awareness under any circumstance and to deftly exercise similarly great degree of holistically formed judgment.

To achieve the sophistication, coherence, and effectiveness necessary for the awareness and judgment required for Information Warfare will require the U.S. military culture to accept at least two conceptual distinctions with which it naturally has trouble.

First, the military must be able to better distinguiah between "efficiency" and "effectiveness" in order to be sure that, in regard to a specific situation or objective, it is not doing the wrong thing well. The need to make such distinctions requires a great effort in developing new—i.e., essentially non-attritively based—measures of merit by which to gauge the new kinds of effectiveness which the Information Warfare concept implies.

Second, Information Warfare requires sophisticated distinctions to be made between hierarchical levels of the cognitive process by which data and information contribute to effective decisions. This is a process which Information Warfare seeks to degrade for the enemy and to preserve and enhance for ourselves. For IW purposes at least, chief among these hierarchical distinctions are those between "awareness" (the lowest level of cognition), "knowledge," and "understanding." One can be aware of something, but not know its specifics. Similarly, one can know something, even very well, but not understand its full implications, especially as they impact and are impacted by specific circumstances.

For example, the West knew a lot about the Soviet Union; but as it turned out, our knowledge far exceeded what we actually understood about it. Similarly, we knew a lot about the North Vietnamese, but there was much we did not understand. An institutional subscription to Information Warfare must be understood to require an intellectual commitment to recognize and act upon these distinctions in terms of doctrine, organization, and intellectual selection/preparation of personnel.

The two principal objectives in Information Warfare must be (1) to degrade adversaries' capacity for understanding their own circumstances, our circumstances, and the circumstances that affect all sides while preserving and enhancing our own capacity for such understanding; and (2) to degrade adversaries' capacities to make effective use of whatever correct understandings they might achieve andto preserve and enhance our own capacities in this regard. As in earlier (i.e., pre-Cold War) history, future conflicts could well be multilateral, with alliances transitory, brief, partial, and calculated often only for the most fleeting advantage. These are yet further practical complications which Information Warfare advocates must directly confront in assessing the rigors of competitive situation awareness and judgment by which Information Age conflicts will be decided.

Achieving and preserving the advantages that will accrue in winning such a competition will be fundamental to success in the future global security competition that is likely to evolve. As such, Information Warfare cannot be pursued as something "exotic" and separate from the mainstream of the command, control, and employment of military forces. Therefore, the ultimate Information Warfare question is this: Is the U.S. national security structure capable of the intellectual and doctrinal suppleness required to pursue an *implicit* set of concerns and issues using highly calculated *specific* means to achieve *explicit* but *coherent* objectives?

Yet again, whether or not the limitations of our previous military experience and the resulting U.S. national security/military culture and intellectual style that it has produced will permit us to effectively meet the doctrinal demands for conceptual and employment coherence which Information Warfare poses must at this point remain an open issue.

Conclusion

Obviously, the post-Cold War era, most notably the aspects of it that comprise the Information Age, requires a new approach to global security. Information Warfare is gaining considerable momentum as the conceptual vehicle with which the United States, especially the military, hopes to meet this challenge. However, the concept's far-reaching and complex implications dictate degrees of intellectual, structural, and procedural coherence that exceed by far anything that the modern U.S. national security and military structures have ever achieved in the past.

For this reason, an objective observer must remain skeptical—if also hopeful—about Information Warfare's historical viability as a new global security for the United States. However, that said, it seems that the only thing more difficult than readying ourselves for Information Warfare would be to conceive of an alternative to it. The Information Age seems to present us with no choice but to pursue Information Warfare wisely and well. It is a concept that is exceedingly subtle in all of its aspects except those of the consequences of failure in its practice.

John Rothrock directs SRI International's Center for Global Strategic Planning. A retired (1990) USAF colonel, his last military position was as a senior fellow in strategy at the National Defense University. While assigned to headquarters of the former USAF Security Service (USAFSS) in the mid 1970s, Rothrock was one of those who developed the early concepts which later evolved into the USAF's Electronic Combat (EC) program. Later, as Chief of Intelligence Planning for the Air Force (1984-1987), Rothrock conceived and initiated USAF's Rapid Application of Airpower (RAAP) situation awareness and targeting support program. He joined SRI after retirement, and has focused since then on a variety of private sector and government projects. These have included work on Information Warfare, post-Cold War space policy, changing global power relationships, and geostrategic implications of various technology trends.

1. Les Aspin, Secretary of Defense, *Annual Report to the President and the Congress.* January 1994, pp. 227-228.
2. This is not to imply that we have now finally adequately developed our Counter Command and Control concepts and capabilities, even at the tactical and lower operational levels. To appreciate the full complexity and potential/implications of information con-

flict on those and also higher planes, see especially V. V. Druzhinin and D. S. Kontorov, *Concept, Algorithm, and Decision* (Moscow: Voinizdat, 1972). This is one of the USAF's "Soviet Military Thought" translation series. Counter C2 and Information Warfare concepts that are not rooted in appreciation of issues raised by Druzhinin and Kontorov probably should be held intellectually suspect. (However, it is not necessary to agree with the authors' decidedly Soviet conclusions about many specific issues.) For more recent, perhaps even deeper discussion of information and its use/manipulation, see also Keith Devlin, *Logic and Information* (Cambridge University Press, 1991). For a less theoretical treatment applicable to the tactical and operational levels, see as well Rothrock, "Counter Command and Control in Conceptual Perspective," *Air University Review*, January-February 1980. This article, while dated in its focus on the Soviet adversary, explores several conceptual issues which probably still warrant consideration.

3. It is in recognition of the complexities that this section addresses that the National Defense University has designated the curriculum it intends to address these issues as a curriculum in "Information-based Warfare." Others are also coming more frequently to use this term to capture the full complexity of the concept.

Export Control as a Proactive Defensive Information Warfare Mechanism

Winn Schwartau

Originally published in Alan Campen, Douglas Dearth, and R. Thomas Goodden (eds.), Cyberwar: Security, Strategy and Conflict in the Information Age *(AFCEA Press, 1996).*

Information Warfare in a commercial or military model is generally categorized as either offensive or defensive, but one can argue for the inclusion of a third category, Proactive Defensive Information Warfare (PDIW), which contains both offensive and defensive characteristics.

Offensive Information Warfare would consist of specifically offensive actions to deactivate opposition infrastructure, ability to communicate, and ability to collect, transmit, or use information. It well might involve the use of passive data collection (insidiousness) through any available means, or the use of mis/disinformation, or any of a number of other approaches which are outlined elsewhere in this book.

Defensive Information Warfare would include countermeasures to defeat any offensive actions on the part of known or unknown adversaries. Hardening of missile silos against secondary EMP effects of a nuclear attack certainly fits into this category: the defensive goal being to maintain availability of an information system to permit an appropriate response. On a smaller, less cataclysmic scale, the use of Tempest shielding to prevent remote eavesdropping of spurious information from information systems is certainly defensive in nature. And so is the use of sophisticated encryption and key management techniques to keep data transmissions and storage media free from breaches of confidentiality and integrity threats.

PDIW techniques, though, do not cleanly fall into either mode, although a case could be made along either line. Such appears to be the case when export control mechanisms such as ITAR and COCOM are employed. A compelling case can be made for this third category to be actively used to protect U.S. military and commercial interests. As we shall see, IW and PDIW are symmetrical, and similar techniques can be used against our own infrastructure by foreign Information Warriors.

ITAR and COCOM export restrictions are intended to keep so-called "sensitive technology" out of the hands of certain policy-chosen third parties. (It is the not the intent of this paper to identify those individuals, groups, or nation-states; these will change from time to time as geopolitical and econo-technical conditions evolve. We will only refer to them for discussion's sake as potential adversaries.) Nonetheless, the commercial sector has made consistent arguments over the last decade, and most notably since the end of the Cold War, that certain export restrictions have inherent points of failure, and thus our export policies should be altered to reflect new realities in a global market.

1. Much of the U.S.-restricted technology is available anyway from foreign companies who may not adhere to U.S. export controls and laws. Therefore, why bother with export controls over such items?
2. History has shown that many restricted export technology regulations have been easily bypassed by less-than-scrupulous manufacturers and through multi-pathed distribution channels.
3. U.S. Customs (and customs of other countries) does not have the ability to perform 100 percent inspections, and often the technology is beyond their scope of expertise to make a determination.
4. Some restricted export technology is only restricted in its final assembled form, thereby permitting legal export of subsystems and components to the potential enemy, wherein the final "export-restricted" product is assembled.
5. American companies have argued that based upon the holes in export policy and enforcement, many export regulations are simply ineffective.
6. Some U.S. companies further argue that the loss to the American economy in import revenues and domestic employment is a greater threat than the export of the technology itself.

This debate has gone on in various arenas for years, but as global availability of advanced fundamental technology proliferates, the efficacy of export restrictions has been further weakened.

The most visible debate to reach the front pages of the conventional media has been over the export control of encryption. For example, Bruce Scheier's book, *Applied Cryptography,* can be exported without restriction, even though it contains detailed source code listings of popular, unclassified encryption algorithms. However, my recent book, *The Complete Internet Toolkit,* is restricted from export because it contains a CD-ROM with almost 70 cryptographic programs.

Detractors of the current export policy maintain that the policy does not inhibit export of restricted technology, and indeed may call more attention to the particular value of the technology. A similar failure can be observed with the export control of Data Encryption Standard (DES) under ITAR, even though DES has been a U.S. public domain standard since 1976. According to a study by the Software Publishers Association, despite attempts at export control, approximately 50 percent of the world's DES products are not made in the United States. What further disturbs U.S. manufacturers is not only the loss of international market share. When a U.S. company uses a non-U.S. DES engine, it is free to import the raw components from countries such as Germany, Taiwan, and Japan, but is restricted from re-exporting them. In some cases, this has caused manufacturing and reassembly of these devices to be moved to non-U.S. soil, where export restrictions are more relaxed.

The emergence of the Internet adds more fuel to the argument that export controls are not effective. This has been borne out in the Justice Department's case against Phil Zimmermann and PGP, which the Department finally dropped.

The ostensible aim of cryptographic export control is to make the U.S. intelligence community's job easier. Given that the NSA is the electronic listening post as the interests of the U.S. dictate, they understandably want to make their job as easy as possible. Intercepting signal transmissions is only one part of their task. The other is to make sense of them. Thus, the more cryptographically encoded transmissions they encounter, the more time, money, and resources they must expend to fulfill their task. It is completely within reason, from their perspective then, to actively promote and lobby for adherence to ITAR in the area of cryptography.

This is clearly one area in which NSA has already taken a PDIW stance. NSA wants to make its job easier, so it expends effort to encourage cryptographic export, but only under certain conditions.

When a cryptographic engine is under export control review for either specific foreign customers or a general license, NSA acts as a reviewing counsel to the Departments of State and Commerce. In some cases, the export is completely denied. Intuitively, such decisions would likely turn on the relative difficulty of decoding such encrypted messages, but the details of export permission/denial are not publicly available. In other cases, though, the NSA will confer with the manufacturer/designer and ask that certain changes to the encryption engine be made.

Some manufacturers allege that the changes instituted by the NSA are designed with two goals in mind, both of which neatly fit into the PDIW concept: (1) changes to the algorithm and encryption engine to make decryption of intercepted messages using that engine simpler; and (2) changes that label the encrypted message with a "flag" so that, upon interception, the NSA knows which process to employ for rapid decryption.

This second approach is subtle, but reminiscent of other signal interception techniques. No manufacturer has suggested that, upon examination of its source code, the NSA alterations actually place a header or tail on the transmission which says, "I am encryption technique XV367, use decryption process F618." That is too obvious a trap, which would not meet the subtler needs of the capable Information Warrior or serious adversary.

Rather, private crypto code analysts maintain that the NSA changes create a cryptographic "signature" which becomes part of the message. Marshall McLuhan's "medium is the message" prediction comes patently to life with such a tactic. When a signal is intercepted and discovered to be somehow encoded, through the use of sophisticated real-time analysis tools the code-breakers determine which encryption algorithm was used. Then, if they so choose, they employ the inverse as a crypto-analytic attack upon the message. This can also be viewed as a subtle form of steganography: the inclusion of a private communication within an open one such that the casual observer cannot determine the meaning of the hidden information, or even that such information exists.

This approach makes total sense, since NSA has spent extensive resources on electromagnetic eavesdropping techniques from keyboards, monitor screens, and printers. They have prepared what are called Digram tables for a myriad of printers, each of which exhibits specific electromagnetic patterns. Thus, when U.S. intelligence places a covert eavesdropping device into an opposition's IT equipment, based upon the device's known patterns, analysis of the actual signal contents becomes an exercise in computing horsepower.

This is an ideal example of PDIW—permit the export of restricted technology but insure that within that exported commodity, a back door is in place which nullifies much of its original purpose.

But these "secret" techniques are fairly open, and the NSA's real or perceived policies, are (rightly or wrongly) deemed to be what their detractors claim them to be: thinly disguised attempts at restricting export of technology through fear, loathing, and disinformation. Therefore, the quality and integrity of NSA-approved exportable U.S. crypto products is suspect to the majority of industrialized nations. A secondary goal is thus achieved: imbue distrust into the approved export products, which will diminish their use.

I suggest that a backlash effect can occur, where independent cryptographic efforts from other countries develop ever harder to crack codes. Only the NSA knows for sure.

As a vehicle of PDIW, NSA control over cryptographic export restriction is like having Ronald McDonald pick the world's best hamburger. However, from a strategic policy standpoint, it makes a lot of sense. And so do other similar instances.

In the late 1960s, Poland wanted to purchase a new telephone system. Obviously, AT&T, with its latest generation of telephone switching equipment, wanted to win the megamillion-dollar contract. However, since Poland was a Soviet-bloc country, export of such technology to it was restricted. However, a deal was reached, a critical part of which the Poles were ignorant. The AT&T equipment would receive export permission if certain alterations to the switching system were made. Poland would never know the difference, since all apparent systemic functionality would be unimpaired.

What was added to the Poland-bound telephone switch was the equivalent of a remote controlled self-destruct switch. The goal was simple and effective. According to knowledgeable sources within the NSA, AT&T made certain modifications to the system that would permit us, the good guys, to remotely access and subsequently shut down the telecommunications infrastructure controlled by this equipment. The hypothetical thinking was that in case of a Soviet incursion into Western Europe through Poland, we (U.S./NATO) could shut down land-based telecommunications in a microsecond.

Similarly, the U.S. military used the media as an unwitting participant in an active mis/disinformation campaign after the Gulf War. Government representatives claimed we used a printer-based computer virus to bring down the Iraqi air defense systems. What we really did was to place a homing beacon within the chips to provide the military with enhanced high technology targets.

A similar approach has been taken with North Korea. Although under severe ITAR and COCOM restriction, North Korea has been able to build a formidable military machine. One of their main military processing centers is run by an old IBM Series 370 mainframe with an old, presumably altered version of the company's operating system. It is claimed that we have the means to deactivate that center through at least two back door channels in the event of heightened readiness or imminent conflict.

The IBM AS-400 series computers are also export restricted to North Korea, but the country has apparently been able to acquire up to a few hundred of them, allegedly from a distribution point in India. These machines are directly tied to the offensive capabilities of that country, and thus of strategic value. Specifically, a denial of service assault upon them would be a prime means to deactivate much of North Korea's military power.

Certainly a very clean, nonlethal (and politically acceptable) method of launching a successfully denial of service attack against these machines is preferable to physical assaults. Again, with the unwitting cooperation of the Indian government, ITAR export permits allowed the export of this advanced technology to India, from where (the planning assumed), the machines would soon find a new home in North Korea.

But these machines are different. They have been chipped with special NSA-manufactured silicon devices that are designed to fail upon command. Either single or multiple silicon critical components, which are presumably difficult to acquire and replace, are carefully chosen as chipping targets. The exact details are likely classified, but the general technique uses a remote high frequency "trigger" signal that the modified chip "hears." Conceptually no more complex than a child's remote control device, the target chip fails, causing a systemic denial of service event. In the event of conflict, the U.S. military obviously gains a significant advantage.

Let's briefly consider how similar PDIW mechanisms can present the United States with both opportunity and risk. From a military and national intelligence standpoint, these techniques meet a number of key criteria:

- Conceptually simple
- Highly efficient
- Reasonably "safe" (nonlethally speaking)
- Insidious and extremely difficult to detect
- Highly targetable

Such techniques will continue to be used more extensively in PDIW for the above reasons. But we now can ask ourselves, just how far beyond the domain of the military and conventional national security should we take this tack? Third-world countries do not have the resources to develop their own technology and must source it from first-world nations, most of whom subscribe to ITAR or COCOM-like policies.

If listening devices, tracking devices, trapdoor software, or self-destruct mechanisms are built into both critical and noncritical U.S.-manufactured export systems (with or without the assistance of the original manufacturer) at what point does the target potential adversary suspect that all U.S.-sourced equipment is so configured? Will this approach cause a shift to purchase of non-U.S. equipment because the equipment is modified for PDIW or merely because it is suspected to be so altered? If so, what effect does this have on export revenues, domestic employment, and strategic advantage?

Similar tactics can be used on greater quantities of U.S. exports, including noncritical items, so that even offshore assembly of systems would be infected with any of a number of embedded weaknesses. For example, if high-speed line printers were outfitted with an electromagnetic detector to read the solenoid signatures as printing occurred, the printer output could be sent to a convenient listening post. The Russians allegedly used this approach (with a cruder implementation) by bugging State Department teletype machines in Moscow in the early 1980s. Upon receipt of the signals, a digram analysis is performed for a real-time reading of the machine's output.

When one considers that the French put listening devices in first class seats of Air France airplanes as part of their national economic intelligence program, we should consider what technologies are available to the United States for similar intelligence gathering or denial of service capability.

On the risk side, the U.S. private sector and government are potentially vulnerable to similar strategies. Much of the technology used in both commercial and classified systems are sourced from the Far East, even though integration and deployment are domestic. Low-level silicon implementations of common functionality are bought on price: they are commodity items. What happens when an insidiously designed piece of hardware or software destined for a critical system (private or government) is remotely triggered to fail? Or if the MTBF is built right in as a form of denial of service through preplanned obsolescence? Worth a second or two of condsideration.

The symmetrical nature of export-control PDIW becomes apparent when we are seen as the potential victim. Commercially available keyboards have been found with preprogrammed silicon chips that insert nasty messages into word processors. Funny? Maybe not so funny in many applications.

The risks are becoming more defined as our reliance upon technology increases daily. The risks to "our side" also increase if our trading partners fear that we may use such techniques on them. There is no clean, simple solution on the horizon.

Nonetheless, part and parcel of quality systems design and security considerations should be an analysis of the defensive postures needed to thwart exported information technology-based PDIW assaults against the United States. The solutions to this conundrum are not simple, implying a greater expenditure of resources to develop identification methods, and then expending the time to perform thorough inspections.

Since such export-control PDIW techniques give us potential advantages as well as point out potential weaknesses, policy must be developed for export controls as they apply to PDIW, and policies must be developed to provide additional protection to our own private and government infrastructures.

Information Warfare Delphi: Characteristics of Information Warfare

Captain Roger D. Thrasher, USAF

In the last few years, Information Warfare has become a widely discussed topic within the Department of Defense and in the civilian world. But anytime you wish to have meaningful discussion on a particular issue, it is vital to have common terms of reference. Such terms serve as a lingua franca and provide a convenient way to converse using shared concepts. Without such terms, communication is often difficult and consensus even more problematic. Such is the situation with Information Warfare. Although most everyone uses the term and many have proposed (differing) definitions for Information Warfare, there is little agreement about the specifics of the term. Alternative terms such as cyberwar, netwar, information-based war, knowledge-based war, command and control warfare, information age war, etc., while possibly more precise, have not yet caught on in general use. So it has proven difficult to settle on one technically, doctrinally, and politically correct definition for Information Warfare.

It may be useful to approach the issue obliquely by discussing the unique aspects of Information Warfare by collecting observations from diverse viewpoints. An attempt was made to do this (as part of a larger thesis research effort) by convening a group of Information Warfare experts to consider, among other topics, the essential nature of information war. This research was conducted using a modification of the Delphi research technique with the following participants from a variety of backgrounds:

- Al Campen; Manager, AFCEA International Press; editor of *The First Information War*
- Vice Admiral Arthur Cebrowski, USN; Joint Staff; Director, J-6
- Peter Cochrane; British Telecom; Director, British Telecom Research Lab
- Dr. Fred Cohen; Management Analytics; author of *Protection and Security on the Information Superhighway*
- James Dunnigan; author of *Digital Soldiers*
- Lieutenant Commander Robert Garigue; Director Intelligence, Se-

579

curity and Operations Automation, Canada; Deputy Program Director, Joint and Strategic Information Systems

- Dr. Fred Giessler; National Defense University; Information Warfare Course Director
- Brigadier General David Gust; U.S. Army; Program Executive Officer, Intelligence and Electronic Warfare
- James Hazlett; SAIC; Senior Analyst
- Ken King; Digital Equipment Corporation; Director, External Research Group Dr. Fred Levien; Naval Postgraduate School; Chair, Information Warfare Academic Group
- Dr. Martin Libicki; National Defense University; author of *The Mesh and the Net*
- Commander Michael Loescher; U.S. Navy; Office of Deputy Assistant Secretary of the Navy (C4I/IW), Director, Information Warfare
- Larry Merritt; Air Force Information Warfare Center; Technical Director Dr. David Probst; Concordia University; Professor of Computer Science
- Winn Schwartau; Interpact; author of *Information Warfare: Chaos on the Electronic Superhighway*
- Robert Steele; CEO, Open Source Solutions
- Colonel David Todd; USAF/XOXT; Chief of Technical Plans

One of several questions put to the Delphi members was about the defining characteristics of Information Warfare. While perhaps a deceptively simple query, the underlying purpose was to elicit discussion on the unique factors of Information Warfare—what makes this type of warfare different from, say, maneuver or attrition warfare.

Campen: The risk in seeking a definition is the temptation to look for correlation with the past, rather than defining differences. I have seen definitions of IW that are useless because they encompass all human endeavor. I argue that the definition of IW must be severely circumscribed if it is to be useful in assessing the impact on policy, doctrine, functions, and organization on civil or military. We must seek out what is different from the past. I submit that difference is dependency upon vulnerable electronic technology. I limit IW to information (data) in electronic form and the hardware and software by which it is created, modified, stored, processed, and moved about. The defining characteristics are dependency upon and vulnerability of electronic information systems. Example: Psyops conducted via printed leaflets is not IW, but radio broadcasts or the electronic manipulation of TV images is. The physical destruction of a telephone exchange is not IW (telegraph lines were cut in the Civil War and submarine cables in WWI), but disabling a switch with a virus is IW.

Cebrowski: The underlying character of Information Warfare is the proliferation of information-based technologies and their associated impact on society and, by extension, on the bedrock issues of national security in the modern age. In warfighting, information-based technologies transcend the target sets of information, information-based processes, and information systems.

Cochrane: The defining characteristic in Information Warfare is when information (in any form, so that includes ideas and philosophies) is supplied, or obstructed, with the aim of causing the information user to make a bad decision, or to confuse/overload their communication or decision-making processes. Examples:

- Knowing what your enemy does not
- Confusing the enemy with false information
- Damaging the information capability access of the opponent or denying him access [to] his own information by jamming communications or hacking computer systems and changing or deleting data
- Interception of communications
- Use of disinformation: propaganda and cultural infiltration

Cohen: The broadest common definition I have been able to get together is: Conflict in which information or information technology is the weapon, the target, the objective, or the method. From now on, I will use IT to indicate "information or information technology."

Dunnigan: Attacking and defending the ability to transmit information.

Garigue: The first thing that comes to mind is the realization that Information Warfare is a consequence of a new and emerging sociotech structure. This emergence is not homogeneous throughout the world. Whereas some western societies are moving rapidly into it, others have not yet started. Modern societies are all presently engaged in building and riding a glass highway. With this in mind we have to face the fact that more and more of our social, economic, political, and cultural transactions are digital in nature and all of them are computer-mediated, which means that in an information society no meaningful event can happen between individuals or organizations without computers and networks. We will have to fulfill our human interactions and commitments through our computerized social networks. We presently, and naively, place a lot of trust in these computer intermediaries that tell us the state of our complex systems. These systems may be cities, financial markets, health, wealth, production, or even distribution. All these sociotech systems are subject to computer control. Computerized networks bridge decision-makers with an ever-increasing array of sensors and effectors that monitor and intercede for us and help us in governing our complex environments. This trend will continue accelerating wherever efficiencies in systems can be found. As with any human-constructed artifact, there are flaws, failings, and limitations. These new, efficient, networked sociotech societies are also, and will always be, flawed. Control over these systems is not more direct and local. Now it is remote and distributed. In open societies, authority to control is conferred by groups onto individuals via legitimate processes in accordance with common values and beliefs. But groups whose goals differ and whose objectives are at odds will try to impose control by force of arguments or might. So now in computer-mediated societies as control has been somewhat centralized within the network layer, we see that there will be a clash of wills for control of that logical space. The fight for control of that space is called Information Warfare.

Giessler: Competing and conflicting information, control, and communication in complex adaptive systems—which all have teleological goals with the ultimate being survival. All systems are involved in Information Warfare—the only question is do they do anything about it? They can be passive or active. IW is all about decisions and the use of information, energy, and material resources to offset disturbances that may drive your system away from the attainment of its objectives—especially the one about survival.

Gust: Definition—after two years of discussion, the Army's Training and Doctrine Command (TRADOC) published FM 100-6, Info Operations. We argued and discussed the definition and who is in charge, even sought and rejected Office of the Secretary of Defense (OSD) staff advice on the definition. I do not believe there is universal agreement on it yet.

Hazlett: Information Warfare is conflict between parties where information or information systems are used to attack and defeat the enemy or when the enemy's use of, or access to, information is attacked.

King: Information Warfare is a conflict between two parties where information technology is the primary means of obtaining a defensive or offensive advantage.

Levien: One of the most critical of these is the fact that it is so imprecise. It obliterates any of the past definitional boundaries of "What is an act of war?" "What is war?" "Who is the enemy?" "Where or which is the enemies' territory or country of national origin?" This now much more difficult assessment of responsibility places new limits on how the military can react against a perceived threat to the country. In fact, it becomes painfully difficult to determine an allowable course of action for a military officer to take when he (or she) is faced with the enormous body of U.S. law that (rightfully) limits and restricts those actions that the military can take against U.S. citizens. In today's world, these same U.S. citizens are inextricably coupled via communications, business association, commercial activity, and just plain vanilla personal interactions with foreign (international?) entities both friendly and hostile. This can and most often does present a legal nightmare for the average military officer to sort out what actions he is permitted to take in this IW environment.

Libicki: Information Warfare is any activity motivated by the need to alter the information streams going to the other side and protect one's own. These range from physical and radioelectronic attack on both systems and sensors (or associated support systems), to cryptography, attacks on computers, and psychological operations.

Loescher: What is new is that information creates and splinters the battle space, enables and defines the killing zone, and provides the means to execute the principles of war. I prefer to call this "war in the info age," which I think is a genuine revolution. In the Navy, the term *info warfare* is being used evolutionarily by some communities to preserve and improve the past—better EW (electronic warfare), better cryptology, etc.

Merritt: This is a good question. These days, there is a lot of press being given to equating IW to network attack (offensive and defensive). In my view, this is a very narrow interpretation and really is not doing the community justice in really working the problem. I think this is why we are now seeing more reference to other terms such as *info dominance* or *info operations.* In my view, IW consists of any action to exploit or affect an adversary's ability to gain a true picture of the battle space or to execute command and control of their forces. Also includes all the same activities associated with protecting our own capabilities. This truly brings in all aspects of EW: network attack, node analysis, intell, recon and surveillance, etc., both terrestrial and space-based. This broad interpretation has been the cause of much controversy that has crossed traditional ricebowls and caused the community to concentrate on particular aspects of the problem.

Probst: Information-based warfare is that branch of warfare information technology that supports two basic pillars of the revolution in military affairs; viz. (1) dominant battlespace knowledge and (2) integrated battlespace management, including pre-engagement battlespace preparation, precision force (including just-in-time strike), and precision logistics. To be effective, these pillars require major advances in modeling and simulation, which in turn require (1) advanced control theory for automated full-spectrum strategic decision-making, precision scheduling, and other information functions; and (2) high-performance data assimilation and analysis for data-intensive predictive modeling and simulation.

Because it relies on high-performance computers and communications, information-based warfare can be disrupted. Defensive Information Warfare tries to make sure that this cannot happen to our forces. Offensive Information Warfare—about which I have some reservations—tries to disrupt the computer-and-communications-based C4ISR (Command, Control, Communications, Computers, Intelligence, Surveillance, and Reconnaissance) of the adversary.

Definitions aside, we can see three embryos of warfare information technology today. These are:

- total situational awareness → integrated battlespace management
- network security → defensive Information Warfare
- the USAF Captain, using SIPRNET (Secret Internet Protocol Router Network), who subverted the Navy's Atlantic Fleet command in September 1995 → offensive Information Warfare

The following is an equivalent vanilla base line for Information Warfare:

- High-performance information-based warfare with dominant battlespace knowledge and precision force—including offensive Information Warfare—will alter the strategic, operational, and tactical levels of war (i.e., it will change the appearance of combat).
- Information infrastructures are now part of the logistics tails of all armed forces, and as such require careful defense.
- Conversely, one may consider degrading the information systems that enhance the military capabilities of the adversary.

Schwartau: I maintain that true Information Warfare is the use of information and information systems as weapons against target information and information systems. I eliminate the call for or use of any bombs or bullets in true info war. IW can attack individuals, organizations, or nation-states (or spheres of influence) through a wide variety of techniques:

- Confidentiality compromise
- Integrity attacks
- Denial of service
- Psyops
- Dis/Misinformation, media, etc.

Most clearly, though, the distinctive feature of pure IW is that it can be so easily waged against a civilian infrastructure in contrast to a military one. This is a new facet of war, where the target may well be the economic national security of an adversary. In addition, though, we have distributed capability to wage war. Today, a small band of antagonists can launch an IW offensive from behind their desks thousands of miles away; or a group of U.S. hackers might choose to declare war on another country, independent of any official U.S. sanction. The capabilities of IW is the issue: how much havoc can I rain down without resorting to bombs and bullets. "A lot" is the answer, and I'm not the only smart guy on the planet.

Steele: The defining characteristics of information are:

- Connectivity (all mediums)
- Content
- Coordination (standards, procurement)
- Communications and computational security
- Context (both cultural and substantive)

Information "warfare" is almost moot or an oxymoron. In this era, failing to be competitive in optimizing the above five aspects of information is tantamount to abdication. At a very simplistic level, Information Warfare can be thought of as an attack on any of the above five elements (e.g., denial of service or corruption of content). On the defensive side, again at a simplistic level, it can be considered in terms of continuity of operations. Unfortunately, our own DoD will never be a serious IW player until it figuresw out that collecting information, and the sensor-to-shooter interface, is the heart of information-based warfare operations.

Todd: With warfare in the information age, our ability to control and exploit the information battlespace will be as much an enabling factor in combined warfare as the ability to control and exploit the air and space battlespace to enable conventional combined terrestrial warfare in the industrial age. Note that I don't use the term *Information Warfare.* The challenge of warfare in the information age is more pervasive than the commonly thought of niches of Information Warfare. But within this category of IW falls our capabilities to attack an adversary's information function (regardless of means), the protection of our information functions (regardless of means), and that IW is a means, not an end.

Synthesis

First, most Delphi participants agreed that much of the current ado about Information Warfare is related to the exploding capabilities of information technology. Rapidly expanding dependence on information technologies is creating a situation where information processing, flows, and stores can be attacked to gain an advantage. But here is where divergence starts to occur. Some felt the focus should be on information technology itself as the method of information war. This posits that only attacking your enemy with nonphysical information technology-based methods constitutes true Information Warfare. Under this view, bombing an early warning radar would not be Information Warfare, while using malicious software to confuse the radar would be Information Warfare, even though the results in both instances might be the same.

Most participants, however, expanded the scope of Information Warfare to focus more generically on the concept of information itself. As historians are fond of pointing out, attacking an adversary's information functions is not new and is not necessarily waged with information technologies. What is important is not the form in which the information is processed, stored, or transmitted, but somehow attacking the actual content of the information. Nor is it important how the information was attacked. Thus, dropping leaflets to impact the mind of a frontline Iraqi soldier would be considered Information Warfare just as much as high-tech radio broadcasts aimed at that same soldier.

There were unique views expressed that merit further examination. One view is that Information Warfare constitutes any action which degrades the capability of the enemy commander's picture of the battle and prevents him from exercising effective command and control. This flavor of Information Warfare is called Command and Control Warfare (C2W) and has been initially designated as the military's battlefield implementation of Information Warfare. This is much more restrictive than the other definitions in that only the commander's information functions are targeted.

A final perspective expressed is that Information Warfare is simply a result of a new and emerging sociotech structure. This structure is characterized by the use of information technology to facilitate the day-to-day transactions of society and by the use of information technology to track the status of complex social and economic systems. Power and control in such a sociotech structure would be more diffuse and distributed and would reside within the network space. The fight for control of the sociotech structure via that space would be called Information Warfare.

Conclusion

Given the diversity of views expressed by the Delphi members, are there any common threads or integrating themes that can be drawn? One key theme is the new and growing dependence on information technology. We now may be able to target and attack the information functions of our adversaries in ways that were not possible until the widespread adoption of information technology. Thus, attacking our enemy's information and information technology vulnerabilities and protecting our own are the essence of Information Warfare. The new Joint Chiefs of Staff definition of Information Warfare takes this view: "Actions taken to achieve information superiority by affecting adversary information, information-based processes, information systems, and computer-based networks while defending one's own information, information-based processes, information systems, and computer-based networks."

The emphasis is on targeting enemy information functions while protecting our own, but does not include our own use of information or information technology for the enhancement of various warfare purposes. Also obvious is the prominence given to attacking and protecting information technologies such as information systems and computer networks.

One issue that remains is whether Information Warfare is also defined by the means used, by the target attacked, or by the purpose for attacking the target. The JCS definition states that the purpose of Information Warfare is information superiority. So if one attacks a computer-controlled drawbridge with a virus for the purpose of taking out that bridge, is that considered Information Warfare? The purpose was clearly not information superiority, although many would still label this an Information Warfare attack. Likewise, disabling a tank by disrupting its microprocessors with an EMP pulse could be considered a strike via Information Warfare means. Thus the sole emphasis on information superiority may be too exclusionary. While certainly information superiority is a major goal of Information Warfare, it can be argued that more traditional warfare purposes can also be served via attacks on vulnerable information technology. If one can disrupt the adversary's economic or warfare functions via attacks on the information technology that he uses to support those functions, then Information Warfare becomes one more means (as is physical destruction) to a particular political or military end (like interdiction, C2W, attrition, economic isolation, etc.).

In summary and at the risk of adding to the confusion of terms, one might break down the subjects of information and warfare into a simple taxonomy. At the top would be *information age warfare*. This term would be comprised of all the aspects of modern and near-future warfare. One of the main features of information age warfare would be *information-enhanced warfare*. This expression recognizes the revolutionary impact of information technology on all functions of war. Another facet would be the overworked term *Information Warfare* as the moniker for attacking an enemy's information functions while protecting one's own.

So is there now a better view of the essential elements of Information Warfare? The answer may be yes, but it is obvious that the full picture has not been revealed yet. The problem of overloading the term *Information Warfare* with different meanings still persists and is likely to for the immediate future.

17

Defense Before Defeat

"Why do today what you can put off till tomorrow."

—PROCRASTINATOR'S PLEDGE

"If we really, really, try, maybe we can ignore it."

—CUSTOMER SERVICE MOTTO

IF I'VE MADE IT sound like the Information Warrior has already won the war . . . well, that was not the intent. He hasn't won. Not yet. But he still *could* if our complacency remains as entrenched as it has been over the last decade and a half. The Information Warrior can be defeated if—and only if—we put our minds to it, and that will require a national effort like we have not seen in years.

We can defeat the Information Warrior. We can render his anti-social, anti-business, and anti-American endeavors futile, but it will take a serious effort on our part. The Information Warrior uses information as a weapon to further erode our personal privacy, and to gain competitive advantage. He uses our information infrastructure as a vehicle for and a target of his Information Weapons. But he can still be defeated.

Like any criminal, the Information Warrior is generally looking for an easy target. If he runs up against roadblocks, he will try to find another weakness until he gets what he wants. The Information Warrior will concentrate his efforts to find the one single weakness in our privacy or our information infra-structure that will permit him to widen the crack in the dike of our defenses. We should expect no less from him because it is in his best interests to do so. He will not pummel his head against the protected walls of Cyberspace when he knows that another open entryway is beckoning him.

The technology, the techniques, and the tools exist to defend against and defeat the Information Warrior. A myriad of companies offer products to protect against viruses, hackers, modem attacks, HERF Guns, and all the other tools in the arsenal of the Information Warrior. Given that the technology exists to protect ourselves on a personal, corporate, and national level, we should try to understand why we remain defenseless. Why has so little been done, and why have the available defensive technologies not been deployed to the extent they should have?

Two reasons—apathy and arrogance.

There is no escaping this fact. After World War II a policy on military defense of the United States and Western Europe was created to reflect the New World Order of 1945. We established that policy to prepare for our adversaries' capabilities *not their presumed intentions*, and today, we must establish a policy to defend our Cyberspace against our adversaries' capabilities, both in the immediate future and for the long term. But both apathy and arrogance stand in the way. I fear that as a result, we will wait until a computer Chernobyl befalls us before we take the threat of Information Warfare seriously.

On a corporate and national level, the danger of procrastination is potentially very dangerous. Thurow writes, "In crisis (Pearl Harbor) or in situations which can be made to look like crisis (Sputnik), Americans respond magnificently. Clear problems (Sputnik, Iraq's invasion of Kuwait) get clear, clean, well managed solutions. America is capable of claiming the twenty-first century for itself. The American problem is not winning—but forcing itself to notice that the game has changed—that it will have to play a new game by new rules with new strategies."[1]

Historians claim that the devastation at Pearl Harbor in

1941 need never have occurred. They maintain that we
received two warnings about an impending attack—one from
the activities of the Japanese at their embassies and from radio
interceptions of their military machine, the second from an
experimental radar system that was being tested in the Pacific.
The radar operator reported what appeared to him to be a
number of aircraft coming our way. Somewhere in the command structure, though, the belief was that the new fangled
radar contraption was not reliable. The brass assumed that the
signals were caused by faulty equipment and chose to ignore
the second warning.

The rest is history. But we're still not listening.

Procrastination is an addictive drug in which all but the
Felix Ungers of the world indulge at one time or another.
Incessant postponement catches up with us sooner or later,
generally at a much higher personal or financial cost. Procrastination is not healthy for this country. Consider the costs:

- Environmental messes—land fills, nuclear waste dumps,
  a disappearing ozone layer—get messier every day
- Failing or weak S&Ls dig themselves deeper and deeper
  holes
- The national deficit is skyrocketing

Each problem we choose to ignore only ends up costing us
more in the long run. We must not allow chaos in Cyberspace
to be added to the list, not when we have before us a way to
avoid the dangers and expenses of moving into Cyberspace
unprepared.

Adequate defenses against every cyberthreat are available.
Just as the technology for the offensive Information Warrior is
cheap and readily available, so the defensive techniques are
well known and available for the asking. Technology alone,
however, will not solve the underlying ailments affecting our
culture. Technology alone does not solve the issue of personal
privacy; technology alone does not solve the problems and
costs to this country caused by international industrial espio-

nage; technology alone does not protect us from a malicious attack against the American economic infrastructure. What is needed, what is absolutely necessary is a national policy which acknowledges the threat to all of us—individually and as a nation—while mapping out a plan for action.

As the Clinton administration prepares to launch us further into the Information Age, with their proposed National Information Infrastructure, one key ingredient is missing: an understanding that such easy access to information can be either good *or* bad. When he was a Tennessee senator, Vice President Albert Gore advocated an electronic superhighway which would tie together more and more computers through faster and denser electronic networks. Those highways are fraught with risks, specifically those of security and privacy.

Having said that, I still believe the National Information Infrastructure is a good idea. We need to walk into Cyberspace with our eyes open. We need to balance pragmatism with our utopian visions. What we need, more than anything, is a National Information Policy, one that will offer America the chance to lead the world into the next century. A policy that will allow us to design our future, not be blindsided by it.

Deterring Information Attacks

Martin C. Libicki, National Defense University

Opinions, conclusions, and recommendations, expressed or implied, are those of the author. They do not necessarily reflect the views of the National Defense University, the Department of Defense, or any other U.S. Government agency.

The many ways in which an information infrastructure of a nation can be defended against attack tend to sort themselves into three types of defense: denial, detection (with prosecution), and deterrence. *Denial* is simply building defenses into information systems so that attacks on them have few if any consequences that cannot be quickly reversed. Individual perpetrators may also be *detected* and subject to the full force of the law (if they can be found and, if necessary, extradited). *Deterrence* assumes that a nation (or similar entity) can be punished for sponsoring such an attack; it works by levying a comparable or greater punishment in return.

Denial and detection are straightforward in theory. No one seriously argues that computer systems should be vulnerable to attack and penetration. As for detection, most cases of hacker warfare are crimes and therefore merit appropriate punishment.[1]

Denial and detection may not be very satisfactory responses, however. Computer systems, some believe, are impossible, or at least very costly, to defend against a determined attack. By one theory, defenses are good up to a point; they can hold back casual attacks. Against full-scale attacks backed by the resources only a nation or similarly financed transnational criminal organization (TCO) can provide, they are less reliable. As for detection, the ease by which hackers can attack a system from anywhere around the globe without leaving virtual fingerprints suggest that the risks of punishment are low. Hackers supported by foreign governments may be detected but later hidden (by TCOs) or found but not extradited (by governments).

Therefore, many argue that deterrence ought to be part and parcel of a nation's information defense strategy. Indeed, according to a poll of Information Warfare experts conducted at a workshop hosted by Evidence Based Research,[2] over two thirds were strongly in favor of the proposition that "The United States [should] have a declarative policy about its response to Information Warfare attacks."

The term *deterrence,* and its cousin *graduated response,* may appear to be leftovers from the Cold War; to the extent that Information Warfare is considered an aspect of strategic warfare, they very well might be.

During the Cold War, the United States developed and adopted a policy of strategic nuclear deterrence; in essence, a warning that those who attack the United States could expect the same in return.[3] It is commonly believed (even if impossible to prove) that deterrence worked—at any rate the American homeland was never attacked by nuclear or conventional weapons. By analogy, analysts have wondered whether a similar strategy might ward off attacks on the nation's critical information systems.

This essay argues that an explicit deterrence strategy against attacks on the nation's information infrastructure is problematic—so much so that there seems little to be gained from making explicit any such policy. It is already widely understood that any state perpetrating harm to the American homeland can expect retaliation of some sort. After the Oklahoma City bombing, an early lead suggested a tie to radical Islamic states. The consensus in the Middle East was that the United States would retaliate in force were such a lead solidified by evidence. For instance, had Iran attacked an information system resulting in casualties (e.g., an unexpected FAA outage, a badly set switch in a rail system), similar retaliation by the United States would be in the offing. Iran might appear surprised that attacks which did not directly injure or kill humans would invite retaliation; but few would believe its protestations.

The United States has never made clear exactly how much harm resulting from a violence incident merits exactly how much retaliation. Sometimes, the identity of the perpetrator makes all the difference. What the United States did to Libya in 1986 would be highly risky applied to a nation with nuclear weapons (e.g., China) or one otherwise capable of causing great mischief (e.g., North Korea). By contrast, U.S. nuclear retaliatory policy was designed to be used against its most powerful foe, the Soviet Union, and could as easily have been used against lesser attackers.

Elements of Deterrence

Dr. Richard Hayes has outlined several prerequisites to the success of a deterrence strategy.[4] Three relate to the issue of explicit deterrence:

- The incident must be well defined.
- The identity of the perpetrator must be clear.
- The will and ability to carry out punishment must be believed (and cannot be warded off).

Two more relate to deterrence-in-kind:

- The perpetrator must have something of value at stake.
- The punishment must be controllable.[5]

In addition, as a third criterion, punishment ought to be proportional to the incident. To mete out a high level of punishment for a modest incident can make the punishment seem like an aggressive act in and of itself; it also removes the flexibility to respond to an adversary who sees little to be lost in moving from a modest to a major incident.

Should information attacks be punished by information counterattacks? Several factors indicate yes. First, punishment in kind makes it more obvious what is being responded to. Until such time (if ever) that Information Warfare attacks can be measured against other attacks, the problem of proportionality remains. How many lives, for instance, are proportional to a disruption in a credit card validation system? By responding in kind, at least a rough symmetry may be maintained. Second, limiting reaction to the same channel keeps the action-reaction cycle within quasi-covert channels. Self-imposed limitations can also keep a lid on however much damage may be done by the most determined Information Warfare attack. This may be far less damage than a conventional war, much less a nuclear war, can cause. An analogy may be drawn to incidents that involve intelligence or diplomatic agents, which are often responded to in kind so as to inhibit specific perpetrating organizations but not invite further retaliation. Conversely, unlike spy-versus-spy exchanges, the perpetrators are not necessarily in the same line of work as their victims (e.g., hackers do not work for stock exchanges). Hacking computers to punish computer hacking also erodes any moral argument the United States may want to make about the evils of hacking in the first place.[6]

The two factors that mitigate against retaliation in kind are asymmetry and controllability. A nation that sponsors an attack on the U.S. infrastructure but that itself lacks a reliable infrastructure to attack cannot be harmed very much and thus will not be deterred by an equal and opposite threat. As a trivial example, North Korea does not have a stock market to take down, and phone service in many Islamic countries is hit-or-miss. If any punishment will suffice, these two considerations do not apply to deterring information.

Controllability is difficult and may remain ever thus. In essence, to predict what an attack on someone's information system will do requires a high degree of intelligence about how to get in it, what to do once inside, and what secondary effects may result from such exploitation. The more complex systems get, the harder it is to predict secondary effects—not only inside the system, but to the world at large. Retaliation may produce nothing, may produce nothing that can be made to look like something, may produce something, may produce everything, may affect third parties (among them neutrals, friends, or the United States). The National Information Infrastructure is becoming, after all, increasingly globalized.

Whether or not retaliation in kind is preferred, doing so has problems, but so does not doing so. Either way, the nuclear-era concept of graduated response in kind lacks the relevance it holds in the nuclear arena.

The remainder of this essay concentrates on the first three factors:

defining the incident, determining the perpetrator, and delivering the retaliation. Eight vignettes illustrate the difficulty of doing all three.[7]

Defining the Incident

In contrast to nuclear events, which are both obvious and rare, hacker attacks—which writ large might constitute Information Warfare—are many and mostly trivial. There may be as many as a half-million break-ins on the Internet every year. Most are homegrown, but some originate from overseas, a fraction of which may be state-sponsored. Most of the half-million do no damage; they are just pranks. Even when damage is done, in many cases it is scarcely beyond annoyance value. Even if either are grounds for individual punishment, it does not necessarily follow that they are grounds for international retaliation. To retaliate against each one will greatly tax the principle of proportionality. The issue in defining the level of an actionable incident is determining how much damage is enough.

Loss of life might be one threshold—clearly a hacker attack on a railroad switch that causes a fatal collision is actionable. Yet, fatalities are often a highly indirect result of actual damage. The only verifiable case of deaths resulting from hacking occurred when the outage of a weather computer was causally related to a marine accident.

Should economic loss beyond a certain threshold trigger retaliation (e.g., stock trades muddled a la Tom Clancy's *Debt of Honor*)? Setting a specific threshold tends to be arbitrary and measuring loss against it is often ambiguous. What is the cost of preventing credit card purchases for a day? Is it the sum of all purchases which would otherwise have been charged; all purchases which otherwise would have been made; all purchases which having been postponed one day were not made another day; the sum of all salaries of people not working? How does one measure the loss of corrupted data? Is it the time required to restore its integrity, or the damage to the integrity of the system so corrupted? Two vignettes illustrate the potential problems involved.

Vignette #1. An American company is bidding against a company of an unfriendly Asian country to supply a telephone system to a third party. A member of the Asian country's intelligence service hacks into the American company's computer, determines what the American company is bidding, undercuts the bid, takes the contract, and thousands of U.S. jobs are lost. Is this an actionable act of Information Warfare—and if so, in what domain? When French intelligence officials were suspected of spying on U.S. firms, the United States retaliated by using its own agents to acquire information on French firms. (Incidentally, they got caught doing so.) During recent trade talks with the Japanese on automobiles, American officials let leak the news that our signals intelligence was able to find valuable information on their negotiation strategy. Was that an act of Information Warfare? If the tables were turned, how could the United States measure the damage done thereby to its interests to determine whether a threshold had been crossed?

Vignette #2. The FAA, over time, suffers from an increasing rate of service outages at its control centers resulting in increasing flight disruptions and attendant economic loss. At some point, someone thinks to check the integrity of its computer system and finds clear signs of hacker intrusion. The hackers are identified unambiguously; unusually enough, so is the time of their first penetration. Even after the operating software is cleaned up, considerable controversy surrounds any attempt to determine what damage, if any, was caused by the hacking. If 1995 is any indication, the FAA's system is heir to an increasing outage rate. Trying to project any such rate into the period that suspicious code was being run to determine what hacking caused (unfortunately it was impossible to link any specific outage to queered, as opposed to otherwise deficient, code) led to a wide variety of estimates, a few of them even positive (that is,

the actual rate of outages exceeded what trend extrapolation would have predicted). Does the hacking have to cause actionable damage, or must it be measured by potential loss of life?

Determining the Perpetrator

If an information attack can be distinguished from background noise and the perpetrator is caught, and a clear chain of evidence pointing to command or at least assistance which can be traced back to a foreign government, then something actionable has taken place. How often can such attacks be unambiguously traced? Perpetrators rarely leave anything as obvious as fingerprints. Invariably, some criminals have habits that increase their chances of being caught—they brag, they return to the scene of the crime, they adopt a specific modus operandi, they do not clean up their signatures—but these are not the hallmarks of professional operators. Because coldly professional hacking incidents (or at least the known ones) are rare, the chances of being able to catch a carefully laid plan are unknowable. And even if the perpetrators are caught, tracing them back to a government is hardly guaranteed: hackers do not wear uniforms, do not require instruments rarely found outside government auspices (e.g., a tank), nor do they need enormous resources to ensure success.[8]

Vignette #3. Jordan begins to feel military pressure from Iraq and the United States ponders intervention on Jordan's side. Suddenly a series of mysterious hacker-caused blackouts plague major American cities. The perpetrator is never identified, but both Hamas and Hezbollah take credit for it. It seems clear, however, that the attack was motivated by Iraq as a warning to the United States not to get involved. Or was it? Iran, to whom the United States is still the Great Satan, would have a double motive—to hurt America and draw it into conflict with its rival, Iraq. Jordan would also want the United States to take the crisis seriously and intervene. So might Israel, which although neutral in the conflict, would be eager to see more U.S. presence just over the horizon and which could not help but benefit if its enemies were to take credit for the attack. To throw in a wild card, North Korea, just having engineered a peace offensive, might have reason to deflect attention onto Iraq and appear to be nice guys in comparison. Or maybe Hamas or Hezbollah was telling the truth after all. The United States lacks the luxury of a single foe who may be assumed to lurk behind every Information Warfare attack. For example, until Libya refused to extradite certain suspects, it was not clear whether Libya, Syria, or Iran was behind the Lockerbie incident.

Vignette #4. As anti-Western sentiment increases in Moscow and Russia seeks to define a foreign policy distinct from the West's, the U.S. telephone system is hit by disruptive outages. The hackers are caught; they are recent immigrants from Russia strongly connected to the emergent Russian Mafia, which in turn have connections to the new government in Moscow. Should Russia be held accountable? Many governments have strong ties to TCOs. To have the choice between perpetrating an attack through its own organs and subcontracting it out, a country would have to take the latter option seriously.[9] The reliability of the subcontractors may be questionable, but once on board, they have internal enforcement mechanisms of their own.

Vignette #5. The same as Vignette #4, except the Russian Mafia are explicitly connected to the KGB. We know this because the Russians have owned up. The KGB outfit responsible is labeled a rogue unit that the government admits it is still trying to control. The outfit, of course, denies it, but cannot lay its hands on any documents showing higher involvement. History is replete with freelancing intelligence units—sometimes on their own account, and sometimes because involving the uniformed military complicates deniability. Russia's rationale looks plausible and so the incident is not considered actionable—but is this accurate? Clearly if a rogue commander were to launch a nuclear weapon, denying responsibility would be much harder. Nations have a responsibility to control dangerous equipments; computers used for hacking hardly qualify as such. Similarly, a rogue battalion invading its neighbor is harder to shrug off because nothing that large, it is understood, can be done without implicit government complicity. But a serious hacking incident need not be that resource-intensive; finding a few bright hackers may suffice.

Certainty of Response

Deterrence policy presumes a tight linkage between incident and response. But how wise a policy would it be to guarantee a specific response regardless of who the perpetrator was? Cold War strategic deterrence was designed for the toughest adversary; any other attackers were an easier included case. With Information Warfare, there is no difficult canonical foe, and thus no lesser included case. Normally, one purpose of demonstrating deterrence is to ensure that similar incidents will not recur. Yet the United

States is vulnerable to such attacks precisely because systems security is so weak (which reflects the perception that damaging attacks are rare). A sufficiently nasty attack would catch people's attention and promote security (or at least tighter access controls and less system dependence).

Afterwards, a second attack would be harder to pull off. Compare the following three vignettes, identical except for their perpetrator.

Vignette #6. A hacker attack on the nation's primary funds transfer system causes the system to shut down while system faults that led to corrupted records are traced down and eradicated. The shutdown of the funds transfer system leads to widespread layoffs, bankruptcies, and a cascading series of panics before order is restored. The crime is linked to agents of the Iranian government. The United States retaliates with air strikes against Iran's nuclear infrastructure, setting back its presumed weapons program by ten years. Iran, in retaliation, attempts to close the Straits of Hormuz, which the United States keeps open to prevent a steep and protracted hike in oil prices. When the dust settles, the consensus emerges that retaliation was nevertheless worthwhile, not so much because it deterred further information system attacks (which it did), but because Iran's nuclear program and threat to oil flow was worrisome. The funds transfer attack was a convenient justification for doing what was otherwise useful.

Vignette #7. It turns out North Korea is responsible for the funds transfer attack. North Korea is in a position to cause considerable damage to South Korea if irked; it probably has nuclear weapons and certainly has the forces to send southward and a history of having done so. Is the United States willing to risk a second Korean War over an incident which could have been thwarted had a few million dollars more been spent on security? Would it be comfortable trying to explain that calculus to other countries? Might it not be more cost effective to pay for serious protection measures for all of its other equally critical systems rather than prepare for retaliation with uncontrollable consequences? In the end, the United States does little (much as South Korea did little in reaction to the assassination of its top officials in Rangoon or the destruction of one of its airliners). Inaction is rationalized by the perception that the government of North Korea probably is not going anywhere and will eventually fall of its own accord.

Vignette #8. This time Serbians are found responsible. Again, retaliation is considered but rejected. Some pressure is put on Serbia to extradite those responsible, but no one expects that such a request will get higher priority than the search for war criminals (where no one expects much success, either). In the end, it is decided that Serbia's enmity toward the United States is situational, not permanent, and that there is no geostrategic rationale for risking armed conflict that escalation to retaliation may cause. Officials are glad that they did not institute a deterrence policy that they would have had to make good on.

Conclusions

The lack of a specific explicit deterrence policy does not prevent the use of retaliation, but the specification of a deterrence policy requires its proponent to respond to what, in the case of information attacks, may be very gauzy circumstances.

It is difficult to see how deterrence can be made to work, but it is easy to see the problems with trying. A declared policy that could not be reliably instantiated would quickly lack credibility. If thresholds are too low or the proof that a nation sponsored terrorism is not sufficiently convincing, then retaliation would make the United States appear the aggressor. If thresholds are too high and standards of proof too strict, then retaliation policy will prove hollow. If the United States retaliates against nations regardless of other political considerations, then it risks unneeded confrontations and escalation; if it is too expedient, then retaliation will appear a cover for more cynical acts.

It may not even be obvious that the United States should react all that vigorously to information attacks. Doing so may tell others that they have hit a nerve—and thus the possibility that a level of pain could be generated which might dissuade us from acting in our other interests, or at least distract us in a crisis. The opposite attitude, that information attacks are problems for those whose defenses are inadequate and not the legitimate concern for the nation's security may play a greater role in dissuading others that the results will be in no way interesting to us and thus to them.[10]

1. Many in the broader computer hacking community would take issue with punishing someone for breaking into computer systems and reading information but otherwise doing no harm. Nevertheless, where the law is clear, most enforcement officials favor prosecution. An analogy may be made to graffiti. By itself, graffiti is minor vandalism. As the New York Police Department has concluded, however, graffiti marks a neighborhood as one in which standards of conduct can be violated with impunity. Not only are residents understandably upset by such indications, but its appearance often presages subsequent, more serious crimes. By analogy, hacker attacks, even those that cause no damage, mark Cyberspace as a lawless environment and thus merit suppression.

2. Dr. Richard Hayes and Gary F. Wheatley, *Information Warfare and Deterrence: A Workshop Report* (Washington, D.C.: NDU Press, 1996).

3. Strategic nuclear deterrence is not the only form of deterrence. So-called tactical nuclear weapons were designed to deny battlefield objectives and to raise the level of destruction so high as to deter battle in the first place. John Mearsheimer has argued in *Conventional Deterrence* (Ithaca, N.Y.: Cornell University Press, 1983), that an aggressor can be deterred by the prospect that vic-

tory will be expensive. As such, it may be wiser for a defender to adopt a military posture designed to prolong war even if that reduces the likelihood of ultimate victory.

4. Hayes, op.cit.,

5. If punishment is taken from a generic menu of responses (e.g., that might be evoked for more traditional terrorism) then these two factors do not differentiate the efficacy of explicitly deterring Information Warfare attacks from explicitly deterring any other attacks, such as terrorist attacks.

6. As differentiated for the legal argument that reprisals in kind may be legitimate in certain circumstances under commonly accepted laws of war.

7. Compare the problems of deterring cyber-terrorism with similar problems in deterring physical terrorism. For physical terrorism, the actionable thresholds are often easier to determine—did were people killed or seriously hurt? (In contrast to cyber-terrorism, it is difficult to imagine incidents that would cause large monetary loss but not casualties.) Finding perpetrators can also be difficult, but at least in this country, the FBI has had pretty good success in large part because physical terrorism leaves physical evidence behind. Finally, the political problem of determining whether to retaliate against a country that sponsors physical terrorism is akin to the same problem applied to cyber-terrorism. By two of the three counts, retaliatory policy against physical terrorism is more problematic than similar policy against cyber-terrorism. Nevertheless, deterrence policy against state-sponsored terrorism has yet to prove conspicuously useful.

8. The requirement that a nation's warriors identify themselves as such (e.g., through uniforms, official gear) reflects the aforementioned laws of war that entitle them, if captured, to be treated as prisoners of war rather than as criminals.

9. The downside is that an organization for sale to the red side may also be for sale to the blue side. Since battle damage assessment for Information Warfare is difficult, blue might induce red's contractor to report back to red that blue's systems were successfully attacked when little damage to blue systems in fact occurred.

10. Whether this attitude can be sustained in a hypersensitive democracy where personal or corporate problems can turn into claims on public resources—military among them—is an entirely different question.

The Use of Cognitive Maps to Visualize Belief Systems About Information Warfare

LCDR Robert J. Garigue, Dept. of National Defence, Canada

This is a research paper written as part of the doctoral program in Information Systems (Carleton University) and does not represent an official position of the Department of National Defence.

Abstract

Reasoning about a new problem such as Information Warfare demands the creation of a cognitive space that offers to the investigator a representation of all the causal links between the main concepts of the domain. Establishing these concepts and their relationships are the results of both a private and public investigation. Cognitive maps have proven their value for the elucidation of new knowledge. This report describes some of the differences involved in the process of constructing static and dynamic cognitive maps. The products of these activities are different types of views. One is a structural representation, the other a declarative functional representation. The static view will be created using pen and paper, the dynamic view will be created with a software package called COPE. A brief discussion as to the findings will be given as a conclusion.

Introduction

To understand something, one must be able to explain it. These explanations are grounded in an abstract representation called a belief system. An explanation need not be scientific, simply justified. This justification could be based on a quantitative method or could come simply from a learned intuition—conscious or not. But how it is grounded is less important than the fact that decision-makers using this belief consider it helpful.

Belief systems can be described as structures that link the significant concepts together. Using phenomenological linkages, we elaborate explanations on the causes and effects of most events that occur in our daily lives. These systems help us make sense of our world as well as determine the boundaries of our understanding of how and why things happen.

These networks of links and nodes representing causality and concepts, are akin to maps that help us navigate the worlds in which we live. Not just in the physical world but also in our abstract worlds that are virtual and temporal. All these worlds have artifacts; natural or humanly

constructed that interact with each other and transform themselves under the actions of our understanding and intentions (Popper). These
interactions extend our maps in unforeseen directions. In other words,
we are able to explore and extend our belief systems by creating new
linkages between known ideas. This associative activity generates new
concepts.

Belief Systems

The expression *l'etre et le devenir* expresses the dialectical creative
tension under which humans operate. What *is* and what *could be* inter-
play and combine as we investigate and mentally construct a representation of the structure of the worlds in which we live. Inevitably, as we
investigate the worlds in order to understand and control them, we continuously transform them.

Under these conditions reality becomes an expression of our interpretation of the present and of what we believe to be possible. In effect,
through the development of these world views, we are in practice creating a present reality in the image of what we think the world can be.

Belief systems are such world views (also referred to as *Weltanschauung,* or a particular viewpoint under examination). They are for us a
way of knowing or having situation awareness. Initially, belief systems
are simply a personal stance. A private internal expression of what
an individual believes his world is all about. But with time, these expressions become public. Individual belief systems can be publicly articulated by the arts and sciences and embedded in mediums through pictures,
language, and text, and become truly independent social artifacts. But now
using software as the medium of expression, belief systems are computationally tractable constructs.

Belief systems expressed in this way are not just open to the process of
public debate and social criticism; through computational analysis, these
world views can elaborate their own logical extensions as well as verify
their internal consistency.

Cognitive Maps

A pictorial representation of causal assertions in the belief system can
be constructed through a graph of points and arrows. The points represent concepts, and the arrows represent the causal links between the
concepts. They are an instance of a knowledge representation structure
and akin to semantic nets. The visual representation makes it easy for
people to see how each of the linked concepts can describe a domain of
understanding as well as how the whole set declares assertions and implications. The product of such a methodology is a structure called a
cognitive map.

Decisions, Causality, and Consequences

One of the benefits of using computer-supported methodologies in
the development of cognitive maps is the range of analysis that can be

done on the assertions. With this system, it is possible to derive formal inferences, which can be used in many ways, such as seeing whether people actually make choices that are consistent with their whole assemblage of stated causal assertions. Such inferences based on a given cognitive map can also be used to offer advice on the implications of specific choices (Axelrod).

Presently in very large and complex structures, computational-based analysis is the best way to evaluate the outcome of a subset of declarations. This concept mapping methodology not only permits the investigation of causality but also permits the evaluation of alternatives through the comparison of consequences.

A simple pen-and-paper approach offers some advantages if the state of the knowledge about the domain of inquiry is small. Initially this approach ensures some internal consistency, and usually static maps capture the main and essential components of the belief systems. However, these advantages are lost as the understanding of the domain increases—large numbers of concepts become rapidly unmanageable. A computational-based method greatly extends this initial structure and yields a more sophisticated and dynamic construct. As the construct is computationally formal it is amenable to a greater range of analysis.

Elaboration of an Unknown Belief System— Information Warfare

A domain of inquiry that is still very new and ill-structured will help show the advantages of the methodology and tool set. Information Warfare is an emergent strategical philosophy, a belief system, which postulates that a new type of warfare will be fought within the information infrastructure of societies. In these battles, information itself as well as the information systems would be considered strategic assets—and therefore targets. As well as information and information systems are the agents of force themselves, they are also regarded as a new variety of weapons and weapon systems. Information Warfare as a strategical theory is still subject to controversy, but it is sufficiently accepted in defense and security organizations around the world for them to spend millions of dollars to develop their capabilities.

A theory of Information Warfare is significant in that it might be the manifestation of a broader paradigm shift. As Thomas Kuhn explained in his treatise *The Structure of Scientific Revolution,* paradigm shifts necessitate a restructuring of all preceding theories within a new conceptual framework. So we need to restructure the notion of conflict within a belief system of Information Warfare. It will have to integrate all the present knowledge we have on warfare and strategy, as well as incorporate these emerging concepts that are specific to a modern digital-based, information-intensive society. Cognitive maps are a way to elaborate and explore such a conceptual framework.

It is important to note that this paper focuses primarily on the meth-

odological and procedural issues of constructing cognitive maps rather
than on the specific investigation of the Information Warfare maps themselves. Some comments on Information Warfare theory will be made to
highlight the relevance of the different approaches to the subject of the
inquiry.

Analysis of a Static Cognitive Map About Information Warfare

An initial and preparatory cognitive map on Information Warfare was
prepared by the author about a year ago to help clarify the problem space
and help in discussions within a group of expert. The fact that that it was
a visual "map" helped expand the scope of the discussions. Several
comments were made to the effect that this was a good way to break down
a very complex problem and to look at how the wide range of concepts
are related to each other.

In looking at Axelrod's requirements for cognitive maps, one could
say that this initial map lacks functionality as it does not have any di-
graph structures. They are simply linkages without consequences. Furthermore, it does not have a full networked structure. However, this
approach is closely related to the "Rich Picture" methodology (Avison
and Wood-Harper), and is still considered a cognitive map. I will simply
qualify it as static. It is essentially a hierarchical structure that shows the
five main supportive knowledge domains (as opposed to organizational
domains). As seen in Figure 1, they are as follows:

Command and Control. This domain encompasses the requirements
for detection, identification, and prosecution of targets, whether physical
or informational. Hence, the requirement to tie sensors to effectors via
processes and models. This domain also would include the decision
models used by decision-makers or the agents acting on behalf of the
human decision-makers.

Information Systems. This domain represents the concepts related to
the notions that information and information systems are both targets
and weapons. They are in effect both the main objects and subjects of
Information Warfare activities and are classed in terms of their functional
control perspective. (It is both a historical and evolutionary perspective).
They are classified as transaction processing systems (TPS), management
information systems (MIS), or more preferably structured and unstruc-
tured decision support systems (DSS), and the latest emergent class of
socio-tech systems (also called semiotic systems) that are akin to World
Wide Web-type architectural constructs.

An important consideration is that the information system domain
also has a classification scheme regarding the types of weapons that can
be used in Information Warfare (Garigue). Briefly, the focal point for
analysis and attack is based on the conceptual framework of computer-
networked mediated decision-making processes. The three classes of
weapons are physical, computational, and semantic. The physical weap-

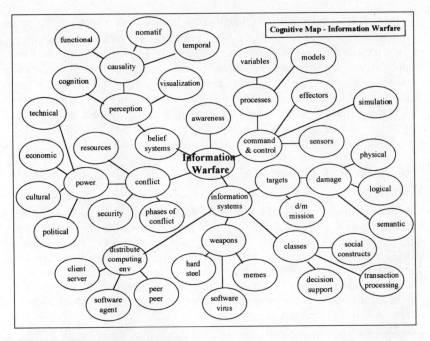

Figure 1. Static Cognitive Map

ons (targeting effectors and sensors) would be hard steel or stealth. The computational weapons could deliver structural and logical attacks via malicious code such as worms, virus, and Trojan horses in order to deny system and service access or deceive other processes. Finally, the semantic weapons target the belief systems of the human decision makers. The class of weapons are memes and dramatic orchestration.

Conflict. In trying to understand the reasons for conflict, one has to examine the relative levels of power (economic, political, cultural, and technical) as well as the relative levels of threat and vulnerability so as to deduce risk. Another important consideration is where along the cooperation/conflict spectrum do the protagonists find themselves. This analysis included all networks (social, cultural, economic, and technical) so as to see the coupling and linkages between them.

Belief Systems. This is a difficult area to represent but needs to be modeled in counterpoint to the command and control domain. This concept helps understanding of the context and processes by which decisions are made. If one takes the point of view that information in context permits the emergence of knowledge, these elements can be seen as building blocks for a knowledge management capability.

Situation Awareness. This domain emerges from the synergistic interaction of the other domains. This new area needs much more applied research. It has a major role to play in all areas related to decision-making.

Constructing Computer-Supported Cognitive Maps

Using the structural, static view of Information Warfare as a stepping stone, a more declarative map was developed by using the COPE software application. The software is designed to hold knowledge about concepts, and encodes it using the cognitive mapping technique. The software can also be used to structure relevant information such as observation, interview data, documentary data, and so forth (Cropper, Eden, and Ackerman). It permits managing a much larger set (1000+) of elements and relationships and enables the manipulation of qualitative data.

Analysis of a Dynamic Cognitive Map About Information Warfare

The main advantage of developing cognitive maps in an interactive way through the use of a dynamic tool is that the iterative process produces a continuous dialogue. The multiple presentations and views combined with the built-in analysis processes spur continuous development and extensions to the map. Not only does the tool set permit storage and concomitant creation of supporting documentation, but it also permits manipulation and analysis of either the total set or just a subset of concepts within the domain of inquiry.

This type of map is completely orthogonal to the static map. At present only the distinct aspect of defensive Information Warfare has been analyzed here. The map shows how system and network vulnerabilities arise as well as their consequences. A concomitant map on the usage of information and information systems as weapons would also need to be depicted to show the full scope of the belief system on Information Warfare. Thus, the map shown in Figure 2 is simply a subset of a larger map. This type of bounding creates sets of concepts that are more detailed and capable. The following sections are some of the main findings with regard to the impact of the methodology on the understanding of the subject of the analysis.

ANALYSIS OF THE DYNAMICS OF CAUSALITY

Head and Tails Analysis. COPE generates a causal view of problems more akin to an input-output analysis (see the high level set in the Appendix), which is very different from the hierarchical and structural interpretation of Information Warfare in the static map. In this map all is cause and effect. Determining the primary and secondary causes as well as the ultimate effects are insights that are not seen and understood from the review of the structural static map even when it was extended into more detail and at a finer level of granularity. For example, Table 1 shows one of the different types of analysis conducted. The heads and tails analysis helps determine which set of final effects are functions of what small set of initial causes. In the static map, these critical concepts, although present, are encapsulated in a different type of abstraction and essentially hidden from public view.

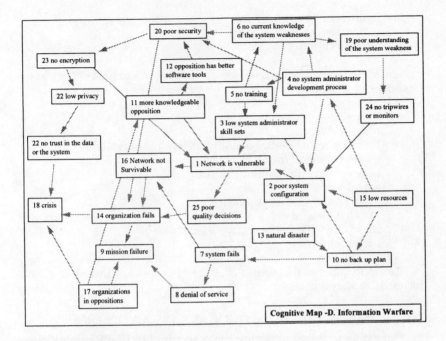

Figure 2. Dynamic Cognitive Map

Table 1. Heads and Tails Analysis

Causes (Tails)	Effects (Heads)
13. Natural disaster	9. Mission failure
15. Low resources	18. Crisis
17. Organizations in opposition	25. Poor-quality decisions

Explanations and Consequences. Another type of analysis—explanations—can generate a series of arguments explaining situations. Here is one of many reasons for the vulnerability of a network. (The format of the argumentation is as per COPE):

1. My network is vulnerable
   may be explained by
3. *Low system administrator skill sets*
   which can be explained by
6. No current knowledge of software weakness available
   which can be explained by
11. More knowledgeable opposition
   which can be explained by
12. Opposition has better software tools
   which can be explained by

20. Poor security
    which can be explained by
23. No encryption

The same type of analysis can be done in reverse to look at the consequences of a situation:

5. No training
   may lead to
6. No current knowledge of software weakness available
   which may lead to
3. Low system administrator skill sets
   which may lead to
11. More knowledgeable opposition
    which may lead to
12. Opposition has better software tools
    which loops to 6

The loop comment indicates that the concepts are linked in a feed forward/back structure.

THE HUMAN-MACHINE DIALOGUE AS A DISCOVERY PROCESS

The dynamic and iterative approach required by COPE can initiate a knowledge elucidation process. Discovery of new concepts for inclusion in the map becomes a by-product of the continual refinement that comes from the dialogue between the system and the users. In many regards the cognitive map is a formal discourse—a thesis—and is maintained by the methodology embedded in COPE. The antithesis comes from the human interpretations and divergences with all its intuitions about the domain of the inquiry. It is these human biases that help spark insight and new concepts.

In order to establish a new belief system that is both efficient and practical, we need to interrogate the logical limit of our assumptions. Functional belief systems are internally coherent and at the same time enable us to see how things happen in the real word. When analysis processes such as explanations or consequences are performed in COPE and give unexpected results, we must resolve these contradictions by theorizing about new concepts. For example, in constructing the Information Warfare dynamic map, several new concepts dealing with system trust and security came to light. Encryption and privacy concepts were found to be required as they determine the level of trust the decision-maker has in the data, the information, and ultimately in the information system itself.

PRIVATE AND PUBLIC CONSENSUS

One other finding from constructing dynamic maps is that the investigator can open his belief system to public criticism. As alluded to earlier, we can operationalize belief systems through cognitive maps. This is not the only approach to articulating a belief system, but the process does permit us to instanciate a publicly accountable and auditable set of rules. In most instances, a public process builds consensus.

KNOWLEDGE CONSTRUCTION

The dynamic cognitive map is considered to be in propositional format: it permits and is a knowledge base. The networked links-and-nodes structure is a rule-based system in which information is structured into knowledge as first order logic proposition:

If this . . . and this . . . and this . . . , then this . . .

As the map keeps extending and creating and linking more and more concepts via the continuing discovery dialogue, its specific formal structure can act as an evolving knowledge representation schema and could eventually become the actual knowledge base of an expert system. It would be interesting to see if these rules can be exported to an expert system shell, where with the help of an inference engine we would have a true expert system. We can see here that the creation of the cognitive map is akin to performing the knowledge acquisition phase during an expert system development project.

DECISION-MAKING

The cognitive map also helps in utility functions analysis. We can make choices and put weights on the links and nodes in order to quantify the causal relationships. We can then choose or prioritize investment plans to counter some possible consequences. We can also add probabilities to the events, and then rank and order probable outcomes. In doing this we are extending the cognitive map to permit the construction of simulations that can support policymaking and investment choices. However, in our example, it is difficult to compare how an investment in the development of new tripwire and monitoring software would be as effective as developing better selection criteria for the system administrator. Through quantification, the map can go from being simply a qualitative view of the world to become a simulation model.

Conclusion

It is clear that the static map created with pencil and paper and the dynamic map created with COPE are two completely different views of the same domain. The static map focuses mostly on structural and hierarchical issues, whereas the dynamic map permits the creation of descriptive and functional views. The static approach presents concepts as a hierarchy of beliefs, whereas the dynamic view presents a value chain of beliefs. However, both approaches have something to offer. They both help in the understanding and elaboration of new problem spaces and need to be worked in conjunction. A better methodology would incorporate both approaches.

Philosophically speaking, knowledge will always have to be presented using different views that capture different ways of knowing a subject. The static view captures what a subject is about. The dynamic view captures how it works. In many respects they are complementary views: two sides of the same coin; each a different world unto itself, but both part of the same reality. As in our review of Information Warfare, it is possible to reach not only shared perspectives, but ones that are also functional.

Avison, D. E. and A. T. Wood-Harper. *Multiview: An Exploration in Information Systems Development.* Oxford: Blackwell Scientific Publications, 1990.

Axelrod, Robert (ed). *Structure of Decision. The Cognitive Maps of Political Elites.* Princeton: Princeton University Press, 1976.

Cropper, Steve, Colin Eden, and Fran Ackerman. "Cognitive Mapping: A User Guide." Working Paper No. 12. Management Science: Theory, Methods, and Practice. University of Strathclyde, September 1989.

Garigue, Robert. "Information Warfare—Developing a Conceptual Framework." Research Paper (http://www.carleton.ca/garigue). June 1995.

Popper, Karl. *The Logic of Scientific Discovery.* New York: Basic Books, 1959.

List of Concepts

1. My network is vulnerable
2. Poor system configuration
3. Low system administrator skill sets
4. No system administrator development process
5. No training
6. No current knowledge of software weakness available
7. System fails
8. Denial of service
9. Mission failure
10. No back-up plan
11. More knowledgeable opposition
12. Opposition has better software tools
13. Natural disaster
14. Organization fails
15. Low resources
16. Network not survivable
17. Organizations in opposition
18. Crisis
19. Poor understanding of system weakness

20. Poor security
21. Low privacy
22. No trust in data or system
23. No encryption
24. No tripwire and monitors
25. Poor-quality decisions

From InfoWar to Knowledge Warfare: Preparing for the Paradigm Shift

Professor Philippe Baumard, University of Paris

Successful firms, such as Intel, maintain an innovative environment, seek continuous performance improvement, favor customer orientation (e.g., through partnerships with customers and suppliers), enhance results orientation, and place speed of creation, defense, and development of value-chains at the core of their strategic focus. To maintain its leadership, Intel developed "war rooms" and encouraged informal relationships that crisscrossed organizational boundaries. Nevertheless, when Intel had to face InfoWar practices, it had to acknowledge that the company failed to prevent and to anticipate large-scale info-destabilization.

New businesses live on the brink of disasters. Yet, "organizations have many stabilizers but quite often lack proper destabilizers."[1] We will argue in this paper that InfoWar (informational arena-based warfare) has been thought within the boundaries of old schemata that will no longer be accurate in the twewnty-first century. These schemata include misconceptions of management, organizations, economics, welfare, and purpose of development. We will investigate, in the footsteps of Hedberg, Jonsson, Starbuck, Steele, Wilensky, and many others design principles that worked and that no longer work. Founding our comments on observations of real-world experiences, we end with recommendations to prepare nations, organizations, and people for the forthcoming paradigm shift: from InfoWar to Knowledge Warfare (K-Warfare).

Why Policymakers Got Trapped in the Information Paradigm

World leaders, who mostly belong to a generation not born with a computer at home, have been strongly influenced by cybernetics. In a cybernetic world, economic and social life is seen as a system: values are categorized, economic systems are modeled, social structures are typologized, and ideologies are invented to put all these systems together. In such a world, policymakers are not long to assume that information is power, and that systematized information is the structure of power itself.

History has been, so far, consistent with such implicit assumptions. Power was centralized, and, therefore, needed centralized intelligence. The world was organized into blocks, and therefore, needed compartmented information. Economic and social systems were hierarchical, and therefore, hierarchical information made sense.

From the start, this cybernetic view of the world was quite erroneous. As Varela and Maturana pointed out,[2] of the neurons that participate in the building of vision, only 20 percent are in the eyes' retinas, whereas 80 percent of them come from other parts of the brain. In other words, 80 percent of our "vision" is internally constructed. Vision is mostly knowledge, not information. Furthermore, this knowledge is mostly tacit; it escapes our individual or collective awareness.[3]

Eventually, people—including policymakers—learn without being aware of what is being learned;[4] code without being aware of coding;[5] and most dramatically, learn without having intended or planned to learn.[6] Most learning is incidental. Emerging Information Warfare doctrines fail to acknowledge this fragility of learning. Mapping without knowing is nonsense. Mapping, as an act of vision, is mostly derived from these 80 percent of neurons in our brains that participate in the construction of images and help us to transform noticed and unnoticed stimuli into sense-making. Such weapons as "private-sector communication satellite constellations that instantly link individuals, on-demand high-resolution imaging spacecraft and rapidly evolving gigabit/sec.-class networks"[7] are no less than phantasmagorias if we neglect to take care of these disturbing—yet remaining—autonomous neurons of our brains.

Indigo, a small firm of less than 12 employees, is an exemplar. Indigo produces and publishes five confidential newsletters, including the *Intelligence Newsletter,*[8] a well-reputed source of intelligence among policymakers in Europe. Myths and rumors circulate, seeing in Indigo's high accuracy a ploy of obscure foreign intelligence. French readers suspect foreign intrusions. Foreign readers suspect French manipulation. In fact, Indigo is nothing else than an efficient "knowledge-refinery,"[9] that is to say a firm purposefully designed for the efficiency of its knowledge generation. Onsite observation shows that "far from being pliable, knowledge generates its own path of transformation, while simultaneously transforming and being transformed by its organizational settings. An implication is that those who would manage knowledge should respect this propensity for autonomous development."[10]

Cautious toward systematized information gathering, Indigo's staff is operating within a "community of practice"[11]—i.e., an intensive and highly contextualized socialization process—and favors HUMINT. The whole organization is focused on sense-making instead of information collection. Intensity and depth of internal and external socializations are considered as the core organizational competitive advantage. The rate of defaults is close to zero. The overall performance, in terms of growth and

ROI, is twice that of similar organizations such as the Economist Intelligence Unit.

To understand such a performance, let us remind that information is not knowledge, and then let us investigate how to deal with knowledge instead of information. As General Francks pointed out, "Vietnam was the first battlefield use of computers. The Univac 1005, which the 25th Infantry Division installed in 1966 at Cu Chi, filled an entire van. Images of the enemy and terrain were captured with conventional cameras and television with light intensification devices, radar, and infrared devices. Sensors and high-altitude reconnaissance scanned 100,000 square miles per hour providing commanders with a heretofore unknown view of the battlefield."[12] Meanwhile, the Vietnamese population was digging underground tunnels. Similarly, the French Foreign Legion was settling its command outposts on hills to dominate battlefields, and meanwhile, Vietnamese soldiers were digging the crops and burying themselves in the face and "vision" of the enemy, proving that neurons from the retinas account for only 20 percent of vision. What was dramatically missing was not information, but knowledge in general, and an adequate form of "knowing" in particular. "We are on the threshold of an era where order can be achieved largely through knowledge, not necessarily through physical order."[13]

Knowledge Versus Information, Knowing Versus Knowledge

Understanding the differences between "knowledge" and "knowing" is essential to a successful entry in this new paradigm. "One contemporary cliche is that more and more turbulent settings are requiring organizations to use more and more knowledge, and that this in turn forces organizations to process more and more information."[14] A knowledge-base is all the learning of people and institutions more or less explicitly encapsulated in minds, brains, models, signals, culture, rules, guidelines. Greek philosophers used to categorize this human knowledge in three ensembles: the *techne,* the embodied technical know-how; the *episteme,* the abstract generalization derived from knowing-how; and the *phronesis,* the wisdom of social practice; i.e., the ability to derive aggregates from social learning.

In modern management literature, the investigation of knowledge within and between organizations is derived from the same twenty-four-centuries-old conceptualization. The conventional view is that relevant knowledge comes from explicit situational analysis; i.e., it is objective knowledge. As Detienne and Vernant pointed out, education in the Judeo-Christian world has been strongly influenced by the pursuit of truth as the sole goal of knowledge generation.[15] Starting in 400 BC, knowledge is systematically understood as objective knowledge, leaving "meaner" forms of knowledge and knowing—such as conjectural knowledge—disregarded and low-grade.

The governmental intelligence cycle itself is a pursuit of objective knowledge. Intelligence generation is driven by an objectivation force that discards unreliable information and sources according to truth-setting rules. As Wilensky put it, the intelligence bodies are overcrowded with "facts-and-figures men," who "introduce a 'rational-responsible' bias." "Facts-and-figures men are preoccupied with rational argument and criteria; their technical competence compels opposing parties to be more careful or honest in their use of information, to match each other expert for expert, fact for fact."[16]

Thus, current doctrines of InfoWar are all implicitly based on a biased assumption that large-scale truth-seeking is superior to depth and differentiation of knowing modes. Such doctrines are based on the belief that the process of organizations and nation's "getting into difficulties" is essentially one of degradation and increasing disutility of their knowledge-base.[17] Yet, when doctrine generators are asked to define such a knowledge-base, they have to face their incapacity to describe and to qualify it.

Knowledge-base, as a matter of fact, is a static concept. It assumes that knowledge can be systematically put in the form of a representation, and neglects all various forms of tacit knowledge in general, and collective tacit knowledge in particular. Thus, the same Judeo-Christian bias applies to the representation of knowledge. Knowledge is assumed to be merely a long-term representation; is seen as a commodity; is talked of in terms of volume and stocks; is described with a vocabulary borrowed from hardware management. In such a biased conception of knowledge, one usually distinguishes short-term or procedural representations that can be immediately acted from long-term or structural representations whose access and development need several apprenticeships.[18]

As a consequence, focus should be on the advancement of "knowing" instead of the accumulation of "knowledge." Development of national intelligence capabilities should therefore target the improvement of interpretational and sense-making skills, instead of pursuing the utopia of the ubiquity of a knowledge seen as a commodity. Such a self-deception has its roots in the reproducibility of information. Redundancy of information is a serious waste of resources in most industrial democracies. For instance, in France, no less than 80 administrative bodies distribute to small and large businesses the same information again and again. This redundant information eventually leads to redundant intelligence administrations, leading to the hypertrophy of bureaucratic and inefficient intelligence bodies.

The 1996 reorganization of the U.S. intelligence community is an exemplar of this lack of focus on "knowing" capabilities and of the exaggerated attention given to the accumulation of "knowledge." In 1992, Ernest R. May "urges the Committee to think of individuals in the Intelligence Community as well as of their organizational boxes."[19] Frank Carlucci, former Assistant to the President for National Security Affairs, underlines that "Congress could render a valuable service if it would lead the intelligence community through the process of cultural change that many of our businesses have gone through."[20] As Orton and Callahan noted, "unwarranted duplication remains a problem; and intelligence remains too isolated from the governmental process it was created to serve."[21]

Focus on knowledge as a commodity versus improvement of knowing can also be observed in the conceptual frameworks that are judged to be a good basis for knowledge-based warfare. Colonel Steven J. Sloboda, formerly in charge of long-range planning for U.S. Space Command, asserts: "Space is literally the fabric upon which we will weave our approach to knowledge-based warfare. Space is the enabling ingredient. Fortunately, the convergence of our experience in space operations, communications networking, and information processing seems to make the move to knowledge-based warfare achievable."[22] Unfortunately, human souls and minds are not fully readable from outer space. The "folk theory" that trust moves not words might well be misleading in a knowledge-based paradigm.

The Vietnam, Gulf, and former-Yugoslavia experiences—three modern war theaters with intensive use of satellite information—are exemplars of the limits of satellite cartography in penetrating human intents. Moreover, such experiences underline the limits of InfoWar. As Dragnich noted, the "so-called information war" that has been proposed "to wage against the Serbs is ridiculous. The Serbs do not need the outside world to tell them that communism and Slobodan Milosevic are bad."[23]

Misconceptions of Management

Thus, management should be designed and understood as primarily a knowledge-generation process. Many companies tend to follow management practices that take the physical world for granted. When the Berlin Wall fell, Finland believed that the announced geostrategic shift would require the acquisition of combat fighters. The market was estimated at around $3 billion. Four French companies—Snecma, Matra, Dassault, and Thomson—and the Defense Administration decide to enter the race for this competitive bid. When the newly settled French Economic Intelligence and Corporate Strategies Commission, at the French Office of Planning, decided to develop a few exemplar case studies, the case of the Mirage 2000-5 was selected.[24] The audit revealed that lack of coordination and knowledge sharing was at the roots of the commercial failure.

Managers who negotiated the contract were chosen according to corporate criteria. Internal competition prevented any attempt of crisscrossed knowledge transfers. Another French firm, the Aerospatiale, which has an in-depth knowledge of the Finland aeronautics market, was not consulted by the competing pool. In the absence of a long-term knowledge strategy, the state was unable to display any capitalization of knowledge on Finland. The lack of longitudinal capitalization of geostrategic knowledge led to the incapability of designing required distinctive attributes in the competitive bid.

In the middle of the negotiation process, the political turmoil in Finland was perceived as an obstacle, whereas the American companies reinforced their coordination and lobbying to use these elections as a leverage for their offer. Indeed, the French consortium was competing with a hypothetical F-16 offer, while the Americans were proposing the F-18. As Wilensky warned, "in all complex social systems, hierarchy, specialization, and centralization are major sources of distortion and blockage of intelligence."[25]

However, it seems that this analysis can be put a step forward. In this intelligence failure, the main cause was the inappropriateness of management practices to a nonmarket environment. The French consortium failed to recognize and acknowledge forces that acted outside the narrow borders of the targeted market. In a transversal environment (that implies geopolitical, geoeconomical, local politics, technology, and society) with a transversal offer (typically a consortium of different firms proposing dual technologies), traditional market management fails to grab critical issues. As R. D. Laing noted, the range of what we think and do is limited by what we fail to notice. If nonmarket knowledge is not integrated in management duties and skills, it is bound to be neglected. Thus, "nonmarket strategies result from a management process that incorporates knowledge of the market and nonmarket environments, information about specific issues, and conceptual frameworks that guide strategy formulation and implementation."[26]

Misconceptions of Organizations

Most organizations are unfit for the management and capitalization of intangible assets in general, and counterproductive in terms of knowledge generation. However true it is that one "must analyze the flow of information along the value chain as well as the movement of goods,"[27] it might be quite insufficient to cope with the new conditions of competitiveness.

The whole concept of value-chain, and the education given to managers on that matter, should be revised. Managers and scholars are used to thinking of organizations as stable contractual bodies, with physical locations (headquarters, plants, departments, etc.), while the new economics call for a focus on industries as systems rather than as buildings and walls. Hedberg introduces the concept of "imaginary organizations" to picture these new economic conditions.[28]

An "imaginary organization" is a knowledge infrastructure concerning markets, potential opportunities, for production and creation of value-chains. Hedberg uses the example of Gant, an American garment brand that was bought by Swedish investors and developed worldwide. Gant has no proprietary plants. The whole organization consists of a team of managers that coordinate market needs and channels with a constellation of independent suppliers. The core competitive advantage of Gant lies in the corporation's ability to coordinate market needs with independent systems' inputs.

Gant uses its knowledge infrastructure to define and find matches between independent production and design capabilities and market needs.

This whole perspective of knowledge infrastructures is likely to be the dominant paradigm in the coming century. Hewlett-Packard in France got rid of local middle management supervisory staff to replace it with a centralized information platform at its headquarters. The "information infrastructure" collects customers' needs and requests, and dispatches the information directly to managers and maintenance engineers' notebook screens through electronic data interchange. Locally, Hewlett-Packard suppressed many subsidiaries and branches. Managers and maintenance engineers work at home, being constantly on the move to meet customers' needs and specifications on sites. The whole organization is transformed in a knowledge-generation node, with many peripheries where action is taking place.

Could such a model be implemented on a national scale, and what would be the social and welfare consequences? It is quite probable that such a knowledge infrastructure could be designed and implemented on a national scale. It would require administrations, large and small corporations, and individuals to share a communal information infrastructure where demands and supplies of tangibles and intangibles would find their matches. In such a perspective, competitive advantage of nations would eventually lie in national ability and speed to generate (and discontinue without social and economic costs) virtual value chains to operate them. Attempts such as the Department of Commerce's Advocacy Center in the United States, and the Committee for Economic Security and Competitiveness (CCSE) attached to the Secretariat General de la Defense National (SGDN) in France, are evidently pursuing such a model.

Both the Advocacy Center and the CCSE pursue an objective of coordination and alertness between administrative bodies and private organizations. However, while the Advocacy Center is located at an operational level with a direct link to the intelligence community, the French CCSE is placed under the authority of the prime minister, and its main focus is a supra-coordination of administrative bodies (Ministries of Finance, Defense, Foreign Affairs, French Office of Planning) that already fulfill, more or less properly, a coordination role. Political ambitions, in France and in the United States, and intelligence communities' internal conflicts, however, are impeding the performance of both the French and American experiences.

Misconceptions of Economics and Welfare

Economic theories mainly failed, for they either never successfully addressed the benevolence issue in economic development or rapidly lost their focus when attempting to grab it. Myths that surround the development of InfoWar or InfoEconomics are mainly myths of malevolence: "cyberwarriors," "viruses," "logic bombs," etc. Whereas we leave the paradigm of economics of forces, physical order, heaviness, and superiority of gender on genius, we tend to bring with us the bad habits of past and history. InfoWar experts and analysts react to the emergence of the knowledge paradigm with a defense attitude toward the unexpected. Whereas a global knowledge infrastructure could have been an opportunity to substitute threat-equilibrium with integrative power,[29] policymakers tend to project ideologies and doctrines that prove to be wrong instead of inventing the conceptual framework that will fit the new economics.

Two biases lie behind the design and mission of these government-level information coordination bodies. The first bias could be pictured as an "intelligentsialization" of the information infrastructure. Both French and American governments have chosen a top-down implementation of their information infrastructure, thus applying obsolete governmental schemata to the management of knowledge. While experts are calling for the development of the largest knowledge-sharing culture possible,[30] national knowledge infrastructure projects are being drawn with an elitist bias. It might occur, around 2010, that such decisions were historical self-deceptions. Doing so, governments tend to confuse information logistics (a structural perspective) with knowledge sharing (an interactionist perspective). In other words, artificial efficiency is reached today because decisionmakers and policymakers who share information already hold the requisite knowledge to make this information actionable. Thus, it gives the illusion that the development of an information structure is a necessary and sufficient condition to attain a national knowledge infrastructure.

On the contrary, such a policy will prove counterproductive. It will eventually create an isolated body of upper-level knowledge, disconnected with the reality of social development and learning, and therefore increasing the gap between people who act, learn, and talk and people being acted upon, learned about, and talked about. Economic performance might be reached through a routinized logistics of generic knowledge amongst business leaders, industrialists, and politicians, but social performance is already doubtful. Research findings suggest that permanent improvement and continuous learning cannot be achieved in situations of disarticulated socialization.[31] Information infrastructures, as designed in American and French projects, favor information exchange, including possible use of information highways, and neglect to design proper socialization devices that would enhance permanent and collective sense-making. Furthermore, such knowledge infrastructures are already perceived by the population as jobs-destructive, in opposition with almost all fourteen points of Deming's principles of continuous transformation.[32] One of these principles says that fear should be driven out so that everyone may work effectively. Surrounded by myths of malevolence, economic-intelligence-sharing infrastructures, on the contrary, announce a quest for economics of coordination costs, worldwide economics of scale, and the birth of a knowledgeable elite with privileged and discretionary access to rising knowledge infrastructures. Hewlett-Packard was an examplar on that point. Local managers disappeared, leaving their place to management technicians "being acted" by electronic data interchange. Many firms, more or less consciously, took this curve. Asea Brown Bovery (ABB) reduced its corporate staff, after its fusion, from more than 4,000 to less than 300 "global managers." Given the fact that middle managers already live and work in suburban areas, the effect is an increasing gap between geographically concentrated conceptual knowledge and geographically dispersed procedural know-how. Instead of encouraging a cooperative culture, knowledge infrastructures may implement a perennial rupture between an exclusive and very small knowledgeable suprastructure, and a very large, fragmented and desocialized, cognitively taylorized substructure.

In Deming's theory, effectiveness is derived from continuous efforts "toward the simultaneous creation of cooperative and learning organization to facilitate the implementation of process-management practices, which, when implemented, support customer satisfaction and organizational survival through sustained employee fulfillment and continuous improvement of processes, products, and services."[33] Similar thinking can be found in intelligence history in general, and in the sixteenth-century Elizabethan doctrine of governmental intelligence in particular: "Elizabeth was intellectually the most enlightened monarch of her time. Francis Bacon writes that she was 'undued with learning,' and 'to the end of her life she sets hours for reading (more than) scarcely any student of her time.' One way to please her was to talk 'In Praise of Knowledge,' as Essex did with his essay, most probably written by Bacon."[34] Queen Elizabeth I's intelligence shadow adviser, Sir Francis Bacon, was the author of the Advancement of Learning in 1605, and also authored an essay entitled "Followers and Friends" in 1597. The other intelligence doctrine advisor, Sir William Cecil, authored a forward-looking memorandum entitled "Matters Necessary to be Done, Troubles That All May Presently Ensue, Things Necessary to be Considered, With Speed, With Foreboding, With Foresight, Plots and Designs."[35] Speed, consistency and sharing of knowledge-generation processes on a large-scale base were already put at the center of national development strategies.

The difference between sixteenth-century Great Britain and current industrial democracies, however, is a fundamental shift from obedience to commitment of the governed. To continue to design information infrastructures in the Elizabethan style is overlooking that knowledge is nowadays widely distributed. "Cooperation, in this context, is synonymous with collaboration among different individuals, groups, or organizations, where all entities are engaging in noncompetitive, mutually beneficial, win-win activities."[36]

Why Shift from InfoWar to Knowledge War: A Case Study

As Wilensky once put it, "information has always been a source of power, but it is now increasingly a source of confusion. In every sphere of modern life, the chronic condition is surfeit of information, poorly integrated or lost somewhere in the system."[37] Roots of such failures can been found (1) in the persistent confusion between knowledge and information, (2) on the large-scale focus that has been given in education to accumulating knowledge-bases versus permanent improvement of the diversity and flexibility of modes of knowing, and (3) in the failure of scientists to integrate in new organizational forms and purposes the advancements of social cognition and collective learning. Yet, "managers are becoming increasingly aware that informed adaptability is at a premium and to attain it they may need different modes of organization to find and solve different types of problems."[38]

Nevertheless, and consistent with a perception of knowledge as a commodity, organization on one side and knowledge on the other side are systematically approached distinctively. Organization theorists propose many alternatives and original organizational forms, but leave managers with the duty of generating adequate knowledge to operate them. Knowledge sociologists put much emphasis on the many forms of socializations that participate in the building of cognitive skills, but are reluctant to study how organizational design and knowledge generation interact.

The German definition of the word *intelligenz* could shed some light on such an intricate issue. The *Wirtschafts-Lexikon,* a principal German dictionary, in defining intelligence, puts "an emphasis on mental processes geared to adaptation, integration, and recognizing significant relationships. These processes are interesting: were we to consider them as characteristics of some organizational form, we would come very near to the 'intelligence system' definition. German thought also recognizes the importance of the perception of causal connection and of capacity for combination."[39] To achieve the integration of knowing and organizing, German authorities have historically put a strong focus on the continuity of education to intelligence in the society. After World War II, the Economic Police were reintegrated in national industrial infrastructures. Today, German students receive education from German generals and senior military officers in most business schools to maintain a longitudinal awareness of the role played by intelligence and military art in the understanding and design of business organizations.

The Perrier case illustrates the importance of "the perception of causal connection and of capacity for combination" so much favored by German intelligence.[40] On July 3, 1989, Perrier and PepsiCo were negotiating the creation of a joint venture in which Perrier would hold 65 percent of the shares. The negotiations were disrupted on July 16. In August 1989, Perrier sold its subsidiary, the Societe Parisienne de Boissons Gazeuses, which distributes Pepsi in France, to its main competitor, Coca Cola. This competitive move was perceived as retaliation. In November 1989, PepsiCo denounced the poor performance of Perrier in the management of its license, announcing the disruption of all contractual arrangements for December 1990. PepsiCo took Perrier to court on November 8, 1990 and announced, a day after, that it would be eventually interested in taking over the soft drink activities of Perrier, if the stock price would be more attractive. Meanwhile, the Coca Cola stock reached the historic price of $72 on November 18, 1989.

On January 19, 1990, a laboratory in Charlottesville, North Carolina discovered traces of benzene in samples of Perrier mineral water. Experts suspected the information to have been transmitted through a mole in a Perrier production plant in Vergeze. "Causal connection" could be made between the test results and the nearby location of a Coca Cola plant. The laboratory manager did not remember having replaced its test equipment, but "combined" information showed strong evidence of all test equipment being graciously replaced by a Coca Cola sponsorship of the laboratory. On February 2, 1990, the Food and Drug Administration warned Perrier that mineral water being distributed in the United States contained benzene.

At that time, Perrier was a potential takeover target. Nestle would eventually be interested, and had made aggressive competitive moves in the European market. In particular, Nestle had managed to sign an exclusivity contract with Walt Disney Europe, walking on traditionally Coca Cola proprietary territory.

On February 5, 1990, the FDA confirmed the presence of benzene in Perrier mineral water. On February 10, Perrier was forced to acknowledge, but reacted very quickly by announcing that all bottles would be withdrawn from the market. On February 12, Perrier's stock lost 14 percent of its value. Suntory, the Japanese distributor of the brand, announced the withdrawal of 10,000 cases from the Japanese market. On February 14, German authorities forbid Perrier mineral water in their markets. The French Commission of Stock Operations (COB) announced an investigation on suspicious stock movements that occurred on February 9. Sales were stopped in the United States, Canada, Japan, Germany, Switzerland, Denmark, and Hong Kong.

This InfoWar could have ended at this event, but Perrier held 25 percent of the American sparkling water market, with annual sales of $500 million. Perrier reacted with great dexterity facing such Info-destabilization. Financial market observers were promptly reassured on the integrity of the natural water source. The human error was fully explained with a worldwide dissemination of accurate counterinformation. Sanitary authorities announced the results of scientific investigations: "The daily consumption of a half-liter of Perrier during 30 years does not increase the risk of cancer." Perrier stock gained 6.3 percent on the Paris stock exchange.

The second phase of this InfoWar began on February 20, 1990. A 36-year-old Athenian woman asked Perrier for 7.5 million francs for the damage caused by the explosion of a bottle that supposedly led to the loss of her eye. Evidence showed that the incident occurred four years before, on August 25, 1986. Several similar court cases appeared in different places: a lawyer in Bridgeport, Connecticut defended a Mrs. Vahlsing; eight similar class action cases appeared in Connecticut and Pennsylvania. Perrier discovered that Kroll, the investigative consultancy that took care of its information in the United States, had withheld key information from its reports.[41] In 1991, Nestle finally took over Perrier.

Very similar cases of InfoWar, such as the Shell-Greenpeace Brentspar's case or the "benzene threat" to Octel Co. in the United Kingdom[42] lead to the same conclusions: (1) an isolated organization cannot cope alone with large-scale Info-destabilization without considerable loss; (2) successful large-scale InfoWars involve interorganizational agreements, and collective manipulations of the worldwide information infrastructure (mass media, scientific institutions, customer groups, etc.); and most importantly, (3) ability to rapidly make sense (i.e., generate knowledge) is superior in counter-fighting InfoWars than systematic collection and compilation of open information already coming from a corrupted or contaminated information infrastructure.

Preparing for the K-Paradigm

Sweden might be an examplar of a country already engaged in preparation for the paradigm shift toward knowledge warfare. In 1977, Dr. Stevan Dedijer started a business intelligence course at Lund University, educating and training many graduate students that would later become take charge of economic intelligence in such groups as Skandia, Volvo, and Ericsson. The latter company has organized a strategic group with the University of Karlstadt that investigates strategic issues of long-distance education and information highways. Members of this group also participated in the 1992 Swedish Ministry of Defense seminars on the application of C4I2 to strategic development. In a well-defined and well-applied strategy, another strategic group that put together economic, social, political, and military leaders such as Lars Hallen (head of scientific attaches), Bjorn Wolrath (AB Skandia CEO), Goran Pagels-Fick (Ericsson), Peter Nygards (State Secretary for Industry), and Jan Foghelin (head of the Defense Research Center Fosvarets Forskningstantalt),[43] started to build an "economic intelligence community" among business leaders in 1991. Originally named BISNES (Business Intelligence and Security Network of Sweden), on a proposed idea from Dedijer, the network adopted a more discreet strategy by inviting for large debriefing sessions economic intelligence thinkers and leaders of the open world. General Pichot-Duclos, head of Intelco, the French InfoWar and Economic Intelligence think tank, was among the early guests of these sessions with businessmen, academia, and the military.

Sweden also holds first rank in systematized intelligence activities in large companies in Europe.[44] Observations compiled by Hedin of Astra-Draco, Electrolux, Ericsson Radio, Gambro, Celsius Tech, Skandia, SCA Graphic, SAS, Telia, and Volvo show a good balance between strategic and operational objectives, a systematic supply-and-on-demand intelligence for corporate management, a focus on information-sharing culture (e.g., systematic community meetings around the BISNES network), and a particular focus on knowledge acquisition processes.[45]

What can be learned from the Swedish experiment? First of all, Sweden's knowledge infrastructure does not seek publicity. Proceedings of the first open conference on Swedish nation-scale economic intelligence were not translated and are not available on any Web servers, although Sweden displays one of the highest rates of electronic information and telecommunications in the world. While Sweden is claiming to be behind with the knowlege warfare agenda, young Swedes can do their military service in economic intelligence activities. Second, the Swedish experiment is culture-driven. Information-sharing has for long been a cultural practice among expatriate Swedes. Emphasis is put on a culture of knowledge-sharing rather than on the constitution of specialized administrative bodies. Third, the core of the Swedish knowledge infrastructure is not hardware-based, but is a "community of practice and sense-making." The BISNES informal network meets regularly, and sense-making is a communal, face-to-face process.

Sweden, however, has favorable conditions that could hardly be met by other countries. It is higly culturally homogeneous and its population is less than 10 million. As with all Scandinavian countries, the level of literacy is one of the highest in the world.

Conclusion

"Making the simple complicated is commonplace; making the complicated simple, awesomely simple, that's creativity."[46] Preparing for the knowledge warfare paradigm requires a strong focus on reengineering the whole education process of industrialized democracies. This is that simple, but policymakers will face strong resistance, especially from academics. Integration of strategic issues assessment should be put as early as possible in education. The current process is cumulative, whereas the required process is interactionist. Instead of thinking of education in terms of sequentiality, policymakers should design education in terms of interconnectivity and interoperability. Many organizations would like today to increase the awareness of strategic issues among their engineers' population and also to increase the awareness of technological issues among their commercial task forces. To do so, they design new systems, centralized economic intelligence units that dispatch technical market information to both communities. Some firms, like Intel, encourage hybrid teams of engineers and managers to fertilize crisscrossed issues. This is a result of taylorized learning and knowing. Emphasis should be on judgment, cognitive skills, cognitive flexibility, incongruity, and ambiguity tolerance at the youngest age. In the knowledge warfare paradigm, strategic advantage does not lie in the concentration of facts and figures, but in the complementarity and singularity of the brains that interpret them. National sense-making capability matters more than electronic information highways.

1. Bo Hedberg and Sten Jonsson, "Designing semi-confusing information systems for organizations in changing environments," *Accounting, Organizations, and Society* 3 (1): 47-64, 1978.

2. F. J. Varela and H. R. Maturana, *L'Arbre de la Connaissance*. Paris: Addison-Wesley, 1994.

3. H. Helmholtz, *Treatise on Physiological Optics* (1867), vol. III. Translated from German by J. P. C. Southall (ed.), New York: Dover, 1962.

4. E. L. Thorndike and R. T. Rock, "Learning Without Awareness of What Is Being Learned or Intent to Learn It," *Journal of Experimental Psychology* 19: 1-19, 1934.

5. L. Hasher and R. T. Zacks, "Automatic Processing of Fundamental Information," *American Psychologist* 48: 1372-1388, 1984.

6. J. G. Jenkins, "Instruction as a Factor of Incidental Learning," *American Journal of Psychology* 45: 471-477, 1993.

7. W. B. Scott, "Information Warfare Demands a New Approach," *Aviation Week & Space Technology,* March 13, 1995, p. 85.

8. http://indigo-net.com/lmr.html. Archives since 1993 are available in English on the Net.

9. J. S. Brown and P. Duguid, "Organizational Learning and Communities of Practice: Toward a Unified View of Working, Learning and Innovation," *Organization Science* 2 (1): 40-57, 1991.

10. W. H. Starbuck, in the preface of P. Baumard, *Organisations Deconcertees. La Gestion Strategique de la Connaissance*. Paris: Masson, 1996 (London: Sage, 1997).

11. J. E. Lave and E. Wenger, *Situated Learning: Legitimate Peripheral Participation*. Cambridge, MA: Cambridge University Press, 1991.

12. General F. M. Francks, Jr., "Winning the Information War: Evolution and Revolution." Speech delivered at the Association of the U.S. Army Symposium, Orlando, FL, February 8, 1994. *Vital Speeches of the Day* 60 (15): 455, 1994.

13. Ibid., p. 456. It is noticeable that Harry Howe Ransom's "Strategic Intelligence" article (1973, General Learning Press), when using the Viet Cong guerilla as an exemplar, and using intelligence estimate NIE 143/53-61, "Prospects for North and South Vietnam," dated 15 August 1961, does not mention the existence of the Vietnamese underground logistics, and suspects the "Bloc to build up the eastern part of south Laos, improving the roads, mountain trails, and airfields, as a major supply channel" (p. 7). This is an exemplar of applying a cultural mode of knowing that projects ethnocentric schemata on a singular reality.

14. Starbuck, op. cit.

15. M. Detienne and J. P. Vernant, *Cunning Intelligence in Greek Culture and Society,* translated by J. Lloyd. Atlantic Highlands, NJ: Humanities Press, 1978.

16. H. Wilensky, "Organizational Intelligence," in *The International Encyclopedia of the Social Sciences,* David L. Sills (ed.), vol. 11. New York: Macmillan & the Free Press, 1967, p. 321.

17. J. C. Spender and P. Baumard, "An Empirical Investigation of Change in the Knowledge Leading to Competitive Advantage."

Research paper presented at the Academy of Management Annual Meeting, Vancouver, August 5, 1995, under the title "Turning Troubled Firms Around: Case-Evidence for a Penrosian View of Strategic Recovery."

18. J. F. Richard, *Les Activites Mentales.* Paris: Armand Collin, 1990.
19. Ernest R. May, statement before the Senate Select Committee on Intelligence, 4 March 1992.
20. Frank Carlucci, testimony before the Senate Select Committee on Intelligence, 4 March 1992.
21. J. Douglas Orton and Jamie L. Callahan, "Important 'Folk Theories' on Intelligence Reorganization," *International Journal of Intelligence and Counterintelligence* 8 (4), 1996.
22. W. B. Scott, "Information Warfare Demands New Approach," *Aviation Week & Space Technology,* March 13, 1995, p. 86.
23. Alex N. Dragnich, "Containing Serbia," Letter to the Editor, *Foreign Affairs* 73 (6) November/December 1994, p. 198.
24. The final report under the presidency of Henri Martre, co-authored by P. Baumard, P. Clerc, and C. Harbulot, was published by La Documentation Francaise in February 1994 under the title *Intelligence Economique et Strategie des Entreprises.* The Mirage 200-5 case study was withdrawn from the final publication.
25. Wilensky, op. cit., p. 323.
26. David P. Baron, "The Nonmarket Strategy System," *Sloan Management Review,* Fall 1995, p. 75.
27. T. A. Stewart, "The Information Wars: What You Don't Know Will Hurt You," Fortune, June 12, 1995, p. 119.
28. Bo Hedberg, *Imaginary Organizations.* New York: Oxford University Press, 1996.
29. For developments on integrative power, see Kenneth E. Boulding, *Three Faces of Power.* London: Sage Publications, 1990.
30. See P. Baumard, "Guerre Economique et Communaute du Intelligence," *La Revue Politique et Parlementaire (Political and Parliementary Review),* Paris, January 1992; P. Baumard, *Strategie et Surveillance des Environnements Concurrentiels,* Paris: Masson, 1991; and C. Harbulot, *La Machine de Guerre Economique,* Paris: Economica, 1993.
31. J. C. Spender and P. Baumard, op. cit.; I. Nonaka and H. Takeuchi, The Knowledge Creating Company: How Japanese Companies Create the Dynamics of Innovation, New York: Oxford University Press, 1995.
32. W. E. Deming, *Out of Crisis.* Cambridge, MA: Massachussets Institute of Technology, Center for Advanced Engineering Study, 1986, pp. 23-24.
33. J. C. Anderson, M. Rungtusanatham, and R. G. Schroeder, "A Theory of Quality Management Underlying the Deming Management Method," *Academy of Management Review* 19 (3): 480, 1994.
34. S. Dedijer, "British Intelligence: The Rainbow Enigma," *Interna-*

tional Journal of Intelligence and Counterintelligence 1 (2): 82, 1989.

35. Quoted by Dedijer, op. cit., p. 83.
36. Anderson, Rungtusanatham, and Schroeder, op. cit., p. 483.
37. Wilensky, op. cit., p. 331.
38. Dale E. Zand, *Information, Organization and Power: Effective Management in the Knowledge Society.* New York: McGraw-Hill, 1981, p. 58.
39. F. T. Pearce and S. Dedijer, "The Semantics of Intelligence." Research Paper, Lund University, February 1976, p. 11.
40. C. Harbulot and P. Gustave, "La Contre-Information ou Comment Repondre—Une Attaque," *Cahiers de la Fonction Publique et de l'Administration* 140: 11-13, November 1995.
41. Source: M. Najman, "Intelligence Economique," a special television broacast, Strasbourg: Arte (Franco-German Television), 1995.
42. D. Knott, "Views Conflict on Benzene Threat," *Oil and Gas Journal,* May 23, 1994, p. 41.
43. Source: "First Large Public Conference on Economic Intelligence in Sweden," *The Intelligence Newsletter* 283: March 7, 1996.
44. H. Hedin, "Business Intelligence Systems: Systematised Intelligence Activities in Ten Multinational Companies," *Journal of the Association of Global Strategic Information,* 1993, pp. 126-136.
45. Lars Bengtsson and Jessica Ohlin, "Strategy Formation and Knowledge Acquisition Process," in Larsson, et al., *Research in Strategic Change: Lund Studies in Economics and Management* 21. Lund University Press, 1993
46. Charlie Mingus, 1977, "Creativity," *Mainliner* 21 (7): 25, 1977, quoted by W. H. Starbuck and P. C. Nystrom, "Designing and Understanding Organizations," in *Handbook of Organizational Design,* vol. 1, Oxford University Press, 1981, p. 9.

Protecting the National Information Infrastructure Against Infowar

**Daniel J. Ryan, SAIC,
and Julie J. C. H. Ryan, Booz Allen and Hamilton**

Our nation's capital is a town in love with buzzwords and jargon, and the defense and intelligence communities are not immune. At their worst, such buzzwords obfuscate and oversimplify, impeding the understanding of issues and their underlying dynamics and thereby subverting the political process. At their best, such words may be "terms of art" that serve as a sort of shorthand to make discussions of policies, practices, and procedures more economical. In any event, in Washington if you know and use the latest jargon, you are perceived as being an insider and can sometimes get your budget increased; otherwise, you're out of luck.

The latest buzzword is *InfoWar,* for "Information Warfare." It's a new term, and it's still evolving. Because it is in vogue, it is being used in many quarters to support arguments pro and con regarding the threat to and vulnerabilities of computers and communications networks, an infrastructure that has its own jargon—Cyberspace or the Information Superhighway or, collectively, the National Information Infrastructure or NII. Ambiguities in usage pose a significant challenge to those responsible for making policy concerning the protection of the NII, defocusing the debate as to what can and should be done to protect it.

Information warfare is, first and foremost, warfare. It is not information terrorism, computer crime, hacking, or commercial or state-sponsored espionage using networks for access to desirable information. These are all interesting and dangerous phenomena that individuals, corporations, and governments face in today's connected, online world, but they are not InfoWar. InfoWar is the application of destructive force on a large scale against information assets and systems, against the computers and networks that support the air traffic control system, stock transactions, financial records, currency exchanges, Internet communications, telephone switching, credit records, credit card transactions, management information systems, office automation systems, the space program, the railroad system, hospital systems that monitor patients and dispense drugs, manufacturing process control systems, newspapers and publishing, the insurance industry, power distribution and utilities, all of which depend heavily on computers.

The distinction is vital; otherwise we have no ability to determine appropriate response options and responding agencies. When CIA employee Aldrich Ames was discovered selling our deepest secrets to our enemies, we did not consider his subversion to have been an act of war eliciting a military response. The bombings of the World Trade Center and the federal building in Oklahoma City were responded to by law enforcement officers, not soldiers and sailors. Without a clear distinction between crime and espionage on the one hand and war on the other, we would quickly find ourselves faced with the prospect of sending the Department of Defense against a 13-year-old who is trying to hack into government computers. There are real issues here that must be solved, including the problems of knowing that an attack is underway, of ascertaining the scope of the attack, and of bringing to bear effective responses. Such issues can be resolved only after an appropriate framework of policies, practices, and procedures has been established based on a clear understanding of the problem to be addressed.

First of all, it is critical to differentiate InfoWar from information-based warfare. From the days of runners carrying tactical information and orders over the plains of Greece, through the eras of signal fires, flags and mirrors and carrier pigeons, to today's use of satellite communications, information has always been a crucial component of military decision-making. The formulation and execution of effective battle plans requires answers to such questions as, "Where are the enemy forces?" "Where are our targets?" "Where are friendly forces?" "What are the intentions of the enemy commanders?" "What is the status of supplies and ammunition needed to prosecute the enemy?" as well as a host of other information. All other things being equal, more timely, accurate, and complete information is a force multiplier and provides a real advantage that reduces casualties and saves equipment and facilities. This is well understood and has been incorporated into our strategic and tactical planning processes.

The concept of information-based warfare formalizes the realization that modern forces are dependent on information and systems that can rapidly and securely provide that information to decision-makers, and that we must maintain and enhance our own information assets while denying that advantage to the enemy. This description of information-based warfare would not surprise Sun Tzu, Alexander the Great, Genghis Kahn, or Clausewitz. What might cause pause to these historical strategists, however, would be the notion of information and information technology as a separate area of warfare independent of guns, tanks, airplanes, and ships.

As information-related technology has evolved, so has its utility to warfare. But it is important to recognize that information technology not only enables modern warfare, it shapes the very way we think about war and its conduct. The state of the art is now at a point where it is possible to conceive of the information infrastructure, content, and technologies as parts of an information dimension to warfare, separate and distinct from other dimensions but subject to similar complexities in strategic and tactical planning as are the more conventional dimensions of air, land, sea, and more lately space. In information-based warfare, we use better, faster, and more complete information to gain an advantage in applying conventional or strategic forces. In InfoWar, the information systems and networks become the battlefield and information itself becomes the target. The Joint DoD-DCI Security Commission said, "Networks are already recognized as a battlefield of the future. Information weapons will attack and defend at electronic speeds using strategies and tactics yet to be perfected. This technology is capable of deciding the outcome of geopolitical crises without the firing of a single weapon." Note that there are three separate parts of this new dimension of warfare: the infrastructure, the content, and the technologies. Each are jointly and severally the weapons and the targets in InfoWar.

This concept—true Information Warfare as opposed to information-based warfare—has captured the attention of many of the world's strategic thinkers from Moscow to Tehran to Chiapas. Nevertheless, such a change in the nature of warfare is hardly new. In World War I, air warfare began to be explored and founded a revolution in warfare. As World War II progressed, the new applications of electromagnetism to warfare led to the "Wizard War," or what is now called electronic warfare. If it seemed like wizardry to the scientists and engineers who invented it, imagine how incomprehensible it must have been to the cavalry and infantry, whose training and experience centered on more tangible dimensions of combat. Two decades ago the need to incorporate the role of space into warfare was recognized. And much as the air power advocates and space and electronic warfare strategists had significant challenges to overcome in their quest to define air, space, and the electromagnetic spectrum as separate and independent dimensions of warfare, InfoWar is facing and must stand up to the skepticism and challenges of the professional warrior community as its strategies and tactics evolve.

The second major problem in protecting the NII in an InfoWar has to do with ownership of the computers and networks that must be protected. Not since the early days of strategic nuclear war has our country's infrastructure been the target for acts of war. In those days we feared that our enemies would strike at population centers in an all-out attempt to destroy our will and our capability to fight. Our counterstrategy was mutual assured destruction (MAD)—"You maybe able to destroy us, but nothing will remain of your country when the dust settles." Later, as the Circular Error Probabilities of our weapons decreased, we shifted to targeting military capabilities rather than population centers. Perhaps as our capability to wage InfoWar improves, selective targeting of infoweapons and malicious code will become possible, but at least for now the target of infoweapons is our information infrastructure and the economy it supports.

Most of that information infrastructure is privately owned and operated rather than under government control. Corporations do not ordinarily fight wars or engage in combat. Most corporations would no more consider the need to develop and pay for the technologies, practices, and procedures that would be needed to defend their proprietary systems and networks against an InfoWar attack than they would have in the 1950s and 1960s developed the technologies, practices, and procedures to protect themselves against a strategic exchange of thermonuclear weapons. The commercial sector expects the Department of Defense to protect them against these threats, just as business expected the War Department and later the Defense Department to protect individuals and commercial interests against attacks by the pirates of Tripoli, the imperialistic Axis nations, and the Soviet "evil empire." This is not to imply that corporations are unconcerned about the protection of their information assets and systems. It is to say that there is a clear difference between the types and scale of threat against which corporations believe it is their responsibility to protect themselves, and the types and scale of threats to which they cannot and should not have to respond.

Nevertheless, the trends are clear:

- More information and more valuable information is being created, stored, processed, and communicated using computers and computer-based systems and networks.

- Computers are increasingly interconnected, creating new pathways to valuable information assets.
- The threat is becoming increasingly sophisticated.

When nation states with powerful capabilities funded by nation-sized budgets are added to the threat mix, individuals and corporations acting alone are completely outclassed and largely helpless.

For the mandarins charged with protecting the nation's security, this is a very difficult problem. For corporate decision-makers, it is simply a question of risk management. Both corporations and individuals naturally strive to eliminate risk. As worthy as that goal my be, we know that complete avoidance of risk is never possible. Even if it *were* possible to eliminate all risk, the cost of achieving that goal would have to be compared against the cost of the possible losses resulting from having accepted rather than having eliminated some or even all of the risk. After all, our economy loses over $300 million in illegal interbank transfers each year, telephone toll fraud exceeds $200 million per year, and credit card fraud tops $3 billion per year, yet these losses are treated as merely costs of doing business. The results of such cost-benefit analyses help individuals and corporations make pragmatic decisions as to whether achieving risk abatement at such a cost is reasonable. A similar analysis leads inexorably to the conclusion that neither an individual nor a corporation can expect to survive an infoWar unscathed, nor could we afford to do so were it even possible. In private industry, our collective ability to operate, and hence the nation's economy, depends upon the NII. No corporation of any size could continue to operate if, for example, the nation's telephone system were successfully targeted in an InfoWar.

Not that the news is all bad. Many of the things individuals and corporations have to do and are doing to defend information assets and systems against white collar criminals, hackers, computer-literate competitors, and even terrorists will provide some measure of protection against an InfoWar attack. We engage in business continuity planning for disaster recovery and we invest heavily in technology to protect our valuable assets, tangible and intangible. We have uninterruptible power supplies to protect us against power outages due to natural disasters, we build beta recovery sites to ensure continuous operations, and we routinely backup our databases. In an InfoWar, we will not be able to protect against the loss of the NII upon which we depend to transact business, but we may be able to protect to some extent our databases, our intellectual capital, and our systems and internal networks.

To minimize the damage that may be expected in a strategic InfoWar, the government needs to do at least two things. First, ensure the ability of the nation to recognize and respond rapidly and effectively to an attack or the threat of an attack. There is no surer deterrence against terrorism or military adventurism by a rogue state than assured and devastating retaliation by the United States. This means protecting the computer systems and communications networks used to mobilize and execute military operations—the Defense Information Infrastructure (DII)—from destructive or denial of service InfoWar attacks, including, if necessary, reducing the military service's reliance on the public switched network and the public power grid, and eliminating other weaknesses that could seriously degrade the ability to mobilize and respond in the event of an attack.

Second, as the government identifies computer and network vulnerabilities and develops the technologies needed to protect the DII, it must share them with the private sector so the knowledge can be used to enhance the security of that part of the NII that is privately owned and operated. Arguments that revealing discovered weaknesses may lead to our enemies correcting those same weaknesses and thereby lessening our own offensive capabilities pale beside the possibility of extensive damage to the NII when corrective action could have been taken. Arguments that access to security technology must be restricted lest it fall into enemy hands fail for like reasons. Those of us that depend upon systems and networks need to know our weaknesses as soon as possible and apply the best available technology to reducing or eliminating vulnerabilities. This will, in turn, lessen the likelihood of a successful attack and hence of any attempt to destroy, corrupt, or exploit our systems and networks.

It would help if there were a coherent set of policies, practices, and procedures applicable across the private sector for protection of information assets and systems. While the government has a pivotal role in securing the nation's information infrastructure, it is extremely unlikely that DoD or the military services will be able to solve the problem acting unilaterally. True, much of the needed security technology has been developed by the Department of Defense and the military services, particularly at the National Security Agency. But too much of the solution must be implemented within the private sector, and that sector, as we all know, is uncomfortable with government intrusions in general, and especially intrusions by the defense and intelligence communities. Since the steps that must be taken to secure the information infrastructure are beyond those likely to result naturally from market forces, some overall approach is needed to foster application of coherent security policies, practices, and procedures across the economy.

If the technological issues were resolved, a system of incentives—tax and otherwise—might work. Unfortunately, there are real problems yet to be resolved with regard to technology. Controls on the use and export of cryptography provide an excellent example. The law enforcement and national security communities, in exercising their missions to protect the security of the nation and the safety of its citizens, rightly see the widespread use of sound cryptography as a problem. These equities are in more or less direct conflict with the equities of individuals and corporations wanting to protect information assets and systems and with those of developers of secure software and hardware systems that would be sold to companies and individuals whose systems comprise the NII. The arguments are too complex to be treated in full here, but amply illustrate the pitfalls of unregulated approaches to securing the information infrastructure.

A body is needed having the power to both make and enforce information security rules that would apply across the private sector. Such bodies are created under the auspices of the Administrative Procedures Act and have both regulatory and adjudicatory authority. One model might be the FCC; perhaps the FCC's charter might even be extended to encompass protection of the information infrastructure, avoiding the unpleasant necessity of creating a new organization in a time of downward budget pressures.

It is the first duty of government to provide for the security of its citizens. One way in which this duty is fulfilled is to provide for the common defense against overwhelming external aggression, whether the weapons are thermonuclear devices and conventional armies or logic weapons and malicious code deployed on our networks. Both corporations and individual citizens rely on the government to deter such aggression, to defend us when deterrence fails, and to retaliate in full force when we have suffered an attack. InfoWar in Cyberspace presents us with new difficulties in both defense and offense, and form the challenge of this decade and the early years of the next century.

America, The Last Empire: Decline or Strength?

Bertil Häggman, Center for Research on Geopolitics

All European empires since the fifteenth century have declined and have had to hand over power to a successor: the Portuguese to the Spanish to the Dutch to the British. After World War II, the American empire has been the leading Western entity.

In his 1990 book *The American Empire,* Geir Lundestad, Director of the Nobel Institute in Oslo looked at the role of the United States from 1945 to 1990. The book came out the year before the Soviet empire collapsed, but Lundestad could already draw the conclusion that there was only one superpower left in the world.

The debate on America's decline started in the 1970s, mainly amongst political economists. Some of the books written about this subject included *The World in Depression* by Charles Kindleberger, *U.S. Power and the Multinational Corporation* (1975) by Robert Gilpin, *The Imperious*

Economy (1982) by David Calleo, *Beyond American Hegemony: The Future of the Western Alliance* (1987), *International Regimes* (1983) edited by Stephen Krasner, and *After Hegemony: Cooperation and Discord in the World Political Economy* by Robert Keohane. They all agreed that the American position was declining. Very few protests against this view were registered; among the writers who took opposing stands were Bruce Russett and Susan Strange, writing separate articles in the journal *International Organization* (1982).

During the presidency of Ronald Reagan, the historian Paul Kennedy's first important book, *The Rise and Fall of the Great Powers—Economic Change and Military Conflict from 1500 to 2000* (1987), reached bestseller status. Kennedy brought the question of American decline into focus, stating quite clearly that America was in decline. A political debate was the result: Kennedy's prediction was rejected not only by President Reagan but by political scientists like Walt Rostow ("Beware of Historians Bearing False Analogies," *Foreign Affairs,* Spring 1988), Samuel Huntington ("The U.S.—Decline or Renewal?" *Foreign Affairs,* Winter 1988), and Joseph Nye (*Bound to Lead—The Changing Nature of American Power,* 1990).

According to Lundestad, most participants in the debate agreed that although America had declined compared to its heyday in the 1950s, the United States was still the strongest power on earth: it had military strength, political organization, and ideological foundation.

In the 1990s, Kennedy has continued his analysis (*Preparing for the Twenty-First Century,* 1993) and Huntington ("The Clash of Civilizations?" *Foreign Affairs,* 1993) has sparked a new debate on the global road ahead. Francis Fukuyama (*The End of History and the Last Man,* 1992) attempted to find the place of America and the American idea in history.

An interesting contribution to the continuing debate on America's role in world history is the posthumously published *The Myth of the West—America as the Last Empire* (1995) by Jan Willem Schulte Nordholt, a leading Dutch expert on American affairs at the time of his death in August 1995. Schulte Nordholt used the heliotropic myth—the old belief that history is the succession of great civilizations developing, like the movement of the sun, from the East to the West. In this myth America is the fulfillment of history, the last empire.

It all started in the Middle East. Orosious, a pupil of Augustine, wrote about two empires that excelled all others, Assyria and Rome: Assyria came earlier, Rome later; Assyria was in the East, Rome in the West. When the former came to an end, the latter had its beginnings. After the fall of Rome, the memory of the Roman Empire was appealed to regularly, but the Roman legacy culminated in the fifteenth century with the Renaissance, which restored classical glory in arts and letters.

Naturally, the thesis of East-to-West development was given new credence when Columbus discovered the New World. Schulte Nordholt asks a fundamental question in this connection: Why were the Europeans the only ones to take the gamble of traveling vast seas to find new land? What was the difference between the Europeans and the Chinese, who also ventured far around to find new land? The Europeans rose above the pretension that they lived in the center of the world; the Chinese did not. The Europeans were the heirs to the Jewish belief that there was no sacredness in nature, and of the Greeks, who had stepped so emphatically beyond the magic circle of cosmic religion and were open to the world around them. Geographic factors also played a role: Europe had bays and coves everywhere and an inland sea, the Mediterranean, that pointed out to the great unknown ocean.

But it was England, a small island, that would make the true transfer of European power to the West. The reason it was England can be found in the victory of the Reformation, as well as in its entire social and intellectual order. The belief that England was the last empire was reflected in poetry and writing from 1600. The English revolution and republic carried the seeds of empire.

English poets did emphasize the importance of dominating the oceans. John Dennis wrote:

> I sing the naval fight, whose triumph fame
> More loudly than our cannons hall proclaim;
> With which heroic force burst Europe's chain
> And made fair Britain Empress of the Main.
> With deafening shouts the English wren the skies,
> While victory hov'ring oer their pendants flies;
> The lust of empire, and the lust of praise,
> Does high and low godlike courage raise.

It is another poem, written by George Berkeley and published in 1752, says Schulte Nordholt, that describes the final phase of the heliotropic myth. The last stanza reads:

> Westward the Course of Empire takes its Way;
> The four first Acts already past,
> A fifth shall close the Drama with the Day;
> Time's noblest Offspring is the last.

Schulte Nordholt also quotes Goethe, one of the Germans open to the new world in the West:

> Amerika, Du hast es besser
> Als unser Kontinent, das alte,
> Hast keine verfallene Schloesser
> Und keine Basalte.
> Dich stoert nicht im Innern,
> zu lebendiger Zeit,
> Unntzes Erinnern
> Und vergeblicher Streit.

Lord Byron foresaw that one day the countries of America would dominate old Europe as Greece and Europe had outstripped Asia.

And the Americans answered to the European predictions. In the beginning of the nineteenth century, the West became the center of American aspirations. The United States turned its back upon the Old World and the principle of the West was clearly expressed in the Monroe Doctrine of 1823. There was one single great theme: constant expansion to the West, and it took about a century for the process to be completed. For the American historian Frederick Jackson Turner, it was self-purification and renewal: "Decade after decade, West after West, this rebirth of American society has gone on."

If America is not the last empire, the question arises: Is there a continuation of the heliotropic myth? With China, Japan, and the Southeast Asian nations rising, will the trail of empire continue over the Pacific Ocean? This theme has been brought up in a book by Kotkin and Kishimoto, *The Third Century: America's Resurgence in the Asian Era* (1988). According to these authors, American history can be divided into three parts: "The nineteenth century, the first part, was the period of isolationism; it was followed by the twentieth, the second part, when attention was fixed upon Europe; and now the third part, which is about to begin, will be Asia's century, because the center of world trade—and civilization—has shifted to the Pacific Ocean."

Schulte Nordholt does not provide any answers to the question of whether the United States is the last empire. But toward the end of the millennium, there are signs that America is rising to the challenge. Dayton showed that there is really only one superpower and that Washington is prepared to take on the responsibility to act not only in the Middle East but in Europe as well. Meanwhile, the important struggle to revive the American economy and balance the budget is continuing. The Clinton administration between 1992 to 1995 failed to provide the vision of a post-Cold War international system. So now the outline of the new system might, though still unclearly, be seen: a possible cooperation between the United States (NAFTA), the European Union (with Germany-France as the core and including Central Europe) and Japan. The land powers China and Russia may form spheres of their own. If the United States manages to restore its strength, the heliotropic myth might after all come true. But the basis of modern power is not military strength, but economic influence. So geopolitical analysis will possibly have to concentrate on the economic sphere. Any state aspiring to superpower or great power status must, however, be willing to defend itself and extend military influence abroad.

18

Outline of a National Information Policy: Defining America's Future

Michael McGreer <mcgreerm@CC.IMS.DISA.MIL> wrote:

The DOD has a special role in society. That role is the use of military force to protect our national interests. In general, this force is used when politics and reason breaks down.

DOD does not, in my opinion, have any other role in the NII except that of a user. And a minor user at that. The national and international user community is orders of magnitude larger.

I have to disagree, perhaps unpopularly so.

The military historically is to use force when reason breaks down, but what's the poor public and NII to do if it finds itself under attack by well organized and financed Information Warriors who break the rules: Instead of pedalling up the Potomac in a submarine or bombing the Statue of Liberty they remotely attack the fly-by-wire systems of aircraft, or impede electronic commerce, or other such nasty deeds?

Relegating the defense of the NII to the FBI or NIST or Commerce implies a weak defense and minimal if any response. If Citibank is taken down (by whatever means) who are they gonna call? Hacker-busters? Let's get real.

On May 14, 1787, George Washington, James Madison, and Benjamin Franklin joined 52 other men representing 12 of the 13 states to, in the words of Alexander Hamilton, "render the Constitution of the Federal Government." Through September of that year, the Constitutional Convention sought to write the instructional manual on how to run the United States of America.

Two hundred years ago, the world was a very different place. The war with England was over and the united States (we were plural then) were preparing for peace. The states needed to forge unity amongst themselves, establish the new country as a viable international partner, and build a strong defense for a secure future. But the most important difference is that the world was a very tangible, very "real" place.

Today, similarities with our founding days abound. The Cold War is over and we are trying to confront peace; we strive for unity amongst our heterogeneous population and we are trying to define the mechanisms by which world trade and electronic commerce will be conducted. But the single greatest difference is that the world today is becoming a "virtual" one, where wealth is no longer necessarily measured in acres of land, but in bits and bytes of information. Wealth and the value added goods of commerce tend to be intangible—a condition that is distinctly anathema to humans.

Unfortunately, we find that for all of the technical progress we have made as the world's leader in technology, little progress has been made in meeting the challenges that widespread technology has unintentionally wrought. As a people and as individuals, we have lost significant amounts of personal privacy. (See "An Electronic Bill of Rights" on page 648 in this book.) We find that the current legal system is having incredible difficulty dealing with multiple challenges as they arrive with the emergence of a third-wave information age society. Ultimately we find that the United States stands on the precipice of another golden age which can equal or exceed our industrial age greatness of a century ago, but we will fail if we do not come to grips with the unpleasant realities we face. We have the first opportunity—and challenge—in over 200 years to define our future that we choose, rather than to be consumed by one we ignore.

That opportunity can define itself in the formal creation of a National Information Policy (NIP; a policy which will provide our country (or any other country who takes a similar route) with a conceptual framework to define success, create wealth, and protect us in a destabilized, decentralized world. As America and the world move into Cyberspace for business, government, entertainment, education, and just about every conceivable activity, we find that we need to develop ground rules of behavior and policy.

Framework of a National Information Policy

To succeed, any NIP framework must recognize two critical facts: (1) Information, as an intangible commodity, is becoming the single most valuable asset of first-world and some second-world countries. (2) Because we have built a complex, interwoven econo-technical infrastructure upon which our society relies for life, sustenance, and success, unanticipated vulnerabilities have arisen that we must accept.

We must understand that none of the burning issues that will comprise an NIP stand alone; instead, each is a piece in a series of enmeshed relationships. What I am suggesting is the necessity to agree upon the resolution of critical issues to develop this framework: issues that will need to be addressed to afford us freedom, growth, and the opportunity for reward.

The Value of Information

If you ask a roomful of people "What is information?" you will get a roomful of answers. For the purposes of this discussion, we will use the term *information* to refer to any sort of data, information, or knowledge. In our physical world, communication of information has historically been via hard copy or word of mouth. We easily relate to these type of transmissions because they are tangible. But today, as intangible information assets proliferate, we have to learn to become accustomed to the new media.

In today's society, information is p-o-w-e-r! Does it also have value? Absolutely! Financial statements today have depreciated worth illustrated as real estate, furniture, hardware, etc., but the information itself is an intangible hidden asset. The value is there. How we calculate that value is the challenge. Government and business rely on the integrity and privacy of their information. In the world of computers and related peripherals, companies have information that is asset intensive. If accounting practices companies suddenly included line items of information assets, would companies' stock rise because of this new methodology?

The noted analyst and writer Peter Drucker stated, "we need an economic theory that puts knowledge into the center of the wealth-producing process." Evaluating the value-added information assets and wealth of information-based companies is impossible with today's normal business models. Lawyers would have a field day if corporations began to itemize information. Protecting information assets would be as impossible as knowing in advance what seven numbers to pick for the Saturday lotto.

An NIP needs to include a method by which information can be recognized to have value and then encourage a model for its evaluation in the wealth-producing process. It will be impossible to develop one technique to fill government, business, and private entities, but we could establish a baseline model that would be accepted by all parties.

Define Information Ownership

The legal concept that possession is nine-tenths of the law suddenly loses meaning when electronic information can be freely distributed to millions of people in seconds. Copyright and patent laws are clear and direct, but how do they relate to Cyberspace when we can copy and transmit television programs, movies, music, and software with the flick of our fingers on a magic button or command? The information highway forces us to make changes to protect ownership and creators of data.

We shall have to depend upon the rules we choose to follow as we explore and resolve information ownership. Think about these questions:

Who owns e-mail that is generated in an office? Our legal system has ruled that e-mail authored by the government (including the White House) is owned by Americans. What about personally generated e-mail. Should the same standard apply?

What about e-mail posted to a BBS? Do I own that information, or is it in the public domain? How do we establish Cyberspace copyright? Can we establish ownership with an electronic copyright for use in Cyberspace?

If I have raw data and you turn it into value-added information organized in a more usable form, who owns the information?

How do we properly define *public domain?* Do we limit it to America, or give ownership to the rest of the world?

Does each person own personal information such as name, address, and social security number? If not, who owns it?

The groundwork of the nature of information needs to be the foundation of an NIP. We must strive for guidelines that are compatible with our political and social systems and that can be interpreted consistently given the realities of Cyberspace.

Define American Cyberspace

Cyberspace has given us an audience without limits. Without defined limits our rights are becoming systematically removed. If Cyberspace is the place in the middle of phones and computer, it is a world without borders. Think of it as being separated into pockets of local or regional spaces, which results in millions of smaller cyberspaces around the globe.

Imagine for a moment that there are only two computers in the world. Cyberspace exists entirely within the connectivity between the two machines. If there was only one network in the world, that would be Cyberspace. By extending that concept, we could say there is a Microsoft cyberspace, an AT&T cyberspace, Winn's cyberspace, and so on. When you log on to your PC, you enter your own small piece of cyberspace and then connect to other cyberspaces. We are not looking at size or distance, but at a fundamental yet intangible environment. Adjoining one cyberspace to another is as simple as opening your front door. That concept can assist us with a base ine to formulate borders of smaller cyberspaces as we begin development of an NIP. On a bigger scale, we could say that Russian cyberspace, Japanese cyberspace, and American cyberspace are distinct entities, with clearly defined electronic borders.

There are two players that make up Cyberspace ownership.

Small-c cyberspaces consisting of personal, corporate, or organizational spaces whose doors are the electronic borders that specify the location of individual cyberspaces. These doors open to the Information Superhighways.

Big-c Cyberspace is the National Information Infrastructure (NII), including all information highways and communications systems. Add this to the small cyberspaces, and then tie it all up with threads of connectivity and you have all of Cyberspace.

Define State Versus Federal Cyberspace

How we define the scope and applicability of the NIP is critical. It must be framed on a national level. We really don't have a choice. State lines may be crossed instantly in Cyberspace, which renders local ordinances moot and makes jurisdictional separation a challenge. If computer fraud takes place within one state, jurisdiction is clear: that particular state would have the authority to sit in judgment. But if I turn on my PC, connect to your personal cyberspace in another state through the dozens of networks located hither and yon, steal information from your company's network, who then sits in judgment? Jurisdiction issues turn into major fiascos of political confusion because those rules are not developed for Cyberspace. We interpret and convolute existing statutes to fit the crime rather than develop legislation which is particular to the ethereal realities of Cyberspace.

Each of the 50 states have different laws regarding computer crimes—50 different sets of laws that would need to relate to American cyberspace. How do we fix this? By authoring a central set of guidelines for jurisdiction with supremacy to function across state lines and within the states where the crime took place. The cooperative jurisdiction of all parties, government, business, and individuals is necessary to establish the rules that will ultimately facilitate the framework of the NIP. We must be flexible enough and have the vision to replace a worn-out system that no longer fits the reality of our world.

Define Who Ought to Be Running Cyberspace

Cyberspace is creating opportunities to make hundreds of billions of dollars in a truly global electronic marketplace. It is also raising control issues over that information and its transmission. Potential markets are expanding daily into third-world countries, making big profits available to first-world suppliers. Domestically, the phone, cable, and entertainment industries are partnering, breaking down formerly adversarial relationships to get their piece of the brobdingnagian global market.

Washington and the Federal Communications Commission are at the center of a war over who will control the information that comes into your home or business. Laws regarding censorship bear down on an electronic population more strictly than with any other form of media. Our national government is literally pole-vaulting into Cyberspace and is concerned with many issues from national security to import and export. It is unfortunate that historically, government and business look at each other with suspicion instead of as a mirroring partnership. With no NIP, we each look for individual political and economic gains with little regard for the effect of our actions upon our nation's security or protection of our citizenry. We must reach a national consensus and not place the nurturing of the NII solely into the hands of either the government or business. We have to develop a realistic partnership.

Define Information as a Strategic Asset

It should be crystal clear that the core of the proposed NIP must be the recognition that information is a major component of our economic and political future. When that consensus is achieved, a number of questions must be addressed.

In the post-Cold War world, it makes sense to value and protect industrial secrets as we do military secrets. Losing industrial information affects the profits of the victim company, which could dictate layoffs, which places financial hardships on families. It also has an undeniable impact on our national economic security.

If such information is stolen by foreign interests, should we not consider that loss an attack against the interests of the United States? For every billion dollars of lost domestic revenue, the government says that 30,000 fewer people will be working. For years, the French government has shown a national determination to seek out and steal foreign information assets in its quest to develop that country's economic well being. In response to their aggression, a group of hackers wants to declare electronic war on France. What should our national response be to cyber-assaults, and does our lack of an NIP encourage vigilantism?

We must define industrial secrets as national economic security assets worthy of protection.

Instead of conventional conflict, the international community often turns to economic sanctions as a method of international enforcement. The NIP needs to provide methods for a national response to international situations. Is the deactivation of an adversary's economy a viable method for enforcement or an alternative to conventional war?

On the other side of the coin, we need to have a clear directive on how we as a nation should react to those who strike our econo-technical infrastructure: telephone switches, airline computers, financial networks, or portions of the power grid. The NIP needs to view information as a national, strategic asset and include protections from information aggressions on all levels.

The NIP must provide for electronic civil defense.

To Spy or Not To Spy

We have no choice—they do it to us. But do two wrongs make a right? The technology available to the CIA, the NSA, and increasingly to individuals, can give us up-to-the-second information of everything that goes on in the world of business development, economy, and politics. We used such capabilities in trade negotiations with the Japanese and likely with other national interests. But should these tactics be part of a formalized policy to benefit our domestic economy and the competitive global position of the United States?

Some say that on the international front, we may create

political storm clouds from such obvious tactics. Others say it is realpolitik to remain competitive. What do we tell our spies? Most are willing to risk their lives for their country; but are they willing to die for GM or USAir or Intel or Microsoft? Once we gather the information, what fair methods can we employ to distribute the information to our advantage? How much proactive spying or intelligence is appropriate to further or national interests?

Our competition has well-thought out policies to advance their interests. More than 100 countries use computers to spy against the United States: Germany's Project RAHAB uses professional hackers to search the global networks for information of value. Until we take a similar stance, we will continue to hold the short end of the stick on a global playing field where our rules ensure that we will be the loser.

Define the Military in Cyberspace

Despite the recent downsizing of the military, we continue to provide the manpower, technology, and funds to do what we feel necessary to keep our nation safe. The military has perfected silent weapons, including those that can extract information from distant computers, hidden computer screens, and virtually all communications on the planet. What else can we do with these capabilities to aid our national economic security?

We have the technology to terminate our opponents and destroy their ability to conduct armed aggression. We also have the ability to wage bloodless conflict. With the technologies available to us, we could direct our adversaries to take notice by closing down their industrial or military infrastructure, combining sanctions and embargoes. We have the response capability, but not yet the political will or direction.

Part of the NIP must define an act of war in Cyberspace. If "bad guy of choice" bombs the Statue of Liberty to the bottom of New York Harbor, we have a plethora of military options.

But if they hit the electronic asset base of a major financial institution, what do we do? Is that war? Do we respond militarily? Does something like that require a national response, or is it something that is solely the company's problem?

Putting the Pieces Together

A National Information Policy will address and answer key questions that will define our future so that every American understands.

1. The economy of the United States is a national security asset worthy of protection by civilian interests, law enforcement, appropriate legislation, and military force, if required. As a nation we have historically protected ourselves against physical incursions onto our shores. We must now stake the same claims for the economic interests of our country.
2. The United States will protect and defend the intellectual wealth of our third-wave society against incursion, theft, or compromise in ways deemed appropriate by law, as above.
3. We define the electronic borders of the United States to be those computers, systems, networks, etc. which are U.S.-controlled, and either lie within the physical borders of the United States or are of economic interest to the United States and its wealth-producing econotechnical industrial base.
4. Models of information ownership will be designed which clearly define who owns what under the virtual conditions of an intangible world.
5. Every reasonable attempt will be made to advance the science and art of economic theory to account for intangible information-based assets.
6. National laws will be redefined to simplify the process

of investigation, forensics, and prosecution of those individuals who commit cyber-crimes across state lines.

7. The United States will develop a policy by which to respond to aggressions against the economic interests or intellectual wealth interests of this country. The concepts of aggression, incursion, sedition, war, and conflict will be redefined to accommodate the realities of an intangible world. We will clearly spell out what actions are not permissible against the United States and develop a range of measured and appropriate responses to these aggressions; including, if necessary, offensive electronic responses in Cyberspace, sanctions, alternative punitive actions, and/or conventional military force.

When it comes to establishing an NIP—our social, ethical, and political response to technology—we don't have all the answers. I certainly don't, and too few of our national leaders are even asking the questions.

So we return to the same question that began this book: Is it the responsibility of government (civilian or military or other) to protect and defend the private sector?

Is a policy of electronic civil defense an appropriate step to take? I certainly think so, and so do most people who have rationally considered the question. The period from May 1995 to May 1996 saw a dramatic increase in sensitivity to the issue amongst military leaders. In 1995 very few of the military and intelligence people thought that an attack against our critical infrastructures justified a strong national (perhaps military) response. In 1996, the nearly universal response was to kick butt, U.S. fashion: "Don't mess with our infrastructure."

Ultimately, with the help of the military or not, the defense of our country is everyone's responsibility.

That means it's up to us.

An Electronic Bill of Rights: In Cyberspace, You Are Guilty Until Proven Innocent

Winn Schwartau

You know, I tend to feel violated when I receive endless masses of junk mail that overflow from my undersized mailbox.

We can all travel back to our school days when we studied the Constitution and the amendments added to it over the last 200 years. Most Americans are acutely familiar with at least a few of those amendments, but perhaps the most familiar of all are the first ten amendments, known as the Bill of Rights.

Today they are the envy of populations worldwide. They were meant to be a strong vehicle to protect our individual freedoms and liberty as our nascent country evolved into a great nation. Many of us forget, however, that as tourists in foreign countries, we are no longer protected by the rights that we take for granted here. In Mexico, there are no civil rights as v.e know them. In England, the press can be summarily banished from publishing information deemed harmful to that country—without the need for a trial or other due process. And those are our friendly neighbors!

While we sit idly by in our idyllic national setting, however, there are great changes occurring around us. Many of those changes are having a distinct impact upon those original rights upon which this nation was founded.

We find that as technology improves our daily existence in ways unimaginable only a decade ago, that same technology has permitted a creeping loss of personal freedoms, liberties, and privacy.

Two hundred years ago, for example, the concept of public records was consistent with the goals of an inchoate democratic society. It meant that I, as an American, could mount my horse, ride down the elm-tree bordered dirt lane, get saddle sores from the 10-mile ride, and freely enter the wooden courthouse. Once there, I could look through the public records and find out who bought the farm next door.

Today, though, with a single request to a professional data banker (or if I have the wherewithal myself), I can dredge up the most private information on most any American, compile it, analyze it, and come to conclusions about that person without his consent or knowledge. Our identities have been reduced to a virtual agglomeration of streams of data which is ripe for the picking with the simplest equipment and a minimum of keystrokes.

In many ways, our greatest national asset, our technology, is also the greatest weakness and vulnerability of our personal privacy. I find a

648

comfortable solution to this complex dilemma in the creation of an Electronic Bill of Rights; a new set of guidelines which firmly and clearly establish the rights of the individual in an intangible, invisible world.

You Own You. This simple concept must be the premise of an Electronic Bill of Rights. You have legal authority over your body. (I hope readers will excuse my not including *Roe v. Wade* issues in this short essay.) If someone strikes you physically, you have both legal and physical defensive recourse. You even have legal authority over your possessions. If someone steals your TV, they can go to jail.

We must establish a parallel set of concepts over the "digital you," that electronic projection which defines who you are and how people perceive you in Cyberspace.

Do you own or have any real control over your electronic identity? Not much, today. Consider that the average American's name is housed within 50,000 or more computer databases along with different facts (or mere opinions) about him. Your name and that information is bought, sold, and traded between five and ten times a day. Is that what we really want? Should a commercial concern with whom you have dealt be permitted to use that data for additional marketing purposes, or sell that information to other private organizations?

I suggest a simple set of guidelines by which we can restore a great deal of our electronic privacy.

1. You own your name, and all of the information that resides along with it. People with whom you deal in commerce may not, without your explicit permission, be able to sell or use your name or its associated data for any purpose. (It is reasonable to exclude legitimate law enforcement needs.) We should perhaps consider the concept of royalty payments to individuals who do not object to being added to an infinite supply of marketing lists.

2. Organizations who hold digital information on you will be required to protect that information according to yet-to-be-determined security criteria. This includes employers and records about their employees, banks who hold critical financial information about you, brokerage firms, doctors, insurance companies, and so on. We have to reestablish confidence on the part of our citizenry.

3. Organizations who have your name in a database must, at least once a year, advise you that you are in their files. At your option, you may request a copy of all files and information they store on you, perhaps at a reasonable fee of a couple of dollars. This is critical because the untamed growth of the "digital you" is where the loss of privacy problem begins.

4. You must have recourse. Today, albeit with great difficulty, the credit reporting bureaus are obligated to release your personal files to you upon request. They are further required to investigate and correct any errors or omissions if you ask. We must extend this concept much further. Insurance companies have access to your medical files but you do not. A single keystroke, an error, can transform a healthy person into a doomed HIV victim, and that person has no simple route for detection or correc-

tion. That is just downright wrong. People and organizations make decisions about you, the individual, based upon opinions, data and human error over which he has absolutely no control.

5. One large grocery chain in Chicago sent letters to its customers who used the store's debit card. "We want to tell you that for the last couple of years we have been secretly collecting information on your purchases. Once we decide, we will let you know what we are going to do with this information." Wrong. They should be able to do nothing more than fill their shelves because I bought all those Ring Dings. I do not want Twinkie and Hostess Cupcake solicitations just because I bought a competing product. An organization should be able to collect only that information about me that is essential to complete the transaction, and once that transaction is completed, all unnecessary information should be deleted unless I give explicit permission otherwise.

These simple concepts are core components of the Electronic Bill of Rights. But we face a number of related issues that must be sorted out before we can say there is equality and privacy in Cyberspace.

Government Privacy. The government keeps a lot of secrets— military secrets, legislative secrets—and they have developed a means to classify those secrets. In general, there are five levels:

- Unclassified. Anything goes, anyone can have it to look at it. We call this open source information.
- Sensitive but Unclassified. Information which should receive some degree of protection, but not a whole lot.
- Classified, Secret, and Top Secret. These are different levels of real secrets, and individuals with access to this information must undergo some degree of scrutiny to be permitted access to it.

The issue I care about is that the information the government holds on you and me—our tax records, medical records, social security files, and so on—are not classified. The general press has covered stories about the abuse of this information when accessed by individuals both inside and outside of government, and then used it for profit, harassment, or even murder.

I would like to see an additional security sensitivity added. It might be called *Personal,* and would be assigned to all private and personal information about Americans that most of us want kept confidential between us and the government.

We would want to assign technical security criteria to that classification which would cover such issues as who can access it, what may be done with it once accessed, how easily it may be moved from one computer to another, and specifically, if it is ever permitted to leave the government's control without explicit permission. In addition, more stringent punitive steps must be available to prosecute those who violate these rules.

This step alone would do a great deal to restore confidence in the privacy rights that Americans want to formally establish.

The First Amendment. The rest of the world envies us for this most precious right—freedom of speech. As Americans we may hate an extremist or opposing or offensive viewpoint, but we defend to the death their right to say it. The denizens of Cyberspace—50 million of us—want to insure that the First Amendment does not become a footnote in history, relegated to the status of a local ordinance .

We have to ask, do we still have the right of free speech as we were taught in school? It depends on the circumstances. If we threaten the President, we can't use the First Amendment as a get-out-of-jail-free card. Bomb jokes at airports and yelling "Fire!" in a movie theater are notable exceptions to the First Amendment's protections. Barring physical threats, we can voice just about any opinion we want: just listen to any politician in a heated campaign.

But there are differences we find in Cyberspace that do not provide clear-cut answers. So I return to the concept that we have to decide what we want, and how we want our country to be in the future; and not to sit by and idly let a chaotic electronic future descend upon us.

Active and Passive Publishing. With the emergence of Cyberspace as a global means of communication, we find there are two very distinct types of publishing: passive and active. All of us with inexpensive hardware can publish our thoughts on the information highway. The active publisher transmits data/information from their electronic address to yours. He sends it to you.

Physically, we are subjected to ever increasing amounts of junk mail and the same thing is occurring in Cyberspace with list servers, spamming, and over-marketing. No matter what we do, we can't escape it! However, we must be good stewards of our technology and stay vigilant that electronic junk mail doesn't eat up our valuable computer resources—especially for those who have to pay by the kilobyte. Active publishing may also mean that you have requested materials such as electronic newsletters which are then actively sent to you.

We meet such issues here as electronic stalking, electronic harassment, and propagandizing entire populations. What recourse do we have when we are subject to endless and perhaps annoying electronic transmissions? Again, we have to decide what behavior is acceptable, which is not, and come to grips with as much as we can within our own national borders.

Now, think of passive publishing in Cyberspace as resembling a large library. The Web perhaps. The librarian compiles information and places it on the server for you to retrieve. If you want it, you have to go after it. You actively solicit and search out the material and then choose to bring it into your domain. In Cyberspace the information may be free to you or you may need to enter a security code, a password, or a credit card if the information is for sale.

The technical differences between the two publishing methods demand that we find appropriate rules for both methods that tie in with the idea of freedom of speech.

Censorship. I don't favor electronic censorship guidelines chosen by the government. I am a great fan of self-censorship (not by intimidation) and personal responsibility. I do not object to the proposed V-chip because it places the responsibility upon the parents or viewer to determine what is acceptable. I do not want the government telling me that *Baywatch* is too racy if I enjoy watching lycra bathing suits in motion.

Censorship is the antithesis to what this country was founded upon and we should aggressively counter the small-minded special interest groups who know best what information is right for you and me. Because, if at first they censor what you don't like, and then they censor what someone else doesn't like, then one day, it might be your turn, and they will censor you. It's a vicious downhill slalom certain to end in disaster, and we must make sure we don't leave the starting gate. Ever.

In 1994, a Tennessee postal inspector electronically ordered adult-oriented materials from a couple (husband and wife) in California, where they were breaking no laws whatsoever. Upon receipt, he indicted them in Memphis, Tennessee, where they stood trial for violation of local obscenity laws—and lost!

In such a fashion, any local yokel ordinance takes legal precedence over that of a distant location, and permits selective remote control enforcement. Is this really what we want, or is it time to lock our personal rights to our physical location?

As a parent of a young girl and boy, I can clearly understand how parents become distraught when their children have complete access to inappropriate materials as they explore the Information Superhighway. In Cyberspace, there is so much R, NC-17, and XXX material available to children that it would make a drunken sailor blush. And much of that material is clearly illegal throughout the entire United States. Do we arrest the country of Denmark because its culture and laws are different? Of course not. Better technical solutions are being developed. We have to learn personal responsibility, engage in better parenting, and quit trying to blame the other guy.

Bad law is not a solution for poor engineering.

The Fourth Amendment. Think about the Fourth Amendment. Its concepts include "the right of the people to be secure in their persons, houses, papers, and effects, against unreasonable searches and seizures." Does that amendment cover information that may be housed on a disk or information you can pick up on the Internet? The amendment is a prime example of decaying legislation which is no longer relevant. Information is not in the same place that it was for our forefathers. Life was simpler then! So what is the litmus test for the need to confiscate information? The American Civil Liberties Union, a watchdog of our personal freedoms, represented by Ira Glasser, stated, "Because of the Supreme Court rulings, the Fourth Amendment has become a relic of formalism: it protects the places where private information used to be, but not the places where it is today."

` We must specifically migrate the concept of the Fourth Amendment into Cyberspace so we all know exactly where we stand.

Providers Versus Publishers. Should an Internet provider be sued or penalized because the content of its computers were in violation of the law? Prodigy was sued because one of its customers placed allegedly libelous statements in a public forum about a financial company. Was that Prodigy's fault? The court said yes, because it was a moderated forum. The implication here is that a forum moderator, say on the subject of Mayan Sun Tanning Lotions, must also be a legal expert on what is a libelous statement or not. I don't think so.

No more than the telephone company is held liable for obscene telephone calls should an electronic provider be responsible for the contents of its computers. Lawrence Livermore Lab computers were found to contain 30,000+ pornographic images, which made it a popular destination for lots of Net surfers. Should they be responsible? The Electronic Bill of Rights must spell it out.

CyberCops. Should we allow police to monitor and eavesdrop data networks, search Cyberspace and come up with incriminating evidence? We have no choice but to draw a line in the sand dictating what is acceptable and unacceptable modus operandi for law enforcement officers. If an e-mail transmission on America Online contained a plan to rob Fort Knox, who would we hold responsible? How much monitoring of Cyberspace do we as a society want? My local police department entrapped and caught an electronic pedaphile while masquerading as a young teen on the Net. We naturally think that is good, but we must choose how far we are willing to go, what rights we are willing to give up in order to maintain a lawful society.

Viruses and the First Amendment. Many of us who have had those dastardly viruses crash our systems have thought about the need to outlaw that type of software. Cyberspace needs to take a hard stand on the issue of malevolent software. The arguments can go on forever. They have the right to write the virus . . . or do they? Suppose serious damages occur from malicious software? How about poor Joe Programmer who inadvertently screws up and his error causes damage? Do we throw him in the slammer?

We have to keep in mind that the only difference between malicious software and a deadly programming error is intent. Let's not make criminals out of experimenters.

National Security. There is a fuzzy line between national security and the rights of our citizens. Our national security defenders want to get their voices heard about freedom of speech and shout when it comes to encryption. The export of excellent cryptography is restricted by the NSA, but I think we will need a definition of "export" and propose means to enforce it in light of the Department of Justice chosing not to indict Phil Zimmermann.

The government has been remarkably slow to develop workable solutions that meet both the legitimate needs of the individual and American interests, and the real needs of law enforcement. Despite years of public debate, only a handful of technical approaches are on the table.

Anonymity and Identity Replication. Kevin Mitnick assumed my electronic identity on the Net to wage a war of words against one of his adversaries. I had a lot of explaining to do to the press. Tantalizing entertainment to some, malicious to others, spoofing identities on the Net occurs with increasing regularity. While most of us probably say spoofing is a bad idea, should it be made illegal? Or do we just ignore it as foolish shenanigans?

And what about electronic anonymity? Through such sites as penet.fi in Finland, any of us can acquire an anonymous identity and surf the Net wildly with the prospect of suffering no personal indignities or repercussions. After all, no one knows who we are.

Guilty Until Proven Innocent. An Electronic Bill of Rights is critical if we are to maintain some semblance of order as we move into the twenty-first century. There are many questions and we have only began to explore the possibilities and endless issues that will be created as we make our great electronic leaps forward.

Have you ever had the experience of a mistake on your credit report? Argue with your bank about an incorrect transaction? Take on the IRS because they miscalculated your 1040? We are judged by others and they base their judgments upon the contents of computers over which we have little or no control, access, or recourse.

We are presumed guilty until we go to the walls supplying our burden of proof of innocence. That is the opposite of the premise on which our legal system is based. If the data entry is incorrect, too bad. We assume the computer is right even when the person who entered the data is wrong.

Taking on the credit bureaucracy means giving yourself plenty of expendable time, because you will be placed on hold, maneuvered through voice mail hell, or sent to the wrong extension by some human operator who really doesn't give a damn about you. In our busy lives, some of us don't take time to review our statements, bank accounts, or credit reports. The creeping control of computers over our lives grows daily and must be placed under arrest until we can design a legal and ethical construct that echoes our beliefs and desires.

The Media. Alvin Toffler once said that if we control the media, we destroy democracy. However, if we don't control it, then they will.

Cyberspace provides an infinite variety of information sources — true news anarchy. The tantalizing migration of big companies into Cyberspace will spawn a shakeout that has occurred within virtually every growth industry since the industrial revolution.

With the media, though, we have to be careful. The FCC regulates how many news outlets a company can have: TV stations, radio stations, newspapers. But what about in Cyberspace? How do we avoid the historical tendency for a few huge companies to dominate a field and in this case control the distribution of information? We are crying out for answers.

Conclusion. As the original Bill of Rights was meant to protect America's citizenry in a physical world, an Electronic Bill of Rights is meant to provide similar protections in the intangible nether world of Cyberspace. What is required is vision—vision to take a look at the future, accept the risks and opportunities to our personal freedoms, and construct and legislate a guide for our future. We must design the future we choose, not accept one that we helplessly slide into.

Our lives are truly open books and the Electronic Bill of Rights I propose closes the book on that abuse.

As an old Chinese proverb says, "If we don't change direction, we are going to end up where we are going." I know that's not what most of us want.

A Declaration of the Independence of Cyberspace

John Perry Barlow, Electronic Frontier Foundation

The Electronic Frontier Foundation (http://www.eff.org/) is a non-profit civil liberties organization working in the public interest to protect privacy, free expression, and access to public resources and information in new media.

Governments of the Industrial World, you weary giants of flesh and steel, I come from Cyberspace, the new home of Mind. On behalf of the future, I ask you of the past to leave us alone. You are not welcome among us. You have no sovereignty where we gather.

We have no elected government, nor are we likely to have one, so I address you with no greater authority than that with which liberty itself always speaks. I declare the global social space we are building to be naturally independent of the tyrannies you seek to impose on us. You have no moral right to rule us, nor do you possess any methods of enforcement we have true reason to fear.

Governments derive their just powers from the consent of the governed. You have neither solicited nor received ours. We did not invite you. You do not know us, nor do you know our world. Cyberspace does not lie within your borders. Do not think that you can build it, as though it were a public construction project. You cannot. It is an act of nature and it grows itself through our collective actions.

You have not engaged in our great and gathering conversation, nor did you create the wealth of our marketplaces. You do not know our culture, our ethics, or the unwritten codes that already provide our society more order than could be obtained by any of your impositions.

You claim there are problems among us that you need to solve. You use this claim as an excuse to invade our precincts. Many of these problems don't exist. Where there are real conflicts, where there are wrongs, we will identify them and address them by our means. We are forming our own Social Contract. This governance will arise according to the conditions of our world, not yours. Our world is different.

Cyberspace consists of transactions, relationships, and thought itself, arrayed like a standing wave in the web of our communications. Ours is a world that is both everywhere and nowhere, but it is not where bodies live.

We are creating a world that all may enter without privilege or prejudice accorded by race, economic power, military force, or station of birth.

We are creating a world where anyone, anywhere, may express his or her beliefs, no matter how singular, without fear of being coerced into silence or conformity.

Your legal concepts of property, expression, identity, movement, and context do not apply to us. They are based on matter. There is no matter here.

Our identities have no bodies, so, unlike you, we cannot obtain order by physical coercion. We believe that from ethics, enlightened self-interest, and the commonweal, our governance will emerge. Our identities may be distributed across many of your jurisdictions. The only law that all our constituent cultures would generally recognize is the Golden Rule. We hope we will be able to build our particular solutions on that basis. But we cannot accept the solutions you are attempting to impose.

In the United States, you have today created a law, the Telecommunications Reform Act, which repudiates your own Constitution and insults the dreams of Jefferson, Washington, Mill, Madison, de Tocqueville, and Brandeis. These dreams must now be born anew in us.

You are terrified of your own children, since they are natives in a world where you will always be immigrants. Because you fear them, you entrust your bureaucracies with the parental responsibilities you are too cowardly to confront yourselves. In our world, all the sentiments and expressions of humanity, from the debasing to the angelic, are parts of a seamless whole, the global conversation of bits. We cannot separate the air that chokes from the air upon which wings beat.

In China, Germany, France, Russia, Singapore, Italy, and the United States, you are trying to ward off the virus of liberty by erecting guard posts at the frontiers of Cyberspace. These may keep out the contagion for a small time, but they will not work in a world that will soon be blanketed in bit-bearing media.

Your increasingly obsolete information industries would perpetuate themselves by proposing laws, in America and elsewhere, that claim to own speech itself throughout the world. These laws would declare ideas to be another industrial product, no more noble than pig iron. In our world, whatever the human mind may create can be reproduced and distributed infinitely at no cost. The global conveyance of thought no longer requires your factories to accomplish.

These increasingly hostile and colonial measures place us in the same position as those previous lovers of freedom and self-determination who had to reject the authorities of distant, uninformed powers. We must declare our virtual selves immune to your sovereignty, even as we continue to consent to your rule over our bodies. We will spread ourselves across the Planet so that no one can arrest our thoughts.

We will create a civilization of the Mind in Cyberspace. May it be more humane and fair than the world your governments have made before.

Davos, Switzerland
February 8, 1996

19

The Future of
Information Warfare

"All the world's a stage . . ."

—WILLIAM SHAKESPEARE

"The wave of the future is coming and there's no fighting it."

—ANNE MORROW LINDBERGH

THE FUTURE IS PROBABLY THE MOST EXCITING PLACE I'll ever visit. Can't wait to get there.

Decades from now, the changes we have seen occur to our econotechnical society over the last few years will be viewed as baby steps into the Information Age. The old adage, today's magic is tomorrow's science, is a truism. We ain't seen nothing yet.

Information technology is going to change, and those changes will deeply affect every segment of society because, as we have seen, the technology has become personal; it creeps into our lives and we have adapted and will continue to adapt to its ever more powerful influence.

There is no reason to assume that each leap in technology will result in purely benign application. No matter what we do, as information technology evolves, there will always be some way to screw things up, either by accident or intentionally. Our job is to predict and minimize the damage. The future of Information Warfare will be largely determined by two factors:

1. New technology. As suggested, a National Information Policy should be able to accommodate as much future

information technology as it possibly can. We know where we are going technically, but there will always be surprises. The future as it appears in the minds' eyes of our gurus and in the research labs of the government and industry will be in our homes tomorrow. We should be prepared.

2. The world is getting wired. Europe and other knowledge-based economies will be following our lead and moving their peoples and cultures into Cyberspace. Information Warfare has largely been an Americocentric phenomenon, but just as we face risks, challenges, and opportunities, so do the countries of the European economic community.

Future Information Technologies

Popular science magazines, the science sections of the general press, and techie television shows peer into their crystal balls in an attempt to divine how life will be lived in five, ten, or fifty years. What we will do, however, is examine future technology from the Information Warrior's standpoint.

The most obvious evolution will be that computers and information systems will get smaller and smaller, faster and faster, more portable, and easier to use. If the current trends in development occur, computer systems ten years from now will be 128 times as powerful as they are today. A mainframe on a desk will be seen as quaint antiquity, and we will even have the power of several mainframes on our person or in our homes. Our personal communicators, or PDAs will have real-time interactive multi-media connections to anyone who has a similar device. Universal translators will spark a revolution in travel and tourism because language will no longer be a barrier.

The future digital storage capacity of computers will make 600 megabyte CD-ROMs look like a thimble of information. IBM has demonstrated the ability to manipulate single electrons and the development of quantum computers is not far behind. Memory density will increase by a factor of 1,000 in the foreseeable future where a nonvolatile memory device the size of a sugar cube could store a good portion of the Library of Congress. In a few years, 100 gigabytes (that's 100,000 megabytes) will be a bare bones necessity for any computer system worthy of the name.

And money. What about money? People who still use cash will do so for only the most pedestrian activities.

National databases will continue to be a sore spot to privacy activists and libertarians. The NCIC database will be expanded to include regional and local criminal databases, making it even more difficult for a lawbreaker to escape detection. The fears of a centralized medical database and centralized banking transactions database and insurance claim database make a National Information Policy all the more urgent—because they are coming.

Colleges and universities will be replaced with a higher educational database that provides personally tailored inter-active instruction and testing. They will prove to be attractive playgrounds for those who think that modifying curriculum, morphing a professor during a lecture, or switching all classes to the Advanced Swahili channel is fun.

These are all fairly predictable outcomes from technologi-cal progress and the risks will be similar to those we face today. But as truly new technology comes about, do we have anything to worry about?

It has been suggested that the ultimate in personal identi-fication is right around the corner. Instead of relying upon easily forged social security cards or medical-history smart cards; or instead of counting upon photographic identification where the face can be customized to match the picture; or rather than requiring voice identification which can be spoofed by the technically literate; why not use our unique DNA strings as the means of absolute identification. At birth, every member of society will have a DNA sample taken, and will be issued a DNA card. If there is a question of identity, scrape a little skin from under a fingernail, shake it up in a portable DNA analyzer and in less than two minutes, positive identification can be established.

But is this a good thing? With data bankers now looking for the ideal customers, or the IRS looking for likely tax cheats, or illegal money-laundering schemes, can DNA mating be far behind? The onging international genome project is mapping the gene structure of man—a mammoth scientific endeavor. We will know which genes carry which diseases, which genes suggest predilections for certain behavior and which others correspond to anticipated appearances for the newborn. If we are each DNAed at birth or DNAed to get a new social security card, not only does the National DNA Identification database know who we are, but also what we are. Insurance computers will ask the DNA computers if we should be insured or if an operation is likely to succeed; they will be able to build DNA-based actuarial tables—kind of takes the fun out of living. Employers will know our genetic dispositions, and future DNA engineers will be able to automatically pair up ideal mates for ideal offspring. The genetically impoverished may be subject to DNA discrimination. It's going to happen, unless we just say no.

Virtual Reality

All of this increased computing power will permit us to build more and more realistic artificial realities in which we may immerse ourselves for business, relaxation, recreation, and education. Mail order and mall stores will offer thousands of Virtual Reality software programs to run virtual reality computers in every home and office. Companies like Nintendo and Sega will own the gaming VR markets with home versions of *Star Trek*'s holodeck. New industries will develop interactive virtual realities for training, education, real-life simulations, an alternative to travel, and perhaps even for cyber-sex, also known as teledildonics.

But the question will be, how much virtual reality is too much? Excessive muscle stimulation can trigger temporary atrophy; what will stimulating all the senses in exaggerated simulations of stress due to the mind? It is said that multimedia accelerates learning; what are the limits of total mental stimulation for extended periods? Will there be a reality endorsed by the AMA and the FDA called Virtual Valium?

In other words, how much information is too much information? VR will likely become an escape vehicle for the economically depressed because it will be an affordable electronic drug. *Fantasy Island* is only a quarter away. Soap operas will never be the same. People addicted to virtual realities— whichever ones they choose—will seek treatment. Sudden religious revelations will increase; so will mental breakdowns. Too much forced virtual reality could be construed as abuse or torture. Virtual reality will cut down on cigarette smoking but can also be used for indoctrination. How much is too much? Will a software company be liable for murder if their virtual reality software overtaxes a weak heart or scares someone to death? Subliminal advertising was eliminated decades ago, but how about subliminal software?

Virtual reality is all about perception, and as technology improves ten or hundred fold, how will we be able to tell what is real and what is not real? Morphing—the visual blending technique made so popular by movies like *Terminator II*— makes the impossible come to life. Finely honed digital visual effects will be indistinguishable from reality. Manipulation of part-real and part-synthesized images will lend confusion to the veracity of multimedia communications. The news media receives a videotape of a massacre or disaster or momentous event. How do they know its real? Today a videotape is pretty good documentary evidence; in the future a Rodney King video might not be believed when image and data fabrication become as easy as using a word processor. Advanced technology covers up a fictional crime in just this way in Michael Crighton's *Rising Sun*.

"I'm from Missouri" will take on new meaning when a

digital identity can be assumed to be no more reliable than are the stories of Elvis sightings in supermarket tabloids. Ersatz information distribution takes on greater importance when we are genetically biased to the axiom, seeing is believing. Given the amount of data required, the security implications of multi-media are immense. Hidden information may be secreted within complex audio and video transmissions, making the modulation of a group of pixels or audio signals to contain secondary codes a favorite technique for future Information Warriors.

The question "Where are you?" will be answered at the push of a button. Global positioning satellites will know, to within a few feet, your exact location. Lives will be saved as personal digital assistants broadcast the location of lost or injured or kidnapped people. But what about employees? Will their every step be tracked to enhance security or to evaluate their performances for promotions? To the dismay of the unions who say the practice is an invasion of privacy, we already track the routes and times of trucks to increase shipping efficiency. Computers already know almost everything about us; will we also decide to add our every location to this list?

Nanomachines are tiny, tiny machines, so small, dozens of them would fit on the head of a pin. Nanoengineers come up with designs for nanomachines to do microminiature jobs. The medical community is exploring nanomachines that will be injected into the body to make repairs on a vein or a muscle or organ. The electronics industry envisions the day when nanomachines will construct other nanomachines to build superminiscule circuits. But ultimately software will drive these Lilliputian cogs and gears, and will be subject to the same deficiencies software suffers today. Nanomachines will be designed to enter environments hostile to humans, and be required to walk to work. Six-legged silicon bugs can already propel themselves today, but to what purposes can such devices be put by the imaginative Information Warrior? What a way to march unseen right into an adversary's electronic infrastructure and do damage at the microscopic level.

Futurists in the bioelectronic industry are looking at ways of merging conventional electronics with living systems to increase speed and density, and reduce power and heat in a new generation of information systems. Widespread commercial applications are not likely to come about for twenty years, but we inch towards such goals with pacemakers and remote triggered electrical stimulation for behavior control. This is about as personal as an information system can get. As information systems are embedded within the human body, the ethical and legal perplexities are only compounded. Will they make us think better and remember more? Or perhaps they will help postpone the aging process by optimizing the body's functions the way yogis alter theirs by slowing down their heartbeat? Or can they be used to manipulate and control the unwilling? Both.

While bio-chips are on the horizon, direct man computer communications is here now. The military calls them SQUIDs, or Super Quantum Interference Devices. SQUIDs are placed on or near a subject's head to detect brainwave pattern activity. The SQUID and the subject learn from each other, so that when, say the pilot of a jet fighter thinks about arming and firing an air-to-air missile, it arms and fires. In the coming years SQUIDs will evolve and will be able to electronically read minds as Hollywood imagined in the Natalie Wood movie *Brainstorm*. When SQUIDs become reversible and can communicate thoughts and information right into the brain, that's when we really have to watch out.

In the future, the ultimate form of Information Warfare may prove to be the direct insertion of information into an adversary's brain from afar. Also known as psychic warfare, the CIA has been studying remote viewing and how it can be used to identify people or objects from the other side of the globe. Parapsychology, including extrasensory perception, far from a science, is seen by the military as a potential means of "soft kill" against enemy soldiers. In the future, will thoughts be read from a distance? Can minds be forced to act in one manner or another or even to shut down by remote devices targeted at specific individuals? We're already examining the possibilities in research on nonlethal weaponry.

But perhaps one of the greatest concerns that we should have is what happens when there are no more secrets. In the world of Information Warfare, that thought makes one group cringe in horror while another views it as the Holy Grail. The movie *Sneakers* proposed the ultimate hacking and intelligence device that made all encryption schemes worthless. Any information, encrypted or not, was no longer a secret.

When surveillance technology reaches the point at which defensive privacy and security mechanisms are no longer effective, there are no more secrets. The satellites will know where you are, what you are doing, what you were saying and to whom. When there are no more secrets, if someone wants to get the electronic goods on you, there will be nothing you can do about it. When there are no more secrets between competing companies, proprietary information will mean less and marketing successes will have to be based upon new criteria. Perhaps we will even see a return to the most ancient computer of all, pen and paper. When there are no more secrets between countries and governments, when we know their every thought and they know ours, the global contest for influence, power, and superiority will be fought on a playing field for which there is no historical precedent.

The World is getting wired. When there are no more secrets, all we will have left is our honor and our integrity.

The other inevitable step in the future of Information Warfare is the increasing globalization of Cyberspace. It is now being populated with the unconnected billions from every continent. Europe is the closest behind the United States in building information superhighways having proposed a $150 billion pan-European project that rivals or exceeds our own NII. As their economic union strengthens, their computing and telecommunications needs will increase. As world trade barriers collapse, extensive communications capabilities will permit even the smallest of companies to trade their wares across the world. When this occurs, European companies and governments will also become targets of Information Warriors.

Europe's history is dramatically different than that of America. Over the centuries their lands have seen seemingly endless political and religious conflicts. Unlike the U.S., each country has had to defend its own soil. History has shown that ethnocentricism and political diversity have been a constant breeding ground for conflict. Economic jealousy founded in accidents of history fuels competition between culturally, politically, and militarily unique nation-states. As the Eastern European countries and former Soviet republics enter the world community, the potential for discord will increase. Packed into a space slightly larger than the United States, over 600 million people occupying almost three dozen countries must peacefully coexist.

European countries have felt the influx of economic and political refugees from the Mideast and Africa, and some political groups are rebelling with stronger nationalistic stances. Many Third World countries view certain European countries with distrust and disdain for former colonialism and the perceived mistreatment of immigrants. These are the very people, who in time, might well act as Information Warriors on behalf of their respective native lands.

Although Information Warfare is somewhat Americocentric today, what holds true for one Information Age society also holds true for others. All will become attractive targets. We see some European cultures making the jump from the early stages of industrialism to the Information Age, bypassing the painful learning curves of behavior and survival in advanced industrial societies. In the search of longterm identity and success, the more technically primitive countries should be expected to make every possible attempt at making the greatest possible progress in the shortest possible time. Information Warfare provides one means to that end.

Europe has been the victim of terrorism for decades. While

technology and information systems have been targets of some terrorist groups, as Europe gets wired, the effect of large scale attacks will increase profoundly. England has already felt the effects. In the terrorist campaign the IRA wages against the British, bombs have been a principal weapon. But one set of bombings in London's financial district shattered windows for blocks and effectively shut down the stock exchange. Losses were estimated to be in the area of one billion dollars, which is a very effective use of a low-tech weapon against a high-tech infrastructure. Conjecture must lead one to the conclusion that direct systemic attacks against the British econotechnical infrastructure are not too distant a probability.

Because Europeans have been subject to terrorist attacks, and because wars have been fought on their home soil, as a people, they are more attuned to the need for security and the right to individual privacy. Seeing armed militia at major airports is not uncommon, and for good reason; security checkpoints make our airports look like an unguarded subway station. As Europe moves into Cyberspace, we can expect them to have a heightened sense of the risks that they face—much more so than Americans do—and be willing to impose the necessary controls as a matter of self-restraint.

The French, for example, are extremely restrictive about what kinds of encryption products are permitted within their borders, suggesting that their government wants to make domestic eavesdropping efforts as easy as possible. The Clipper Chip proposal met with nearly universal derision when we suggested that the same system might be used throughout Europe. The bottom line was, the U.S. was not going to dictate unilaterally a world-wide encryption scheme; especially one designed in a technical and political void by the National Security Agency. No way. One fear was that the U.S. had built in a back door that would allow our government to surreptitiously read international communications.

From a global standpoint, America's First Amendment and

Bill of Rights is a local ordinance. European law enforcement agencies do not have to follow the same rules that ours do. Citizens of many European countries much more accustomed to benevolent socialist policies tend to trust their governments and assume that they will not abuse their rights. On the other hand, child pornography is legal in some countries, but vocal criticism of some governments is subject to arbitrary censorship. The rules are different.

Moreover, Europeans have already voiced concern over the United States' lax handling of personal data. Threats have been voiced that unless protection of such data is enhanced to levels that meet European standards, multinational businesses will be reluctant to or prohibited from transporting data and information into American-based computer systems. That alone could be a blow to expanded trade and commercial activities across the Atlantic.

Nation-states will by necessity develop their own National Information Policies to further their own interests and to protect their assets and their citizens. Some countries have already implemented policies in the form of state-sponsored espionage, nationalistic electronic protectionism, and enhanced privacy rights for their peoples. But over time, conflicts over policies and practices in Cyberspace are bound to result, just as they do in all forms of business and political undertakings. As we develop our own National Information Policies, it will do us well to consult with our international trading partners to promote early discussions on global agreements.

In the United States, the National Security Agency sets the standards by which computer security is measured, and in Europe, a coalition of England, Germany, Belgium, and the Netherlands has established a corresponding set of criteria. The U.S., Canada, and Europe are attempting to find a compromise so that our respective pieces of Cyberspace can talk to each other in a manner that provides for the privacy and security each side desires. Japan has its own sets of specifications, and as we all meet in Cyberspace, a common global means of establishing privacy and security will be even more necessary.

As NAFTA has broken down trade barriers between the U.S., Canada, and Mexico, we should insure solidarity on the Global Network. Over the years GATT has helped to increase international trade from a few billion to trillions of dollars in annual trade. Similarly conceived cybertreaties will be constructed when we realize just how much sense they make.

If the United States, the countries of Europe, other knowledge-based societies, and emerging ones have their own best interests at heart, internationalizing Cyberspace should become a political priority.

Conscientious and creative use of the Global Network during the colonization of Cyberspace will be an economic windfall to the world's economy well into the twenty-first century. Cooperation and compromise will have to occur on many fronts by all participants. America can give our concepts of freedom of speech and freedom of the press to the global village. International standards of personal privacy might be based upon the European precedents to the ultimate benefit of new democratized societies. Surely we will find a common reason to outlaw industrial and economic espionage. Perhaps law enforcement agencies will be given the political ability to coordinate investigation and prosecution of computer crimes, espionage, and cybercrimes on the Global Network.

Given the vision and collective political wisdom of countries whose leaders have had to build entire economies from scratch, it is only a matter of time before they tackle the same issues we in the United States face today. The nations of Europe must look at their own migratory paths in the next decade as much as we should build our policies and practices based upon our national considerations.

In the coming years we will see amazing technology permeate every facet of our lives, some of which will be welcomed, some of which will be less well received, and some of which will be used against us. We will see personal empowerment increase in significance as technology and information become the media for influence. We will see the world shrink even more than it already has in the last two decades. This new virtual world we are building will be as real to our descendants as this physical one is to us.

The future is what we make it. Let's make it a good one.

Afterword: Practical Proactive Security and Privacy

EVEN A FEW defensive measures can reduce your chances of being victimized by an Information Warrior. Remember that the more barriers you raise—the harder you make their job—the greater the chance of them moving on and leaving you alone.

Defending the Digital You

With a little bit of effort, each of us can take a stand to protect our individual electronic privacy. As of today there is no absolute means to avoid prying eyes; public records are still legally available to anyone with an interest in the private details of your life. But you can at least make sure that what some of the computers say about you is accurate.

One of the first steps is to look into how the credit reporting bureaus portray your financial worthiness. The three big credit reporting agencies—TRW, Equifax, and Trans Union—are all required by the Fair Credit Reporting Act to provide you with a free copy of your own credit reports. Get them!

There are a number of books on the subject of how to interpret or repair what the credit reports say about you; they are worth the investment. Most cities now have credit repair businesses that claim to be able to fix your credit reports; be very, very careful. For every legitimate credit repair company, there are ten more than can actually cause more damage—and they charge husky fees for the opportunity. Fixing your own credit is difficult. The credit agencies have a firmly ensconced system that discourages complaints. They tend to act as though you are guilty until proven innocent, but you are protected by law and have very clear rights. Take advantage of those rights.

The first step is to write letters to TRW, Equifax, and Trans Union, requesting a copy of your report. Make sure you request your files from all three; they are competitors and sell their services to different banks and companies across the country. Just because you fix one credit report doesn't mean the others are fixed as well, so you have to go through the same steps with all three. Within about a month, you will receive copies of your credit reports. Each company uses a slightly different format. Analyze the reports and look for whatever discrepancies and errors you find. The next step is the tough one. You are going to have to prove the errors!

Write back to the credit agency and detail exactly why you think the credit report is wrong. Be as specific as possible. When I first went through this process a number of years ago I found on my report:

- Debts that were never mine. I challenged these, asking the companies claiming the debts for substantiation. If the credit agency receives no response from the company, the negative information is removed.
- Negatives from years and years ago. All negatives older than seven years (ten years for bankruptcies) can be deleted. Many companies don't keep active records for more than a couple of years, so if you dispute their

digital allegations, it may simply be too complicated for them to respond. In this case, you win, and the negative is pulled.

- Inaccurate late payments. These are almost impossible to defend if the credit issuer says you were late. When it's their word against yours, you lose. Substantiate as much as possible with canceled checks, old credit card statements, etc.

- A totally wrong accusation. Although I was able to back up my case with extensive documentation, the offending party still refused to admit their error. The credit agency changed my alleged debt from a negative to a neutral, but it was still there. I spent the better part of a year pressuring the credit agency to see the common sense of my argument that a satisfied debt that never *was* a debt still made me look like a deadbeat. Only after I spoke to people at the executive level did my credit report get fixed.

You may feel that the credit agency is not responding properly. Push them to live up to their legal responsibility. Perhaps the information they received by the credit grantor is wrong. Don't hesitate to go straight to the bank, the credit card company, or whomever you disagree with. They have the power and control to update your credit profile by directly reporting an error or resolution of a dispute to the credit reporting agency. Negotiate. Get everything in writing and double check with the credit agency that the error has been repaired.

Sometimes the negative is technically accurate, but there are mitigating circumstances. By law the credit bureaus have to let you add a one-hundred word explanation for each item on your report. Take advantage of your rights. When your credit file is pulled, at least your version of the story will be told as well.

If you don't get satisfaction from the front-line people at the credit agencies, insist on speaking to management. Supervisors are merely clerks with a title and they still don't have the authority to make things right. I asked one supervisor at Equifax, "Can't you see the problem here? It's just a matter of common sense." To which she replied, "We don't use any of that here." How right she was. It took a month to find a vice president authorized to use common sense.

Go to the bookstore, pick up a copy of a credit repair book, and then go for it. It will be frustrating. You might get writer's cramp and cauliflower ear, but you have to stick with it. In the end, it's the only mechanism you have to set this part of your digital profile right.

Make sure your medical files, which provide another detailed picture of your life and upon which insurance companies rely, are accurate. The Medical Information Bureau is the place to start. Privacy groups say that the MIB makes you jump through hoops to get results, but they too have to follow the Fair Credit Reporting Act.

FREEDOM OF INFORMATION ACT

The government keeps extensive records on each of us, and you have a legal right to see many of them. Under the Freedom Of Information Act, you can write to government agencies such as the FBI and request that they provide you with copies of your records and files. In the letter, identify yourself as completely as possible, including social security number, address, date and place of birth, and previous addresses. In the case of the FBI, mail your request to: FBI Headquarters, J. Edgar Hoover Building, Tenth and Pennsylvania Ave., Washington, D.C., 20535. Make sure that you also ask for any files which may be held by field offices in specific cities; you might want to send copies of your FOIA request to those offices as well. Make sure you have your letters notarized. You can also write to the CIA and the Justice Department in search of what the government has on you.

DATABASES

When you apply for credit, ask that your name be kept off mailing lists sold to other companies. In some cases you can make the request verbally; in others, a letter may be required. For your existing accounts, ask the company to delete your name from their marketed mailing lists. If enough companies comply, the volume of junk mail you receive will shrink by half in just a few months.

You can also have your name removed from direct marketing mailing lists. The Direct Marketing Association will tag your name with a "Don't Solicit" message—meaning no junk mail or junk phone calls—but that doesn't necessarily mean you will be erased from their computers.

Joe Apter, President of Telephonic Info, says that the best way to maintain privacy in the electronic world is to stay out of computers. Easier said than done. That would mean no checking accounts, no savings accounts, no credit cards, no charge accounts, no magazine subscriptions. If you drive, the DMV computer's got you; if you pay taxes, you're in the IRS and Social Security computers. Apter adds that today some banks will cooperate with their customers' desires to enhance their personal privacy. Ask your bank, Apter advises, if they will add a code to your account that will keep your files private from all except lawful governmental access.

Lastly, you can join any of the many personal privacy and advocacy groups dealing with these issues on both a social and political level. You can write your Congressperson expressing your concerns and how you think they should be dealt with. Let the White House know, too. These days, even the President has an E-mail address. Remember, you have a voice.

As we continue our migration into Cyberspace, the rules and laws will change, and it is our personal responsibility to stay on top of developments. Keep informed of your rights. Subscribing to a personal privacy journal will help you stay current on the latest developments. If enough people feel that their personal electronic privacy is important, if they make their voices heard by the political powers that be, and if the advocacy groups receive enough support, then there is room for hope that the current situation will improve. But it won't happen if we sit idly by, waiting for the other guy to take care of our problem.

A few more common sense steps will make it harder for you to become a victim:

- Guard your social security number with a vengeance—it may well be your most valuable piece of personal information. Even though it is often available from public sources, don't make a snoop's job any easier. If someone asks for it at a retail establishment, you don't have to give it to them! If someone calls and asks for your social security number—unless you know who it is, why they need it, and if they're entitled to know— don't give it out.

- Be careful of telephone scam artists who offer you a free prize if you'll just answer a few questions. The information they ask for can be exceedingly personal and you have no obligation to provide it.

- Check your bank statements carefully—especially ATM withdrawals—and make sure that no one can see you enter your PIN number at public bank machines.

- Be careful when using telephone credit cards. Shoulder surfers love nothing more than people who don't hide their access codes.

- Giving out credit card numbers on the phone should be done judiciously.

- Don't expect any privacy on the Internet unless you use encryption. PGP has become very popular for secure communications and several products are based upon it.

- The rule of thumb is, don't say anything on the telephone you wouldn't want seen in the newspaper. Encrypted mobile and home cellular phones will soon be priced for the mass market, if you want true privacy.

And watch out for those baby monitors: ours has picked up some great gossip from the neighbor's phones!

- Personal computer users should *always* practice safe computing.

Defending Against Class 2 Information Warfare

Corporate America has the ability to protect itself against the Information Warrior, if only it will take action. Many of the weaknesses that businesses experience are self-induced and easily fixed—any company can protect its information assets to reduce the chances of a successful attack and to minimize any damages.

When it comes to Information Warfare, there is no way to insure that a company is absolutely invulnerable to attack. Even the military, with all the money it spends on security efforts, has experienced severe breaches to its information infrastructure. The goal here is to build in enough proactive defenses to dissuade most, if not all, attacks.

Consider the conventional thief. Does he attempt to rob the house with the most security or the least? A house with no security is a much more inviting target than a house with a security system, a big dog, and locks on the windows. The bank with light security will be higher on the hit list than the bank with an armed guards and a vault that closes itself when a threat becomes apparent. So it goes with electronic information assets.

The first step any organization can take is to recognize that information is critical to its success. Some companies may decide at the board level that without adequate information asset protection, the company—or its board members—may be legally liable if they become a victim of Information Warfare. In a litigious society insufficient protection is inexcusable. Other companies may worry about a slump in customer confidence if customers' privacy or assets are compromised.

Whatever the motivation on the company's part, a high-level, management-mandated decision to protect information assets is the first step to corporate security in the Information Age. Any effort to protect information assets must include a corporate-wide policy which clearly spells out the importance of information—and access to that information—to the financial well-being of the company. Developing a corporate policy is a comprehensive effort requiring the mandate of top management, the support of middle management and the compliance of every employee. Without policy, there is no security.

Depending upon the organization, the actual methods for information asset protection will differ but all the following measures should be considered:

- Examine legal liabilities. A corporate counsel should provide input into the development of any security policy, since the law is constantly changing and many of the current legal cyberbattles are being fought on old legal footings. There is little case law in these areas, but examining the legal culpability of an organization is essential to determining its defensive postures.
- A comprehensive risk analysis should be performed by the audit and MIS departments on a regular basis. They should evaluate the risk to the company if computer systems fail, from either intentional or accidental forces. How long can the company function without computer services? What will the ultimate cost to the company be in real dollars? A risk analysis should examine everything from the effects of a virus attack to the severing of high speed communications.
- A Security Profile Analysis, an empirical technique I developed, examines the company's networks from the bad guys' perspective. An SPA looks at myriad components—from network systems to employee behavior—to determine how an Information Warrior might be able to penetrate your facility or compromise your information assets. This is a very enlightening exercise—most

companies discover they don't know what they have or even what their networks look like.

- An employment screening process should be considered. It might be worth asking permission of your potential hires to examine their personal records—even though you could do so legally without their permission—to avoid falling into the trap of becoming a clandestine antipersonnel Information Warrior yourself. Any personnel databanking should be well thought out, have a specific purpose, be unbiased, and remain within the legal limits of state and federal statutes.

- Establish a clear set of ethical guidelines for your company and your employees. The rules by which you wish to operate your piece of Cyberspace should be understood by everyone under your company's aegis and will help set a positive example for your employees.

- Join several security organizations and participate in their annual conferences. Don't just send your technical staff: the highest level management should attend and become involved. The costs of attending these events are minimal and the opportunity they provide for social networking between companies and security practitioners is invaluable.

- Adhere to the copyright restrictions on all company software and applications. The penalties are severe for illicit copying of software, on both the personal and corporate level. The Software Publisher's Association is an excellent source for current policies and actions.

- Make security awareness, education, and training an ongoing part of all employee programs. The fundamentals of protecting company information should be covered and covered again through electronic and written communications, video support materials, and interactive computer training. Getting your employees on your side is worth every penny it costs.

- Examine how your garbage disposal is handled. Dumpster diving yields quick, inexpensive results for those on the search for lazily discarded information. Shredders or a burn bag may be necessary to keep sensitive data truly private.

- Backup your system. Determine which files you can not live without and make sure that the hard disks on all PCs, networks, servers, and hosts are regularly backed up. If you don't, you will pay the price—sooner or later.
- Plan for natural disasters. Large companies use what are called Hot Sites. When the World Trade Center was bombed, floods raged through Chicago, Andrew leveled South Florida, and an earthquake struck San Francisco, major companies minimized their downtime by implementing their off-site disaster recovery plan.
- Plan for the Information Warrior. If your systems suddenly undergo attack from an unauthorized intruder, what should you do? If a breach of confidential information occurs, the company should have a plan to respond, including the possible notification of the authorities. Planned reactions can speed up recovery in the event of intentional system failures.
- Consider establishing a data classification system for your organization. Applying military-think with "unclassified," "secret," "top secret" and such isn't necessarily the way to go; there's an easier way. A company essentially has three kinds of information:

1. General company information—lists, designs, customers, and pricing.
2. Information on employees, including a fair amount of private information that cannot be legally released to third parties.
3. Information on customers and suppliers.

When considering information assets in this way, we can assign a degree of sensitivity to each category. Your information assets will fit into one of the following data sensitivity definitions:

1. Loss of this information can cause a near-fatal blow to the company. This information should be accessible to the fewest people possible.
2. Loss of this information would cause severe, though not irreparable, harm to the company. Take extra effort to protect it.
3. If this information gets out it would hurt, but no serious damage would occur.
4. This information is often already public and anyone's for the asking. Who cares?

Whatever system or definitions a company might choose, learning what information assets it controls, who uses them, and how well protected they are is an invaluable undertaking.

- Coordinate your physical and electronic security efforts. They are stronger working hand in hand and may be less expensive to implement. Teach guards that floppy disks are as valuable as calculators and computer hardware. For very sensitive facilities, consider installing bulk erasers into the entrance and exit paths to make sure no unauthorized electronic data goes in or out.
- Test the physical security of your plant from time to time.
- Test the electronic security of your systems with a penetration analysis. Security budgets often double after one of these!
- Take advantage of the wide variety of techical solutions for security problems covered in this book.

PRACTICE SAFE COMPUTING

- Using antiviral software to minimize the risk of infection. Using two or more competing software packages that utilize both scanning and heuristic or behavior-based detection mechanisms will greatly reduce the chances of being hit with a virus. Software applications such as word processing, databases, and graphics should only be permitted to enter a company's computers from specific places within the network. Users should be restricted from loading their own software into the networks without authorization.

- PC security software will help to control the importing and exporting of software applications and sensitive company data in and out of workstations. Determine what, if any, company data may go home with employees and effect the security controls to reflect those choices.

- Use access-control software and hardware controls to limit access to network resources or data. A clerk should not have access to financial or design information, but the CFO will need the ability to access accounting centers throughout the organization. With so much connectivity between offices, controlling access to vital corporate functions is an absolute must.

- Look for creeping modem growth—an ideal way to sneak company data out of your control. Use a demon dialer to identify any surreptitious modems that could be costing the company a fortune in lost information.

- Implement an audit system. Audit software monitors and records how employees or others are using information resources. If there is a compromise or attack, audit trails will help give a backwards road map to the source.

   Watch out, however, for overusing keystroke monitoring audits. Efficiency experts once considered using this method to see who got the most work done, but the Department of Justice strongly recommends against it as a possible invasion of privacy at the workplace. Let someone else be the test case.

   Be careful of E-mail monitoring. Some take the position that since the network is owned by the company, the company should be able to do anything it wants including reading personal employee E-mail. Others insist that employees must be given some degree of privacy at the workplace. Get legal advice before taking any steps.

The biggest conundrum is how to investigate the electronic files of an employee suspected of sabotage. Is breaking the law the only route to protecting your company? Make sure you document everything, and involve your lawyer.

- If you are connected as a host to the Internet, get a firewall. A firewall isolates you from the network, excepting those people you want admitted or want to let surf the 'net. This is one surefire way to protect the corporate jewels.

ENCRYPTION

- Encryption is the ultimate means of information asset protection. If properly implemented, encryption will foil almost any attack short of a nationally-sponsored effort. Encryption can be used to protect any information asset, whether stored on tape or disk, or while in transit on a communications link.

Generally, encryption should be seriously considered on all intercompany transmissions. If data are being sent across the Global Network, either by Internet or fax, encryption will thwart almost any attempt at illicit eavesdropping over telephone lines or leased lines. Even small companies (such as law firms that handle sensitive information) should seriously consider adding encryption to their communications.

Encrypting data on a local area network is becoming increasingly popular, as is encryption of data stored on hard disks, file servers, and bigger computers. Laptops are stolen at alarming rates, so adding encryption to them is an inexpensive alternative to losing sensitive information.

All international data and faxes with any sensitivity should be encrypted. Period. Assume all international voice communications to be public; someone is listening.

Picking an encryption method can be confusing, and there are as many opinions are there are choices. Many proprietary encryption algorithms claim both high strength and high performance, but selecting a reliable one is a difficult proposition. Keep in mind that stronger algorithms are slower in software and more expensive in hardware, while weaker algorithms can be implemented inexpensively with little impact on performance. DES is still a middle-of-the-road approach, but will be decertified by the government in 1997. Efforts are afoot to create a Triple-DES standard, which will save billions in replacing existing systems.

Whatever means of encryption is selected, make sure the key management system is both easy and strong. RSA's public key encryption has become an almost de facto standard because of its ease and its strength. Other key management schemes are automatic and require little or no human intervention. The Internet is embracing Phil Zimmerman's Pretty Good Privacy, or PGP. Dozens of products exist to solve just about any encryption problem you care to solve.

- Don't rely on passwords alone to protect the front door of your piece of Cyberspace. They are the weakest form of identification you can use. At a minimum, try to implement passphrases instead. The password KILA-BUNI or the PIN 1009188 is harder to remember than a longer passphrase such as "My blue dog is bright red," but passphrases are much harder to guess or discover. If you do use passwords and passphrases, changing them on a regular basis is one of the smartest things an individual or an organization can do. When someone leaves the company, make sure that one of the first things you do is delete his user ID and password from all systems.

  Stronger authentication is more expensive, but you get

what you pay for. Physical ID plus a password requires the user to identify him-or herself twice, once with something they know (the password) and once with something they own (a card or token). For high security applications consider using biometric identification based upon a fingerprint, a retinal scan, or facial infrared imaging.

- Display a warning screen that states company policy whenever someone signs onto a company computer. The Department of Justice has suggested wording that states that the use of company computers is restricted to those with specific approval, and all other access or use is prohibited. Using an on-screen warning for both onsite users and those calling in from a remote computer site puts the company in a better legal position if any breaches end up in court.

- *Never* use the default security specifications that come in products you buy and install. Always, always, always change them. The Information Warrior knows that most of us leave them in the factory default condition, making illicit entry or compromise all the easier.

- Configure security policy to your needs and coordinate those needs among all security people throughout the company. The mainframe people and the LAN people and the communications people all need to be working from the same play book.

- See if the internal phone system or PBX is connected to your computer networks. If it is, make sure that the security is strong. The boundary between phone fraud and computer crime is becoming increasingly fuzzy—in Cyberspace, everything connects to everything.

The bottom line is to put up enough barriers against the Information Warrior so that unless he is really after you, he'll go knocking on the next door and leave you alone. The casual 'net-surfing hacker looking to hone his skills on your MIPS will move on to his next victim if he runs up against tough security.

All these precautions can pay off in more ways than one. You may want to consider using the enhanced security of your company as a marketing tool. Depending upon the nature of a company's business, strong security or enhanced personal privacy guidelines can be attractive to potential customers.

This chapter offers only a small list of the security issues and options that an individual or company can consider when attempting to protect personal or institutional information assets. As technology improves for both sides in the Information Wars, and as the National Information Infrastructure grows and matures, the issues will change and relative risks will increase and decrease. Security and privacy issues will also change, and we must have a flexible enough mechanism and infrastructure to react rapidly to the risks and vulnerabilities.

Above all, we must remember that only when we as a country are successful in enacting a National Information Policy will our personal, professional, corporate, and national security needs be adequately and clearly addressed.

The resources section of this book provides a list of companies, publications, associations, government, and underground resources valuable to anyone interested in any facet of security and privacy. Some of these resources are for training and education, some are very technical, and some provide excellent product information. Everyone from the tenderfoot security beginner, to nontechnical management, to human resources, to the experienced professional should find resources that address their needs.

Perhaps the best resource of all is you. Use it wisely.

The Ten Commandments of Computer Ethics

1. Thou shalt not use a computer to harm other people.
2. Thou shalt not interfere with other people's computer work.
3. Thou shalt not snoop around in other people's computer files.
4. Thou shalt not use a computer to steal.
5. Thou shalt not use a computer to bear false witness.
6. Thou shalt not copy or use proprietary software for which you have not paid.
7. Thou shalt not use other people's computer resources without authorization or proper compensation.
8. Thou shalt not appropriate other people's intellectual output.
9. Thou shalt think about the social consequences of the program you are writing or the system you are designing.
10. Thou shalt always use a computer in ways that insure consideration and respect for your fellow human being.

SOURCE: Computer Ethics Institute, Washington, D.C.

Resources:
Who Ya Gonna Call?

SOMEWHERE IN THIS LIST you will find what you're looking for. Refer to http://www.infowar.com for updates and revisions. Any additions? Any corrections? Send them to: betty@infowar.com.

Credit Reporting Agencies

Trans Union Consumer
  Relations Center
208 South Market
Wichita, KS 67202
800-879-2674

CBI Equifax Credit Information
  Services
PO Box 740256
Atlanta, GA 30374
800-879-4094

TRW National Consumer Assistance Center
PO Box 749029
Dallas, TX 75374
800-392-1122

For credit repair, make sure you go to all three companies, not just the first one that responds. These guys' computers don't talk to each other—they're competitors. You have clear rights under the Fair Credit Reporting Act.

Privacy

Mail Preference Service, PO Box 3861, New York, NY 10163-3861

If you'd like your name removed from junk mail lists, write to these guys. Only those companies who are members of the Direct Marketing Association are said to honor your requests. Thus, the riff-raff of direct mail will still probably reach you.

Beth Givens, Project Director
Center for Public Interest Law
University of San Diego
5998 Alcala Park
San Diego, CA 92110
Voice: 619-260-4160
Fax: 619-298-5681
e-mail: bgivens@acusd.edu
Privacy Rights Clearinghouse Hotline (CA only): 619-298-3396
U.S.: 800-773-7748

If you need help with a privacy issue, call the Hotline. Their fact sheets are online, and the one of most interest to InfoWar readers is "Coping With Identity Theft: What to Do When an Imposter Strikes." The Web address is http://pwa.acusd.edu/.

Telephone Preference Service
PO Box 9014
Farmingdale, NY 11735-9014

As you might expect, this organization is supposed to tell direct marketing firms not to solicit you on the phone. The privacy groups says it helps, but not a lot.

Medical Information Bureau
PO Box 105 Essex Station
Boston, MA 02112
617-426-3660
330 University Avenue
Toronto, Ontario M5G 1R7 Canada
416-597-0590

Often used by data brokers, insurance companies, employers, and investigators. Like the credit agencies, it is subject to the Fair Credit Reporting Act.

Security and Privacy Organizations

National Computer Security
Association
10 S. Courthouse Avenue
Carlisle, PA 17013
717-258-1816 (www.ncsa.com)

Open Source Solutions
11005 Langton Arms Court
Oakton, VA 22124
703-242-1700

ISSA
401 N. Michigan Avenue
Chicago, IL 60611
312-644-6610

MIS Training Institute
498 Concord Street
Framingham, MA 01701
508-879-7999

Privacy International
666 Pennsylvania Avenue
Washington, DC 20003
202-544-9240

Computer Professionals for
Social Responsibility
666 Pennsylvania Avenue
Washington, DC 20003
202-544-9240

ftp.cpsr.org
American Society for Industrial
Security
1655 N. Fort Myer Drive
Arlington, VA 22209
703-522-5800

Software Publishers Association
1730 M Street, NW
Washington, DC 20036
202-452-1600

Sometimes affectionately called the software police, the SPA monitors and assists in software copyright violations.

Electronic Frontier Foundation
666 Pennsylvania Avenue
Washington, DC 20003
202-544-9237

Computer Ethics Institute
11 Dupont Circle, NW
Washington, DC 20036
202-939-3707

What's right and what's wrong, morally speaking.

Security and Privacy Publications

Info Security News
498 Concord Street
Framingham, MA 01701
508-879-7999

Virus Bulletin
21 The Quadrant Abingdon Science Park
Abingdon, Oxfordshire 0X14 3YS UK
011-44-235-555139

Privacy Journal
PO Box 28577
Providence, RI 02908
401-274-7861

Computers and Security
Mayfield House
256 Banbury Road
Oxford OX2 7DH UK
011-44-865-512242
562 Croydon Road
Elmont, New York 11003 USA

Computers and Security is an erudite, academic journal for advanced security practitioners.

The Computer Law and
  Security Report
Mayfield House
256 Banbury Road
Oxford OX2 7DH UK
011-44-865-512242
Elsevier
655 Avenue of the Americas
New York, NY 10010 USA
212-989-5800

Data Pro Research
600 Delran Parkway
Delran, NJ 08075
800-328-2772

Security Management
1655 N. Fort Myer Drive
Arlington, VA 22209
703-522-5800

PIN Magazine
PO Box 11018
Washington, DC 20008
301-652-9050

Personal Identification News focuses on means of identifying people: from passwords to smart cards to biometrics. Annual conference.

Cryptologia
17 Alfred Road W.
Merrick, NY 11566
516-378-0263

Monitoring Times
PO Box 98
Brasstown, NC 28902
704-837-9200

Everything about radio and cellular and eavesdropping and scanning the airwaves.

International Journal of Intelligence
PO Box 411
New York, NY 10021
212-737-7923

Occasional good articles about information security and intelligence concerns.

EMC Technology
State Road 625
PO Box "D"
Gainesville, VA 22065
703-347-0030

EMC Technology are the experts in electromagnetic control from TEMPEST to shielding to HERF. Very technical.

Security Magazine
1350 E. Touhy
Des Plaines, IL 60018
708-635-8800

Heavy on physical security and video surveillance. Growing into information security.

Computer Security Digest
150 N. Main
Plymouth, MI 48170
313-459-8787

News briefs and topical odds and ends.

Low Profile Newsletter
PO Box 84910
Phoenix, AZ 85701
800-528-0559

Privacy-related issues and news.

Internet World
11 Ferry Lane W.
Westport, CT 06880
203-226-6967

Zine all about living on the Internet. Great for beginners and net-surfers alike.

Wired
544 Second Street
San Francisco, CA 94107
415-904-0660

A super-flashy high gloss zine destined to become the upscale standard for cybernauts.

CCS (Counter Spy Shop)
630 Third Avenue
New York, NY 10017
212-557-3040

Countersurveillance and privacy-enhancement technologies and products for individuals and businesses.

Underground Resources

MAGAZINES

2600: The Hacker Quarterly
PO Box 99
Middle Island, NY 11953
516-751-2600

One of the hacker's bibles and the subject of debate on Capitol Hill. Take a trip to the other side.

Gray Areas
PO Box 808
Broomall, PA 19008-0808

Focuses on fringe topics of interest to hackers.

Mondo 2000
PO Box 10171
Berkeley, CA 94709

The original "cyberculture" zine.

Axcess
4640 Cass Street #9309
San Diego, CA 92169

Mondo-type style and information.

Black Ice
PO Box 1069
Brighton BN2 4YT UK

Mondo/Wired style with British flair.

Boing Boing
11288 Ventura Boulevard #818
Studio City, CA 91604

For do-it-yourself cyborgs.

FringeWare Review
PO Box 49921
Austin, TX 78765

Articles of a cyberpunk bent, catalog of FringeWare Products.

Nuts & Volts
430 Princeland Court
Corona, CA 91719

The best magazine available for hardware-oriented hackers.

Intertek
13 Daffodil Lane
San Carlos, CA 94070

An informative and serious cyberpunk magazine.

Consumertronics
2011 Crescent Drive
PO Drawer 537
Alamogordo, NM 88310
505-434-0234

How to rip off the electric company; computer phreaking; credit card scams; and other assorted extreme pieces of information.

American Eagle Publications
PO Box 41401
Tucson, AZ 85717
602-888-4957

Highly controversial publications that discuss how to write computer viruses.

ELECTRONIC MAGAZINES

Phrack Magazine
603 W. 13th #1A-278
Austin, TX 78701
(www.infowar.com for archives)

The definitive hacker publication. For electronic copy, E-mail phrack@well.sf.ca.us and ask to be added to the list.

Computer Underground Digest
E-mail: tk0ju2@mvs.cso.niu.edu
(ask to be added to list)

A regularly published digest covering topics related to the underground side of computing.

The following are three Open Source resources, but they frequently carry information on IW:

The Open Source Professional List
Eliot A. Jardines, Moderator
E-mail: opensrce@fcc.com

A moderated electronic discussion list revolving around a preselected monthly topic. Potential subscribers should send a brief statement to the above E-mail address stating who they are, what they do, and what their open source interests are.

The Open Source Homepage
http://www.eajardines.com/os.html

Provides on-line Open Source-related resources, reviews, articles, links, and the Open Source Professional List monthly topic statements.

The Open Source Quarterly (ISSN 1087-1748)
Eliot A. Jardines, Publisher
34 Thompson Street
Fairfield, CT 06432-4349
$40.00 per year (4 issues)

A compilation of the Open Source Professional List monthly discussion topics, plus Open Source-related articles and columns.

HACKER MEETINGS

PumpCon. Philadelphia, October. Raided for two straight years. Information circulated on the Net a few months prior.

SummerCon. The famous yearly private hacker gathering. By invitation only.
E-mail: summercon@stormking.com.

HoHo Con. Texas, December. The largest, wildest hacker con we've got.
E-mail: hohocon@zero.cypher.com

DefCon. Las Vegas, Summer. More organized than the rest, the granddaddy of hacker cons.
http://www.defcon.org

You owe it to yourself and your company to check these out. Outrageous, anarchistic, chock-full of information. See how the other side lives by going one-on-one with the underground.

2600 Hacker Meetings. First Friday of every month at the following locations. Everyone is invited—hackers to professionals to law enforcement to those without a clue.

2600 Enterprises
PO Box 99
Middle Island, NY 11953-0099
516-751-2600
E-mail: 2600@well.sf.ca.us

Government Resources

National Institute of Standards and Technology
Computer Security Labs
Gaithersburg, MD 20899
301-975-2000

NIST sets standards and works closely with the NSA in information security. Get their catalog of publications, including the Rainbow Series of computer security pamphlets. They have a free BBS and newsletter, the CSL Bulletin. The Computer Security Publications booklet is invaluable.

National Computer Security Center
9800 Savage Road
Fort Meade, MD 20755
301-859-4371

This reasonably open section of the NSA sets security standards for the government. They evaluate and certify computer and communications security products. Technical, exacting, and academic in nature, they also have an annual conference. Authors of the Orange Book and Red Book. Dockmaster is their BBS for qualified security folks.

CANADA

Goverment Services Canada (GSC)
Industrial and Corporate Security Branch
Hull, Quebec, Canada

EUROPE

British Embassy
3100 Massachusetts Avenue, NW
Washington, DC 20008
202-462-1340

For up-to-date sources on British government security efforts. They have made available in the past the Information Technology Security Evaluation Criteria (ITSEC) in coordination with Germany, Belgium, and the Netherlands.

Computer Security Branch
Information Technology Division
Department of Trade and Industry
Room 847 Kingsdale House
66-74 Victoria Street
London SW1E 65W UK

ITSEC and other government security documents.

Commission of the European Communities
Directorate-General XIII
Information Industries and Innovation Directorate F
RACE Programme and Development of Advanced Telematics
   Services
rue de la Loi 200
B-1049 Brussels, Belgium

Part of the ITSEC group.

European Computer Manufacturers Association
114 Rue du Rhone
CH-1204 Geneva, Switzerland
011-41-22-735-3634

The ECMA is a standards group comprised of a wide range of security standards. Write for a catalog of their offerings.

Electronic Resources

The Global Network provides a wide range of services to those interested in these areas.

The President of the United States
president@whitehouse.gov
vicepresident@whitehouse.gov

On the Internet, subscribe or ftp to:

comp.risks	comp.security.announce
alt.security	misc.security
alt.security.index	de.comp.security
bit.listserv.security	comp.security.misc

alt.security.ripem
alt.security.keydist
alt.security.pgp
comp.security.unix
alt.privacy
comp.society.privacy
alt.privacy.clipper
alt.os.multics

alt.cellular
comp.virus
alt.hackers
alt.hackers.malicious
alt.hackers.cough.cough.cough
alt.cyberpunk
alt.2600
alt.society.cu-digest

If you can get to the IRC (Internet Relay Chat), look for the hacker discussion groups and join in or just listen. New newsgroups pop up all the time, and have their own forums on numerous large BBSs.

Net Hangouts for Hackers

#hack　　IRC channel with hacking discussions
#warez　 IRC channel with software piracy discussions
#phreak　IRC channel with phone fraud discussions

Security-Related Electronic Mailing Lists

Computer Emergency Response Team
E-mail: cert@cert.org
(ask to be put on list)

A periodic maling of security-related problems affecting Internet users.

The Firewalls
E-mail: majordomo@greatcircle.com
(in body of message write "SUBSCRIBE FIREWALLS.")

The best mailing list going for issues dealing with securing systems through the implemention of system firewalls.

The BugTraq
E-mail: bugtraq@crimelab.com
(ask to be put on list)

Serious security-related discussions pinpointing actual bugs, their invocations, and workarounds.

Reporting Computer Crimes

If you are the victim of any kind of computer crime or other violation in cyberspace, report it. Make sure your documentation is as complete as possible, and be specific to make sure you speak to the right people who also speak computerese. If there's any question about who to report it to, call your local police department, your state police, or the FBI and ask for help. While most computer crimes do invite investigation, jurisdiction is sometimes confusing, so you may have to stick with it until you find the right group.

Please, please, please, report computer crimes. You'll help the next guy if you do.

Computer Emergency Response Team—Coordination Center
Software Engineering Institute
Carnegie Mellon University
Pittsburgh, PA 15213
412-268-7090
E-Mail: cert@cert.org

A federally funded organization to reactively and proactively promote security. As a centralized repository for technical problems, system-wide breaches, or attacks, especially on the Internet, they can generate a national response in minutes.

Federal Bureau of Investigation
National Computer Crime Squad
J. Edgar Hoover Building
10th and Pennsylvania Avenue
Washington, DC 20535.

For interstate crimes and those concerning federal interest computers, international incidents, and computer crimes in general. If in doubt, call them, and they'll point you in the right direction. Contact your local bureau office; its number is in the phone book.

U.S. Secret Service
Electronic Crimes Branch
1800 G Street, Room 900
Washington, DC 20223
202-435-5850

For computer and communications crimes involving federal interest computers, presidential threats, counterfeiting, and general computer intrusions. Does not investigate classified security breaches. Coordinates with the FBI for jurisdiction and often the two agencies share cases.

For any computer crimes that involve your communications equipment or were allegedly committed over the telephone lines, contact any of the following and make a formal complaint.

Local telephone company
Regional Bell operating company
Cellular carrier
Long distance carrier or other service provider

If you don't know the number, call the Operator and ask who handles such things. If you don't get satisfaction, be persistent. The security, fraud, or investigations unit should be able to help you.

More Mail Lists, News Groups, etc.

www.infowar.com

EmergencyNet NEWS Services (ENN)
E-mail: enn@emergency.com
http://www.emergency.com

An electronic news service that specializes in news stories that involve law enforcement, fire, EMS, medical, disaster, terrorism, intelligence, military, and national security topics. An excellent resource!

rec.games.pbm
http://www.pbm.com/lindahl/pbm.html

A newsgroup for discussing play-by-mail games (ordinary mail and E-mail); both wargames and non-wargames.

IWR Daily Update
Tempest Co.
PO Box 15095
Boston, MA 02215-0002
617-266-5637
Fax: 617-266-7680
E-mail: tempest@tempestco.com
http://www.tempestco.com

IWR is the only open sources resource that provides daily and priority updates on the ever-changing events taking place in the the world of both public and private sector intelligence. In today's day and age it is no longer acceptable to find out what happened a month after the fact. IWR provides timely information that is not constrained by page limits. IWR's release schedule and page size is determined by events, not by preordained schedules. By providing the subscriber with three different elements (quarterlies, special reports, and updates), the subscriber has access to near-real-time intelligence, brief reports, and analytical pieces.

RISKS

Direct requests to request@csl.sri.com (majordomo) with one-line "SUBSCRIBE." (www.infowar.com for archives)
Security/privacy issues. Excellent!!!!

Intelligence Newsletter
E-mail: oschmidt@dialup.francenet.fr

Olivier Schmidt and his entire team of international correspondents specialize in information on security and intelligence and have created this online electronic fortnightly.

Cloaks and Daggers Open Discussion of Intelligence (Academic)
Rudolf Kies, Ph.D., Moderator <kies@sure.net>
<cloaks> on listserv@sjuvm.stjohns.edu
<bit.listserv.cloaks-daggers>
<listserv@listserv.net> (www.infowar.com for archives)

We don't spy on anyone—we just watch those who do.

Cipher—Electronic Magazine from the IEEE Computer
Society's TC on Security and Privacy
Carl Landwehr, Editor
Subscriptions: cipher-request@itd.nrl.navy.mil (not automated) with subject line "subscribe."

Hypertext browsers may prefer to read *Cipher* that way. It can be found at URL http://www.itd.nrl.navy.mil/ITD/5540/ieee/cipher.

Privacy Digest
Subscriptions are by an automatic listserv system; for subscription information, please send a message consisting of the word *help* in the body to privacy-request@vortex.com.

URLs to Check Out

Crypto
http://www.cosc.georgetown.edu/denning/

Crypto-Log (TM)
http://www.enter.net/chronos/cryptolog.html

A guide to Internet resources on cryptography—more than 500 links on everything from algorithms to vulnerabilities are listed. This site contains an annotated collection of over 400 pointers to everything available on the Web regarding cryptography, including programs, source code, reports, and research.

CryptoAPI
http://www.microsoft.com/intdev/

A mailing list (discussion list) for Microsoft Cryptographic API (CryptoAPI), which provides services that enable application developers to add cryptography to their Win32 applications.

Privacy
http://www.epic.org/privacy/medical/ (medical privacy)

Public Law
"Public International Law":
http://www.ecel.uwa.edu.au/law/links/fauburn/
Francis Auburn—Australia fauburn@ecel.uwa.edu.au

Hackers
Netta Gilboa, President
http://www.gti.net/grayarea

Covers in-depth topics such as virus writers, phone phreaks, a break-in at the Well, and numerous hacker conventions.

HACKWATCH.COM
http://www.ireland.iol.ie-kooltek

Home page for Hack Watch News and Syndicated HackWatch. Hack Watch News is the only European signal security newsletter and Syndicated HackWatch is a subset that is published in various magazines throughout Europe and the U.S. Syndicated Hack Watch is also available in the following usenet groups: alt.satellite.tv.crypt, alt.satellite.tv.europe, rec.video. satellite.europe, rec.video.satellite.dbs. A number of dial-up BBSs carry HackWatch. The electronic version of Hack Watch News is available only from Special Projects BBS (+353-51-50143).

Hackers Catalog from Telecode
PO Box 6426
Yuma, AZ 85366-6426
520-726-2833
Fax: 520-726-2833
E-mail: Telecode@aol.com

Civil Defense
http://www.ndu.edu/ndu/inss/strforum/forum46.html
http://www.infowar.com

"Defining Civil Defense in the Information Age." Government, InfoWar, a little bit of everything.

MEGATERMS: Military Terms and Acronyms, V. 4.1
contact Mike Bandor
E-mail: bandorm@jcave.com

Currently 22,700 terms and acronyms.

http://www.fedcenter.com
Capt. Roger Thrasher

A super resource to check out the servers of our government.

Air Chronicles (US Air Force Web site)
http://www.cdsar.af.mil/

Airborne Electronic Warfare Systems Department
http://www.code802.nwscc.sea06.navy.mil/

C4I HORIZON '95
http://infosphere.safb.af.mil/rmip/h95top.htm

DISA Center for INFOSEC (CISS).
http://www.disa.mil/ciss/ciss.html

"The Center for Information Systems Security's goal is to create and manage a unified, fully integrated information systems security program for all DII systems. CISS acts as the focal point for assuring availability, integrity and confidentiality of DII Automated Information Systems (AIS) information."

Electronic Privacy Information Center (EPIC)
E-mail: info@epic.org
http://cpsr.org/cpsr/privacy/epic/privacy_resources.faq

Online guide to privacy resources. EPIC is a public interest research center in Washington, D.C.

Federation of American Scientists (FAS)
http://www.clark.net/pub/gen/fas

Conducts analysis and advocacy on science, technology, and public policy, including nuclear weapons, arms sales, biological hazards, secrecy, and space policy. FAS is a privately funded nonprofit policy organization whose Board of Sponsors includes half of America's living Nobel laureates.

The definitive site for Information Warfare:
http://www.infowar.com.

Information Warfare
http://www.rain.org/lonestar/infowar.htm

Information Warfare: The Invisible War
http://www.seas.gwu.edu/student/kimc/

Management Analytics
http://all.net/books/iw/top.html

Information Warfare books and resources.

Institute for the Advanced Study of Information Warfare (IASIW)
http://www.psycom.net/iwar.1.html

A virtual nongovernmental organization formed to facilitate an understanding of information warfare with reference to both military and civilian life.

Intelligence Reform Project
http://www.clark.net/pub/gen/fas/irp/
http://www.infowar.com

Internet Security Issues
http://www.cs.albany.edu/ault/security/

Line of Site
Real Trends
9200 Centerway Road
Gaithersburg, MD 20879

U.S. Military Sites on the Internet (an address book of about 350 URLs pertaining to the U.S. military). This is a no-frills, cut-to-the-heart-of-the-matter publication, presenting welcome relief for those of us who are tired of wading through pages of photos and descriptors just to find one URL. Listings are in alphabetical order and there is even space for writing in additions or comments. Periodic updates will be available from the publisher—electronic transmission is available. Send cash, check, or money order for $12 plus $3 shipping and handling. Be sure to include your full mailing address.

National Computer Security Association (NCSA)
http://www.ncsa.com

NCSA's mission is to foster improvement in all aspects of worldwide digital security, reliability, and ethics by providing key services to three principal constituents: end-users of digital technologies, computer and communications industry product developers and vendors, and computer and information security experts.

National Military Intelligence Association (NMIA)
http://www.cais.com/NMIA/HomePage.html

National Security Agency (NSA)
http://www.nsa.gov:8080

National Technical Information Service (NTIS)
http://www.fedworld.gov/ntis/ntishome.html

Naval Postgraduate School: Joint C4I Systems Curriculum
http://www.stl.nps.navy.mil/c4i

Office of the Director of C4I (Information Systems for Command, Control, Communications, and Computers)
http://www.army.mil/disc4-pg/disc4.html

Reto E. Haeni's Information Warfare Home Page
http://www.seas.gwu.edu/student/reto/infowar/info-war.html

S. D. James' Information Warfare Home Page
http://vislab-www.nps.navy.mil/james/info_war.html

Security (Web site with resources)
http://www.southwind.net/miked/security.html

Third Wave Revolution: Netwars and Activists, Power on the Net
http://www.teleport.com/jwehling/OtherNetwars.html

U.S. Air Force Air Intelligence Agency
http://www.dtic.dla.mil/airforcelink/pa/factsheets/Air_Intelligence_
  Agency.html

U.S. Army Digitization Master Plan
http://fotlan5.fotlan.army.mil/..ADMP/adotoc.html

U.S. Army Research Laboratory
http://www.brl.mil/EA/ARL_homepage.html

Joint Doctrine Home Page
http://www.dtic.mil/doctrine/index.html

The Joint Chiefs of Staff have opened up this site for general access. This is a fine site with lots of information, as well as access to the Joint Electronic Library.

U.S. Navy Warfare Systems and Sensors Research Directorate
http://www.nrl.navy.mil/code.5000.html

USA FA 53
http://www.seas.gwu.edu/seas/fa53/index.html

Serving uniformed service automation and acquisition professionals; systems automation.

C4I-Pro Archives
http://www.infowar.com
http://www.stl.nps.navy.mil/lists/c4i-pro/date.html

Computer Underground Digest (CUD)
http://www.utopia.com/mailings/cud

An open forum dedicated to sharing information among computerists and to the presentation and debate of diverse views.

Cypherpunks archive by thread
http://infinity.nus.sg/cypherpunks/

Best of Security List
http://www.connectnet.net.au/BoS/

Archive by thread.

Forum on Risks to the Public in Computers and Related Systems (Committee on Computers and Public Policy)
Peter G. Neumann, Moderator
http://catless.ncl.ac.uk/Risks/
http://www.inforwar.com

The RISKS Forum is a moderated digest. Its Usenet equivalent is comp.risks.

Privacy, Security, Crypto, Surveillance archive (from EFF)
http://www.eff.org/pub/Privacy/

Glossary of Information Warfare Terms

A very basic list that will be expanded on http://www.infowar.com.
AIA: Air Intelligence Agency at Kelly Air Force Base
AFIWC: Air Force Information Warfare Center
C2W: Command-and-control warfare. Command systems, rather than commanders, are the chief target, as in Persian Gulf War.
C4I: Command, Control, Communications, Computers, and Intelligence.
Copernicus: The code name under which the Navy plans to reformulate its command and control structures in response to the realization that information is a weapon. Through Copernicus, warfighters will get the

information that they need to make tactical decisions. The architecture of Copernicus was designed by Vice Admiral Jerry O. Tuttle.

DES: Data Encryption Standard *DISA:* Defense Information Security Administration. Military organization charged with resposibility to provide information systems support to fighting units.

DoD: Department of Defense

Van Eck monitoring: Monitoring the activity of a computer or other electronic equipment by detecting low levels of electromagnetic emissions from the device. Named after Dr. Wim van Eck, who published on the topic in 1985.

EMP/T Bomb: A device similar to a HERF gun, but many times more powerful.

EW: Electronic warfare

GCCS: Global Command and Control System.

HERF: High Energy Radio Frequency, as in HERF gun—a device that can disrupt the normal operation of digital equipment such as computers and navigational equipment by directing HERF emissions at them.

IBW: Intelligence-based warfare

INFOSEC: Protection of classified information that is stored on computers or transmitted by radio, telephone, teletype, or any other means.

IW/C2W: Information warfare/command and control warfare

JC2WC: Joint Command and Control Warfare Center.

NAIC: National Air Intelligence Center at Wright Patterson Air Force Base

NSA: National Security Agency. This agency is charged with the tasks of exploiting foreign electromagnetic signals and protecting the electronic information critical to U.S. national security.

RMA: Revolution in Military Affairs. The realization by the military that information, and information technologies, must be considered as a weapon in achieving national objectives via military activity.

SIGINT: The interception and analysis of electromagnetic signals

TEMPEST: Military code name for activities related to van Eck monitoring, and technology to defend against such monitoring.

Bibliography

A compilation from many contributors. Thank you! And a special thank you to Dr. Dan Kuehl from NDU (kuehld@ndu.edu) and Bruce Hocka (hocka@carlisle-em2.army.mil).

We will add to the list as we update. See http://www.infowar.com.

"Winning the Information War." Advance Planning Briefing for Industry, United States Army Communications-Electronics Command, Ft. Monmouth, New Jersey. Symposium held May 11-12, 1994, Ocean Place Hilton Resort and Spa. Agenda and description of sessions, 10 pages.

Alberts, David S. and Richard E. Hayes. "The Realm of Information Dominance: Beyond Information Warfare," in First International Symposium on Command and Control Research and Technology, National Defense University, 19-22 June 1995. Washington, DC: National Defense University, 1995, pp. 560-565.

Allard, Col. Kenneth C. *Command, Control, and the Common Defense: Key Study of Command and Control from the Strategic, Macro Level.*

Arquilla, John and David Ronfeldt. "Cyberwar Is Coming!" (Copyright 1993 by Taylor & Francis, Bristol, PA.) Originally published in *Journal of Comparative Strategy* 12 (2): 141-165.

Basalla, George. *The Evolution of Technology.* Cambridge: Cambridge University Press, 1988.

Bauer, Martin (ed.). *Resistance to New Technology: Nuclear Power, Information Technology and Biotechnology.* Cambridge: Cambridge University Press, 1995.

Benedikt, Michael (ed.). *Cyberspace: The First Steps.* Cambridge: MIT Press, 1991. Some extremely interesting theoretical and conceptual thinking about cyberspace as a place or an environment.

Bjerknes, Gro, Pelle Ehn, and Morten Kyng (eds.). *Computers and Democracy: A Scandinavian Challenge.* Aldershot, UK: Avebury, 1987.

Bowers, C. A. *The Cultural Dimensions of Educational Computing: Understanding the Non-Neutrality of Technology.* New York: Teachers College Press, 1988.

Braverman, Harry. *Labor and Monopoly Capital: The Degradation of Work in the Twentieth Century.* New York: Monthly Review Press, 1974.

Bucciarelli, Louis L. *Designing Engineers.* Cambridge: MIT Press, 1994.

Bud-Frierman, Lisa (ed.). *Information Acumen: The Understanding and Use of Knowledge in Modern Business.* London: Routledge, 1994.

Busey, Adm. James B., IV, USN (Ret.). "Information Warfare Calculus Mandates Protective Actions." Presidents Commentary. *Signal* (official publication of AFCEA), October 1994, p. 15.

Button, Graham. *Technology in Working Order: Studies of Work, Interaction, and Technology.* London: Routledge, 1993.

Clark, Howard W. and Saundra K. Wallfesh. "Measuring Effectiveness of Theater Information Warfare/Command and Control Warfare Campaigns." FIESTACROW 95 (Command and Control Warfare in Joint Operations track). Association of Old Crows, San Antonio, TX, April 1995.

Campen, Alan D. *The First Information War: The Story of Communications, Computers, and Intelligence Systems in the Persian Gulf War.* Fairfax, VA: AFCEA International Press, October 1992. An anthology of studies of communications in the Gulf War.

Cockburn, Cynthia. *Machinery of Dominance: Women, Men, and Technical Know-How.* Boston: Northeastern University Press, 1988.

Collins, Harry M. *Artificial Experts: Social Knowledge and Intelligent Machines.* Cambridge: MIT Press, 1990.

Cook, Lt. Col. Wyatt C., "Information Warfare: A New Dimension in the Application of Air and Space Power." 1994 CJCS Strategy Essay Writing Contest Entry, Lieutenant, 37 pages.

Cooley, Mike. *Architect or Bee?: The Human Price of Technology.* London: Hogarth Press, 1987.

Defense Information Systems Agency. "Defensive Information Warfare (DIW) Management Plan," 15 August 1994, Version 1.2, four sections and appendices.

DeLanda, Manuel. *War in the Age of Intelligent Machines.* New York: Zone Books Swerve edition, 1991. An analysis of the relationship between chaos theory, technology, and warfare.

Dreyfus, Hubert L. *What Computers Can't Do: A Critique of Artificial Reason.* New York: Harper & Row, 1972.

Faulkner, Wendy and Erik Arnold (eds.). *Smothered by Invention: Technology in Women's Lives.* London: Pluto Press, 1985.

Feenberg, Andrew. *Critical Theory of Technology.* New York: Oxford University Press, 1991.

FitzGerald, Mary C., "Russian Views on Information Warfare." *Army* 44 (5): 57-60, May 1994.

Franks, Frederick M. Jr., "Winning the Information War: Evolution and Revolution." Speech at the Association of the US Army Symposium, Orlando, FL, February 8, 1994. Copyright City News Publishing Company Inc., 1994. 11 pages.

Garigue, Robert. "On Strategy, Decisions and the Evolution of Information Systems." Technical Document. DSIS DND Goverment of Canada, 1992

Garigue, Robert. "Information Warfare—Theory and Concepts" Report 4/95. Office of the Assistant Deputy Minister—Defence Information Services. DND Goverment of Canada.

Garigue, Robert. *Information Warfare—Developing a Conceptual Framework.* Version 2.1—Working Document. Doctoral Research. Decision Analysis Laboratory, Carleton University, Canada, 1995-1996

Green, Eileen, Jenny Owen, and Den Pain (eds.). *Gendered by Design: Information Technology and Office Systems.* London: Taylor and Francis, 1993.

Habermas, Jurgen. *The Theory of Communicative Action,* vol. 2. "Lifeworld and System: A Critique of Functionalist Reason." Boston: Beacon Press, 1987.

Hacker, Sally. *Pleasure, Power, and Technology: Some Tales of Gender, Engineering, and the Cooperative Workplace.* Boston: Unwin Hyman, 1989.

Heidegger, Martin. *The Question Concerning Technology and Other Essays.* Translated from the German by William Lovitt. New York: Harper & Row, 1977.

Information Society Journal 8 (1). Published quarterly by Taylor & Francis. Basingstoke, UK: Burgess Science Press, 1992.

Johnson, Craig L. "Information Warfare—Not a Paper War." Special Report, *Journal of Electronic Defense,* August 1994, pp. 55-58.

Johnson, Frederick C. and Floyd C. Painter. "The Integration of Warfare Support Functions." Technology Analysis, Warfare Integration, C31:1988, pp. 176-182.

Kahin, Brian and Janet Abbate (eds.). *Standards Policy for Information Infrastructure.* Cambridge: MIT Press, 1995.

Kahin, Brian and James Keller (eds.). *Public Access to the Internet.* Cambridge: MIT Press, 1995.

Kelly AFB (TX). "EW Expands into Information Warfare." *Electronic Warfare, Aviation Week & Space Technology,* October 10, 1994, pp. 47-48.

Kraft, Michael E. and Norman J. Vig (eds.). *Technology and Politics.* Durham: Duke University Press, 1988.

Kraut, Robert E. (ed.). *Technology and the Transformation of White-Collar Work.* Hillsdale, NJ: Erlbaum, 1987.

Lea, Martin (ed.). *Contexts of Computer-Mediated Communication.* New York: Harvester Wheatsheaf, 1992.

Libicki, Martin. "What Is Information Warfare?" Institute for National Strategic Studies, ACIS Paper 3, August 1995. ISSN 1071-7552.

Lilienfeld, Robert. *The Rise of Systems Theory: An Ideological Analysis.* New York: Wiley, 1978.

Lukacs, Georg. *History and Class Consciousness: Studies in Marxist Dialectics.* Translated from the German by Rodney Livingstone. Cambridge: MIT Press, 1971. Originally published in 1923.

Lum, Zachary A. "Linking the Senses." *Journal of Electronic Defense,* August 1994, pp. 33-38.

Luoma, William M. "Netwar: The Other Side of Information Warfare." Paper submitted (8 February 1994) to the Faculty of the Naval War College in partial satisfaction of the requirements of the Department of Joint Military Operations. 42 pages.

MacKenzie, Donald and Judy Wajcman (eds.). *The Social Shaping of Technology: How the Refrigerator Got Its Hum.* Milton Keynes: Open University Press, 1985.

Melzer, Arthur M., Jerry Weinberger, and M. Richard Zinman (eds.). *Technology in the Western Political Tradition.* Ithaca: Cornell University Press, 1993.

Mumford, Lewis. *Technics and Civilization.* London: Routledge, 1946.

Munro, Neil. *The Quick and the Dead: Electronic Combat and Modern Warfare.* Good introduction to EW.

National Research Council's System Security Committee. *Computers at Risk: Safe Computing in the Information Age.* An unemotional examination of the threat and our vulnerabilities.

Negroponte, Nicholas. *Being Digital.* New York: Knopf, 1995.

Nelson, Andrew, et al. *The Art of War.* Sun Tzu paraphrased into modern parlance by the faculty of the School of Information Warfare & Strategy.

Nelson, Andrew. "The Art of Information Warfare." Private publication by author, 1995, p. 75.

Noble, David F. *America by Design: Science, Technology, and the Rise of Corporate Capitalism.* Oxford: Oxford University Press, 1977.

Noble, David F. *Forces of Production: A Social History of Industrial Automation.* Oxford: Oxford University Press, 1986.

"Preparing for the 21st Century: An Appraisal of US Intelligence." Published 1 March 1996. Available at www.access.gpo.gov/int. Gives a good overview of the whole intel community. Appendix B lists the duties and functions of each department/agency/congressional committee involved in intelligence collection, production, and oversight.

Roos, John G. "Info Tech Info Power." *Armed Forces Journal International,* June 1994, pp. 31-36.

Rosenberg, Nathan. *Inside the Black Box: Technology and Economics.* Cambridge: Cambridge University Press, 1982.

Rothschild, Joan (ed). *Women, Technology, and Innovation.* Oxford: Pergamon, 1982.

Schuler, Douglas and Aki Namioka (eds.). *Participatory Design: Principles and Practices.* Hillsdale, NJ: Erlbaum, 1993.

Schwartau, Winn. *Information Warfare: Chaos on the Electronic Superhighway.*

Science Application International Corporation (SAIC), "Planning Considerations for Defensive Information Warfare—Information Assurance." 16 December 199, 61 pages.

Sclove, Richard E. *Democracy and Technology.* New York: Guilford Press, 1995.

Slatta, Michelle and Joshua Quittner. *Masters of Deception: The Gang That Ruled Cyberspace.* Would you feel better if it was the KGB instead of teenagers roaming through our telephone systems and databanks?

Sovereign, Michael G. and Dr. Ricki Sweet. "Evaluating Command and Control: A Modular Structure." Technology Analysis, Evaluating C2, C:31 1988, pp. 156-161.

Star, Susan Leigh (ed.). *The Cultures of Computing.* Oxford: Blackwell, 1995.

Stoll, Clifford. "The Cuckoo's Egg: Tracking a Spy Through the Maze of Computer Espionage." New York: Doubleday, 1989. Classic story of "the Hannover Hacker." See also his 1995 *Silicon Snake Oil: Second Thoughts on the Information Highway,* which is a contrarian view of the Internet revolution's effect on society.

Strassmann, Paul. *The Politics of Information Management.* Of the few "gods of information", Paul is one of them

Street, John. *Politics and Technology.* New York: Guilford Press, 1992.

Suchman, Lucy A. *Plans and Situated Actions: The Problem of Human-Machine Communication.* Cambridge: Cambridge University Press, 1987.

Thompson, Paul. *The Nature of Work: An Introduction to Debates on the Labour Process,* 2nd ed. London: Macmillan, 1989.

Tobias, Sheila. *Overcoming Math Anxiety.* New York: Norton, 1978.

Toffler, Alvin and Heidi. *War and Anti-War: Survival at the Dawn of the 21st Century.* Boston: Little, Brown, 1993. Especially chapters 20-21, pp. 190-212. The book that in many ways started the discussion of IW.

Van Crevald, Martin. *The Transformation of War.* Forecasts the end of war as we know it as we enter an era of non-Clausewitzian and lower intensity conflict. See also his *Command in War* for his thesis of the importance of styles of command and its relationship to C2W. See also his *Technology and War: From 2000 BC to the Present,* especially chapters 16 and 18, pp. 235-249, 265-283, for his assessments concerning military technology.

Wajcman, Judy. *Feminism Confronts Technology.* University Park: Pennsylvania State University Press, 1991.

Winner, Langdon. *The Whale and the Reactor: A Search for Limits in an Age of High Technology.* Chicago: University of Chicago Press, 1986.

Yates, JoAnne. *Control Through Communication: The Rise of System in American Management.* Baltimore: Johns Hopkins University Press, 1989.

MONOGRAPHS

Dunn, Richard J. *From Gettysburg to the Gulf and Beyond.* NDU Press.

Hutcherson, Lt. Col. Norman B. *Command and Control Warfare: Putting Another Tool in the Warfighter's Database.* Air University Press.

Libicki, Martin C. *The Mesh and the Net: Speculations on Armed Conflict in a Time of Free Silicon.* Institute for National Strategic Studies (INSS), NDU Press.

Molander, Roger C., Andrew S. Riddle, and Peter A. Wilson. *Strategic Information Warfare: A New Face of War.* RAND, MR-661.0-OSD, November 1995.

Ronfeldt, David F. *Cyberocracy, Cyberspace, and Cyberology: Political Effects of the Information Revolution.* RAND

Sullivan, General Gordon R. and Colonel James M. Dubik. *War in the Information Age.* Army War College Strategic Studies Institute.

What Is Information Warfare? Institute for National Strategic Studies (INSS), NDU Press.

Monographs produced at Air University's School of Advanced Airpower Studies: Major Jason B. Barlow, "Strategic Paralysis, An Airpower Theory for the Present"; Major Thomas E. Griffith, Jr., "Strategic Attack of National Electrical Systems"; Major Gerald Hust, "Taking Down Telecommunications"; Major Steven M. Rinaldi, "Beyond the Industrial Web: Economic Synergies and Targeting Methodologies."

ARTICLES

Alleyne, Mark D. "Thinking About the International System in the Information Age: Theoretical Assumptions and Contradictions." *Journal of Peace Research* 31 (4): 407-424.

Anderson, James: "Chugging up the Onramp of the Info Interstate." *Foreign Service Journal,* March 1995.

Arnold, H. D., J. Hukill, J. Kennedy, and A. Cameron. "Targeting Financial Systems as Centers of Gravity: Low Intensity to No Intensity Conflict." *Defense Analysis* 10 (2): 1994.

Arquilla, John "The Strategic Implications of Information Dominance." *Strategic Review,* Summer 1994.

Berkowitz, Bruce D. "Warfare in the Information Age." *Issues in Science and Technology* 12, Fall 1995.

Black, Peter. "Soft Kill: Fighting Infrastructure Wars in the 21st Century." *Wired* July-August 1995.

Bugliarello, Dr. George. "Telecommunications, Politics, Economics, and National Sovereignty: A New Game." *Airpower Journal* 10 (1), Spring 1996.

Chairman JCS Instruction (CJCSI) 3210.1. "Joint Information Warfare Policy." January 1996. Classified Secret.

Cohen, Eliot. "What to do About National Defense." *Commentary* November 1994.

Davis, Major Norman C. "An Information-Based Revolution in Military Affairs." *Strategic Review* 24 (1), Winter 1996, pp. 43-53.

Defense Science Board Study, Summer Study Task Force Report. "Information Architectures for the Battlefield: Information in Warfare and Information Warfare. Defense Technical Information Center (DTIC) #AD-A285745, October 1994. Unclassified.

"Defense Technology." *The Economist,* June 10, 1995, pp. 5-20.

Department of Commerce, "Global Information Infrastructure: Agenda for Cooperation." GPO, 1995.

Department of Defense Directive (DODD) 3600.1. Taproot for all DOD IW activities and efforts. classified Top Secret (currently under revision)

DiNardo, Richard L. and Daniel J. Hughes. "Some Cautionary Thoughts on Information Warfare." *Airpower Journal* 9 (4), Winter 1995.

Dunlop, Col. Charles L. "How we Lost the War of 2007." *The Weekly Standard* 1 (19), 29 January 1996.

Emmett, Sq. Ldr. Peter C. "Software Warfare: The Emerging Future." *Royal United Services Institute Journal,* December 1992. See also his "Information Mania—A New Manifestation of Gulf War Syndrome?" *Royal United Services Institute Journal,* February 1996, pp. 19-26.

Fitzgerald, Mary. "Russian Views on Electronic Signals and Information Warfare." *American Intelligence Journal,* Spring-Summer 94; similar article in *Army,* May 1994.

Glynn, Patrick. "Quantum Leap." *The National Interest,* Spring 1995, pp. 50-57.

JCS Memo of Policy (MOP) 3., "Command and Control Warfare." March 1993. Unclassified. Taproot for all JCS C2W activities and efforts.

Jensen, Col. Owen. "Information Warfare: Principles of Third Wave War." *Airpower Journal,* Winter 1994.

Jensen, Lt. Col. Richard M. "Information War Power and Air Power: The View Through an Historical Prism." Harvard Program on Information Resource Policy.Johnson, Craig. "Information War—Not a Paper War." *Journal of Electronic Defense,* August 1994.

Joint Publication 3-13.1, "Joint Doctrine for Command and Control Warfare." March 1996. Unclassified.

Kraus, George F. Jr.: "Information Warfare in 2015." *US Naval Institute Proceedings,* vol. 121/8/1/110, August 1995.

Lafferty, Brad, et al. "The Effect of Media Information on Enemy Capability: A Model for Conflict." *Proteus: A Journal of Ideas,* Spring 1994. Authors were a student research group at the Air Command and Staff College.

Lewonoski, Mark C. "Information War." *Essays on Strategy IX.* NDU Press.

Libicki, Martin C. and CDR James A. Hazlett. "Do We Need an Information Corps?" *Joint Force Quarterly,* Autumn 1993.

Mann, Col. Edward: "Desert Storm: The First Information War." *Airpower Journal,* Winter 1994.

Morgan, Richard A. "Military Use of Commercial Communication Satellites: A New Look at the Outer Space Treaty and Peaceful Purposes." *Journal of Air Law and Commerce,* Fall 1994, pp. 239-326.

Morris, Chet and Janet, and Thomas Baines. "Weapons of Mass Protection: Nonlethality, Information Warfare, and Airpower in the Age of Chaos." *Airpower Journal,* Spring, 1995.

National Joint Security Commission. "Redefining Security." December 1994. Unclassified.

Naval Studies Board. "Report on Information Warfare." February 1995. Secret.

Neuman, Johanna. "The Media's Impact on International Affairs, Then and Now." *SAIS Review* 16 (1): 109-123, Winter-Spring 1996.

Nye, Joseph S. Jr. and William A. Owens. "America's Information Edge." *Foreign Affairs,* March-April 1996, pp. 20-36.

Office of Technology Assessment, US Congress. "Information Security and Privacy in Network Environments." GPO, 1994.

OSD Net Assessment. "The Military Technical Revolution: A Preliminary Assessment." September 1992. Secret.

Power, Richard. "CSI Special Report on Information Warfare." *Computer Security Institute,* 1995.

Rhode, CDR William E. "What Is Info War?" *US Naval Institute Proceedings* vol. 122/2/1/116, February 1996.

Rothrock, John. "Information Warfare: Time for Some Constructive Skepticism." *American Intelligence Journal,* Spring-Summer 1994.

Ryan, Lt. Col. Donald E. "Implications of Information-Based Warfare." *Joint Force Quarterly,* Autumn-Winter 1994-1995.

SAIC (sponsored by DISA). "Planning Considerations for Defensive Information Warfare—Information Assurance." December 1993. Unclassified.

Schneider, Major Michael W. "Electromagnetic Spectrum Domination: 21st Century Center of Gravity or Achilles Heel?"

Security Policy Board. "White Paper on Information Infrastructure Assurance." December 1995.

Smith, Major Kevin B. "The Crisis and Opportunity of Information War."

Spacecast 2020. "Leveraging the Infosphere: Surveillance and Reconnaissance in 2020." *Airpower Journal,* Summer 1995.

Stein, George J. "Information Warfare." *Airpower Journal,* Spring 1995.

Stix, Gary: "Fighting Future Wars." *Scientific American,* December 1995, pp. 92-98.

Struble, Lt. Cmdr. Daniel. "What Is Command and Control Warfare?" *Naval War College Review,* Summer 1995, pp. 89-98.

System Security Study Committee, Computer Science and Telecommunications Board, Commission on Physical Sciences, Mathematics, and Applications, National Research Council; "Computers at Risk: Safe Computing in the Information Age." Washington, DC: National Academy Press, 1991. An unemotional examination of the threat and our vulnerabilities.

Szafranski, Col. Richard. "A Theory of Information Warfare: Preparing for 2020." *Airpower Journal,* Spring 1995.

Wake Forest Law Review, Spring 1995; nine articles devoted to the Information Superhighway, Cyberlaw, and legal issues related to Information Warfare; for legal issues, see also Lawrence Lessig, "The Path of Cyberlaw," *Yale Law Review* 104, 1995.

"When Waves Collide: Future Conflict." *Joint Force Quarterly,* Spring 1995.

Wicks, Wendy (ed.). "Government Information and Policy: Changing Roles in a New Administration." National Federation of Abstracting and Information Services, 1994.

GAO REPORTS

"Communications Privacy: Federal Policy and Actions." GAO/OSI-94-2, November 1993.

"Computer Security: Virus Highlights Need for Improved Internet Management." GAO/IMTEC-89-57, June 1989.

"Computer Security: Unauthorized Access to a NASA Scientific Network." GAO/IMTEC-90-2, November 1989.

"Computer Security: Hackers Penetrate DOD Computer Systems." GAO/T-IMTEC-92-5, November 1991.

"Economic Espionage: The Threat to US Industry." GAO/T-OSI-92-6, April 1992.

"Information Superhighway: An Overview of Technology Challenges." GAO/AIMD-95-23, January 1995.

"Telecommunications: Interruptions of Telephone Service." GAO/RCED-93-79FS, March 1993.

Who's Who in Information Warfare

THIS LIST IS A VERY SHORT representation of people who are active in the field of Information Warfare. It expands daily and we had to stop somewhere. Please refer to http://www.infowar.com for current listings.

Mark Aldrich
GRCI Infosec Engineering
1900 Gallows Road, Vienna, VA 22182
703-506-5000 X5415
E-mail: maldrich@ccmail.va.grci.com

John I. Alger, Dean
School of Information Warfare and Strategy
National Defense University, Fort McNair, Washington, DC
202-685-3629, X365
E-mail: algerj@ndu.edu
http://198.80.36.91/ndu/inss/staff/alger.html

Dr. Alger served in the U.S. Army for more than 22 years. He saw two tours of duty as an airborne infantryman in Vietnam, taught military history at West Point, was the Associate Dean of Faculty and Academic Programs at the National War College, and concluded his active military service as the Chief of Political-Military Affairs on the Army Staff. His publications include *The Quest for Victory: The History of the Principles of War.*

Axel Anaruk, National Program Manager
Cray Research, Inc.
5005 LBJ Freeway, Suite 800, Dallas, TX 75244
214-383-2342 Fax: 214-934-0072
E-mail: axel.anaruk@cray.com

IW execution-vs.-policy experienced. Air Force IW: assessing command and control systems, recommending counters/countermeasures, developing support mechanisms and procedures to apply to IW mission planning (then called C2W). Assessed effectiveness of and recommended improvements to tactical combat intelligence systems. Planned and assisted architecting systems for Air Force and Joint exercises CONUS and OCONUS. Now providing tools and architectures for IW from an industry perspective; specifically, high performance computing applied to increasing the speed of the processing part of own OODA while getting inside the other guy's loop.

Robert C. Ashworth, Major, USMCR
Sr. Principal Systems Analyst, Digital Systems Research
7301 Rivers Ave., Suite 230, N. Charleston, SC 29406
803-764-2933 Fax: 803-764-2933
E-mail: (DSR) ashworth@dsr.com
(NISE East) ashwortr@nosc.mil (USMC) gitm0j@mqg1.usmc.mil

Ashworth has over 10 years of Information Systems Security experience in direct support of DoJ, DoN, and joint-service DoD organizations. During his career, he has led Information System Security support teams while in the Marine Corps, and while supporting government-sponsored organizations with Booz, Allen & Hamilton and with Digital Systems Research. He provides analyses for protection against external IW attacks. His experience includes supporting all facets of establishing activity-wide InfoSec programs, assisting with system design reviews, providing certification and countermeasure testing, and conducting risk analyses for information systems of varying levels of complexity and classification. Additionally, as a major in the USMCR, he developed courses and provided experienced consultation with other instructors for the initial Computer Security curriculum at the USMC Computer Sciences School. Currently, he provides the USMC with InfoSec policy development and review support.

Robert Ayers
E-mail: ayersb@ncr.disa.mil

Stewart A. Baker, Esq., Partner
Steptoe & Johnson
330 Connecticut Ave. NW, Washington, DC 20036-1795
202-429-6413 Fax: 202-429-3902
E-mail: sbaker@steptoe.com
http://www.us.net/steptoe/baker.htm

Practice includes issues relating to encryption and export controls, online transactions, digital signatures, electronic surveillance, and government regulation of international trade in high-technology products; advice and practice under the antidumping and countervailing duty laws of United States, European community, Canada and Australia, U.S. Foreign Sovereign Immunities Act, and Foreign Corrupt Practices Act; edited ABA's *Canadian Law Newsletter;* co-chair, International Law and National Security Committee of the American Bar Association; Chair, Task Force on International Notarial Issues of the ABA's Section of International Law and Practice; member, E-100 Working Party on Legal and Regulatory Matters of the U.S. Council for International Business; member, Defense Science Board's Task Force on Information Warfare Defense.

John Perry Barlow
Electric Frontier Foundation
barlow@eff.org
http://www.eff.org/barlow

Former cattle rancher, former Grateful Dead lyricist, and current vice-chair of the Electronic Frontier Foundation.

Bruce Barnett, Computer Scientist
GE Corporate Research and Development Center
PO Box 8, 1 River Road, Schenectady, NY 12301
518-387-5220 Fax: (518) 387-4042
E-mail: barnett@crd.ge.com

Research in security, network management, network analysis, distributed applications, expert systems, and performance.

Philippe Baumard
16, rue du Pont aux Choux, 75003 Paris, France
0-11-33-1-40-27-80-53 Fax: 0-11-33-1-45-17-05-88
E-Mail: pbaumard at paris9.dauphine.fr

Assistant Professor, Ecole Superieure des Affaires, University of Paris-XII; Professor of Strategic Management, ESSEC International Management Development (IMD); Professor of Comparative Economics, Institute of Patrimony Management, University of Paris-Dauphine; Professor of Organizational Behavior, Ecole Superieure de Commerce de Paris; Professor of Strategic Management, HEC (Hautes Etudes Commerciales), International Track; Consultant, Economic Intelligence, Corporate Strategies Large Organizations (USA, France).

Anita D'Amico Beadon, Ph.D.
Manager, New Information Warfare

Northrop-Grumman Advanced Technology & Development Center
Mail Stop C33-06, Bethpage, NY 11714
516-575-9059 Fax: 516-575-0679
E-mail: anita_beadon@atdc.northgrum.com

I am an experimental psychologist by training. For years I've been leading research projects and groups in everything from maritime simulation to space station displays/control to digital cartography. We have put together a team of people to expand our business base in information warfare.

Jim Bell, CEO
Optigreen
7214 Corregidor, Vancover, WA 98664
360-696-3911
E-mail: jimbell@pacifier.com

Electronic, chemical, computer, and radio consulting. Specializes in system subversion.

Major Mats Bjore, Senior Analyst
Swedish Armed Forces
Humlevagen 9, 18694 Vallentuna, Sweden
46-8-51240735
E-mail: 73064.325@compuserve.com

Practical and theoretical OSINT, research in IW- and IM- related to intelligence methods.

Debbie Blair, Public Affairs Director
Church of Scientology International
6331 Hollywood Blvd., Suite 1200, Los Angeles, CA 90028
213-960-3500 Fax: 213-960-3508
E-mail: Blair_CSI@wow.com

Hugh V. Blanchard, Intelligence & Information Operations Analyst
Military Professional Resources, Inc.
Hotel Chamberlin, Suite 701, Fort Monroe, VA 23651
804-723-8053 Fax: 804-723-4089
E-Mail: vtpe95a@prodigy.com

Retired from service in 1995 after service as enlisted soldier, NCO, and commissioned officer in Military Intelligence. Current work is deeply involved in the Army's initial study of Information Operations and the development of an IO Action Plan.

William Boni, Manager
Intelligence & Information Protection Services
Amgen
1840 Dehavilland, 9-1-H, Thousand Oaks, CA 91320
805-447-6192 Fax: 805-447-6945
E-mail: bboni@ix.netcom.com

Interested in issues surrounding economic and industrial espionage, criminal hacking/"cracking," high technology terrorism and all associated countermeasures. Job responsibilities include advising senior management and staff of the world's largest biotechnology company on effective countermeasures to safeguard proprietary information/ technology and intellectual property against the full range of threats in the global economy. Responsible for designing and implementing technology to protect the global network and corporate information systems.

Donald L. Buchholz, Communications Specialist
TEXCOM, Inc.
801 Water St., Suite 500, Portsmouth, VA 23704
804-397-0035 X212 Fax: 804-397-2813
E-mail: buchholz@infi.net, d_buchholz@nise-p.nosc.mil

Contractor currently working with NISE EAST Code 535, SHF Satellite Systems. Perform installation design and installation of SHF Baseband Systems and equipment integration, which involves most facets of C4I less operational aspects.

Col. Alan D. Campen, USAF (Ret.)
14305 Shelter Cove Rd., Midlothian, VA 23112
804-739-9828
E-mail: AlanC3398@aol.com

Manager of AFCEA International Press and adjunct professor, School of Information Warfare and Strategy, National Defense University. Formerly Director of Command and Control Policy, office of Undersecretary of Defense for Policy; vice president C3I, BDM Corp; contributing editor *The First Information War* (1992) and *Cyberwar: Security, Strategy and Conflict in the Information Age* (1996).

Timothy A. Campen, Deputy Director
National Drug Intelligence Center
319 Washington Street, Johnstown, PA 15901
814-867-4662 Fax: 814-532-4686
E-mail: tcampen@interramp.com

Deputy Director for technical support division for United States Department of Justice, National Drug Intelligence Center. Responsible for offensive and defensive IW. Provide technology and strategies for high-confidence automated intelligence systems and networking. Available to contribute to decisive information warfare working groups and advisory boards.

Col. Howard W. Clark (Ret.)
Director of Information Warfare Analysis
Dynamics Research Corporation
60 Frontage Road, Andover, MA 01810.
508-475-9090 X2934 Fax: 508-475-8657
EMail: hclark@s1.drc.com
HWCSr@aol.com

Director of Information Warfare Analysis. Program manager and technical lead of team comprised of former tri-service, Joint Staff Officer-qualified, senior officers. Developing IW aspects of national and theater-level campaign planning, bringing the tools of IW to bear for the Joint Chiefs of Staff and theater commanders and their major subordinate commanders. Five years program manager for IW government customers. Focus areas include the development and evaluation of IW and C2W organizations, material requirements, concepts, doctrine, tactics, techniques and procedures. Design lead for IW/C2W simulation development. Army service: 30 years Infantry; strategist; war planner; Senior Army Planner for Joint Affairs. Brigade Command; two Infantry combat tours in Vietnam. Education includes M.A. in Political Science, Northwestern University, 1971, and year-long Senior Executive Fellowship at Harvard University Center for International Affairs.

John W. Cobb, Ph.D.
Coordinator; Scientific Computing and Strategic Planning Office of Computing and Network Management
Oak Ridge National Laboratory/Lockheed Martin Energy Research
MS-6486 BLDG.-62MIT, Oak Ridge, TN 37831-6486
423-576-5439 Fax: 423-241-5722
E-mail: cobbjw@ornl.gov
http://www.ornl.gov/ocnm/Cobbdata.html

Dr. Cobb is a computational plasma physicist by training. His current duties include managing and coordinating different scientific computing and strategic planning activities at the Oak Ridge National Laboratory, a Department of Energy multi-purpose national energy research lab. His interests in IW are in the broadest terms. He is particularly interested in small-scale warfare activities directed by small groups and targeted at small portions of the network either to gain unauthorized access to data or to corrupt data, particularly data with economic relevance. He is also interested in limits on information technology imposed by fundamental physical principles.

Steven Cobb, Director of Special Projects
NCSA
10 S. Courthouse Ave., Carlisle, PA 17013
717-258-1816 Fax: 717-243-8642
scobb@ncsa.com

Prolific author and speaker on numerous subjects including computer security.

Dr. Frederick B. Cohen, President
Management Analytics
PO Box 1480, Hudson, OH 44236
216-686-0090 Fax: 216-686-0092
E-mail: fc@all.net

Dr. Cohen is known for his work on information protection. He has authored over 50 scientific articles and several widely read books.

Guy L. Copeland, Director, Technology
Computer Sciences Corporation
3001 Centreville Rd., Herndon, VA 22071
703-471-3044 Fax: 703-471-3145
E-mail: gcopelan@csc.com
www.csc.com

Lead representative for CSC's CEO, Van B. Honeycutt in the President's National Security Telecommunications Advisory Committee (NSTAC) for CSC's contribution to studies and analyses and the generation of advice and recommendations to the President. NSTAC issues explicitly include network security, information security and information assurance, the defensive aspect of information warfare. Co-Chairs the NSTAC's NII Task Force and it's Standards Liaison Group and is a member of its Information Assurance Task Force, its Network Security Group and its National Security/Emergency Preparedness Group. Within CSC, he provides CSC management with advice on emerging information and telecommunication technologies, including those which will affect information assurance.

Dr. Myron L. Cramer, Principal Research Scientist
Georgia Tech Research Institute
Georgia Institute of Technology
400 Tenth St., Atlanta, GA 30332-0840
404-894-7292 Fax: 404-894-8636
E-mail: myron.cramer@gtri.gatech.edu

Leads Competitive Information Technologies Group specializing in competitive applications of information technologies and information warfare. Also leads GTRI New Initiatives Group in Secure Information Systems developing and applying advanced methods of security for commercial and government automated information systems. Member of inter-agency Joint Information Warfare Threat Analysis Working Group currently characterizing threats to networked systems. Over 26 years of academic and professional experience in conducting and managing research programs in electronic warfare, intelligence, sensor technologies, and signal processing. Originated concept of computer viruses as a new form of electronic warfare against networked command and control systems.

Paul Dare, Information Warfare Manager
Boeing Defense & Space Group
Seattle, Wa 98124
206-773-1401 Fax: 206-773-6624
E-mail: darph900@ccmail.ca.boeing.com

Working new business aspects of IW as it pertains to military and Boeing products. Twenty-three years in software-hardware-systems-communications development, most in classified military programs.

Simon Davies, Director
Privacy International
London School of Economics
Visiting Fellow, Department of Law
University of Essex, UK
E-mail: Davies@privint.demon.co.uk

Shane Daniel Deichman, Head, Intelligence Systems
NCCOSC RDT&E Division 4122 working for First Marine Expedition-
   ary Force (I MEF)
CG, I MEF, G-2/Systems
Box 555300, Camp Pendleton, CA 92055-5300
619-553-2767 Fax: 619-725-9126
E-mail: deichman@nosc.mil
http://www.adnc.com/web/shane

Interested in historical perspectives of information warfare, and how the lessons of the great military theorists (Clausewitz, Jomini, Sun Tzu, etc.) are applicable in the realm of IW. Also, the use of disinformation — and methods of overcoming such vulnerabilities.

Dorothy E. Denning, Professor, Computer Science Department
Georgetown University
225 Reiss Science Building, Washington, DC 20057-1232
202-687-5703 Fax: 202-687-1835
E-mail: denning@cs.georgetown.edu
http://www.cosc.georgetown.edu/denning

Dr. Denning has been an active researcher in the area of computer crime and information security since 1973. Her recent work is focused on finding an international approach to encryption that will meet the data protection needs of users and the law enforcement, public safety, and national security needs of nations. She has been reviewing different approaches to key escrow encryption, including the government's Clipper/Capstone system, and has co-developed a taxonomy of key escrow encryption systems. She is also studying application of the Global Positioning System (GPS) to information security. She is the author of *Cryptography and Data Security* and over 80 papers on cryptography, database security, intrusion detection, hackers, inference, information flow, and other security topics.

Matthew G. Devost, Systems Engineer
Science Applications International Corporation, M/S 1-2-6
1710 Goodridge Dr., McLean, VA 22102
703-287-7604 Fax: 703-356-2534
E-mail: matthew_devost@cpam.saic.com

IW researcher for various government and private organizations. Author of thesis "National Security in the Information Age," May 1995 (University of Vermont, Burlington). Work in all areas of IW, but especially interested in political and national security dimensions of IW and Information Terrorism.

Dale Ellis, Computer Programmer/Analyst/USAF
7575 Sentry Blvd., Tinker AFB, OK 73145
405-734-3850 Fax: 405-734-4372
E-mail: ellisd@bldg284.awacs.af.mil

Experienced in deception and covert information collection. Experienced in CI/CE operations and covert

Ron Ewald, President
MarTech Strategies
407-723-5979

MarTech Strategies is a consultancy and information service provider operating in international telecommunications. MarTech has designed and developed a number of models and databases that detail critical and sensitive data and information about major users, knowledge and global information technology hubs, facilities used to link them, and Metropolitan Area Networks (MANs); essentially Schwartau's "maps of cyberspace," including those of more than 100 national communication infrastructures.

Bruce Cana Fox, Design Specialist
Lockheed Martin Skunk Works
1011 Lockheed Way, Palmdale, CA 93599-2732
805-572-4374 Fax: 805-572-4398
E-mail: bfox@ladc.lockheed.com

Designer of computer systems for combat aircraft, including Integrated Mission Systems, Information Display Systems, and Satellite Communications systems.

LCDR Robert J. Garigue
Department of National Defence/DISO
National Defence Headquaters
MGen Pearkes Blvd., Ottawa, Canada K1A 0K2
613-992-6855 Fax: 613-992-1469
E-mail: garigue@dgs.dnd.ca

Considered by many senior officers in the Department of National Defence as the "enfant terrible" of Command and Control, Garigue is the Deputy Program Director for Joint and Strategic Information Systems. Previously, he was Strategic Information Technology Specialist in the Office of the Assistant Deputy Minister, Defence Information Service Organization (DISO). He is a member of the "Panel of Experts" on IW at the Privy Council Office and Scientific Advisor for a number of Departmental R&D projects that focus on advanced information systems issues. He has served on Canadian and Royal Navy Submarines as Operations and Weapons Officer. He completed his undergraduate degree at L'Ecole des Hautes Etudes Commerciales (HEC) in Quantitative Analysis and his M.S. in Computer Information Systems at the Claremont Graduate School (California). He is presently doing research for his Ph.D. in Information Systems (Carleton University) in the areas of Computational Epistemology, Knowledge Management, Intelligent Software Agents, and Strategic Decision Support Systems.

Mark Gembicki, Executive Vice President
WarRoom Research
1134 Veranda Ct., Baltimore, MD 21223
Voice/Fax: 410-437-1106
E-mail: WarRoom2@aol.com

WarRoom Research is a unique organization specializing in the research and development of WarRoom systems. The company is divided into three groups which support a WarRoom throughout a lifecycle, as well as providing a variety of stand-alone services.

Beth Givens, Project Director
Privacy Rights Clearinghouse
University of San Diego Center for Public Interest Law
5998 Alcala Park, San Diego, CA 92110
Voice 619-260-4160 Fax: 619-298-5681
E-mail: bgivens@acusd.edu
http://www.acusd.edu/prc

Project Director of the Privacy Rights Clearinghouse, located at the University of San Diego's Center for Public Interest Law. The Clearinghouse was established July 1992 and has been funded primarily by the California Public Utilities Commission's Telecommunications Education Trust. The project maintains a toll-free complaint/information line on technology-related privacy issues and is available to California consumers. The Clearinghouse is the first endeavor of its kind in the country. Givens holds a master's degree in telecommunications policy from the Annenberg School for Communication, University of Southern California (1987). She has a background in library and information services, specializing in computerized information systems and network development (M.L.S., University of Denver, 1975).

Dr. Ivan Goldberg, Director
Institute for the Advanced Study of Information Warfare
1346 Lexington Ave., New York, NY 10128
212-876-7800 Fax: 212-737-0473
E-Mail: Psydoc@PsyCom.Net
http://www.psycom.net/iwar.1.html

Dr. Goldberg is a psychiatrist in private practice and on the faculty of Columbia University. The founder of PsyCom.Net, a telecommunications service for mental health professionals. Chief professional activity is treating people with "treatment-resistant" mood disorders, especially manic depression. The topic of IW and especially its close relationship to PsyOps is also an interest.

R. Tom Goodden, DPA, CEO/President
The Goodden Consultancy Inc.
108 W. South Street, Carlisle, PA 17013
717-258-8262 Fax: 717-241-6223
E-mail: gooddent@pa.net

Thirty years' experience in global telecommunications and intelligence analysis and consulting. Developed U.S. Army War College curriculum on IW. Adjunct Professor at JMIC. Consultant to DoD on foreign trends in telecommunications. Consultant to industry on IW, electronic warfare, threat systems, competitor analysis, market development.

Sarah Gordon, Security Analyst
Command Software Systems
1061 E. Indiantown Rd., Suite 500. Jupiter, FL 33477
407-575-4239 (Fax) 407-575-3026
E-mail: sgordon@dockmaster.ncsc.mil, sgordon@commandcom.com

Works in Research and Development of F-PROT Professional Anti-Virus Software. Her work has been profiled in the European *Wall Street Journal,* the *New York Times,* and *Virus Bulletin.* Invited speaker at diverse Computer Security Conferences such as those hosted by the NSA/NIST/NCSC, and DEFCON. She has worked since 1985 educating users on Computer Security issues. Her work has been published in many computer trade publications, and she is the winner of the 1994 IFIP Technical Committee 11 award for her work in Ethics and Technology. Her specialties are computer viruses, UNIX security, and ethical implications of technology.

Frank A. Graves, Information Systems Engineer
Science Applications International Corp.
1710 Goodridge Dr., McLean VA 22102
703-821-4527 Fax: 703-760-0911
E-mail: frank.graves-1@cpmx.saic.com
http://www.saic.com

John Guinasso
Data Systems Security Inc.
4960 Almaden Expressway, MS237, San Jose, CA 95118
408-323-8556 Fax: 408-323-8557
jcg@wcdssi.com
http://www.scruznet.com/jcg/dssi.htm

Data Systems Security is a data and information security service company. To provide the best service possible, DSSi has teaming partners from top Network and Computer Security consultants in the industry. The primary goal of DSSi is to secure clients from internal and external information and data technology intrusion. Our highly experienced security experts have specialized skills to test, discover, and repair of security vulnerabilities on a wide array of technology platforms in multiple industries. Our experts leverage specific skills through a focused consortium to drive a "best of breed" approach to maximize customer security needs. These experts are consistent contributors to industry security trends and are keynote speakers at prominent security forums around the globe.

Bertil Haggman, LL.M.
Center for Research on Geopolitics (CRG)
PO Box 1412, S-25114 Helsingborg, Sweden
Voice/Fax: +46-42-217171
E-mail: bertil.haggman@helsingborg.se

Main interest is psychological defense aspect of IW but also the influence of IW capabilities on the balance of power in the world (geopolitics). Author of a large number of books, articles and research papers in the fields of geopolitics, international terrorism, psychological warfare, disinformation, and vulnerability of modern high technology societies. Volunteer officer, Swedish Psychological Defense.

Dr. H. T. "Terry" Hawkins, Deputy Director
Nonproliferation & International Security Division/Programs
Mail Stop 650
Los Alamos National Laboratory, Los Alamos, NM 87544
505-665-1259 Fax: 505-665-4109
E-mail: hthawkins@lanl.gov

Alan R. Heminger
Associate Professor of Information Resources Management
Graduate School of Logistics and Acquisition Management
Air Force Institute of Technology/LAR
2950 P St., Wright Patterson AFB, OH 45433-7765
513-255-7777 X3353 Fax: 513-476-7988 DSN: 986-7988
E-mail: aheminge@afit.af.mil

As Professor of Information Resource Management for the USAF, much of my teaching and research touches on issues that are relevant to the concepts of IW. I have academic and applied background in the use of information for strategic planning and the use of group support systems.

M. Hewitt, H. B. Earhart Fellow
Center for Defense and Strategic Studies
Southwest Missouri State University
901 S. National, Springfield, MO 65804
417-836-4137 Fax: 417-836-6667
E-mail: mhewitt006@aol.com
http:// www.smsu.edu/contrib/dss/index.htm

Current research emphasizes the relationship between national security strategy and emerging technology, including the information sciences. Professional and academic experience includes institutional management of information systems, international relations, and national security studies.

Robert D. Hickman, Test Support Division Chief
Joint Interoperability Test Command, DISA
Commander JITC, Attn: JTBA, Ft Huachuca, AZ 85613-7020
520-538-5105 DSN: 879-5105; Fax: 520-538-5204/0371 DSN: 879-5204/0371
E-mail: hickmanr@fhu.disa.mil, hickman@primenet.com
JITC Homepage: http://164.117.224.252/

Primary interest lies in Joint and Combined Interoperability of Tactical C4I systems. Have worked in joint/combined interoperability testing and certification program for the past 24 years, including operational exercise evaluations and distributed testbed evaluations. Most efforts have been with the information exchange interfaces such as digital data links TADILs), message text formats (USMTF and VMF), and imagery (NITF). Joint efforts have been in accordance with DODD 4630.5, DODI 4630.8, and CJCSI 6212.01 Compatibility, Interoperability, and Integration of Command, Control Communications, Computers, and Intelligence Systems. Combined efforts have been in accordance with the Pacific Command Combined Interoperability Program (PACOM CIP) and the Allied Data System Interoperability Agency (ADSIA) NATO Common Interface Standards (NCIS) NATO Interoperability Planning Document (NIPD) efforts.

Capt. John Hudanich, USAF
INFOSEC Technology Office
Emission Security R&D Program Manager
Rome Laboratory/ERC-1
31 Grenier St., Hanscom AFB, MA 01731-3010
617-377-2071 Fax: 617-377-2563
E-mail: hudanich@rl.af.mil
http://www.infosec.rl.af.mil

Stephen M. Jarrett
Strategic Technologies Team
Rockwell-Collins Avionics and Communications Division
350 Collins Rd. NE, M/S 120-133, Cedar Rapids, IA 52498
319-395-3651 Fax: 319-395-2136
E-mail: smjarret@cacd.rockwell.com

Graduate of the U.S. Naval Academy (1972). Completed 17 years of sea duty, three years as Captain of Nuclear Ballistic Missile Submarine *USS Daniel Boone* in 1991. Awarded the President's Award as Honor Graduate of the College of Naval Warfare at the U.S. Naval War College in 1992. Assistant for Space CNO N-60C for Navy Space and Electronic Warfare Directorate and Joint Exercise and Flagship Coordinator for the C4I systems for the Navy prior to transitioning to Rockwell in 1993. At Rockwell he acted as the Joint Advanced Strike Technology representative on the JAST architecture review board. He presently performs advanced concept planning for the Collins Avionics and Communication Division of Rockwell.

Jay J. Kahn, Senior INFOSEC Engineer
The MITRE Corporation
1820 Dolly Madison Blvd., McLean, VA 22102-3481
703-883-6622 Fax: 703-883-1245
E-mail: jkahn@mitre.org

The MITRE Corporation is a not-for-profit, federally chartered research and development center supporting the Department of Defense. MITRE is involved in the entire spectrum of IW activities, including Security Engineering and Acquisition Support; formulation of national defense policy; standards development; the development of criteria; trusted product evaluations; research into guards, trusted authentication, and distrusted systems; prototyping such as for the compartmented-mode workstation and digital signatures; security tools development; risk analysis; and vulnerability analysis.

Major David M. Kennedy, US Army
550 Main St., Cincinnati, OH 45201-1159
513-684-2698 Fax: 513-684-3800
E-mail: (personal) 73157.2722@compuserve.com

US Army military police officer and Certified Information Systems Security Professional. Interests include protection of information systems and investigation of security violations. Assistant SysOp for the National Computer Security Association's forum on CompuServe, GO NCSAFORUM.

Henry M. Kluepfel, CPP, Vice President
SAIC
1 Exchange Place, Suite 10000, Jersey City, NJ
201-309-3080 Fax: 201-309-3078
E-Mail: hanklue @cpqm.saic.com
hanklue@aol.com

Carlo Kopp
Multiprocessor Research Group
Department of Computer Science
Monash University, Clayton, 3168, Australia
+61-3-905-5229
E-mail: Carlo.Kopp@cs.monash.edu.au
http://www.cs.monash.edu.au/carlo

One of Australia's foremost proponents of IW. Graduated with first class honors in Electrical Engineering in 1984 from University of Western Australia. Completed M.S. in Computer Science in 1966 and is currently working on a Ph.D. in the same discipline at Monash University in Melbourne, Australia. He has over a decade of diverse industry experience, including the design of high speed communications equipment, optical fiber receivers and transmitters, communications equipment including embedded code, UNIX computer workstation motherboards, graphics adaptors and chassis. More recently, he has consulted in UNIX systems programming, performance engineering, and system administration. Actively publishing as a defense analyst in Australia's leading aviation trade journal, *Australian Aviation*. Recognized authority on the application of modern military technology to operations and strategy. Work on electronic combat doctrine, electromagnetic weapons doctrine, laser remote sensing, and signature reduction has been published by the Royal Australian Air Force since 1992. Most important work has been the development of a doctrinal model for the offensive use of electromagnetic weapons in strategic warfare.

Klaus-Peter Kossakowski, CERT Manager
DFN-CERT
Vogt-Koelln-Strasse 30, D-22527 Hamburg, Germany
+49-40-54715-261 Fax: +49-40-54715-241
E-mail: kpk@cert.dfn.de, kossakowski@informatik.uni-hamburg.de)
http://www.cert.dfn.de/kpk/eng

Received degree from the University of Hamburg in the field of Information Science, concentrating on networks, communication, and computer security. Among the first members of the Virus Test Center, Hamburg (1988), personally working on the phenomenon of malicious programs in networks. Since then has worked in the field of network security. Engaged with the DFN-CERT (the first German Computer Emergency Response Team for an open network) since its conception, he started his official work in January 1993, taking over responsibility for administration and organization. He is a member of the Internet Society and the German "Gesellschaft fuer Informatik e. V." - GI.

Col. C. R. Krieger, USAF (Ret.), Systems Analyst
Dynamics Research Corporation
Frontage Rd., Andover, MA 01810
508-475-9090 X3091 Fax: 508-475-8657
E-mail: ckrieger@s1.drc.com, crk@world.std.co

IW Analyst (someone has to do the work). Developing IW aspects of national and theater-level campaign planning, bringing the tools of IW to bear for Joint Chiefs of Staff and theater commanders and their major subordinate commanders. Focus areas include the development and evaluation of IW and C2W organizations, material requirements, concepts, doctrine, tactics, techniques and procedures. Evaluator of IW/C2W simulation development.

James Leveque, Director, Departmental Public Affairs
Department of National Defence
National Defence Headquarters
101 Colonel By Drive, 12CBN, Ottawa, Ontario, K1A 0K2, Canada
613-996-8959 Fax: 613-992-3418
E-mail: jameslev@magi.com
aa246@issc.debbs.ndhq.dnd.ca

Main interests are industrial espionage; use of national media (by foreign powers) for propaganda purposes; issues management.

Martin C. Libicki, Senior Fellow
National Defense University
Fort McNair, Washington, DC
202-685-3837 X521 Fax: 202-685-3664
libickim@ndu.edu
http://www.ndu.edu/ndu/inss/staff/libicki.html

Specialist in RMA, IW, and information technology standards. He has written about the RMA in "The Revolution in Military Affairs" (*Strategic Forum* 11), "The Next Enemy" (*Strategic Forum* 35), "The Mesh and the Net" (*McNair Paper* 28), and "DBK and Its Consequences" in *Dominant Battlespace Knowledge*. He authored the Information Technologies chapter of *Strategic Assessment 1995* and the Emerging Military Instruments chapter of *Strategic Assessment 1996*. He has also written "What Is Information Warfare?," summarized in *Strategic Forum* 28.

David F. Linowes
University of Illinois at Urbana-Champaign
College of Liberal Arts and Sciences
308 Lincoln Hall
702 South Wright St., Urbana, IL 61801
Voice 217-333-0670 Fax: 217-333-5255

Professor Linowes is the distinguished Boeschenstein Professor of Political Economy and Pubic Policy Emeritus and is a champion of employees' rights in the workplace.

David A. McClung, Program Manager, Information Warfare Division
Applied Research Laboratories (ARL:UT)
University of Texas at Austin
PO Box 8029, Austin, TX 78758-4423
512-835-3374 Fax: 512-835-3774
E-mail: dmcclung@arlut.utexas.edu
http://www.arlut.utexas.edu/itgwww/

Interested in modulation, estimation, detection, forward error correction, spread spectrum, and RF issues in communications and electronic warfare. Over 20 years experience in R&D, engineering, test and evaluation, and operation of communications, navigational, information, and EW systems literally from the foxhole to the White House provides operational insight to applied research. ARL:UT is a DoD university research laboratory. Specific capabilities/interests of the Information Warfare Division include custom software and associated computer hardware to support C4I modeling simulation, planning, test and evaluation. Strengths in the areas of distributed computing, three-dimensional graphics, rule-based systems, object oriented design, and large systems integration have enabled our division to apply state-of-the-art research to build medium-to-large simulation and tactical systems. Our development process supports rapid design/build/ deployment of systems to satisfy critical DoD requirements.

David McMunn, President
McMunn Associates Inc./Borders Unlimited Corporation
1604 Spring Hill Rd., Suite 200, Vienna, VA 22182-1609
703-827-4126/4128 Fax: 703-827-4120
E-mail: mcmunn@aol.com

As consultant to Departments of Defense, Justice, and Energy and the Intelligence Community, as well as several Fortune 200 companies, addresses IW concerns in counterterrorism, counter-WMD proliferation, international law enforcement, and civil maritime contexts. Previously served as White House Director for Border Security (1990-1991), Atlantic Fleet Director for Intelligence (1986-1989), and on Vice President's Task Force on Combatting Terrorism (1985-1986).

Wayne Madsen, Security Analyst
Computer Science Corp.
Systems Group
3170 Fairview Park Dr., Falls Church, VA 22042
703-876-1000
E-mail: wmadsen777@aol.com

Consultant, author, and speaker relating to the Internet and security issues. Also writes for Elsevier Science Publications.

Lt. CMDR Jim Manley, USN (Ret.)
C4I Systems Development Projects Leader
Teknowledge Corporation
1810 Embarcadero Rd., Palo Alto, CA 94303
415-424-0500 X439 Fax: 415-493-2645
jmanley@teknowledge.com
http://www.teknowledge.com/HIBURST/

Former Naval Intelligence officer with a B.S. in engineering from the U.S. Naval Academy and M.S. in computer science from the U.S. Naval Postgraduate School. He leads the development of software in C4I systems for the Advanced Research Projects Agency (ARPA) and commercial products at Teknowledge Corporation. He has significant experience in the development of application, communications and database software for secure environments and is currently leading the development of object-oriented, distributed, knowledge-based situation assessment software for C4I and commercial users operating in bandwidth-limited environs. He is interested in all aspects of IW to include both offensive and defensive measures in both military and commercial application areas and welcomes a dialog with others having interests in any of the above areas.

Sammy Migues, Staff Scientist
PRC, Inc.
1500 PRC Drive, McLean, VA 22102
703-883-8872 Fax: 703-883-8328
E-mail: migues_sammy@prc.com
http://www.c3i.wsoc.com (PRC Enterprise Assurance Group)

Efforts aim at protecting integrity of the enterprise (a local collection of systems and LANs) and remote access to the enterprise (InfoWar Defend) from a myriad of attacks by various threat agents (InfoWar Attack). Use a set of capability processes and models to apply defensive techniques uniformly across a wide variety of commercial and government scenarios.

Louis R. Moore, Senior Analyst
RAND
1700 Main St, PO Box 2138, Santa Monica, CA 90407-2138
310-393-0411
E-mail: Louis_Moore@rand.org
http://www.rand.org/

Interests: Incorporating effects of Information Operations including IW into simulations.

Major Paul Moscarelli, USAF
33 Sherbrooke Rd., Newton, MA 02158
617-332-7259
e-mail: pmoscare@emerald.tufts.edu

A B-52 pilot turned graduate student at the Fletcher School of Law and Diplomacy at Tufts University. Fields of study: International Security Studies, International Information and Communication, and International Political Economy. Currently reviewing IW literature. I intend to do further research in the field.

Kenneth S. Moser, CNA, MIS Director
APICS
5553 Winford Ct., Fairfax, VA 22032
703-323-7846 Fax: 703-237-4316
E-mail: kenneth.moser@industry.net

Almost 15 years' experience as a network administrator on VAX, many flavors of UNIX, AppleTalk, NetWare, and a little Windows NT. Currently working on CSE and hope to complete Eastern Michigan University's masters program in Information Security sometime in 1997. Write monthly columns on computing issues for two magazines and am active online. Have generally been assigned computer security duties by default, but largely pursued them as an avocation—hope to make it a bigger part of my career in the future.

N. Munro, Reporter, *Washington Technology*
3513 Woodside Rd., Alexandria, VA 22310
703-960-5724 Fax: 703-848-2353
E-mail: nmunro@technews.com

Munro has broken numerous IW-related stories since 1988, authored a book on electronic warfare, and written several freelance pieces for publications such as the *Washington Post.*

Captain Dennis G. Murphy, USN
Submarine Communications Program Manager (PMW 173)
Space and Naval Warfare Systems Command (SPAWAR)
2451 Crystal Dr., Suite 500, Arlington, VA 22245-5200
703-602-8871 Fax: 703-602-3899
murphyd@smtp-gw.spawar.navy.mil
www.spawar.navy.mil/pmw173/173index.html

Program Manager for the Submarine Communications Program Office (PMW 173) responsible for design, development, acquisition, and life cycle support of all antennas, radios, baseband switching, and data distribution on all classes of U.S. nuclear powered submarines. This includes the following RF bands: ELF, VLF, LF, HF, VHF, UHF, SHF, EHF. The Submarine Communications Master Plan, which describes the Navy's plan to provide full telecommunications connectivity to submarines, is located on the PMW 173 WWW Homepage.

Roger Nebel
HomeCom Communications, Inc.
8201 Greensboro Dr., Suite 100
McLean, VA 22102
703-610-6845 Fax: 703-847-5404
E-mail: nebel@homecom.com
http://www.homecom.com

Vice President, Director, HomeCom Communications, Inc., an Atlanta-based Internet applications development firm. Head of the Internet Security Services division based in McLean, VA. HomeCom is a leader in providing Internet-based solutions for business and government. The Internet Security division provides risk assessment, penetration testing, boundary protection, and secure electronic commerce consulting and integration services.

Jerry A. Nepodal, Senior Scientist/Project Manager
MRJ, Inc.
10560 Arrowhead Dr., Fairfax, VA 22030-7305
703-277-1849 Fax: 703-385-4637
E-mail: jnepodal@mrj.com

With 20 years of experience in information technology and C4I system architectures and processes, my appreciation and respect for the ramifications of IW continually grows. The exponentially improving technology and methods to execute IW make it imperative that forums for exchanging ideas continue to mature. We, as a society and as professionals engaged in this arena, will be faced with significant challenges. I look forward to participating in the formulation of solutions and the harnessing of this technology for constructive contributions to our world.

Peter G. Neumann, Principal Scientist
SRI International Computer Science Lab
Menlo Park, CA 94025-3493
415-859-2375 Fax: 415-859-2844
Neumann@CSL.SRI.com, RISKS@CSL.SRI.COM
http://www.CSL.SRI.com

No solicitors or commercial misuses, please.

Charles M. O'Herin, Director, Business Operations Systems
New Definitions, Inc.
PO Box 44989, Tacoma, WA 98444
Consultant
O'Herin Enterprises
PO Box 7002, Tacoma, WA 98407
Voice/Voice-mail/Fax: 206-761-0443
E-mail: cmoherin@wolfenet.com

Over 25 years of experience managing, defining, engineering, reengineering high technology programs or information management organizations and systems. Over six years as independent small business owner providing consulting services from these experiences. Over five years providing consulting services to a national laboratory as principal or senior investigator supporting experiments of C4I organizations or systems and multilevel security operations and systems.

Capt. John R. Paron, USN (Ret.), Senior Systems Analyst
Dynamics Research Corporation
1755 Jefferson Davis Hwy, Suite 802, Arlington, VA 22202
703-412-2812, X6071 Fax: 703-412-2819
E-mail: jparon@s1.drc.com

IW Analyst. Developing IW aspects of national and theater-level campaign planning, bringing the tools of IW to bear for Joint Chiefs of Staff (JCS) and theater commanders and their major subordinate commanders. Focus areas include the development and evaluation of IW and C2W organizations, material requirements, concepts, doctrine, tactics, techniques, and procedures. Evaluator of IW/C2W simulation development. Thirty years' Navy service.

George J. Pinkham, Jr., Senior Engineering Associate
Hughes Technical Services
3980 Sherman St., Suite 200, San Diego, CA 92110-4324
619-683-8719 Fax: 619-298-9032
E-mail: gpinkham@msmail3.hac.com

Training design and implementation. Development Engineering. Have worked in the AEGIS, ACDS Block 1, SSDS, WDS Mk. 14, and WDS Mk 2. Have taught AEGIS, STANDARD Missile, CIWS, HARPOON, TOMAHAWK, C2P (Link 16 C2P for ACDS) Model 5.

MSgt. Bob Potter, Deployable C4 Force Manager
HQ Air Combat Command/SCXX
180 Benedict Ave., Suite 209, Langley AFB, VA 23665-1993
804-764-5736 Fax: 804-764-6435
E-mail: potterb@hqaccsc.langley.af.mil

Validates and projects deployable C4 force structure and equipage to support deployed USAF operations in combat and operations other than war.

Willard George Preussel, Senior Staff Engineer
Dynetics, Inc.
1000 Explorer Blvd, Huntsville, AL 35806
205-922-9230 X218 Fax: 205-922-9029
E-mail: preussel@dynetics.com
http://ns.dynetics.com

Manages Dynetics C4I programs, most of which involve the foreign intelligence field. Served at Missile and Space Intelligence Center 1966-1982, Assistant for Cryptologic Programs, National Intelligence Systems, OSDC3I 1982-84, Dynetics since 1984. Particular interests include air defense C4I systems (nationality independent), RF weaponry (particularly HPM), space and terrestrial military communications trends and systems, and various IW threats.

Peter V. Radatti, President/CEO
CyberSoft, Inc.
1508 Butler Pike, Conshohocken, PA 19428
610-825-4748 Fax: 610-825-6785
E-Mail: radatti@cyber.com
URL:www.cyber.com

Has been working on UNIX and network-based software attack problems since 1988. After three years of development he designed and published VFind, the world's first antivirus package for UNIX. Released at the UNIX Expo International 1991 in NYC, it is also the world's first heterogeneous antivirus package. VFind simultaneously scans for UNIX, MSDOS, Macintosh, Amiga, NT, and Macro attack programs. Includes CVDL pattern matching language and RSA MD5-based cryptographic integrity tool. Will port to any system, Internet ready.

Marcus J. Ranum
Firewall Colporteur
3018 Guilford Ave., Baltimore, MD 21218
410-889-8569
EMail: mjr@clark.net
http://www.clark/net/pub/mjr

The principal author of several major Internet firewall products, including DEC SEAL, TIS Gauntlet, and TIS Internet Firewall Toolkit. Ranum has been managing UNIX systems and network security for over 13 years, including configuring and managing whitehouse.gov. He is a frequent lecturer and conference speaker on computer security topics.

F. Patrick Roll, IW/C2W Program Manager
Integrated Systems Control (ISC)
350 Centre Pointe Dr., Virginia Beach, VA 23462
804-671-2562 Fax: 804-499-5502
E-mail: proll@iscvb.com

The IW/C2W section at ISC consists of team of experienced operators schooled in all five elements of C2W. Situated within the C4I Division, it is involved in development of Naval C2W doctrine, tactics, procedures, and techniques. The team is also well grounded in the C2W support areas of reconnaisance/surveillance systems and C4I architectures, and has conducted numerous IW/C2W studies and analysis for CNO and JCS.

Col. John E. Rothrock, USAF (Ret.)
Director, Center for Global Strategic Planning
SRI International
1611 N. Kent St., Arlington, VA 22209
703-247-8570 Fax: 703-247-8537
john_rothrock@sri.com
JRothr9879@aol.com

During his 26-year military career, from which he retired in 1990, Rothrock focused substantially on applications of advanced information technology as a force multiplier. He served in Vietnam (1969-1970) as chief of a combat interrogation team, with extended attachments to U.S. ground forces. Concepts that he developed in the 1970s as Chief of Combat Applications for the USAF Security Service (predecessor to today's Air Intelligence Agency) came to form much of the conceptual basis for the Air Force's Electronic Combat program. Joining SRI International upon his military retirement, Mr. Rothrock assumed directorship of the Center for Global Strategic Planning. He continues to write and speak frequently for both U.S. and international audiences on strategic applications of advanced technology and other geo-strategic issues. Rothrock speaks German and conducts research in Russian.

Earle L. Rudolph, Jr. Program Manager, Information Systems
Texas Instruments
1745 Jefferson Davis Highway, Suite 605, Arlington, VA 22202
703-413-1159 Fax: 703-413-6025
E-mail: erudoph
mimi@magic.itg.ti.com
erudolph@erols.com

Daniel Joseph Ryan
380 Forelands Rd., Annapolis, MD 21401
On AT&T dial 0-700-DAN-RYAN Fax: 703-824-6113
E-mail: Ryan_D@acm.org
http://www.c3i.saic.com/GWISS/docs/pmo/ryan/index.html

Corporate Vice President and Division General Manager of Science Applications International Corporation. Previously, Ryan served as Executive Assistant to the Director of Central Intelligence with responsibility as Executive Secretary and Staff Director for the Joint DoD-DCI Security Commission. Earlier, he was Director of Information Systems Security for the Office of the Secretary of Defense.

Julie J. C. H. Ryan
380 Forelands Rd., Annapolis, MD 21401
Voice 703-902-6839
Fax: 703-902-6942
E-Mail: Ryan_Julie@bah.com

Senior Associate at Booz, Allen & Hamilton where she is a member of the Intelligence Client Service Team providing consulting services to the Intelligence Community, developing new business, and responding to client requirements. She also serves as a member of the Naval Studies Board of the National Academy of Sciences. Prior to rejoining Booz, Allen, Ryan served as Senior Staff Scientist at TRW Systems where she specialized in information warfare applications, as Associate at Welkin Associates advising the Intelligence Community.

Ben Samman, Infosec Consultant
928 Franklin St. #333, Oakland, CA 94607
510-893-0680
E-mail: samman@cs.yale.edu

Specializes in user and machine authentication and integration of cryptography into existing applications.

James C. Settle
PO Box 2235, Springfield, VA 22152-2235
703-569-0011 Fax: 703-569-0012
e-mail settle@netcom.com
http://ourworld.compuserve.com/homepages/Settle

Retired from the FBI as head of the National Computer Crime Squad. As Director of Information Security Services with I-NET, Inc., he worked with government agencies and companies ranging in size from five nodes to networks operating hundreds of nodes, assisting them in securing their networks. He presently is the CEO of Settle Services in Technology, LLC. Has appeared on *Nightline,* CNN, the Discovery Channel, French National Television, Fuji Television, and many other radio, television, and print media on computer and network security. He is a keynote speaker and panel moderator at conferences including Computers Freedom and Privacy, Business Forum (Cophenhagen) National Computer Security Association, DEFCON III, Information Systems Security Association, CERT/FIRST, and many others.

Nick Simicich, Internet Security Consultant
IBM Global Consulting
32 SW 12th Way, Boca Raton, FL 33486
407-443-2578 Fax: 407-392-4008
E-mail: Nick_Simicich@bocaraton.ibm.com
http://scifi.maid.com/njs.html

Member of IBM's security consulting team specializing in Internet activities. IBM can provide anything from emergency response services to firewall installation. Personal specialties include IP protocol layer scanning/attacking, firewall installation verification, and web server verification.

Luigi Spagnuolo, Chief
Rome Laboratory, USAF
31 Grenier St., Hanscom AFB, MA 01731-3010
617-377-4249 Fax: 617-377-2563
spagl@rl.af.mil
http://infosec.rl.af.mil

The Information Security (INFOSEC) Technology Office Information Warfare technologies include Computer Security (COMPUSEC), Emission Security, Communications Security (COMSEC) and Secure Voice. The Information Security (INFOSEC) Technology Office conducts C4 systems security research and development in three areas of IW: Emission Security, Communications Security, and Secure Voice. The office defines and evaluates alternative concepts and/or products that can provide the security services required to reduce the risk of hostile technological exploitation of Air Force Systems. Customers supported by these efforts include the Air Force Information Warfare Center, CIA, NSA, National Security Telecommunications and Information Systems Security Agency, DOD Digital Voice Processing Consortium, Speakeasy, and major ESC SPO's: F-22, HaveQuick, JTIDS, Sincgars, Iceland Air Defense System (IADS).

Capt. Lars Starbuck, Information Warfare Officer
Field Command, Defense Nuclear Agency FCDNA/FCRCI
1680 Texas St. SE, Kirtland AFB, NM 87117
505-846-2220 Fax: 505-846-4265
E-mail: starbuckl@fc.dna.mil

Clark Staten
Emergency Response & Research Institute
6348 N. Milwaukee Ave., Suite 312, Chicago, IL 60646
Fax: 312-631-4703
E-Mail: sysop@emergency.com
http://www.emergency.com

Collection and analysis of open source intelligence. Interface capabilities between military and civilian emergency service agencies. Development and cooperation in civilian/emergency service intelligence networks. Computer security and virus issues. The use of WWW/Internet resources for integrated psy-ops and public education purposes. Psychological aspects of open source information.

Robert D. Steele, President
Open Source Solutions, Inc.
11005 Langton Arms Ct., Oakton, VA 22124-1807
703-242-1700 Fax: 703-242-1711
E-mail: ceo@oss.net
http://www.oss.net/oss

Founder of Open Source Solutions, a not-for-profit educational corporation chartered in Virginia and serving as the international clearinghouse for information about open sources, systems, and services, including security. The original advocate for increased use of open sources by national intelligence communities, and a noted commentator on national corporate information strategies and IW as a larger strategic issue encompassing electronic home defense and good intelligence, not just offensive interruption of services.

David S. Stodolsky, Ph.D., Guest Researcher
University of Copenhagen
Tornskadestien 2, st. th., DK-2400 Copenhagen NV, Denmark
45-38-33-03-30 Fax: 45-38-33-88-80
E-mail: david@arch.ping.dk, david@euromath.dk
PGP KeyID: B830DF31

My major interest in the IW area is artificial immune systems. I was the first to propose (on Virus-L) the use of what are now called "kill" signals to combat computer viruses. (See Kephart, *IEEE Spectrum* 30 (5): 20-26, 1993.) In a paper being revised for publication in *Methods of Information in Medicine,* I describe a Contagion Vigilance Automation System which uses security mechanisms also applicable to control of infectious agents affecting computers.

Charles Swett
Acting Deputy Director for Low Intensity Conflict Policy
Office of the Assistant Secretary of Defense for Low Intensity Conflict
The Pentagon, Room 2B525, Washington, DC 20301
703-693-5208 Fax: 703-693-0615
E-mail: swett@interramp.com

Frank R. Swift
Unclassified Computer Security Coordinator; ACPPM for LLNL
Lawrence Livermore National Laboratory
7000 East Avenue L-315, Livermore, CA 94550-6514
510-422-1463 Fax: 510-423-0913
E-mail: uncl@llnl.gov
http://www.llnl.gov/cso

I am interested in measuring performance of computer protection systems, auditing/monitoring attacks, developing attack/intrusion signatures and analysis of volumetric data to provide indicators of inappropriate use, and attacks by both the internal and external users in order to curtail waste, fraud, and abuse and to combat the espionage threat.

Richard Szafranski
Colonel, USAF (Ret.)
334-215-0635 Fax: 334-215-0524
E-mail: rsz@mont.mindspring.com, rsz@toffler.com

National security analyst, consultant, and strategist with Toffler Associates.

Capt. William J. "Buzz" Szarek
Chief, Theater Battle Management C4I Systems Security
Air Force Information Warfare Center/EAS
Kelly AFB, TX 78243-7036
210-977-3113 Fax: 210-977-4814

Computer security advisor and team leader to all C4I systems supporting joint air combat operations for theater commanders and battle staffs. Supervises team of officers responsible for developing, analyzing and validating system specifications, security tests and evaluations. Manages contractors supporting security system upgrade programs. Identifies security deficiencies and ensures rapid implementation of countermeasures protecting information processed, stored, or transported through the TBM.

Jeffrey Voas, Vice President, Research
Reliable Software Technologies #250
21515 Ridgetop Cir., Sterling VA 20166
703-404-9293 Fax: 703-404-9295
jmvoas@RSTCORP.com
http://www.rstcorp.com

Vice President of Reliable Software Technologies overseeing the research initiatives of the company. Currently the principal investigator on research initiatives for ARPA, NASA, National Institute of Standards and Technology, U.S. Air Force, and National Science Foundation. He has published over 70 journal and conference papers in the areas of software testability, software reliability, debugging, safety, fault-tolerance, design, and computer security. Before co-founding RST, Voas completed a two-year postdoctoral fellowship sponsored by the National Research Council at Langley Research Center. His research during this position yielded techniques for predicting software testability, new software metrics based on semantic rather than syntactic information, software debugging, design techniques for improving software testability, and computer virus detection schemes. Voas has served as a program committee member for numerous conferences, and will serve as Conference Chair for COMPASS '97. Voas has co-authored *Software Assessment: Reliability, Safety, Testability* (John Wiley & Sons, ISBN 0-471-01009-X), and has served on several international panels that were convened in the areas of testability, testing, reliability, security, and privacy. In 1994, the *Journal of Systems and Software* ranked Voas sixth among the 15 top scholars in Systems and Software Engineering. Voas is a member of IEEE and received a Ph.D. in computer science from William & Mary in 1990.

Bill Waddell, Senior Systems Engineer
U.S. Army War College (DynCorp Contractor)
Operations Group
Carlisle, PA 17013
717-245-4222 DSN 242-4222; Fax: (717) 245-4463
E-mail: waddellw@csl-emh2.army.mil

I am contracted to write the Army War College curriculum in C2W and Information Operations. I am a retired Navy Officer (aviator, not wire head) with joint operational experience and am a 1991 graduate of the Naval War College.

A. Bruce Walter, C3I/EW Program Development Manager
Sanders, Inc., Division of Lockheed Martin
1725 Jefferson Davis Hwy., Suite 403, Arlington, VA 22202-4102
703-413-5868 Fax: 703-413-5888
E-mail: bruce.walter@lmco.com

Specializes in high performance defense electronics systems for airborne, shipboard, submarine, and ground based applications. Interested in applications of existing and future systems to C3I, electronic warfare, command and control warfare, and IW.

Elin Whitney-Smith, Ph.D.
Institute for Change and Learning
George Washington University
212 Seventh St. SE, Washington, DC 20003
202-543-1527
E-mail: elin@tmn.com

Dr. Smith is a confessed cypernetician interested in change in complex systems. This has led to interests in the impact of information technology on organizational, social, economic and culture change, and the evolution of ecological systems.

Col. G. I. Wilson, USMC (OSD Pentagon)
1600 S. EADS 201-S Arlington, VA 22202
703-695-0092 Fax: 703-693-5371
E-mail: wilsongi@aol.com, 72447.2602@compusrve.com

Was the driving force in introducing OSINT to the I Marine Expeditionary Force Command Element. Published article in *Marine Corps Gazette*—"Uncorking the Information Genie"—that has caused various Marine Corps C4I offices to look at open source and COTS technologies. Considered by many as one the Corps' most bold and innovative thinkers and doer with regard to integrating open source, IW, OpSec, OpDep, InfoSec, ComSec, and maneuver warfare. Has written and published extensively in military journals: maneuver warfare, fourth-generation warfare, cellular technology, special operations, and other military topics. Recently recommended for a meritorious service medal for efforts pertaining to naval expeditionary intelligence, OSINT, ONI LNO, NRaD LNO, and INMARSAT.

Ira Winkler, Director of Technology
National Computer Security Association
10 S. Courthouse Ave., Carlisle, PA 1703
winkler@ncsa.com

World leader in the fields of IW, Industrial Espionage, Penetration Testing, and Social Engineering, and an invited speaker around the world. He will be running the NCSA Certification Laboratory and will be responsible for the NCSA Firewall Certification program.

Footnotes

Introduction

1. Submitted testimony, Subcommittee on Technology and Competitiveness, Committee on Science, Space and Technology, U.S. House of Representatives. June 27, 1991.
2. *Computers at Risk: Safe Computing in the Information Age.* National Academy Press, 1991. p. 7.

Chapter 1

1. David Halberstam, *The Next Century*, Avon Books, 1992, p. 131.
2. *St. Petersburg Times*, September 6, 1992.
3. Steven Emerson, *The New York Times*, April 7, 1993.
4. Conversations with FBI Special Agent Jim Kallstrom, June 6, 1993.
5. *Time* Magazine, July 5, 1993, p. 24.
6. David Long, *Anatomy of Terrorism*, Free Press, 1990, p. 5.
7. *Ibid.*, p. 6.
8. Emerson, *The New York Times.*
9. "Terrorism in the USA," House Task Force on Terrorism and Unconventional Warfare report, January 25, 1991.
10. *Time* Magazine, July 5, 1993, p. 25.
11. Long, p. 7.
12. *Ibid.*, p. 11.
13. *New York Post*, July 2, 1992, page 1.
14. House Task Force on Terrorism and Unconventional Warfare, July 1, 1992.
15. *Ibid.*
16. *Ibid.*
17. "Narco Terrorism and the Syrian Connection," House Task Force on Terrorism and Unconventional Warfare report, August 23, 1991.
18. Long, p. 123.
19. *Ibid.*, p. 124.

20. Nixon, p. 25.
21. Count de Maranches and A. Andelman, *The Fourth World War*, Morrow, 1992, p. 266.
22. *Ibid.*, p. 24.
23. Lester Thurow, *Head to Head: The Coming Economic Battle Among Japan, Europe and America*. William Morrow and Co., 1992, p. 21.
24. *Wall Street Journal*, Sept. 24, 1993, p. R27.
25. *Ibid.*, p. 122.
26. Thurow, p. 23.
27. Peter Drucker, *Post Capitalist Society*, Harper Business, 1993, p. 96.
28. *Ibid.*, p. 4.
29. Nixon, p. 124.
30. Drucker, p. 8.
31. Shintaro Ishihara, *The Japan That Can Say No*, Simon and Schuster, 1991, p. 50.
32. Thurow, p. 31.
33. *Ibid.*, p. 31.
34. Nixon, p. 124.
35. Ronald Kessler, *Spy Vs. Spy*, Simon and Schuster, 1988, p. 12.
36. Nixon, p. 93.
37. Nixon, p. 94.
38. Nixon, p. 94.
39. John P. Mello, Jr., "Espionage! Are the Spooks Targeting Your Business?" *ISP News*, Volume 3 Number 5, September/October 1992.

Chapter 2

1. Quoted by David Ahl in a 1982 interview.
2. "Artificial Life Gets More Vivacious," *Wall Street Journal*, Dec. 23, 1992.
3. Douglas Hofstadter, *Godel, Escher, Bach*, Vintage Press, 1980, p. 26.
4. R. Buckminster Fuller, *Synergetics*, Macmillan Publishing, 1975, p. 3.
5. Winn Schwartau, *Terminal Compromise*, Inter. Pact Press, 1991.
6. Hudson Briefing Paper, February, 1992, Hudson Institute, Herman Kahn Center.
7. Joel Kurtzman, "The Death of Money," Simon and Schuster, 1993, p. 11.
8. *Ibid.*, p. 51.
9. *Ibid.*, p. 65.
10. *Ibid.*, p. 26.
11. *Ibid.*, p. 183.

Chapter 3

1. Daniel Boorstein, *The Discovers*, Random House, 1983, p. 500.
2. Bruce Sterling, *The Hacker Crackdown*, Bantam, 1992, p. 7.
3. *Ibid.*, p. 8.
4. *Wall Street Journal*, Dec. 23, 1992, p. B6.
5. Thomas P. Hughes, *American Genesis*, Viking, 1989, p. 450.
6. Charles A. Reich, *The Greening of America*, Bantam, 1971, p. 92.
7. Hughes, p. 452.
8. David Aheff, *Game Over*, Random House, 1993.
9. "Law and Disorder," *Virus Bulletin*, April 1993.
10. Kurtzman, p. 107.
11. *Ibid.*, p. 113.

Chapter 5

1. Leonard Lee, *The Day the Phones Stopped*, Donald I. Fine, Inc., 1991.
2. Tom Forester & Perry Morrison, "Computer Ethics", Basil Blackwell, Ltd. U.K., 1990.
3. Forester & Morrison p. 74.

4. Forester & Morrison p. 74.
5. Forester & Morrison p. 74.
6. Lee, p. 11.
7. Lee, p. 111.
8. Lee, p. 114.
9. Lucy Reilly, *Washington Technology News*, August 27, 1992.
10. Lee p. 96.
11. Reilly, *Washington Technology News*.
12. Forester & Morrison p. 78.
13. Hofstadter, p. 17.
14. Lee, p. 109.
15. Lee, p. 261.
16. National Computer Security Association.
17. Company prospectus, September 1992.
18. *Ibid.*
19. James Daly, *Computerworld*, March 1, 1993.
20. Mark Ludwig, *The Little Black Book of Computer Viruses*, American Eagle Publications.
21. *Ibid.*
22. *Ibid.* back cover.
23. Private Interview
24. *The New York Times*, January 5, 1994, C1.
25. "In House Hackers," *Wall Street Journal*, August 27, 1992.
26. Kurtzman, p. 181.
27. Kurtzman, p. 187.
28. Hansell, "Cash Machines Get Greedy," *The New York Times*, Feb 18, 1994.
29. Lee, p. 115.
30. Lee, p. 47.

Chapter 6

1. Private conversation with company officials.
2. Dave Powell, "Plugging the Leaks in Data Networks," *Networking Management*, May 1992.
3. Timothy Haight, "Network Security," *Network Computing*, July 1991. (From a diagram supplied by Enigma Logic, Concord, CA.)
4. Gary Anthes, *Computer World*, November 30, 1992.
5. Mark Kellner, *Federal Computer Week*, October 22, 1990.
6. Kevin Power, *Government Computer News*, August 3, 1992.
7. Terry Quindlen, *Government Computer News*, November 25, 1991.
8. *Hactic*, issue 16-17, 1992.
9. *Ibid.*
10. *Ibid.*, Quindlen.
11. Peter Lewis, "A Rise in Internet Break-Ins Sets off a Security Alarm," *The New York Times*, February 5, 1994; John Burgess, "Break-Ins Hit Huge Network of Computers," *The Washington Post*, February 4, 1994.
12. *Security Insider Report*, November 1992.
13. *2600 The Hacker Quarterly*, Summer 1992, Devil's Advocate.
14. *New York Times*, July 9, 1992.
15. Mike Alexander, *Computerworld*, May 14, 1990.
16. Presidential National Security Decision Directive-42.
17. *Monitoring Times*, July 1993
18. Radio Shack, Executive Offices Memorandum from Bernard S. Appel, November 11, 1987.
19. *The New York Times*, June 9, 1991.
20. *Monitoring Times*, September 1992.
23. *Radio Electronics*, October, 1986.

24. *Satellite Dealer*, June 1986.
25. *Ibid.*
26. *Ibid.*
27. *Ibid.*
28. *The State of Security in Cyberspace*, Stanford Research Institute, 1992.

Chapter 7

1. *ISP News*, October 1992.
2. *"Now! It Can Be Told,"* September 30, 1991.
3. Wim van Eck, "Electromagnetic Radiation from Video Display Units: An Eavesdropping Risk?" PTT Dr. Neher Laboratories, Leidschendam, Netherlands, April 16, 1985.
4. *Ibid.*
5. BBC Television, "High Tech Spies," produced by John Penycate.
6. Author interview with NSA-approved Tempest engineers, June 1991.
7. Author interviews with Bob Carp, November and December 1992.
8. "Beyond van Eck Phreaking," *Consumertronics*, 1988.
9. "CRT Spying: A Threat to Corporate Security?" *PC Week*.
10. Author interview with Don Delaney, November and December 1992.
11. Private conversations, May 1991.
12. "Eavesdropping on the Electromagnetic Emanations of Digital Equipment: The Laws of Canada, England and the United States," Christopher Seline, June 7, 1990. Privately distributed document.
13. Private conversations with NSA officials, November 1992, Washington, D.C.
14. David Johnston, "Tailed Cars and Tapped Telephones: How U.S. Drew Net on Spy Suspects," *The New York Times*, February 24, 1994.

Chapter 8

1. Lee Dembart, "Hide and Peek," *Reason*, November 1993.
2. NCSA White Paper on Encryption Export Control Policy in the United States, January 10, 1994.
3. Michael Weiner, "Efficient DES Key Search," Bell Northern Research, August 20, 1993.
4. NCSA Security Conference, June 10, 1993, Washington, D.C.
5. Edmund Andrews, "U.S. Plans to Push Computer Coding Police Can Read." *The New York Times*, February 5, 1994.

Chapter 10

1. Warren Getler, "Drug Warriors," *World Monitor*, October 1992, p. 38.
2. *Ibid.*, p. 39.
3. Thomas B. N. Ricks, "Nonlethal Arms: New Class of Weapons Could Incapacitate Foe Yet Limit Casualties—Military Sees Role for Lasers, Electromagnetic Pulses, Other High-Tech Tricks—Sticky Roads, Stalled Tanks," *Wall Street Journal*, January 4, 1993.
4. Neil Munro, "Microwave Weapon Stuns Iraqis," *Defense News*, April 15, 1992.
5. Ricks, *Wall Street Journal*.
6. "Space and Electronic Warfare, A Navy Policy Paper on a New Warfare Area," by LCDR M. S. Loescher, from the Office of Chief of Naval Operations.
7. Private conversations.
8. Lee, p. 56.

9. *Ibid.*, p. 179.

10. *Ibid.*, p. 182.

11. *EMC Technology*, February 1991.

12. E.R. Van Keuren, et al., *Utilization of High Power Microwave Sources in Electronic Sabotage and Terrorism*, Maxwell Labs, 1992.

13. E.R. Van Keuren, et al., *Implications of the High Power Microwave Weapon Threat in Electronic System Design*, Maxwell Labs, 1992.

14. Van Keuren, *Utilization*.

15. E.R. Van Keuren, "Electronic Terrorism and Sabotage: An Historical Perspective," draft paper, 1992.

16. James W. Rawles, "High Technology Terrorism," *Defense Electronics*, January 1990.

17. Private conversations with FAA contractors and suppliers.

18. Sharon Begley, et al., Newsweek, July 26, 1993. "Mystery Stories at 10,000 Feet."

19. *Ibid.*, Begley

20. Brochure from EMC.

Note: "Los Alamos Explosive RF Weapon Technology Development," by James W. Toeus, "A High Intensity Single Pulse Microwave Source for Defense Applications," by Michael Fazio, "Microwave Hardening Technology," by Drs. Robert Smith and Lamar Allen, and "Evaluation of a Miniaturized Coaxial Spark Gap," by Sergey Krimchanskey and Robert Garver were sources for much of Mr. Van Heuren's work.

Chapter 11

1. Conversation with Rop Gonggrijp, April 1992, Amsterdam, Netherlands.

2. Sterling, p. 68–70.

3. Indictment, U.S. District Court, Southern District of New York, received, July 9, 1992.

4. Court Exhibit #3, U.S. vs. Lee, received from U.S. Attorney, December 11, 1992.

5. "The Mad Hacker's Tea Party," *Now! It Can Be Told*, September 30, 1991.

6. Sterling, p. 313.

Chapter 12

1. A Paramount film, released in 1992.

2. Comments at the Computer Professionals for Social Responsibility Conference, June 7, 1993.

3. Jane Meinhardt, "Huge Credit Card Record Theft Uncovered," *St. Petersburg Times*, June 27, 1992.

4. William Carley, "In House Hackers," *Wall Street Journal*, August 27, 1992.

5. *Ibid.*, Forester & Morrison, p. 14.

6. *Ibid.*, Carley.

7. *Ibid.*, Carley.

8. *Information Week*, May 11, 1992.

9. Forester & Morrison page 9.

10. *Ibid.*, Carley.

11. Tim Rioche, "Two Charged With Computer Fraud in Credit Scam," *St. Petersburg Times*, January 26, 1993.

12. James Daly, "Notorious Hacker Charged with Stealing Fed Secrets," *Computerworld*, December 14, 1992.

13. "Computer Maker Blamed for Breakdown," *St. Petersburg Times*, April 30, 1993.

14. *Federal Computer Week*, January 13, 1992.

15. James Smith, "SSA Employees Accused of Selling Personal Data," *Government Computer News*, January 6, 1992.

16. *St. Petersburg Times*, November 13, 1992.

17. Mike Rothmiller and Ivan G. Goldman, *The L.A. Secret Police: Inside the LAPD Elite Spy Network*, Simon and Schuster, 1992, p. 166.

18. Anthony Kimery, "Big Brother Wants to Look Into Your Bank Account," WIRED, December 1993.

19. Jeffrey Rothfeder, *Privacy For Sale*, Simon and Schuster, 1992, p. 124.

20. *Ibid.*, p. 202.

21. *Security Insider Report*, May 1993.

22. *Information Week*, August 9, 1993.

23. Mark Barroso, "The Missing Files of Harry Lee Coe III," *Creative Loafing*, September 9, 1993.

24. John P. McPartlin, "GAO: FBI Breach Is An Inside Job," *Information Week*, August 9, 1993.

25. Rothfeder, p. 137.

26. Rothmiller and Goldman, p. 21.

27. *Ibid.*, p. 21

28. *Ibid.*, p. 112.

29. *Ibid.*, p. 79.

30. *Ibid.*, p. 111.

31. Rothfeder, p. 52.

32. *Ibid.*, p. 54.

33. Forester & Morrison, p. 9.

34. Forester & Morrison, p. 52.

35. Rothfeder, p. 123.

36. *Ibid.*, p. 175.

37. *Ibid.*, p. 112.

38. *Ibid.*, p. 80.

39. *Ibid.*, p. 95.

40. *St. Petersburg Times*, September 26, 1993.

41. "A Spy In the House of Hate," *Chic*, November 1993.

42. Rothfeder, p. 91.

43. Alvin and Heidi Toffler, *War and Anti-War*, Little, Brown and Co., 1993.

44. Rob Kelly, "Borland Releases Spy Case Details," *Information Week*, March 15, 1993.

45. Kevin Kelly, "There's Another Side to the Lopez Saga," *Business Week*, August 23, 1993.

46. Elizabeth Heichler, "Airline Hacking," *Computerworld*, January 18, 1993.

47. *Ibid.*

48. William Conley, "Global Spy Networks Eavesdrop on Projects of Petroleum Firms," *Wall Street Journal*, January 6, 1994.

Chapter 13

1. Closed door Congressional session. *Time*, July 19, 1993.

2. Winn Schwartau, "Fighting Terminal Terrorism," *Computerworld*, January 17, 1991.

3. John Gantz, "Meta-Virus Set to Unleash Plague on Windows 3.0 Users," *Infoworld*, April 1, 1991.

4. "Iraqi Virus Hoax," *Security Insider Report*, April, 1992.

6. "Now It Can Be Told," September 30, 1991.

7. Space and Electronic Warfare, Policy Paper developed by the Office of the Chief of Naval Operations, June 1992, p. 2.

8. *Ibid.*

9. RFP No: DAAL01-93-R-2900, Closing Date: 28 SEPTEMBER 92, U.S. Army LABCOM, Fort Monmouth, NY 07703-5601.

10. Toffler, p. 150.

Chapter 14

1. Judi Hassen, "Access to Medical Files Reform Issue," *USA Today*, July 27, 1993.

2. Editorial, "Full Disclosure," Summer 1992.

3. Telephonic Info promotional literature.

4. Mitch Betts, *Computerworld*, August 9, 1993.

5. *Computerworld*, August 9, 1993.

6. Private communications, September 20, 1993. (In early 1994, he won the first round of lawsuits.)

Chapter 15

1. Mello.

2. U.S. Dept. of State publication 10017, November 1992.

3. Hughes, p. 9.

4. Speech to the National Press Club, April 3, 1990.

5. *Washington Times*, February 9, 1992.

6. Peter Schweizer, *Friendly Spies*, Atlantic Monthly Press, 1993

7. *Ibid.*, p. 34.

8. *Ibid.*, p. 259.

9. *Ibid.*, p. 123.

10. Private interviews, September 1993.

11. Bill Gurtz, "French Spooks Scare Firms," *Washington Times*, February 9, 1992.

12. Schweizer, p. 96.

13. *Ibid.*, p. 97.

14. *Ibid.*, p. 98.

15. *Ibid.*, p. 110.

16. *Ibid.*, p. 290.

17. *Ibid.*, p. 5.

18. *Ibid.*, p. 17.

19. *Ibid.*, p. 158.

20. *Ibid.*, p. 161.

21. *Ibid.*, p. 163.

22. *Nashville Tennessean*, October 9, 1993, page E1.

23. Kurtzman, p. 107.

24. Kurtzman p. 107.

25. "Cold War Treachery Revealed," *Time*, July 5, 1993.

26. Schweizer, p. 256.

Chapter 16

1. "Space and Electronic Warfare," policy paper, Office of the Chief of Naval Operations, June 1992.

2. Count de Maranches, p. 204.

Chapter 17

1. Thurow, p. 257.

Index

Automated systems
  in big business, 82
  downside of, 82

Babbage, Charles, 81
Baby Bells, 184
Baby monitors, and privacy, 677
Baker, Stewart A., 408
Banks
  ATMs, 226, 227–228, 387–388,
    676
  computer crimes against,
    105–106, 283–284, 334–335,
    373, 387–389, 529–531
  computer problems of, 107,
    149–150, 151
  and Data Encryption Standard,
    236
  integrity of information of, 133
  and Van Eck radiation detection,
    231
  vulnerability of, 105–106,
    149–150, 226, 227–228,
    283–284
Barbarians at the Gate (film), 522
Barlow, John Perry, 71, 655
Baumard, Philippe, 611
Baven, Mark, 231
BBSs. *See* Bulletin board systems;
  Hacking groups
Beard, Tom, 395–396
Bell, Alexander Graham, 97
Bell, Jim, 420
Bell Company, 97
Biegelman, Martin, 387
Bill of Rights. *See also*
  Constitution, U.S.
  electronic, 648–657
Billsf (hacker), 352
Binary Schizophrenia, 38, 100–105
  computer viruses and, 155
  conditions giving rise to, 99–100
  governmental, regarding
    cryptography, 242
  inaccurate credit card records
    and, 474

manifestations of, 100–105
use of term, 99–100
as weapon of Information
  Warfare, 106
Bio-cybernetics, 244–247
Bio-chips, 664
Black, Percy, 341
Blackmail, 132, 134
Boeing, 16–18, 518–519
Boorstein, Daniel, 96
Boren, David, 516
Brandt, Willy, 525
Bretton Woods Agreements (1944),
  84
British Airways, 399–400
Bugging methods, 474–475
Bulletin board systems (BBSs), 640,
  697–698. *See also* Hacking
  groups
  ownership of information on, 640
Bush, George, 187
Business organizations. *See*
  Corporations

Campen, Al, 8
Canada, security resources in, 696
Cantwell, Maria, 18, 242
Capabilities, technological, versus
  intentions, 39–40
Capitalism, three schools of, 61–65
Capstone, 238, 241
Carp, Bob, 226–227
Carter, Jim, 226
Casey, Diane, 378–379
Cassette players, on airplanes, 284
Catia software program, 519
CB radios, destructive use of, 193
CD players, on airplanes, 284, 285,
  286
Cellular phone calls, 676
  ESN readers for, 192–193
  interception of, 191–193, 194
Central processing unit (CPU)
  chips, 255–257
Chaos, creation of, by global

National Security Agency (*cont.*)
  National Computer Security Center, 696
National Security Decision Directive 42, 187–188
Native American cryptographers, 233
NATO, 62
Navy, U.S., 430
  and electronic-based weaponry, 280, 281
  Space and Electronic Warfare policy, 430
Network analyzers, 177
Networks. *See also* Global Network; Local area networks; Telecommunications networks
  break-ins of, 176, 181–197
  destruction of, 181
  lack of security of, 175–176, 181, 244
  sniffing, 177–180
  superhighway of, to Information Warriors, 180–181, 591
New World Order, 35
  components of, 52
  economic realities of, 61–62
  economic warfare as part of, 29, 58–70
  military defense policy, 589
Nixon, Richard, 28, 60, 62, 84, 513
Noe, Frans, 374
NORAD, 49

O'Hearn, Betty G., 247
Operation Sundevil, 187
Operations centers, physical security of, 34
Ownership of information, 640–641, 646

Parker, Don, 184, 194
Passive sniffers, 178–181
Passive techniques, 137–138
Passwords. *See also* Identification

access to, 177, 180–181, 186, 349
authentication of, 684
PBXs, 196
PC Virus Control Handbook, The (Jacobson), 170
Peros, Mike, 380–381
Personal (Class 1) Information Warfare, 9–10, 473–512
  axioms of, 473
  methods of, 474
  power of, 478, 479–485
Personal computers, 79, 98–99
  on airplanes, 284–286
  cost of, 80
  of future, 659–660
  safe computing practices for, 677, 681–683
Personal privacy. *See* Privacy, personal
Peterson, Padgett, 59–60, 239
PGP (Pretty Good Privacy), 242, 247–253, 676
Phone phreaks, 38, 134, 184, 185–186, 352
Phrack, 39
Political action groups, in Information Warfare, 396–397
Politicians, in Information Warfare, 395–396
Postcapitalist society, Drucker on, 61–62
Poulson, Kevin, 204, 375
Print media, 110–111
Privacy, personal, 29, 30, 486–501, 507–512, 675. *See also* Personal (Class 1) Information Warfare
  advocacy groups for, 675
  data banks and, 649–650
  employees and, 391–392
  in future, 663
  government employees and, 379, 382–384
  invasion of, 33, 34, 39, 229–230, 394–395, 473–485